Contemporary Cases
in U.S. Foreign Policy

Contemporary Cases in U.S. Foreign Policy

From Terrorism to Trade

Fourth Edition

Ralph G. Carter, *Editor*
Texas Christian University

CQ PRESS

A Division of SAGE
Washington, D.C.

CQ Press
2300 N Street, NW, Suite 800
Washington, DC 20037

Phone: 202-729-1900; toll-free, 1-866-4CQ-PRESS (1-866-427-7737)

Web: www.cqpress.com

Cover design: www.thedesignfarm.com
Typesetting: C&M Digitals (P) Ltd.

♾ The paper used in this publication exceeds the requirements of the American National Standard for Information Sciences—Permanence of Paper for Printed Library Materials, ANSI Z39.48-1992.

Printed and bound in the United States of America

14   13   12   11   10   1   2   3   4   5

Library of Congress Cataloging-in-Publication Data

Contemporary cases in U.S. foreign policy : from terrorism to trade / Ralph G. Carter, editor. — 4th ed.
　　p. cm.
　Includes bibliographical references and index.
　ISBN 978-1-60426-731-0 (pbk. : alk. paper) 1. United States—Foreign relations—1989—Case studies. I. Carter, Ralph G.
　E840.C66 2011
　327.73—dc22

2010034104

Contents

PART I   INTERVENTION POLICY

*The "war on terrorism" had its origins in the early 1990s, escalated
with the 1998 bombings of the U.S. embassies in Kenya and Tanzania,
and came into full fruition with the terrorist attacks on New York City
and the Pentagon on September 11, 2001. As a result, two U.S.
administrations made war on Osama Bin Laden's al Qaeda network
and the Taliban regime in Afghanistan that provided it sanctuary.
Following years of warfare in Afghanistan, the Obama administration
employed a surge strategy against the Taliban in order to pacify the
country sufficiently to allow U.S. troops to begin coming home.*

*A number of neoconservatives who previously advocated the
overthrow of the Saddam Hussein regime in Iraq emerged as key
officials in the George W. Bush administration. Following the
September 11 attacks and the initial retaliation against Afghanistan,
they again advocated regime change in Iraq. Relying on their
interpretations of the president's commander in chief powers and a
congressional authorization to use force, White House officials
conducted the invasion and subsequent occupation of Iraq with as
little input from outsiders as possible. President Obama's controversial
troop surge sought to stabilize the country so U.S. forces could be
drawn down.*

September 11 terrorist attacks both pushed that issue to the bottom of the government's agenda and changed the nature of the debate. The already difficult issues regarding how to deal fairly with legal and illegal immigrants combined with fears about the need to tighten the country's borders against potential terrorist penetration. Despite early promises by the Obama administration to take up comprehensive immigration reform, intransigence on all sides continues to prevent a resolution of these issues.

PART III ECONOMIC AND TRADE POLICY

In 2007 a housing bubble burst in the United States. As a result, more and more banks and financial institutions became the holders of "toxic" assets, the actual values of which were unknown. Not knowing their true exposure from these bad loans, banks and financial institutions cut back on other lending to protect themselves, thereby creating a credit crisis that quickly spread around the world. The outgoing Bush administration had to find a way to bail out the banks to make credit available again, and the new Obama administration had to find a way to coordinate international responses to promote global economic recovery.

For five decades, the United States has maintained a unilateral embargo against the Castro regime in Cuba. The embargo has failed to push first Fidel Castro and now his brother, Raúl, from power, and it has become a lightning rod for U.S. interest groups. Some Cuban American groups see dropping the embargo as rewarding the Castros for their intransigence (and abetting communism), while some U.S. industries shut out of Cuban markets maintain that a unilateral embargo only punishes U.S. businesses and not their foreign competitors.

Thirty years after the United States and China established economic relations, the two continue to exchange complaints about each other's trade practices. China moved from the status of a "strategic partner" under the Clinton administration to a "strategic competitor" under the Bush administration. Now the Obama administration must find a way to deal with China as an emerging economic power, finding the appropriate balance between protecting U.S. economic interests while taking advantage of all China offers.

The George H. W. Bush, Clinton, George W. Bush, and Obama administrations have struggled with the issue of how to respond to global climate change. The U.S. government's reluctance to reduce fossil fuel emissions to the levels dictated by the 1997 Kyoto Protocol led some states and cities to set their own emissions reduction targets. For its part, the Obama administration sought to participate in a follow-up Copenhagen Protocol, but due to the widely varying positions taken by both developed and developing states, the administration was only able to obtain informal, voluntary pledges of future emissions reductions.

Despite the United States' characterization of itself as "a nation of laws," it has long wanted to protect U.S. officials and citizens from frivolous prosecution by the United Nations' International Criminal Court. President Bill Clinton was enthusiastic about the court so long as indictments had to be approved by the UN Security Council— where the United States could protect itself with a veto. George W. Bush rejected the idea of the court, and Barack Obama has shown that he is not keen on signing treaties the Senate is unlikely to approve. All the while, the International Criminal Court continues to take on new cases.

What legal rights do detainees in the "war on terrorism" have? Are they prisoners of war, criminals, or something else? The Bush administration's policies that such detainees largely lacked legal rights have been generally overturned by the courts. The Bush administration subsequently sought to try such detainees before military tribunals, but the Obama administration has maintained that the U.S. criminal court system should be able to handle such trials in most cases.

Preface

The terrorist attacks of September 11, 2001, and events thereafter demonstrate that post–cold war expectations for a more peaceful world built on a foundation of liberal democracies are, at best, premature. Military conflicts and national security issues continue to occupy the spotlight, while less traditional foreign policy concerns have also emerged. Human rights, trade matters, and the U.S. role in the international community have moved to the forefront, as foreign policy making has become a much more complex and crowded affair than it was during the cold war.

Just as the types of foreign policy issues that seem important have changed, the relative roles played by different policy makers have been in flux as well. Although presidents still occasionally act unilaterally—as in decisions to use military force—presidential preeminence in overall foreign policy making has diminished. Domestic and international groups, nongovernmental organizations, and members of Congress now actively challenge the executive branch's ability to direct foreign policy. In the post–cold war period, public opinion also seems to play a greater role in policy makers' decisions.

This historic shift in the policy process raises a number of questions: Can international institutions contain terrorism or ethnic and religious violence? How can the United States protect its citizens and interests from global terrorist threats? Are unilateral U.S. responses appropriate for global threats, or do they just compound the problem? Will disgruntled domestic actors define new enemies or foreign policy challenges? Will the international economy be marked by trade wars between regions and free trade within them? What is more important to U.S. foreign policy: human rights or corporate profits and market share? These questions and similar concerns prompted the conception of this book.

Each of the fifteen case studies included here speaks to a foreign policy process that has become more open, pluralistic, and deeply partisan. With the dramatic increase in the number of congressional subcommittees in the 1970s, followed by the explosive growth of the electronic media in the 1980s and 1990s, individuals and groups now have more points of access through which to participate in policy making. These new actors have their own needs, interests, and agendas. They are more partisan in their behavior as well, with Democrats and Republicans vying to put their own foreign policy agendas or policy alternatives forward. In short, U.S. foreign policy making now resembles U.S. domestic policy making: it is overtly political.

Most of the cases in this volume reflect the reality of jurisdictional competition between the president and Congress (and at times the courts) over the control and direction of foreign policy in the contemporary era. Not only do members of the president's opposition party regularly challenge his foreign policy initiatives, but even members of his own party resist executive leadership when they think that the White House tramples on legitimate congressional responsibilities or that the public overwhelmingly opposes administrative policies. Such circumstances have often led to "bad blood" between the branches, a situation that cannot help but strain the policy-making process. White House controversies—or fundamental changes in governmental direction, such as the 2008–2009 bailouts of banks and financial institutions—can further weaken presidential power. These themes combine to reveal the chinks in the armor of the presidential preeminence model of foreign policy making.

Using Case Studies in the Classroom

Although many excellent U.S. foreign policy texts exist, most fall short in their coverage of recent events and debates. This book aims to cover contemporary incidents, so that instructors can raise issues confronting today's policy makers. Each case study is an original work written expressly for this volume and is organized in a format that emphasizes the substance of events. A textbook's general description of foreign policy making simply cannot capture all of the intricacies, nuances, and subtleties involved in the events chronicled here. The cases starkly reveal the human dimension of policy making and also help instructors show how administrations often take pains to attempt to do things differently than their predecessors. In addition to showing students the human, political, and organizational faces of policy making, these case studies also introduce them to the wide variety of issues and actors found in the post–cold war and post–September 11 period. Students are presented with a "good story," full of compelling characters and daunting challenges, and information on the relevance of issues and why particular policy choices were made.

The pedagogical benefits of the case study approach have spurred its use within the international studies community, joining military, business, public policy, and public administration schools that have long used this approach. For college graduates to compete and perform effectively in the real world, they must first see the world as it is. Simplified models of reality may be necessary at times, but they are rarely sufficient in and of themselves. Theoretical models alone do not capture the messy nature of foreign policy making. If instructors are to facilitate an understanding of the political arena, in which everything seemingly affects everything else, they must confront students with the policy-making dynamics that real-world cases illustrate. Were policy makers trying to make rational choices? Were they trying to balance power concerns on a regional or global basis? Were they more responsive to external threats or opportunities, or to internal political pressures at home? Were they reacting to widely shared perceptions of reality? Did analogies mold their decisions, or were they merely used to convey or defend decisions to the public? These and other theoretical concerns are addressed through the case study method.

Case studies also promote critical thinking and encourage active intellectual engagement. None of their recognized advantages can be realized unless students ask themselves why things occurred as they did. Reasoning, considering alternatives, deciding on one alternative rather than another, and communicating the reasoning behind a choice are skills that are integral to lifelong learning and success in any professional career.

Because different educational environments—for example, seminars versus large lecture courses, upper-level courses versus introductory classes—require different teaching approaches, this collection includes a number of aids to help students and instructors get the most out of each case study. "Before You Begin"—a series of critical questions at the beginning of each case—serves as a touchstone, giving students ideas to consider and later review. Each case includes a brief chronology noting the important events covered and a list of key figures in the case. Our shared goal here is to walk a fine line: to encourage students to think without telling them what to think. To provide instructors with guidance in using the studies, the online, password-protected instructor's manual (**http://ccusfp.cqpress.com**) includes a section on the nuts and bolts of case-based teaching as well as separate entries for analyzing and discussing each case study.

The Cases

The case studies in this book were selected to illustrate two important realities of the post–cold war and post–September 11 period: (1) the range and diversity of the old and new issues facing U.S. foreign policy makers and (2) the variety of the participants in the current policy-making process. The first set of cases concerns the ongoing questions of when and how the United States should intervene militarily. Military interventions have always been considered "high politics"—decisions typically made in the White House. As the "war on terrorism," Iraq intervention, and Colombia intervention cases show, presidents still largely dominate these issues. However, as always, domestic criticism arises swiftly if presidential policies are not seen as successful.

Changing national security and defense challenges prompted another set of cases. How to deal with nuclear weapons proliferation in North Korea, and potentially Iran, has bedeviled policy makers at both ends of Pennsylvania Avenue during the Clinton, Bush, and Obama administrations. After a series of contentious issues marked U.S.-Russian relations during the Clinton and Bush administrations, President Barack Obama sought a highly publicized "reset" of those relations, beginning with a new START Treaty. Also early in his presidency, Obama was confronted with a new piracy challenge in the waters off Somalia, as well as with continuing controversial issues left over from the prior administration, such as the best way to pursue immigration reform in an environment marked by security concerns and an electronic eavesdropping program designed to protect the public from terrorist attacks. Regarding the third set of cases, many observers predicted that the hallmark of the post–cold war period would be a new emphasis on trade and more cooperative international initiatives, but all of that almost came apart during the global financial crisis of 2008–2009. The Bush and Obama responses were to bail out threatened financial institutions and to press for more global economic stimulus efforts, respectively. In a context of more interdependent trade relationships, the question arises as to why the United States maintains a fifty-year-old embargo of Cuba. The case of how to deal with China shows a variation from engagement (under Clinton) to competition (under Bush) to something in between (under Obama). In each instance, an administration's policy toward China pits a variety of domestic groups (and their congressional advocates) against each other. In this case, business interests generally prevailed over the human rights, labor, and environmental groups lobbying to deny China permanent normal trade relations with the United States.

The last set of cases focuses on the difficulties the United States currently faces in its dealings with a range of international organizations. The complexities of the issues, pressures from interest groups, and divisions within Congress have prevented the United States from doing as much regarding combating global climate change as President Obama would prefer. Congressional pressures and Defense Department concerns forced the Clinton, Bush, and Obama administrations to forgo cooperation with the new International Criminal Court. The final case study highlights the politics of the detention of people rounded up in the United States after the attacks of September 11; enemy combatants captured in Afghanistan and held at Guantánamo Bay, Cuba; U.S. citizens declared enemy combatants by the president; and detainees in U.S.-run prisons in Iraq. Whereas the Bush administration claimed that the president, as commander in chief, has the authority to deal unilaterally with the first three sets of detainees, the Supreme Court ruled otherwise, holding that such detainees could not be denied access to U.S. courts and lawyers. Their legal status is still in limbo. These are a few examples of the wide range and diversity of U.S. foreign policy making in the post–cold war and post–September 11 era.

Acknowledgments

As is usually the case in publishing, this book benefits from the efforts of many individuals. First, my thanks go to the authors of the case studies. Not only were they willing to write the studies requested, but they also graciously agreed to make the changes that the CQ Press editors and I suggested. Much appreciated is the timeliness with which they produced their chapters, particularly as the situations covered in some cases continued to evolve as they wrote. Second, a number of colleagues and friends provided valuable assistance at various stages of this process. In addition to the many who reviewed previous editions, I must thank Randall Blimes, Cooper Drury, Mary Durfee, Lindsay Heger, and Laura Zanotti for their reviews, which guided this new edition. I have also benefited from helpful feedback from many members of the Active Learning in International Affairs Section of the International Studies Association. Having good help when you need it is a treasure, and this volume is better as a result of their respective contributions.

Luckily for me, the professionals at CQ Press have also been great partners. Elise Frasier guided this edition and was consistently helpful and supportive. Careful copyediting by Talia Greenberg further improved the writing. Gwenda

Larsen took great care in shepherding the book through the production process and into print.

Finally, I must thank those closest to me. First, Nita has been wonderful throughout the long life of this project. Her advice, understanding, and encouragement, particularly on the many nights and weekends when I had to work, helped me keep my focus on the job at hand. Her consistent support has been instrumental to the successful completion of this project. Second, I also need to thank my extended family and friends. They too have been supportive and understanding when my work pulled me away at times. I am truly fortunate to be surrounded by such caring individuals.

Contributors

RALPH G. CARTER is a professor in and former chair of the political science department at Texas Christian University. His research interests center on how U.S. foreign policy is made, with particular attention to the role of Congress. He is the coauthor of *Making American Foreign Policy* (1994, 1996) and *Choosing to Lead: Understanding Congressional Foreign Policy Entrepreneurs* (2009), and in 2010 he served as an associate section editor for the *ISA Compendium Project*. Carter is a past president of both the International Studies Association's Foreign Policy Analysis Section and Midwest Region. He served as one of the inaugural editors of *Foreign Policy Analysis* and is the 2006 recipient of the Quincy Wright Distinguished Scholar Award by ISA Midwest. He holds a PhD from Ohio State University.

LINDA CORNETT is associate professor and chair of political science at the University of North Carolina, Asheville, where her classes include international organization, international political economy, and the political economy of development. She earned her bachelor's degree from Transylvania University, Lexington, Kentucky, and a master's and PhD in political science from the University of Washington, Seattle.

LOUIS FISHER is scholar in residence at the Constitution Project. Previously he worked at the Library of Congress as a specialist on constitutional law and separation of powers. He received his doctorate at the New School for Social Research in 1967 and is the author of many books, including *Presidential War Power* (2nd ed. 2004), *Constitutional Conflicts between Congress and the President* (5th ed. 2007), and (with Katy Harriger) *American Constitutional Law* (8th ed. 2009).

FRÉDÉRICK GAGNON is a professor in the Department of Political Science at the University of Quebec at Montreal. He is the director of the Center for United States Studies of the Raoul Dandurand Chair, at the same university, and was visiting scholar at the Woodrow Wilson International Center for Scholars (Washington, D.C.) and at the Center for American Politics and Citizenship (University of Maryland) in 2006, and visiting professor at the Center for Canadian-American Studies at Western Washington University in 2008. His research and teaching interests focus on the U.S. Congress, American foreign policy, legislative-executive relations, congressional and presidential elections, U.S. culture wars, and Quebec-U.S. relations. He is the author of a French-language textbook on the U.S. Congress

(*Le Congrès des États-Unis*, 2006). He is currently preparing a book on the influence of the chairs of the Senate Foreign Relations Committee since 1945.

MARK GIBNEY is Belk Distinguished Professor at the University of North Carolina–Asheville. His recent publications include *International Human Rights Law: Returning to Universal Principles* (2008) and the edited volume *Human Rights and Extraterritorial Obligations* (2010). He also has two forthcoming books. The first (with Sabine Carey and Steve Poe) is *The Politics of Human Rights: The Quest for Dignity;* the second is an e-book, *The Global Refugee Crisis.* Since 1984, Gibney has directed the Political Terror Scale (PTS), one of the world's leading human rights datasets (www.politicalterrorscale.org).

PATRICK J. HANEY is professor of political science at Miami University, Oxford, Ohio. His teaching and research interests are U.S. foreign and national/homeland security policy. He is the author of *Organizing for Foreign Policy Crises: Presidents, Advisers, and the Management of Decision Making* (2002) and the coauthor of *The Cuban Embargo: The Domestic Politics of American Foreign Policy* (2005).

RYAN C. HENDRICKSON is professor of political science at Eastern Illinois University. His research and teaching interests focus on American military action abroad and leadership at NATO. He is the author of *The Clinton Wars: The Constitution, Congress, and War Powers* (2002) and *Diplomacy and War at NATO: The Secretary General and Military Action after the Cold War* (2006). He received a PhD from the University of Nebraska, Lincoln.

JENNIFER S. HOLMES is an associate professor of political economy and political science at the University of Texas at Dallas. Her major area of research is violence and development, with an emphasis on Latin America and Southern Europe. She is the author of *Terrorism and Democratic Stability* (2001, 2006), *Terrorism and Democratic Stability Revisited* (2008), and *Guns, Drugs, and Development in Colombia* (2008), and the editor of *New Approaches to Comparative Politics: Insights from Political Theory* (2003) and *Latin American Democracy: Emerging Reality or Endangered Species?* (2008). Holmes's articles have been published in *Terrorism and Political Violence, Latin American Politics and Society, Bulletin of Latin American Research, International Journal of Social Economics, Studies in Conflict and Terrorism, International Journal of Public Administration,* and *Revista de Estudios Colombianos.*

STEVEN W. HOOK is professor and chair of the Department of Political Science at Kent State University. He is the author of *National Interest and Foreign Aid* (1995), *American Foreign Policy since World War II* (18th ed. 2010), and *U.S. Foreign Policy: The Paradox of World Power* (3rd ed. 2011). He is editor of *Foreign Aid toward the Millennium* (1996), *Comparative Foreign Policy: Adaptation Strategies of the Great and Emerging Powers* (2002), and *Democractic Peace in Theory and Practice* (2010). His articles have appeared in journals such as *World Politics, International Studies Quarterly, International Interactions, Foreign Policy Analysis,* and *Asian Survey.* Hook is a past president of the Foreign Policy Analysis Sections of the International Studies Association and the American Political Science Association.

MICHAEL P. INFRANCO teaches international politics and government courses in the Department of Political Science at Washington State University and international law to graduate students at Troy University's Malmstrom Air Force Base campus. His research interests include American foreign policy, Middle Eastern politics, intergroup conflict, and international law. In 2006 he retired as a lieutenant commander from the U.S. Navy Reserve; he holds a graduate diploma in National Security and Strategic Studies from the U.S. Naval War College (1996). Infranco is a combat veteran and has an expeditionary medal for his participation in Ernest Will missions in the Persian Gulf during the Iran-Iraq War. He has also participated in several international exercises and conferences, such as Ulchi Focus Lens 93 (defense of South Korea) and a Korean security conference at International Christian University in October 2003. He received his PhD from Washington State University in May 2005.

DONALD W. JACKSON was recently retired as the Herman Brown Professor of Political Science at Texas Christian University. His research over the past few years has focused on transnational and international dimensions of the rule of law, especially on the protection of human rights. In 1998 he was an observer at the UN conference that led to the adoption of the Rome Statute and the creation of the International Criminal Court.

PATRICK JAMES is professor of international relations and director of the Center for International Studies at the University of Southern California (PhD, University of Maryland, College Park). James specializes in comparative and international politics. His interests include the causes, processes, and consequences of international conflict, crisis, and war. He also focuses on Canada, most notably with respect to constitutional dilemmas. James is the author of eighteen books and more than one hundred articles and book chapters. Among his honors and awards are the Louise Dyer Peace Fellowship from the Hoover Institution at Stanford University; the Milton R. Merrill Chair in Political Science at Utah State University; the Lady Davis Professorship of the Hebrew University of Jerusalem; the Thomas Enders Professorship in Canadian Studies at the University of Calgary; the Senior Scholar Award from the Canadian Embassy, Washington, D.C.; the Eaton Lectureship at Queen's University in Belfast; the Quincy Wright Scholar Award from the Midwest International Studies Association; and the Eccles Professorship of the British Library. He is a past president of the Midwest International Studies Association and the Iowa Conference of Political Scientists and currently is Distinguished Scholar in Ethnicity, Nationalism, and Migration for the International Studies Association (ISA). He is vice president, 2005–2007, and president, 2007–2009, of the Association for Canadian Studies in the United States, and vice president, 2008–2009, of the ISA. James served a five-year term as editor of *International Studies Quarterly.*

THOMAS D. LAIRSON is Gelbman Professor of International Business and professor of political science at Rollins College in Winter Park, Florida. His courses focus on East Asia, and he has written on international political economy, Chinese business, Asian economic growth, and technology and economy. He served as the first Ford Foundation Professor of International Relations in Hanoi, Vietnam, in 1994 and will serve as a Fulbright Fellow in Singapore in 2011. Lairson earned his PhD from the University of Kentucky.

JEFFREY S. LANTIS is professor of political science and chair of the international relations program at the College of Wooster, Wooster, Ohio. His teaching and research interests include foreign policy analysis and international cooperation and conflict. A 2007 Fulbright Senior Scholar in Australia, he is the author of several books, including *The Life and Death of International Treaties* (2009), as well as numerous journal articles and book chapters. He is a past president of the Active Learning in International Affairs Section of the International Studies Association. He earned his PhD from Ohio State University.

FRANKLIN BARR LEBO is an A.B.D. PhD candidate and adjunct instructor in the Department of Political Science at Kent State University. His research and teaching interests center on East Asia, along with matters pertaining to international peace, security, and sustainability studies. Lebo received his JD from the University of California, Hastings College of the Law, and is a licensed attorney in the state of Ohio. He is also the dean of academic affairs for Minds Matter of Cleveland, a multi-state nonprofit dedicated to helping underprivileged students gain admission to college. Lebo is the coauthor (with Steven W. Hook) of "Development/Poverty Issues and Foreign Policy Analysis" in *The International Studies Encyclopedia* (2010).

PETER LEHR is a lecturer in terrorism studies at the Centre for the Study of Terrorism and Political Violence at the University of St. Andrews, Scotland. A regional specialist on the Indian Ocean, Lehr focuses his teaching and research on maritime safety and security (including piracy and maritime terrorism), political violence and terrorism, and organized crime. He is the editor of *Violence at Sea: Piracy in the Age of Global Terrorism* (2007) and the coeditor (with Rupert Herbert-Burns and Sam Bateman) of *Lloyd's MIU Handbook of Maritime Security* (2009). Currently, he is working on a book on piracy from ancient to modern times. He earned his PhD from the University of Heidelberg, Germany.

ERIC MOSKOWITZ is associate professor of political science and urban studies at the College of Wooster, Wooster, Ohio. His research interests center on presidential decision making, the public policy-making process, and racial politics. He has also published on housing and neighborhood policy and contemporary U.S. decision making on foreign policy. He received his PhD from Indiana University.

ÖZGÜR ÖZDAMAR is an assistant professor in the Department of International Relations at Bilkent University, Turkey. His research interests include foreign policy analysis, international relations theories, and energy security. He also specializes in Middle Eastern and Black Sea politics.

RODGER A. PAYNE is professor of political science at the University of Louisville and director of the Grawemeyer Award for Ideas Improving World Order. His research interests include U.S. foreign policy, global environmental politics, and state policy responses to nuclear and biological weapons proliferation. He is the coauthor (with Nayef H. Samhat) of *Democratizing Global Politics* (2004). He holds a PhD from the University of Maryland, College Park.

SEAN PAYNE is a doctoral candidate in the School of Urban and Public Affairs at the University of Louisville. His research interests include environmental politics, international development, and urban policy.

THOMAS PRESTON is professor of political science at Washington State University and a Faculty Research Associate at the Moynihan Institute of Global Affairs at the Maxwell School, Syracuse University, and at CRISMART (the National Center for Crisis Management, Research, and Training), part of the Swedish National Defense College in Stockholm, Sweden. His research interests focus on security studies, foreign affairs, and political psychology. He is the author of *The President and His Inner Circle: Leadership Style and the Advisory Process in Foreign Affairs* (2001) and *From Lambs to Lions: Future Security Relationships in a World of Biological and Nuclear Weapons* (2007/2009) and coauthor of *Introduction to Political Psychology* (2004/2010). He holds a PhD from Ohio State University.

MARC R. ROSENBLUM is associate professor of political science at the University of New Orleans and a senior policy analyst at the Migration Policy Institute (MPI) in Washington, D.C. In 2006 Rosenblum was a Council on Foreign Relations Fellow detailed to the office of Sen. Edward Kennedy during the Senate immigration debate, and he was involved in crafting the Senate's immigration legislation in 2006 and 2007, before serving as a member of President Obama's Immigration Policy Transition Team in 2009. His current work at MPI focuses on the U.S. immigration policy debate, migration and U.S. labor markets, and U.S.-Mexican and U.S.-regional migration issues. Rosenblum is the author of a 2004 book, *The Transnational Politics of U.S. Immigration Policy*, and more than twenty-five academic journal articles, book chapters, and policy briefs on immigration, immigration policy, and U.S.-Latin American relations. He is currently completing a book on the history of U.S. immigration policy, and is the coeditor of the forthcoming *Oxford University Press Handbook of International Migration*.

JAMES M. SCOTT is a professor and department head of political science at Oklahoma State University. He is the coauthor (with Ralph G. Carter) of *Choosing to Lead: Understanding Congressional Foreign Policy Entrepreneurs* (2009) and the author, coauthor, or editor of four other books and more than forty articles, chapters, and other publications. A former president of both the International Studies Association's Midwest Region (2000) and its Foreign Policy Analysis Section (2001), he is currently a coeditor of *Foreign Policy Analysis*.

Introduction

Ralph G. Carter

The Greek philosopher Heraclitus may have been the first person to put in writing the notion that "the only constant is change."[1] Since the days of the Greek city-states, foreign policy has involved reacting to both threats and opportunities that arise in a changing international environment. However, the pace of those changes in the international system has varied considerably over time. From 1947–1989, there were only incremental changes in the issues typically perceived as most important by U.S. foreign policy makers. The cold war rivalry dominated their discussions, and regardless of the subjects involved, most foreign policy–related issues sooner or later came down to the question: How does this affect our relations with the Soviet Union and its allies?[2]

When the cold war rivalry ended with the fall of the Berlin Wall and the fragmentation of the Soviet Union, some expected a new international system marked by more harmonious relationships among states. Instead, a period of rapid and at times violent change ensued. Fundamental questions arose about how to deal with Russia and the former Soviet republics. Were they friends, allies, competitors, or rivals? Without the glue of anticommunism as a bond, the United States and its traditional allies and trading partners faced the task of forging similar new relationships. Again, fundamental questions arose: Should NATO continue to expand? What should the U.S. relationship be with the European Union? Were EU states friends or "friendly competitors"? What were the United States' interests in, and thus relationships with, the nations of Africa, Asia, and Latin America?

Global issues that had long been overshadowed by the cold war now moved to the forefront of U.S. foreign policy. How should the United States react to regional conflicts, the challenges involved in nation building, attempted genocide, poverty, and threats to the environment? How much should the United States depend on international organizations in the pursuit of its goals? What place should international actors like NATO, the United Nations, the World Bank, the World Trade Organization, and the

International Monetary Fund have in U.S. foreign policy? Should the United States lead these international organizations, or should it act as a "first among equals" in a team-like environment?

The September 11, 2001, terrorist attacks on New York City and the Pentagon brought home the message that many of those beyond U.S. borders were fundamentally opposed to the main currents of U.S. foreign policy, if not to the basic themes in U.S. culture itself. If Americans thereafter needed any additional reminders that all are affected by events in other countries, the consequences of the global recession of 2007–2009 reiterated that message.

As the international environment has changed, so have U.S. foreign policy processes. These changes in the internal policy-making process are as evident as the changes in the external environment. Understanding the dynamics of this process is the goal of this volume.

The "Old" Foreign Policy System

With the exception of a few periods of "thaw," the cold war dominated U.S. foreign policy from 1947 until the fall of the Soviet Union in late 1991. The threat of nuclear war between the U.S.- and Soviet-led blocs put a premium on national security policy, and the U.S. foreign policy process evolved to meet that threat. As commander in chief, the president was at the heart of this process. Moreover, the National Security Act of 1947 gave the chief executive considerable assistance by creating a unified Defense Department as well as the Central Intelligence Agency, National Security Council, and the post of national security adviser.

Not surprisingly during this period, the focus of the policy-making process became the presidency and the executive branch. This process was well represented by the presidential preeminence model of foreign policy making, which views foreign policy as the result of decisions and actions by the president and his closest advisers and relevant other officials in the executive branch.[3] Other theoretical approaches were developed within the presidential preeminence model to reflect the processes by which presidential administrations made foreign policy. These included seeing their actions and decisions as:

- optimal choices of a rational calculation of costs and benefits;
- choices between various bureaucratic routines appropriate to the situation; or
- the result of political processes played out within the administration by actors with differing degrees of power and interests in a particular issue.[4]

Members of Congress, interest groups, the media, and the public were seen as playing little or no role in the making of foreign policy.[5]

The "New" Foreign Policy System

The post–cold war era triggered changes in the ways in which U.S. foreign policy is made. With the exception of the war power, the ability of the president to play a predominant role in shaping policy diminished, and the roles played by a host of other actors increased.[6] Two factors were crucial to these changes. First, the global economy became more interdependent, and decisions made elsewhere had greater influence on the United States. In short, intermestic issues—those that occur in the international environment but are reacted to as if they are domestic policy issues—are more common than was previously the case. Take, for example, the possible ways of formulating policy toward China: Should U.S. policy be defined primarily as national security policy, thus mobilizing the State and Defense Departments to rein in China's ability to threaten U.S. security interests? Should it increasingly be defined as trade policy, mobilizing officials in the Commerce Department, national and state chambers of commerce, trade groups, and U.S.-based multinational corporations that want to sell more to the enormous Chinese market? Should China policy be defined as monetary policy, thus empowering the Treasury Department and possibly the Federal Reserve to be major players? Should China policy be seen as "jobs policy," thus mobilizing members of the Labor Department and labor unions, whose members and leaders fear the loss of U.S. jobs to lower-paid Chinese workers? Should it be defined as human rights policy, thus mobilizing the State Department's under secretary for global affairs (under whose jurisdiction human rights issues fall) and such interest groups as Amnesty International, Human Rights Watch, and Freedom House? In short, how an issue is defined determines who will play active roles in the resolution of the matter.

Second, during the cold war foreign and national security policy was deemed too important and too risky to let nonexperts play a significant role. Primary policy-making actors included the president, his close White House advisers, and key officials from the foreign and defense bureaucracies—the members of the National Security Council and their staff, the State Department, the Defense Department, and the Central Intelligence Agency and other parts of the intelligence community. Congressional and public roles were generally relegated to supporting the actions of the White House, except in those instances of a major policy mistake or when no policy emerged from the White House.[7]

With the exception of protecting the United States from al Qaeda and its supporters, there is now no clear domestic political consensus regarding the central aims of U.S. foreign policy. Without widely shared norms to exclude their participation, more and more domestic actors can be expected to try to shape foreign policy. Hence one can expect more foreign policy activity by members of Congress through legislation and other actions that administrations often resent (such as holding critical committee hearings, using oversight roles to monitor the administration's foreign policy performance, requiring extensive briefings and reports by administration actors, and making speeches critical of administration policy). Members of the opposition party can particularly be expected to challenge the president's foreign policy in terms of ends pursued and means employed. Interest groups and other nongovernmental organizations will become more involved as well, lobbying government officials on behalf of their policy preferences, using the written and electronic media to get their policy positions before the public and government officials, engaging in letter-writing campaigns to influence officials, using campaign contributions to help friendly officials get elected, and so on. Members of the media and other pundits will use their access to editorial pages, television, and the expanding constellation of news and information outlets to influence foreign policy in their preferred direction. Grassroots activists, online bloggers, public opinion pollsters, and others who claim to represent the public will also become involved. Even the ability of the president to control his own administration may weaken, as bureaucratic actors become more active in policy making or find themselves the targets of other actors.[8]

Thus the unifying theme of this volume is that the U.S. foreign policy process is becoming more open, more pluralistic, and more intensely partisan. It resembles more the decade leading up to World War II than the four decades that followed the war. One leading scholar summarizes the current period as follows:

> [T]here now seems to be a *post–cold war dissensus* predicated on societal disagreement on the nature and extent of U.S. leadership, policy disagreement on the proper role, strategy, goals, and instruments of U.S. foreign policy, and procedural decentralization away from presidential leadership to more widely diffused involvement of actors from a wider circle of bureaucratic agencies, members of Congress, and nongovernmental actors.[9]

In short, the foreign policy process is becoming more like the domestic policy process, and thus it is becoming more political. As President Bill Clinton said in

1995, "The more time I spend on foreign policy . . . the more I become convinced that there is no longer a clear distinction between what is foreign and domestic."[10] More actors are involved, and they have their own foreign policy needs, interests, and agendas. Although the president still has impressive formal and informal foreign policy roles and powers, he is now less able to dominate foreign policy processes and outcomes than was the case during the cold war.[11] Presidential foreign policy "wins" may be less frequent than previously was the case, and they will almost always represent hard-fought victories.

A number of other themes unify this volume. Jurisdictional competition between the president and Congress over the control and direction of foreign policy is commonplace. Even members of the president's own party will resist his policies if they think the White House is trampling on the legitimate jurisdictional responsibilities of Congress to legislate policy or appropriate funds. The opposition party can be expected to challenge the president's wishes, and does so often. For example, during the 1990s congressional Republicans developed a visceral dislike for President Clinton. It seemed that Republican Party leaders Trent Lott, Dick Armey, and Tom DeLay, along with powerful committee chair Jesse Helms, opposed nearly anything Clinton supported. White House scandals, including the Monica Lewinsky affair and allegations of illegal campaign contributions, gave critics another reason to oppose Clinton's policy goals. The high-water mark of their opposition was Clinton's impeachment. More recently, the Democratically controlled Congress of 2006–2008 seemed just as skeptical of the George W. Bush administration, particularly when the White House refused to share requested information and documents with Congress or invoked executive privilege in the face of congressional subpoenas to get top administrative officials to testify under oath on Capitol Hill. Now, in the Obama era, former vice president Dick Cheney has been quick to criticize many of the new president's foreign and national security policy decisions, and many congressional Republicans have done so as well. Partisan attacks between the two branches cannot help but strain the policy-making process. The themes discussed here reveal some of the chinks in the presidential preeminence model of policy making.

The Case Study Approach

One often hears statements like "Today Washington announced . . ." or "The United States responded by. . .". Such pronouncements obscure the fact that individuals "announce" and decide how to "respond." Saying "The United

States decided to do *X*" is shorthand for the more accurate statement that a number of people acting in the name of the state decided to do *X*, usually for a variety of different reasons. Case studies are perhaps the best way to illustrate how such individuals cooperate, compete, and often compromise in order to produce foreign policy.

The fifteen studies that comprise this volume are teaching cases. The definition of a teaching case is that it tells the story of what happened, "who was involved, what they contended with, and, sometimes, how it came out."[12] Rather than provide analysis of why things happened as they did, teaching cases rely on the reader to determine why individuals took the stances or engaged in the actions discussed. They vividly illustrate how policy making brings together individuals who see matters from different perspectives and who are motivated by an assortment of goals and objectives. Such cases also help show that these policy makers live in a political environment in which everything affects everything else; foreign policy decisions are not made in a vacuum. They affect and are affected by other foreign and domestic policy issues at the time the policy is devised and into the foreseeable future. Like the rest of the political process, foreign policy making can be a messy affair, and case studies help illustrate the process realistically.

One advantage of the cases in this volume is their contemporary nature. Textbooks usually cover the broad themes and theoretical issues involving foreign policy making, but often do not have many contemporary illustrations of what happens or how things play out in the policy-making process. These cases focus on issues and events that confronted U.S. policy makers from the last decade of the twentieth century through the first decade of the twenty-first century. A second advantage of these studies is their range. They were chosen to represent the array of external challenges and opportunities, substantive issues, internal political situations, and policy-making dynamics that seem likely to repeatedly confront U.S. foreign policy makers in the post–cold war and post–September 11 world.

Each case study offers a unique perspective on the events, issues, and policy makers involved, but beyond their uniqueness are patterns in the influences at work. Where do the causal factors for U.S. foreign policy arise? According to realists and neorealists, the answer typically lies beyond U.S. borders. These observers see foreign policy as a state's reaction to events taking place in an international system based on anarchy and lacking a strong legal structure. In essence, states can be expected to pursue their self-defined interests in ways that are, at least at some level, rational.[13] On the other hand, advocates of liberalism argue that what happens within a state's borders also matters, often as much as (or maybe more than) the external situations foreign policy makers face. Thus for liberals and neoliberals, a central belief is "*state structures matter: the structure of their domestic governments and the values and views of their citizens affect their behavior in international affairs.*"[14] According to this point of view, one cannot ignore who is in the government, what they think, and what motivates them. In short, different administrations and Congresses will react differently to similar external events. The cases in this volume illustrate the importance of such external and internal factors and help in understanding what U.S. officials have been dealing with in the post–cold war and post–September 11 eras. In this respect, they provide a realistic understanding of how policy is actually made. They serve as reminders that people often have to make quick decisions based on less-than-complete information, and they help hone critical thinking skills in preparation for real-world situations.[15]

Each case opens with a section titled "Before You Begin," which poses questions about that particular case. These questions help in organizing thoughts and directing attention to important issues. All the cases follow a similar internal organization. Each introduces the case, provides background information, relates relevant events, and offers a conclusion that should help in identifying some of the broader issues or themes involved. Each study is accompanied by a chronology of events and a list of key actors.

Case-based teaching requires class participation. Instructors ask questions, and students are expected to discuss what happened and, more important, determine why it happened as it did. Such active learning requires that students come to class prepared to contribute to an informed discussion of the case assignment, including putting themselves in the place of the major actors in order to assess issues and events. Why did policy makers do what they did? What internal or external factors affected their decisions? Was the option selected their only option? If not, why was that option chosen over others? What could be gained, and what could be lost? Students will get the most from this approach if they come to class having carefully thought about such things in addition to having reviewed the questions in "Before You Begin." Such preparation will make for a better understanding of the real world of foreign policy making.

As the cold war was ending, some observers of international politics began speculating about the nature of the post–cold war world. Many offered the optimistic assessment that international conflict would decline, and widely shared liberal values would become the new glue of international politics.[16]

Unfortunately, violent conflict did not disappear, and versions of capitalism were embraced more widely than commitments to liberal values like democracy and human rights.[17] U.S. foreign policy still consequently must deal with difficult issues involving the use of military force and how to protect national interests in an uncertain environment. The first three cases in this volume focus on matters involving U.S. decisions about whether and how to participate in military interventions. In chapter 1, Frédérick Gagnon and Ryan Hendrickson examine the efforts by the Clinton, Bush, and Obama administrations to respond to the terrorist threat represented by Osama Bin Laden and the Afghanistan Taliban. In chapter 2, Jeffrey Lantis and Eric Moskowitz review the Bush administration's efforts to employ coercive diplomacy against, and then topple, the Iraqi regime of Saddam Hussein, as well as the Obama administration's efforts to disengage from that conflict. In chapter 3, Jennifer Holmes looks at the efforts by the Clinton, Bush, and Obama administrations to stanch the flow of illegal drugs into the United States by helping the Colombian government fight drug traffickers—a decision that many felt risked U.S. involvement in Colombia's long-standing civil war and severely provoked the anti-American Chávez regime next door in Venezuela.

The next six case studies examine defense and security issues (broadly defined) facing the United States. In chapter 4, Thomas Preston and Michael Infranco chronicle the U.S. efforts to promote a negotiated settlement over Iran's nuclear weapons program, a case posing the fundamental question of whether or not a "rogue" regime should be readily engaged or made to prove its good faith first. In chapter 5, Patrick James and Özgür Özdamar examine the dynamics involved in the Clinton, Bush, and Obama administrations' efforts to confront the threat posed by North Korean nuclear weapons. In chapter 6, Ralph Carter and James Scott detail the poor relationship that developed between the United States and Russia after the end of the cold war and the Obama administration's goal to "reset" the relationship in a more positive direction. In chapter 7, Peter Lehr reveals how the problem of modern-day piracy in the waters off the Somalia coast has grown to become a serious national security and commercial threat and how the Obama administration responded to its first piracy challenge. As a response to the global terrorist threat, the Bush administration relied on warrantless wiretapping of overseas phone calls made by U.S. citizens or residents to gain intelligence information. That effort, as well as the Obama administration's efforts to reconcile national security needs and the protection of civil liberties, is the focus of Louis Fisher's work in chapter 8. In chapter 9, Marc Rosenblum details the political dynamics behind efforts by both the Bush and Obama administrations to reform U.S. immigration policy—both by those who wanted to tighten up the rules for the sake of national security and those who wanted to liberalize them in the name of fairness.

Some observers thought the post–cold war world would be an era characterized by heightened international trade, so the next selection of case studies focuses on trade issues. In chapter 10, Thomas Lairson details how the Bush and Obama administrations reacted to the recent global economic crisis. In chapter 11, trade issues are the focus as Patrick Haney examines why the United States still maintains a trade embargo of Cuba. A range of trade-related issues come to the fore in chapter 12, where Steven Hook and Franklin Lebo look at the impact of a wide array of interest groups across the last three administrations' decisions regarding trade with China.

A more liberal world would be one marked by a greater reliance on international organizations, institutions, and law. The last section of this volume examines how U.S. approaches to multilateral policies mesh with the concerns of others in dealing with system-wide international issues. In chapter 13, Rodger Payne and Sean Payne focus on how the Clinton, Bush, and Obama administrations have reacted to the challenges of global climate change. In chapter 14, Donald Jackson and Ralph Carter illustrate the Clinton, Bush, and Obama administrations' political dilemma when faced with the issue of how to react to the creation of the new International Criminal Court and the possibility that U.S. citizens might be tried before it for war crimes, crimes against humanity, or genocide. In chapter 15, Linda Cornett and Mark Gibney trace the evolution of Bush administration decisions concerning the detention of "enemy combatants" captured in the "war on terrorism" and how the Obama administration has sought to modify those controversial decisions.

These cases represent the wide range of actors, interests, and issues comprising contemporary U.S. foreign policy. The conclusion returns to the book's primary unifying theme—that in the post–cold war period, U.S. foreign policy making is becoming increasingly open, pluralistic, and partisan. New issues have made their way onto the policy agenda, and many newcomers—agencies, interests, and constituencies—have become involved in addressing them. In short, U.S. foreign policy making looks increasingly like U.S. domestic policy making, and in a world marked by increasing interdependencies among states, perhaps that is to be expected.

Notes

1. See "The Only Thing Constant Is Change," *The Daily Philosopher*, www.thedaily philosopher.org/daily/000011.php.

2. Richard Melanson, *American Foreign Policy since the Vietnam War: The Search for Consensus from Richard Nixon to George W. Bush,* 4th ed. (Armonk, N.Y.: M. E. Sharpe, 2005).

3. James M. Scott and A. Lane Crothers, "Out of the Cold: The Post–Cold War Context of U.S. Foreign Policy," in *After the End: Making U.S. Foreign Policy in the Post–Cold War World,* ed. James M. Scott (Durham: Duke University Press, 1998), 1–25.

4. Graham Allison and Philip Zelikow, *Essence of Decision: Explaining the Cuban Missile Crisis,* 2nd ed. (New York: Longman, 1999).

5. See, for example, Samuel P. Huntington, *The Common Defense: Strategic Programs in National Politics* (New York: Columbia University Press, 1961); Roger Hilsman, *To Move a Nation* (New York: Doubleday, 1967); Morton Halperin, *Bureaucratic Politics and Foreign Policy* (Washington, D.C.: Brookings Institution, 1974); John Steinbruner, *The Cybernetic Theory of Decision: New Dimensions of Political Analysis* (Princeton: Princeton University Press, 1974); Roger Hilsman, *The Politics of Policy Making in Defense and Foreign Affairs,* 2nd ed. (Englewood Cliffs, N.J.: Prentice Hall, 1990); and Allison and Zelikow, *Essence of Decision.*

6. See Ralph G. Carter and James M. Scott, *Choosing to Lead: Understanding Congressional Foreign Policy Entrepreneurs* (Durham: Duke University Press, 2009); James M. Lindsay and Randall B. Ripley, "How Congress Influences Foreign and Defense Policy," in *Congress Resurgent: Foreign and Defense Policy on Capitol Hill,* ed. Randall B. Ripley and James M. Lindsay (Ann Arbor: University of Michigan Press, 1993), 17–35; James M. Lindsay, *Congress and the Politics of U.S. Foreign Policy* (Baltimore: Johns Hopkins University Press, 1994); and virtually all of the selections in Scott, *After the End.*

7. For more on policy vacuums and policy corrections, see Carter and Scott, *Choosing to Lead.*

8. Scott and Crothers, "Out of the Cold"; James M. Scott, "Interbranch Policy Making after the End," in Scott, *After the End,* 389–407.

9. Scott, "Interbranch Policy Making after the End," 405.

10. Quoted in Ralph G. Carter, "Congress and Post–Cold War U.S. Foreign Policy," in Scott, *After the End,* 129–130.

11. See Carter, "Congress and Post–Cold War U.S. Foreign Policy"; Jerel Rosati and Stephen Twing, "The Presidency and U.S. Foreign Policy after the Cold War," in Scott, *After the End,* 29–56.

12. John Boehrer, quoted in Vicki L. Golich, "The ABCs of Case Teaching," *International Studies Perspectives* 1 (2000): 12.

13. There are lots of sources for realism and neorealism. For reasonably concise discussions of these topics, see David A. Lake, "Realism," in *The Oxford Companion to Politics of the World,* ed. Joel Krieger (Oxford: Oxford University Press, 1993), 771–773; or Allison and Zelikow, *Essence of Decision,* 30–33.

14. Allison and Zelikow, *Essence of Decision,* 39 (emphasis in original).

15. Laurence E. Lynn Jr., *Teaching and Learning with Cases: A Guidebook* (New York: Chatham House Publishers/Seven Bridges Press, 1999), 2.

16. See Francis Fukuyama, "The End of History?" *National Interest* 16 (Summer 1989): 3–16.

17. See Samuel P. Huntington, *The Clash of Civilizations and the Remaking of World Order* (New York: Simon and Schuster, 1996).

1 The United States versus Terrorism: From the Embassy Bombings in Tanzania and Kenya to the Surge in Afghanistan

Frédérick Gagnon and Ryan C. Hendrickson

Before You Begin

1. What is the traditionally accepted view of Congress's exercise of war powers during the cold war and after September 11, 2001? How does that view compare to Congress's role leading up to military action in 1998, 2001, and 2009?

2. In the days prior to military action in 1998, 2001, and 2009, how did the diplomatic challenges differ for Presidents Bill Clinton, George W. Bush, and Barack Obama?

3. Is Congress's decision to endorse military action against those involved in the September 11 attacks a victory for Congress's war powers? If so, why?

4. Which advisers seem to have the most significant influence on Presidents Clinton, Bush, and Obama's decisions regarding terrorism and Afghanistan? Why?

5. Did President Clinton's military action in 1998 have a "diversionary" intent? What evidence supports such a view? What evidence challenges it?

Introduction: Striking Back at Terrorism

The public, the media, and most members of Congress sometimes are not privy to the process in which U.S. use of force decisions are made. Although Presidents Bill Clinton, George W. Bush, and Barack Obama appear to have vastly different interests in policy matters, and certainly have divergent views of the appropriate role for the United States in international affairs, many similarities exist in the ways they made decisions as commander in chief. On August 20, 1998, when Clinton launched missile strikes against alleged facilities of Osama Bin Laden in Sudan and Afghanistan, and on October 7, 2001, when Bush set in motion Operation Enduring Freedom against the Taliban and al Qaeda in Afghanistan, nearly all the critical military decisions were made by the executive branch. In 2009 Obama's "strategic review" of

Bush's Afghanistan policy and decision to expand the war on terrorism in Afghanistan and Pakistan were also made primarily by the executive branch, with limited input from other actors. Unlike many other foreign policy issues in the post–cold war and post-9/11 environments, the center of action concerning terrorism is the White House.

Background: Terrorism and Presidential Powers

The U.S. Constitution grants Congress the power to declare war, as well as other enumerated powers associated with the military. The president is given the explicit authority to act as commander in chief. Most constitutional scholars agree, however, that the president is empowered to use force without congressional approval to "repel sudden attacks" against the United States.[1] In other instances, the president must obtain Congress's approval prior to using force.

For much of U.S. history, Congress's war powers have been respected by the commander in chief.[2] With the cold war's onset and the widely accepted belief that the Soviet Union and communism represented a threat to the United States, the president's perception of his power as commander in chief became increasingly one of omnipotence. Since 1945 presidents have asserted broad military powers with few recognized limitations. Because members of Congress agreed that communism should be checked, and because it was politically safer to let a president assume full responsibility for U.S. military endeavors, Congress often deferred to executive branch unilateralism in actions by the president as commander in chief.[3] This practice remained the norm until the 1973 passage of the War Powers Resolution, which was designed to reassert the authority that many felt Presidents Lyndon Johnson and Richard Nixon had usurped from Congress during the Vietnam War.[4] The resolution requires that the president "consult with Congress in every possible circumstance" prior to and after the introduction of U.S. forces into hostilities (P.L. 93-148). Despite its intent, the War Powers Resolution has been a failure. All presidents since 1973 have maintained that it is unconstitutional—arguing that it illegally limits their power as commander in chief—and Congress has often failed to enforce it.[5] The Clinton presidency is a good example of this dynamic. Clinton viewed his powers as commander in chief broadly, maintaining that congressional approval was not required for him to take military action.[6] Clinton's outlook is evidenced by U.S. military actions against Iraq, NATO air strikes in Bosnia and Kosovo, military deployments to Haiti and Somalia, and the use of force against Bin Laden, all of which occurred without specific congressional approval.

U.S. Embassy Bombings in Tanzania and Kenya: Clinton Strikes Osama Bin Laden

On August 7, 1998, 263 people, including 12 Americans, were killed in simultaneous truck bomb explosions at the U.S. embassies in Nairobi, Kenya, and Dar es Salaam, Tanzania. Immediately after the bombings, experts from the Federal Bureau of Investigation (FBI) and the Central Intelligence Agency (CIA) rushed to East Africa to determine responsibility for the attacks. The evidence quickly pointed to Osama Bin Laden, a name most Americans had never heard of but who was no stranger to the U.S. intelligence community. Bin Laden was born in 1957 into a wealthy, conservative family in Saudi Arabia with connections to the Al Saud, the Saudi royal family. In the 1980s, he left Saudi Arabia to go to Afghanistan and support the *mujahidin,* the fighters who were resisting the Soviet takeover and occupation of Afghanistan with critical military assistance from the United States. Toward the end of the Afghan war, Bin Laden established an organization of radical Muslims that would become the foundation for al Qaeda, a network of supporters willing to advance their fundamentalist version of Islam using any means necessary. He then moved to Saudi Arabia and Sudan and was suspected of being involved in the bombing of the World Trade Center in New York City in February 1993. The State Department added al Qaeda to its list of terrorist organizations in 1997. One of the first statements by Bin Laden to generate international attention occurred on August 23, 1996, when he publicly issued a *fatwa,* or decree (usually by a recognized religious leader), calling for a *jihad* (struggle or holy war) against the United States to oppose its military presence in Saudi Arabia that began with the 1991 Persian Gulf War. In 1998 Bin Laden once again caught the eye of the world when on February 23 he issued a second *fatwa* in a fax to a London-based Arabic newsletter. In the communication, he made three central points: the United States should leave the Muslim holy land; the United States should end the "great devastation inflicted" upon the Iraqi people through its continuation of economic sanctions; and the United States was engaged in a religious and economic war against Muslims, while simultaneously serving Israel's interests vis-à-vis the Muslim world. The truck bombings at the U.S. embassies in Kenya and Tanzania occurred less than six months later.

A week after the attacks, on August 14, Director of Central Intelligence (DCI) George Tenet presented his agency's analysis—a "judgment about responsibility"—to President Clinton. According to the CIA, additional evidence suggested that Bin Laden was planning another attack on Americans and that an important gathering of Bin Laden associates would take place in

Timeline

The Clinton, Bush, and Obama Administrations' Strikes against Osama Bin Laden

August 23, 1996	Osama Bin Laden issues his first *fatwa* against the United States.
February 23, 1998	Bin Laden issues his second *fatwa* against the United States.
August 7, 1998	Bombs explode at the U.S. embassies in Nairobi, Kenya, and Dar es Salaam, Tanzania.
August 14, 1998	Director of Central Intelligence George Tenet presents his agency's assessment that Bin Laden and his al Qaeda network were behind the attacks on the embassies.
August 17, 1998	President Bill Clinton admits to the nation that he misled the public about having an extramarital relationship with White House intern Monica Lewinsky.
August 20, 1998	In a 2:00 a.m. telephone conversation with national security adviser Sandy Berger, Clinton authorizes strikes against Bin Laden. Missiles are launched on alleged al Qaeda sites in Afghanistan and Sudan.
Mid-September 1999	The Clinton administration initiates "the plan," consisting of broader covert operations intended to gather intelligence on Bin Laden and disrupt al Qaeda.
October 12, 2000	Al Qaeda launches a suicide boat attack against the USS *Cole* while it is docked in Aden, Yemen. Seventeen Americans are killed.
September 11, 2001	Al Qaeda operatives hijack four commercial aircraft, flying two into the World Trade Center towers and crashing another into the Pentagon. The fourth aircraft crashes in a field in Pennsylvania. The death toll is 2,995.
September 14, 2001	The Senate passes S.J. Res. 23, authorizing George W. Bush to use all necessary and appropriate force against those associated with the September 11 strikes on the United

	States. The House of Representatives responds the following day by passing the resolution.
September 15–16, 2001	President Bush holds meetings with foreign policy principals at Camp David to discuss military operations in retaliation for the September 11 attacks.
October 6, 2001	Bush gives final approval for military action against Afghanistan.
October 7, 2001	The United States launches Operation Enduring Freedom against the Taliban and al Qaeda in Afghanistan.
December 7, 2001	The Taliban lose Kandahar, the last major city under its control.
August 2003	NATO takes control of security in Kabul, its first-ever operational commitment outside Europe.
October 2006	NATO assumes responsibility for security across the whole of Afghanistan, taking command in the east from a U.S.-led coalition force.
April 2008	NATO leaders meeting in Bucharest say peacekeeping mission in Afghanistan is their top priority. They pledge a "firm and shared long-term commitment" there.
September 2008	President Bush sends an extra 4,500 U.S. troops to Afghanistan, in a move he described as a "quiet surge."
February 2009	President Barack Obama announces the dispatch of seventeen thousand extra U.S. troops in Afghanistan.
March 2009	President Obama unveils a new U.S. strategy for Afghanistan and Pakistan to combat what he calls an increasingly perilous situation.
December 2009	President Obama announces the dispatch of thirty thousand extra U.S. troops in Afghanistan. He also declares that the United States will begin withdrawing its forces by 2011.[a]
June 2010	Gen. Stanley McChrystal is relieved of command of American and NATO forces in Afghanistan.

[a] For a complete timeline, read BBC, "Timeline: Afghanistan," http://news.bbc.co.uk/2/hi/1162108.stm.

Afghanistan on August 20, 1998. At the meeting with Tenet, Clinton gave tentative approval to a military response and authorized his senior military advisers to move forward with operational plans.[7]

The bombings and their aftermath occurred at a difficult time for Clinton. On August 17, he testified to the Office of the Independent Counsel and a grand jury, by videoconferencing, that he had had an extramarital relationship with former White House intern Monica Lewinsky. Later that evening, in a national address, Clinton admitted that he had "misled" the American people about his relationship with Lewinsky.[8] After his address, Clinton and his family left for a vacation, but planning continued for military strikes against Bin Laden. On Wednesday, August 19, while on Martha's Vineyard, Clinton discussed the strikes with Vice President Al Gore. Senior leaders in Congress were also notified of possible military action. Throughout the day, Clinton spoke on four occasions by phone with his national security adviser, Samuel "Sandy" Berger, who was in Washington. In a call around 2:00 a.m. Thursday, Clinton gave final approval for the strikes.

Beginning on August 20 around 1:30 p.m. EST, seventy-nine cruise missiles were launched at targets in Sudan and Afghanistan from ships stationed in the Arabian and Red Seas. The Sudanese targets included the al-Shifa pharmaceutical plant, which the United States alleged was a chemical weapons factory. Six other sites were struck simultaneously in Afghanistan. Secretary of Defense William Cohen declared that al-Shifa was chosen because Bin Laden was heavily involved in Sudan's military-industrial complex and had an interest in acquiring chemical weapons.[9] In discussing the sites hit in Afghanistan, Gen. Henry Shelton, chairman of the Joint Chiefs of Staff, said that one "base camp" that served as the headquarters for Bin Laden's organization was struck.

Approximately twenty-five minutes after the strikes, Clinton addressed the nation, providing four justifications for his actions. First, he announced that "convincing evidence" pointed to Bin Laden's responsibility for the attacks on the embassies. Second, the president pointed to Bin Laden's history of terrorist activities. Third, Clinton argued that "compelling information" suggested that Bin Laden was planning another attack against the United States. Fourth, he said that Bin Laden sought to acquire chemical weapons.[10] In a second address to the nation later that evening, Clinton expanded on Bin Laden's previous declarations and activities and said that his senior military advisers had given him a "unanimous recommendation" to go forward with the strikes.[11] In mentioning the unanimous recommendation Clinton may have been anticipating the reaction from the public, 40 percent of whom believed that the Monica

Lewinsky scandal may have influenced the decision to strike. Administration officials responded vehemently with denials that any link existed between the president's domestic troubles and the strikes at Bin Laden.[12] Though many Americans thought the "Lewinsky factor" may have entered into the decision to use force, 75 percent still supported the strikes.[13]

Consulting Congress

The night before the attacks, Berger phoned Speaker of the House Newt Gingrich, R-Ga., and Senate Majority Leader Trent Lott, R-Miss., and presented them with the evidence implicating Bin Laden. Senate Minority Leader Tom Daschle, D-S.D., also received a phone call before the strikes.[14] Berger attempted to call House Minority Leader Richard Gephardt, D-Mo., who was traveling in France. Clinton also phoned these leaders, with the exception of Gephardt, as he flew back to Washington to deliver his second address to the nation.[15] DCI Tenet notified, at minimum, Sen. Bob Kerrey, D-Neb., a member of the Senate Intelligence Committee, in advance of the strikes, which Kerrey strongly supported.[16] Other reports contend that Gingrich had been consulted and was privy to intelligence on Bin Laden before Berger's first phone calls were made.[17]

In retrospect, it is clear that the most senior leaders in Congress of both parties knew of the impending strikes. White House spokesperson Michael McCurry purposely noted that all requirements of the War Powers Resolution were met, including its consultation mandate.[18] In the aftermath of Clinton's strikes against Bin Laden there were no complaints about violations of the War Powers Resolution or Congress's war-making powers. Congress gave broad support to the president on constitutional grounds.

Although these strikes were the last overt military effort to kill Bin Laden before the terrorist attacks of September 11, 2001, the Clinton administration did not give up the hunt for Bin Laden. Before Clinton left office, he authorized five different intelligence operations aimed at disrupting al Qaeda's planning and preempting terrorist activities.[19]

The most comprehensive intelligence operation was known simply as "the plan" and went into effect around mid-September 1999. The plan sought to focus more attention on human intelligence gathering and expand the CIA's efforts to recruit well-qualified operatives who could be placed on the ground in Afghanistan to gather intelligence on Bin Laden. Another critical element of the plan was to develop and use the Predator, an unmanned aerial vehicle with intelligence-gathering and military strike capabilities. On at least two occasions before September 11, and perhaps a third, the Predator sighted Bin Laden.[20] Former counterterrorism coordinator Richard A. Clarke maintains that on Clinton's orders, the United States had submarines in place with cruise missiles ready for use against Bin Laden, but apparently not at times when "actionable intelligence" and military capability existed at the same time.[21]

From a policy-making perspective, the National Commission on Terrorist Attacks Upon the United States, or the 9/11 Commission, made one especially important finding regarding the Clinton administration's counterterrorism policies: Senior officials of the National Security Council (NSC) and the CIA "differ[ed] starkly" in their assessment of the administration's objectives in regard to Bin Laden and therefore what types of actions they should be pursuing. NSC staffers, including Berger, maintained that the administration's policies were clear; authorization had been given to kill Bin Laden. In contrast, CIA officials asserted that the administration had sought the capture of Bin Laden and that only under certain conditions could he be killed.[22] Although misunderstandings or differences existed among key agencies regarding the effort to get Bin Laden, it is clear that the center of action for counterterrorism decisions and use of force was at the White House, with critical assistance provided by the CIA, and that military action was the preferred means of addressing these newfound terrorist challenges.

September 11: Authorization of Force and the War on Terrorism

President George W. Bush was made aware of the events that unfolded on September 11 while visiting with children at Emma E. Booker Elementary School in Sarasota, Florida. Upon hearing that an aircraft had crashed into the Pentagon, Bush later said, he thought to himself, "We're at war. . . . Somebody is going to pay."[23] After the session with the children ended, Bush's Secret Service detail quickly escorted him to *Air Force One*. As it was not considered safe to fly the president back to Washington immediately, Bush was flown to Offut Air Force Base in Omaha, Nebraska. From there, he spoke by phone with members of his National Security Council, including DCI Tenet, who reported that Osama Bin Laden was behind the attacks.[24] By early evening, Bush was back at the White House, where deliberations began on how to address the crisis.

The constitutional dynamics and the authority of the president to respond to the September 11 attacks with military action were considerably different from Clinton's strikes against Afghanistan in 1998. Because the United States was directly attacked on its soil, most constitutional experts would concur that the Constitution allowed Bush, as commander in chief, to respond with force in defense of the nation. In addition, Article 51 of the United Nations Charter permits all member states to act in self-defense if attacked.[25] The Bush administration, however, quickly turned to Congress for formal authorization for the use of force. The public was strongly in favor of a military response, and by approaching Congress the administration could avoid raising constitutional questions about the legitimacy of its forthcoming military actions. At the same time, legitimate constitutional questions existed in terms of whom the United States would be at war with. Part of the difficulty of this issue is that the enemy is not easily defined, identified, or targeted.

When Bush administration officials first met with congressional leaders and their senior staff members on September 12, congressional staffers were initially struck by the sweeping nature of the administration's force authorization proposal. Its request included the authority to "deter and pre-empt any future acts of terrorism or aggression against the United States" and essentially unrestricted financial resources for military responses, which would infringe on Congress's constitutional authority to appropriate money.[26] Key legislators, such as Senate Majority Leader Daschle and Sen. Robert C. Byrd, D-W.Va., thought it was Congress's duty to avoid giving the president "a blank check to go anywhere, anytime, against anyone."[27] During deliberations over the language of the resolution, administration officials agreed to eliminate *pre-empt* and replace it with *prevent*.[28] The request for unlimited spending powers was deleted.[29] As of late evening on September 13, final agreement on the resolution language had not been reached.[30]

On the morning of September 14, Daschle and Senate Minority Leader Lott met with their respective caucuses. Later that morning, the Senate approved, 98–0, S.J. Res. 23 (P.L. 107-40), granting the president sweeping powers to initiate military action. The key provision of the resolution concerning force authorization stated:

> That the President is authorized to use all necessary and appropriate force against those nations, organizations, or persons he determines planned, authorized, committed, or aided the terrorist attacks that occurred on September 11, 2001, or harbored such organizations or persons, in order to prevent any future acts of international terrorism against the United States by such organizations or persons.

The process by which this resolution was crafted and eventually voted on is uncharacteristic in that it was not passed from a formal committee of the

House or Senate, and there was no public debate on the constitutional merits of the resolution. The White House consulted with Congress and revised its original proposal based on congressional input, but all in private sessions. A day after the Senate approved the resolution the House did so as well, in a 420–1 vote. Rep. Barbara Lee, D-Calif., was the only member of Congress who voted against the measure, maintaining that it provided a "blank check" to the president and granted him "overly broad powers."[31]

In most cases, senators and representatives commented on the resolution after the vote. A number of senior Democratic senators heralded the resolution as a victory for the principle of checks and balances. There is no doubt that Congress forced some important changes in the resolution's language, exercised and demanded its constitutional prerogatives on appropriations, and even inserted a reference to the War Powers Resolution. Congress also limited the administration's military response to only those "nations, organizations, or persons" associated with the September 11 attacks. These "congressional demands" were noted by senators Carl Levin, D-Mich., and Joseph Biden, D-Del., among others.[32] Regardless, the resolution language remained quite broad and granted considerable discretion to the president to determine who is responsible for the attacks and how an organization or individuals may be related to the events of September 11. It was easy to interpret the resolution in a number of equally legitimate ways. The process was constitutional, with the White House seeking congressional authority to act and the House and Senate voting to grant such authority. At the same time, however, some observers maintain that Congress abdicated much of its war power through the resolution's broad and ambiguous language and by granting the president excessive discretion as commander in chief.[33]

These interactions appear to be the last instance prior to the decision to use force against Afghanistan and al Qaeda when Congress played a substantive role. It is difficult to find any meaningful congressional input between the House vote on September 15 and the initiation of Operation Enduring Freedom on October 7, where a member of Congress had a role in determining whom to go to war against or when to respond militarily.

Whom to Strike

When administration officials first met with the president to discuss the September 11 attacks and devise a response, there was a great deal of confusion and difference of opinion over what should be done.[34] The first weekend following the attacks, Bush convened the principals at Camp David to begin planning for a broad war on terrorism. On the first day of the meetings,

Saturday, September 15, Secretary of Defense Donald Rumsfeld and Deputy Secretary of Defense Paul Wolfowitz pressed for making Iraq a target of the planned military response. Secretary of State Colin Powell made the case that Bin Laden should be the sole focus of the response, in part because he believed that international support existed for attacking Bin Laden but not Iraq. General Shelton was surprised that Iraq was even in consideration and also favored a military response only against Bin Laden. Tenet and Vice President Dick Cheney focused their attention on Bin Laden. Andrew Card, White House chief of staff, also voiced the opinion that al Qaeda should be the target of the response.[35] During these discussions, national security adviser Condoleezza Rice acted as the president's central coordinator at planning sessions. She absorbed information and views and then consulted privately with Bush on the options.[36]

Bush made the decision on September 15 to focus the administration's response on al Qaeda only. After Bush returned to the White House on Monday, September 17, he told his senior principals that Iraq would not be a target for a military response at that time. Former administration officials confirm that it was Bush's view that it was not the appropriate time to strike Iraq, although Bush felt that Iraq was somehow complicit in the September 11 attacks.[37] With Iraq no longer a target, and apparently with heavy input from George Tenet, the Taliban and al Qaeda were increasingly viewed as one entity, ending any lingering debate over whom to strike. The Taliban had come to power in 1996 and governed Afghanistan under an extreme interpretation of the *sharia,* or Islamic law.[38] It provided sanctuary for Bin Laden in 1996, when he was expelled from Sudan, and protected him after the 1998 strikes on the U.S. embassies in East Africa. The Taliban also gave him communications equipment and security guards. In exchange, Bin Laden helped the Taliban train its military and expand its political control over Afghanistan, and he also provided financial assistance to Mullah Omar, leader of the Taliban.[39]

On September 17, Bush instructed Colin Powell to issue an ultimatum to the Taliban: either turn over Bin Laden or face severe consequences from the United States. On Sunday, September 23, the CIA assessed that Mullah Omar would side with Bin Laden and refuse to give up the al Qaeda leader. That, indeed, was what happened.[40]

When to Attack

After they decided whom to attack, the question plaguing the Bush administration, and especially President Bush, was when to initiate the strikes. In the first days after September 11, Secretary Rumsfeld offered that it would take at least sixty days to get the military in place and ready for a major offensive. Gen. Tommy Franks, head of Central Command, concurred but more conservatively estimated that it could take several months.[41] President Bush wanted to be aggressive in time and strategy and avoid any comparison with President Clinton's military strikes. He felt that Clinton's strikes amounted to little more than "pounding sand" with cruise missiles.

Bush was attracted to one of the strategies presented by General Shelton. The plan Bush preferred entailed the launch of cruise missiles, air raids on Taliban and al Qaeda defenses, and the use of Special Operations Forces, and thus the insertion of "boots on the ground," all working in concert to combat al Qaeda and the Taliban. In addition, the CIA was to enlist the support of anti-Taliban groups in the northern and southern regions of Afghanistan to attack the Taliban with the assistance of Special Operations Forces and CIA operatives.

As the military plans moved forward, the need for diplomatic allies in the Middle East quickly became clear. To insert Special Operations Forces and to attack from the south, the United States needed access to military bases in the Persian Gulf. Oman, one of the best U.S. allies in the region, had assisted the Clinton administration with the use of its bases in the 1998 air strikes on Iraq. Although Oman did not immediately rush to assist the Bush administration, it ultimately agreed to lend its support, as did Bahrain and the United Arab Emirates. To Secretary Powell's surprise, Pakistani president Gen. Pervez Musharraf, who had had friendly relations with the Taliban, agreed almost immediately to Bush's multiple diplomatic, intelligence, and military requests.[42]

The biggest operational and diplomatic obstacle was securing staging areas for combat and search and rescue operations north of Afghanistan. To obtain permission to operate from military bases in some of the former Soviet republics, the administration requested the assistance of Russian president Vladimir Putin in making diplomatic overtures in the region. Putin, who exercised considerable diplomatic influence with nearly all of the former republics, agreed on the condition that U.S. actions were only temporary and did not represent a long-term military presence in the region.[43]

This Central Asian element was the final piece of the puzzle needed before a military response could be initiated. Uzbekistan—whose president, Islam Karimov, did not have good relations with President Putin—was a preferred site. In responding to the U.S. request, Karimov initially demanded NATO membership, a $50 million loan, and what amounted to a full-fledged security guarantee from the United States. Although the United States did not grant

Karimov's every wish, the Uzbeks signed on to assist the United States on October 3. The military launched its first strikes on the Taliban on October 7. The Taliban regime was brought down 102 days after the terrorist attacks of September 11, and American support for conduct of the war remained near 90 percent for the duration of the fighting in 2001.[44]

After the Initial Strikes

During the initial military strikes on the Taliban and al Qaeda in Operation Enduring Freedom in 2001, war planning directed by the White House, Secretary of Defense Donald Rumsfeld, and the commanding officer for the United States Central Command, Gen. Tommy Franks, had already begun for a possible invasion of Iraq.[45] These actions have led to the argument that U.S. war efforts in Afghanistan suffered from a lack of attention from the rest of the Bush administration, as its central foreign policy ambition and challenge focused first on removing Saddam Hussein from Iraq and then on containing the civil war that ensued in Iraq.[46] Whether this critique is accurate or not, for the remainder of Bush's presidency the U.S. military presence in Afghanistan grew steadily, reaching approximately thirty-two thousand troops by December 2008.[47] During these years, much of the Bush administration's strategic approach to Afghanistan focused on utilizing the North Atlantic Treaty Organization (NATO) to build support for the new Afghan government and on lobbying the NATO allies to conduct more aggressive combat operations against the Taliban and al Qaeda.

In the aftermath of the Taliban's immediate defeat in 2001, the United States turned to the United Nations Security Council to negotiate the presence of an international peacekeeping force in Kabul. UN Security Council Resolution 1386 permitted the presence of UN peacekeepers in Kabul, and created an International Security Assistance Force (ISAF) that sought to provide security for the interim national government. Simultaneously, while this and other diplomatic initiatives unfolded, U.S. military efforts persisted as well. One of the largest military strikes against the Taliban occurred in March 2002 in Operation Anaconda, where U.S. forces struck the Taliban in the Shahi-Kot Valley. At the time, the strikes inflicted considerable damage on Taliban forces, but by some accounts forced the Taliban into the mountainous regions of western Pakistan for refuge.[48] This migration was significant in that it gave the Taliban a new sanctuary to regroup outside of Afghanistan in a region of Pakistan outside of governmental control. This location caused tactical and diplomatic challenges for the military operation that remain in place today.

NATO's formal role in Afghanistan came at the urging of primarily Canada, Germany, and the United States, who sought a continuity of command for ISAF through NATO rather than the national leadership transitions that came under UN auspices.[49] On August 11, 2003, NATO agreed to take over ISAF. Over the next three years, the peacekeeping mission expanded to include thirteen Provincial Reconstruction Teams (PRTs), which were small groups of civilians and military personnel who spread out across northern and western sections of Afghanistan. The PRTs were deployed to help in the reconstruction of schools and roads, and more generally sought to provide support for economic growth and the national government, which eventually included approximately ten thousand troops from the NATO allies.[50]

Over the course of 2001 to 2006, the U.S. military presence grew gradually as well, as military efforts continued to focus on finding and killing members of the Taliban and al Qaeda. These efforts, though, were dwarfed by the war in Iraq that began on March 20, 2003, which generally consumed the Bush administration for the rest of its tenure. During these same years, Congress was similarly focused on Iraq and otherwise not closely tracking military events in Afghanistan, which is best characterized by the few congressional hearings devoted to Afghanistan and the limited oversight devoted to NATO operations by members of Congress.[51] Nonetheless, the Bush administration continued to work through NATO to wage this war. On July 31, 2006, after intense U.S. lobbying, NATO agreed to oversee the entirety of the Afghan military operation, which now included NATO participation in combat operations along with the PRTs. In agreeing to this revised and more extensive presence in Afghanistan, four NATO members—Canada, the Netherlands, the United Kingdom, and the United States—agreed to wage combat operations in the south. While this new policy indicated that NATO was capable of adapting to new security threats, the change also highlighted the profound differences in how each ally viewed its role in Afghanistan. Some of the allies, notably Germany and Italy, contributed hundreds of peacekeepers to more peaceful regions of Afghanistan in the north and west. These allies, along with other NATO partners, also placed "national caveats" for the kind of military engagement that their countries would permit. Such restrictions included strict prohibitions on the use of force, restriction on aircraft flights during the night, limited patrols that could only be conducted in armed personnel vehicles, and distance limitations on how far patrols could travel from their military bases.[52]

These caveats, and the ensuing casualties that occurred with British, Canadian, and Dutch military forces, produced new and serious diplomatic tensions within NATO. Those states who were experiencing casualties often challenged those allies deployed in safer regions to take on combat operations.[53] Frustration was also evident in the Bush administration, which was well displayed when Secretary of Defense Robert Gates suggested that some of the current allies did not have the necessary military skills and professionalism to engage in counterinsurgency operations, which later resulted in diplomatic protests from the Netherlands and a subsequent apology from the United States.[54] Although NATO secretary general Jaap de Hoop Scheffer consistently noted that Afghanistan was NATO's number one priority, the NATO allies continued to adopt very different military approaches for the remainder of the Bush administration, which led to ongoing diplomatic fissures within the alliance.

Despite the ongoing U.S. military operations and NATO's increased military and peacekeeping presence, by the end of the Bush administration most analysts, including U.S. intelligence agencies and the Department of Defense, concluded that the Taliban had successfully regrouped and was capable of waging increasingly advanced military attacks on U.S. and NATO forces.[55] In 2008 the United States suffered 155 casualties in the conflict, the highest number of deaths in one year since the war began. Sen. Barack Obama's presidential campaign often noted that Bush's efforts in Iraq had moved the United States away from what Senator Obama viewed as the real source of global terrorism, which was centered in Afghanistan.

Obama's AfPak Strategy and Troop Surges

When Barack Obama won the 2008 U.S. presidential election, the United States had been fighting terrorism in Afghanistan for more than seven years. The new president did not wait long before starting to implement the changes he had promised during the presidential campaign. As Obama argued during the campaign: "Now is the time for a responsible redeployment of our combat troops that . . . refocuses on Afghanistan."[56] According to Obama, the war in Iraq had distracted the United States from the more important fight against al Qaeda and the Taliban. Obama believed the United States had to change its strategy in Afghanistan in order to win the war against those he labeled "violent extremists."

Obama softened George W. Bush's tone and has been less inclined to use terms such as *evil, brutal,* or *murderers* to define al Qaeda and the Taliban. However, the policies he adopted in the first months of his presidency illustrate his determination to use military force as he deems necessary. In February Obama declared that he would send an additional seventeen thousand American troops to Afghanistan in the spring and summer of 2009.[57] The president also announced a new "comprehensive" strategy on March 27, 2009, addressing what his administration believed are the major factors that have caused security in Afghanistan to deteriorate since 2006.[58] The strategy—dubbed the "AfPak" strategy—starts with what the White House calls a "clear, concise, attainable goal": "disrupt, dismantle, and defeat al Qaeda and its safe havens."[59] Moreover, it treats Afghanistan and Pakistan as two countries but one challenge. According to Obama, it is imperative to focus more intensely on Pakistan than in the past, and to increase "U.S. and international support, both economic and military, linked to Pakistani performance against terror."[60] For example, in terms of military cooperation, the Obama presidency has coincided with greater U.S. assistance to the Pakistani army in its push against militants in South Waziristan by providing surveillance video and intelligence gleaned from CIA-operated unmanned aircraft.[61] While it was the first time Islamabad had ever accepted such help from the United States, some have criticized Obama's decision to put Pakistan on the same level as Afghanistan in the war against al Qaeda and the Taliban. For instance, former Pakistani president Pervez Musharraf argued that Pakistan is different from its neighbor, which has no government and is completely destabilized.[62] But United States Special Envoy for Afghanistan and Pakistan Richard Holbrooke—who is believed to be the one who coined the term *AfPak*—provided a different interpretation in March 2009, arguing that the terrorists who attacked New York are in Pakistan, not in Afghanistan.[63]

Obama's "AfPak" strategy is detailed in a White Paper published by the White House in March 2009. The paper is the product of an overarching sixty-day inter-agency review of the situation in Afghanistan, chaired by South Asian expert Bruce Riedel and cochaired by Richard Holbrooke and Under Secretary of Defense for Policy Michele Flournoy.[64] The paper states that Obama's objectives in Afghanistan and Pakistan are the following: (1) disrupt terrorist networks in Afghanistan and especially Pakistan to degrade any ability they have to plan and launch international terrorist attacks; (2) promote a more capable, accountable, and effective government in Afghanistan that serves the Afghan people and can eventually function, especially regarding internal security, with limited international support; (3) develop increasingly self-reliant Afghan security forces that can lead the counterinsurgency and counterterrorism fight with reduced U.S. assistance; (4) assist efforts to enhance civilian control and stable constitutional government in Pakistan and a vibrant economy that provides opportunity for the people of Pakistan; and (5) involve the international community to actively assist in addressing these objectives for Afghanistan and Pakistan, with an important leadership role for the UN.[65]

When one looks at how the decisions to reshape U.S. strategy in Afghanistan have been made by the Obama administration, one can see two striking similarities between the Democratic president and his two predecessors. On one hand, just like Clinton and Bush, Obama has made the White House the center of action concerning terrorism. Indeed, during the first year of the Obama presidency, the key players of the debate on Afghanistan have been the president himself, Defense Secretary Robert Gates, United States Special Envoy for Afghanistan and Pakistan Richard Holbrooke, commanders of U.S. and allied forces in Afghanistan David Mckiernan (until June 2009) and Stanley A. McChrystal (from June 2009 to June 2010), Vice President Joseph Biden, Secretary of State Hillary Rodham Clinton, Chairman of the Joint Chiefs of Staff Mike Mullen, Commander of the U.S. Central Command David Petraeus, White House Chief of Staff Rahm Emanuel, and White House national security adviser James Jones.[66] On the other hand, just like the members of the Clinton and Bush administrations, Obama's advisers have not always agreed on U.S. strategy to fight terrorism in Afghanistan. In White House sessions, military leaders and civilian officials have clashed over questions of strategy and troop levels, especially in October and November 2009, after the U.S. troops experienced one of their deadliest months in Afghanistan. The rift between Obama and some of his advisers became obvious when General McChrystal, after a four-hour September meeting with Mullen and Petraeus, asked for forty thousand more troops to better protect the Afghan people and train security forces, and pressured the president in public to reject Vice President Biden's proposals to switch to a strategy more reliant on drone missile strikes and special forces operations against al Qaeda.[67] Biden, who has been Obama's "in-house pessimist" or "bull in the china shop" on Afghanistan from the moment the president took office, said he did not favor abandoning Afghanistan, but has recommended to leave the U.S. force in this country roughly to what it was in February 2009 (a total of sixty-eight thousand troops).[68] According to Biden, al Qaeda has reconstituted in Pakistan and the United States must concentrate its efforts and resources there. In marketing his strategy, the vice president has pointed out that Washington spends approximately $30 in Afghanistan for every $1 it spends in Pakistan.[69]

While some members of the Obama administration, such as Rahm Emanuel and James Jones, are believed to share Biden's pessimism about Afghanistan, others expressed doubts about the vice president's plan and aligned themselves with General McChrystal, who was later relieved of his command on June 23, 2010, for derogatory comments made by him and his military staff about senior White House officials that were published in *Rolling Stone* magazine. Indeed, while Jones said a troop buildup would not be welcome, and while Emanuel told Obama early in 2009 that the war in Afghanistan could threaten his presidency, Hillary Clinton and her close ally Richard Holbrooke stated that they would back McChrystal's request.[70] Robert Gates appeared more skeptical of further troop increases at first, especially because he thought it could fuel resentment the way the Soviet occupation did in the 1980s. However, he finally backed McChrystal's plan after the general convinced him that the goal of U.S. forces was to protect civilians in major Afghan cities from Taliban attacks, not to dominate Afghanistan like the Soviet Union tried to do during the invasion.[71]

In December 2009, after nine formal war meetings and three months of intense debate within his administration, the president finally announced that he would deploy thirty thousand additional troops to Afghanistan within six months to break the Taliban's momentum. The main mission of these new troops would be to kill insurgents, protect population centers in the south and east of Afghanistan, and speed up training of Afghan security forces in order to hand over control of the mission to Afghan authorities.[72] In a move that illustrated Obama's willingness to address the critics of those who dubbed the war "Obama's Vietnam," the president also stated that the troop surge did not mean an open-ended commitment. Indeed, Obama declared that his goal was to end the war successfully and quickly, and that after eighteen months, U.S. troops would begin to come home.[73]

Two days after Obama announced his policy, Sens. John Kerry, D-Mass., and Richard Lugar, R-Ind., who hold the positions of chairman and ranking minority member in the Senate Foreign Relations Committee, proved that members of Congress did not want to remain silent or passive in the debate on Afghanistan and Pakistan. Kerry and Lugar held public hearings during which Hillary Clinton, Robert Gates, and Michael Mullen were invited to give more details about Obama's "AfPak" strategy.[74] These hearings were not the first ones Kerry and Lugar had held since Obama took office. For instance, in May 2009 Kerry set up a debate on Afghanistan within the committee and expressed concerns about the deteriorating security situation in most of the country.[75] Kerry, who was believed to share Biden's pessimism on surging the troops in Afghanistan, also played a fundamental role in the passage of the Enhanced Partnership with Pakistan Act of 2009 in October 2009. The key provisions of this law, which has also been dubbed the "Kerry-Lugar bill," are to provide Pakistan $1.5 billion in annual economic assistance for five years and renewable for another five.[76] One key goal of the bill is to counter widespread anti-American sentiment in Pakistan by helping Pakistan's civilian government deliver essential services to its population.[77]

In addition to Kerry and Lugar, Sens. Carl Levin, D-Mich., and John McCain, R-Ariz., who hold the positions of chairman and ranking minority member in the Senate Armed Forces Committee, have also organized multiple hearings on Obama's policies in Afghanistan and Pakistan. For instance, on February 26, 2009, the committee held a hearing on "Strategic Options for the Way Ahead in Afghanistan and Pakistan," during which Senator McCain shared Obama's position that the United States needed a troop surge in Afghanistan and a regional strategy to fight al Qaeda and the Taliban.[78] On December 2, 2009, Levin and McCain also invited Hillary Clinton, Robert Gates, and Michael Mullen to discuss Obama's strategy with the full committee. During this meeting, McCain criticized Obama for his decision to set an arbitrary date to begin withdrawing U.S. forces from Afghanistan.[79]

In the House, chairmen of the Permanent Select Committee on Intelligence (Rep. Sylvestre Reyes, D-Tex.) and of the Committees on International Affairs (Rep. Howard L. Berman, D-Calif.) and on Armed Services (Rep. Ike Skelton, D-Mo.), have been some of the most dynamic congressional actors in the debate on "AfPak." For instance, the three took part in an October 2009 White House meeting to discuss General McChrystal's troop-surge proposal. While Berman said he would consider other options before backing McChrystal, Reyes and Skelton advised Obama to follow his recommendation. Skelton even sent a six-page letter to Obama in which he implored the president to "give the general what he needs."[80] Other House Democrats such as Rep. John Murtha (Penn.) and Speaker Nancy Pelosi (Calif.) also expressed concerns about Obama's decision to escalate the war.[81] However, the debate between the White House and Congress on the war in Afghanistan revealed that members of Congress have little control over Obama's decisions beyond the money to pay for it. Indeed, there was little doubt, in January 2010, that the $30 billion Obama has said his troop surge will require over the year would be approved[82]—unless the war deteriorates to a point where the American people can no longer accept it.

Conclusion: Presidential Leadership in the War on Terrorism

As of July 2010 Osama Bin Laden and Mullah Omar remained at large. In December 2009 national security adviser James Jones declared that the al Qaeda chief is "somewhere inside North Waziristan, sometimes on the Pakistani side of the border, sometimes on the Afghan side of the border."[83] He has continued to communicate through audiotapes sent to members of the Arab news media over the years, and Mullah Omar's efforts to reorganize remnants of the Taliban have been effective.[84] In November 2009, Omar issued a message in which he rejected peace negotiations while Western forces remain in Afghanistan.[85] Such a statement and the alleged attempted plane-bombing against the United States on December 25, 2009, by a twenty-three-year-old Nigerian man reminded Washington and its allies that the war could last longer than Obama would want it to.

In the Clinton, Bush, and Obama administrations' military actions against al Qaeda, the White House has been the heart of the policy-making process, with limited formal input from others. This finding contrasts sharply with most other cases in this book—and in general with U.S. foreign policy making in the post–cold war era—in which multiple bureaucratic officials, individual members of Congress, and individuals outside of government often play critical roles. Although Congress has considerable formal leverage through the War Powers Resolution and the Constitution to demand a substantive role for itself in matters concerning the decision to go to war, it is largely the president who controls the policy-making process regarding such a decision. Bush and Clinton, to different degrees, consulted with Congress, but in their formal communications with Capitol Hill, they asserted essentially unlimited powers as commander in chief, as had all presidents during the cold war. Obama was less inclined to assert unlimited powers as commander in chief, and he consulted with key members of Congress during his policy review on Afghanistan. However, it seems fair to argue that Congress had little direct leverage over Obama. Formally, members of Congress could rely on the power of the purse and refuse to finance Obama's surge plan; instead, most members of Congress supported President Obama, with only a handful of liberal Democrats openly challenging either of Obama's troop surges.

The national security advisers of Clinton and Bush played key roles prior to the use of force. Sandy Berger and Condoleezza Rice, respectively, acted as primary confidants, consulting privately with the commander in chief. It appears that the national security adviser was the most trusted principal among all senior-level foreign policy decision makers in both administrations. Obama's national security adviser also played an important role during the debate on Afghanistan. However, it seems fair to say that other political actors at least matched James Jones's influence, especially Secretary of Defense Robert Gates, who toward the end of the White House debate about the troop surge was instrumental in shaping a plan that would bridge the differences between Hillary Clinton, Joseph Biden, and others.

The public widely supported the military actions of Bill Clinton and George W. Bush. Although many people suspected that Clinton's strikes on al Qaeda may have been a "diversionary military action" related to the Lewinsky scandal, his approval ratings remained high in the days following the strikes.[86] President Bush's political approval ratings soared soon after the September 11 tragedy and remained exceptionally high during the war in Afghanistan. As for Obama, the unveiling of his new military strategy revealed that Americans were not overly confident about the war. Only time will tell whether the public ends up favoring Obama's policy or not, but it seems fair to argue that Afghanistan could be a key issue in the elections to come.

Key Actors

Samuel "Sandy" Berger   National security adviser, principal adviser to President Clinton leading up to strikes in 1998 against Osama Bin Laden and his network in Sudan and Afghanistan.

Joseph Biden   Vice president, President Obama's "in-house pessimist" and most outspoken critic about an expansive troop-surge policy in Afghanistan.

Osama Bin Laden   Leader of al Qaeda, which was responsible for the bombings of U.S. embassies in Nairobi, Kenya, and Dar es Salaam, Tanzania, and the September 11 attacks.

George W. Bush   President, principal decision maker for initiating Operation Enduring Freedom against the Taliban and al Qaeda in 2001 in Afghanistan.

Richard A. Clarke   Counterterrorism coordinator for Presidents Clinton and Bush.

Bill Clinton   President, principal decision maker for strikes against Bin Laden in 1998.

Hillary Rodham Clinton   Secretary of state, advocate for a troop surge in Afghanistan during the first months of the Obama presidency.

Rahm Emanuel   White House chief of staff, expressed opposition to an expansive troop surge in Afghanistan during the first months of the Obama presidency.

Robert Gates   Secretary of defense, helped President Obama shape a troop-surge plan that would bridge the differences between Hillary Clinton, Joseph Biden, and others.

Richard Holbrooke   United States Special Envoy for Afghanistan and Pakistan, coined the term *AfPak* during the first months of the Obama presidency.

James Jones   White House national security adviser, expressed opposition to an expansive troop surge in Afghanistan during the first months of the Obama presidency.

Stanley A. McChrystal   Commander of U.S. and allied forces in Afghanistan, most aggressive advocate for a troop surge in Afghanistan during the first months of the Obama presidency; relieved of his command due to unprofessional military conduct.

Barack Obama   President, principal decision maker for increasing the war effort against the Taliban and al Qaeda after January 2009.

Condoleezza Rice   National security adviser, principal adviser to Bush in the lead-up to attacking the Taliban and al Qaeda in Afghanistan in 2001.

Hugh "Henry" Shelton   Chairman of the Joint Chiefs of Staff under Clinton and Bush, provided Bush with options for striking the Taliban and al Qaeda after the September 11 attacks.

George Tenet   Director of the Central Intelligence Agency under Clinton and Bush, exercised great influence in determining whom to strike after the September 11 attacks on the United States.

Paul Wolfowitz   Deputy secretary of defense, most aggressive advocate for military strikes on Iraq immediately after September 11.

Notes

1. Charles A. Lofgren, "War-Making under the Constitution: The Original Understanding," *Yale Law Journal* 81 (1972): 672–702.
2. Francis D. Wormuth and Edwin B. Firmage, *To Chain the Dog of War* (Urbana: University of Illinois Press, 1989).
3. Ryan C. Hendrickson, *The Clinton Wars: The Constitution, Congress, and War Powers* (Nashville: Vanderbilt University Press, 2002).
4. Robert David Johnson, *Congress and the Cold War* (Cambridge: Cambridge University Press, 2006), 190–193.
5. Michael J. Glennon, "Too Far Apart: The War Powers Resolution," *University of Miami Law Review* 50 (1995): 17–31; Edward Keynes, "The War Powers Resolution: A Bad Idea Whose Time Has Come and Gone," *University of Toledo Law Review* 23 (1992): 343–362.
6. Hendrickson, *The Clinton Wars*, 104.
7. "Press Briefing with National Security Advisor Berger on U.S. Strikes in Sudan and Afghanistan," August 20, 1998, http://secretary.state.gov/www/statements/1998/980820.html.

8. Bill Clinton, "Address to the Nation on Testimony before the Independent Counsel's Grand Jury," Weekly Compilation of Presidential Documents, August 28, 1998, 1638, available at www.gpoaccess.gov/wcomp/index.html; James Bennet, "Testing of a President: The Overview," New York Times, August 18, 1998, A1.

9. Defense LINK News, "DoD News Briefing," August 20, 1998, www.defenselink .mil/news/Aug1998/t08201998_t820brfg.html.

10. Bill Clinton, "Remarks on Departure for Washington, D.C., from Martha's Vineyard, Massachusetts," Weekly Compilation of Presidential Documents, August 28, 1998, 1642.

11. Bill Clinton, "Address to the Nation on Military Action against Terrorist Sites in Afghanistan and Sudan," Weekly Compilation of Presidential Documents, August 28, 1998, 1643.

12. For example, see Secretary of State Madeleine Albright's statements, "Interview on NBC-TV Today Show with Katie Couric," August 21, 1998, http://secretary.state.gov/www/statements/1998/980821.html.

13. For polling data, see Marck Z. Barabak, "The Times Poll," Los Angeles Times, August 23, 1998, A1; Bruce Westbrook, "War or a 'Wag'?" Houston Chronicle, August 25, 1998, 1; Marcella Bombardieri, "Wagging Dog? Fine, Some Say," Boston Globe, August 22, 1998, A8.

14. Office of the Press Secretary, "Press Briefing by McCurry in Gaggle," August 20, 1998, www.clintonpresidentialcenter.org/legacy/082098-press-briefing-by-mccurry-ingaggle.htm; see also Chuck McCutcheon, "Lawmakers Back Missile Strikes Despite a Bit of GOP Skepticism," CQ Weekly, August 22, 1998, 2289.

15. McCutcheon, "Lawmakers Back Missile Strikes."

16. "National Commission on Terrorist Attacks Upon the United States, Eighth Hearing," March 24, 2004, http://9-11commission.gov/archive/hearing8/9-11Commis sionHearing-2004-03-24.htm.

17. Office of the Press Secretary, "Press Briefing by McCurry in Gaggle"; see also McCutcheon, "Lawmakers Back Missile Strikes," 2289.

18. See Office of the Press Secretary, "Press Briefing by McCurry in Gaggle."

19. Bob Woodward, Bush at War (New York: Simon and Schuster, 2002).

20. Tenet maintains that it is likely that two sightings occurred, but Richard A. Clark, former counterterrorism coordinator, maintains that there were three occasions. "Testimony of Richard A. Clarke before the National Commission on Terrorist Attacks Upon the United States," March 24, 2004, 3, http://9-11commission.gov/hearings/hearing8/ clarke_statement.pdf.

21. Ibid.

22. National Commission on Terrorist Attacks Upon the United States, "Intelligence Policy," staff statement no. 7, March 24, 2004, 8–9, http://9-11commission.gov/hearings/hearing8/staff_statement_7.pdf.

23. Quoted in Woodward, Bush at War, 17.

24. Ibid., 26–27.

25. One forceful advocate of this view is Robert F. Turner, "The War on Terrorism and the Modern Relevance of the Congressional Power to 'Declare' War," Harvard Journal of Law and Public Policy 25, no. 2 (2002): 519–537.

26. Quoted in David Abramowitz, "The President, the Congress, and Use of Force: Legal and Political Considerations in Authorizing Use of Force against International Terrorism," Harvard International Law Journal 43, no. 1 (2002): 73.

27. Tom Daschle (with Michael D'Orso), *Like No Other Time: The Two Years That Changed America* (New York: Three Rivers Press, 2003), 124.

28. Abramowitz, "The President, the Congress, and Use of Force," 73.

29. *Congressional Record,* September 14, 2001, S9424.

30. Dave Boyer, "Some Lawmakers Call for War on Terror," *Washington Times,* September 14, 2001, A13.

31. Barbara Lee, "Why I Opposed the Resolution to Authorize Force," *San Francisco Chronicle,* September 23, 2001.

32. *Congressional Record,* September 14, 2001, S9416, S9417, S9423.

33. Nancy Kassop, "The War Power and Its Limits," *Presidential Studies Quarterly* 33, no. 3 (2003): 513–514.

34. An excellent account about the White House deliberation is provided in Woodward, *Bush at War.* See also Ron Suskind, *The Price of Loyalty: George W. Bush, the White House, and the Education of Paul O'Neill* (New York: Simon and Shuster, 2004); and Richard A. Clarke, *Against All Enemies: Inside America's War on Terror* (New York: Free Press, 2004).

35. Woodward, *Bush at War,* 83–91.

36. Ibid., 158; David Halberstam, *War in a Time of Peace: Bush, Clinton, and the Generals* (New York: Scribner's, 2001), 404–409.

37. Woodward, *Bush at War,* 99. Woodward's account squares with the recollection of former Treasury secretary Paul O'Neill. See Suskind, *The Price of Loyalty,* 184–187.

38. Shawn Howard, "The Afghan Connection: Islamic Extremism in Central Asia," *National Security Studies Quarterly* 6, no. 3 (2000): 28–29.

39. James S. Robbins, "Bin Laden's War," in *Terrorism and Counterterrorism: Under the New Security Environment,* ed. Russell D. Howard and Reid L. Sawyer (Guilford, Conn.: McGraw-Hill/Duskin, 2004), 396; George Tenet, "Written Statement for the Record of the Director of Central Intelligence Before the National Commission on Terrorist Attacks Upon the United States," March 24, 2004, 6–7, http://9-11commission.gov/hearings/hearing8/tenet_statement.pdf.

40. Woodward, *Bush at War,* 99, 121.

41. Ibid., 32, 43. For more details about Tommy Franks's role in the planning of the war, see Gen. Tommy Franks, *American Soldier* (New York: HarperCollins, 2004), 255–262.

42. Woodward, *Bush at War,* 115–117, 59.

43. Ibid., 117–118.

44. RAND Corporation, "Operation Enduring Freedom: An Assessment," Research Brief, 2005, 1, www.rand.org/pubs/research_briefs/2005/RAND_RB9148.pdf. See also Richard Morin and Claudia Deane, "Most Americans Back U.S. Tactics; Poll Finds Little Worry over Rights," *Washington Post,* November 29, 2001, A1.

45. Michael R. Gordon and Bernard E. Trainor, *COBRA II: The Inside Story of the Invasion and Occupation of Iraq* (New York: Pantheon Books, 2006): 19–23; Thomas E. Ricks, *Fiasco: The American Military Adventure in Iraq* (New York: Penguin Books, 2007), 32–34.

46. Sean Kay, "From COIN to Containment," ForeignPolicy.com (September 1, 2009), http://afpak.foreignpolicy.com/posts/2009/09/01/from_coin_to_containment.

47. Kirk Semple, "U.S. Plans a Shift to Focus Troops on Kabul Region," *New York Times,* December 7, 2008, A1.

48. Eric Schmitt and Thom Shanker, "A Nation Challenged; Strategy; Afghans' Retreat Forced Americans to Lead a Battle," *New York Times,* March 10, 2002, 1.

49. Wallace J. Thies, *Why NATO Endures* (Cambridge: Cambridge University Press, 2009), 304; Sean M. Maloney, "The International Security Assistance Force: The Origins of a Stabilization Force," *Canadian Military Journal* 4 (Summer 2003): 4–7.

50. Michael J. McNerney, "Stabilization and Reconstruction in Afghanistan: Are PRTs a Model or a Muddle?" *Parameters* 35 (Winter 2005–2006): 32–46; Sean M. Maloney, "Afghanistan Four Years On: An Assessment," *Parameters* 35 (Autumn 2005): 21–32.

51. Ryan C. Hendrickson, "L'OTAN et George W. Bush: Perspectives du Congrès américan sur la transformation de l'alliance," *Études internationales* 38, no. 4 (2007): 475–499.

52. Vincent Morelli and Paul Belkin, "NATO in Afghanistan: A Test of the Transatlantic Alliance," *Congressional Research Service,* August 25, 2009, 10–11.

53. Mike Blanchfield, "U.K. Minister Blasts Dion's Stance on Afghanistan: NATO Needs to 'Get Real,' " *National Post,* December 12, 2006, A6; Bruce Campion-Smith, "Lack of NATO Help Slammed," *Toronto Star,* November 16, 2006, A06.

54. Judy Dempsey, "Defense Secretary, Facing Criticism, Hails NATO's Forces in Afghanistan," *New York Times,* January 18, 2008, A10.

55. Mark Massetti and Eric Schmitt, "U.S. Study Is Said to Warn of Crisis in Afghanistan," *New York Times on the Web,* October 9, 2008; Mark Mazzetti, "Military Death Toll Rises in Afghanistan as Taliban Regain Strength," *New York Times,* July 2, 2008, A6.

56. Barack Obama, "Obama's Remarks on Iraq and Afghanistan," *New York Times,* July 25, 2008, www.nytimes.com/2008/07/15/us/politics/15text-obama.html?page wanted=print.

57. Helene Cooper, "Putting Stamp on Afghan War, Obama Will Send 17,000 Troops," *New York Times,* February 17, 2009, www.nytimes.com/2009/02/18/washington/18web-troops.html.

58. Kenneth Katzman, "Afghanistan: Post-Taliban Governance, Security, and U.S. Policy," *Congressional Research Service,* October 6, 2009, 26.

59. The White House, "What's New in the Strategy for Afghanistan and Pakistan," March 27, 2009, www.whitehouse.gov/the_press_office/Whats-New-in-the-Strategy-for-Afghanistan-and-Pakistan.

60. Ibid.

61. "U.S. Drones Aiding Pakistani Military Offensive," *Fox News,* October 23, 2009, www.foxnews.com/politics/2009/10/23/drones-aiding-pakistani-military-offensive.

62. Spiegel interview with Pervez Musharraf, "Obama 'Is Aiming at the Right Things,'" *Spiegel Online,* June 7, 2009, www.spiegel.de/international/world/0,1518, 628960,00.html.

63. Pascale Mallet, "Les États-Unis énoncent leurs priorités en Afghanistan," *La Presse,* March 21, 2009, www.cyberpresse.ca/international/moyen-orient/200903/21/01-838918-les-etats-unis-enoncent-leurs-priorites-en-afghanistan.php.

64. Katzman, "Afghanistan: Post-Taliban Governance, Security, and U.S. Policy," 26.

65. The White House, "White Paper of the Interagency Policy Group's Report on U.S. Policy Toward Afghanistan and Pakistan," March 27, 2009, 1, www.whitehouse.gov/assets/documents/Afghanistan-Pakistan_White_Paper.pdf.

66. "Key Players in the U.S. Debate on Afghanistan Policy," *Los Angeles Times,* October 17, 2009, www.latimes.com/news/nationworld/world/la-fg-afghan-players17-2009oct17,0,3331018.story.

67. Alex Spillius, "White House Angry at General Stanley McCrystal Speech in Afghanistan," *The Daily Telegraph,* October 5, 2009, www.telegraph.co.uk/news/world

news/northamerica/usa/barackobama/6259582/White-House-angry-at-General-Stan
ley-McChrystal-speech-on-Afghanistan.html.

68. Peter Baker, "Biden No Longer a Lone Voice on Afghanistan," *New York Times*,
October 13, 2009, www.nytimes.com/2009/10/14/world/14biden.html; Peter Baker,
"How Obama Came to Plan for 'Surge' in Afghanistan," *New York Times*, December 6,
2009, www.nytimes.com/2009/12/06/world/asia/06reconstruct.html?_r=2&scp=5&sq=
afghan%20surge&st=cse.

69. A. B. Stoddard, "Biden's Moment," *The Hill*, October 28, 2009, http://thehill
.com/opinion/columnists/ab-stoddard/65273-bidens-moment.

70. *Los Angeles Times,* "Key Players in the U.S. Debate on Afghanistan Policy."

71. "Q. and A. on Obama's Afghan Plan," *New York Times*, December 7, 2009, http://
thecaucus.blogs.nytimes.com/2009/12/07/q-and-a-on-obamas-afghan-plan.

72. "Obama's War," *The Economist*, December 2, 2009, www.economist.com/world/
unitedstates/displayStory.cfm?story_id=15004081&source=features_box1; Sheryl Gay
Stolberg, Helene Cooper, and Brian Knowlton, "Obama Aides Make Case for Afghan
Plan," *New York Times*, December 2, 2009, www.nytimes.com/2009/12/03/world/
asia/03policy.html?_r=1&hp.

73. Barack Obama, "Remarks by the President in Address to the Nation on the Way
Forward in Afghanistan and Pakistan," *The White House*, December 1, 2009, www.white
house.gov/the-press-office/remarks-president-address-nation-way-forward-afghani
stan-and-pakistan.

74. See U.S. Senate Foreign Relations Committee, "Afghanistan: Assessing the Road
Ahead," December 3, 2009, http://foreign.senate.gov/hearings/hearing/20091203.

75. John Kerry, "Chairman Kerry Opening Statement at Hearing On Afghanistan-
Pakistan Strategy, " U.S. Senate Committee on Foreign Relations, May 21, 2009, http://
foreign.senate.gov/testimony/2009/KerryStatement090521a.pdf.

76. U.S. Public Law 111-73, "Enhanced Partnership with Pakistan Act of 2009,"
October 15, 2009, http://frwebgate.access.gpo.gov/cgi-bin/getdoc.cgi?dbname=111_
cong_public_laws&docid=f:publ073.111.pdf.

77. Omar Waraich, "How a U.S. Aid Package to Pakistan Could Threaten Zardari,"
Time Magazine, October 8, 2009, www.time.com/time/world/article/0,8599,1929306,00
.html.

78. See U.S. Senate Committee on Armed Services, "Hearing to Receive Testimony
on Strategic Options for the Way Ahead in Afghanistan and Pakistan," February 26,
2009, http://armed-services.senate.gov/Transcripts/2009/02%20February/A%20Full%
20Committee/09-05%20-%202-26-09%20(2).pdf.

79. John McCain, "Statement of Senator McCain," *Hearing to Receive Testimony on
Afghanistan*, U.S. Senate Armed Forces Committee, December 2, 2009.

80. S. A. Miller, "Key Democrats Align with Military on Afghan Buildup," *Washington Times*, October 9, 2009, www.washingtontimes.com/news/2009/oct/09/key-demo
crats-align-with-military-on-buildup.

81. Karen DeYoung, "Lawmakers Scrutinize New Afghan Strategy," *Washington Post*,
December 3, 2009, www.washingtonpost.com/wp-dyn/content/article/2009/12/02/
AR2009120201013.html.

82. Ibid.

83. Syed Saleem Shahzad, "Osama Can Run, How Long Can He Hide?" *Asia Times*,
December 12, 2009, www.atimes.com/atimes/South_Asia/KL12Df03.html.

84. Hassan M. Fattah, "Bin Laden Re-emerges, Warning U.S. while Offering 'Truce,'" *New York Times,* January 19, 2006. See also Amir Shah, Associated Press, "Taliban Leader Said to Be Reorganizing Group," *Fort Worth Star-Telegram,* September 22, 2003, 6A.

85. Tom Coghlan, "Taleban Leader Mullah Omar Gets on Message with Speech Aimed at West," *The Times,* November 26, 2009, www.timesonline.co.uk/tol/news/world/Afghanistan/article6932459.ece.

86. For an argument expressing doubt about the diversionary theory for these strikes, see Ryan C. Hendrickson, "Clinton's Military Strikes in 1998: Diversionary Uses of Force?," *Armed Forces and Society* 28 (2002): 309–332.

2 The Return of the Imperial Presidency? The Bush Doctrine and U.S. Intervention in Iraq

Jeffrey S. Lantis and Eric Moskowitz

Before You Begin

1. Has the "imperial presidency" model been resurrected more than a decade after the end of the cold war?

2. Why did the Bush administration decide to invade Iraq and topple Saddam Hussein in 2003? How did the events of September 11 translate into justification in 2003 for a preemptive war against Iraq?

3. What leaders were particularly influential in shaping the decision to invade Iraq, and what domestic opposition did they face?

4. Why was it so difficult for Congress to have any significant impact on presidential plans for war?

5. What links can you draw between the decision-making process and outcomes in the Iraq war?

6. What are the long-term implications of a doctrine of preemption for U.S. foreign policy?

Deterrence—the promise of massive retaliation against nations—means nothing against shadowy terrorist networks with no nation or citizens to defend. Containment is not possible when unbalanced dictators with weapons of mass destruction can deliver those weapons or missiles or secretly provide them to terrorist allies. . . . We must take the battle to the enemy, disrupt his plans, and confront the worst threats before they emerge. In the world we have entered, the only path to safety is the path of action. And this nation will act.

—President George W. Bush,
2002 Graduation Speech at West Point

Introduction

The terrorist attacks of September 11, 2001, represented a watershed moment for U.S. foreign policy. September 11 enabled the executive branch to assume an unusual amount of influence over security policy making. President George W. Bush and his advisers used that influence in a variety of ways, including implementing a new strategy calling for preemptive strikes against potential enemies. The United States would rely most often on the unilateral exercise of power, rather than on international law and organizations, to achieve its security objectives. Some observers suggest that the Bush doctrine, the larger war on terrorism, and the Iraq war (2003–2010) represent the resurgence of the "imperial presidency."

Background: The Rise of the Imperial Presidency

Historian Arthur M. Schlesinger Jr. coined the term *imperial presidency* to describe the dominance of the executive branch in U.S. policy making during the cold war. Schlesinger identified a pattern of steady accumulation of power in the executive branch, especially "under the demand or pretext of an emergency." By the early 1970s, he argued, "the American president had become on issues of war and peace the most absolute monarch (with the possible exception of Mao Tse Tung of China) among the great powers of the world."[1] Schlesinger viewed this as an *un*constitutional usurpation of authority through "the appropriation by the Presidency, and particularly by the contemporary Presidency, of powers reserved by the Constitution and by long historical practice to Congress."[2] Another scholar, Michael Beschloss, concurred: "The founders never intended to have an imperial president. Always worried about tyranny, they drafted a Constitution that gives the president limited authority and forces him to use his political skills to fight for influence as he squeezes laws out of Congress and prods the American people to think in new ways."[3]

The imperial presidency may have blossomed in the first decades of the cold war, but political winds shifted in the 1970s as Americans grew weary of the war in Vietnam and executive excess. The Watergate scandal and resignation of President Richard Nixon in 1974 seemed to mark the demise of the cold war imperial presidency. A resentful Congress and a mobilized nation consciously began to check the power of the executive branch. Succeeding presidents faced resistance from mobilized institutions that constrained their latitude in foreign

Timeline

U.S. Intervention in Iraq

August 2, 1990	Iraq invades Kuwait.
August 8, 1990	President George H. W. Bush announces that the United States is sending troops to Saudi Arabia in response to the Iraqi invasion of Kuwait; the UN Security Council later passes a resolution authorizing the use of force if Iraq does not withdraw from Kuwait by January 15, 1991.
January 17, 1991	UN-sanctioned multinational forces launch an air war against Iraq.
February 24–28, 1991	After a six-week air campaign, the multinational forces launch a ground war against Iraqi forces. Iraqi troops quickly retreat from Kuwait under a withering coalition attack, and Bush decides to end the war after one hundred hours.
March 1991	Iraqi president Saddam Hussein brutally puts down a Shia revolt in southern Iraq and a Kurdish revolt in the north. After much criticism, the Bush administration sets up "no-fly" zones over Iraq to restrain further Iraqi military actions against these groups.
April 3, 1991	The UN Security Council passes Resolution 687, which requires the Iraqi government to allow international inspections of all its weapons facilities and to destroy all weapons of mass destruction (WMD).
December 1998	Iraq ends all cooperation with UN weapons inspections. Without Security Council approval, President Bill Clinton orders Operation Desert Fox, a four-day bombing campaign of Iraqi military installations.
September 15, 2001	In a meeting of the war cabinet, Deputy Secretary of Defense Paul Wolfowitz proposes including Iraq as a target of the U.S. military response to the September 11 terror attacks. Secretary of

	State Colin Powell objects, arguing that an international coalition could only be built for an attack against the Taliban and al Qaeda in Afghanistan. George W. Bush agrees that Afghanistan should be the immediate target, though he indicates that Iraq will be reconsidered later.
January 29, 2002	In the State of the Union address, Bush denounces Iraq, Iran, and North Korea as an "axis of evil." He declares that the United States will act preemptively against nations with WMD that threaten the United States. He focuses particularly on Iraq.
Summer 2002	Debate about regime change in Iraq rages in the Bush administration. The momentum for war appears to be growing; Powell, the secretary of state, warns Bush about the political and economic consequences in the Middle East if the United States unilaterally acts against Iraq.
October 11, 2002	Congress passes a joint resolution authorizing Bush to use any means he deems appropriate to enforce Security Council resolutions against Iraq and to defend U.S. national security.
November 8, 2002	The Security Council unanimously passes Resolution 1441, warning Iraq of serious consequences unless it submits immediately to unrestricted weapons inspections.
March 19–20, 2003	After an ultimatum for Saddam Hussein to surrender goes unheeded, U.S. and coalition forces launch air and missile attacks on Iraq.
March 20, 2003	U.S. and coalition forces invade Iraq.
May 1, 2003	Bush announces that all major combat operations in Iraq have been successfully concluded, at a historic appearance on the USS *Abraham Lincoln* under a banner proclaiming "Mission Accomplished."
June 28, 2004	Paul Bremer, head of the Coalition Provisional Authority, hands over sovereign authority to an interim Iraqi government.

(continued)

Timeline *(continued)*
U.S. Intervention in Iraq

December 15, 2005	Iraqis elect a permanent government, with the Shia-led United Iraqi Alliance winning a plurality of the seats. Nouri al-Maliki, of the Shiite Dawa Party, is selected prime minister.
December 6, 2006	The Iraq Study Group issues its report calling for an aggressive diplomatic effort and a phased withdrawal of U.S. troops.
January 10, 2007	President Bush announces plans for a "New Way Forward," which includes a surge of 21,500 additional troops to Iraq.
November 2008	The United States accepts a status of forces agreement with Iraq that commits the United States to withdraw all of its troops from Iraq by December 31, 2011.
February 27, 2009	President Obama announces that all U.S. combat troops will be removed from Iraq by August 31, 2010, yet unrest in the country continues.

policy making. The international security environment was also uncertain, and Washington officials seemed to share a basic consensus that the United States should tread carefully in global affairs in the post–cold war era. When George W. Bush entered office in 2001, Beschloss characterized him as the United States' first truly "post-imperial president," given the controversy surrounding the 2000 election, public attitudes favoring restraint in foreign affairs, and the relative peace in the world.

U.S. Foreign Policy after September 11

The attacks of September 11 became a catalyst for fundamental transformations in U.S. foreign policy. Key tenets of cold war strategic culture no longer appeared adequate. The United States suddenly seemed vulnerable. Shaping U.S. responses to the terrorist threat would call into question key concepts and practices in foreign affairs, including hegemony and multilateral cooperation.

The Bush administration decided to interpret September 11 as a transformative moment for the country. President Bush and his top advisers believed that the attacks represented a "moment of destiny" for the nation. Moreover, they recognized that the attacks had reduced the public's resistance to risk taking and its casualty aversion. National security adviser Condoleezza Rice characterized this new era as similar to the period from 1945 to 1947, where events "started shifting the tectonic plates in international politics." She argued it was "important to try to seize on that and position American interests and institutions and all of that before they harden again."[4]

The administration began to define new avenues for foreign and security policy. The president received congressional support for a broadly worded resolution that authorized him "to use all necessary and appropriate force against those nations, organizations, or persons he determines planned, authorized, committed, or aided the terrorist attacks that occurred on September 11, 2001, or harbored such organizations or persons, in order to prevent any future acts of international terrorism against the United States by such nations, organizations, or persons." The resolution did not prompt much congressional debate, yet this was the beginning of what Ivo Daalder and James Lindsay have termed "a revolution in American foreign policy." Bush's advocacy of "the unilateral exercise of American power" and his emphasis on "a proactive doctrine of preemption and [de-emphasis of] the reactive strategies of deterrence and containment" set the path for a dramatic new phase in U.S. foreign policy.[5]

Decision Making and the Iraq War

The idea to invade Iraq as part of a global war against terrorism was first raised with the president just days after the September 11 attacks. The option was shelved at the time, but it remained under discussion in secret meetings over the next year. Each time the Iraq option was discussed, it gained broader support inside the administration.[6]

On September 15, 2001, President Bush held a meeting of his principal national security advisers, including Rice, Vice President Richard Cheney, Secretary of State Colin Powell, Secretary of Defense Donald Rumsfeld, Deputy Secretary of Defense Paul Wolfowitz, Director of Central Intelligence (DCI) George Tenet, and Chairman Richard Myers of the Joint Chiefs of Staff. Rumsfeld and Wolfowitz reportedly brought along briefing papers that identified "three potential sets of targets: Taliban, al Qaeda, and Iraq."[7] When given the opportunity, Wolfowitz argued that Iraqi president Saddam Hussein was a tyrant who represented a direct threat to U.S. national security; that his regime supported international terrorism; that Iraq sought to develop weapons of mass destruction (WMD) that could be used against U.S. allies, including Israel; and that he might have been involved in the September 11 plot.[8]

In fact, Iraq had been a primary U.S. security concern since the Persian Gulf War in 1991. After the war, officials in the George H. W. Bush administration authored a Defense Policy Guidance that called for a firm stand against the Iraqi leader and other adversaries and stated that "American power ought to be vigorously asserted to bring order to a potentially disintegrating post–Cold War world."[9] As part of Iraq's 1991 surrender, the United Nations (UN) conducted regular inspections of suspected WMD sites (through 1998). After the war, the Iraqi leader had cracked down on insurgent groups and political opponents. In response, the United States and its allies established "no-fly" zones over parts of northern and southern Iraq to help protect those groups. U.S. and British planes patrolled the zones from 1991 to 2003, engaging in periodic exchanges of fire with Iraqi antiaircraft missile batteries. In May 1991, President Bush also signed secret orders for the CIA to spend more than $100 million on covert operations to "create the conditions for removal of Saddam Hussein from power."[10]

In September 2001, however, there was little support among the president's other advisers at Camp David for the Iraq option. When Wolfowitz continued to make his argument, Bush had his chief of staff, Andrew Card, take Wolfowitz aside to tell him to allow the discussion to move on to other, more immediate policy alternatives.[11] Nevertheless, Bush reportedly told his national security adviser the next day that the first target of the war on terrorism was Afghanistan: "We're putting Iraq off," he said, "but eventually we'll have to return to that question."[12] In late November 2001, the president told Rumsfeld to update war plans for Iraq. Senior administration officials later said that Bush "understood instantly after September 11 that Iraq would be the next major step in the global war against terrorism, and that he made up his mind" on Iraq "within days, if not hours, of that fateful day."[13]

But first the administration moved forward with plans to strike the Taliban and al Qaeda in Afghanistan. Bush launched the war against Afghanistan with strong congressional and public support. U.S. and British troops, aided by forces from other countries, conducted a rapid series of campaigns against the Taliban. Special operations troops worked in concert with groups in the Northern Alliance and quickly took control of key regions of the country. By December 2001 the war in Afghanistan seemed nearly over, though Osama Bin Laden and other top leaders of al Qaeda remained at large.

Even before the war in Afghanistan wound down, battle lines had been drawn within the Bush administration over Iraq. Administration officials were divided into two camps: those who favored an invasion of Iraq and those who favored intensified efforts to contain Iraq.[14] In 2002 the camp supporting the invasion of Iraq included Rumsfeld, Cheney, and Wolfowitz. Also sharing their perspective were I. Lewis "Scooter" Libby, Cheney's chief of staff; Zalmay Khalilzad, deputy national security adviser on Iraq; Stephen Hadley, deputy national security adviser; and Wayne Downing, White House counterterrorism adviser. Some members of this faction had been pressuring the government to topple the Iraqi leader since the early 1990s. The call for an attack on Iraq was an important part of the agenda of a group of so-called neo-conservatives, or "neo-cons," inside (and outside) the Bush administration, who were affiliated with a think-tank called the Project for the New American Century (or PNAC).

Secretary Rumsfeld was a key player in planning the Iraq invasion. He has been described as a "masterful bureaucratic infighter who ruthlessly gained control over the major decisions [of the Iraq war] and marginalized colleagues." The secretary "operated in a secretive fashion [allowing] him to increase control over information that acted to distort and complicate the policy-making process."[15] Rumsfeld was advised by the Pentagon's Defense Policy Board, a private group of consultants led by neo-conservatives including former Pentagon official Richard Perle, former CIA director James Woolsey, and *Weekly Standard* editor William Kristol, the chair of PNAC. In February 1998 eighteen prominent neo-conservatives from PNAC had sent President Bill Clinton an open letter warning that Saddam Hussein posed an immediate threat to the United States and calling for U.S. support for a popular insurrection in Iraq. They called specifically for the Clinton administration to recognize an exile group, the Iraqi National Congress, as the provisional government of Iraq.[16] Neo-conservatives persuaded Congress to pass the Iraq Liberation Act in 1998, a "piece of legislation that made regime change in Iraq the official policy of the United States."[17] Many of those neo-conservatives were later drafted by Cheney to serve in top positions in the Bush administration. They sought U.S. international hegemony and the democratization of the Middle East. In their calculation, the overthrow of the Iraqi leader could be the catalyst for change. After achieving regime change in Iraq, Perle suggested the United States could more easily intimidate other dangerous states such as Iran and Syria to fall in line by simply delivering "a short message. . . . 'You're next.' "[18]

After September 11, Secretary Rumsfeld created a new office in the Pentagon, the Counterterrorism Evaluation Group—later known as the Office of Special Plans—that was to provide the secretary with advanced analysis of intelligence on Iraq and links between Middle Eastern states and terrorist networks. Critics charged that this office was created to find evidence of what Wolfowitz and Rumsfeld already "believed to be true—that Saddam Hussein had close ties to al Qaeda, and that Iraq had an enormous arsenal of chemical, biological, and possibly even nuclear weapons that threatened the region and potentially, the United States."[19]

Dick Cheney was, "by common consent, the most powerful vice president in history."[20] And he seemed especially preoccupied with the September 11 attacks and possible links between Saddam Hussein and al Qaeda. Wolfowitz commented that Cheney was "someone whose view of the need to get rid of Saddam Hussein was transformed by September 11, by the recognition of the danger posed by the connection between terrorists and WMDs, and by the growing evidence of links between Iraq and al Qaeda."[21] Soon after September 11, "Cheney immersed himself in a study of Islam and the Middle East," meeting with scholars to discuss whether "toppling Saddam would send a message of strength and enhance America's credibility throughout the Muslim world."[22] His staff was also heavily focused on Iraq, working closely with Rumsfeld and the Pentagon in investigating links between Iraq and al Qaeda and building the case for war. Secretary Powell later said that he had "detected a kind of fever in Cheney. [Cheney] was not the steady, unemotional rock that he had witnessed a dozen years earlier during the run-up to the Gulf War. The vice president was beyond hell-bent for action against Saddam. It was as if nothing else existed."[23]

The group within the administration opposed to an outright invasion of Iraq included State Department officials, who became strong advocates of containment as an alternative, along with some military leaders. Powell was the leading voice for moderation in the cabinet during the winter months of 2001 and 2002. He was supported by Richard Armitage, deputy secretary of state, Richard Haas, director of policy planning, and retired army general Anthony Zinni, the department's adviser on the Middle East. DCI Tenet also worried about the implications of an invasion for U.S. international security. State Department officials argued that the United States should support a renewed international program of WMD inspections in Iraq and ideally should build a multilateral coalition of countries willing to authorize more stringent UN Security Council resolutions and possibly even threaten the use of force against Saddam Hussein's regime. Thus, while there was a growing consensus that the

Iraqi leader should be removed from office, there remained significant disagreement on the means to that end.

Secret Plans

The two camps secretly debated Iraqi policy throughout the fall of 2001. Rumsfeld and Cheney reportedly kept Iraq alive in "freewheeling meetings of the principals," where they discussed possible ties between so-called rogue states, such as Iraq, and terrorist groups. One senior official said of those meetings, "The issue got away from the president. He wasn't controlling the tone or the direction. . . . [Some members of the administration] painted him into a corner because Iraq was an albatross around their necks."[24] On November 21, 2001, while the war in Afghanistan continued, the president ordered Secretary Rumsfeld and Gen. Tommy Franks, head of Central Command (CENTCOM), to begin secretly updating war plans for Iraq. Bush would later say that this order was "absolutely" the first step in taking the nation to war.[25] Between December 2001 and September 2002 Franks would meet with President Bush eight times to present ever more detailed Iraq war plans.

Bush's State of the Union address in January 2002 gave him a platform to articulate the evolution of his foreign policy objectives. In the address, the president's articulation of an "axis of evil"—Iran, Iraq, and North Korea—suggested that there were obvious enemies in the war on terrorism. A few weeks later, the president secretly directed the CIA to begin developing plans for supporting military efforts to overthrow the Iraqi regime. The CIA received almost $200 million for covert activities against Baghdad.[26] President Bush reportedly set a deadline of April 15, 2002, for his advisers to develop a "coagulated plan" for dealing with Iraq. He told top officials that he was ready to "take out Saddam."[27]

This new push to develop an operational plan led to serious debates in 2002 over the nature and scope of the operation. Administration officials discussed a number of options for toppling the Iraqi leader, including "providing logistical and intelligence help to [his] enemies in hopes of inciting a mutiny within his military circle; providing air and limited ground support for an assault by opposition groups; or an outright American invasion."[28] CIA officials informed the president that covert action alone could not achieve regime change in Iraq. Civilian leaders at the Pentagon and officials on the National Security Council (NSC) favored an option in the spirit of the "Afghanistan model"—using several thousand Special Forces soldiers and concentrated airpower to support opposition groups' efforts to defeat the Iraqi army. Wolfowitz and Downing were among the most outspoken advocates for the invasion plan, believing that light and technologically advanced forces could swiftly overrun Iraqi opposition.[29] At one point, Rumsfeld argued that perhaps as few as 125,000 troops could win the war.

The Joint Chiefs of Staff and General Franks of CENTCOM argued strongly against the Pentagon's civilian leadership during this period. The military brass believed that any operation in Iraq would require overwhelming force to confront Iraq's established army. Military leaders were very concerned about Iraq's potential use of chemical or biological weapons and the possibility of prolonged urban warfare. They also questioned the reliability of the Iraqi National Congress as a leader of insurgent forces and the adequacy of plans for a postwar occupation regime. At one point General Franks articulated a plan calling for 380,000 troops for the invasion and occupation. "Nobody knew how long U.S. forces would need to be in Iraq, so CENTCOM war planners wrote that the occupation would last as long as ten years."[30] State Department officials joined the military brass in trying to resist a rush to invade.

To make matters worse, the NSC did not adequately manage the decision process. Kim Holmes, an assistant secretary of state in the Bush administration, said that she observed fights and disagreements about foreign policy decisions "everywhere, constantly" during this period.[31] Critics charged that Rice was not sufficiently engaged in her management role, opting instead to serve as confidante to the president. According to one report, Rice's management of the NSC, "the principal coordinator and enforcer of presidential decision-making," was severely lacking. Another State Department official said, "If you want a one-word description of the NSC since January 21, 2001, [it is] dysfunctional."[32] Because Rumsfeld and Cheney had a close personal relationship, they often teamed up to "roll over national security advisor Rice and Secretary of State Powell" on Iraq policy making.[33]

Finally, though the subject of postwar planning for Iraq seems (in hindsight) to be just as important as war planning, it received far less attention in the buildup to the invasion. The State Department had started a postwar planning initiative in 2002, but its efforts were quickly swept aside by the Pentagon leadership. Rumsfeld successfully argued that his department should be in charge of postwar planning and the occupation. The president signed National Security Presidential Directive NSPD-24 on January 20, 2003, establishing an Iraq Postwar Planning Office in the *Defense* Department.[34] Pentagon leaders blocked input from other agencies. Retired general Jay Garner was appointed to head postwar planning initiatives, but months of preparation only revealed more potential problems. One analysis from a planning simulation in Washington in late February 2003—just one month before the invasion—warned, "Current force packages are inadequate for the first step of securing all major urban areas, let alone for providing interim police. . . . We risk letting much of the country descend into civil unrest [and] chaos whose magnitude may defeat our national strategy of a stable new Iraq."[35] Even though Rumsfeld had primary authority, through NSPD-24, the secretary seemed aloof and uninterested in postwar planning, while at the same time micromanaging the war plans.

The Hot Summer

Summer 2002 was a critical period for Bush administration decision making on Iraq. Officials publicly maintained that there were no war plans on the president's desk, but evidence began to mount that an invasion was in the works. At the graduation ceremony of the U.S. Military Academy at West Point on June 1, the president gave a speech that hinted that he had already made up his mind on Iraq. Faced with threats of attack from terrorist groups and rogue states, Bush argued:

> The gravest danger to freedom lies at the perilous crossroads of radicalism and technology. When the spread of chemical and biological and nuclear weapons, along with ballistic missile technology—when that occurs, even weak states and small groups could attain a catastrophic power to strike great nations. . . . They want the capability to blackmail us, or to harm us, or to harm our friends—and we will oppose them with all our power.[36]

Secretary of Defense Rumsfeld also continued to manipulate the policy-making process. According to interviews with former administration members, "Instead of engaging the debate with the rest of the principals and the NSC process, Rumsfeld sought to secure a direct line to Bush. . . . Rumsfeld would assert that the chain of command, which he characterized as running from combatant commanders, to him, to the president, superseded the NSC process."[37] When other members of the administration complained that they were being shut out of the decision process, deputy national security adviser Stephen Hadley reportedly told them "the real work was being done upstairs [in the White House] with the president, Cheney, and Rumsfeld."[38]

The issue came to a head at an August 5 meeting of the NSC. General Franks briefed the president and his advisers on war plans for Iraq, including a new plan for faster mobilization and strikes. At the end of the briefing,

Secretary Powell requested time alone with the president and Rice to address his reservations. Powell frankly expressed his concerns about the potential negative consequences of an invasion. He told the president, "You are going to be the proud owner of 25 million people. You will own all their hopes, aspirations, and problems. You'll own it all."[39] Powell and Armitage privately called this "the Pottery Barn rule: You break it, you own it." The secretary went on to warn that an attack on Iraq would "suck the oxygen out of everything. This will become the first term."[40] The best approach, Powell argued, was for the United States to push for UN and allied support.

President Bush, over the next few days, appears to have decided on a two-track strategy. Track one would authorize military deployments and call-ups of reserves to amass troops in the Persian Gulf region for an attack against Iraq. Track two would focus on diplomacy at the United Nations. Should the UN efforts fail, the diplomacy would nevertheless help build international, congressional, and public support for track one. This second track remained controversial inside the administration. Some officials, possibly including the president, simply "didn't believe diplomacy would or could take care of the threat Saddam posed. Going to the UN was a means, not an end."[41] Neoconservatives in the administration did not want another UN resolution creating new arms inspections in Iraq, fearing that the Iraqi leader would manipulate the inspection process and sidetrack U.S. efforts at regime change. Meanwhile, others in the Bush administration believed there was a chance that a refurbished United Nations inspection regime could work.

Given the disarray inside the administration, it was no surprise that debates over the tracks broke out into the open. State Department officials leaked their concerns to the press, questioning whether the administration had already decided upon an invasion. Leading Republicans also began to question publicly the merits of a rush to invade. Brent Scowcroft, the national security adviser under the elder Bush, published an op-ed article warning "an attack on Iraq at this time would seriously jeopardize, if not destroy, the global counter-terrorist campaign we have undertaken."[42] Republican leaders in Congress had concerns about whether the administration had adequately prepared the military or the public for the scope of the undertaking.

In late August, invasion supporters pushed back. Rice gave an interview to the BBC in which she emphasized the growing moral imperative for the United States and its allies to topple Saddam Hussein: "This is an evil man, who left to his own devices, will wreak havoc again on his own population, his neighbors and if he gets weapons of mass destruction and the means to deliver them on all of us. There is a very powerful moral case for regime change."[43] Vice President Cheney contributed to the war momentum, declaring in an August 26 speech to the convention of the Veterans of Foreign Wars, "We must take the battle to the enemy. . . . There is no doubt that Saddam Hussein now has weapons of mass destruction; there is no doubt that Saddam is amassing them to use against our friends, against our allies, and against us. . . . Many of us are convinced that Saddam will acquire nuclear weapons fairly soon."[44]

Secretary Powell was blindsided by Cheney's bold assertions. Powell, who was on vacation, had not been briefed on the vice president's speech. He was particularly angered because weeks earlier the president's top advisers had unanimously agreed to take the Iraq issue to the United Nations. Cheney's public assertion that inspections would not prevent Iraq from acquiring WMD was contrary to Bush's yearlong insistence that inspectors should be allowed to resume their work. Powell characterized Cheney's action as "a preemptive attack" on the policy process.[45]

Powell returned to Washington and requested another meeting with Bush to try to convince him of the need for the United States to work with the international community on the Iraq issue. He argued that the United States could gain international support by formulating a UN Security Council resolution to clamp down on Iraq and force compliance with UN demands. The president reassured Powell that he would pursue a new round of diplomacy. The night before Bush's September address to the UN General Assembly, Powell convinced Rice that the president should include the following statement in his speech: "We will work with the UN Security Council for the necessary resolutions, but the purposes of the United States should not be doubted. The Security Council resolutions will be enforced."[46]

Bringing the War to the Home Front: Speaking with One Voice

By mid-August 2002 the public and Congress both sensed that war with Iraq was inevitable, but there was also deep-seated skepticism. Prominent congressional Republicans, including House Majority Leader Richard Armey, R-Texas, and Sens. Chuck Hagel, R-Neb., and Richard Lugar, R-Ind., questioned the wisdom of a unilateral, preemptive attack on Iraq. Other congressional representatives, back in their districts for the summer recess, were finding their constituents uncertain about a potential invasion. A *Washington Post*/ABC News poll showed a slip in public support for a war, and only 45 percent of the public thought Bush had a clear policy on Iraq.[47]

On August 26, the White House seemed to respond to new questions by asserting that the president needed no authorization from Congress to pursue a preemptive attack against Iraq. Such a strike was validated, a spokesman argued, by the president's constitutional role as commander in chief, the 1991 congressional authorization of the Persian Gulf War, and the 2001 congressional authorization to use force against those involved in the September 11 assault. One administration official said, "We don't want to be in the legal position of asking Congress to authorize the use of force when the president already has that full authority." The administration also feared restrictions that Congress might impose on the president's flexibility to move against Iraq.[48]

Many in Congress rejected the president's argument. Sen. Arlen Specter, R-Pa., insisted that the war was "a matter for Congress to decide. The president as commander in chief can act in an emergency without authority from Congress, but we have enough time to debate, deliberate and decide."[49] Sen. Robert Byrd, D-W.Va., argued that the Persian Gulf War resolutions "ceased to be effective once Iraq capitulated to U.S. and allied forces in April 1991." Sen. Max Cleland, D-Ga., maintained that the September 11 use-of-force resolution was "not some blank check to go after any terrorists in the world."[50] Others in Congress conceded the president's legal position but believed it would undermine the war's political support. Said Sen. John McCain, R-Ariz., "I believe technically the president is not required to come to Congress; politically, I believe it would be foolish not to."[51]

Significant congressional opposition (even among Republicans) coupled with volatile public attitudes ultimately led the White House to seek congressional approval to act against Iraq. The administration began to make its case to the nation and to Congress through frequent appearances by administration officials on television talk shows, in testimony at congressional hearings, and closed-door briefings for congressional leaders. On September 4, Bush met with a congressional delegation to make the case for the use of force against Iraq and to ask for an authorizing resolution. The president told them he wanted congressional approval soon—before the end of the October recess and before midterm elections—and without conditions.

The Search for Support

Bush's speech to the UN General Assembly on September 12 was designed to address both tracks of policy developed by the White House. While the president offered an olive branch—negotiations with the UN Security Council to reach a multilateral resolution of the Iraq situation—he also issued strong words of warning to Iraq and other nations. Marking the one-year anniversary of the September 11 attacks, he said:

> Our principles and our security are challenged today by outlaw groups and regimes that accept no law of morality and have no limit to their violent ambitions. . . . In one place—in one regime—we find all these dangers, in their most lethal and aggressive forms, exactly the kind of aggressive threat the United Nations was born to confront. . . . The conduct of the Iraqi regime is a threat to the authority of the United Nations, and a threat to peace. . . . Are Security Council resolutions to be honored and enforced, or cast aside without consequence? Will the United Nations serve the purpose of its founding, or will it be irrelevant?[52]

Eight weeks later, on November 8, the UN Security Council unanimously approved Resolution 1441, authorizing a new round of weapons inspections in Iraq. In late fall 2002, dozens of UN inspectors returned to Iraq for the first time in four years.

The UN address was a turning point for Bush in his efforts to build popular support at home for war. Major media outlets noted the overwhelmingly favorable congressional response to the speech and suggested that it had generated momentum for quick approval of a resolution authorizing force.[53] The White House sent its formal draft of a resolution to Congress one week after the UN address. It authorized the president "to use all means that he determines to be appropriate, including force, in order to enforce the United Nations Security Council Resolutions . . . [to] defend the national security interests of the United States against the threat posed by Iraq, and restore international peace and security in the region [the Middle East]."[54]

The draft had been designed to give the president maximum flexibility. Reaction in Congress was generally positive, though some were troubled by the breadth of authority requested. In particular, the phrase "restore international peace and security in the region" seemed to authorize the president to undertake, at his discretion, other military interventions throughout the Middle East. The White House indicated a willingness to negotiate but insisted that Bush would not accept conditions that required another round of UN or congressional approval.

By late September, the executive and legislative branches were engaged in a tug of war over the resolution. Some Democrats pulled back, fearing that the president's insistence on quick passage was being used for partisan advantage in the upcoming election. Senator Byrd spoke out against "this war hysteria

[that] has blown in like a hurricane."[55] Meanwhile, the White House shifted rhetorical focus to national security and the war on terrorism. Rumsfeld publicly asserted that the U.S. had "bulletproof" evidence linking Saddam Hussein to al Qaeda.[56] According to one analysis, themes of war and security made up more than two-thirds of the content of Bush campaign speeches in the fall of 2002.[57] Bush's strategy appeared to be having success, with polls showing voters more concerned about Iraq than the economy, despite a significant decline in both the stock market and consumer confidence.

Some Democrats in Congress capitulated to the pressure, while others fought back. Several admitted to the *Washington Post* that many Democrats who opposed the president's confrontational strategy toward Iraq would "nonetheless support it because they fear[ed] a backlash from voters."[58] Others wanted to meet the president's deadline so as to eliminate the war as an election issue and be able to focus on more politically promising domestic issues.[59] Yet other Democrats felt the tone of the Republican campaign had become so harsh that they had to stand up. Both the president and the vice president suggested several times on the campaign trail that congressional Democrats were not adequately concerned about national security.[60] In response, Senate Majority Leader Tom Daschle, D-S.D., angrily defended the patriotism of Democrats, charging, "This is politicization pure and simple."[61]

The president sought to mollify Democrats at a September 26 meeting with congressional leaders. He publicly declared, "The security of the country is the commitment of both political parties."[62] The White House also circulated a new compromise resolution in Congress, with the regional security clause eliminated, language invoking the War Powers Act inserted, and a new clause requiring the president to inform Congress promptly of his determination that diplomatic efforts were insufficient.

The new version of the resolution was generally well received in Congress. Nonetheless, Sen. Joseph Biden, D-Del., and Senator Lugar, with the support of several other moderate senators, sought to narrow the resolution's justifications for war from the laundry list of UN resolutions to a single justification: Iraq's failure to destroy its WMD. Biden admitted, however, that he probably would vote for even an "imperfect" resolution so as not to undermine the president in the international arena. He added, "I just can't fathom the president going it alone. If I'm wrong, I've made a tragic mistake."[63] The White House saw making WMD the sole justification for war as too restrictive. Bush wanted the flexibility to remove the Iraqi leader from power regardless of whether he was disarmed. The president declared, "I don't want to get a resolution which ties my hands."[64]

House Minority Leader Richard Gephardt, D-Mo., also suggested revisions to the White House, which found them far less restrictive than those of Biden and Lugar. On October 2, the White House announced that it had come to an agreement with Gephardt and the Republican Party leadership in the House on a new draft resolution. Gephardt explained his endorsement by arguing, "We had to go through this, putting politics aside, so we have a chance to get to a consensus that will lead the country in the right direction."[65] The agreement isolated Daschle, the only major congressional leader who had not come to terms with the White House, and diminished Biden and Lugar's bargaining position.

Bush built on the momentum from the Gephardt agreement with a speech televised on October 7, in which he called for Congress to pass the authorizing resolution. He made the case that Iraq was an urgent threat "because it gathers the most serious dangers of our age in one place." In supporting the principle of a preemptive strike, he argued "we cannot wait for the final proof—the smoking gun—that could come in the form of a mushroom cloud." Bush went on to say that congressional passage did not mean that war was imminent. Rather, a resolution would show "the United Nations and all nations that America speaks with one voice."[66]

The momentum of the Gephardt-Bush agreement and the October 7 speech seemed to sweep away much of the centrist opposition to the revised resolution. Two major Republican dissenters, Armey and Lugar, quickly fell into line with the president, and Daschle indicated that he too was now inclined to vote for the resolution. Within several days, others on the fence began to do the same. Sen. Evan Bayh, D-Ind., a strong supporter of regime change in Iraq and a cosponsor of the administration resolution, explained the Democratic shift: "The majority of the American people tend to trust the Republican Party more on issues involving national security and defense than they do the Democratic Party. We need to work to improve our image on that score by taking a more aggressive posture with regard to Iraq, empowering the president."[67]

On October 10, the House approved the resolution 296–133, with 127 Democrats and 6 Republicans opposed. The vote was less consensual than expected. Observers saw it as a sign of Democratic dissatisfaction with Gephardt's position and a reaction to the late release of a CIA letter concluding that Iraq was only likely to use WMD against the United States in response to an attack.[68] Early the next day, the Senate voted overwhelmingly, 77–23, in support of the resolution. The most impassioned opposition came from Senator Byrd, who deplored Congress's failure to be faithful to its constitutional duties, asserting, "We can put a sign on top of this Capitol: Gone home, gone fishing, out of business."[69] Senator Daschle summed up the case for supporting the president's resolution: "I believe it is important for America to speak with one voice at this critical moment."[70]

Final Preparations

The Bush administration publicly praised the congressional authorization and supported efforts by international weapons inspectors in Iraq (track two). Behind the scenes, however, the administration was heavily engaged in war preparations. As fall turned to winter, the United States prepositioned more than one hundred thousand troops in the Persian Gulf and called up National Guard and reserve units. It appears that President Bush made his final decision to authorize the war in fall 2002, even as weapons inspectors continued their work in Iraq. In October the Joint Chiefs of Staff sent a strategic guidance memo to combat planning officers in the field, telling them in essence that "a war with Iraq [should] be considered part of the war on terror."[71] CIA director Tenet was also convinced that war was inevitable based on a private conversation with the president in which Bush told him, "We're not going to wait." In a discussion with CIA officials on November 4, Tenet was "asked if it really looked like war with Iraq: 'You bet your ass,' Tenet said bluntly. 'It's not a matter of if. It's a matter of when. The president is going to war. Make the plans. We're going.' "[72]

That winter the president was briefed on the contents of Iraq's twelve-thousand-page declaration to the United Nations rebutting WMD charges. The administration dismissed Iraq's evidence as implausible. In early January 2003 the president told Rice privately, "This [international inspections] pressure isn't holding together. Time is not on our side here. . . . We're going to have to go to war." Rice interpreted this as the president's final decision: "He had reached the point of no return."[73]

The International Community and the Impending War

The world seemed to come together following the attacks of September 11. U.S. allies in NATO invoked Article V of the Washington Treaty, defining the events as an attack on the entire alliance. In the Afghan war, European countries provided logistical support for operations, emergency food aid, refugee assistance, and stabilization forces.

International cooperation on Iraq was another matter, however. By fall 2002, U.S. and allied perceptions of threats to security began to diverge. Many in the Bush administration, especially the neo-conservatives, argued that terrorism, tyranny, and the spread of WMD were the fundamental threats to U.S security. While sympathetic, other world leaders saw their own "homeland security" as economic stability and the management of ethnic and religious tensions. To some, the most pressing issue in the Middle East continued to be the Israeli-Palestinian conflict, not regime change in Iraq.

Relations between the United States and its NATO allies soured in 2002, as the Bush administration pushed a more interventionist foreign policy around the globe. Faced with resistance to an invasion of Iraq, the Bush administration demonstrated its willingness to go its own way on international security issues. On January 20, 2003, after intense debate, the Europeans made it clear that they would not go beyond Resolution 1441 to endorse an invasion of Iraq based merely on a lack of cooperation with weapons inspectors. Insiders have suggested that this was a turning point for Powell, who felt ambushed by the timing and intensity of international criticism. On February 5, Powell outlined to the UN Security Council suspected WMD sites in Iraq and purported links between Saddam Hussein and al Qaeda. The world listened with interest, but European diplomats argued that Powell had presented no "new" evidence of Iraqi violations.

The Iraq War

On March 17, hours after dropping plans to gain a Security Council resolution authorizing war against Iraq, President Bush issued a public ultimatum to the Iraqi leader: Go into exile within forty-eight hours or risk attack from the United States and its allies. The president made it clear that he expected war and believed that he had a strong base of congressional and public support.[74] In a poll taken hours after the president's speech, 66 percent of Americans said they approved of the ultimatum and the choice of going to war against Iraq if Saddam Hussein did not leave office; 68 percent of respondents said that they believed the United States had done "everything in its power" to reach a diplomatic resolution.[75]

U.S. and coalition forces launched "Operation Iraqi Freedom" on March 19, 2003, and ground troops advanced rapidly into Iraq. The main contingent of ground troops invaded from the south, coupled with a massive aerial bombardment. Invading forces faced challenges such as bad weather, long and insecure supply lines, and hit-and-run attacks, but they made steady progress northward through the country. In early April, U.S. and coalition forces rushed into Baghdad and forced a general surrender of Iraqi forces. On May 1, aboard the USS *Abraham Lincoln,* President Bush stood before a banner proclaiming "Mission Accomplished" and declared the "end of major combat operations" in Iraq.[76] His administration's policy of preemptive attack had proven successful. Iraq had been liberated from a tyrannical dictator, and the threat of a rogue regime with WMD had been eliminated. The president's made-for-television spectacle was a powerful symbol of the modern imperial presidency.

However, the war and its consequences proved more difficult to control than its imagery. No evidence of an active WMD program was ever found. Intelligence reports used by the Bush administration in making its case for urgent action proved false. Critics charged that the administration had "cooked the books" in favor of war. In particular, they asserted that the Pentagon's Office of Special Plans manipulated intelligence to influence public opinion and legitimate the administration's Iraq policies. Most experts now believe that Iraq's WMD capacity did not survive the 1991 Persian Gulf War and subsequent international inspections.[77]

Furthermore, the limitations of postwar occupation planning soon became apparent. Many Bush administration officials simplistically believed that coalition forces would be greeted as liberators of Iraq, but that did not occur. Moreover, U.S. and allied forces were not deployed in sufficient numbers to provide security throughout the country. Jay Garner and his postwar administration arrived in Baghdad to find deteriorating conditions and very few resources with which to restore order. In the three weeks that followed the fall of the Iraqi government, unchecked looting gutted almost every major public institution in Baghdad. When questioned about the chaos, an exasperated Rumsfeld said, "Stuff happens! Freedom is untidy."[78] Things quickly went from bad to worse, as an insurgency against coalition forces gained momentum.

Some of the consequences of the Iraq war might have been recognized with a more coherent policy-making process. There is no doubt that the tough interagency struggle leading up to the war fostered bitter disagreements between departments in the aftermath of the invasion.[79] Secretary Rumsfeld had fought hard for Pentagon control of the postwar situation, and excluded many regional experts from the process. When Jay Garner tapped State Department experts to help him with postwar planning, Rumsfeld had them removed from the team because they had previously written or said things "that were not supportive" of the Pentagon's plan.[80]

In May 2003, in an effort to stabilize Iraq, Bush and Rumsfeld replaced Garner as head of the Coalition Provisional Authority (CPA) with Paul Bremer, an experienced diplomat. While Bremer brought new resources to rebuild Iraq's infrastructure, he was also responsible for two of the most controversial occupation initiatives: the de-Baathification of the Iraqi government and the disbanding of the Iraqi army. These actions alienated hundreds of thousands of Iraqis and destroyed an indigenous Iraqi security force. Bremer's actions were part of Rumsfeld's plan to control postwar Iraq, but they had never been cleared at the interagency level. Critics have charged that these actions helped foment the popular insurgency that further destabilized Iraq, and Garner later called them "tragic decisions."[81]

Although "major combat operations" were supposedly over, attacks against coalition troops actually increased. More than a thousand U.S. soldiers were killed and several thousand were injured between spring 2003 and fall 2004. Facing the reality of the postwar occupation of Iraq, U.S. public opinion eroded. An April 2004 poll indicated that 46 percent of Americans believed that the United States "should have stayed out of Iraq." One year after the president's announcement of the end of major combat operations, his overall approval rating stood at 46 percent, down from a high of 89 percent just after the September 11 attacks.[82] But despite public doubts about the war, Iraq never became a central issue in the 2004 presidential election, perhaps because both Democratic nominees had voted to authorize the president's use of force in Iraq.

In spite of the change in public sentiment, President Bush and top officials maintained a resolute attitude. Indeed, the president was determined to proceed toward restoration of order in Iraq and the consolidation of democracy. Chairman of the Joint Chiefs of Staff Richard Myers observed:

> When any doubt started to creep into the small, windowless Situation Room, the president almost stomped it out. Whether it was alarming casualties, bad news, the current decision on the timing of Iraqi elections, some other problem, or just a whiff of one of the uncertainties that accompany war, the president would try to set them all straight. "Hold it," Bush said once. "We know we're doing the right thing. We're on the right track here. We're doing the right thing for ourselves, for our own interest and for the world. And don't forget it. Come on, guys."[83]

But the situation continued to worsen between 2004 and 2006, even as the Bush administration struggled to prop up a new unity government in Iraq. In late April 2004, the press reported on stories and photographs of prisoner abuse by U.S. soldiers at the Abu Ghraib prison outside Baghdad. Attacks on U.S. troops continued to rise. According to a May 2006 secret report by the intelligence division of the Joint Chiefs, the insurgency had gained momentum from 2004 to 2006. Attacks on coalition forces were at their highest level with more than three thousand in May 2006, and the Joint Chiefs report correctly predicted rising violence in the coming year.[84]

Searching for an Endgame: "Tell Me How this Ends"[85]

By 2006 the Bush administration's policies in "postwar" Iraq had become untenable given the growing and complex pattern of violence emanating from Baathist insurgents, Sunni jihadists, and Shiite militias, and with U.S. casualties and economic costs continuing to rise in Iraq. 2006 was also an election year in the United States, and the White House reluctantly agreed that spring to the creation of a bipartisan commission, the Iraq Study Group (ISG), to reevaluate U.S. options in Iraq. Meanwhile, Republican Party prospects seemed to dim. A *New York Times*/CBS News poll taken just before the election showed that the war in Iraq was the most important issue for voters. Thirty-four percent of the public believed the war should be Congress's first priority. No other issue even reached 10 percent in the poll. Moreover, only 29 percent of the respondents supported Bush's handling of the war in Iraq, and almost 70 percent believed that he had no plan to end the war.[86]

The election brought a stunning victory for the Democrats, who gained control of the Senate by a margin of 51–49 and the House 233–202. Not a single Democratic incumbent was defeated in the House. On December 6, 2006, the ISG issued its report. The opening sentence set the tone: "The situation in Iraq is grave and deteriorating." Despite its scathing critique of the situation, the report rejected drastic policy change in the form either of a significant increase in, or an immediate withdrawal of, U.S. troops. But it refused to accept staying the course, either. Instead, the report called for an aggressive diplomatic offensive involving all of Iraq's neighbors, internal political reform in Iraq, and a shift in the role of the U.S. military from direct combat to training Iraqi forces—with the goal, subject to conditions in Iraq, of removing U.S. combat forces by spring 2008.[87]

In public comments, President Bush acknowledged that the ISG report was "worthy of serious study," but he was clearly not comfortable with two of its most significant recommendations: negotiations that included Iran and Syria and setting a timetable for the removal of combat troops.[88] He indicated that he would wait for studies ongoing in his administration before making any decisions about future policy directions. In fact, in September 2006, concerned with both the security situation in Iraq and the political situation in the United States, the administration had begun a review of Iraq policy. The review was kept secret because White House officials believed it "would amount to political suicide to announce a broad reassessment of Iraq strategy" prior to the elections. But without such a review, "they would be forced to accept the conclusions of the final report of the Iraq Study Group."[89]

Apparently, by late September the White House began to wonder whether staying the course was still a viable option, and it appears that the president decided Donald Rumsfeld, a staunch defender of current policies, would be replaced after the election.[90] The pace of the administration's policy review quickened in November. Deputy national security adviser J. D. Crouch was tasked with coordinating reassessments already under way by the National Security Council, the Joint Chiefs of Staff, and the State Department. The goal was to complete the review by mid-December so as to have policy alternatives to compete with the ISG report. But the administration found it difficult to build a consensus on a new policy and soon announced that no new policy would be forthcoming before early 2007.[91]

Much of the military leadership, including the Joint Chiefs of Staff; Gen. John Abizaid, head of Central Command; and Gen. George Casey, commander of the coalition forces in Iraq, were highly resistant to any significant increases in troop levels.[92] They believed that an increase would only encourage the Iraqi government to postpone making necessary political, economic, and military reforms. On the other hand, national security adviser Stephen Hadley consistently supported a troop surge to regain control of the security situation in Baghdad, arguing that viable political reforms could not be achieved without that security.[93]

Bush had never seriously considered beginning to withdraw troops from Iraq. By early December the president was leaning toward some type of surge.[94] Bush's final views were shaped by a White House meeting with retired general Jack Keane, who not only strongly supported an increase in troop levels but confidently outlined a new strategy for the troops based on counterinsurgency doctrine. A White House aide later told Keane, "The meeting in the Oval Office turned out to be decisive, in terms of your presentation. . . . You did two things in there that I haven't seen. You gave them a vision, a way ahead, and you gave them courage."[95]

The president was disappointed with the Joint Chiefs' opposition to a significant troop surge. He was said to have come away from a meeting with them on December 13, 2006, thinking that the chiefs "were trying to manage defeat rather than find a way to victory."[96] Bush was quoted as warning them: "What I want to hear from you is how we are going to win . . . not how we're going to leave."[97] By the end of December, the Joint Chiefs, as well as Casey and Abizaid, accepted a troop surge. But Bush also agreed to a permanent increase of ninety-two thousand soldiers to relieve the stress on the military created by deployments in Iraq and Afghanistan.[98] For years Rumsfeld had stymied calls for an increase in the permanent force levels of the army and the marines. Moreover, Bush accepted the military's request that the new Iraq policy include greater emphasis on economic development and political reform, as well as assurances from the Maliki government that it would provide sufficient Iraqi forces to assist U.S. troops and that military operations would be permitted in Shiite neighborhoods.

In early January 2007, as the nation waited for Bush's Iraq policy address, word leaked out that the president was replacing the U.S. diplomatic and military leadership in Iraq—the U.S. ambassador to Iraq, the commander of coalition forces in Iraq, and the head of Central Command. Perhaps most important, Gen. David Petraeus, who had been responsible for revising the army's counterinsurgency policy and who enthusiastically supported a troop surge, was to be the new commander of forces in Iraq. A senior official in the administration commented, "The idea is to put the whole new team in at roughly the same time, and send some clear messages that we are trying a new approach."[99]

That "new way forward" was announced on January 10. The president admitted that his old course had failed, but his new plan did not resemble the recommendations of the ISG report: there was no time frame for withdrawal or even reduction of troops, and there was no ambitious diplomatic initiative to draw Iraq's neighbors into a peace process. Instead, arguing that the mission in Iraq was too important to be abandoned, the president announced that a "surge" of five more brigades (about 21,500 combat troops) would be sent to Iraq. Controlling sectarian violence and providing physical security would become the primary goal of U.S. forces. There would also be an extensive economic development effort to enhance the lives of Iraqis, and the government of Iraqi prime minister Nouri al-Maliki would be given a series of political reform benchmarks to achieve, although, unlike the ISG recommendations, no sanctions were threatened for failure to achieve them.

Most Democrats and some Republicans in Congress denounced the troop increase as a rejection of both the bipartisan ISG recommendations and the public will as expressed in the fall election. An overnight *Washington Post*/ABC

News poll found that 61 percent of the public opposed the president's plan.[100] Congress struggled to respond to Bush's initiative, but congressional Democrats were divided. A number of recourses were considered, including a nonbinding resolution opposing the troop increase; a repeal of the original legislation authorizing the use of force in Iraq and its replacement with another, more narrowly drafted, conditional authorization; an appropriation of funds for the war that put conditions on the use of troops in Iraq, such as stipulating a deadline or goal for the removal of combat soldiers; and a refusal to appropriate any future funds for the war.

Each of those options raised political, military, and constitutional problems, however. Some members of Congress rejected a nonbinding resolution as a meaningless symbol that would do nothing to end the war. Others thought that placing restrictions, including time limits, in legislation not only would infringe on the president's constitutional role as commander in chief, but would put the military at risk by limiting the president's ability to make rapid adjustments to changes on the ground. Strong opponents of the war thought conditional appropriations would still let the war continue for too long. Conditional legislation also had the liability of being subject to presidential veto. All sides agreed that Congress had the constitutional authority to refuse to appropriate any future funds for the war, but that had the serious political liability of leaving members open to charges of failing to support the troops.

President Bush's need in spring 2007 for a $97 billion supplemental appropriation for the wars in Iraq and Afghanistan provided opponents with a vehicle to limit the combat role of U.S. troops in Iraq. But Democratic leaders' attempts to require a timetable for a planned troop withdrawal could not muster the two-thirds vote necessary to override a presidential veto in the House, nor could they gather a consistent sixty-vote majority in the Senate. At the end of May, the Democratic leadership in both houses conceded defeat and agreed to drop any troop withdrawal language from the appropriation bill funding the Iraq war through September 30, 2007. The only concession that Congress was able to win from the Bush administration was the inclusion in the legislation of benchmarks of military, economic, and political progress in Iraq. The bill required that President Bush provide a report to Congress evaluating the progress on those benchmarks on July 15 and September 15—a plan designed to assuage concerns about presidential accountability by both opponents and moderate Republicans.

General Petraeus saw a need to produce quick results in Iraq to meet both the needs of the political process in Washington and the military manpower constraints that made it unlikely that the surge could continue indefinitely. On the political side, he worried, "The Washington clock is moving more rapidly than the Baghdad clock. . . . So we're obviously trying to speed up the Baghdad clock a bit and to produce some progress on the ground that can perhaps . . . put a little more time on the Washington clock."[101] On the troop question, he recognized that all of the surge troops, ultimately numbering about thirty-one thousand, would not arrive until June 2007, and yet they would probably have to rotate out of Iraq by the summer of 2008. Furthermore, the new counterinsurgency strategy entailed not only a surge in the number of troops but a change in military and political policy in Iraq. Much of the new military strategy could not be put into play until all the troops arrived. It would necessitate a different mix of population-centric and enemy-centric tactics.[102] The new approach would combine a continued, but more focused, attack on the most violent insurgent and sectarian militias with a new emphasis on a far more sustained effort to make secure population centers. The population-centric component would require that troops be moved from large forward bases isolated from Iraqis into smaller bases in their neighborhoods.

The last and most crucial component of the new strategy was to encourage the political reconciliation of the three major warring factions within Iraq—Sunni, Shia, and Kurd. In particular, it would require that the Maliki government, which was perceived by many Iraqis as a pro-Shia government, balance more fairly the needs of the three groups. But such reconciliation was not likely to occur until all sides felt more physically secure.

The first half of 2007 did not go well in Iraq. Violence against both Iraqi civilians and U.S. troops sharply escalated. Petraeus recalled the spring of 2007 as a "horrific nightmare."[103] More American troops (904) died in Iraq in 2007 than in any other year of the war. In addition, almost twenty-four thousand Iraqi civilians were killed.[104] But by the late summer, as the strategy became more fully operational, violence began to diminish significantly. Both troop and civilian casualties were cut in half over the last six months of 2007. Most analysts attributed this significant decline to a number of factors, including the increase in the number of troops; the change to a more population-centric strategy; and, perhaps most important, the successful outreach to insurgent Sunni militias that resulted in almost one hundred thousand of them being placed on the American payroll.[105]

In September 2007 Petraeus and Crocker were required by Congress to report on conditions in Iraq. The Joint Chiefs used this deadline to push within the administration once more for rapid combat troop reductions. But prior to the hearings, Petraeus met personally with Bush and convinced him that the counterinsurgency strategy was working and that surge levels should only slowly be reduced by July 2008. Petraeus later testified in the congressional hearings that there had been significant military progress in Iraq, with incidents of violence down over 45 percent from its high point in December 2006. Nonetheless, he said the situation was fragile, and a precipitous drop in U.S. troop levels could have "devastating consequences."[106] He then recommended the gradual surge withdrawal approved by Bush. Both Crocker and Petraeus were less definitive about the improvement in the political situation in Iraq, though they noted the promise of local efforts in reconciliation and government reform.[107]

While most Democrats and some Republicans were still troubled by the lack of a clear strategy to militarily disengage successfully from Iraq in the near term, Petraeus seemed to have bought the new counterinsurgency policy more time on the Washington clock. In 2008 there would be no serious attempt in Congress to set a timetable for disengagement,[108] the security situation in Iraq would continue to improve, and the annual civilian and military violence levels in Iraq would decline in both 2008 and 2009.[109]

Ironically, the most effective impetus for a troop withdrawal timetable came from within the *Iraqi* political process. By the middle of 2007 the Maliki government announced that it would not accept an extension of the UN mandate for the multinational forces in Iraq beyond 2008. Iraqis saw the end of the UN mandate as an important recognition of their renewed national sovereignty. Without a UN mandate, there would be no legal basis for the presence of U.S. troops on Iraqi soil. Consequently, the United States and Iraq would need to negotiate a bilateral "status of forces agreement" for the governance of U.S. troops in Iraq. As the various Iraqi political factions jockeyed for political position for the provincial and national elections scheduled for 2009, the Maliki government sought to use the status of forces agreement to legitimize itself as a government independent of U.S. influence. Maliki sought more Iraqi control over the use and regulation of U.S. troops in Iraq. In addition, under "intense domestic pressure" he insisted on a timetable for withdrawal that would allow him to frame the agreement as one that would set the conditions for "Americans leaving Iraq."[110] In July 2008, Maliki seemed to support Democratic presidential candidate Barack Obama's plan to withdraw troops sixteen months after Obama's inauguration.[111] Faced with the expiring UN mandate and recognizing Maliki's precarious domestic political position, the Bush administration acquiesced and signed an agreement in November 2009 that unconditionally required the United States to remove its combat troops from Iraqi cities by June 30, 2009, and to withdraw all of its troops from Iraq by December 31, 2011.[112]

Obama's War in Iraq

The war in Iraq moved into its second presidential administration on January 20, 2009. Barack Obama took office with fourteen combat brigades still in Iraq. He had campaigned on withdrawing all combat troops there by the spring of 2010. Obama had also indicated that he would increase U.S. military forces in Afghanistan. Given the sharp constraints on U.S. military personnel, these two goals were intertwined. On his first full day in office Obama met with the military leadership and his national security advisers to discuss plans for the prompt withdrawal of combat troops. Obama faced a tension between his electoral base and the military field commanders (General Petraeus, the new commander of CENTCOM and responsible for both Iraq and Afghanistan, and Gen. Raymond Odierno, who replaced Petraeus as commanding general in Iraq). The electoral base expected Obama to keep his promise of a steady sixteen-month withdrawal from Iraq, while Odierno and Petraeus were in favor of a much slower and phased pullout. While presidents are loathe to alienate their electoral base, Obama also had to consider the consequences of disregarding military advice and then taking the blame if the fragile Iraqi stability unraveled.

During these January discussions, Odierno with Petraeus's support recommended to Obama a very slow decline of troop strength that would remove only two brigades over the next six months and then evaluate conditions on the ground. Odierno was particularly concerned that there be a sufficient U.S. force present during the Iraqi national elections, which were scheduled to be held at the beginning of 2010.[113] Obama indicated that he wanted a more rapid military retraction. A month later Obama announced he had approved a plan to bring out all the combat troops by August 2010, three months later than his sixteen-month campaign promise. Most of the withdrawals would take place after the Iraqi national elections. This nineteen-month time frame was a compromise between those who favored a fairly rapid, sixteen-month withdrawal and others who believed it should take place much more gradually. In the end, Obama advisers "said they believed that they had reached an accommodation that would satisfy both the military and a public eager to get out of Iraq, while relieving the strain on the armed forces and freeing up resources for Afghanistan."[114]

Conclusion

The Iraq war has provided some important lessons for U.S. foreign policy in the post–September 11 era. In many ways, an ongoing war on terrorism lends itself to an imperial presidency. The Bush doctrine and the wars in Afghanistan and Iraq all suggest the ability of a very strong executive to dominate U.S. foreign policy decision making. The Iraq war and its aftermath also demonstrate some of the problems that result from executive branch dominance in foreign policy making. A highly personalized and aggressive executive decision process, especially with an acquiescent Congress, appears prone to making decisions without an adequate range of information. The result can be a series of flawed decisions, including, in the case of U.S. military action against Iraq, underestimating the danger of intervening without adequate international support, failing to make adequate preparations for the occupation of Iraq, and only belatedly recognizing that the occupation strategy in effect was failing.

The constraints on an imperial president can be quite limited. Despite losing the 2006 congressional elections, Bush was still able to go against public opinion and impose a troop surge in 2007. The limits on Congress's ability to influence the situation were also seen in that decision. Party loyalty among congressional members of the president's party and the president's veto power normally limit Congress's ability to check the president. The most potent constitutional tool available to Congress, a funding cutoff, is under most circumstances too blunt a political tool to wield effectively. It may be that an imperial president can only be checked by his own electoral fate, the presidential two-term limit, or the abandonment of his cause by his own party. These are all slow processes.

The result was, by many accounts, an ill-conceived war with no conclusive end in sight. While the levels of violence have been greatly reduced in Iraq since the end of 2007, and many casual observers have concluded that the surge was a success, the situation is much more complex. For Petraeus and Crocker the solution to the spiraling chaos of Iraq in 2006–2007 was not military but political. The strategic purpose of the surge was to provide enough physical security for all sides in Iraq that they would then have the space to work out a political reconciliation.[115] At this writing, there has been some progress in that regard. Reasonably peaceful provincial elections were held in January 2009. The Iraqi government also accepted into the Iraqi security forces some of the former Sunni insurgents who had aligned with the U.S. forces in 2007 and 2008. Modest steps were also taken to provide amnesty, pensions, and jobs opportunities for former members of the Baath Party and the army. But many of the most important issues for reconciliation had yet to be achieved by early 2010. For these reasons, Thomas Ricks argued that "the surge did not work. Militarily, or tactically it did. It improved security. But its stated goal was to create a breathing space in which a political breakthrough could occur and that did not happen."[116] Many difficult issues remained, including sharing of oil revenues, a new federalist governing arrangement for Iraq, and sectarian differences between Sunni, Shia, and Kurdish populations in Iraq. Most disturbingly, the closely contested March 2010 Iraqi parliamentary elections had yet to produce a viable majority coalition as of late August 2010. The Iraqi political system appeared fragile and stalemated.

Moreover, this uncertainty has come at a high price. By 2009 the war had already cost the United States over $850 billion, with continuing costs, including refurbishing depleted military equipment and the long-term care of wounded veterans, estimated at two trillion dollars.[117] The human cost included over 4,300 American troops killed and more than 30,000 wounded, plus an Iraqi society with over 100,000 civilians killed and 4 million people displaced from their homes.

Key Actors

George W. Bush   President, saw the need after the September 11 attacks for the United States to adopt a policy of preventive strikes against nations that presented a potential security threat; believed that Iraq was such a threat.

Richard Cheney   Vice president, strongly believed that Iraq, because it allegedly possessed weapons of mass destruction and had links to al Qaeda, posed an immediate threat to the security of the United States and that diplomacy would not produce an adequate response.

Stephen Hadley   National security adviser in the second term of the Bush administration, was a strong proponent of a surge after the 2006 election.

Barack Obama   President, who campaigned for the presidency in 2008 on a platform of removing all combat troops from Iraq in sixteen months and refocusing U.S. efforts to restabilize Afghanistan.

David Petraeus   Commanding general of the Multi-National Forces in Iraq, led the counterinsurgency strategy with the surge troops in 2007–2008; later served as head of Central Command (CENTCOM) and succeeded Gen. Stanley McChrystal as commander of surge operations in Afghanistan in 2010.

Colin Powell   Secretary of state, argued within the administration that the threat from Iraq could be contained with beefed-up UN weapons inspections and cautioned against the United States intervening militarily in Iraq without international support.

Condoleezza Rice   National security adviser and central foreign policy adviser to President George W. Bush, had difficulty coordinating the policy process within the administration because of strong and conflicting personalities and policy positions; became secretary of state in the second term.

Donald Rumsfeld   Secretary of defense, argued that a transformed U.S. military with precision-guided munitions and a smaller, lighter strike force was the appropriate option to remove the allegedly imminent Iraqi threat.

George Tenet   Director of central intelligence, was skeptical about the need for an invasion of Iraq but later provided intelligence reports that helped the president make the case for war.

Paul Wolfowitz   Deputy secretary of defense, a long-time proponent of a preventive military strategy in general and the use of military force to achieve regime change in Iraq in particular.

Notes

1. Arthur M. Schlesinger Jr., *The Imperial Presidency* (Boston: Houghton Mifflin, 1973), ix.

2. Ibid., viii.

3. Michael Beschloss, "The End of the Imperial Presidency," *New York Times,* December 18, 2000, A27.

4. Nicholas Lemann, "The Next World Order: The Bush Administration May Have a Brand New Doctrine of Power," *New Yorker,* April 1, 2002, www.newyorker.com/ fact/ content/?020401fa_FACT1 (accessed January 12, 2004).

5. Ivo H. Daalder and James M. Lindsay, *America Unbound* (Washington, D.C.: Brookings Institution Press, 2003), 2.

6. Bob Woodward, *Plan of Attack* (New York: Simon and Schuster, 2004).

7. Michael R. Gordon and Bernard E. Trainor, *Cobra II: The Inside Story of the Invasion and Occupation of Iraq* (New York: Pantheon, 2006), 16.

8. Bryan Burrough, Evgenia Peretz, David Rose, and David Wise, "The Path to War," *Vanity Fair,* May 2004, 236.

9. Michael J. Mazarr, "The Iraq War and Agenda Setting," *Foreign Policy Analysis* 3 (2007): 2.

10. Quoted in Jane Mayer, "The Manipulator," *New Yorker,* June 7, 2004, 61.

11. Bill Keller, "The Sunshine Warrior," *New York Times Magazine,* September 22, 2002, 48; Bob Woodward, *Bush at War* (New York: Simon and Schuster, 2002), 85.

12. Woodward, *Plan of Attack,* 26.

13. Quoted in Glenn Kessler, "U.S. Decision on Iraq Has Puzzling Past," *Washington Post,* January 12, 2003, A1.

14. Lawrence F. Kaplan, "Why the Bush Administration Will Go After Iraq," *New Republic,* December 10, 2001, 21.

15. Stephen Benedict Dyson, " 'Stuff Happens': Donald Rumsfeld and the Iraq War," *Foreign Policy Analysis* 2009, vol. 5, 327, and 333–334.

16. Seymour M. Hersh, "The Iraq Hawks," *New Yorker*, December 24, 2001, 58.

17. David Rieff, "Blueprint for a Mess," *New York Times*, November 2, 2003, A1.

18. Richard Perle, "Should Iraq Be Next?" *San Diego Union-Tribune*, December 16, 2001, www.aei.org/article/13478 (accessed January 22, 2010).

19. Seymour M. Hersh, "Selective Intelligence?" *New Yorker*, May 12, 2003, www.newyorker.com/printable/?fact/030512fa_fact (accessed January 11, 2004).

20. Gordon and Trainor, *Cobra II*, 38.

21. Quoted in Michael Elliot and James Carney, "First Stop, Iraq," *Time*, March 31, 2003, 177; Daalder and Lindsay, *America Unbound*, 130.

22. Daalder and Lindsay, *America Unbound*, 130.

23. Woodward, *Plan of Attack*, 175.

24. Kessler, "U.S. Decision on Iraq Has Puzzling Past."

25. Woodward, *Plan of Attack*, 1–3.

26. Susan Page, "Iraq Course Set from Tight White House Circle," *USA Today*, September 11, 2002, 5A-6A; Woodward, *Bush at War*, 108, 329; Evan Thomas, "Bush Has Saddam in His Sights," *Newsweek*, March 4, 2002, 21.

27. Elliot and Carney, "First Stop, Iraq," 173.

28. Christopher Marquis, "Bush Officials Differ on Way to Force Out Iraqi Leader," *New York Times*, June 19, 2002, A1.

29. Woodward, *Plan of Attack*, 72–73.

30. Gordon and Trainor, *Cobra II*, 26.

31. Quoted in Dyson, " 'Stuff Happens,' " 332.

32. Glenn R. Kessler and Peter Sleven, "Rice Fails to Repair Rifts, Officials Say," *Washington Post*, October 12, 2003, A1.

33. Mark Hosenball, Michael Isikoff, and Evan Thomas, "Cheney's Long Path to War," *Newsweek*, November 17, 2003, 29.

34. Gordon and Trainor, *Cobra II*, 112.

35. Quoted in Bob Woodward, *State of Denial* (New York: Simon and Schuster, 2006), 125.

36. "President Bush Delivers Graduation Speech at West Point: Remarks by the President at the 2002 Graduation Exercise of the United States Military Academy," West Point, New York, June 1, 2002, www.whitehouse.gov/news/releases/2002/06/print/20020601-3.html (accessed January 22, 2004).

37. Dyson, " 'Stuff Happens,' " 334.

38. Woodward, *Plan of Attack*, 230.

39. Ibid., 150.

40. Ibid.

41. John Diamond et al., "Bush Set Sights on Saddam after 9/11, Never Looked Back," *USA Today*, March 21, 2003, 8A.

42. Brent Scowcroft, "Don't Attack Saddam," *Wall Street Journal*, August 15, 2002, A14.

43. Glenn Kessler, "Rice Lays Out a Case for War in Iraq," *Washington Post*, August 26, 2002, A1.

44. Elizabeth Pond, *Friendly Fire: The Near-Death of the Transatlantic Alliance* (Washington, D.C.: Brookings Institution Press, 2004); see also "Vice President Speaks

at VFW 103rd National Convention," www.whitehouse.gov/news/releases/2002/08/20020826.html (accessed January 12, 2004).

45. Woodward, *Bush at War*, 44, 161.

46. *Frontline*, "The War Behind Closed Doors," www.pbs.org/wgbh/pages/frontline/shows/iraq.

47. Dana Milbank, "White House Push for Iraqi Strike Is on Hold," *Washington Post*, August 18, 2002, A1.

48. Mike Allen and Juliet Eilperin, "Bush Aides Say Iraq War Needs No Hill Vote," *Washington Post*, August 26, 2002, A1.

49. Ibid.

50. Miles Pomper, "Bush Hopes to Avoid Battle with Congress over Iraq," *CQ Weekly*, August 31, 2002, 2255.

51. Allison Mitchell and David Sanger, "Bush to Put Case for Action in Iraq to Key Lawmakers," *New York Times*, September 4, 2002, A1.

52. "President's Remarks at the United Nations General Assembly," www.whitehouse.gov/news/releases/2002/09/print/20020912-1.html (accessed July 31, 2003).

53. Dan Balz and Jim VandeHei, "Bush Speech Aids Prospect for Support by Congress," *Washington Post*, September 13, 2002, A32.

54. "Text of the Proposed Resolution," *Washington Post*, September 20, 2002, A21.

55. U.S. Congress, *Congressional Record*, September 20, 2002, 148:S8966.

56. Eric Schmitt, "Rumsfeld Says U.S. Has 'Bulletproof' Evidence of Iraq's Links to Al Qaeda," *Washington Post*, September 28, 2002, A9.

57. Dana Milbank, "In President's Speeches, Iraq Dominates, Economy Fades," *Washington Post*, September 25, 2002, A1.

58. Jim VandeHei, "Daschle Angered by Bush Statement," *Washington Post*, September 26, 2002, A1.

59. Milbank, "In President's Speeches."

60. Ibid.

61. VandeHei, "Daschle Angered."

62. Todd Purdum and Elisabeth Bumiller, "Congress Nearing Draft Resolution on Force in Iraq," *New York Times*, September 27, 2002, A1.

63. David Nather et al., " 'One Voice' Lost in Debate over Iraq War Resolution," *CQ Weekly*, September 28, 2002, 2500.

64. "Bush Rejects Hill Limits on Resolution Allowing War," *Washington Post*, October 2, 2002, A1.

65. Quoted in Louis Fisher, "Deciding on War against Iraq: Institutional Failures," *Political Science Quarterly* 18, no. 3 (2003): 403.

66. Karen DeYoung, "Bush Cites Urgent Iraqi Threat," *Washington Post*, October 8, 2002, A1.

67. John Cushman, "Daschle Predicts Broad Support for Military Action against Iraq," *New York Times*, October 7, 2002, A11.

68. "CIA Letter to Senate on Baghdad's Intentions," *New York Times*, October 9, 2002, A12.

69. Dana Milbank, "For Many, a Resigned Endorsement; Attack Authorized with Little Drama," *Washington Post*, October 11, 2002, A6.

70. James VandeHei and Juliet Eilperin, "House Passes Iraq War Resolution," *Washington Post*, October 11, 2002, A1.

71. Thomas Ricks, *Fiasco* (New York: Penguin, 2006), 66.

72. Woodward, *State of Denial,* 89.

73. Woodward, *Plan of Attack,* 254.

74. Richard W. Stevenson, "Bush Gives Hussein 48 Hours, and Vows to Act," *New York Times,* March 18, 2003, A1.

75. CNN, "Poll: Two-Thirds of Americans Support Bush Ultimatum," www.cnn .allpolitics.printhis.clickability.com/pt/cpt?expire=1&fb=Y&urlID=5736455&action= cpt& partnerID=2001 (accessed May 6, 2003).

76. Peter Baker, "The Image Bush Just Can't Escape," *Washington Post,* May 4, 2007, http://www.washingtonpost.com/wp-dyn/content/article/2007/05/03/AR2007050 302138.html (accessed August 30, 2010).

77. Hersh, "Selective Intelligence?"; Burrough et al., "The Path to War," 294.

78. Harvey Rice and Julie Mason, "America at War; Anarchy Reigns in Baghdad," *Houston Chronicle,* April 12, 2003, 1.

79. *Frontline* interview with Richard Clarke, January 23, 2006, www.pbs.org/wgbh/ pages/frontline/darkside/interviews/clarke.html (accessed November 20, 2009).

80. Quoted in Dyson, " 'Stuff Happens,' " 338.

81. Woodward, *State of Denial,* 219; see also Ricks, *Fiasco,* 158–165.

82. Richard W. Stevenson and Janet Elder, "Support for War Is Down Sharply, Poll Concludes," *New York Times,* April 29, 2004, A1; see also Marist College Institute for Public Opinion Poll, quoted in Kenneth T. Walsh, "A Case of Confidence," *U.S. News and World Report,* November 17, 2003.

83. Woodward, *State of Denial,* 371.

84. Quoted in ibid., 472.

85. Gen. David Petraeus to journalist Rick Atkinson in 2003 as reported in Atkinson's *In the Company of Soldiers* (New York: Henry Holt and Co., 2004), 6.

86. Adam Nagourney and Megan Thee, "With Election Driven by Iraq, Voters Want New Approach," *New York Times,* November 2, 2006, 1A.

87. Iraq Study Group, *Iraq Study Group Report* (New York: Vintage, 2006), xiii.

88. Peter Baker and Robin Wright, "Bush Appears Cool to Key Points of Report on Iraq," *Washington Post,* December 8, 2006, A1.

89. David Sanger et al., "Chaos Overran Iraq Plan in '06, Bush Team Says," *New York Times,* January 2, 2007, A1.

90. Ibid.

91. Michael Fletcher, "Bush Delays Speech on Iraq Strategy," *Washington Post,* December 13, 2006, A12.

92. Linda Robinson, *Tell Me How This Ends* (New York: Public Affairs, 2008); Thomas Ricks, *The Gamble: General David Petraeus and the American Military Adventure in Iraq, 2006–2008* (New York: Penguin Press, 2009); and Sanger et al., "Chaos Overran Iraq Plan."

93. Glenn Kessler, "Bush's New Plan for Iraq Echoes Key Parts of Earlier Memo," *Washington Post,* January 11, 2007, A13.

94. Michael Abramowitz and Peter Baker, "Embattled Bush Held to Plan to Salvage Iraq," *Washington Post,* January 21, 2007, A1.

95. Linda Robinson, *Tell Me How This Ends*, 35.

96. Ibid.

97. Sanger et al., "Chaos Overran Iraq Plan."

98. Ann Scott Tyson and Josh White, "Gates Urges Increase in Army, Marines," *Washington Post,* January 12, 2007, A14.

99. Robin Wright and Michael Abramowitz, "Bush Making Changes in His Iraq Team," *Washington Post,* January 5, 2007, A1.

100. Michael Abramowitz and Robin Wright, "Bush to Add 21,500 Troops in an Effort to Stabilize Iraq," *Washington Post,* January 11, 2007, A1.

101. Ricks, *The Gamble,* 148.

102. Robinson, *Tell Me How This Ends.*

103. Ricks, "Understanding the Surge in Iraq and What's Ahead," *Foreign Policy Research Institute E-Notes,* www.fpri.org/enotes/200905.ricks.understandingsurgeiraq .html (accessed May 4, 2009).

104. Brookings Institution, *Iraq Index,* www.brookings.edu/iraqindex (accessed December 11, 2009).

105. Robinson, *Tell Me How This Ends,* 324–326; Ricks, "Understanding the Surge in Iraq and What's Ahead."

106. Peter Baker and Jonathan Weisman, "Petraeus Backs Initial Pullout," *Washington Post,* September 11, 2007, A1.

107. William Branigin, Robin Wright, and Peter Baker, "Petraeus, Crocker Argue Iraqi Government Needs Time," *Washington Post,* September 11, 2007, A1.

108. John Donnelly, "2008 Legislative Summary: Conduct of the Iraq War," *CQ Weekly,* December 8, 2008, 3264.

109. Brookings Institution, *Iraq Index,* December 11, 2009, www.brookings.edu/ iraqindex.

110. Karen DeYoung, "U.S., Iraq Scale Down Negotiations Over Forces," *Washington Post,* July 13, 2008, A1.

111. Sudarsan Raghaven and Dan Eggen, "Iraq Points to Pullout in 2010," *Washington Post,* July 22, 2008, A1.

112. Mary Beth Sheridan, "Iraq Head, Top Cleric Back 2011 Exit by U.S.," *Washington Post,* November 16, 2008, A1.

113. Peter Baker and Thom Shanker, "Obama Meets with Officials on Iraq, Signaling His Commitment to Ending the War," *New York Times,* January 22, 2009, A1.

114. Peter Baker and Elisabeth Bumiller, "Obama Favoring Mid-2010 Pullout in Iraq, Aides Say," *New York Times,* February 25, 2009, A1; Karen DeYoung, "Obama Sets Timetable for Iraq," *Washington Post,* February 28, 2009, A1.

115. Robinson, *Tell Me How This Ends;* Ricks, *The Gamble.*

116. Ricks, "Understanding the Surge in Iraq and What's Ahead."

117. James Glanz, "The Economic Cost of War," *New York Times,* February 28, 2009, A1; *Iraq Study Group Report,* 32.

3 Colombia and U.S. Foreign Policy: Coca, Security, and Human Rights

Jennifer S. Holmes

Before You Begin

1. What should the United States do about drug smuggling?

2. Did Plan Colombia help or hinder the U.S. goals of promoting trade, democracy, and regional stability in Latin America?

3. Do Colombia's concerns with its social stability and democracy conflict with the strategic or political concerns of the United States? Where do they converge, or where do they conflict?

4. Does U.S. policy address Colombian social stability and democracy? What concerns do U.S. lawmakers prioritize?

5. Why has U.S. aid to Colombia tended to be predominantly military in nature? Is this the most appropriate type of assistance?

6. Should human rights in Colombia be a prominent concern in crafting U.S. foreign policy where the drug trade is involved? Who is interested in this issue?

7. Is drug trafficking fundamentally a question of supply or of demand? Which aspect of the problem does U.S. policy address?

8. How did the September 11 attack on the United States alter the foreign policy of President George W. Bush toward Colombia?

Introduction: The Colombian Challenge

Colombia has been designated "public enemy number one" in the debate over illegal drugs in the United States. When Colombia reached its peak of cocaine production in 2001, it alone provided about 75 percent of all the cocaine consumed in the world. In 2003, 90 percent of all cocaine in the United States either originated in Colombia or passed through it.[1] Despite spending billions of dollars in a sustained effort to eradicate coca production and some of the lowest production levels in a decade, Colombia still cultivates half of all coca in the Andean region and produces half of the global cocaine supply. Opium poppies (used in heroin production) and marijuana are also grown in Colombia.[2]

U.S. presidents have attempted to deal with drug smuggling in various ways. President Ronald Reagan declared the drug trade a national security threat and launched his so-called war on drugs. Supplemented by First Lady Nancy Reagan's "Just Say No" domestic campaign against U.S. consumption of illegal drugs, Reagan focused on production, processing, and trafficking abroad. Under President George H. W. Bush, the "Andean Initiative" provided some Latin American countries with military support, economic assistance, and law enforcement advice to curb production and trafficking. Countries that did not cooperate faced possible U.S. military intervention, as Panama experienced in 1989.[3] President Bill Clinton noted that drug production and trafficking put Colombia's progress in peril, while fueling addiction and violence in the United States and elsewhere.[4] Having reallocated some interdiction funds to programs targeting demand in face of substantial congressional resistance, in his second term Clinton shifted policy, reverting to a supply side strategy. "Plan Colombia," a comprehensive strategy developed in coordination with the Colombian government, dramatically increased U.S. assistance, but it did not allow counternarcotics aid to be used directly for counterinsurgency purposes. Increasing involvement by Washington heightened concerns within the human rights community and in Congress about U.S. involvement in the Colombian conflict. After the September 11 attacks, President George W. Bush adopted an approach overtly combining counterinsurgency and counternarcotic strategies in Colombia. President Barack Obama faces increasing calls for change of U.S. policy toward Colombia.

Background: The Colombian Producer State

Before the 1991 Constitution, political participation had been limited in Colombia, although it is one of Latin America's oldest democracies. After fighting a brutal civil war, the Liberal and Conservative Parties agreed to a power-sharing arrangement, known as the National Front, which lasted from 1958 until 1974. Until 1986, "adequate and equitable" representation was guaranteed to both formerly warring parties. The dominance of these two left little room for others. Since the 1960s Colombian governments have faced rebel insurgencies.[5] Since the 1970s Colombia has also been struggling against an illegal drug industry with expansive networks that have penetrated the economy and

Timeline
U.S. Aid to Colombia

1986

With congressional passage of P.L. 99-570, the United States adopts the process of certifying aid recipients on the basis of their efforts to stem the illegal drug trade. If not certified, countries risk forfeiting U.S. economic and military assistance.

1989

President George H. W. Bush's Andean Initiative provides Colombia and other South American nations with military and economic assistance and law enforcement advice to curb the production and trafficking of illegal drugs.

1994

Rumors circulate that Colombian president Ernesto Samper Pizano's election campaign had received millions of dollars from the Cali drug cartel.

1995

For the first time, Colombia fails to gain U.S. certification as a cooperating partner in the war on drugs, but receives a national security waiver.

1996

The United States decertifies Colombia but does not grant a national security waiver or impose sanctions.

1997

The United States decertifies Colombia and issues a list of drug-fighting measures that the Colombian government must implement in order to receive assistance, which is granted. The Leahy amendment is passed, restricting units of security forces from receiving U.S. aid if the secretary of state determines that the unit has committed human rights violations, a measure that threatens aid to Colombia.

1998

Colombia fails to gain certification but is issued its second national security waiver. Andrés Pastrana is elected president.

February 1999

The United States certifies Colombia as a partner in the war on drugs.

October 1999	Pastrana proposes Plan Colombia, a program to reduce drug cultivation, strengthen Colombia's political and judicial institutions, and gain the upper hand against the guerrillas opposed to the government. Pastrana's government seeks U.S. and international assistance to carry out the $7 billion program.
January 2000	Clinton proposes $1.6 billion in aid for Plan Colombia.
March 2000	The House of Representatives approves $1.7 billion in aid for Plan Colombia.
June 2000	The Senate approves $934 million in aid for Plan Colombia. House and Senate conferees agree on $1.3 billion with a certification provision.
August 2000	Clinton waives the requirement that Colombia meet human rights standards and implement drug-fighting measures before aid dollars and equipment can be released. Colombia is certified as a partner in the war on drugs.
January 2001	George W. Bush assumes office as president.
September 11, 2001	Al Qaeda attacks the United States, flying hijacked passenger planes into the World Trade Center towers and the Pentagon.
February 20, 2002	Peace talks between the Colombian government and the Revolutionary Armed Forces of Colombia (FARC) break down, and government forces reassert control over the land it had granted the organization.
August 2002	P.L. 107-206 is passed, allowing Colombian counternarcotics aid to be used for counterinsurgency purposes. The Andean Trade Preference Act (P.L. 107-210) is renewed.
August 7, 2002	Alvaro Uribe Vélez takes office as president.
May 2003	Bush designates the United Self-Defense Groups of Colombia (AUC) and the FARC as significant foreign narcotics traffickers.

(continued)

Timeline *(continued)*
U.S. Aid to Colombia

February 2004	Forty leaders of the FARC and AUC are placed on the U.S. list of international drug traffickers.
March 2004	Bush proposes increasing the personnel cap for Plan Colombia to eight hundred soldiers and military advisers and six hundred civilian contractors.
March 23, 2004	President Uribe visits Washington and requests a new, multiyear counterinsurgency and counternarcotics package through 2009.
July 2004	The government begins peace talks with the AUC. AUC leader Salvatore Mancusco addresses the Colombian Congress.
February 2006	Colombia and the United States sign a free trade agreement, but the U.S. Congress does not approve it.
May 2006	President Uribe is elected to a second term. The Colombian Constitution had been amended to allow presidential reelection.
December 2006	The Andean Trade Preference Act is extended through June 2007.
March 2007	The unfolding Colombian "paragate" scandal reaches Uribe's cabinet, forcing his foreign minister to resign and implicating Colombia's army chief and head of domestic intelligence.
May 2008	Fourteen paramilitary leaders are extradited to the United States because of charges of drug trafficking.
December 2009	The Andean Trade Preference Act is extended for another year.

politics. Adding to the conflict are privately funded paramilitary armies with varying degrees of loyalty to the Colombian government and military.

The activities of the various guerrilla groups, drug cartels, and paramilitaries have made Colombia one of the most violent nations in the world. The damage done to the country and the people has been horrendous. More than two million of Colombia's forty-three million citizens have fled their country since 1985, and countless bombings have rocked its cities. In addition to civilian deaths, thousands of police officers, hundreds of journalists and judges, and even presidential candidates and Supreme Court justices have been murdered since 1985.[6] Additionally, more than four million people have been forced to flee their homes because of the conflict since 1985.[7]

Politics and Drugs

Two left-wing guerrilla groups are currently actively engaged in the Colombian violence. The largest and best equipped is the Revolutionary Armed Forces of Colombia (FARC). Estimates of peak membership were as high as eighteen thousand members, although current estimates are as low as eight thousand. The FARC wants to overthrow the government to create a democracy inspired by Marxist notions of social justice. The group finances its organization by extorting money from businesses, including from drug traffickers, in areas under its control. The Army of National Liberation (ELN) is another, smaller guerrilla group involved in political violence. Its members number four thousand to five thousand and gained notoriety by bombing the pipeline that carries most of Colombia's export oil from the eastern plains to the Caribbean.[8]

In response to these guerrilla groups, paramilitary groups formed. The most notorious confederation of paramilitaries was the United Self-Defense Groups of Colombia (AUC), which was led by Carlos Castaño. The fifteen thousand–strong AUC secured funding from landowners, businessmen, and drug dealers[9] with the aim of protecting their lives and property from the guerrillas.[10] The group reorganized in 2002 in preparation for talks with the government. In December 2002 the AUC declared a unilateral cease-fire with the government, and in 2003 some of its constituent groups began to disband. As peace talks progressed in 2004, however, the leaders responsible for purging the organization's drug funding either were assassinated (Rodrigo Franco) or disappeared (Carlos Castaño), creating uncertainty about the cohesion and motivation of the remaining AUC leadership. The last block demobilized in 2006, with approximately 34,000 former paramilitaries participating in this collective process.[11] Concerns remain about whether or not paramilitaries have actually demobilized or if some are regrouping.[12] Suspicions also remain about government complicity with paramilitary violence.[13] Former guerrilla fighters have demobilized as well. The Colombian army tallied 2,638 demobilized guerrillas in 2009, creating a total of 20,555 individual demobilizations since August 2002.[14]

Colombian drug traffickers have also been involved in the violence plaguing the country. The drug trade in Colombia began with the small-scale cultivation of marijuana in the 1960s; by the 1970s some Colombians had begun to process and export cocaine. The necessary chemical supplies were imported from Europe, and cocaine paste was brought in from Peru and Bolivia. The final product was then smuggled into the United States. By 1982 the drug trade accounted for 10 percent to 25 percent of Colombia's exports. At that point, however, the trade did not appear to be a threat to Colombian democracy.[15]

A few groups initially controlled the trade. One of the major traffickers was the Medellín cartel, headed by Pablo Escobar and Jorge and Fabio Ochoa. The cartel was arguably at its strongest in the middle to late 1980s. When Escobar was killed in a shootout with Colombian police in December 1993, the Cali cartel took over most cocaine production. Less violent than the Medellín cartel, the Cali organization focused its attention on legalizing parts of its operations and moving into legitimate businesses. President Ernesto Samper Pizano was rumored to have received $6 million from legal Cali businesses during his 1994 campaign. Nevertheless, Samper pursued an antidrug strategy. The major cartel kingpins were all jailed by 1996, though they received relatively light sentences.[16]

In addition to the well-known Cali and Medellín cartels, many other independent organizations produced, refined, and smuggled drugs. Sometimes the smaller groups cooperated or coordinated their activities with the larger operations.[17] With law enforcement targeting the Cali and Medellín cartels, others quickly arose to meet demand. A large number of cocaine labs were destroyed and the eradication of opium was stepped up in 1996, but the successes were short-lived. In the words of David Gaddis, the resident U.S. Drug Enforcement Administration (DEA) chief in Colombia, "The head of the mother snake was chopped off . . . but now we have to chase baby poisonous snakes, which can be . . . just as venomous."[18] Between 1993 and 1999 the potential acreage of the coca harvest almost quadrupled.[19]

The business of drugs is far-reaching and complicated, and in the case of Colombia it has profoundly affected preexisting social dynamics. Before the emergence of drug trafficking, there had been an ongoing struggle between traditional landowners and popular groups concerning unused *latifundios* (large estates or ranches), demands by peasants for title to property, and disagreements over state-supported rural modernization programs. Until the 1970s the large landowners usually won in such disputes. The drug trade changed the pattern by introducing competition from the narco-traffickers, who had invested in land. By the 1980s armed protection of *haciendas* was reinforced, "so that in the middle of that decade almost all of the struggle for land had been eliminated through a combination of military harassment and paramilitary terrorism" of the peasants.[20] The spread of the drug trade removed any obstacles before it, including judges, police, and so forth. The result was growth in criminal elements and a change in the dynamics of the traditional conflict over land.

The rise of the drug trade also affected the operations of guerrillas opposed to the government and their control over territory. Bloody conflicts between narco-traffickers and guerrillas are common in guerrilla-controlled areas that traffickers have taken over for cultivation and processing. Some have tried to characterize the guerrillas as little more than another drug cartel. For example, Gen. Barry McCaffrey, President Clinton's director of the Office of National Drug Control Policy, called the FARC the "principal organizing entity of cocaine production in the world."[21] According to Marc Chernick, director of the Andean and Amazonian Studies Program at Georgetown University:

> However, this is a gross distortion of the situation in Colombia. The guerrillas do not constitute another "cartel." Their role in the drug trade is in extorting a percentage of the commercial transaction of coca and coca paste, just as they do with many other commercial products in the areas in which they operate, be it cattle, petroleum, or coffee.[22]

The nature of the trafficker-guerrilla relationship is significant because some policy makers have tried to link the guerrillas with the cartels in an effort to justify the use of drug war funds for counterinsurgency purposes. In areas where guerrillas remain strong, sometimes a pragmatic relationship develops in which the producers and traffickers usually pay tribute to the guerrilla groups.[23] At other times, some guerrilla groups or fronts have become directly involved in aspects of cultivation, processing, and trafficking.

Controlling the Drug Trade and Violence

Since the late 1970s the Colombian government has tried to craft political and military solutions for the rebel and drug conflicts, but few of these efforts have enjoyed lasting success. President Julio César Turbay Ayala (1978–1982) relied on the military and paramilitary units to control guerrilla violence. President Belisario Betancur (1982–1986) initiated talks that resulted in the establishment of the leftist Unión Patriótica by former FARC members. Their demobilization was not accepted by all parties, and paramilitary groups killed more than six thousand Unión Patriótica members. From the perspective of the left, the government did little to protect the newly incorporated party or to pursue the paramilitaries that targeted its members. Consequently, a 1984 cease-fire agreement between the government and the FARC failed. Rural and urban violence escalated under President Virgilio Barco Vargas (1986–1990). President César Gaviria Trujillo (1990–1994) attempted to restart talks with guerrilla insurgents, holding extensive negotiations in 1991 and 1992, but the discussions did not produce an agreement.

The Colombian government's response to the drug trade has varied. The United States had demanded the right to extradite Colombian citizens and charge them in U.S. courts, on the grounds that the Colombian judicial system was too weak and corrupt to prosecute traffickers effectively. President Turbay signed an extradition treaty in 1979, but no extraditions were requested until the Betancur administration. Once extraditions began, they created cycles of drug violence, in which the narco-traffickers would attack government and public targets, followed by state retaliation, followed by more violence, and so on. The situation became so bad that President Gaviria halted the extraditions. In 1991 he tried a policy of voluntary submission to justice, by which drug traffickers would be allowed to legalize their assets if they pled guilty to a few offenses and agreed to serve short sentences. During the Samper administration (1994–1998), the Colombian Congress passed an asset forfeiture law and allowed the extraditions of drug traffickers to the United States to resume. Even so, Colombia's relationship with the United States was severely strained by allegations that Samper accepted drug-tainted campaign money.[24]

In 1998 newly elected president Andrés Pastrana (1998–2002) launched attempts to combat the drug problem and the guerrilla conflict. He initiated talks with the FARC and the ELN for the first time in eight years. Both were offered safe havens, free from government interference, as a precondition to the peace talks. The FARC received forty-two thousand square kilometers of land in the center of Colombia, and the ELN was to control approximately five thousand square kilometers, although that zone was never fully implemented because of local and paramilitary resistance. At the end of Pastrana's term, peace talks broke down and the safe havens were abolished. In 1999 Pastrana proposed a six-year program called "Plan Colombia," whose provisions included promoting alternative development in coca-growing areas, strengthening Colombia's political and judicial institutions, and regaining the initiative in the conflict with the guerrillas. The estimated cost of the program was more than $7 billion. The government committed $4 billion to the effort and requested aid from the European Union and the United States.[25]

President Alvaro Uribe Vélez introduced the "Democratic Security and Defense Strategy" shortly after being elected in 2002. Its main goal was to restore the rule of law and a climate of security through a coordinated effort by the security forces and the judiciary. Uribe declared a "state of internal commotion" that gave him emergency powers, implemented a 1.2 percent war tax on assets, and proposed antiterrorism legislation. In March 2004 the government reintroduced the Search Bloc police unit to hunt drug traffickers in the south. It specifically targeted the Norte de Valle drug cartel in much the same way that government forces earlier went after the Medellín cartel.[26] Also in 2004 Uribe initiated peace talks with the AUC. Uribe's government has extradited individuals to the United States for prosecution, with the concurrence of the Colombian Supreme Court.[27] In May 2008, fourteen paramilitary leaders were extradited to the United States. One of them, Diego Alberto Ruiz Arroyave, was sentenced in 2009 to seven and a half years for trying to buy weapons such as anti-aircraft missiles in return for cocaine.[28] Uribe was reelected in 2006 and is considering running for a third term.

Pre-Clinton U.S. Policy

There are two basic ways to fight drug use. One is to reduce the demand for drugs by increasing education and treatment programs. The other is to attack the supply by reducing drug production and targeting trafficking. U.S. foreign policy toward Colombia has focused on supply-side tactics. A main component of this strategy has been tying aid, trade concessions, and external credits to the Colombian government's compliance with the U.S. supply reduction goals, resulting in the militarization of antidrug campaigns.[29]

In 1989 the U.S. military presence in Colombia was minor, as was U.S. assistance. After drug traffickers assassinated Luis Carlos Galán, the leading presidential candidate, the United States decided to strengthen the Colombian military and jump-start the war on drugs. Within a day, President George H.W. Bush released $65 million in stockpiled Defense Department weapons and supplies to Colombia. Congress quickly approved a $200 million line of credit from the U.S. Export-Import Bank to the Colombian military. Three weeks later, Bush announced $261 million more in aid for Bolivia, Colombia, and Peru, as part of his Andean Initiative. By 1992 U.S.-Colombian efforts had begun to concentrate on attacking the drug traffickers and cartels directly by focusing on the kingpins instead of on crop eradication. As U.S. policy came to rely more heavily on military and police efforts to combat the traffickers, many observers, including the U.S. General Accounting Office, became concerned that the United States would be drawn into counterinsurgency operations in the long-standing conflict between the Colombian government and the rebels.[30]

In 1999, according to the State Department's Bureau for International Narcotics and Law Enforcement Affairs, U.S. drug policy in Colombia had three main goals: to eliminate the cultivation of illegal drugs, including opium, coca, and marijuana; to strengthen Colombia's ability to disrupt and dismantle major drug trafficking organizations and prevent their resurgence; and to destroy the cocaine and heroin processing industries.[31] These goals needed to be accomplished without undermining regional stability or the already embattled Colombian democracy.

The Clinton Drug Policy

When asked by an MTV interviewer during the 1992 presidential campaign if he had ever tried marijuana, candidate Bill Clinton responded that he had, but "I didn't inhale." Clinton's comment undermined his credibility to pursue an antidrug strategy. The distrust increased after December 7, 1993, when Clinton's surgeon general independently suggested that the government study the idea of legalizing some drugs as a way to reduce violent crime. Despite the president's press secretary stating that such a study was not even being considered,[32] many thought that the administration did not take the drug problem seriously. Clinton initially pursued a different balance of supply-side and demand-side efforts. Between September 1992 and September 1995 he reduced interdiction efforts and eliminated a thousand antidrug positions, shortened mandatory sentences for traffickers, and proposed cutting 80 percent of the staff of the Office of National Drug Control Policy and reducing the number of Drug Enforcement Agency agents by 227. Republicans viewed this policy as responsible for an increase in the supply of drugs from Colombia.[33] When they charged that Clinton's policy was evidence of a lack of commitment to an antidrug strategy, administration officials protested that the statistics they cited took the president's policy out of context. Robert Gelbard, assistant secretary of state for international narcotics and law enforcement affairs, clarified some of the funding reductions:

> The President's 1995 National Drug Control Strategy continues our shift in focus to the source countries, so we are taking a more surgical view of how to destroy major transit and transshipment operations. Both concentrations are occurring against the backdrop of enhanced efforts to strengthen anti-narcotics institutions of cooperating countries so they can shoulder more of the drug control burden.[34]

The truth was that although some programs suffered cutbacks, others had an increase in funding. In 1993 the international counternarcotics budgets of most U.S. agencies were cut. Gelbard's budget, for example, was reduced by 30 percent. But overall, Clinton's aid request for drug control for fiscal year 1994 rose to $13.2 billion, an increase of $1.1 billion from the previous year. Five areas were to receive more money, including drug prevention, drug treatment, drug-related criminal justice, drug-related research, and other international programs. Funding for interdiction, however, was cut by $94 million and anti-drug intelligence programs were cut by $600,000. Some members of Congress, such as Rep. Donald Manzullo, R-Ill., believed that the cuts reflected a lack of emphasis on interdiction by the administration, even though Clinton's stated policy was to shift funding from "transit zone interdiction" to stopping pro-duction in the source countries.[35]

In addition to disagreements over the components of Clinton's antidrug strategy, many House Republicans were also angry at delays in delivering promised aid to Colombia. Rep. Dan Burton, R-Ind., said, "It is unfortunate that the Congress has had to fight tooth and nail with the administration, from the State Department to the United States Embassy and our Ambassador in Bogotá, in an attempt to try to get some form of assistance down to the brave people who are fighting the war on drugs."[36] In another example, Burton, along with Reps. Ben Gilman, R-N.Y., and Dennis Hastert, R-Ill., was upset about the lack of aid—specifically, getting UH-1H "Huey" helicopters to the Colombian national police in a timely manner.

Clinton received high marks for appointing Barry McCaffrey, a retired four-star U.S. Army general, to head the White House Office of National Drug Control Policy, a move that many saw as an attempt by Clinton to build up his credentials in the war on drugs.[37] McCaffrey took over as "drug czar" in February 1996, but his appointment did not produce the positive effects the president had hoped for. In fact, McCaffrey contributed to interbranch squabbling by accusing some in Congress of attempting to micromanage U.S. foreign policy toward Colombia.[38] Adding to the dissension, Secretary of State Madeleine Albright emphasized supporting the peace process with the guerrillas. Some in the Pentagon favored an approach that focused on the military, and many Republicans in Congress preferred more aid to the Colombian national police.[39]

Congressional opinion would ultimately be important in crafting policy. Not only did Congress's control over spending allow it to determine how much aid would be sent to Colombia, but it could challenge presidential decisions under a certification policy adopted in 1986 (P.L. 99-570) based on Section 490 of the Foreign Assistance Act of 1961. Amendment of the act gave Congress a more active role in forging policy in regard to drug-producing and drug transit countries. It required the president, on March 1 of each year, to select one of three options for drug-producing and transit countries: (1) to certify a country as fully cooperating to meet the goals of the UN Convention against Illicit Traffic in Narcotic Drugs and Psychotropic Substances, also known as the Vienna Convention; (2) to decertify a country as uncooperative but grant it a national security waiver, so that it would not suffer sanctions; or (3) to decertify a country and impose sanctions. Sanctions could include an end to most U.S. aid and votes against loans for that country in multilateral economic and development organizations. Depending on the country, other sanctions could be imposed, such as the elimination of its sugar quota for the U.S. market or a cutoff of tourist visas to the United States. The president could also levy trade sanctions; for example, he could deny preferential tariff treatment granted by the Andean Trade Preference Act of 1991, increase tariffs generally, or withdraw the United States from any pre-clearance customs arrangements. Congress could overturn the president's decision within thirty days.[40]

Until 1995 Colombia had always received full certification. In 1995 Sen. Jesse Helms, R-N.C., sponsored an amendment to prohibit federal aid to Colombia until it began to fight more effectively against drug production and corruption. Despite Helms's efforts, Colombia received a national security waiver that year. In 1996 Clinton again decertified Colombia, but sanctions were not applied, and the government received the year's aid allocation. President Samper's acceptance of Cali cartel money for his campaign seemed to be the reason for the decertification. In 1997 Colombia was decertified and given six months to improve its drug-fighting efforts before a decision on sanctions would be made. The United States demanded the extradition of Colombian nationals (especially the Cali kingpins), full implementation of asset forfeiture and money laundering laws, implementation of a bilateral agreement on maritime law enforcement (to aid in interdiction efforts), tightened security for Colombian prisoners, the use of more potent herbicides for drug crop eradication, and better efforts against corrupt officials.[41] Colombia did not meet the demands but received aid nonetheless.

Another notable event of 1997 was the passage of an amendment sponsored by Sen. Patrick Leahy, D-Vt. His amendment to the Foreign Operations Act for Fiscal Year 1998 stated, "None of the funds made available by this Act may be provided to any unit of the security forces of a foreign country if the Secretary of State has credible evidence that such unit has committed gross violations of human rights." Passage of the amendment was an acknowledgment of unofficial ties between the Colombian military and right-wing paramilitary groups in fighting the guerrillas, and it would later be included, in varying ways, in other security assistance programs. Difficulty in applying it would arise, however, over the definitions and compositions of military units. Representative Burton, among others, criticized the administration for not granting Colombia a national security waiver in 1996 and 1997. Samper's term ended in August 1998, and that year Colombia failed certification but was granted a national security waiver. In 1999, 2000, and 2001, under President Pastrana, Colombia would again receive full certification.

Plan Colombia: Aid in 2000–2001

Congressional criticism followed President Clinton's Colombia policy into the new millennium. Some Republicans, such as Sen. Mike DeWine, R-Ohio, wanted to shift the balance of funding away from education and prevention and back to supply-side efforts. Congress (in P.L. 105-277) added $870.2 million in extra monies for the drug war for fiscal year 1999. Again, many Republicans accused Clinton of not taking the problem seriously enough.[42] Political pressure continued to build for a stronger U.S. response to the Colombian drug problem, culminating in U.S. support for Plan Colombia.

On January 10, 2000, Representative Hastert, who was now Speaker of the House, gave a speech in Chicago to the Mid-America Committee for International Business and Government Cooperation on the need to increase funding to Colombia. "Aggressive diplomacy, military assistance, continued military cooperation, intelligence activities, and counterdrug assistance will be necessary if we are to deter this growing threat. . . . The Republican-led Congress stands ready to support such a comprehensive strategy, but time is not on Colombia's side."[43] Building on congressional support for Plan Colombia, the next day Clinton announced plans to increase aid to Colombia, proposing a $1.6 billion package designed to create two antidrug battalions (of one thousand troops each) within the Colombian military, control Colombian airspace, and wipe out coca fields.[44] The most expensive aspect of the 2000 plan was the allocation of sixty-three UH-1H Huey combat helicopters for use by antinarcotics forces in southern Colombia, where the FARC was strong.

Resistance

Criticism of the aid package focused on two matters. Many opponents were concerned that U.S. aid was being used for counterinsurgency purposes, thereby involving the United States in another country's civil war. Some critics asked why Plan Colombia focused counternarcotics actions in southern Colombia, a traditional rebel stronghold, instead of the northern regions, where paramilitaries sympathetic to the government were active in the drug trade. Brian E. Sheridan, the assistant secretary of defense for special operations and low-intensity conflict, asserted that there was no evidence to support the suspicion that the true purpose of U.S. aid was to assist Colombia in its internal conflict. "We are working with the Colombian government on counternarcotics programs. We are not in the counterinsurgency business," contended Sheridan.[45] An earlier congressional staff report presented a somewhat different view:

> [T]he United States has tried to describe a bright line separating counterdrug and counterinsurgency support to Colombia, with no direct assistance for counterinsurgency. That line remains in law. Circumstances, however, are pushing the limits, making it difficult on the ground to make distinctions between insurgents and traffickers.[46]

Others wanted to make sure that U.S. aid would not be used to benefit groups implicated in human rights violations. For example, Senator Leahy implored Clinton, "We at least need to see a concerted effort by the Colombian army to thwart the paramilitary groups, who are responsible for most of the atrocities against civilians, and a willingness by the Colombian armed forces to turn over to the civilian courts their own members who violate human rights."[47] Because of the complexity of the Colombia situation, it was impossible to ascertain with total certainty whether U.S. aid was being used for counterinsurgency efforts, at least indirectly. Part of the controversy involved whether the Colombian military had ties to paramilitary groups, such as Castaño's AUC, which was responsible for some 75 percent of the political killings. Human Rights Watch, in its *World Report, 2000,* documented ties between the Colombian army's Fourth Brigade and the Castaño group. Castaño's men were reportedly able to exchange civilian corpses for weapons from the brigade. The army would then dress the corpses as guerrillas and claim that they had been killed in combat.[48] The State Department, in its *1999 Country Reports on Human Rights,* acknowledged that Colombian "security forces actively collaborated with members of paramilitary groups by passing them through roadblocks, sharing intelligence, and providing them with ammunition."[49] Many human rights groups, as well as congressional Democrats, contended that the 2000–2001 aid package did not do enough to break these ties and prosecute paramilitary collaborators.

In response to critics, the Clinton administration reduced the amount of aid requested for Colombia from $1.6 billion to $1.3 billion for 2000.[50] To appease the Pentagon, it dropped the request for sixty-three rebuilt, Vietnam-era Huey helicopters and requested instead thirty newer, more expensive, and more sophisticated Sikorsky UH-60 L Blackhawk helicopters for combating drug trafficking.[51]

Congressional Passage

Despite the vocal opposition of critics, the administration's modified proposal had solid support in the House. One of its most enthusiastic supporters was Speaker Hastert, who said, "The bill we're considering today is about our children and whether we want our children to grow up in a society free from the scourge of drugs."[52] Few wanted to be portrayed as condoning drug smuggling, but some spoke out against the aid package. Rep. David Obey, D-Wis., invoked the Vietnam War: "This is the camel's nose under the tent for a massive long-term commitment to a military operation. I detest Vietnam analogies under most circumstances, but in this case there is a very real parallel."[53] Rep. Maxine Waters, D-Calif., objected for humanitarian reasons: "This bill gives money to drug traffickers who kill other drug traffickers and murder innocent civilians."[54] In the end, the House approved more aid for Colombia than the administration requested—$1.7 billion. On March 30, 2000, the House rejected an attempt to lower the amount by a vote of 239–186. It then passed the appropriations bill of which the Colombia aid was a part, 263–146.[55]

In the Senate, Sen. Slade Gorton, R-Wash., and Sen. Paul Wellstone, D-Minn., criticized the Colombian military's human rights record and declared that the aid package would pull the United States into Colombia's civil war.[56] Gorton stated, "There has been no consideration of the consequences, cost, and length of involvement. . . . This bill says let's get into war now and justify it later."[57] One of the concessions made to allay such fears was to limit the number of American military personnel in Colombia to five hundred at any one time, with exceptions made for carrying out a possible rescue mission.[58] The bill the Senate approved called for supplying Huey helicopters rather than the Blackhawks.[59]

Ultimately, on June 22 the Senate approved, 95–4, a Colombian aid package totaling $934 million, just slightly more than half of the $1.7 billion the House had approved. Majority Leader Trent Lott, R-Miss., called for giving Colombians "the aid they need, the equipment that they need to fight these massive narcotics traffickers themselves." Additionally, Sen. Chris Dodd, D-Conn., argued, "This package may not be perfect, but our delay in responding to a neighbor's call for help is getting old. . . . When we step up and offer the Colombian democracy a chance to fight for themselves, we're not only doing it for them, we're doing it for ourselves."[60] House and Senate conferees met and split the difference.[61] The final package of $1.319 billion contained the requirement that the government of Colombia obtain a national security waiver to receive the aid if it could not meet six conditions:

- The president of Colombia must issue a written order requiring that all military personnel facing credible allegations of human rights violations be tried in civilian courts.
- The commander general of the Colombian armed forces must promptly suspend those members facing credible allegations of human rights violations or of participating in paramilitary groups.
- The Colombian armed forces must fully cooperate with the investigations of civilian authorities in the search for those accused of human rights violations.
- The Colombian government must actively prosecute in civilian courts paramilitary leaders and members and any military personnel who assist them.
- The Colombian government must craft a plan to rid the country of all coca and poppy production by 2005.
- The Colombian armed forces must develop and deploy a judge advocate general corps in field units to investigate military personnel misconduct.[62]

The majority of aid to Colombia under the 2000–2001 plan went to the police ($363.1 million) and the armed forces ($589.2 million). The remaining $238 million in the package went for alternative development, aid to the displaced, human rights, judicial reform, law enforcement, and peace efforts. The final package included the Blackhawks.[63]

But controversy did not end with the passage of the package. Clinton continued to be pressured to withhold aid because of human rights violations. Senator Wellstone wrote the president on July 28:

> At present, the President of Colombia has issued no directive requiring that Colombian armed forces personnel accused of human rights violations will be held accountable in civilian courts, nor has the Colombian military taken the firm, clear steps necessary to purge human rights abusers from its ranks or ensure that its personnel are not linked to paramilitary organizations. . . . [Y]our Administration cannot and should not certify Colombia to receive assistance.[64]

Representatives from thirty-three nongovernmental organizations, including Amnesty International, the Washington Office on Latin America, and numerous church groups, requested that Colombia not be certified because of its lack of compliance with the human rights provisions of Section 3201 of the supplemental aid package. In an open letter to President Clinton on July 31, the groups stated, "A certification or waiver that ignores this critical human rights situation will send a clear message . . . that the United States' commitment to human rights does not go beyond empty rhetoric."[65]

The groups further noted that the Colombian government had not met several of the conditions. First, officers had not been dismissed from duty or referred to civilian authorities for trial, despite credible accusations of army-paramilitary collusion. Second, the Colombian government had not enforced its own law that officers accused of human rights violations should be tried in civilian courts, even though the Colombian Constitutional Court had ruled that human rights cases must be heard in civilian courts. Third, the groups charged that the Colombian government had not acted to restrain the paramilitary groups or protect the population from attacks. Their letter concluded, "We have raised serious questions about [the current aid policy's] efficacy as counter-narcotics policy. . . . It will be an unqualified disaster, however, if the human rights conditions prove meaningless at the very outset."[66] In the end, Colombia met only one of the U.S. requirements. Nevertheless, in August

Clinton waived the requirement that the conditions of the aid be met, stating that the grave situation in Colombia dictated that aid could not be delayed any longer.[67] In this instance, drug control was the defining characteristic of the national interest; human rights were not.

Just a week after passage of the package, Speaker Hastert announced that he was reviewing a request for an additional $99.5 million in aid to provide more aircraft, ammunition, and other equipment to the Colombian police. Seventeen conservative lawmakers, including Burton and Gilman, wanted more aid to the police to be included in the foreign assistance bill for the new fiscal year. They favored the police because they believed that they were less implicated in human rights violations and more effective at fighting drugs than the military.[68]

The Policy of George W. Bush

The September 11 attacks on the United States altered the atmosphere of debate about Colombia and U.S. policy toward it. What was previously viewed as a government under siege by internal forces was now viewed as an ally fighting terrorism from within. In an October 15, 2001, press conference at the Organization of American States, Francis X. Taylor, State Department coordinator for counterterrorism, stated:

> The FARC, the AUC, and the ELN are on the [U.S. government's] list [of terrorist groups] because they participate in terrorist activities and they get the same treatment as any other terrorist group, in terms of our interest in going after them and ceasing their terrorist activities.[69]

Thus began the shift in U.S. policy toward Colombia.

Insurgency: The New Terrorism

In the new atmosphere of fighting terrorism, one observer noted, public "officials from both countries must frame Colombia's problems along antiterrorism lines to assume continued United States support."[70] Similarly, Secretary of State Colin Powell stated on October 25, 2001: "There's no difficulty in identifying [Osama Bin Laden] as a terrorist. . . . Now, there are other organizations that probably meet a similar standard. The FARC in Colombia comes to mind." This change in perspective meant that the Bush administration would actively pursue a policy of blending counternarcotics aid with counterinsurgency aims.

On Capitol Hill, Rep. Cass Ballenger, R-N.C., chairman of the House Subcommittee on the Western Hemisphere, stated on April 11, 2002, "Let's face it, the FARC, ELN and AUC are terrorists who support their activities with drug money. Although they do not have the reach of al Qaeda or Hamas, they do have international reach, which includes smuggling drugs out of Colombia and into the United States and Europe."[71]

Peace talks between the Colombian government and the FARC broke down on February 20, 2002, the day the FARC hijacked an airliner, taking its fifth member of Colombia's Congress hostage. At midnight, government forces began to reestablish authority in the area previously given over to FARC control as a precondition for peace talks. According to the government, the FARC never intended to negotiate in good faith, but instead used the zone as a platform for promoting attacks. The FARC accused the government of militarily blockading the zone and of not aggressively pursuing paramilitary groups.

Following the White House lead, the House of Representatives passed Resolution 358 on March 6, 2002, pledging "to assist the Government of Colombia to protect its democracy from United States–designated foreign terrorist organizations." This shift in rhetoric was followed by a change in policy. An August 2, 2002, emergency request for counterterrorism funding contained a clause allowing the Colombian government to use all current and previously appropriated counternarcotics assistance for counterinsurgency purposes in a "unified campaign against narcotics trafficking [and] against activities by organizations designated as terrorist organizations such as the Revolutionary Armed Forces of Colombia (FARC), the National Liberation Army (ELN), and the United Self-Defense Forces of Colombia (AUC)."[72] Thus the previous distinction between counterinsurgency and counternarcotics activities was erased. Moreover, the Clinton-era policy of prohibiting intelligence sharing other than for counternarcotics purposes—as set out in Presidential Decision Directive 73—was revised to allow the sharing of paramilitary and guerrilla intelligence with Colombian officials, regardless of whether a drug connection existed.[73]

This shift intensified opposition from those who believed that the Colombian situation had the potential to become a Vietnam-like quagmire. "This is a major policy change. . . . We could find ourselves engulfed in a morass that would eat up American soldiers like we have not seen in years," warned Rep. Ike Skelton, D-Mo.[74] Rep. Jim McGovern, D-Mass., agreed: "The United States will be plunging head first into a grinding, violent and deepening civil war that has plagued Colombia for nearly four decades."[75] Opposition aside, the Bush administration aggressively moved against drug and guerrilla leaders. On August 26, 2003, the former head of the Medellín cartel, Fabio Ochoa Vasquez, was sentenced to more than thirty years in federal prison by a federal judge in Miami.[76] On May 29, 2003, the FARC and the AUC were designated by Bush as "significant foreign narcotics traffickers." In February 2004, forty leaders of the FARC and AUC were placed on the U.S. list of international drug traffickers, and many were indicted in the United States.[77]

Continuing Plan Colombia 2002–2005: The Andean Regional Initiative and the Andean Counterdrug Initiative

The 2002, 2003, 2004, and 2005 aid packages are generally criticized by opponents for being too focused on military and counternarcotics assistance, with too little attention paid to social and economic conditions, human rights, and environmental concerns. President Bush's 2002 request for the Andean Regional Initiative (ARI)—his administration's funding program for Plan Colombia, launched in April 2001—totaled $882.29 million. Of this amount, Colombia was to receive $399 million, with $146.5 million allocated for socio-economic aid and $252.2 million for military and police aid. The House (H.R. 2506) allotted the ARI $826 million, $52 million less than Bush's request. The House debate included three notable, unsuccessful amendments. Rep. Nancy Pelosi, D-Calif., proposed to cap Colombian military aid at $52 million and allocate the remainder to an infectious diseases child survival account. An amendment by Rep. Steven Rothman, D-N.J., proposed suspending fumigation efforts until they could be proven safe. An amendment by Rep. David Obey proposed to shift all ARI counternarcotics funding to domestic drug treatment programs. The Senate (S.R. 107-58) only allocated the ARI $698 million, $184 million less than Bush wanted. The bill included demands for verifying the safety of aerial fumigation and eradication programs and human rights certification.[78] In the end, the Bush administration received $782 million to pursue "strengthening democracy, regional stability, and economic development"[79] but was limited by three human rights conditions. These included a second round certification for 40 percent of the aid and no national security waiver provision, a requirement that the State Department provide assurances about the safety of fumigation practices, and a cap of four hundred U.S. military personnel and four hundred civilian contractors to support Plan Colombia. The total for all programs to Colombia in 2002 was $367 million in military and police aid and $147 million in social and economic aid.[80]

President Bush's 2003 request included $979.8 million for the ARI, including $537 million for Colombia. In the end, Colombia received $284 million for eradication and interdiction programs, $149.2 million for social and economic programs, and a renewed Air Bridge Denial Program (an air interdiction effort), all limited by human rights certification. In the supplemental fiscal 2003 Emergency Wartime Supplemental Appropriations Act (P.L. 108-11), Colombia received an additional $37 million for presidential security, police aid, support for displaced people, and aerial eradication programs. It also was granted $93 million to protect the Cano-Limon pipeline.[81] A two-stage human rights certification provision was included: 25 percent of the aid was held in two parts for the secretary of state's certification that Colombia was prosecuting human rights violators within the police and military and to ensure that the Colombian military had severed ties to the paramilitary organizations and was actively pursuing them. Another provision threatened to reclaim helicopters if they were used in support of paramilitary operations. The law also contained a provision for withholding 80 percent of the eradication budget until the State Department certified that health and environmental guidelines and standards were met. The 2003 aid program maintained the cap on four hundred military personnel and four hundred contractors for Plan Colombia. The unified campaign continued, but concern about a Vietnam-style entanglement was clear in the conference report. It warned that the authority to conduct a unified campaign "is not a signal . . . for the United States to become more deeply involved in assisting the Colombian Armed Forces in fighting the terrorist groups, especially not at the expense of the counternarcotics program, but to provide the means for more effective intelligence gathering and fusion, and to provide the flexibility to the Department of State when the distinction between counternarcotics and counterterrorism is not clear cut."[82] Making such distinctions continues to be difficult. In March 2007, the U.S. embassy in Colombia confirmed a report that Colombian and U.S. troops had participated in an unsuccessful joint operation to rescue three U.S. military contractors held by the FARC since their surveillance aircraft went down in February 2004.[83]

For fiscal year 2004, President Bush requested $990.7 million for the ARI, with $731 million of the assistance set aside for the Andean Counterdrug Initiative (part of the ARI beginning with funds allocated in fiscal year 2002). Bush requested $463 million for Colombia, including $150 million for social and economic programs and $313 million for narcotics interdiction and eradication programs. The House (H.R. 2800) fully funded the ACI at $731 million. The Senate Appropriations Committee (S.B. 1426) allotted only $660 million. The House (H.R. 2673) raised the cap on the number of military personnel to five hundred and maintained the unified campaign of counternarcotics and counterinsurgency aid.[84] The ACI was ultimately funded at $731 million, with Colombia receiving $332 million in military and police aid and $136 million for socioeconomic programs. The 2004 package retained the unified campaign language, maintained the cap on personnel at four hundred, and had similar human rights and fumigation certification provisions.

The 2005 request for the ACI, the last anticipated year of the original Plan Colombia funding, was $462.8 million, with approximately two-thirds going to police or military aid and the remaining third to economic or social development. The military cap was raised to eight hundred from four hundred, and the civilian to six hundred from four hundred. Rep. Jan Schakowsky, D-Ill., charged, "It seems that the Bush administration's solution to dealing with the world is to deploy more U.S. soldiers and guns for hire, while refusing to seek real, lasting solutions."[85] The announcements coincided with a visit by President Uribe to Washington to ask the Bush administration and Congress for a new multiyear package of counterinsurgency and counternarcotics aid through 2009.[86] Additional 2005 funding included $348.3 million for the Colombian foreign military financing, antiterrorism, Department of Defense (DoD), and AirWing programs. The 2006 ACI funding was similar at $469.5 million, although the amount for alternative development increased slightly. Also included was $20 million in support for paramilitary demobilization, subject to certification by the secretary of state that the demobilized had actually renounced violence and were fully cooperating with the Colombian authorities. Additional 2006 funding included $247 million for the Colombian foreign military financing, DoD, and AirWing programs. During debate, Rep. Jim McGovern, D-Mass., sponsored an amendment to H.R. 5308 that would have cut military aid to Colombia by $100 million. "This policy has failed as an antidrug policy," he said. "It has failed as a human rights policy, and it has failed to have any impact whatsoever in reducing the availability, price or purity of drugs in the streets of America."[87] Although the amendment failed 189–234, it reflects growing concern in the House. Leahy amendment human rights language and fumigation safety certification provisions were contained in both years' packages.[88]

Each year from 2002 to 2006, Secretary of State Powell, and later, Secretary of State Condoleezza Rice, certified that Colombia had met its human rights obligations. A portion of the aid package is withheld until the secretary of state certifies that human rights conditions have been met. Each time the country has been certified, however, congressional opponents and human rights groups have objected. The human rights debate became particularly heated in 2002, when a cable signed by former ambassador Myles Frechette surfaced detailing comments made in 1997 by Representative Hastert. In the cable, Hastert was quoted as telling Colombian police and military leaders that human "rights concerns were overblown" and decrying the "leftist-dominated" Congresses that "used human rights as an excuse to aid the left in other countries." A Hastert spokesperson later tried to affirm his commitment to human rights but failed to reassure activists about Hastert's sincerity.[89] Human rights groups and their supporters ultimately succeeded in maintaining the restrictions. One Colombian unit was decertified in 2003 because of the lack of an effective and transparent investigation into a 1998 incident in Antioquia, Colombia.[90]

Two additional policy changes occurred under George W. Bush. First, as was the case during the Clinton administration, under President Bush trade politics were linked to the fight against drugs in Colombia. In December 2001 the Andean Trade Preference Act expired. That act, which lowered tariffs on certain products from Andean countries, was an important part of the program to make legal crops an attractive alternative for Colombian farmers. Senate Majority Leader Tom Daschle, D-S.D., successfully pressed for a renewal and expansion of the act, which was passed in August 2002 (P.L. 107-210) with an expiration date of December 2006. Instead of preferring a permanent extension of the Andean Trade Preference Act, U.S. trade representative Robert Zoellick announced that the administration would pursue more comprehensive trade talks with Andean nations in 2004.[91] Bilateral agreements were signed with Peru in December 2005 and Colombia in July 2006, but only the Peruvian agreement has been approved by the U.S. Congress. While the APTA was nearing expiration and the new bilateral trade agreements were not yet ratified, the act was extended through mid-2007. Second, the drug certification policy changed in 2002 and 2003. Under the new law (P.L. 107-228, Section 706), the president submits to Congress by September 15 each year a list of major drug-producing or trafficking countries and, from among them, an additional list of countries that have "failed demonstrably . . . to make substantial efforts." These countries would potentially suffer sanctions. Moreover, the old prerogative of

Congress to override the president's determinations has been eliminated. This modified U.S. certification process is now supplemented by the Organization of American States' program, the Multilateral Evaluation Mechanism (MEM).[92]

As early as 2002 there was talk of "Colombia fatigue" and the need for an "exit strategy."[93] Before the fall 2006 elections, many were ready to support changes; an amendment to H.R. 5522 proposed shifting $30 million from aerial eradication in Colombia to global refugee relief. Amendment cosponsor Rep. Jim Leach, R-Iowa, said his support was based on "a belief that a military emphasis of this kind carries many counterproductive consequences." In response to statements that increased eradication was a sign of success, amendment sponsor Representative McGovern rebutted, "Yes, eradication has dramatically increased, but it has changed nothing."[94] Despite debate, ACI funding remained consistent with previous years at $465 million, with $306.5 million going to police and military and $151 million to social and economic development or rule of law programs. Democratic control of Congress after the November 2006 elections raised hopes of many to increase pressure to pursue a different mix of policies, although no radical change of policy has occurred.

At the same time, President Uribe began circulating a new six-year plan titled the Strategy of Strengthening Democracy and Social Development (2007–2013), which proposes a much heavier emphasis on social and economic programs, as opposed to military and police aid. Meanwhile, concurrent with paramilitary demobilization, new evidence emerged of ties between high-ranking Colombian officials and paramilitaries—as human rights groups have long alleged—in an unfolding scandal dubbed "paragate." Top officials or politicians charged and held for collaboration with paramilitaries' intelligence directors, governors, military officers, and, as of September 2009, thirty-nine members of Congress, are under investigation and twenty-nine detained.[95] Although some believe that uncovering these ties demonstrates Uribe's resolve to eradicate paramilitary links, others worry about the depth of the scandal and Uribe's sincerity in prosecuting so many members of his governing coalition. These events may significantly change the tone of U.S. congressional debate in the future.

Barack Obama: Change or More of the Same?

Many of the same issues from Plan Colombia have resurfaced with President Obama's 2010 aid package for Colombia, which includes $675 million, with approximately $252 million in economic and social aid and $423 million in military and police aid.[96] With the end of an agreement for U.S. forces to use an Ecuadorian Pacific coast base for counternarcotics and military operations, the United States negotiated with Colombia in 2009 to increase its military presence in Colombia, signifying continuity if not an intensification of existing regional strategy, despite vociferous protests from Venezuela, Nicaragua, and Ecuador.[97] However, frustration in Congress is increasing. For example, the Conference Report on H.R. 3288, Transportation, Housing and Urban Development, and Related Agencies Appropriations Act, 2010, bans any U.S. aid to the Colombian Departamento Administrativo de Seguridad (DAS) or successor organizations because of the allegations of collusion with paramilitary groups and illegal surveillance and wiretapping of Colombians. Existing certification requirements on eradication and human rights are maintained.

Despite these restrictions, some in Congress have pushed for fundamental change in U.S. policy. Some advocate more emphasis on domestic demand reduction. For example, in the debate over the 2009 Omnibus Appropriations Act, Rep. Dennis Kucinich, D-Ohio, argued that "money directed to domestic demand reduction efforts . . . is more effective at reducing drug consumption and curtailing the flow of illicit drugs into the country."[98] Others have called for a reevaluation of U.S. aid to Colombia. In a letter to Secretary of State Hillary Rodham Clinton, Sens. Russell Feingold, D-Wis., Chris Dodd, D-Conn., and Patrick Leahy, D-Vt., described a dire "deterioration of the rule of law and basic rights in Colombia." They highlighted ongoing scandals involving the DAS, harassment of human rights activists, erosion of checks and balances, and insufficient accountability for the *falsos positivos* scandal in which up to 1,700 innocent civilians were killed but disguised as guerrilla fighters to inflate body counts in order to secure promotions and other rewards. They were dismayed by the State Department's September 2009 certification of Colombia for meeting human rights conditions of U.S. aid. Instead, they advocated "that the administration send an unambiguous signal that these abuses are unacceptable and that stopping them is a priority and a prerequisite for our continued partnership with the Colombian government." Additionally, they called for more assistance to judicial and law enforcement programs, alternative development, a peace process with the FARC, and a reduction of aerial eradication programs and military aid.[99] These concerns echo calls for a fundamental change in U.S. drug policy from the Partnership of the Americas Commission, convened by the Brookings Foundation. This report unequivocally calls the war on drugs a failure and recommends full comparative evaluation of all available policies and more attention to alternative development, harm reduction, and demand reduction, in addition to more effective hemispheric dialogue and interdiction efforts.[100]

Resistance from congressional Democrats over labor rights and the assassination of union leaders (thirty-nine in 2009) has also resulted in the stalling of approval for the free trade agreement with Colombia, despite the support of the president and secretary of state.[101] In lieu of the permanent free trade agreement with Colombia, Congress passed another extension of the Andean Trade Preference Act in December 2009.

Conclusion: Supply or Demand—New Players, Unforeseen Events, and a New Agenda

President Clinton faced political pressure from Republicans in Congress and human rights groups as he crafted a drug policy toward Colombia. Originally, Clinton tried to pursue a policy that included more demand-side efforts and a reduction in interdiction activities, but Republicans dubbed him "soft on drugs." Unwilling to weather conservative criticism of a new policy approach, he returned to a supply-side policy, symbolized by the appointment of General McCaffrey and the size of the 2000–2001 aid package. Clinton was also pressured by members of Congress and nongovernmental groups who feared that military aid to Colombia would result in more human rights violations. In the end, Clinton made concessions to both sides by increasing funds for the military and police and by including human rights provisions in aid packages.

President George W. Bush significantly changed U.S. policy, openly allowing counternarcotics aid to be used for counterinsurgency purposes. This shift reignited the debate about U.S. intervention in other countries' internal affairs and drew negative comparisons to the conflict in Vietnam. Human rights concerns persisted and were joined by worries about the effects of aerial eradication on the environment and people. The Republicans' loss of control of Congress increased hopes for significant changes in U.S. policy, especially given the unfolding para-politics scandal. However, President Obama has not yet fundamentally changed U.S. policy, although concern continues to grow in Congress, especially among Democrats.

The debate over Colombian drug policy exemplifies the conflict over intervention in Latin America in the post–cold war era and the increasing complexity of crafting foreign policy. Fighting communism in the region is no longer the priority; instead, new threats, such as the drug trade, are considered more important. Nonetheless, old concerns about entanglement and intervention remain. In addition, nongovernmental organizations, such as Amnesty International, are becoming more effective in making their voices heard in the policy debate and are making human rights an issue that Congress and the president cannot ignore. Whether human rights groups have succeeded in changing politics to include safeguarding civilians, or policies pay only lip service to that ideal, is debatable.

U.S. concerns about international terrorism have allowed governments to label people and organizations previously engaged in guerrilla campaigns, independence movements, and other strictly internal conflicts as terrorists. It is clear that no president can easily control the content of foreign policy. Political capital must be expended to promote the president's foreign policy agenda, as in other policy arenas. The present configuration of U.S. policy in Colombia demonstrates how lobbying by particular industries, nongovernmental activism, old-fashioned politics, and unforeseen events all shape foreign policy.

Key Actors

Cass Ballenger   Representative, R-N.C., chairman of the House Subcommittee on Western Hemisphere Affairs, headed efforts in the House to secure Colombian aid packages under President George W. Bush.

Dan Burton   Representative, R-Ind., wanted Colombia to receive a national security waiver in 1996 and 1997 to allow U.S. assistance to be disbursed despite Colombia's being denied certification as a partner in the war on drugs; supported more aid to the Colombian national police.

George W. Bush   President, eliminated the distinction between counternarcotics and counterinsurgency assistance for Colombia.

Bill Clinton   President, wanted to shift drug policy to strike a balance between suppressing demand and interdicting supply.

Hillary Rodham Clinton,   Secretary of state under President Barack Obama.

Chris Dodd,   Senator, D-Conn., opponent of continued military aid to Colombia.

Russell Feingold,   Senator, D-Wis., opponent of continued military aid to Colombia.

Ben Gilman   Representative, R-N.Y., supported more aid to the Colombian national police.

Dennis Hastert   Speaker of the House, R-Ill., strong proponent of additional military aid to Colombia.

Jesse Helms   Senator, R-N.C., chairman of the Senate Foreign Relations Committee from 1995 to 2001, critic of aid to Colombia because of corruption concerns.

Patrick Leahy   Senator, D-Vt., advocate of including human rights provisions in foreign aid bills.

Barry McCaffrey   Retired U.S. Army general, director of the Clinton administration's Office of National Drug Control Policy; advocate for a supply-side approach to combat drug smuggling.

Jim McGovern   Representative, D-Mass., critic of supply-side drug policy.

Andrés Pastrana   Colombian president, struggled to regain confidence of the United States; devised Plan Colombia to deal with Colombia's drug and guerrilla problems.

Ernesto Samper Pizano   Colombian president, plagued by allegations of ties to drug traffickers because of Cali cartel contributions to his electoral campaign.

Alvaro Uribe Vélez   Colombian president, pursued hard-line approach against insurgents and narco-traffickers, pursued peace talks with the paramilitaries, requested a new U.S. multiyear aid package through 2009.

Paul Wellstone   Senator, D-Minn., advocate of human rights in Colombia, who died in 2002.

Notes

1. According to Paul E. Simons, acting assistant secretary of state for international narcotics and law enforcement affairs, in a hearing before the Senate Drug Caucus, 108th Cong., 1st sess., June 3, 2003, www.state.gov/g/inl/rls/rm/21203.htm.

2. United Nations Office on Drugs and Crime's 2009 *Colombia Coca Cultivation Survey.*

3. For an excellent overview of U.S. drug policy from Nixon to Bush, see Bruce M. Bagley and William O. Walker, eds., *Drug Trafficking in the Americas* (Coral Gables: University of Miami, North-South Center, 1996).

4. White House, Office of the Press Secretary, "Statement by the President (Plan Colombia)," November 10, 1999.

5. On contemporary Colombian history and politics, see Harvey Kline, *State Building and Conflict Resolution in Colombia, 1986–1994* (Tuscaloosa: University of Alabama Press, 1999).

6. Rafael Pardo, "Colombia's Two-Front War," *Foreign Affairs* 79, no. 4 (July/August 2000): 65.

7. CODHES, Consultoría para los Derechos Humanos y el Desplazamiento, Bogotá, Colombia, March 2008.

8. Bruce Bagley, "Drug Trafficking, Political Violence, and U.S. Policy in Colombia in the 1990s," *Mama Coca,* January 5, 2001, www.mamacoca.org/bagley_drugs_and_violence_en.htm.

9. "Carlos Castaño afirma que envi—instructores a las Autodefensas Unidas de Venezuela," *El Tiempo,* June 30, 2002. See Mauricio Aranguren Molina, "Las Autodefensas y el Narcotráfico," in *Mi confesión: Carlos Castaño Revela Sus Secretos* (Bogatá: Oveja Negra, 2002).

10. Carlos Castaño, letter to Anne Patterson, U.S. ambassador to Colombia, October 26, 2001, www.semana.com/imagesSemana/documentos/aucannepatterson.doc.

11. EFE, "Colombian Paramilitary Group: We Are Ready to Demobilize," March 5, 2004; 2008 Human Rights Report: Colombia.

12. Human Rights Watch, "Paramilitaries' Heirs: The New Face of Violence in Colombia," February 3, 2010, www.hrw.org/node/88060 (accessed February 14, 2010).

13. One of the most serious allegations is that Jorge Noguera, head of the Colombian intelligence agency DAS (Department of Administrative Security), passed the names of numerous trade union activists and a sociologist to the paramilitaries to be murdered. Simon Romero, "Scandal over Spying Intensifies in Colombia," *New York Times,* September 16, 2009. Shortly afterwards, the Colombian government disbanded the DAS and distributed the six thousand workers to other intelligence agencies due to this scandal and others involving illegal wiretapping and surveillance.

14. "In 2009, 2,638 Guerillas Demobilized," *Ejército Nacional,* January 5, 2010, www.ejercito.mil.co/index.php?idcategoria=237329.

15. Francisco Thoumi, "Why the Illegal Psychedelic Drug Use Industry Grew in Colombia," in Bagley and Walker, *Drug Trafficking in the Americas.*

16. Alejandro Reyes, "Drug Trafficking and the Guerrilla Movement in Colombia," in Bagley and Walker, *Drug Trafficking in the Americas.*

17. Fabio Castillo, *Los Nuevos Jinetes de la Cocaína* (Bogotá: Oveja Negra, 1996).

18. Andrew Selsky, "Colombia DEA Chief Discusses Targets," Associated Press, January 23, 2004.

19. Department of State, *1999 International Narcotics Strategy Report.*

20. Reyes, "Drug Trafficking and the Guerrilla Movement in Colombia," 125.

21. Scott Wilson, "U.S. Drug Chief Tries to Boost Colombian Resolve," *Washington Post,* November 21, 2000, A22.

22. House Committee on International Relations, *U.S. Narcotics Policy toward Colombia,* hearing, 104th Cong., 2nd sess., 1996, 47.

23. Ibid., 122. See also Roberto Steiner, "Hooked on Drugs: Colombian-U.S. Relations," in *The United States and Latin America: The New Agenda,* ed. Victor Bulmer-Thomas and James Dunkerley (London: Institute of Latin American Studies, University of London, 1999), 171.

24. For an in-depth overview of the responses to the guerrilla and drug conflict, see Reyes, "Drug Trafficking and the Guerrilla Movement in Colombia," and Steiner, "Hooked on Drugs."

25. A copy of Plan Colombia is available at www.usip.org/library/pa/colombia/adddoc/plan_colombia_101999.html#pre.

26. Reuters, "Colombia Revives Cartel-Busting Police Squad," March 5, 2004.

27. Amanda Iacone, "Colombia's High Court Will Allow Cartel Figure's Extradition to U.S.," *Miami Herald,* November 22, 2002; Jason Webb, "The Colombian Supreme Court Voted to Allow the Extradition of Victor Patiño Fómenque, a Notorious Cali Cartel Chief Who Faces Drug Charges in South Florida," Reuters, April 23, 2002. Nelson Vargas Rueda of the FARC was returned to Colombia in mid-2004 after U.S. authorities determined that he was the wrong man. See Sibylla Brodzinsky and Jay Weaver, "U.S. Drops Case against Suspected FARC Guerrilla," *Miami Herald,* July 8, 2004.

28. Associated Press, "Colombian Paramilitary Member Sentenced in Houston," June 2, 2009.

29. Bruce M. Bagley, "Myths of Militarization: Enlisting Armed Forces in the War on Drugs," in *Drug Policy in the Americas,* ed. Peter Smith (Boulder: Westview Press, 1992).

30. General Accounting Office audits in 1992 and 1993 revealed that counternarcotics funds were being illegally used for counterinsurgency operations. The GAO concluded that this practice would likely continue because of the complexity of the Colombian situation. See Government Accountability Office, "The Drug War: Counternarcotics Programs in Colombia and Peru," T-NSIAD-92-9, Washington, D.C., February 20, 1992; Government Accountability Office, "The Drug War: Colombia Is Implementing Antidrug Efforts, but Impact Is Uncertain," T-NSIAD-94-53, Washington, D.C., October 5, 1993.

31. Bureau for International Narcotics and Law Enforcement Affairs, fact sheet, April 23, 1999.

32. Stephen Labaton, "Surgeon General Suggests Study of Legalizing Drugs," *New York Times,* December 7, 1993.

33. U.S. Congress, *Congressional Record,* June 21, 2000, S5509.

34. House Committee on International Relations, Subcommittee on the Western Hemisphere, *A Review of President Clinton's Certification Program for Narcotics Producing and Transit Countries in Latin America,* hearing, 104th Cong., 1st sess., 1995, 33.

35. House Committee on Foreign Affairs, Subcommittee on International Security, International Organizations, and Human Rights, *U.S. Anti-Drug Strategy for the Western Hemisphere,* joint hearing, 103rd Cong., 2nd sess., 1994.

36. House Committee on Government Reform and Oversight, Subcommittee on National Security, International Affairs, and Criminal Justice, *International Drug Control Policy: Colombia,* hearing, 105th Cong., 2nd sess., 1998, 22.

37. See, for example, "Choice of General as Drug Fighter Gets Enthusiastic Response," *New York Times,* January 28, 1996.

38. Stanley Meisler, "House OKs $3.2 Billion Measure to Bolster the Fight against Drugs," *Los Angeles Times,* September 17, 1998, 8.

39. Miles A. Pomper, "Hastert Leads the Charge in Colombia Drug War," *CQ Weekly,* September 11, 1999, 2094.

40. "International Drug Trade and the U.S. Certification Process: A Critical Review," proceedings of a seminar held by the Congressional Research Service and prepared for the Senate Caucus on International Narcotics Control, 104th Cong., 2nd sess., September 1996. The Andean Trade Preference Act of 1991 provided economic support to countries struggling to eliminate drug production by expanding the trade opportunities for legal crops. The ten-year program empowered the president to grant duty-free treatment to selected imports from Bolivia, Colombia, Ecuador, and Peru.

41. Statement by Assistant Secretary of State for Inter-American Affairs Jeffrey Davidow, *International Drug Control Policy: Colombia,* 19.

42. Jonathan Peterson, "Albright Pushes Anti-Drug Plan in Visit to Colombia," *Los Angeles Times,* January 15, 2000, A9. Despite Colombia's decertification, aid to its military and police had doubled from $68.6 million in 1993 to $136.4 million by 1997. (There had been decreases in 1995 and 1996 to $51.4 million and $73.9 million, respectively.) See also "Last Minute Spending Signals Shift in Drug War," *Congressional Quarterly Almanac,* 1998, 2–118.

43. Miles A. Pomper, "Clinton's Billion Dollar Proposal for Colombian Anti-Drug Aid Fails to Satisfy Republicans," *CQ Weekly,* January 15, 2000, 90.

44. Peterson, "Albright Pushes Anti-Drug Plan."

45. Larry Rohter, "Cocaine War: A Special Report; A Web of Drugs and Strife in Colombia," *New York Times,* April 21, 2000.

46. Senate Caucus on International Narcotics Control, *On Site Staff Evaluation of U.S. Counter-Narcotics Activities in Brazil, Argentina, Chile, and Colombia,* staff report, 105th Cong, 2nd sess., January 28, 1998, 19.

47. Pomper, "Clinton's Billion Dollar Proposal," 91.

48. Human Rights Watch, *World Report, 2000,* www.hrw.org/wr2k.

49. Department of State, Bureau of Democracy, Human Rights, and Labor, *1999 Country Reports on Human Rights,* February 25, 2000, www.state.gov/www/ global/ human_rights/99hrp_index.html.

50. Ester Schrader, "Congress Agrees on Funding for Colombia," *Los Angeles Times,* June 23, 2000, A1.

51. Tim Golden, "Colombia and Copters and Clash over Choice," *New York Times,* March 6, 2000.

52. Janet Hook and Ester Schrader, "Colombia Aid Package Gets House Approval," *Los Angeles Times,* March 31, 2000, A22.

53. Ibid.

54. Eric Pianin, "House Approves Additional $4 Billion for Defense; Nearing Passage, $12.6 Billion Emergency Spending Bill Has Funds for Colombia, Non-Emergencies," *Washington Post,* March 30, 2000, A6.

55. Hook and Schrader, "Colombia Aid Package." Included in the House bill was an endorsement of the administration's switch from the Huey helicopters to the Blackhawks. Intense lobbying efforts by the companies that make the helicopters helped influence the details of the final aid package. United Technologies, the Connecticut-based company that builds the Blackhawk, had contributed more than $700,000 to Republican and Democratic members of Congress between the 1996 and 1998 elections. Golden, "Colombia and Copters."

56. Karen DeYoung, "Colombia Aid Nears Approval in Senate; Lawmakers Back Bigger U.S. Military Role in Drug Fight," *Washington Post,* June 22, 2000, A1.

57. Anthony Lewis, "Abroad at Home: Into the Quagmire," *New York Times,* June 24, 2000.

58. Eric Schmitt, "$1.3 Billion Voted to Fight Drug War among Colombians," *New York Times,* June 30, 2000.

59. DeYoung, "Colombia Aid Nears Approval."

60. Ester Schrader, "Congress Agrees on Funding for Colombia," *Los Angeles Times,* June 23, 2000, A1.

61. Ibid.

62. Military Construction Appropriations Act, 2001, P.L. 106-246, Sec. 3201.

63. DeYoung, "Colombia Aid Nears Approval."

64. Available at www.ciponline.org/colombia/072801.htm.

65. Available at www.ciponline.org/colombia/073101.htm.

66. Ibid.

67. Marc Lacey, "Clinton Defends Colombia Outlay," *New York Times,* August 31, 2000, A1.

68. Eric Pianin and Karen DeYoung, "House Considers More Aid for Colombia; $99.5 Million Package Would Include Aircraft, Ammunition to Fight Drug War," *Washington Post,* September 9, 2000, A2.

69. Francis X. Taylor, press conference, Organization of American States, Washington, D.C., October 15, 2001, www.oas.org/OASpage/eng/videos/pressconference10 _15_01.asf. The AUC was added to the list in 2001, but the ELN and the FARC were on the list even before September 11. They were officially designated as subject to Executive Order 13224 of September 23, 2001, on October 31, 2001. See www.fas.org/irp/news/2002/03/fr031902s.html.

70. Arlene Tickner, "Colombia and the United States: From Counternarcotics to Counterterrorism," *Current History,* February 2003, 81.

71. Rep. Cass Ballenger, R-N.C., "U.S. Policy toward Colombia," statement before the House Committee on International Relations, Subcommittee on the Western Hemisphere, 107th Cong., 2nd sess., April 11, 2002, wwwc.house.gov/international_relations/107/ball0411.htm.

72. P.L. 107-206, H.R. 4775, http://frwebgate.access.gpo.gov/cgi-bin/getdoc.cgi ?dbname=107_cong_public_laws&docid=f:publ206.107.pdf.

73. Ingrid Vaicius and Adam Isacson, "The 'War on Drugs' Meets the 'War on Terror'" (Washington, D.C.: Center for International Policy, February 2003).

74. Speech by Rep. Ike Skelton, *Congressional Record,* May 23, 2003, H2998.

75. Speech by Rep. Jim McGovern, *Congressional Record,* May 23, 2003, H2997.

76. Jerry Seper, "Colombian Drug Lord Draws 30 Years in Prison; Ochoa Reneged on Promise Not to Return to Narcotics Trade," *Washington Times,* August 27, 2003, 3A.

77. Treasury Department, "Treasury Takes Action against FARC/AUC Narco-Terrorist Leaders in Continued Effort to Halt Narcotics Trafficking," press release js-1181, February 19, 2004, www.ustreas.gov/press/releases/js1181.htm.

78. K. Larry Storrs and Nina M. Serafino, Congressional Research Service, *Andean Regional Initiative (ARI): FY 2002 Assistance for Colombia and Neighbors,* Report for Congress, October 31, 2001.

79. White House, Office of the Press Secretary, "Andean Regional Initiative," fact sheet, March 23, 2002, www.state.gov/p/wha/rls/fs/8980.htm.

80. Vaicius and Isacson, "The 'War on Drugs' Meets the 'War on Terror.'"

81. Paul E. Simons, acting assistant secretary of state for international narcotics and law enforcement affairs, in a hearing before the Senate Drug Caucus, 108th Cong., 1st sess., June 3, 2003, www.state.gov/g/inl/rls/rm/21203.htm.

82. K. Larry Storrs and Connie Veillette, Congressional Research Service, *Andean Regional Initiative (ARI): FY2003 Supplemental and FY2004 Assistance for Colombia and Neighbors,* Report for Congress, August 27, 2003, 4.

83. Associated Press, "U.S., Colombians Conduct Operation," *Fort Worth Star-Telegram,* March 11, 2007, 18A.

84. Storrs and Veillette, *Andean Regional Initiative.*

85. Bloomberg Newswire, *New York Daily News,* "Bush: Add Troops in Colombia," March 23, 2004.

86. Center for International Policy, "Plan Colombia 2?," press release, March 22, 2004, www.ciponline.org/colombia/040322memo.htm.

87. Speech by Rep. Jim McGovern, *Congressional Record,* June 28, 2005, HR 5308.

88. Connie Veillette, "Colombia: Issues for Congress," Congressional Research Service, Library of Congress, January 4, 2006, 24.

89. "Declassified Document Says Hastert Downplayed Human Rights Concerns in Colombia," *CongressDaily,* May 3, 2002.

90. State Department, Daily Press Briefing, January 14, 2003, www.stategov/r/pa/ prs/ dpb/2003/16641.htm.

91. Jerry Hagstrom, "Zoellick: Colombia, Peru, Ecuador and Bolivia Next FTAs," *CongressDaily,* November 18, 2003, 9.

92. Raphael Perl, "Drug Control: International Policy and Approaches," Congressional Research Service, Library of Congress, updated February 2, 2006.

93. Michael Shifter and Vinay Jawahar, "Latin America Daily Brief," *Oxford Analytica,* August 22, 2003.

94. Latin American Working Group, "House Increases Aid to Colombia before Uribe Visit, Senate Freezes Funds over Human Rights Concerns," June 13, 2006, www .lawg.org/ countries/colombia/fy07debate.htm.

95. INDEPAZ, cited in "Para-Politics in Colombia's Congress: Updated Count," www.cipcol.org/?p=663.

96. Just the Facts, http://justf.org/Country?country=Colombia&year1=2005&y ear2=2010.

97. Simon Romero, "Increased U.S. Military Presence in Colombia Could Pose Problems with Neighbors," *New York Times,* July 22, 2009.

98. Speech by Rep. Dennis J. Kucinich, *Congressional Record,* February 25, 2009, Omnibus Appropriations Act, 2009.

99. January 21, 2010, letter to the Honorable Hillary Rodham Clinton from Sens. Russell Feingold, D-Wis., Chris Dodd, D-Conn., and Patrick Leahy, D-Vt.

100. "Re-Thinking U.S.-Latin American Relations: A Hemispheric Partnership for a Turbulent World," Report of the Partnership for the Americas Commission, Brookings Institution, November 2008.

101. Matthew Bristow, "Congress Won't Pass U.S.-Colombia Free-Trade Pact in '10—U.S. Envoy," *Nasdaq Dow Jones,* January 26, 2010.

4 The Nuclear Standoff between the United States and Iran: Seeking a Diplomatic Path through a Minefield of Mutual Distrust

Thomas Preston and Michael P. Infranco

Before You Begin

1. What have been the trends and patterns in U.S.-Iranian relations over the past five decades? Why do history and context matter in foreign policy decision making for U.S.-Iranian relations?

2. How does each actor, the United States and Iran, view the other, and are those perceptions accurate? Could the perceptions be changed?

3. How has the Obama administration differed in its approach to negotiations with Iran from the previous Bush administration? Is there potential for a breakthrough on the nuclear standoff?

4. What are the domestic political constraints, especially in Iran after the contested presidential election in June 2009, that may prevent both countries from improving their relations or compromising on the nuclear issue?

5. How does the current war in Afghanistan and waning American presence in Iraq affect U.S.-Iranian relations? Do they aggravate the current impasse in nuclear negotiations?

6. How has the reelection of Mahmoud Ahmadinejad affected U.S.-Iranian relations? Does the current Iranian political leadership bode well for the future of U.S.-Iranian relations?

7. What are the policy approaches of the United States, United Nations, European Union, and Iran regarding the nuclear issue?

8. How have the United States and its European allies sought to communicate their view about the impermissibility of a wide-scale Iranian nuclear-enrichment program to the United Nations and world community?

9. How can the Obama administration successfully bring along China and Russia to apply pressure on Iran to agree to the International Atomic Energy Agency (IAEA) nuclear reprocessing agreement or face tougher Security Council sanctions?

10. What were the roots of the Iranian nuclear program? What negotiating strategy may influence Iran to desist from developing nuclear weapons? Does it really matter, in terms of regional stability, whether Iran obtains nuclear weapons?

Introduction: The Clenched-Fist Metaphor and the Problem of Diplomatic Constraints

In his January 2009 inaugural address, President Barack Obama announced that the United States was prepared to extend a hand in friendship to those adversarial states who "are willing to unclench" their fists.[1] This statement represented a significant departure from the hard-line negotiating approach favored by the previous Bush administration. Obama was intent on reinvigorating America's image abroad, and in particular, establishing a new direction in the United States' relationship with the Islamic world. It was also an explicit recognition that the Bush policy of nondirect negotiations over Iran's nuclear enrichment program (and its implied threats of military force) had failed to produce any substantive results with Tehran. Instead, the Iranian program had steadily expanded its nuclear facilities and developed new technologies (like IR-2 centrifuges) that hastened the Persian state's ability to produce enriched uranium for nuclear fuel or bombs. Indeed, in a direct criticism of the previous approach, Bush representative Nicholas Burns lamented that in order for negotiations to work, diplomats must meet face to face. As Burns observed, "I worked for three years, day in and day out, on Iran and never got to meet an Iranian diplomat. . . . The policy did not work."[2]

Yet Obama faces an equally difficult task following the political quagmire of post-election Iran, in which the government has continued to suppress political dissent, deep fissures have emerged within the clerical community, and the long-term political stability of the country itself has been called into question. Obama's new strategy had been buoyed by popular support abroad, especially among Middle Eastern Muslims, in large part because it departed so substantively from George W. Bush's 2002 "axis of evil" policy direction. The approach was predicated on the belief that direct negotiations with Iran had greater potential to yield a resolution to the nuclear standoff. Unfortunately, the strategy's implementation was soon undercut by the political disorder within Iran surrounding the June 2009 contested presidential election, in which Supreme Leader Ali Khamenei declared then-President Mahmoud Ahmadinejad the winner even before the official recount. Many Iranian protesters believed the election was fraudulent and that conservative mullahs, in collusion with

Ahmadinejad and the Iranian Republican Guard, had stolen the election through vote rigging.

This string of events created a considerable problem for the Obama administration. In effect, opponents of Obama's direct-negotiation approach claimed the United States would be acquiescing to an illegitimate regime by dealing directly with Ahmadinejad. Several hard realities now confronted the White House as it sought to reverse the direction and pace of Iran's nuclear program while maintaining international support for any enhanced sanctions that might be required. There were the ongoing military conflicts in Afghanistan and Iraq that could easily be destabilized by Tehran in the event of hostilities. There was also the problem of an overstretched U.S. military, declining public support for the existing wars, and the fact that Iran had an opaque (and well-dispersed) nuclear program impossible to preempt or destroy with air strikes alone. Not only would military force likely be ineffective, it would certainly undercut the Iranian reform movement itself, provide justification for a conservative crackdown, and scuttle allied support for harsher UN sanctions. Yet, for U.S. domestic politics and public opinion, accepting a "nuclear" Iran and negotiating with a dictatorship in Tehran were also seen as largely unacceptable—creating a difficult policy problem for Obama.

From Iran's standpoint, there were long-standing security concerns regarding its own regional security, especially given the existing U.S. military presence in neighboring Iraq and Afghanistan, alongside a strong, nationalistic desire (even among the Iranian public) to pursue a nuclear program and not be dictated to by the international community. For Ahmadinejad, appealing to Iranian nationalism serves to distract from the continuing reform movement protests and maintain the support of Supreme Leader Ayatollah Khamenei and other conservative allies critical to his political survival. Thus, in some respects, Ahmadinejad needs the impasse over Iran's nuclear program to continue, but only at a low simmer. Considering the constraints facing both sides, it becomes easy to see why the current standoff over Iran's nuclear program has become so enormously complex and difficult to resolve diplomatically.[3]

Background: Patterns of Intervention and Mutual Antagonism

A defining tendency in U.S.-Iranian relations has been a long-standing pattern of American intervention in Iran's domestic affairs. In 1953 the United States backed the overthrow of Iranian prime minister Mohammad Mossadeq's

Timeline

U.S.-Iranian Relations and the Nuclear Issue

August 1953	A U.S.-supported coup overthrows democratically elected Iranian prime minister Mohammed Mossadeq and the pro-American Shah is restored to power.
1970s	The Shah of Iran institutes a nuclear program with both civilian and military components.
Mid-1978 through 1979	Iranian revolution overthrows the Shah, who is replaced by Ayatollah Khomeini.
October– November 1979	The Shah is admitted into the United States; Iranian students seize U.S. embassy in Tehran.
April 1980	The United States breaks off diplomatic relations with Iran; U.S. hostage rescue mission fails.
September 1980	Iraq invades Iran, beginning the Iran-Iraq War (1980–1988); the United States supports Iraq.
Mid-1985	Iran begins a secret centrifuge enrichment program.
1987	Iran acquires drawings of centrifuges and component parts from A. Q. Khan smuggling network.
May 1995	President Bill Clinton signs an executive order prohibiting trade with Iran.
August 1997	Moderate cleric and reformer Mohammad Khatami becomes president of Iran.
1999	After assembling and testing centrifuges, Iran enriches uranium for the first time.
June 2001	U.S. Senate extends economic sanctions on Iran an additional five years.
January 29, 2002	President George W. Bush gives his "axis of evil" speech.
August 14, 2002	Opposition group of exiles reveals that Iran has clandestine uranium enrichment facility and heavy water plant.

(continued)

Timeline *(continued)*

U.S.-Iranian Relations and the Nuclear Issue

September 12, 2003	The International Atomic Energy Agency (IAEA) calls on Iran to suspend all enrichment-related activity.
October 21–23, 2003	Iran agrees to halt all enrichment and reprocessing activities after negotiations with France, Britain, and Germany.
March 13, 2004	IAEA criticizes Iran for failing to report centrifuge research or suspend all activities.
April 29, 2004	Iran announces it is starting to convert uranium, the step preceding actual enrichment.
September 18, 2004	IAEA tells Iran to cease uranium conversion and implicitly threatens referral to UN Security Council.
November 15, 2004	After further negotiations with the European Union (EU), Iran agrees to cease uranium enrichment.
August 2005	Ahmadinejad becomes Iran's president, campaigning on a pro-nuclear platform.
September 2, 2005	IAEA announces that Iran has not fully cooperated with the agency, despite repeated requests and visits from inspectors.
January 12, 2006	Europeans call off nuclear talks with Iran.
February 4, 2006	IAEA board votes to report Iran to the UN Security Council.
April 11, 2006	Iran announces that it has succeeded in enriching uranium.
May 2006	Ahmadinejad sends his letter to President Bush.
June 2006	UN sanctions are delayed to give Iran time to consider a new package of U.S. and European incentives to end its nuclear program; Iran rejects the proposal and is given an August 31 deadline to implement "full and sustained suspension" of its nuclear activities.

October 2006	North Korean nuclear test; Iran refuses to condemn it and sets up second centrifuge cascade.
December 2006	Security Council unanimously passes resolution banning import or export of materials and technology used in uranium enrichment, reprocessing, or ballistic missiles.
March 2007	Security Council unanimously passes resolution banning all arms exports to Iran and freezing assets of Iranians linked to its military or nuclear program.
April 2007	Ahmadinejad boasts Iran is capable of enriching uranium on an industrial scale.
April 2008	Ahmadinejad tours the Natanz site to publicize the testing of a new generation of centrifuges, the IR-2, which may have the capability to enrich uranium at a much faster rate.
January 2009	Barack Obama is inaugurated president of the United States, promising to "extend a hand [to hostile states] if . . . [they] are willing to unclench [their] . . . fist[s]."
June 2009	President Ahmadinejad is reelected in a contested election that is followed by months of street protests challenging the authority of the Islamic Republic's ruling elite.
July 2009	Iranian government's brutal crackdown against political protesters and reformers. Hundreds are jailed and tortured in Evin prison.
September 2009	Iran discloses the existence of the Qum nuclear facility. The site had gone unreported to the IAEA.
October 2009	Iran rejects an IAEA plan to reprocess enriched uranium in Russia and then assemble the uranium fuel into rods in France to be sent back to Iran for use in a medical research facility in Tehran.
November 2009	The Iranian government approves the building of ten additional uranium enrichment facilities in violation of UN demands, which ordered Iran to stop its nuclear program.

democratically elected government, an action sparked by Mossadeq's efforts to nationalize Iran's oil industry, taking ownership away from British companies. The United States subsequently reinstalled the autocratic Shah of Iran, who preserved foreign rights to Iran's oil fields. Although the United States saw Mossadeq's overthrow through the cold war lens of East-West competition and the need to prevent the spread of communism, to Iranians it epitomized U.S. interference in their internal affairs and imperial ambitions in their country. Hostility toward the United States for reinstalling the Shah continued long after his overthrow in the 1979 Iranian revolution. Indeed, it is revealing that a key Iranian demand during the subsequent hostage crisis, when militant students seized the American embassy and its staff, was an apology for the 1953 overthrow and a U.S. pledge never again to interfere in Iran's domestic affairs. Since that time, American policy makers have not restored diplomatic relations, have encouraged dissident groups, have spoken favorably of regime change, and have depicted Iran as a rogue state intent on shirking international law to advance its Islamic revolutionary agenda and destabilize the region. The Iranians have responded with unremitting hostility of their own, condemning the "Great Satan," pursuing improved military capabilities, and working to undercut American influence in the Middle East.

The origins of the conflict can be traced to the rise of the Shah of Iran, Mohammad Reza Pahlavi, who replaced his father on the Iranian throne during World War II. After he was deposed by the Iranian people during the early 1950s and Mossadeq elected, the Shah was returned to power in 1953 in a U.S.-backed coup.[4] In return for substantial American military and economic aid, the Shah provided both a steady stream of oil and an important pro-Western ally in the Persian Gulf to help block Soviet expansionism. Iran's strategic position and resources continued to make it a high-priority ally for American presidents throughout the Shah's reign. However, the Shah's rule was also marked by corruption, brutality, and political repression. The Shah's secret police and intelligence service, known as the SAVAK, was particularly hated by the population. It ruthlessly helped maintain the Shah's one-party rule through the torture and execution of thousands of political prisoners, suppression of political dissent, and alienation of the religious masses.[5] U.S. training and support of the SAVAK served to further cultivate anti-Americanism in the decades prior to the Iranian revolution. Moreover, the Shah's efforts to modernize Iran and follow a Western model of development angered the country's conservative religious leaders, who saw Western influences as an affront to their fundamentalist Islamic faith.

Inspired by the fundamentalist cleric Ayatollah Ruhollah Khomeini, whose pro-Islamist and anti-Western message struck a special chord with the Iranian masses, violent demonstrations erupted throughout the country in mid-1978. By January 1979, the Shah (now terminally ill with cancer) abdicated his Peacock Throne and went into exile, and Khomeini returned from exile. The Shah moved first to Egypt, then to Morocco, and by February 1979 was ready to accept an earlier American offer of asylum. On February 14, however, Iranian students "temporarily" overran the American embassy and held U.S. personnel for "several hours," prompting U.S. government concern for all the Americans there. When President Jimmy Carter's Special Coordinating Committee met to discuss the situation, it concluded that if the Shah was permitted to enter the country there might be an Iranian backlash that could threaten U.S. personnel in the country. As a result, Carter decided to rebuff the Shah's request for admission into the United States, but administration officials remained split over the matter. Secretary of State Cyrus Vance argued against receiving the Shah, but national security adviser Zbigniew Brzezinski and a cadre of friends (including former secretary of state Henry Kissinger) pushed for the Shah's admission. Time and the Shah's health interceded in his favor, and Carter eventually acquiesced to the Shah's entry after being told that his life could only be saved by medical facilities in New York.[6] The Shah arrived in October 1979, received medical treatment, and was encouraged to leave. He eventually traveled to Egypt, where he died in July 1980. But the damage to U.S.-Iranian relations had been done. On November 4, 1979, thousands of Iranian students overran the U.S. embassy and seized 66 American hostages (53 of whom would be held for some 444 days).

The ensuing hostage crisis would humiliate and destroy the Carter presidency and cause a rupture in U.S.-Iranian relations that has lasted to the present day. The two countries still do not have diplomatic relations, and the three-decade freeze, in which the relationship has remained set in a mode of mutual hostility and antipathy, is the backdrop against which the current nuclear dispute is playing out. During the hostage crisis, U.S. efforts to negotiate with the Iranians were complicated by the fact that no one knew who had authority to discuss the hostages. Indeed, Iranian president Abolhassan Bani-Sadr negotiated with Carter for months before admitting he had no authority to release the hostages. Infuriated, Carter authorized a rescue mission, the ill-fated Desert One operation, which ended in disaster in the Iranian desert with a fatal collision between U.S. aircraft on an improvised runway. Despite all the sanctions the United States had to deliver, including freezing all Iranian assets, halting all military sales, breaking diplomatic relations, and so forth, Iran refused to budge on its demands that the United States release its assets, apologize for past misdeeds, and return the Shah (and, after his death, his wealth) to Tehran. Only the full-scale invasion of Iran by Saddam Hussein's Iraq in September 1980 (the start of a bloody eight-year war of attrition) and the election in November 1980 of Ronald Reagan, who had campaigned on a promise to unleash massive military retaliation on Iran if the hostages were not released, convinced the Iranians finally to resolve the crisis. Thus on Carter's last day in office, in January 1981, the United States released a "ransom" of some of Iran's frozen financial assets, and the hostages were freed.

U.S.-Iranian Relations from the Reagan through Clinton Years

The U.S.-Iranian relationship continued to deteriorate during the Reagan administration, with the Americans throwing their support behind Iraq in its war with Tehran (even though Iraq was the aggressor). But with concerns about the spread of Iran's radical Islamist politics to the moderate, Sunni states of the Gulf, which the United States depended upon for oil (such as Saudi Arabia and Kuwait), Washington saw supporting Iraq as the lesser of two evils. The United States provided Iraq with economic support and military supplies, as well as sensitive satellite intelligence on Iranian military movements, while encouraging the wealthy Gulf states to bankroll the Iraqi war effort to the tune of hundreds of billions of dollars throughout the 1980s.[7] The Reagan team essentially established a long-term policy of containment of Iran, which subsequent administrations continued. Obviously, given the enormous casualties that the eight-year war inflicted on Iran, which some estimates place as high as one million, and its economic costs of upwards of $350 billion,[8] it is unsurprising that U.S. support for Saddam's Iraq created further hostility toward America among the Iranian people.

With Iraq winning the conflict and its economy in shambles, Iran went to the United Nations (UN) to negotiate a cease-fire with Iraq. The Iranian leadership's feelings toward America at that point were clear, with Khomeini, frustration boiling over, declaring, "God willing . . . we will empty our hearts' anguish at the appropriate time by taking revenge on the Al Saud [monarchy] and America."[9] Relations remained frosty between Iran and the George H. W. Bush and Clinton administrations, both of which claimed that Iran was sponsoring terrorism (through its financial and military support of groups such as Lebanon's Hezbollah and the Palestinian Hamas). Both American presidents suspected that Tehran might be pursuing nuclear weapons.

All U.S. and Iranian leaders must deal with the reality that domestic political constraints encourage hostile policies toward one another and that appearing tough toward the other is usually rewarded. It has also become a pattern of U.S.-Iranian relations that any move toward moderating the corrosive nature of the current relationship meets significant roadblocks. For example, in seeking to deter Iran from sponsoring terrorism abroad or pursuing weapons of mass destruction (WMD), President Clinton found himself caught between a desire to implement an anti-Iranian trade embargo during the mid-1990s and growing political pressure to pursue a more extreme, regime-change policy. Following the pattern of Reagan's containment policy, Clinton hoped to separate the Middle East into friendly, moderate states versus the more radical, fundamentalist ones—thereby isolating Iran and putting pressure on it to alter its behavior. Clinton noted, "I am convinced that instituting a trade embargo with Iran is the most effective way our nation can help curb Iran's drive to acquire devastating [nuclear] weapons and its continued support for terrorist activities."[10] However, in the months leading up to the trade embargo vote, pressure increased on Clinton to adopt an even tougher policy. Aside from growing intelligence concerns about Iran's progress toward nuclear weapons (that were leaked to the press), Speaker of the House of Representatives Newt Gingrich, R-Ga., stated, "The eventual forced replacement of Iran's Islamic regime is the only long-term strategy that makes sense."[11] The United States adopted both the trade embargo and a policy implicitly supporting regime change.

Iran's Nuclear Program

The Iranian nuclear program began during the mid-1970s under the Shah. He embarked on an ambitious effort involving establishment of a nuclear weapon design team and covert efforts to obtain the know-how and materials required, as well as plans to construct twenty-three nuclear power reactors.[12] The Shah openly said Iran would have nuclear weapons "without a doubt and sooner than one would think."[13] Documents found after the Iranian revolution revealed that the Shah's government and Israel discussed plans to adapt an Israeli surface-to-surface missile for use by Tehran to carry nuclear warheads.[14] Iran began a clandestine uranium enrichment program in 1985 and sought to develop a scientific cadre capable of pursuing a weapons program; fifteen thousand to seventeen thousand Iranian students were sent abroad to study nuclear-related subjects.[15] Iran also actively recruited nuclear technicians from the former Soviet Union and other countries, offering salaries of up to $20,000 a month to hire skilled (but impoverished) nuclear scientists.[16] In addition to building a gas centrifuge uranium enrichment program at Natanz, which former International Atomic Energy Agency (IAEA) director general Mohamed El Baradei described as "sophisticated," Iran acknowledged intending to build both a forty-megawatt thermal heavy-water reactor at Arak and a fuel fabrication plant for the reactor at Esfahan.[17] The pilot plant at Natanz was designed to hold about one thousand centrifuges and produce ten to twelve kilograms of weapons-grade uranium per year. The main enrichment facility at Natanz was envisaged to hold up to fifty thousand centrifuges and produce about five hundred kilograms of weapons-grade uranium annually (enough for twenty-five to thirty nuclear weapons per year). This facility, if operated at full capacity, could "produce enough weapons-grade uranium for a nuclear weapon in a few days."[18] In addition, Pakistan (through the illegal A. Q. Khan smuggling network) provided Iran not only with advanced centrifuge technology and advice, but also with essential data on bomb design.[19] In total, this infrastructure has the capability (if completed) to transform Iran rapidly into not only a nuclear weapon state, but one with a substantial arsenal.

As the program's development demonstrates, Iran's interest in nuclear weapons has continued regardless of the nature of the current regime.[20] In April 2008, Iranian president Mahmoud Ahmadinejad toured the sprawling Natanz site with then–Defense Minister Mostafa Mohammad Najjar, which was odd given that Iran has claimed that the enrichment of uranium is for peaceful purposes (though the tour may have been a showcase for domestic audiences). The photos of the visit show Ahmadinejad walking between cascades of P-1 centrifuges of Pakistani design. Yet the real value of the photos from an intelligence standpoint showed Ahmadinejad "viewing a disassembled IR-2" next-generation centrifuge of Iranian design, which could speed up the enrichment process by four times.[21]

Estimates within the U.S. intelligence community about Iran's nuclear program have varied widely (in some ways mirroring the worst-case assumptions found in prewar Iraqi WMD estimates). For example, the CIA reported in January 2000 that Iran might be able to make a nuclear weapon, but other intelligence agencies hotly disputed the claim.[22] Estimates of Iranian nuclear capabilities routinely overestimated the speed of Tehran's progress, with U.S. and Israeli intelligence in 1992–1993 predicting an Iranian nuclear bomb by 2002, and in 1995 predicting a bomb within "7–15 years."[23] Although a presidential commission reported in March 2005 that U.S. "intelligence on Iran is inadequate to allow firm judgments about Iran's weapons programs," an

August 2005 National Intelligence Estimate (NIE) concluded that Iran was "determined to build nuclear weapons" but unlikely to possess them until 2010–2015.[24] But although the speed and scope of the program are subject to conjecture and debate, the intelligence services of Israel, Germany, Britain, and the United States all agree on the fundamental point that Tehran has "a long-term program to manufacture nuclear weapons."[25] In the views of many experts, Iran already possesses the basic nuclear technology, infrastructure, and expertise to build weapons and lacks only adequate stockpiles of fissile material to become a nuclear state.[26]

However, Tehran signed the Nuclear Non-Proliferation Treaty and placed its existing civilian nuclear power industry under IAEA inspection. As a result, Iran found itself not only under greater scrutiny from the IAEA but also subject to substantial supplier state restrictions on the importation of technology for its declared civilian nuclear power industry. By treaty, Iran is obligated to report all nuclear activities to the IAEA, and when rumors surfaced regarding a hidden program, Tehran (after intense outside pressure) was eventually forced to allow inspectors into the country in October 2003. Unfortunately for Tehran, the inspections revealed a long-running Iranian nuclear program that had effectively concealed itself from outside scrutiny for decades and which, unmolested, had the potential to provide it with substantial weapons capabilities. Although the U.S. position on Iran remained hostile, befitting Iran's status within the "axis of evil," Britain, France, and Germany embarked on a five-year diplomatic effort to peacefully resolve the dispute over Iran's nuclear program. These efforts, combined with the diplomatic impasse during the first year of the Obama presidency, have yet to produce an acceptable settlement to both sides.

The Bush Approach: Lost Opportunities after September 11

It should be noted that in the months following the September 11 attacks, the Bush administration had an opportunity to expand cooperation with the government of Iranian president Mohammad Khatami. Khatami, a reformer, believed that a window of opportunity had opened. Mohammad Hossein Adeli, a deputy at the Iranian Foreign Ministry, began intense contacts with higher officials in the Iranian government. Adeli explains, "We wanted to truly condemn the [September 11] attacks but we also wished to offer an olive branch to the United States, showing we were interested in peace."[27] Adeli was even able to convince Supreme Leader Ali Khamenei that the proposals would be productive. A Khamenei assistant noted, "The Supreme Leader was deeply suspicious of the American government. . . . But [he] was repulsed by these [September 11] terrorist acts and was truly sad about the loss of the civilian lives in America."[28]

In the weeks following the September 11 attacks, American and Iranian representatives met several times in Switzerland. The Iranian delegation was pushing for action because it was opposed to the Taliban government and had supported elements of the opposition Northern Alliance (also an ally of the United States against the Taliban and al Qaeda). Jim Dobbins, President Bush's first envoy to Afghanistan, worked extensively with the Iranian diplomatic leader, Javad Zarif (a University of Denver graduate). Zarif was instrumental in convincing the Northern Alliance delegate, Yunus Qanooni, to accept Hamid Karzai, a Pashtun from the south, as the new president of Afghanistan and to form a coalition government. According to Dobbins, "The Russians and the Indians had been making similar points. . . . But it wasn't until Zarif took him aside that it was settled." Iran also committed $500 million to rebuild Afghanistan. A critical moment was approaching in which the United States and Iran had common interests and the will to open up dialogue on a number of issues, but a series of gaffes destroyed the moment. One week after the Iranian pledge to provide aid to Afghanistan, Iran was included in the "axis of evil" speech. Former Bush speechwriter Michael Gerson suggests that it was former national security adviser Condoleezza Rice's idea to add Iran to that speech. For Mohammad Adeli, the speech immediately marginalized the Iranian officials who were seeking better relations with the United States. Adeli comments, "The speech exonerated those [hard-liners] who had always doubted America's intentions."[29]

There had also been a history of American legislative antagonism toward Iran. In July 2001, prior to the September attacks, the Senate approved legislation extending sanctions against Iran for another five years—a move that undercut efforts by moderate Iranian president Mohammad Khatami to improve relations with Washington and emboldened hard-liners. In October 2006, Congress passed and President Bush signed into law the Iran Freedom Support Act, which placed sanctions on countries that have helped Iran's nuclear program, even if the technical support was legal under the Nuclear Non-Proliferation Treaty (NPT).[30] Critics noted the similarity of this legislation to the 1998 Iraq Liberation Act, which helped to provide the Bush administration with some authority to take action in the buildup to the 2003 war.

Before leaving office, it became obvious to President Bush that military action against Iran's nuclear facilities would only complicate his government's efforts at trying to achieve stability in Iraq and Afghanistan. In January 2009, senior American officials disclosed that Bush had denied Israeli requests for special bunker-buster bombs and to fly over Iraq to strike the Iranian Natanz nuclear complex.[31] Late in his presidency, Bush became convinced that a strike against Iran would "prove ineffective, lead to the expulsion of international inspectors and drive Iran's nuclear effort further out of view."[32] In its place, Bush directed a covert program to sabotage the Iranian nuclear program.

In sum, the Bush presidency could be characterized as a period of missed opportunities with recurring episodes of conflict and misunderstanding. Domestic constraints on both sides have added to the diplomatic malaise. Since 1979, any U.S. president seeking to soften policy toward Iran, normalize relations, or engage in direct talks has risked attack by domestic opponents of such moves. Similarly, in Iran, limited efforts by two Iranian presidents—Ali Akbar Hashemi Rafsanjani during the 1990s and Mohammad Khatami prior to 2005—to improve U.S.-Iranian relations brought both men under attack at home from conservative clerics, who forced them to maintain the existing hostile pattern. Both sides are trapped with a hostile image of the other, locked into place like a bug in amber by the historical relationship they share and by strategic and political factors that make it almost impossible to escape.

U.S.-Iran Nuclear Standoff (2005–2009): The European Union and United Nations as Negotiating Agents

Over the course of the Bush years, the Europeans viewed diplomacy as the best way to resolve the dispute, to maintain international support for whatever sanctions might be necessary, and to avoid provoking a conflict that might cause Iran to leave the Nuclear Non-Proliferation Treaty and cease cooperation with the IAEA. Whereas the United States left the direct diplomatic efforts to the Europeans and refused to discuss incentives for Iran, it did not discourage Britain, Germany, and France from pursuing their efforts, judging that any later efforts to gain international support for harsher measures against Tehran would require an effort at diplomacy first (especially after the controversial lead-up to the Iraq war).[33]

In June 2005, hard-line conservative Mahmoud Ahmadinejad was elected president of Iran, replacing the moderate reformist Khatami. And while maintaining that Iran's nuclear program was not intended to develop weapons, Ahmadinejad, even as he exited the polls on election day, left no doubt about his position on the issue, stating: "Nuclear energy is a result of the Iranian people's scientific development and no one can block the way of a nation's scientific development. . . . This right of the Iranian people will soon be recognized by those who have so far denied it."[34] Over the following months, Iran began to adopt a much tougher stance in its negotiations with the Europeans and the IAEA. Although Ahmadinejad became the visible, public face of this more confrontational approach, he was not entirely responsible for the shift, since this policy is actually decided not by the president but by the supreme leader, Ayatollah Ali Khamenei.[35] Tehran not only refused to comply with the IAEA's demand to halt its uranium conversion program (which it had restarted in defiance of the agreement previously reached with Britain, Germany, and France) but stated that "making nuclear fuel for civilian purposes was its right under the Nuclear Nonproliferation Treaty (NPT)."[36] By beginning work again at its uranium conversion facilities in Isfahan, where raw uranium is converted into a gas that can later be fed into centrifuges for enrichment, Iran explicitly rejected giving up its right to develop nuclear fuel indigenously.[37] Iranian officials warned the West that Iran would not negotiate over its uranium conversion plants but said it was still willing to discuss the uranium enrichment facilities at Natanz in future talks.[38] The governing board of the IAEA responded to the Iranian actions by setting a deadline of September 3, 2005, for Iran to "reestablish full suspension of all enrichment related activities."[39]

When Iran failed to comply with the new deadline, the United States and its European allies found their options limited. Although not immediately referring Iran to the UN Security Council, the Western allies sought a tough new IAEA resolution accusing Iran of "noncompliance" with treaties governing its nuclear program. Russia and China still objected to the IAEA draft proposal, since it signaled that Iran's case would eventually be sent to the Security Council—a step they were unwilling to take—and blocked this move to punish Iran. For its part, Iran continued to say it was willing to continue negotiations with the Europeans but did not back away from its earlier declaration that referral to the UN might lead to its withdrawal from the NPT.[40] This long dance between Iran and the IAEA had been under way since inspectors first discovered that Iran was clandestinely enriching uranium in 2003. Between June 2003 and September 2005 the IAEA board passed seven resolutions criticizing Iran's activities and urging it to grant unfettered access to inspectors.[41] Still, although Iranian nuclear activities continued to be suspicious, the IAEA was unable to prove conclusively that Iran was pursuing a weapons program—despite its lack of cooperation with inspectors and its failure to provide a full accounting of its efforts to acquire centrifuges for uranium enrichment or an explanation for the discovery of recently produced plutonium, which was inconsistent with Tehran's claims that its plutonium separation experiments only ran between 1988 and 1993.[42] In the absence of conclusive proof, Russia, India, Brazil, South Africa, and many developing countries opposed U.S. and European calls for a referral of Iran to the Security Council, where sanctions (either military or economic) could be imposed.[43]

With international pressure on Tehran growing and the United States and Europeans adopting a more united front over the nuclear issue, Ahmadinejad upped the ante in January 2006, announcing that Iran would reopen its massive uranium enrichment complex at Natanz after a fourteen-month halt in operations. That facility had sparked the original crisis over the Iranian nuclear program, when it was revealed in February 2003 that inspectors discovered plans for more than fifty thousand centrifuges at the site—enough when fully constructed to produce fuel for up to twenty nuclear weapons per year. Not only did the Western allies send messages to Tehran warning against such a move, but Russia and China did as well—a stark warning to Iran that the resistance of those two states to a referral to the Security Council might be waning.[44] Nevertheless, within days Iran broke open the internationally monitored seals on three of its nuclear facilities, clearing the way for uranium enrichment and derailing any new negotiations with the Europeans. Combined with Iran's harsh rhetoric, its actions met general condemnation by the international community. One European diplomat commented, "The Iranians have behaved so remarkably badly, it's hard to believe that the international community will do anything other than put them in front of the ultimate court of international public opinion (the UN Security Council). . . . That is where the Iranians are heading."[45] For their part, the Iranians defended their actions as peaceful and involving research activities permitted them under the NPT.[46] Later, during a press conference following a meeting with his French and British counterparts, the German foreign minister, Frank-Walter Steinmeier, noted, "Our talks with Iran have reached a dead end. . . . From our point of view, the time has come for the UN Security Council to become involved."[47] Pressing its advantage, the United States announced its full support for the European action, with Secretary of State Rice declaring Iran's actions "have shattered the basis for negotiation."[48]

In response to the renewed movement toward referring it to the Security Council, Iran turned up the heat still further in April 2006 by announcing its nuclear engineers had advanced to "a new phase in the enrichment of uranium" allowing it to speed ahead production of nuclear fuel on an industrial scale. In a nationally televised broadcast, Ahmadinejad declared that "Iran has joined the nuclear countries of the world," leading the White House to announce that the United States would work with the Security Council "to deal with the significant threat posed by the regime's efforts to acquire nuclear weapons." Given that earlier in the week Bush had repeated his "stated goal" not to allow "the Iranians to have a nuclear weapon, the capacity to make a nuclear weapon, or the knowledge as to how to make a nuclear weapon," Ahmadinejad's announcement represented a serious setback for U.S. foreign policy.[49]

Although nuclear analysts quickly dismissed Iran's claims as exaggerated "political posturing," meant to invoke Iranian nationalism to firm up domestic political support for Ahmadinejad and convince the international community that Iran's nuclear advances were inevitable, that did nothing to reduce growing international concern about the program.[50] Iran refused to answer IAEA questions about the existence of a previously unknown, secret uranium enrichment program (based on P-2 centrifuges obtained on the black market through the A.Q. Khan network) unwisely disclosed weeks earlier by Ahmadinejad. Declaring the new technology would increase fourfold the amount of uranium Iran could enrich, Ahmadinejad rejected a UN deadline to suspend the nuclear program and a proposal by Moscow to enrich uranium for Iran on Russian soil, declaring that sanctions would hurt Western nations more than Iran.[51] In response, the United States announced it would ask the Security Council to require Iran to stop enrichment based on Chapter Seven of the UN Charter, the section making resolutions mandatory and opening the way for either sanctions or military action—a move opposed by both Russia and China.[52]

Over the following months, with no movement on either the diplomatic or the sanctions front, the Europeans began pressing Bush to make a "dramatic gesture" to reenergize talks, rally world opinion against Iran, and avoid having the Americans blamed for not doing their utmost to defuse the crisis.[53] An eighteen-page letter from Ahmadinejad to Bush in May 2006, although filled with religious language and declarations that Western democracy had failed, was seen by many foreign policy experts as an attempt by the Iranian leader to open a new dialogue.[54] After an internal White House debate, in which Secretary Rice overcame the skepticism of Vice President Dick Cheney to convince Bush of the need for "a third option" apart from "either a nuclear Iran or an American military action," the president agreed to engage in substantive talks with Iran—the first major negotiations in the twenty-seven years since the hostage crisis. Although Cheney and other hard-line officials were "dead set against it" and preferred a strategy to isolate Iran enough to force "regime change," they were finally persuaded that if a military response was eventually necessary, it would be easier to gain international approval if efforts at negotiation preceded it.[55] As a result, in June 2006 punitive action by the Security Council was shelved until Iran had a chance to respond to a new package of incentives (still minus U.S. security guarantees) presented by the United States, Europe, Russia, and China.[56] Although the Iranians immediately stated that they would "not negotiate over our nation's natural nuclear rights," they struck a slightly conciliatory tone by noting that they were "ready to hold fair and unbiased dialogue and negotiations over mutual concerns within the context of a defined framework," and Ayatollah Khamenei (long an opponent of direct talks with Washington) gave his blessing to talks "if there was respect for mutual interests."[57] In response to the Iranian rejection of the package of economic incentives, the UN Security Council issued a call for Iran to implement a "full and sustained suspension" of its nuclear activities by August 31 or face sanctions.[58]

Iran ignored those calls, and after North Korea's nuclear test in October 2006, the European Union (EU) supported limited UN sanctions against Iran after it had rejected suspending its enrichment program as a precondition for starting new talks.[59] The IAEA followed by reporting that Iran had successfully set up a second centrifuge cascade and was continuing to expand its enrichment capabilities, though then–IAEA director El Baradei maintained, "The jury is still out on whether they are developing a nuclear weapon."[60] Although Iran suggested that "France organize and monitor the production of enriched uranium inside Iran" (a proposal rejected by the West as falling short of Security Council demands for a freeze on all nuclear activities), Tehran maintained its position that it would not comply with the UN demands and refused to condemn North Korea for its nuclear test.[61] Raising tensions further, Ahmadinejad declared in November 2006 that Iran's program was nearing the milestone of mastering the nuclear fuel cycle and that "we can have our celebration of Iran's full nuclearization this year."[62] The announcement increased Western concerns, since mastering the fuel cycle implies the ability not only to enrich uranium but also to reprocess plutonium from spent fuel, potentially providing Iran with two sources of material for nuclear weapons.

Finally, in December 2006 the Security Council unanimously passed a resolution against Iran, banning the import or export of materials and technology used in uranium enrichment, reprocessing, or ballistic missiles. Although the measure was softened to gain Russian and Chinese support (and excluded any sanctions against the Bashehr nuclear power plant being built by Russia in southern Iran), it still froze the assets of twelve Iranians and eleven companies involved in Tehran's nuclear and ballistic missile programs.[63] That led to friction with U.S. allies in Europe, who resisted subsequent Bush administration demands to increase financial pressure on Iran by curtailing exports, loan guarantees, and many business transactions because of their far greater commercial and economic ties with Tehran.[64] The Europeans believed they were being asked to sacrifice far more than the Americans for the sanctions (given limited U.S. business interests), and their resistance provided Tehran with a continued economic lifeline in the face of the UN penalties. For example, in February 2007 Russia announced that it would consider OPEC-like cooperation with Tehran on sales of natural gas, and President Vladimir Putin observed that "the people of Iran should have access to modern technologies, including nuclear ones . . . they should choose a variant that will guarantee Iran access to nuclear energy" while complying with their NPT commitments to avoid weaponization.[65] One of the greatest hurdles for the United States in marshaling international support for harsh economic sanctions remains the reality that other states have tremendous economic interests in Iran and much to lose from such measures—ranging from the Russians and Chinese, who fear losing access to Iranian oil and gas, to the Europeans, who have long-standing business interests with Tehran.

Even so, in the face of Iran's continued defiance, on March 24, 2007, the Security Council unanimously passed Resolution 1747 barring all arms exports to Iran and freezing the financial assets of twenty-eight Iranians linked to its military and nuclear programs. This action provoked Khamenei to warn that were new sanctions passed, "Iran would strike back against any threats or violence." Not only was the nuclear program "more important than the nationalization of oil in 1958," he said, but "if they want to treat us with threats and use of force or violence, the Iranian nation will undoubtedly use all its capabilities to strike the invading enemies."[66] Ahmadinejad warned that if pressure on Iran was not ended, he would consider halting all cooperation with the IAEA, observing that the West "should know that the Iranian nation will defend its right and that this path is irreversible."[67] According to Under Secretary of State Nicolas Burns, the United States was "trying to force a change in the actions and behavior of the Iranian government," and whereas the sanctions "immediately focused on the nuclear weapons research program," they were also "trying to limit the ability of Iran to be a disruptive and violent factor on Middle East politics."[68] Two U.S. carrier battle groups were sent to the Persian Gulf as a veiled threat to Iran. Nevertheless, in April 2007 Ahmadinejad boasted that

Iran was capable of "enriching uranium on an industrial scale," with a newly operational site containing 1,300 centrifuges enriching small amounts of uranium at an underground facility in Natanz.[69] The United States intended to try gradually increasing the severity of sanctions against Iran, while refusing to take military options off the table, but Iran showed no willingness to give in and speeded up its installation of centrifuges. In 2007 it was estimated that there was a growing likelihood of perhaps eight thousand centrifuges being added at Natanz, which would have been enough to enrich sufficient fissile material for at least two nuclear weapons a year.[70]

Throughout 2008 and 2009, Iran moved to expand its nuclear enrichment facilities—and, evidently, to improve its technology with regard to nuclear weapons. Ahmadinejad's visit to Natanz in April 2008 showcased the new-generation IR-2 centrifuges, which may have enhanced capability to separate out U-235 for fuel or bombs. The key to the IR-2's success is in its carbon fiber construction, which is lighter and potentially more capable than the P-1 and P-2s (of Pakistani design).[71] What was especially intriguing were the forty-eight photos released to the Western press, including one of Ahmadinejad standing next to a disassembled IR-2.[72]

Later, in fall 2009, Iran disclosed to the IAEA that it had not reported an enrichment site near the city of Qum, within the confines of a Revolutionary Guard base. The underground plant has been estimated to eventually hold "3,000 centrifuges" of the P-1 type.[73] The new disclosure, coupled with the fact that Iran's nuclear program has been dispersed and literally gone underground, caused great concern in the West. U.S. Defense Secretary Robert Gates noted that a military strike "would only slow Iran's nuclear ambitions by one to three years."[74] Iran's tunneling capability has been enhanced substantially. The Qum site, about one-half complete, is "buried inside a mountain."[75] The Iranian Revolutionary Guard Corps owns construction firms that do much of this tunneling. Finally, in October 2009, the IAEA reported that Iran had acquired "sufficient information to be able to design and produce a workable atom bomb."[76] According to the report, nuclear experts suggest that the Iranian Ministry of Defense "'aimed at the development of a nuclear payload to be delivered using the Shahab 3 [medium-range] missile system.'"[77] These facts point to a possible Iranian nuclear weapons capability in the future. Despite UN Security Council sanctions, and an engaged West seeking accommodation over the enrichment issue, Iran stayed the course on its nuclear path. The EU is now in step with the Obama administration in dealing with Iran. When the Qum site was disclosed both British prime minister Gordon Brown and French president Nicolas Sarkozy quickly condemned Iran's deception. Sarkozy implied Iran would have two months beyond October to comply with the IAEA, and Brown warned that "the international community has no choice today but to draw a line in the sand."[78]

The Obama Approach and the Challenges of Post-Election Iran

Barack Obama was elected president of the United States in November 2008 and campaigned on a pledge to open direct negotiations with the Iranians over the nuclear standoff. Obama's plan diverged sharply from that of the Bush administration. In his inaugural address, and later in the Cairo Address, Obama hinted at the possibility of the UN reaching accommodation with Iran by allowing it to retain some limited nuclear enrichment capability for peaceful purposes. Obama explained, "Any nation—including Iran—should have the right to access peaceful nuclear power if it complies with its responsibilities under the Nuclear Non-Proliferation Treaty."[79] This was a clear departure from the Bush administration policy of nonengagement and denial of Iran's ability to enrich uranium. Obama sent a letter to Ayatollah Khamenei, the real power broker in Iranian politics, outlining a framework for talks to resolve the stand-off. However, this strategy was frustrated by the failure of Iran to accept a proposed IAEA reprocessing deal, its persistent human rights abuses after the contested presidential election, and the lack of will on the part of the UN Security Council to place added pressure on Iran.

In the IAEA proposal that Iran rejected in October 2009, Tehran was to send 2,600 pounds of its enriched uranium to Russia for reprocessing, and then on to France for assembly into fuel rods—a move that would have significantly reduced the amount of material that could be diverted for weapons purposes. The fuel rods would then be sent back to Iran for use in a medical research facility in Tehran. In July 2009, Obama travelled to Moscow to meet with Russian president Dmitry Medvedev to persuade the Kremlin to cooperate in placing pressure on Iran to accept limits on its enrichment program. Obama cancelled the deployment of the ABM system in Eastern Europe in the hopes of a quid pro quo from Moscow. However, by October 2009, Russian foreign minister Sergey V. Lavrov stated, "Threats, sanctions and threats of pressure in the current situation, we are convinced, would be counterproductive."[80] As one of Iran's closest trading partners, Russia insisted that Iran had made good faith efforts to deescalate the conflict. Nevertheless, Moscow was dismayed by the disclosure in September of the Iranian Qum nuclear site—yet another new, undisclosed enrichment facility, and a discovery that increased its willingness to consider some additional sanctions.

For its part, China has also resisted tough new sanctions against Iran. China has "invested heavily in Iranian oil and gas reserves" and has been wary that sanctions may adversely affect its commercial relationship with Tehran.[81] Chinese-Iranian trade has escalated in recent years with "Iran awash in Chinese products . . . and [Iran supplying] . . . 15 percent of China's oil."[82] These facts, taken in concert with Iranian counteroffers of an incremental reprocessing agreement in December 2009, effectively kept China from moving toward the position of the Western powers. In this proposal, Iranian foreign minister Manouchehr Mottaki announced Iran would "hand over 400 kilograms, or 882 pounds, of uranium initially—about a third of the amount proposed in the draft agreement reached under United Nations auspices in October [2009]—in exchange for an equivalent amount of enriched material to fuel a medical research reactor."[83] Critics argued this was simply a technique to divide the UN Security Council.

Obama also faced the difficulty of negotiating with Iran in the aftermath of the June 2009 contested presidential election and the brutal crackdown that followed. On June 12, 2009, Iranians went to the polls to elect a new president, which pitted the incumbent Ahmadinejad against several reformer candidates, including former prime minister Mir Hussein Moussavi (whose position on nuclear enrichment did not diverge substantially from Ahmadinejad's). Moussavi had a wide following and was clearly expected to challenge Ahmadinejad in the polls. However, by early nightfall on election day, Ahmadinejad was announced as the overwhelming victor. Given Moussavi's popularity, and clear evidence of irregularities, many supporters saw the election results as a sham, provoking tens of thousands of dissenting Iranians into the streets. Khamenei quickly backed Ahmadinejad, though many reformers and clerics alike believed the election had been stolen. Almost immediately, Iranian police and Basij militiamen began to violently suppress the street demonstrations. Over the course of several weeks, hundreds were jailed with reports of torture, rape, and murder in prisons. For Americans, the drama played out on June 20 when a young woman, Neda Agha-Soltan, was gunned down during an antigovernment rally. The images showed a woman dying in the streets and opened up cracks in the regime, leading Iranians to see their own government as illegitimate and repressive.

In sum, Obama now faces a regime that has "circled the wagons" and is divided from within, greatly complicating diplomacy. Interwoven into this internal instability is the historic animosity and suspicion between Washington and Tehran. Indeed, many Iranians believe the nuclear issue is simply a means for the United States to keep Iran down and continue its hegemony over the region. As Karim Sadjadpour notes, "'Khamenei still believes the United States wants to go back to the patron-client relationship and the nuclear issue is being used for that.'"[84] Moreover, Khamenei recognizes the politically precarious position of his government and is likely to be reluctant to negotiate from a position of weakness. Thus Obama faces the monumental tasks of avoiding any perceived involvement in Iranian domestic affairs, convincing Russia and China to bring pressure on Tehran over enrichment, and overcoming the historical suspicions that make compromise by either side difficult.

Conclusions and Policy Options

Assuming that no extreme measures are taken militarily against Iran in the near future, how might it be possible to resolve the nuclear impasse? Obama campaigned on a platform of opening up direct dialogue with Iran, yet over his first year in office was unable to achieve a breakthrough. At the same time, Ahmadinejad's hold on the presidency has weakened and he has increasingly leaned on the Revolutionary Guard for support. Moreover, whether he wants to work out an agreement with the IAEA is still unclear. First, he is beholden to Ayatollah Khamenei, the real center of power in Iran, who favors continuing the nuclear program. And with the current domestic political turmoil, it seems unlikely that Khamenei or Ahmadinejad would seriously compromise on an issue so important to their conservative constituencies. On the surface it would appear that Iran's strategy is to delay concessions (or make limited ones to stave off significant sanctions) for as long as possible in order to allow the nuclear program to become a *fait accompli*. Iranian negotiators were able to hold off certain sanctions when it proposed a half-hearted counteroffer of gradual reprocessing, knowing that the Europeans and Americans would balk at that arrangement. By November 2009, Iran simply dismissed the plan as unworkable because "it did not trust Russia and France . . . [who] under . . . the plan would further refine and mold the low-enriched uranium . . . to follow through on the deal."[85]

In the absence of any agreement, the United States may have to negotiate a deal similar to the 1994 Agreed Framework with North Korea: one that could slow the pace of Iran's nuclear development, permit more substantive IAEA inspections, and allow diplomacy time to work. Though the agreement with North Korea was imperfect, without it the world would likely have seen either a general war on the Korean peninsula (which the Pentagon estimated would inflict a million casualties) or a North Korean regime with enough fissile material for at least two hundred weapons (instead of the nine to twelve it likely possesses).[86] If the choice becomes one of launching a major war or making "lemonade from lemons" by adopting a deal that merely slows Iran's nuclear progress, it is likely the latter will be the preferred option.

A more serious problem may be that the Europeans and the Obama administration have drawn a line in the sand, placing the deadline for Iranian agreement at the end of 2009. As we begin the second half of 2010 with no agreement in sight, the UN Security Council may now be called on to place additional sanctions on Iran, a move certain to increase Iranian intransigence. There is still no sense of what Russia and China will do in this case, but both have resisted backing Tehran into a corner. Thus, reengaging in another diplomatic effort may help in a number of ways. First, a limited reprocessing deal would at least buy the IAEA more time to delay the Iranian nuclear program and allow more thorough onsite inspections. The second, more vital point is that Iran is changing, albeit slowly. Most Iranians were born after the revolution, and there is a younger generation that desires more personal and political freedom to choose their own future. The contested election exposed deep cleavages within Iranian society, even within the clerical community itself. Speaking at Tehran University in July 2009, former Iranian president Rafsanjani "assailed the government's handling of the post-election unrest" and argued that the government had "lost the trust of many Iranians."[87] In a word, the seeds of dissent have been firmly entrenched in Iranian society, and the legitimacy of the existing regime has been shaken. The reform movement is likely a slow-motion avalanche, one that may eventually address the threat posed by Iran's nuclear program if time can be bought through diplomacy.

While the Obama administration searches for answers, it is important that military options (though not the threat of them) be taken off the table. Given that Iran is years away from developing nuclear weapons, precipitate military action is not called for at this point.[88] Moreover, the potentially extreme consequences of such action, given Iran's unquestioned ability to disrupt stability in both Iraq and Afghanistan, and the overstretched condition of the U.S. military, make it utterly unrealistic at present. Though the EU has now largely adopted the U.S. view that only sanctions will alter Iran's behavior, this approach must include carrots as well as sticks. Realistically, demanding complete Iranian capitulation on the nuclear issue given the current context is only likely to result in either conflict or a continuation of the current, ineffectual pattern of negotiations with Tehran. That pattern—of U.S.-UN threats and sanctions, Iranian defiance, and the inability to take strong UN action (because of U.S. military constraints and the unwillingness of veto-wielding council members to acquiesce to it)—will inevitably lead to more tension in the region; even greater hostility between the United States and Iran; and, in the long run, an Iranian nuclear program outside of IAEA supervision providing Tehran with both civilian and military capabilities.

Key Actors

Mahmoud Ahmadinejad   Iran's current president (2005–present), a conservative opposed to the social reforms pushed by Khatami, has strongly pursued a more aggressive negotiating position in support of Iran's continued nuclear enrichment program, which he claims is for peaceful purposes. Ahmadinejad was victorious in the contested presidential election of June 2009. His internal position was weakened due to street protests challenging his legitimacy in the aftermath of the election.

George W. Bush   U.S. president, took a hard line on negotiations with Iran over its nuclear program, demanding that Iran stop nuclear enrichment before negotiations could go forward.

Jimmy Carter   U.S. president during the Iranian revolution and the hostage crisis.

Bill Clinton   U.S. president, signed an executive order in 1995 prohibiting trade with Iran to force it to stop supporting terrorism and developing a nuclear weapons program.

Supreme Leader Ali Khamenei   Iran's current supreme leader, wields tremendous power to step into the political process and make important decisions for the country. He has strongly supported Iran's nuclear program and has been largely opposed to normalizing relations with the United States.

Mohammad Khatami   Iranian president (1997–2005), tried unsuccessfully to reform the political system and establish better relations with the West.

Ayatollah Ruhollah Khomeini   Iranian revolutionary leader, became Iran's first supreme leader. His anti-Western policy became the inspiration behind the Iranian revolution and the storming of the American embassy in Tehran.

Mir Hussein Moussavi   Former Iranian prime minister and presidential challenger to Ahmadinejad. Moussavi lost the June 2009 contested presidential election, but quickly became the symbol of resistance to the Iranian regime. His followers have continued to engage in political dissent throughout the country.

Barack Obama   Current U.S. president, who campaigned on a platform of opening up dialogue directly with the Iranian government. His clinched-fist metaphor was intended to send a message to the Iranian government that the United States desired a less confrontational and more cooperative relationship with the Islamic republic. After the contested election, his position became much more difficult due to resistance to negotiations within the U.S. government.

Ali Akbar Hashemi Rafsanjani   Former Iranian president and powerful cleric who has challenged the legitimacy of the current Iranian regime; viewed the June 2009 presidential election as fraudulent.

Ronald Reagan   U.S. president, adopted a containment strategy versus Iran and supported Iraq in its war against Tehran (1980–1988).

Notes

1. Barack Obama, "Inaugural Address," January 21, 2009, www.whitehouse.gov/blog/inaugural-address.

2. Roger Cohen, "The Making of an Iran Policy," August 2, 2009, www.nytimes.com/2009/08/02/magazine/02Iran-t.html.

3. See Thomas Preston, *From Lambs to Lions: Future Security Relationships in a World of Biological and Nuclear Weapons* (Boulder: Rowman and Littlefield, 2007).

4. See William J. Daugherty, "Jimmy Carter and the 1979 Decision to Admit the Shah into the United States," AmericanDiplomacy.org, January 2003, www.unc.edu/depts/diplomat/archives_roll/2003_01-03/daugherty_shaw.

5. GlobalSecurity.org, "Ministry of Security SAVAK," www.globalsecurity.org/intell/world/iran/savak.htm.

6. Daugherty, "Jimmy Carter."

7. John King, "Arming Iraq and the Path to War," March 31, 2003, www.parstimes.com/news/archive/2003/arming_iraq.html.

8. Farhang Rajaee, *The Iran-Iraq War: The Politics of Aggression* (Gainesville: University Press of Florida, 1993), 1.

9. Ibid.

10. Moshahed Hossein, "U.S. Strategy Tries to Isolate Iran," May 1995, web.archive.org/web/20030103132635/www.netiran.com/Htdocs/Clippings/FPolitics/950515XXFP02.html.

11. Ibid.

12. Seymour M. Hersh, "The Iran Game," *New Yorker,* December 3, 2001, 42–50; Elaine Sciolino, "Nuclear Ambitions Aren't New for Iran," *New York Times,* June 22, 2003, WK 4.

13. Sciolino, "Nuclear Ambitions," 4.

14. Ibid.

15. Terrence Henry, "Nuclear Iran," *Atlantic Monthly,* December 2003, 45.

16. Ibid.; Jack Boureston and Charles D. Ferguson, "Schooling Iran's Atom Squad," *Bulletin of the Atomic Scientists* 60, no.3 (May/June 2004): 31–35.

17. David Albright and Corey Hinderstein, "Iran, Player or Rogue?" *Bulletin of the Atomic Scientists* 59, no.5 (September/October 2003): 54–56.

18. Ibid.

19. Hersh, "The Iran Game," 50; William J. Broad, David E. Sanger, and Raymond Bonner, "A Tale of Nuclear Proliferation: How Pakistani Built His Network," *New York Times,* February 12, 2004, A1.

20. For a detailed discussion of Iran's postrevolution pursuit of nuclear, biological, and chemical weapons, see Gregory F. Giles, "The Islamic Republic of Iran and Nuclear, Biological, and Chemical Weapons," in *Planning the Unthinkable: How New Powers Will Use Nuclear, Biological, and Chemical Weapons,* ed. James J. Wirtz, Peter R. Lavoy, and Scott D. Sagan (Ithaca, N.Y.: Cornell University Press, 2000), 79–103.

21. William J. Broad, "A Tantalizing Look at Iran's Nuclear Program," April 28, 2008, www.nytimes.com/2008/04/29/science/29nuke.html.

22. James Risen and Judith Miller, "No Illicit Arms Found in Iraq, U.S. Inspector Tells Congress," *New York Times,* October 3, 2003, A1.

23. Joseph Cirincione, *Deadly Arsenals: Tracking Weapons of Mass Destruction* (Washington, D.C.: Carnegie Endowment for International Peace, 2002), 257. Indeed, a January 2005 briefing to the Israeli Knesset by Meir Dagan, head of the Mossad intelligence agency, warned that Iran could build a bomb in less than three years and, if it successfully enriched uranium in 2005, could have a weapon two years later. See BBC News, http://news.bbc.co.uk/go/pr/fr/-/2/hi/middle_east/4203411.stm, January 24, 2005. By August 2005, Israeli intelligence had adjusted its estimate to Iran's having the bomb as early as 2008, "if all goes well for it," but probably by 2012. Orly Halpern, "New Estimates on Iranian Nukes," *Jerusalem Post,* August 1, 2005, jpost.com/servlet/Satellite ?pagename=Jpost/JPArticle/ShowFull&cid=1122776414371&p=1101615860782.

24. Douglas Jehl and Eric Schmitt, "Data Is Lacking on Iran's Arms, U.S. Panel Says," *New York Times,* March 9, 2005, A1; Steven R. Weisman and Douglas Jehl, "Estimate Revised on When Iran Could Make Nuclear Bomb," *New York Times,* August 3, 2005, A8. Agreeing with this assessment, London's International Institute for Strategic Studies concluded that Iran would not be expected to build nuclear weapons before the next decade.

25. Alan Cowell, "Nuclear Weapon Is Years Off for Iran, Research Panel Says," *New York Times,* September 7, 2005, A11. See Cirincione, *Deadly Arsenals,* 255. The IAEA, after two years of inspections, has stated it has not found evidence of any weapons program. See Jehl and Schmitt, "Data Is Lacking on Iran's Arms."

26. Cirincione, *Deadly Arsenals,* 255.

27. Michael Hirsh, Maziar Bahari, et al., "Rumors of War," *Newsweek,* February 19, 2007, 30.

28. Ibid., 31.

29. Ibid.

30. Azar Nafisi, "The Veiled Threat," *The New Republic,* February 22, 1999, 27.

31. David E. Sanger, "U.S. Rejected Aid for Israeli Raid on Iranian Nuclear Site," January 11, 2009, www.nytimes.com/2009/01/11/washington/11iran.html.

32. Ibid.

33. Steven R. Weisman, "U.S. in Talks with Europeans on a Nuclear Deal with Iran," *New York Times,* October 12, 2004, A16.

34. David E. Sanger, "Iranian Upset, U.S. Challenge," *New York Times,* June 26, 2005, A1.

35. Nazila Fathi, "Iran Tells Europe It's Devoted to Nuclear Efforts and Talks," *New York Times,* August 4, 2005, A6.

36. Nazila Fathi, "Iran Warns the West Not to Use the U.N. to Penalize It," *New York Times,* September 12, 2005, A7.

37. Nazila Fathi, "Iran Rejects European Offer to End Its Nuclear Impasse," *New York Times,* August 7, 2005, A11.

38. Nazila Fathi, "Iran's New Leader Turns to Conservatives for His Cabinet," *New York Times,* August 15, 2005, A3.

39. Thomas Fuller and Nazila Fathi, "U.N. Agency Urges Iran to Halt Its Nuclear Activity," *New York Times,* August 12, 2005, A8.

40. Steven R. Weisman, "West Presses for Nuclear Agency to Rebuke Iran, Despite Russian Dissent," *New York Times,* September 23, 2005, A6.

41. Mark Landler, "Nuclear Agency Expected to Back Weaker Rebuke to Iran," *New York Times,* September 24, 2005, A3.

42. Mark Landler, "U.N. Says It Hasn't Found Much New about Nuclear Iran," *New York Times,* September 3, 2005, A3.

43. Steven R. Weisman, "Wider U.S. Net Seeks Allies against Iran's Nuclear Plan," *New York Times,* September 10, 2005, A3.

44. Elaine Sciolino, "Iran, Defiant, Insists It Plans to Restart Nuclear Program," *New York Times,* January 10, 2006, A11.

45. Steven R. Weisman and Nazila Fathi, "Iranians Reopen Nuclear Centers," *New York Times,* January 11, 2006, A1.

46. Ibid.

47. Richard Bernstein and Steven R. Weisman, "Europe Joins U.S. in Urging Action by U.N. on Iran," *New York Times,* January 13, 2006, A1.

48. Ibid.

49. Nazila Fathi, David E. Sanger, and William J. Broad, "Iran Reports Big Advance in Enrichment of Uranium: U.S. Warns of 'Significant' Arms Threat as Tehran Says It Will Defy the UN," *New York Times,* April 12, 2006, A1.

50. William J. Broad, Nazila Fathi, and Joel Brinkley, "Analysts Say a Nuclear Iran Is Years Away," *New York Times,* April 13, 2006, A1.

51. David E. Sanger and Nazila Fathi, "Iran Is Described as Defiant on 2nd Nuclear Program," *New York Times,* April 25, 2006, A6.

52. Elaine Sciolino, "U.N. Agency Says Iran Falls Short on Nuclear Data," *New York Times,* April 29, 2006, A1.

53. Steven R. Weisman, "U.S. Is Now Ready to Meet Iranians on Nuclear Plan," *New York Times,* June 1, 2006, A1.

54. Michael Slackman, "Iranian Letter: Using Religion to Lecture Bush," *New York Times,* May 10, 2006, A1; David E. Sanger, "U.S. Debating Direct Talks with Iran on Nuclear Issue," *New York Times,* May 27, 2006, A1.

55. David E. Sanger, "Bush's Realization on Iran: No Good Choice Left except Talks," *New York Times,* June 1, 2006, A8.

56. Thom Shanker and Elaine Sciolino, "Package of Terms (No Sanctions Included) for Iran," *New York Times,* June 2, 2006, A12.

57. Ibid.

58. Elissa Gootman, "Security Council Approves Sanctions against Iran," *New York Times,* December 24, 2006, A8.

59. "Europeans Back Gradual Steps against Iran's Nuclear Program," *New York Times,* October 18, 2006, A11.

60. David E. Sanger, "U.N. Official Says Iran Is Testing New Enrichment Device," *New York Times,* October 24, 2006, A8.

61. Elaine Sciolino, "Iran's Proposal to End Nuclear Standoff Is Rejected by the West," *New York Times,* October 4, 2006, A6; Navila Fathi, "Iran Defies Call to Drop Nuclear Plans," *New York Times,* October 13, 2006, A11.

62. William J. Broad and Nazila Fathi, "Iran's Leader Cites Progress on Nuclear Plans," *New York Times,* November 15, 2006, A8.

63. Gootman, "Security Council Approves Sanctions."

64. Steven R. Weisman, "Europe Resists U.S. on Curbing Ties with Iran," *New York Times,* January 30, 2007, A1.

65. Steven Lee Myers, "Pact with Iran on Gas Sales Is Possible, Putin Says," *New York Times,* February 2, 2007, A8.

66. Nazila Fathi, "Iran Says It Can Enrich Uranium on an Industrial Scale," *New York Times,* April 10, 2007, A3.

67. David E. Sanger, "Atomic Agency Confirms Advances by Iran's Nuclear Program," *New York Times,* April 19, 2007, A10.

68. Jon Sawyer, "War with Iran? Congress Says OK," *Los Angeles Times,* October 29, 2006, M1.

69. Sanger, "Atomic Agency Confirms Advances."

70. David E. Sanger, "Inspectors Say Iran Is Advancing on Nuclear Front," *International Herald Tribune,* May 15, 2007, A1.

71. Broad, "A Tantalizing Look at Iran's Nuclear Program."

72. Ibid.

73. David E. Sanger and William J. Broad. "U.S. and Allies Warn Iran over Nuclear 'Deception,' " September 26, 2009, www.nytimes.com/2009/09/26/world/middle east/26nuke.html.

74. William J. Broad, "Iran Shielding Its Nuclear Efforts in Maze of Tunnels," January 6, 2010, www.nytimes.com/2010/01/06/world/middleeast/06sanctions.html.

75. Ibid.

76. William J. Broad and David E. Sanger, "Report Says Iran Has Data to Make a Nuclear Bomb," October 4, 2009, www.nytimes.com/2009/10/04/world/middleeast/04nuke.html.

77. Ibid.

78. Sanger and Broad, "U.S. and Allies Warn Iran Over Nuclear 'Deception.' "

79. Barack Hussein Obama, "Cairo University Address," June 4, 2009, www.white house.gov/the_press_office/Remarks-by-the-President-at-Cairo-University-6-04-09.

80. Mark Landler and Clifford J. Levy, "Russia Resists U.S. Position on Sanctions for Iran," October 14, 2009, www.nytimes.com/2009/10/14/ . . . /14diplo.html.

81. Ibid.

82. Roger Cohen, "The Making of an Iran Policy," August 2, 2009, www.nytimes .com/2009/08/02/magazine/02Iran-t.html.

83. Robert F. Worth, "Iran Avows Willingness to Swap Some Uranium," December 13, 2009, www.nytimes.com/2009/12/13/ . . . /13iran.html.

84. Roger Cohen, "The Making of an Iran Policy," August 2, 2009, www.nytimes .com/2009/08/02/magazine/02Iran-t.html.

85. Borzou Daragahi, "Nuclear Fuel Won't Go Abroad, Iranians Say," November 19, 2009, latimes.com/news/nation-and-world/la-fg-iran-nuclear19-2009nov19,0,6854982 .story.

86. See Preston, *From Lambs to Lions.*

87. Robert F. Worth, "Tehran Losing Iranians' Trust, Ex-Leader Says," July 18, 2009, www.nytimes.com/2009/07/18/world/middleeast/18iran.html.

88. Ibid.

5 The United States and North Korea: Avoiding a Worst-Case Scenario

Patrick James and Özgür Özdamar

Before You Begin

1. Why has North Korea been trying for more than two decades to achieve a nuclear weapons capability?

2. If incentive-based diplomacy had been pursued initially, would it have had a chance of resolving the issue before North Korea acquired nuclear weapons?

3. Is the Agreed Framework a good arrangement? Is the agreement an example of appeasement or of diplomatic and peaceful management of an international problem?

4. How did President George W. Bush's labeling North Korea a member of the "axis of evil" change U.S.–North Korean relations? How did five years of confrontation policy by the Bush administration contribute to security in East Asia and the world?

5. Was the deal reached in February 2007 another form of "appeasement" or a new hope for resolution of the issue? Did this deal send the wrong message to other states hoping to produce nuclear weapons?

6. Which foreign policy options are available to the Obama administration in dealing with North Korea?

7. What does U.S. policy on North Korea teach us about nuclear proliferation in general?

Introduction: Surprising Intelligence

In March 1984 satellite images of North Korea revealed a nuclear reactor under construction at Yongbyon, one hundred kilometers north of the capital, Pyongyang. The photographs shocked the Reagan administration, as this small but militarily powerful communist country in East Asia might be preparing to produce some of the world's deadliest weapons. The images also showed a reactor-type chimney rising from the site. In June 1984, additional intelligence identified a cooling tower, limited power lines, and electrical grid connections for the local transfer of energy. Analysts suggested that the reactor probably used uranium and graphite, both of which were available locally. This evidence could not establish conclusively that North Korea had the capacity to produce nuclear weapons; further intelligence in 1986, however, showed the construction of buildings similar to reprocessing plants used for separating plutonium, a step needed to produce atomic weapons. That same year, new photographs revealed circular craters of darkened ground, assumed to be the residue of high-explosive tests. The pattern suggested a technique used to detonate a nuclear device. A check of earlier photographs revealed the aftereffects of similar tests since 1983.[1]

When intelligence sources discovered construction in 1988 of a fifty-megawatt-capacity reactor—one much larger than the reactor photographed in 1984—the United States became even more alarmed. Estimates held that the older, smaller reactor could produce enough plutonium for up to six weapons a year, whereas the larger plant would make enough for up to fifteen weapons. Finally confident of the existence of a nuclear program, the administration of George H. W. Bush approached Soviet and Chinese officials in February 1989 and Japanese and South Korean authorities in May 1989 about putting pressure on North Korea to meet its obligations as a member of the International Atomic Energy Agency (IAEA). The administration specifically wanted North Korea to sign a safeguards agreement allowing inspections of its nuclear facilities.[2] Thus began more than two decades of roller-coaster U.S.–North Korean relations concerning nuclear nonproliferation.

Background: North Korea's Nuclear Quest

The Korean Peninsula was ruled as a single entity from the time the Shilla Kingdom unified it in the seventh century until the end of World War II.[3] Japan colonized Korea in 1910, but when Japan surrendered in 1945, the Soviet Union and United States temporarily divided Korea at the 38th parallel. Thus a communist system evolved in the north, and a capitalist system in the south. Soon thereafter, the peninsula experienced the Korean War. Fought between communist North Korea (Democratic People's Republic of North Korea, DPRK) and anticommunist South Korea (Republic of Korea, ROK) for domination of the peninsula, the war lasted from June 1950 to July 1953 and stands out as a major proxy war between the United States and Soviet Union.[4] The principal combatants included on one side Australia, Canada, South Korea,

Timeline

Key Developments in U.S.–North Korean Relations

1977	The Soviet Union supplies North Korea with a small, experimental nuclear reactor.
March 1984	Satellite images of North Korea reveal a nuclear reactor under construction at Yongbyon, one hundred kilometers north of the capital, Pyongyang.
1985	North Korea accedes to the Nuclear Non-Proliferation Treaty (NPT).
1988	U.S. intelligence identifies the construction of a large-capacity reactor in North Korea.
1989	The United States leads in calling on North Korea to meet its obligation to sign a safeguards agreement with the International Atomic Energy Agency (IAEA).
September 1991	The United States announces its withdrawal of tactical nuclear arms from the Korean Peninsula.
December 1991	North Korea and South Korea sign the Basic Agreement, concerning the end of hostilities between them, and the Joint Declaration on the Denuclearization of the Korean Peninsula, agreeing to forgo nuclear weapons–related activities.
January 1992	North Korea concludes a safeguards agreement with the IAEA.
1993	The crisis over North Korea's nuclear program escalates.
March 1993	Political and military issues erode North Korea's relations with South Korea and the United States. As a result, North Korea declares its intent to withdraw from the NPT in ninety days.
June 1993	The United States eases tensions with North Korea by offering to hold high-level talks on nuclear issues. The North suspends its withdrawal from the NPT.
January 1994	The CIA asserts that North Korea may have built one or two nuclear weapons.

June 13, 1994	North Korea announces its withdrawal from the IAEA.
June 15, 1994	Former president Jimmy Carter negotiates a deal in which Pyongyang confirms its willingness to freeze its nuclear program and resume high-level talks with the United States.
June 20, 1994	The Clinton administration sends a letter to the North Korean government stating its willingness to resume high-level talks if the North Koreans proceed in freezing their nuclear program.
July 8, 1994	North Korean leader Kim Il Sung dies. He is succeeded by his son Kim Jong Il.
October 21, 1994	The United States and North Korea sign the Agreed Framework in Geneva. The agreement involves dismantling Pyongyang's nuclear program in return for heavy oil supplies and light water reactors.
March 1995	Japan, South Korea, and the United States form the Korean Peninsula Energy Development Organization (KEDO) as part of the Agreed Framework.
1996–2000	North Korea and the United States hold several rounds of talks concerning the North's missile program. Washington suggests that Pyongyang adhere to the Missile Technology Control Regime (MTCR). The talks prove unproductive.
August 1998	North Korea generates unfavorable international attention by testing the Taepodong 1 rocket, which flies over Japan. The missile has a range of 1,500 to 2,000 kilometers.
June 15, 2000	At a historic summit, North Korea and South Korea agree to resolve the issue of reunification for the Korean Peninsula.
June 19, 2000	Encouraged by the Korean summit, the United States eases sanctions on North Korea.
January 29, 2002	President George W. Bush labels North Korea a member of a so-called axis of evil. The North Korean government reacts negatively.

(continued)

Timeline *(continued)*

Key Developments in U.S.–North Korean Relations

October 3–5, 2002	James Kelly, assistant secretary of state for East Asian and Pacific affairs, visits North Korea and informs officials that the United States is aware of its clandestine nuclear program.
October 16, 2002	North Korea admits to having had a clandestine program to enrich uranium (and plutonium) for nuclear weapons development.
November 2002	KEDO stops shipping oil to North Korea. The IAEA asks North Korea for clarification on its nuclear program.
December 2002	North Korea responds to KEDO's oil stoppage by restarting its frozen nuclear reactor and orders IAEA inspectors out of the country.
January 10, 2003	North Korea withdraws from the NPT.
April 2003	At a meeting held in Beijing with China, South Korea, and the United States, North Korea announces that it has nuclear weapons.
2003–2004	Negotiations involving China, Japan, North Korea, Russia, South Korea, and the United States fail to produce any effective results.
July 4–5, 2006	North Korea conducts seven missile tests, including a long-range Taepodong 2.
July 15, 2006	The UN Security Council unanimously votes to impose sanctions that ban selling missile-related material to North Korea by all member states.
October 3, 2006	North Korea conducts its first nuclear detonation test ever. The world condemns this provocative act.
October 14, 2006	The UN Security Council unanimously votes to impose both military and economic sanctions on North Korea to protest the nuclear test.

February 13, 2007	Announcement comes from the six-party talks, continuing in Beijing, that North Korea has agreed to freeze its nuclear reactor in Yongbyon in return for economic and diplomatic concessions from the other parties.
June 2008	As an important step in the denuclearization process, North Korea announces its nuclear assets.
October 2008	United States removes North Korea from its sponsors of terrorism list; in return, North Korea agrees to allow inspectors in its key nuclear sites.
April 2009	North Korea fires a rocket carrying a satellite. Suspected for testing a long-range missile by regional countries and criticized by the UN Security Council, North Korea declares it will no longer participate in six-party talks.
May 2009	North Korea tests a nuclear device for the second time in its history, protests from all around the world.
January 2010	North Korea claims to work for ending hostilities with U.S. and a nuclear-free Korean peninsula.

Turkey, the United Kingdom, the United States, and other allies under a UN mandate, and on the other side North Korea and the People's Republic of China. The Soviet Union sided with North Korea, but it did not provide direct military support in the form of troops.[5] After three years of fighting, a ceasefire established a demilitarized zone (DMZ) at the 38th parallel, a demarcation still defended by substantial North Korean forces on one side and South Korean and U.S. forces on the other. More than fifty years after the fighting, the adversaries have yet to sign a peace treaty.

North Korea is ruled by one of the last remaining communist regimes and has had only two leaders in more than a half-century: Kim Il Sung, from 1948 till his death in 1994, and his son Kim Jong Il, who succeeded him. The Korean Worker's Party of North Korea is the last example of a classic Stalinist, communist party. The regime in North Korea is extremely autocratic, and the country has perhaps the most closed political system in the world.[6] After decades of mismanagement, the North relies heavily on international food aid to feed its population and avert mass starvation.[7] It is estimated that nearly two million people may have died of famine from 1995 to 1998.[8]

Despite severe economic crises over the last two decades and widespread famine, North Korea continues to feed one of the largest armies in the world, with more than a million personnel.[9] In addition, North Korea's interest in nuclear power apparently began in the 1960s, when Kim Il Sung asked China to transfer nuclear technology to North Korea after China's first nuclear tests. Chinese leader Mao Zedong rejected such requests in 1964 and in 1974. The Soviet Union also refused to transfer nuclear technology to North Korea, but in 1977 the Soviets gave it a small, experimental reactor and insisted that it be placed under IAEA safeguards.[10] In all likelihood the North persisted in efforts to go nuclear for two primary reasons: the Korean War experience and South Korean efforts to obtain nuclear weapons. During the war, North Korea experienced the threat of U.S. nuclear power, a menace that remained in Pyongyang's consciousness after the war concluded. According to one observer, "No country has been the target of more American nuclear threats than North Korea—at least seven since 1945." South Korea had attempted to gain nuclear weapons in the 1970s, but the United States prevented it from doing so. That venture by the South strongly influenced North Korean policy makers' security perceptions and pushed them toward seeking the nuclear option. In 1995 Walter Slocombe, U.S. under secretary of defense for policy in the Clinton administration, itemized the threats that North Korea's going nuclear poses, saying that it

- could be coupled with the oversized conventional force to extort or blackmail South Korea and greatly increase the costs of a war on the Korean Peninsula;
- could ignite a nuclear arms race in Asia;
- could undermine the Nuclear Non-Proliferation Treaty (NPT) and the IAEA safeguards system of inspections; and
- could lead to the export of nuclear technologies and components to pariah states and terrorists worldwide, and could project the nuclear threat across most of Northeast Asia if the government was successful in upgrading missile delivery systems.[11]

For these reasons, nuclear proliferation by North Korea became one of the foremost foreign policy challenges for the United States in the late twentieth century, and it continues to be in the current century.

The Policy of George H. W. Bush

In the 1980s and early 1990s most senior officials in the first Bush administration—including national security adviser Brent Scowcroft, his deputy and later CIA director Robert Gates, Secretary of State James Baker, Secretary of Defense Dick Cheney, and Under Secretary of Defense Paul Wolfowitz—believed that diplomatic means would not work with North Korea. Domestic political reasons, such as pressure to focus on the economy, along with Congress's and the foreign policy establishment's obvious distaste for dealing with North Korea, reinforced their reluctance to employ cooperative measures. Because Washington did not want to engage in diplomatic give-and-take, it adopted a crime-and-punishment approach that arguably led to crisis and subsequent deadlock.[12] In other words, from 1989 through 1992 the United States primarily, though not exclusively, used the stick rather than the carrot to deal with North Korea.

The Bush administration relied on the IAEA to monitor North Korea's nuclear program and the UN Security Council to enforce compliance with the NPT, to which North Korea had acceded in 1985 on the advice of the Soviet Union.[13] Although Pyongyang was supposed to sign the IAEA safeguards treaty within eighteen months of signing the NPT, it delayed for six years and signed the agreement only in January 1992. In other words, through various actions (or inaction) the North Korean government gave the impression that it had an ongoing interest in producing nuclear weapons.

Efforts by the Bush administration significantly influenced North Korea's ultimate signing of the IAEA safeguards agreement. By 1990 South Korea and the United States both worried that North Korea might already have developed one or two nuclear weapons. Unknown to U.S. officials, Soviet intelligence also had been receiving signals about the North Korean project. A KGB document from February 1990 (revealed in 1992) suggested that the North actually had completed a bomb:

> Scientific and experimental design work to create a nuclear weapon is continuing in the DPRK. . . . According to information received, development of the first atomic explosive device has been completed at the DPRK Center for Nuclear Research, located in the city of Yongbyon in Pyongan-pukto Province. At present there are no plans to test it, in the interests of concealing from world opinion and from the controlling international organizations the actual fact of the production of nuclear weapons in the DPRK. The KGB is taking additional measures to verify the above report.[14]

Beginning in 1991, South Korea and the United States implemented different elements of an integrated political, economic, and military campaign designed to persuade North Korea to allow inspections of its nuclear facilities. U.S. actions appear, however, to have been somewhat ad hoc, developing according to circumstances,[15] most notably in reaction to getting nowhere by using the stick alone.

During 1991 U.S. strategy concerning North Korean nuclearization consisted of four primary elements. The first was an unequivocal statement of a reduced U.S. military position on the Korean Peninsula.[16] In 1990 the United States had initiated limited troop withdrawals from South Korea as part of its East Asian Strategic Initiative (and had taken steps to ease the trade embargo on the North). Then, in part because the cold war was coming to an end, the United States announced in September 1991 the withdrawal of nuclear warheads, shells, and bombs from South Korea.[17] Second, Washington reaffirmed its security relationship with South Korea, to convince the North Koreans that delaying inspections would gain them nothing; this was conceived as an assertive element to balance the more pacific announcement about its forces and nuclear arsenal. Third, the annual U.S.–South Korean Team Spirit Military Exercise, which had been condemned by North Korea as provocative, was suspended for a year. Fourth, U.S. officials agreed to begin to direct talks with North Korea, albeit only for a single session, with more to follow if North Korea cooperated and allowed nuclear inspections.[18]

This diplomatic approach produced some relatively positive consequences. In December 1991 North Korea and South Korea began talks at the level of prime minister that resulted in two agreements, which were welcomed by the United States. The Basic Agreement, signed on December 10, appeared to provide a strong basis for ending hostility between the two Koreas. Its main terms are as follows:

- Mutual recognition of each other's systems and an end to mutual interference, vilification, and subversion.
- Mutual efforts "to transform the present state of armistice into a solid peace," with continued observance of the armistice until this is accomplished.
- A mutual commitment not to use force against each other and the implementation of confidence-building measures and large-scale arms reductions.
- Economic, cultural, and scientific exchanges, free correspondence between divided families, and the reopening of roads and railroads severed at the border.[19]

After signing the Basic Agreement, the North and South reached a nuclear accord in only six days. The Joint Declaration on the Denuclearization of the Korean Peninsula states that both countries agree not to "test, manufacture, produce, receive, process, store, deploy or use nuclear weapons" or "process nuclear reprocessing and enrichment facilities."[20]

In January 1992 North Korea concluded a safeguards agreement for inspection of its nuclear facilities by the IAEA, another result of a diplomatic initiative. At the end of April, almost everything stood ready for inspections to begin at Yongbyon.

Some observers argue that the fundamental lesson from the negotiations was that diplomacy works when dealing with North Korea about its nuclear program, so such an approach should continue. According to this line of argument, the gradual, nuanced strategy of pressure and incentives had persuaded the North to allow inspections.[21] Other observers argue, however, that the Bush administration had not provided any substantial incentive to the North to truly convince policy makers there to comply fully with the agreement. In fact, they say that the administration's handling of North Korea caused the deadlock that led to the more serious upheavals years later.[22] This line of argument also suggests that North Korea actually wanted to open direct talks with the United States, to obtain assistance to ameliorate its economic problems, and to build light water reactors to solve its energy problem.[23] Quite possibly because of a reluctance to show the carrot, the Bush administration preferred to ignore North Korea's true goals.

Analysis of the situation in greater depth suggests that it is very likely that North Korea attempted to use its nuclear program as a bargaining chip to lure the United States into direct talks and into supplying it with light water reactors. The United States and South Korea, however, perceived the nuclear threat to be real. The differences between Washington's and Pyongyang's perceptions of the North's nuclear program stood during this phase as the main obstacles to a genuine resolution of North Korean nuclearization. Administration hawks—among them the national security adviser, Brent Scowcroft, and Under Secretary of State for Political Affairs Arnold Kanter—lobbied hard for military action against North Korea. In a more general sense, the administration had assembled a foreign policy team whose members believed that diplomacy would be wasted on North Korea because its leadership understood only the use of force. This view may have been indicative of a Munich syndrome, a disposition against appeasement of presumably dangerous states. Approaching elections also encouraged the Bush administration to play hardball with North Korea.

The agreements reached between the two Koreas, along with the North's announcement that it would allow IAEA inspections, represented two quite positive developments in terms of nonproliferation and peace on the Korean Peninsula. As early as February 1992, however, CIA director Gates alleged—and, it turned out, with good reason—that the North had not been honest about its nuclear program. After Pyongyang accepted inspections, the head of the IAEA, Hans Blix, traveled to North Korea in May 1992 for a guided tour of its nuclear facilities in advance of the formal IAEA inspection teams. Although North Korea aimed to show Blix the most nonthreatening aspects of its program, large buildings suspected of being used for processing plutonium turned out to be exactly that. Blix's visit served to confirm suspicions that the North's nuclear weapons program might still be active. Later in 1992 the IAEA revealed that North Korea had not been truthful about its activities. Pyongyang had declared that it had processed ninety grams of plutonium for research purposes only. Analysis by the IAEA, however, revealed that it had processed plutonium at least three times—in 1989, 1990, and 1991. A sample of nuclear waste, supposedly from the separation process, did not match any of the separated plutonium, which led the IAEA to believe that more plutonium than was revealed had to have been produced. Neither the IAEA nor the CIA, however, could determine how much plutonium the North possessed at the time.[24]

In 1993 the dialogue between North Korea and the actors trying to denuclearize it gradually began to collapse. In January the IAEA began informing the international community that it might ask to inspect two other suspected North Korean sites, an unusual measure for the organization. The CIA provided the IAEA with photographs of certain sites that had not been inspected and that it thought might contain the hidden plutonium. North Korea, as anticipated, rejected further inspections on the grounds that the suspected structures were only conventional military buildings and that permitting further IAEA inspections would be a breach of sovereignty and a threat to North Korean security. The IAEA's desire for additional investigations isolated North Korea and set back the newly developing relations between Pyongyang and the world.

Despite the cooperation agreements between the North and South, by February 1993 growing evidence of the North's undocumented nuclear activities, combined with other events, reduced hopes for an amicable solution to the problem of North Korean nuclearization. In fall 1992 South Korea had revealed evidence of a North Korean spy ring in the ROK. The South Korean Agency for National Security Planning (ANSP) asserted that a conspiracy against the

South—involving labor organizations and even lawmakers in the National Assembly—intended to disrupt its politics to facilitate unification with the North in 1995, an action that was viewed unfavorably in the South. The ANSP alleged that more than four hundred people were involved in the spy operation. North Korea rejected the allegations.

Although South Korea had a legitimate right to investigate espionage against it, the timing of the announcement could not have been worse in the context of long-term relations with the North. Bilateral talks and cooperation were canceled and their future prospects significantly damaged. As might have been expected, the suspended Team Spirit military exercises resumed. In spite of the spy ring incident, it is difficult to understand why South Korea and the United States would renew the military exercise. North Korea had long protested Team Spirit and had even used it as an excuse for delaying imminent IAEA inspections. Put simply, the gains hard won by diplomacy were lost as a result of the Team Spirit exercises. In fact, just a day before the exercises began, the "Dear Leader," Kim Jong Il, heightened tensions all around when he ordered that "the whole country, all the people and the entire army shall, on March 9, 1993, switch to a state of readiness for war."[25]

Thus the diplomatic "spring" of 1992 gradually eroded in 1993. After six months of IAEA inspections, the North had obtained no tangible benefits from the process: no economic aid, no direct talks with the United States, no broader dialogue with the South, and no ability to verify that U.S. nuclear weapons had in fact been withdrawn from the South. The increasing demands from the IAEA and South Korea to allow short-notice inspections of virtually any military site in North Korea, combined with the spy ring incident and Team Spirit, led some observers to speculate that the South's moves were designed to force the North to back away from negotiations.[26] Despite all of these developments, it is not possible to place full blame for the disintegration of relations in 1993 with South Korea or the United States. The North had apparently violated international agreements and did not want to make additional concessions on denuclearization. The absence of any sign by the United States that it might be interested in rapprochement might also have contributed to the shift toward disintegrating relations. North Korea's actions ultimately influenced U.S. and South Korean policy makers to revert to a hard-line approach.

Withdrawal from the NPT and Reactor Refueling

The Clinton administration inherited a developing crisis in its first days in office. By January 1993, North Korea already had begun maneuvering around IAEA inspections. The administration did not, however, make any significant policy shifts, choosing instead to retain Bush administration policies, which stressed adherence to the NPT. This legalistic approach merely held that North Korea had certain obligations under the NPT and must therefore fulfill them. Direct talks with the North or benefits related to nonproliferation might come if the North complied with inspection requirements.

Secretary of Defense Les Aspin and officials from his office suggested initiating direct contact with Pyongyang in the form of a high-level delegation in early 1993 and offering the North Koreans concrete benefits as incentives to cooperate. They argued that if North Korea still refused to cooperate after getting the carrot, then the United States would use the stick of sanctions and possibly even military action. For the Clinton administration, this represented not appeasement but a rather balanced approach. One U.S. official described the policy as a "sugar-coated ultimatum."[27] President Bill Clinton did not pursue this option at first, because it seemed like rewarding the North for not doing something it should have already done. The conservative media and some members of Congress had been attacking the administration for its seemingly left-of-center disposition toward gays in the military, and conservatives argued that perceived weakness in dealing with North Korea was unacceptable among much of the public.

The first crisis for the Clinton administration began in March 1993 when, during the Team Spirit exercises, Pyongyang asserted that such operations endangered nonproliferation efforts and threatened its security. It announced its opposition to additional nuclear inspections on its territory, claiming that the IAEA worked for U.S. interests. That same month, North Korea stated its intention to withdraw from the Nuclear Non-Proliferation Treaty in ninety days. Both the Clinton administration and the South Korean government of Kim Yong Sam were relatively new in March 1993 and not well prepared for such a development, but with the support of South Korea, the United States eased tensions by offering to hold talks with Pyongyang on nuclear issues. In return, North Korea suspended its withdrawal from the NPT in June. Thus the Clinton administration effectively adopted the Defense Department's previously articulated approach of direct, high-level talks, and North Korea attained one of its goals: to sit at the negotiating table with the United States. With this success, the North proposed to relinquish its entire nuclear program in return for light water reactors. The United States acknowledged the North's interest but then stated that it should first comply with IAEA inspections and renew its dialogue with South Korea. The dialogue with the United States continued in

1993 but did not resolve any existing problems. The IAEA continued to have difficulties with North Korea. The IAEA referred the issue to the UN Security Council and even claimed that it would be better for North Korea to be excluded from the NPT than to compromise the treaty's integrity.[28]

The North ignited another crisis as the international community discussed what to do about matters already under review. While ideas about how to punish North Korea for its nuclear program preoccupied leading members of the world community, Pyongyang declared in May 1994 that the reactor would be refueled. This meant removing the existing rods, from which weapons-grade plutonium could then be produced.[29]

The Carrot

In response to North Korea's decision to refuel, in early summer 1994 President Clinton threatened to halt the U.S. dialogue and impose economic sanctions, which would significantly damage the North's already terrible economy. He also considered air strikes. The North announced that sanctions would mean war.[30] Before implementing punitive action, the administration decided to take a diplomatic tack. Former president Jimmy Carter had previously communicated to the White House his interest in visiting North Korea to seek a peaceful solution to the looming nuclear crisis. The Reagan and Bush administrations had earlier rejected his requests to travel to North Korea.[31] This time, however, Carter found support in the Oval Office. A White House official referred to Carter's visit as an opportunity for "a face-saving resolution" to the tensions.[32] Clinton did not designate Carter as an official U.S. representative, so he would travel to North Korea with the status of a private citizen. The State Department, however, briefed him and dispatched a career Foreign Service officer to accompany him. State Department spokesperson Michael McCurry pointed out that Carter would not be "carrying any formal message from the United States."[33]

The Carter mission had two primary goals: to defuse the immediate tensions related to the North Korean nuclear program and to jump-start the talks between the United States and North Korea. Carter left for Pyongyang on June 12, North Korea announced its withdrawal from the IAEA on June 13, and on June 16 the Clinton administration laid out its vision of economic sanctions. Madeleine Albright, the U.S. ambassador to the United Nations, called for restricting arms exports from North Korea, cutting UN assistance, and encouraging further diplomatic isolation. These measures would be followed by economic sanctions if the North did not comply with the IAEA inspection regime.

Carter's diplomatic efforts, however, yielded positive results, with North Korea expressing a willingness to freeze its nuclear program and resume high-level talks with the United States. On June 20 the United States sent a letter to Pyongyang officially proposing such talks.[34]

The Carter visit elicited both praise and criticism. Conservatives perceived it as appeasement, and even some Democrats in the administration became outraged when Carter renounced the possible use of sanctions. One point cannot, however, be ignored: Carter's visit prevented the use of force and perhaps a war with enormous costs. According to one State Department official, "If Jimmy Carter had not gone to Korea, we would have been damned close to war."[35] If the prevention of war is the criterion of success, then at least for the short term Carter's mission must be regarded as a success indeed. Carter's efforts led both sides to conclude that negotiations constituted the best option available to them, but Kim Il Sung's death on July 8 delayed the start of talks that month. They instead began on August 5.

The Agreed Framework and KEDO

On October 21, 1994, the United States and North Korea signed the Agreed Framework to resolve the issues surrounding Pyongyang's nuclear program. The agreement included a bilateral structure for negotiations—which represented a major change in the nature of U.S.–North Korean relations—and was to be implemented in phases, allowing the two sides to assess each other's compliance at each step before moving on to the next. The Agreed Framework required North Korea to undertake the following:

- Eliminate its existing capability to produce weapons-grade plutonium.
- Resume full membership in the NPT, including complying completely with its safeguards agreement with the IAEA, which mandates the inspectors to investigate suspected nuclear waste sites and to place any nuclear material not previously identified under IAEA safeguards.
- Take steps to consistently execute the Joint Declaration on the Denuclearization of the Korean Peninsula.
- Engage in a dialogue with the South.

The Korean Peninsula Energy Development Organization (KEDO)—a consortium of Japan, South Korea, and the United States officially established in March 1995 to coordinate the agreement—was by 2003 to provide two 1,000 megawatt, light water reactor power plants (priced around $4 billion) and supply North Korea with 500,000 tons of heavy oil annually to compensate for the capacity forfeited by freezing its graphite-modulated reactors. The United

States and North Korea agreed to open liaison offices in each other's capitals and reduce barriers to trade and investment. The United States also agreed to provide formal assurances that it would not threaten North Korea with nuclear weapons.[36] North Korean negotiator Kang Sok Ju remarked to his American counterpart, Robert Gallucci, that the North's bargaining chip was continuing production of plutonium and preventing IAEA inspections if the United States did not comply with the agreement. In turn, U.S. leverage rested on the prospect of establishing political and economic ties valuable to North Korea.[37]

The Agreed Framework was a loose agreement in the sense that its implementation was left to the states' own volition. Implementation initially ran rather smoothly. In August 1998, however, North Korea launched over Japan a Taepodong 1 rocket with a range of 1,500 to 2,000 kilometers. Pyongyang announced that the rocket had successfully placed a small satellite into orbit, but that claim was contested by the U.S. Space Command. Japan responded to this invasion of its air space by suspending the signing of a cost-sharing agreement for the Agreed Framework's light water reactor project until November 1998. The development came as a shock to the U.S. intelligence community, which admitted being surprised by North Korea's advances in missile-staging technology. On October 1, 1998, U.S.–North Korean missile talks held in New York made little progress. The United States requested that Pyongyang terminate its missile programs in exchange for the lifting of some remaining economic sanctions. North Korea rejected the proposal, asserting that the lifting of sanctions was implicit in the Agreed Framework.

On November 12, 1998, President Clinton appointed former secretary of defense William Perry as his policy coordinator on North Korea. A policy review that Perry undertook noted that the situation in East Asia was not the same as it had been in 1994, when the Agreed Framework was signed. He observed that the North's missile tests had substantially increased Japanese security concerns and that the passing of North Korea's leadership to Kim Jong Il had created further uncertainty. On a more positive note, the new South Korean president, Kim Dae Jung, had embarked on a policy of engagement with North Korea. Based on his policy review, Perry ultimately devised a two-path strategy. The first path involved a new, comprehensive, and integrated approach to negotiations. In return for the North's full compliance with the NPT, Missile Technology Control Regime, and export of nuclear and missile technologies, Japan, South Korea, and the United States would reduce pressures that the North perceived as threatening. Perry argued that reduction of those threats would give the regime confidence about coexisting with other states in the region. If the North did as it should, according to Perry, the United States should normalize relations and relax sanctions.

Perry's second path focused on what to do if North Korea did not want to cooperate. If there was no chance of continuing relations with the North, the United States would sever relations, contain the threat, and enforce the provisions outlined in the first path.[38] Perry's report also observed that the North had complied with the NPT and had not produced plutonium in the preceding five years, which provided grounds for encouragement about the feasibility of the first path.

Overall, the first five years of the Agreed Framework revealed a mixed record. The North did not advance in producing nuclear weapons, but it did significantly improve its missile technology. The United States supplied crude oil as agreed, but the light water reactors remained far from being finished as scheduled. Maintaining the Agreed Framework was not to be an easy job.

The Critics

Clinton's policy of "engagement" met severe criticism in Congress and from conservative columnists. Critics argued that it was unacceptable to compromise with a so-called rogue state that threatened U.S. allies. From that point of view, unless the North capitulated, coercion in general, sanctions in particular, and even military action would be preferred to negotiation. Moreover, considering North Korea's economic problems, any deal effectively supported an already sinking regime. Putting together a deal such as the Agreed Framework, according to critics, was immoral and set a terrible precedent for other rogue states.[39] In an October 1994 letter to Clinton, four Republicans on the Senate Committee on Foreign Relations summed up the more critical view of policy at the time: "We are left wondering how to distinguish such a deal from U.S. submission to North Korean nuclear blackmail."[40] Other concerns focused on the timing of reciprocal concessions and actions under the framework.

Clinton administration officials and supporters of the Agreed Framework responded that although the United States made some concessions, the outcome, if successful, would meet U.S. strategic objectives. Key achievements for the United States as a result of the agreement were enumerated as follows: (1) being able to estimate the amount of plutonium produced by the North in the past and dismantling any nuclear weapons already produced; (2) convincing North Korea to halt its nuclear program; (3) keeping North Korea within the NPT and its safeguards agreement; (4) enticing the North out of international isolation; and (5) supporting stability and security in the region.[41]

Largely through Ambassador Gallucci, the administration also countered the critics with six arguments. First, the framework did not amount to appeasement or, even worse, submission to blackmail because North Korea had made even more concessions than the United States. Second, the conditions the North agreed to fulfill met U.S. objectives, such as its remaining within the NPT and respecting obligations under the safeguards agreement. Third, the agreement pertained to the North's past nuclear program and aimed to find plutonium already produced. Fourth, whether Pyongyang met the requirements of the safeguards agreement could be verified by IAEA and U.S. assets, and no benefits would be provided before proof of full compliance. Fifth, the agreement needed to be viewed as a compromise, meaning that significant but not unreasonable costs were entailed to obtain such benefits as reduction of the threat of nuclear proliferation and instability in Northeast Asia. Sixth, the agreement set a precedent only to the degree that other situations involve similar elements, an unlikely event.[42]

The United States, like other great powers before it, has tended toward a basic action-reaction pattern: "Our first reaction to somebody's doing something we don't like is to think of doing something unpleasant to them."[43] In partial contrast to that generalization, the Clinton administration's Agreed Framework with North Korea on nuclear proliferation serves as an example of incentive-based diplomacy. Despite some legitimate criticisms, by signing the framework the United States accomplished its immediate goals at a bearable cost. The agreement, despite the political and financial problems of domestic criticism and the cost of supplying crude oil to North Korea, functioned until (for better or worse) President George W. Bush designated North Korea, Iraq, and Iran an "axis of evil" in 2002.

The Policy of George W. Bush

Dialogue with North Korea slowed as the new George W. Bush administration took some time to review policy toward it in early 2001. Although Republicans, including some Bush aides, engaged in harsh rhetoric about the North, after three months of review, the president announced in June 2001 that his administration would stick with the basic outlines of the existing policy in the form of the Agreed Framework. Lobbying by Japan and South Korea, combined with Secretary of State Colin Powell's successful fending off of the more conservative Bush advisers, were influential in bringing about this decision.[44]

Although the administration reaffirmed its intent to supply the two light water reactors that the framework specified in return for North Korea's restraint of its nuclear development, it found domestic opposition to fulfilling that requirement difficult to bear. From the beginning of the administration, some members of Congress and commentators in academia and the media argued repeatedly that one of the two reactors should be replaced with a thermal power station. The reasoning was that nuclear weapons–grade plutonium could be extracted from them. Another, hidden reason might have been the increasing cost of the heavy oil the United States had provided to North Korea since 1995, and which it was slated to continue to provide until the new reactors were completed. Because of the financial and organizational problems related to KEDO, analysts expected the reactors to be finished around 2010.

Republican partisans did not want to fund a regime that they believed was hostile to the United States. The South Korean government, which bore 70 percent of the construction costs for the two reactors, maintained its opposition to their replacement with thermal power stations because: (1) that would violate the most critical agreement between the United States and the North; (2) it would further delay the project and result in additional costs; and (3) it would be impossible for North Korea to extract plutonium of nuclear weapons grade from the light water reactors because, although extraction remains theoretically possible, it would not be able to obtain the extremely sophisticated reprocessing technology needed. North Korea also opposed such a change in the Agreed Framework. Although the Bush administration initially gave no indication of a significant change in U.S. policy, the simple act of reviewing the agreement was enough to upset the North. On March 17, 2001, the North Korean Central Broadcasting Station issued the following warning: "If the Bush administration feels it burdensome and troublesome to perform the Geneva Agreed Framework, we don't need to be indefinitely bound by an agreement that is not honored. We will go on our way in case the agreement is not honored."[45] *Rodong Sinmun,* the state-controlled newspaper, observed, "North Korea would take 'countermeasures' if the United States does not perform its obligations under the agreement. We will also demand compensation for the delay in construction of the LWRs [light water reactors]."[46] At the end of 2001, there appeared to be reason to believe that bilateral talks would continue, although the North was suspicious of a renewed dialogue.

Another year of tense relations between the United States and North Korea unfolded in 2002. The attacks of September 11, 2001, on the United States transformed the Bush administration's foreign policy into one that would deal with unfriendly regimes more decisively, and if necessary, unilaterally and forcefully. The watershed event of 2002 for U.S.–North Korean relations occurred on January 29, when President Bush, in his State of the Union address, accused North Korea of being one of three members of a so-called axis of evil that threatened U.S. and even world security. In this highly controversial speech, Bush described North Korea as "a regime arming with missiles and weapons of mass destruction, while starving its citizens. . . . The United States of America will not permit the world's most dangerous regimes to threaten us with the world's most dangerous weapons."[47] Bush's speech sent shock waves around the world, as leaders waited to see what it might mean in practice.

Shortly after the speech, the State Department and the U.S. ambassador to South Korea, Thomas C. Hubbard, insisted that the president's statement did not represent a policy shift. The United States, according to them, remained fully open to resuming bilateral talks with North Korea without any preconditions.

North Korea, however, responded harshly and directly to the speech with rhetoric aimed to match Bush's:

> Mr. Bush's remarks clearly show what the real aim [sic] the U.S. sought when it proposed to resume talks with the DPRK recently. . . . We are sharply watching the United States [sic] moves that have pushed the situation to the brink of war after throwing away even the mask of "dialogue" and "negotiation." . . . The option to strike impudently advocated by the United States is not its monopoly.[48]

Thus, with Bush's speech and Pyongyang's reaction to it, what guarded hopes there were for a renewed diplomatic exchange between the United States and North Korea disappeared, at least for the foreseeable future.

In South Korea and Japan, various political groups accused the United States of destroying the North-South dialogue and threatening the peace in East Asia. Although the State Department, and Secretary Powell himself, asserted on several occasions that the United States was ready to resume a dialogue with North Korea at "any time, any place, or anywhere without preconditions," that did not convince the North Koreans.[49] A memorandum from President Bush stated that he would not certify North Korea's compliance with the Agreed Framework; because of national security considerations, however, Bush waived the provision that would have prohibited Washington from funding KEDO.[50] Continuation of that support under such hostile conditions, however, did not bring North Korea back to the negotiation table.

The United States warned North Korea in August 2002 to comply as soon as possible with IAEA safeguard procedures. The North replied that it would not do so for at least three more years. Developments that fall raised the tension between the United States and North Korea and led to the confrontation that continues today. In October, James Kelly, assistant secretary of state for East Asian and Pacific affairs, visited North Korea and presented U.S. concerns about its nuclear program as well as its ballistic missile program (which at the time the North Koreans themselves had delayed), export of missile components, conventional force posture, human rights violations, and overall humanitarian situation. Kelly informed Pyongyang that a comprehensive settlement addressing these issues might be the way to improve bilateral relations. North Korea called this approach "high-handed and arrogant" and maintained its noncooperative stance.[51]

More important, the United States announced on October 16 that North Korea had admitted to the existence of a clandestine program to enrich uranium (in addition to plutonium) for nuclear weapons, after Kelly had informed the North Koreans that the United States had knowledge of it. Such a serious violation of the Agreed Framework raised immediate and intense reactions around the world. In November, KEDO announced the suspension of oil deliveries, and the IAEA asked North Korea for clarification on its nuclear program. North Korea rejected these demands and announced that because of the halt to KEDO's supply of oil, it would reopen the frozen nuclear reactors to produce electricity. In December, North Korea cut all seals on IAEA surveillance equipment on its nuclear facilities and materials and ordered inspectors out of the country.

North Korea continued to abrogate its international agreements with the announcement of its withdrawal from the NPT on January 10, 2003. The following month, the United States confirmed that North Korea had in December restarted a nuclear reactor previously frozen by the Agreed Framework. The North also conducted two missile tests in February and March 2003.[52] Perhaps most ominous was an incident in which North Korea sent a fighter jet into South Korean airspace and shadowed a U.S. reconnaissance plane.[53]

Trilateral talks among China, North Korea, and the United States in April 2003 and six-party talks (with Japan, Russia, and South Korea) in September 2003 and February 2004 did not bring a resolution to the crisis.[54] Little was produced diplomatically in 2004 and 2005. Leaders of the two nations occasionally railed against each other, while diplomats achieved next to nothing. In August 2004, in response to President Bush's portraying Kim Jong Il as a "tyrant," North Korea described the president as an "imbecile" and a "tyrant that puts Hitler in a shade." Then on September 28, North Korea announced that it had produced another nuclear weapon from eight thousand spent fuel rods for self-defense against U.S. nuclear threats. On September 13, 2005, six-party talks resumed. On September 19, another "historic" statement was issued that North Korea agreed to give up its nuclear activity and rejoin the NPT. This time the good atmosphere did not even survive a day: on September 20, North Korea declared it would not give up its nuclear program if light water reactors were not supplied. This eventually ended the fifth round of six-party talks, without progress, a month later.[55]

The international community experienced a more turbulent year concerning the North Korean nuclear program in 2006. Two major acts by the DPRK shocked observers: on July 4 and 5, the DPRK test-fired seven missiles including a Taepodong 2, whose suspected range covers the western coast of the United States. The UN Security Council responded quickly, on July 15, 2006, with unanimous Resolution 1695, which demanded that North Korea return to the six-party talks without precondition, comply with the September 2005 joint statement "in particular to abandon all nuclear weapons and existing nuclear programmes," and return to the NPT and IAEA safeguards soon. In addition, the Security Council required all member states "to exercise vigilance and prevent missile and missile-related items, materials, goods and technology being transferred to DPRK's missile or WMD programmes."[56]

North Korea's response to the sanctions was even more provocative. On October 9, 2006, North Korea conducted its first nuclear weapon test ever. Sending shock waves around the world, the DPRK administration argued that the test was against "U.S. military hostility." The UN Security Council adopted Resolution 1718, condemning the action and demanding similar compromises from the DPRK. The UN also imposed military and economic sanctions.[57]

There were contending commentaries and intelligence about this test. On October 13, U.S. intelligence asserted that the air sample obtained from the test site contained radioactive material; yet the size of the explosion was less than one kiloton, which is quite small compared to nuclear detonations by other states, which usually ranged from ten to sixty kilotons.[58] On the other hand, a recent comment by CIA director Michael Hayden suggests that the October 2006 test was a failure, and the United States does not recognize North Korea as a nuclear weapon–maintaining state.[59] Obviously, the DPRK conducted some kind of a nuclear detonation, but the success of the test is open to debate.

While the international community was upset by the latest developments in the DPRK's nuclear program and the failure of diplomacy at the six-party talks, the world was stunned, once again, with a new development: on February 13, 2007, "The Third Session of the Fifth Round of the Six-Party Talks" issued a statement that North Korea had agreed to a new arrangement. According to this, "yet another" historic agreement,

1. The DPRK will shut down and seal the Yongbyon nuclear facility in sixty days, including the reprocessing facility, and invite back IAEA personnel for monitoring and verifications.
2. The DPRK will discuss with other parties a list of all its nuclear programs.
3. The DPRK and the United States will start bilateral talks aimed at solving issues between them and advance toward full diplomatic relations. In this context, the United States will begin the process of removing the DPRK from its state sponsor of terrorism list and terminate its application of the Trading with the Enemy Act to the DPRK.
4. The DPRK and Japan will start bilateral talks aimed at taking steps to normalize their relations.
5. The parties agree to send economic, energy, and humanitarian assistance to the DPRK. Initially, fifty thousand tons of heavy fuel oil will be given to DPRK within the next sixty days.[60]

During 2007 and 2008, there were major developments in the denuclearization of North Korea. In July 2007, North Korea shut down its Yongbyon reactor in return for fuel aid by the South. In June 2008 the country announced it dismantled the cooling tower of the same facility. In return, the United States removed North Korea from its state sponsors of terrorism list. However, with North Korea launching a rocket on April 5, 2009, U.S.–North Korean relations worsened again. Protesting the UN Security Council's condemnation of the rocket launch, North Korea declared it would not participate in six-party talks and would not be bound by any agreement signed before. On May 25, 2009, North Korea made a second nuclear test, generating protests from all around the world. As of February 2010, there has not been a substantial development in U.S.–North Korean relations toward a resolution of the issue.

Critics of George W. Bush's Policies

The international community welcomed the new 2007 agreement, but it was publicly criticized by U.S. policy makers across the political spectrum. The most frequently expressed objection was that, despite the fact that Republicans had voiced their contempt for the Agreed Framework of 1994 for a decade, the new deal that the Bush administration agreed to looked almost identical to it; that is, North Korea would suspend its nuclear program in return for economic and diplomatic incentives by the other parties. Perhaps the only difference was that now North Korea seemed to have achieved greater nuclear capabilities than before. Therefore many analysts asked what had been the use of the confrontation policy that the Bush administration had followed for five years, which simply gave North Korea additional time to build more weapons. A South Korean regional expert's comment was informative: "We have lost four or five years and now we have to start again with North Korea—except the situation is worse because they have now tested a nuclear device."[61]

Critics of the Bush administration were not the only ones dissatisfied with the agreement. John Bolton, a Republican and former U.S. ambassador to the UN, criticized the deal harshly: "It sends exactly the wrong signal to would-be proliferators around the world: If you hold out long enough and wear down the State Department negotiators, eventually you get rewarded. . . . It makes the [Bush] administration look very weak at a time in Iraq and dealing with Iran it needs to look strong."[62] Many Republicans in Congress also criticized the deal on similar grounds.

The Bush administration rejected the assertion that the agreement was an example of appeasement because it was based only on staggered incentives. That is, if North Korea did not fulfill the requirements, it would not receive any economic or diplomatic concessions. However, one should also remember that the heavily criticized Agreed Framework was based on similar terms. In sum, it could be argued that the confrontation policy of the Bush administration ended up favoring the North Korean regime. Between 2007 and North Korea's missile and nuclear device tests in 2009, the agreement seemed to work quite well. However, with apparent escalations from the North Korean side, the talks and dismantling of nuclear reactors have been curbed. A solution to the problem seems more difficult than before.

The Obama Administration and North Korea

In the first year of the Obama administration, North Korea did not appear to be at the top of the foreign policy agenda. Obama's election rhetoric, i.e., engagement with hostile nations, took a setback with North Korea's second nuclear test. Although Secretary of State Hillary Rodham Clinton used harsh rhetoric and warned the country, President Obama and his administration seemed only to hope that North Korea would rejoin the six-party talks by itself.

Of course, the Obama administration inherited a multiparty diplomatic process from the previous administration that has been suspended due to the North's behavior in early 2009. Yet the administration seemed to focus heavily on other issues such as Afghanistan, and did not seem to pay much attention to the Korean peninsula. Only after a crisis over a sunken warship began in 2010 between the North and South, the Obama administration became involved in the Korean affairs.

Conclusion: Options

North Korea's nuclear status has been an issue of varying salience in U.S. foreign policy for the last two decades. Presidents have used a range of tactics, from the stick to the carrot and varying combinations thereof, to cope with North Korea's quest for status as a nuclear power. It is not clear that any particular approach can be labeled an unqualified success. However, the dealings of various administrations with North Korea have one characteristic in common: their inclination to repeat the same mistakes over and over again: "U.S. administrations have a tendency to start from scratch in their dealings with North Korea—and then relearn, step by step, the tortuous lessons."[63]

The George W. Bush administration significantly changed U.S. policy on North Korean nuclear proliferation, replacing engagement with confrontation, which led to the breakdown of bilateral relations and undermined the gains of the Agreed Framework of 1994. North Korea's uncompromising attitude and provocative behavior did not help the situation. Opponents of the Clinton administration's way of dealing with North Korea raised valid arguments concerning the likelihood that Pyongyang could be trusted to implement the framework and relinquish its quest for nuclear weapons. The Bush administration's undermining of the Agreed Framework without providing a better alternative, however, hurt the United States and its allies. As North Korean vice foreign minister Kim Gye Gwan noted, North Korea can develop a nuclear arsenal without the limitations of any international agreement or monitoring: "As time passes, our nuclear deterrent continues to grow in quality and quantity."[64] Free from the limitations of the Agreed Framework, North Korea may have quadrupled its arsenal of nuclear weapons.[65] Currently, North Korea is estimated to have six to eight nuclear bombs.

None of the options for the future is without difficulties. One option is to do nothing: accept the North as a nuclear power (as is done with India, Israel, and Pakistan) and hope not to aggravate the situation. That entails the danger of North Korea's developing long-range missiles that can hit U.S. soil or selling nuclear material to terrorists. Moreover, allowing the North to have nuclear weapons would set an unacceptable precedent for future cases of nuclear proliferation. Japan and South Korea, for example, might want to produce such weapons in response to the North Korean threat. The presence of multiple nuclear powers in Asia could lead to an enormously costly war in the region and place China in a difficult position in terms of choosing a side. Countries like Iran may also use North Korea as an example of legitimate nuclear programs.

Second, the North Korean nuclear facilities could be destroyed, if that is still feasible strategically. Such an action might cause collateral damage and radioactive fallout over China, Japan, and South Korea. Third, sanctions and international pressure, led by China, Japan, Russia, and the United States, could eventually pressure North Korea into giving up its nuclear program. The North, however, already is being pressed hard, and escalation of such tactics could lead to another war on the Korean Peninsula.

The fourth option is trying to make the February 2007 deal work in a way that would provide assurances to the North Korean regime about its security and deliver the economic and diplomatic aid that the country desperately needs. This could fit into President Obama's engagement policy promises during his election campaign. However, judging from two decades of U.S.–North Korean relations on the nuclear issue, no carrot policy seemed to work perfectly. North Korea as a military dictatorship prefers benefits of nuclear deterrence over economic and political gains. Perhaps a significant leadership change in North Korea may lead to positive developments. Therefore the United States and the rest of the world should closely observe who will be the next leader of North Korea after Kim Jong-Il, whose health reportedly has been deteriorating in the last few years. Only a North Korean leader who really wants to cooperate can change the outcome. From U.S. foreign policy makers' perspective, North Korea seems to be an unsuccessful example.

Key Actors

George H. W. Bush   First U.S. president to deal with North Korea as a nuclear problem, employed a confrontation policy and avoided direct talks.

George W. Bush   President, publicly referred to the Korean leadership as part of a so-called axis of evil (along with Iran and Iraq), hastening the breakdown of relations and of implementation of the Agreed Framework.

Jimmy Carter   President, actions as a self-appointed ambassador to help ease tensions between the United States and North Korea in summer 1994 led to a resumption of talks that produced the Agreed Framework.

Bill Clinton   President, advocated engagement and direct negotiation with North Korea.

Robert L. Gallucci   Ambassador-at-large and chief U.S. negotiator during the 1994 crisis with North Korea.

International Atomic Energy Agency   UN agency that promotes safe, secure, and peaceful nuclear technologies for member states; active in keeping the North Korean nuclear program in check.

Kim Il Sung   The "Great Leader" of North Korea from 1948 to 1994; chairman of the Korean Workers' Party, which has ruled the country for more than five decades.

Kim Jong Il   The "Dear Leader" of North Korea since 1994; successor of Kim Il Sung, his father, and general secretary of the Korean Workers' Party and chairman of the National Defense Committee.

Korean Peninsula Energy Development Organization   Grouping of Japan, South Korea, and the United States, established in 1995 to advance implementation of the Agreed Framework; was to provide North Korea with heavy fuel oil and light water reactors in return for dismantling its nuclear program.

William J. Perry   U.S. North Korea policy coordinator and special adviser to President Bill Clinton, reviewed North Korean policy in 1999.

Notes

1. David Reese, *The Prospects for North Korea's Survival*, International Institute for Strategic Studies Adelphi Papers 323 (Oxford: Oxford University Press, 1998).

2. Ibid.

3. AsianInfo.org, "Korea's History/Background," www.asianinfo.org/asianinfo/korea/pro-history.htm.

4. Encyclopedia4u.com, "Korean War," www.encyclopedia4u.com/k/korean-war.html.

5. Wikipedia, "Korean War," http://en.wikipedia.org/wiki/Korean_War.

6. TheFreeDictionary.com, "Korean Communist Party," http://encyclopedia.thefreedictionary.com/Korean%20Communist%20Party.

7. Central Intelligence Agency, "North Korea," *World Factbook*, www.cia.gov/cia/publications/factbook/geos/kn.html.

8. May Lee, Associated Press, "Famine May Have Killed Two Million in North Korea," August 19, 1998, www.cnn.com/WORLD/asiapcf/9808/19/nkorea.famine.

9. Facts on International Relations and Security Trends, http://first.sipri.org/index.php.

10. Reese, *The Prospects for North Korea's Survival*, 42.

11. Walter B. Slocombe, "The Agreed Framework with the Democratic People's Republic of Korea," *Strategic Forum* 23 (Washington, D.C.: National Defense University,

Institute for National Strategic Studies, 1995), www.ndu.edu/inss/strforum/SF_23/forum23.html.

12. Leon V. Sigal, *Disarming Strangers: Nuclear Diplomacy with North Korea* (Princeton: Princeton University Press, 1998).

13. Ibid.

14. Michael J. Mazarr, *North Korea and the Bomb: A Case Study in Nonproliferation* (New York: St. Martin's Press, 1995), 56–57.

15. Ibid.

16. Ibid.

17. Curtis H. Martin, "The U.S.–North Korean Agreed Framework: Incentives-Based Diplomacy after the Cold War," in *Sanctions as Economic Statecraft: Theory and Practice*, ed. Steve Chan and A. Cooper Drury (New York: St. Martin's Press, 2000).

18. Mazarr, *North Korea and the Bomb*.

19. Reese, *The Prospects for North Korea's Survival*, 45.

20. Ibid., 46.

21. Mazarr, *North Korea and the Bomb*.

22. Sigal, *Disarming Strangers*.

23. In terms of nonproliferation, light water reactors are preferred to the North Korean graphite-modulated reactors because producing the necessary waste for the development of nuclear weapons is much more difficult.

24. Mazarr, *North Korea and the Bomb*.

25. Ibid., 98.

26. Ibid.

27. Ibid., 102.

28. Reese, *The Prospects for North Korea's Survival*.

29. Ibid.

30. Sigal, *Disarming Strangers*.

31. Rod Troester, *Jimmy Carter as Peacemaker: A Post-Presidential Biography* (Westport, Conn.: Praeger, 1999), 76.

32. D. Jehl, "U.S. Is Pressing Sanctions for North Korea," *New York Times,* June 11, 1994, A7, cited in Troester, *Jimmy Carter*, 76.

33. Stone, "Citizen Carter, the Statesman," *USA Today*, June 15, 1994, A4, as cited in Troester, *Jimmy Carter*, 76.

34. Troester, *Jimmy Carter*.

35. Sigal, *Disarming Strangers,* 132.

36. Thomas L. Wilborn, "Strategic Implications of the U.S.-DPRK Framework Agreement," U.S. Army War College, Washington, D.C., April 3, 1995, www.milnet.com/korea/usdprkp1.htm#B22.

37. Reese, *The Prospects for North Korea's Survival.*

38. William J. Perry, "Review of United States Policy toward North Korea: Findings and Recommendations," unclassified report, Washington, D.C., October 12, 1999, http:// bcsia.ksg.harvard.edu/publication.cfm?program=CORE&ctype=book&item_id=6.

39. Wilborn, "Strategic Implications."

40. Alfonse D'Amato, Jesse Helms, Mitch McConnell, and Frank Murkowski, October 19, 1994, in Wilborn, "Strategic Implications," 6.

41. Wilborn, "Strategic Implications."

42. Ibid.

43. R. Fisher, *International Conflict for Beginners* (New York: Harper and Row, 1970), as quoted in Martin, "The U.S.–North Korean Agreed Framework."

44. John Diamond, "On Foreign Policy Bush Moving to Clinton Views," *Chicago Tribune,* June 8, 2001.

45. Yonhap News Agency, *North Korea Handbook* (Armonk, N.Y.: M. E. Sharpe, 2003), 553.

46. Ibid.

47. Donald G. Gross, "Riding the Roller-Coaster," *Comparative Connections: An E-Journal on East Asian Bilateral Relations,* April 2002, www.csis.org/pacfor/cc/0201Qus_skorea.html.

48. Ibid., 1.

49. Arms Control Agency, "Chronology of U.S.–North Korean Nuclear and Missile Diplomacy," fact sheet, June 2003, www.armscontrol.org/factsheets/dprkchron.asp.

50. Ibid.

51. Ibid.

52. Ibid.

53. Donald G. Gross, "Tensions Escalate in Korea as the U.S. Targets Iraq," *Comparative Connections: An E-Journal on East Asian Bilateral Relations,* April 2003, www.csis.org/pacfor/cc/0301Qus_skorea.html.

54. Donald G. Gross, "In the Eye of the Beholder: Impasse or Progress in the Six-Party Talks?" *Comparative Connections: An E-Journal on East Asian Bilateral Relations,* April 2004, www.csis.org/pacfor/cc/0401Qus_skorea.html.

55. BBC News Web site, "Timeline: North Korea Nuclear Stand-Off," http://news.bbc.co.uk/2/hi/asia-pacific/2604437.stm (accessed April 9, 2007).

56. United Nations Web site, "Security Council Condemns Democratic People's Republic of Korea's Missile Launches," July 15, 2006, www.un.org/News/Press/docs/2006/sc8778.doc.htm.

57. "Resolution 1718 (2006)," IAEA News Center, October 14, 2006, www.iaea.org/NewsCenter/Focus/IaeaDprk/unscres_14102006.pdf.

58. Associated Press, "U.S. Confirms North Korea's Nuclear Test," October 16, 2006, www.iht.com/articles/ap/2006/10/16/america/NA_GEN_US_NKorea.php.

59. Lee Jin-woo, "U.S. Judges N. Korean Nuclear Test Failure," *Korea Times,* March 28, 2007, http://times.hankooki.com/lpage/nation/200703/kt2007032821284011990.htm.

60. Ministry of Foreign Affairs of PRC, "Initial Actions for the Implementation of the Joint Statement," February 13, 2007, www.fmprc.gov.cn/eng/zxxx/t297463.htm.

61. Jun Bong-geun, of the Institute of Foreign Affairs and National Security in Seoul, as quoted in "The End of a Long Confrontation?" by Charles Scanlon, BBC News, February 13, 2007, http://news.bbc.co.uk/2/hi/asia-pacific/6357853.stm.

62. "Rice Calls North Korean Deal 'Important First Step,' " CNN News, February 13, 2007, www.cnn.com/2007/WORLD/asiapcf/02/13/nkorea.talks/index.html.

63. Scanlon, "The End of a Long Confrontation?"

64. Charles L. Pritchard, "What I Saw in North Korea," *New York Times,* January 21, 2004.

65. Ibid.

6 Hitting the Reset Button: Changing the Direction of U.S.-Russian Relations?

Ralph G. Carter and James M. Scott

Before You Begin

1. Why did the U.S.-Russian relationship deteriorate in the post–cold war era?

2. What changed to cause these regimes to reach out to each other?

3. Who initiated this outreach to the other, and why?

4. What were the goals on each side for this new process of engagement?

5. What was accomplished in this outreach?

6. Why did it take so long to achieve any tangible results?

Introduction

The George W. Bush administration often followed an approach in which the United States would refuse to engage "rogue" or problematic regimes unless specified preconditions were met, arguing that to engage them without preconditions gave them added legitimacy. Yet with "change we can believe in" as the mantra of the 2008 presidential campaign, Barack Obama promised a new emphasis on engagement with other international actors. Confident in American "soft power" and the potential for persuasion, Obama believed the United States should be willing to talk with anyone, and thus his administration would reach out to both friends and enemies. Despite the end of the cold war and the nominal friendship of the two former rivals, the U.S.-Russian relationship had been tense at times since 1991 and seemed to be growing more so. Shortly after arriving in office, the Obama administration announced its desire to "hit the reset button" on the U.S.-Russian relationship. "Resetting" relations between major powers—and longtime rivals—proved far more difficult than senior administration officials ever imagined.

Background: A Bumpy Post–Cold War Ride

When the cold war ended with the dissolution of the Soviet Union in 1991, a brief moment of euphoria was followed by a period marked by missed opportunities and misperceptions.[1] Facing an economic collapse far worse than the Great Depression of the 1930s, Russians expected significant foreign economic assistance in their time of need. Not only did they believe they merited economic aid from wealthy Western states based on the wretched economic conditions they faced, but they also believed they would be "rewarded" by the capitalist West for their abandonment of communist ideology. However, while some aid was forthcoming, particularly from Germany, the amount of U.S. aid provided during the George H. W. Bush administration was widely perceived as too little, too late by Russian elites. President Bush and other senior U.S. officials felt it would not be prudent to engage Russia with a large infusion of foreign aid until the true colors of the new regime had been revealed. While President Boris Yeltsin proclaimed his friendship with the United States, other Russian elites were calling for a reestablishment of the former Russian empire, and some Russian military officials were saying the real U.S. aim was to cripple the new Russian regime so it could never be a rival again. Thus, in a very short time, the seeds of mistrust had been planted.

If Russians hoped for a more responsive administration when Bill Clinton took office, they were to be disappointed. At a summit conference in Vancouver in April 1993, Clinton and Yeltsin agreed to the creation of a U.S.-Russian Joint Commission on Economic and Technological Cooperation. Led by U.S. vice president Al Gore and Russian prime minister Viktor Chernomyrdin, the Gore-Chernomyrdin Commission (as it became known) later expanded to include eight different committees to structure cooperation across a variety of policy issues.[2] With that structure in place, Clinton delegated Russian issues to Gore and the commission, and except for moments of attention to a few major issues, Clinton's personal approach to Russian concerns became almost one of benign neglect.

Despite these perfunctory efforts at cooperation, alliance politics quickly became a point of friction. When the Soviet Union dissolved, its military alliance—the Warsaw Pact—did as well, and the Russians could not understand why NATO continued on as before. In the 1992–1995 Bosnian civil war, NATO began out-of-area operations for the first time. As a historical ally of the Serbs, the Russians were upset when NATO launched air strikes against Serbian forces and then sent peacekeeping forces to Bosnia after the war.[3] Russian

Timeline

Key Developments in Post–Cold War U.S.-Russian Relations

December 1991	With the dissolution of the Soviet Union, the Russian Federation is the most important component of the old USSR left standing.
1992	The George H. W. Bush administration's foreign assistance package for Russia is seen as "too little, too late" by most Russian elites, some of whom interpret the U.S. offer as an American hope for Russia's economic failure.
1992–1995	NATO alarms the Russians by intervening in the Bosnian civil war against Russia's traditional ally Serbia. Russia demands to participate in the peacekeeping force in Bosnia following the war's end, and NATO agrees to allow Russian troops as part of the peacekeeping component.
April 1993	New U.S. president Bill Clinton and Russian president Boris Yeltsin create a U.S.-Russian Joint Commission on Economic and Technological Cooperation (the Gore-Chernomyrdin Commission) to coordinate U.S.-Russian cooperative relations.
1997	Over Russia's objections, NATO invites Hungary, Poland, and the Czech Republic to join the alliance. NATO seeks to pacify Russian objections by providing Russia more economic aid and inviting Russia to join the Group of Seven major industrial nations (G-7).
1999	Over Russia's objections, NATO conducts a bombing campaign against Serbia for its ethnic cleansing operations in the Serbian province of Kosovo. With the war's end, Russian peacekeeping troops in Bosnia race into Kosovo and take control of the major international airport there, establishing a presence as peacekeepers without authorization from NATO.

(continued)

Timeline *(continued)*

Key Developments in Post–Cold War U.S.-Russian Relations

2002	Over Russia's objections, NATO invites former communist Eastern European states Bulgaria, Romania, Slovakia, and Slovenia as well as former Soviet states Latvia, Lithuania, and Estonia to join NATO.
2002–2003	Russia opposes the George W. Bush administration's efforts to get UN authorization of the use of force against Iraq and may have provided Iraq with information on U.S. military plans prior to the 2003 invasion of Iraq.
2005	Local Russian security forces in Perm force a three-hour standoff when they demand the right to inspect the military aircraft carrying a delegation of U.S. senators, one of whom is freshman senator Barack Obama.
2006	Russia hires a U.S. public relations firm to improve its image.
January 2007	Over Russian objections, the Bush administration announces an antiballistic missile system to be based in Poland and the Czech Republic to protect allies in Europe from a missile attack from a rogue Middle Eastern state.
Late 2007–early 2008	Russian combat aircraft come provocatively close to U.S. airspace in Alaska eight times.
February 11, 2008	A Russian bomber twice flies over the aircraft carrier *USS Nimitz* in the Pacific, and three other Russian bombers are in the area.
February 18, 2008	Over Russia's objections, the United States recognizes Kosovo's independence from Serbia.
April 3, 2008	Over Russia's objections, NATO invites Albania and Croatia to join the alliance and notes former Soviet republics Georgia and Ukraine will join the alliance at some later date.

August 7–12, 2008	Russian troops defeat Georgian forces in a war over the status of Georgia's breakaway provinces Abkhazia and South Ossetia.
Late January 2009	Russian president Dmitry Medvedev calls and writes newly inaugurated U.S. president Barack Obama, seeking to improve U.S.-Russian relations.
February 7, 2009	At a security conference in Munich, U.S. vice president Joe Biden says the new administration seeks to "press the reset button" on relations with the Russians.
February 13, 2009	U.S. under secretary of state William Burns meets with Russian officials in Moscow regarding major items to be on the "reset" agenda, which include a new replacement for the START Treaty, a new bilateral commission to coordinate relations, and support for Russia's entry into the World Trade Organization.
February 15–19, 2009	Both President Obama and Defense Secretary Robert Gates publicly emphasize that if Russia could help neutralize the threat of Iran's nuclear weapons program, there would be no need for a missile defense system in Poland and the Czech Republic.
March 1, 2009	Obama clarifies that any changes regarding European missile defense would be contingent on changes in Iran's behavior, not on a deal with Russia. Medvedev denies that there is a deal to support increased sanctions against Iran in return for the United States dropping plans for missile defense systems in Poland and the Czech Republic.
March 6, 2009	U.S. secretary of state Hillary Rodham Clinton meets with Russian foreign minister Sergei Lavrov in Geneva to discuss the "reset" agenda, which is mistakenly translated into Russian as the "overloaded" or "overcharged" agenda.
Mid–late March 2009	Medvedev announces a new Russian military rearmament program, Lavrov says that NATO is still an anti-Russian alliance, and the Russian deputy foreign minister declares that missile defense in Europe has to be linked to the negotiations for the new START II Treaty.

(continued)

Timeline *(continued)*

Key Developments in Post–Cold War U.S.-Russian Relations

April 2, 2009	Obama and Medvedev meet in London for the Group of Twenty (G-20) major economies meeting and profess their desire for a new START II Treaty.
April 5, 2009	In a speech in Prague, Obama calls for a nuclear-free world.
Mid-April–June 2009	Russia sends thousands more troops to Abkhazia and South Ossetia and conducts military exercises near the Georgian border.
July 6, 2009	Obama meets in Moscow with both President Medvedev and Prime Minister Vladimir Putin. Medvedev is noncommittal regarding Obama's pressure to reenergize the "reset" effort while Putin presses a long list of Russian grievances against the United States.
Mid-July 2009	Russian military training exercises take place near the Georgian border while U.S. and Georgian military forces undertake exercises inside Georgian territory.
July 24, 2009	Following a trip to reassure Ukrainian and Georgian leaders of U.S. support, Vice President Joe Biden tells a reporter that Russians need to accept the U.S. positions regarding the new START II Treaty, because their economic and human growth rate problems are so dire that the Russians cannot sustain themselves in the image they prefer.
July 27, 2009	The State Department announces that the United States is pursuing improved relations with India and China through bilateral presidential commissions on the U.S.-Russian model, thereby signaling the Russians that Russia may not be the prime focus of the Obama administration.
August 4, 2009	Medvedev calls Obama to wish him a happy birthday and to urge greater efforts by negotiators so a new START II Treaty can be ready by the December target date.
August 12, 2009	Putin announces that Abkhazia will get nearly $500 million in additional military aid.

September 17, 2009	Obama announces that, due to setbacks in Iran's long-range missile program, the United States will discontinue the Bush administration's plan for missile defense systems to be based in Poland and the Czech Republic and instead rely on shorter-range and more mobile antimissile systems that can be positioned closer to Iran.
September 18, 2009	Russian officials announce that their prior decision to place short-range missiles and strategic bombers in the Russian territory of Kaliningrad next to Poland is rescinded.
September 25, 2009	Medvedev says Russia is willing to consider new sanctions against Iran.
Fall 2009	Negotiations on the new START II Treaty face stumbling blocks regarding on-site verification, sharing of telemetry data, and other issues.
December 2009	Meeting at the UN Climate Conference in Copenhagen, Obama and Medvedev generally agree on the numbers of warheads and launchers to be allowed under the new START II Treaty. U.S. negotiators think the negotiations are essentially over.
January 2010	The Russian side insists on linking missile defense issues to the START II Treaty, and Romania's announcement that it will host short-range interceptor missiles in the new Obama missile defense system alarms Russian elites.
February 24, 2010	Medvedev calls Obama to press for incorporation of missile defense concerns in the START II Treaty. Obama resists that change.
March 13, 2010	Medvedev calls Obama and agrees to the concept of separate statements, to be signed along with the START II Treaty, that clarify their positions regarding missile defense and the START II Treaty.
April 8, 2010	Obama and Medvedev sign the START II Treaty in Prague.
May 2010	For the first time, U.S. military forces participate in Moscow's Victory Day Parade on May 9, 2010, celebrating the Russian victory over German fascism in World War II.

troops were subsequently allowed to participate in the NATO peacekeeping mission in Bosnia.[4]

NATO's eastward creep continued when, at the 1997 NATO summit conference in Madrid, three former Warsaw Pact members were invited to join NATO.[5] NATO's goal in inviting Poland, the Czech Republic, and Hungary to join the alliance was to preserve and institutionalize the democratic reforms undertaken in those states, but Russians saw this as an anti-Russian alliance creeping closer to their borders. U.S. and NATO leaders sought to assuage Russian concerns by increasing economic assistance to Russia and inviting Russia to participate as a nonvoting member in the Group of Seven advanced industrial countries. With Russia's inclusion, the G-7 became known as the G-8.

Not only did Poland, the Czech Republic, and Hungary join NATO formally in 1999, but that year NATO engaged in a bombing campaign against the Serbian-dominated Yugoslavian government in the war over the Serbian province of Kosovo. The Russian government bitterly opposed NATO's intervention in the Kosovo war, and following a cease-fire, Russian peacekeeping troops in Bosnia entered Kosovo and took up an unauthorized presence at its main international airport.[6] Russian foreign policy makers saw a link between NATO's willingness to intervene in Kosovo and a possible future NATO intervention in Chechnya, a breakaway Islamic province where the Russian army was accused of serious human rights violations. New Russian president Vladimir Putin's harsh military response to crush the Chechen militants was not challenged by the United States following September 11, 2001, as new U.S. president George W. Bush accepted Putin's definition that Chechen militants were Islamic terrorists and thus fit under Bush's call for a global war on terrorism.

The fact that they agreed on the global war on terrorism did not mean the Bush and Putin administrations agreed on other matters, and in many ways U.S.-Russian relations deteriorated further during the Bush years. NATO expansion arose again. In 2002 Bulgaria, Romania, Slovakia, and Slovenia—all former communist states in east central Europe—were invited to join NATO. More upsetting to the Russians was the fact that three former republics of the Soviet Union—Estonia, Latvia, and Lithuania—were also invited to join. Putin's regime vigorously but unsuccessfully opposed the expansion of NATO into what the Russians saw as their historic sphere of influence. Those seven states became new NATO members in 2004, and NATO continued to press closer to Russian borders by targeting the Balkans and Caucasus for further expansion. In 2007 Albania and Croatia were scheduled for inclusion in NATO (which later happened in 2009), and Bush pushed for former Soviet republics Ukraine and Georgia to be included as well. Due in large part to Russian opposition, Ukraine and Georgia were not accepted as members at the same time as Albania and Croatia, but NATO declared they would be included at some future point.[7]

Other national security differences arose. Although Putin endorsed Bush's call for a global war on terrorism, Russia opposed the Bush administration's emphasis on preempting foreign threats before they could attack the United States. To the Russians, this amounted to a U.S. attempt to create a unipolar world, which they opposed.[8] Along with France and China, Russia refused to approve a UN Security Council resolution authorizing the use of force against Iraq in 2002.[9] When the United States and its allies prepared to invade Iraq in 2003, Russia not only opposed the use of force, but reports indicated that Russian diplomats forwarded information on U.S. military strategy and troop movements to Saddam Hussein's regime.[10]

Iran proved to be another major point of disagreement between the U.S. and Russian governments. Throughout his presidency, George W. Bush pushed for tighter economic sanctions against Iran as long as it continued to refuse to allow international inspection of its nuclear program. Putin resisted such sanctions, perhaps in part due to the many Russian commercial contracts with Iran—including Russia's building of a nuclear reactor there.[11] Bush also proposed an antiballistic missile (ABM) defense system to protect Europe from long-range, intercontinental ballistic missiles (ICBMs) launched by Iran. Yet Putin saw the positioning of the radar installation in the Czech Republic and the interceptor missiles in Poland as a threat to Russian national security that would have to be countered. He proposed that the ABM system be relocated closer to Iran in Azerbaijan, one of the former Soviet republics, but Bush declined the offer.[12]

By early 2008, already tense relations were strained even further. Angry over U.S. recognition of Kosovo as an independent state and NATO's flirtation with Ukraine and Georgia, Putin threatened to target missiles at the Ukrainian capital if it joined NATO, and in February a Russian bomber twice flew over the USS *Nimitz* in the Pacific, only to be escorted away by U.S. fighters. This followed eight similar instances of provocative Russian flights near Alaskan airspace in the prior six months. The Bush administration responded to Russia's unwillingness to support new sanctions against Iran by refusing to sign an already negotiated treaty to allow Russia to share in the lucrative business of storing spent civilian nuclear fuel. On the campaign trail, presidential hopefuls

John McCain, Hillary Clinton, and Barack Obama criticized President Bush for being too soft on Putin for his actions abroad and repression of human rights at home.[13] In April, Bush and Putin met in the Russian Black Sea resort town of Sochi for a summit conference. Michael McFaul, a Stanford professor and adviser on Russia to the Obama campaign, wanted to know why Bush would waste time talking to lame-duck president Putin when he could wait a month and talk to newly elected president Dmitry Medvedev instead.[14]

By this time, the Russians were clearly intrigued with Obama as a presidential candidate. Konstantin Kosachev, a Russian parliamentarian, said, "Barack Obama looks like the candidate that can be expected to take the greatest strides towards Russia. Unlike McCain he's not infected with any Cold War phobias."[15] However, after the Russians invaded Georgia in August 2008 to protect the separatist enclaves of Abkhazia and South Ossetia from a Georgian military advance, both candidates Obama and McCain called for a cease-fire and UN Security Council action, and Obama called for Russia to respect Georgian territory.[16]

In sum, as President-elect Obama prepared to enter office, U.S.-Russian relations were already poor and getting worse. Obama had experienced the tensions personally as a freshman senator in 2005 when, on his first trip to Russia with other members of the Senate Foreign Relations Committee, Russian security forces in the city of Perm demanded the right to board and inspect the U.S. military aircraft on which they were flying. The senators refused, a three-hour standoff ensued before Washington and Moscow officials could override the local authorities, and the Russian Foreign Ministry later apologized to the U.S. delegation.[17] By 2006 the Russian government realized its image in the United States was so poor it hired an expensive public relations firm to try to rebrand Russia as a progressive, growing power, and it spent millions of dollars over the next two years in the effort to create a more positive image.[18] Yet while the Russians sought to present a better image, their actions often alarmed the West. Although Russian leaders said they preferred a multipolar world to any resumption of the cold war, they spent much of 2008 taking more aggressive steps in their own national interests. The most challenging of these was going to war with Georgia. However, they also sought to modernize their military, find new naval bases abroad, increase their capabilities to project force abroad, and double their defense spending (after accounting for inflation). They expanded their arms sales abroad by initiating sales to Algeria, Brazil, Cuba, Lebanon, Saudi Arabia, and Venezuela.[19] President Medvedev later said that by late 2008 "I felt that we had reached a dead end and had almost slid to the level of a cold war."[20] Due to the actions on both sides, U.S.-Russian relations were like a simmering pot. For Obama, the question was how to reduce the heat.

Phase I: Courtship, January 2009–Mid-March 2009

President Obama was inaugurated on January 20, 2009. Less than a week later, Dmitry Medvedev called him and suggested that two "young, new presidents" should be able to work together. Medvedev followed up the call with an eight-page letter to Obama and another phone call to discuss substantive issues affecting U.S.-Russian relations. Obama's initial response was to list Iran's nuclear program, nuclear proliferation, and Middle East matters as issues where their interests coincided.[21] On February 7, at an international security conference in Munich, Vice President Joe Biden said the Obama administration wanted to "press the reset button" on relations with Russia. "The last few years have seen a dangerous drift in relations between Russia and members of our alliance," he added. "The U.S. and Russia can disagree but still work together where its interests coincide." In his view, those issues included nuclear programs in Iran and North Korea as well as assistance to the NATO effort in Afghanistan. He was concerned that the previous month the president of Kyrgyzstan had announced that the United States would no longer be able to use the Manas airbase to resupply NATO troops in Afghanistan.[22] Later, at the Munich conference, Biden met with Russian deputy foreign minister Sergei Ivanov, who asked if the "reset" initiative was real. Biden assured him it was, and the two then had a substantive discussion of the issues involved in Afghanistan, Iran, and arms control.[23]

In a February 13 visit to Moscow, Under Secretary of State (and former ambassador to Russia) William Burns met with Russian leaders. They quickly agreed on major elements of a "reset" agenda: a new treaty to replace the expiring Strategic Arms Reduction Treaty (START), recreating bilateral committees to promote cooperation similar to those of the Gore-Chernomyrdin Commission, and U.S. support for Russia's entry into the World Trade Organization (WTO). Burns added that if the Russians could help reduce the threat from Iran's nuclear weapons program, the need for an ABM system in Europe could be reconsidered. Yet beyond these positives, there were obstacles to overcome. The United States would have to overlook the fact that Russia had offered Kyrgyzstan $2.1 billion to put the Manas airbase off-limits for the resupply of NATO forces in Afghanistan. The Kyrgyz decision then allowed Putin to offer

NATO an overland route to Afghanistan through Russia, which could put resupply at risk of Russian interference or blockage. (A subsequent U.S. offer to increase aid to Kyrgyzstan renewed the U.S. right to use the airbase.) Also, Russia's repression of human rights (such as the suppression of dissidents, murder of opposition journalists, etc.) would have to be overlooked or decoupled from the "reset" initiative. The Russian government was still allowing hawkish messages in state-controlled media outlets that portrayed Russia as surrounded by enemies and listing the United States among them. Reports also indicated that Russia was making military preparations to "finish the job" of regime change in Georgia by toppling the government of Mikheil Saakashvili by force the following summer. Finally, the plummeting Russian economy could mobilize public opposition to the Medvedev/Putin regime and deprive Russia of the funds to undertake new initiatives.[24]

Despite these potential obstacles, the momentum was still positive. In mid-February, Obama sent Medvedev a letter offering to reconsider the Polish/Czech ABM system if Russia could help with the issue of Iran's nuclear program. On February 19 at a NATO defense ministers' meeting in Krakow, Secretary of Defense Robert Gates told reporters there would be no need for the controversial ABM system were it not for the threat of missile attacks from Iran. He said he had told the Russians the same thing in 2008.[25] This positive signal was matched the next day in Moscow, when Iranian defense minister Mostafa Mohammad Najjar arrived for talks on the delivery of an S-300 anti-aircraft missile system Iran had already contracted to purchase from Russia. Russian officials told him the S-300 deal, which both the United States and Israel had opposed, was on hold.[26] By the end of the month, Obama administration officials were putting together a formal package of potential issues that would structure U.S.-Russian relations on a firmer foundation. These included restoration of the NATO-Russia Council, suspended with the start of the Georgian war in the summer of 2008; negotiation of a replacement to START; and cooperation on Iran, help with Afghanistan, and possible reconsiderations of missile defense in Europe.[27] On March 1, Medvedev was similarly optimistic when he told reporters in Spain that he expected the United States and Russia to deal with the issue of missile defense in Europe "in a more inventive and partnership-like" way now that the new administration was in place.[28]

These positive statements generated pushback from critics at home, and both Obama and Medvedev held press conferences on March 1 to clarify their positions. Obama said that any decision about missile defense in Europe would be based on estimations of Iran's threat to Europe, not on any deal with Russia.

He said the United States remained steadfast in its position of defending Poland and the Czech Republic from missile attacks, with shorter-range Patriot missile batteries even if the Bush administration's more ambitious long-range missile defense program was scrapped. For his part, Medvedev told reporters that Russia would continue building a nuclear reactor in Iran and continue opposing harsher sanctions against the Iranian regime; he also denied that there was a deal in which the Russians would change their position in return for a favorable decision on missile defense in Europe. Medvedev said he hoped Obama's common sense would lead him to conclude that canceling the Polish/Czech ABM system was the right thing to do, regardless of Russian actions elsewhere.[29]

On March 5, 2009, NATO foreign ministers met in Geneva and decided to resume relations between NATO and Russia, which had been broken off following the August 2008 war with Georgia. The next day in Geneva, Secretary of State Clinton met Russian foreign minister Sergei Lavrov for the first time. Clinton talked of the need for a "fresh start" in U.S.-Russian relations, and policy areas identified as part of the potential "reset" agenda included the following: Iran (linking Russian help with Iran's nuclear program with stopping the ABM system in Poland and the Czech Republic, stopping the Russian sale of S-300 missiles to Iran, seeking Russian support for additional economic sanctions against Iran), Afghanistan (proposing an international conference to try to bring peace and stability there and seeking NATO resupply of Afghanistan through Russian airspace), START (both sides wanted to reduce strategic nuclear warheads, but the Russians wanted to reduce stored warheads and delivery vehicles in addition to deployed warheads and delivery vehicles), and NATO expansion (both Georgia and Ukraine had been promised membership at some point in the future, but Russia opposed their entry into NATO).[30] Their two hours of talks began awkwardly. Clinton presented Lavrov a symbolic reset button as a gift, but State Department translators had gotten the Russian word for "reset" wrong. Instead, it was identified as the "overloaded" or "overcharged" button rather than the "reset" button. Both laughed off the somewhat prophetic incident.[31] Clinton said that both sides needed to "translate words into deeds." Lavrov agreed that all issues needed to be addressed, but he took the opportunity to criticize the U.S. recognition of Kosovo, and he defended the Russian sale of missile components to Iran.[32]

In contrast to Lavrov's somewhat pessimistic remarks, in mid-March Medvedev told a visiting group of American scholars that the recent successful Iranian launch of a satellite was alarming and should raise real concerns on the part of both the U.S. and Russian governments. He appeared to be signaling the United States that a deal could be made, with greater Russian pressure on Iran in return for changes in missile defense in Europe. At about that same time, reports surfaced that the Obama administration was considering whether to slow down the pace for NATO membership for Ukraine and Georgia and to push for repeal of the Jackson-Vanik Amendment, which imposed U.S. trade sanctions on Russia and other countries accused of human rights violations.[33] Thus the momentum of the "reset" initiative still seemed positive.

Phase II: Reality Sets In, Mid-March–July 2009

Beginning in mid- to late March, pessimistic signals seemed as likely as more optimistic ones. On March 17, Medvedev announced that Russia would begin a large-scale military rearmament program, and would upgrade Russia's nuclear forces beginning as soon as the START agreement expired in December 2009.[34] Three days later, Medvedev told a visiting delegation of former U.S. cabinet secretaries led by Henry Kissinger that he was hoping the Obama administration would live up to its pledge to "reset" relations. Yet the same day, the Russian deputy foreign minister told reporters that the European ABM issue had to be linked to START negotiations.[35]

At a meeting in Brussels over March 21–22, Foreign Minister Lavrov told a group of current and past European policy makers his view of things. He felt that the West had lied to Russia and that NATO was still a threat to Russia and should be replaced by the Organization for Security and Cooperation in Europe (OSCE). He went on to imply that if Europe made too many demands on Russia, there were plenty of customers in Asia for the Russian natural gas now purchased by Europeans. He finished his remarks by questioning the assumption that Iran's nuclear program was meant for military purposes.[36]

With these more ominous tones surfacing, Obama struggled to maintain progress. In early April, he and Medvedev met during the G-20 economic summit in London, where they renewed their pledge to complete an arms treaty to replace START I when it expired in December.[37] On April 5, Obama used an opportunity in Prague to issue the call for a nuclear-free world.[38] However, such efforts soon met new challenges in the form of renewed conflict between Russia and NATO over aggressive Russian actions in Georgia. Just two weeks after the hopeful statements at the G-20 meeting, Russia sent thousands of troops, with air and armor support, to Abkhazia and Ossetia; added an additional deployment in early June; and conducted large-scale military exercises close to the Georgian border in late June.[39] At the same time, Russia used its power as one of the permanent members of the UN Security Council to veto a resolution extending the stay of UN peacekeepers in Georgia.[40] NATO responded with joint military exercises with Georgian forces, which Russian leaders immediately denounced.[41] Thus, on the eve of a planned summit conference between Obama and Medvedev in Moscow, tensions were growing. Indeed, one Russian diplomat took advantage of a gathering of Western visitors to tick off a series of grievances that Russia held against the United States, including the U.S. failure to provide significant aid during the 1990s, support for Chechen "terrorists" after September 11, NATO's expansion to Russia's borders, and provocative missile defense system plans for Poland and the Czech Republic. According to the Russian diplomat, "America owes Russia, and it owes a lot, and it has to pay its debt."[42]

The Moscow summit began on July 6, 2009, just one day after the Russian military exercises on the Georgian border ended. President Obama sought to reestablish momentum toward the "reset," as well as play on potential dissension or competition between President Medvedev and Prime Minister Putin, in part by casting Medvedev as the reasonable partner and Putin as the obstructionist. Hence, Obama devoted significantly more time and attention to Medvedev during the summit.[43] However, as veteran journalist Jim Hoagland reported, while Obama and his advisers sought to treat Medvedev as a Russian version of Obama, other indicators pointed to the Medvedev-Putin strategy as a high-level "good cop—bad cop" pair, with the "two leaders acting as separate lobes of the same brain. Putin represents the vengeful, hostile-to-change and sensitive-to-slight part of the Russian personality, while Medvedev personifies the impressive intellectual and literary interests of the Russian elite."[44]

At the same time Obama was seeking to engage with Medvedev, he was also delivering a grim message about the U.S. view of the road ahead toward a meaningful reset. While pressing for progress on nuclear arms and other matters, Obama also pressed Medvedev to respect Georgia's territorial integrity and said the United States did not accept the idea of a privileged position for Russia among the former Soviet republics.[45] In a speech at the summit, he also rejected the idea of a Russian sphere of influence in the former Soviet republics and indicated U.S. support for the future inclusion of Georgia and Ukraine in NATO.[46] While Obama was warmly received, such comments were not. Medvedev offered praise for Obama's new approach to diplomacy, but refrained from making any concessions or commitments. Putin, on the other hand, was more direct, challenging Obama with a list of slights and grievances during their meeting together.[47] Just a week after the summit, both the United States and Russia conducted military exercises near Georgia (with the United States coordinating with the Georgian military), even as UN peacekeepers left Georgia, where they had been stationed for sixteen years to help reinforce the cease-fire between Russia and Georgia.[48] Hence, by mid-summer, optimism over a speedy "reset" in relations had given way to the realities of cold, hard interests and diverging perspectives.

Phase III: Fault Lines Reappear, July–August 2009

In the aftermath of the Moscow summit, efforts toward resetting U.S.-Russian relations entered a third phase, in which both presidents contended with a complex set of conflicting interests and cross-pressures. Both presidents found themselves struggling to balance pressures at home and from abroad, while maintaining positive momentum toward resetting U.S.-Russian relations.

One issue concerned countries around Russia's perimeter. Just two weeks after the Moscow summit, Mikheil Saakashvili, Georgia's president, asked the United States for advanced defensive weapons in the face of Russian troops massed in Abkhazia and South Ossetia. While the Obama administration did not make such a commitment, the news did little to ease the growing tensions.[49] At the same time, Lech Walesa and Václav Havel, the well-known former leaders of Poland and the Czech Republic, sent an open letter to Obama, urging him not to forget Eastern Europe in the process of "resetting" relations with Russia. These highly regarded individuals articulated the growing concern in countries of the region that Russia's needs—and U.S. interests in improved relations and progress on arms control—would be prioritized above the rest of the region.[50]

The United States responded in several ways. In one track, administration officials painted an optimistic and reassuring picture of progress. For example, Assistant Secretary of State Philip Gordon told a hearing of the House Foreign Affairs Subcommittee on Europe that the Obama administration was open to the idea of possible Russian admission to NATO, stressing that NATO was neither an anti-Russian alliance nor a strategic threat to Russia. Similarly, Celeste Wallander, Deputy Assistant Secretary of Defense for Russia, told the subcommittee that Russia made it clear that it wanted to cooperate with NATO despite differences over Ukraine and Georgia.[51]

Other officials provided further positive and reassuring signals. For example, Alexander Vershbow, Assistant Secretary of Defense for International

Security Affairs, told a hearing of the House Armed Services Committee that the Obama-Medvedev summit had gone better than anticipated, stressing agreements to allow shipments of both lethal and nonlethal cargoes across Russian airspace to resupply NATO forces in Afghanistan and pledges of cooperation on nuclear nonproliferation as examples. Vice Adm. James A. Winnefeld Jr., director for strategic plans and policy for the U.S. Joint Chiefs of Staff (JCS), told the committee that these and other summit agreements would improve military-to-military cooperation with the Russians and help reduce tendencies to see the U.S.-Russian military relationship in zero-sum terms. Vershbow also announced that a U.S. military team had traveled to Russia for discussions on the establishment of an early warning system in Russia to evaluate missile threats from places like Iran and North Korea. According to Vershbow, these discussions were partly intended to reduce paranoia and worst-case scenario assumptions among Russian elites about U.S. actions and intentions in Europe.[52]

At the same time, Vice President Joe Biden was dispatched to Georgia and Ukraine, where he delivered a number of key messages. In Kiev, Biden told his hosts, "As we reset the relationship with Russia, we reaffirm our commitment to an independent Ukraine."[53] Biden also renewed U.S. support for Ukraine's entry into NATO. However, he also urged Ukrainian leaders to end their factional in-fighting and commit to a package of political and economic reforms recommended by the International Monetary Fund and Western governments.[54] In Georgia, Biden sharply criticized Russia's military intervention and expressed U.S. support, but also stressed the U.S. view that Georgia could not pursue a military solution to the problem. He also urged speedier democratic reforms, and offered further U.S. support for Georgia's entry into NATO, saying, "We understand that Georgia wants to join NATO. We fully support that aspiration."[55]

Biden sparked controversy in his post-visit remarks to the press. In typical fashion, the vice president was especially candid, telling the *Wall Street Journal* that while it would be unwise to embarrass them publicly, Russia's poor economy gave its leaders little choice but to go along with the U.S. position on a START extension. As Biden put it, they "have a shrinking population base, they have a withering economy, they have a banking sector and structure that is not likely to be able to withstand the next 15 years, they're in a situation where the world is changing before them and they're clinging to something in the past that is not sustainable."[56] While the *Wall Street Journal* congratulated Biden for his candor in the controversial interview, the *Los Angeles Times* decried his remarks, albeit honest, as "appallingly ill-advised" and "counter-productive" to the president's goal of resetting U.S.-Russian relations.[57] Russian newspapers and Russian leaders alike also objected to Biden's remarks. Secretary Clinton tried to downplay Biden's remarks in an interview on the NBC program *Meet the Press*, where she noted that the Obama administration considered Russia a great power and said, "Every country faces challenges. We have our own challenges, Russia has their challenges. There are certain issues that Russia has to deal with on its own."[58]

In another signal that revealed the delicate balancing act in which the Obama administration was engaged, the State Department's daily press briefing on July 27, 2009, announced that the Obama administration was pursuing high-level reengagement discussions with the governments of China and India, with structured presidential and secretarial participation—just like the approach to the Russians at the Moscow Summit on July 6–8. Russian leaders interpreted this as a signal that closer U.S.-Chinese and U.S.-Indian relations would lessen the American need for closer ties with Russia, as well as the fact that Russia had not been singled out for a privileged relationship as many in Russia had perceived at the Moscow Summit.[59]

Russian leaders responded to this mixed bag of signals, assurances, carrots, and sticks with their own mixed bag. On the one hand, Medvedev called Obama on the phone on August 4 to wish him a happy birthday and to push the idea that both of them should order their negotiators to increase the pace of their work so START II could be ready in December.[60] Russian foreign minister Sergei Lavrov also asserted that U.S.-Russian differences over the Georgian war were resolved and would not impair U.S.-Russian relations, as indicated by the Moscow Summit in July.[61]

At the same time, Russian officials continued to take a more combative tone and assert their interests. For example, in spite of his positive assessment, Lavrov also asserted that Georgia was trying to destabilize the entire Caucasus region by inviting U.S. participation in the EU's mission monitoring the Georgia-Abkhazia-South Ossetia borders.[62] Russian deputy foreign minister Grigoriy Karasin criticized the U.S. decision to sell "defensive" arms to Georgia, noting Georgia's aggression of the past year and calling it "a strange way to promote democracy."[63] Prime Minister Putin visited Abkhazia (his first visit since Russia recognized Abkhazia's independence) and pledged Russian military support in the case of a future Georgian attack. He also urged the OSCE and UN to recognize Abkhazia's independence. Putin also announced a $463 million military assistance package to help safeguard the Abkhazia border with Georgia and $350 million in economic development aid to Abkhazia. He accused the United States of encouraging other states to recognize Georgia's claim to Abkhazia and South Ossetia.[64] Additionally, in early August Medvedev posted an open letter on his Kremlin Web site to Ukrainian president Viktor Yushchenko. In it he listed a number of Russian complaints against Ukraine, including its efforts to join NATO over Russian objections.[65] These and other statements prompted the Obama administration to deny that U.S. support for Georgia or Ukraine was aimed at Russia or involved lethal military assistance.[66]

Amidst this impasse, both presidents faced stirrings of domestic political opposition. For example, in Russia Medvedev faced signs of public concern. According to the Russian Public Opinion Research Center, a July 18–19 poll showed 54 percent of Russians expected U.S.-Russian relations to improve following the recently completed summit meeting in Moscow.[67] Similarly, on the anniversary of the war in Georgia, a poll showed that, while most respondents believed Western countries supported Georgia in an effort to push Russian influence out of the Transcaucasus region, for the first time slightly more Russians held Georgia to blame for the conflict (35 percent) than the United States (34 percent). Previous polls had put the number holding the United States to blame at 49 percent.[68] In the United States, rumblings from members of Congress signaled to the Obama administration that patience was ebbing and that more progress in resetting U.S.-Russian relations was desired. For example, Rep. Robert Wexler, D-Penn., chairman of the House Foreign Affairs subcommittee on Europe, pressed for progress on arms control negotiations while resisting Russian pressure in the region, and fellow committee member Rep. Dana Rohrabacker, R-Calif., stressed that Russia had been taken for granted since the end of the cold war and relations needed to be mended.[69]

Phase IV: ABM Reset—An Opening and Opportunity, August–October 2009

By the late summer, the Obama administration was forced to come to grips with the complicated realities of U.S.-Russian relations and difficulties in overcoming the differences that had plagued the relationship since the heady optimism at the end of the cold war. With prospects for a quick "reset" fading, the administration considered options to spur progress and produce tangible gains. After intense deliberation, Obama elected to change U.S. missile defense plans to better address Iran's threat and capabilities. Driven by new intelligence and the Defense Department's assessment and recommendation, the decision also carried the prospect of focusing Russian leaders on two areas of potential cooperation that would help make the reset a reality: START II negotiations and cooperation to address Iranian nuclear programs.

According to press reports, the missile defense shift was "years in the making,"[70] and U.S. officials strenuously denied that they were simply accommodating Russian objections.[71] However, Obama also noted, "If the byproduct of it is that the Russians feel a little less paranoid and are now willing to work more effectively with us to deal with threats like ballistic missiles from Iran or nuclear development in Iran, you know, then that's a bonus."[72]

With review and discussion stretching back into the early months of the administration, the critical period occurred in August and early September of 2009. At that time, new and updated intelligence assessments on Iran were provided to top officials in the White House, Defense and State Departments, and elsewhere. This intelligence indicated that Iran had experienced expensive setbacks in its ICBM research and development program and was opting instead to produce larger numbers of short- and medium-range missiles that, when launched in large numbers, could threaten Europe and the Middle East. The new intelligence on the setbacks in the Iranian ICBM program caused Secretary Gates to reverse his prior endorsement of the Bush administration's Poland/Czech-based ABM system. He also had an ally in the new under secretary of state for arms control and international security, Ellen Tauscher. While a member of Congress, Tauscher had used her position as a subcommittee chair on the House Armed Services Committee to stop authorizations for funding the Poland/Czech-based ABM system until the Defense Department produced successful tests of the system.[73] As Gates put it, he did not want the United States committed to a defense system against Iranian ICBMs when the real threat was Iranian shorter-range missiles.[74]

Obama and his top foreign policy advisers met on September 10 to consider the new intelligence and review missile defense plans, while also considering a 2006 study commissioned by Gates in his capacity as defense secretary for the Bush administration. At that meeting, officials discussed an "upper tier" system that combined long-range interceptor missiles in California and Alaska with ten interceptor missiles in Poland, and a "lower tier" system that featured a combination of shorter-range, already deployed, or capable of deployment missiles: the Aegis seaborne SM-3 missiles, the Terminal High Altitude Air Defense System (THAAD) about to be deployed to Israel, and Patriot antimissile batteries already deployed. Defense Department experts recommended the "lower tier" system, as its components were considerably cheaper and capable of being deployed years earlier. In the meeting, Marine Gen. James Cartright, vice chairman of the JCS, raised objections to the "upper tier" system, based on his prior service in charge of the Pentagon's missile and space weapons programs. He believed the Defense Department was about to embark on a very expensive investment to meet an Iranian ICBM threat that might never materialize. He was a persuasive opponent of the status quo, as was Defense Secretary Gates.[75] After discussion, the president made the decision to abandon the planned "upper tier" system in favor of the "lower tier" option based on more mobile systems located closer to Iran and the Middle East, and both Poland and the Czech Republic were so advised, although they had been consulted on the matter earlier.[76] The president's announcement of the decision came on September 17 (see Box 6.1).

Although the official line was that the missile defense decision was not linked to Russian concerns or the desire to facilitate progress in U.S.-Russian relations, privately U.S. administration officials acknowledged the connections. In particular, policy makers expressed their hopes that Russia would cooperate on UN sanctions directed against Iran's nuclear program and, especially, that the decision to cancel the ABM system in Poland/Czech Republic would facilitate progress on a START II Treaty.[77]

If so, the administration initially appeared to be swiftly rewarded. Medvedev immediately praised the decision and said, "We will work together to develop effective measures against the risks of missile proliferation, measures that take into account the interests and concerns of all sides and ensure equal security for all countries in European territory."[78] According to observers, the Obama decision to scrap the ABM system in Europe opened the door for Russian cooperation on the new START agreement and nuclear nonproliferation, which Russian elites saw as linked. Russian commentators expected the Medvedev regime to reciprocate quickly, and they praised the Obama administration for taking Russian views into consideration. Furthermore, Russian Foreign Ministry sources said the Americans expected Russia to support tougher UN sanctions on Iran and to stop delivery of the S-300 antiaircraft missile defense system to Iran.[79] As military expert Viktor Baranets explained on a Russian government-controlled television news program, in addition to pressure for Russian help on Iran:

> We can say that today is an historic day because a real step towards real reset was made. . . . By taking this step, which we welcome, Obama at the same time has put us in a difficult situation. Such steps never come free of charge. Naturally, Russia will have to pay for it in a big way. I can't rule out concessions in the nuclear missile department.[80]

Box 6.1 President Obama on Revising U.S. ABM Plans in Europe,
September 17, 2009

The best way to responsibly advance our security and the security of our allies is to deploy a missile defense system that best responds to the threats that we face and that utilizes technology that is both proven and cost-effective.

In keeping with that commitment, and a congressionally mandated review, I ordered a comprehensive assessment of our missile defense program in Europe. And after an extensive process, I have approved the unanimous recommendations of my Secretary of Defense and my Joint Chiefs of Staff to strengthen America's defenses against ballistic missile attack.

This new approach will provide capabilities sooner, build on proven systems, and offer greater defenses against the threat of missile attack than the 2007 European missile defense program.

This decision was guided by two principal factors. First, we have updated our intelligence assessment of Iran's missile programs, which emphasizes the threat posed by Iran's short- and medium-range missiles, which are capable of reaching Europe. There's no substitute for Iran complying with its international obligations regarding its nuclear program, and we, along with our allies and partners, will continue to pursue strong diplomacy to ensure that Iran lives up to these international obligations. But this new ballistic missile defense program will best address the threat posed by Iran's ongoing ballistic missile defense program.

Second, we have made specific and proven advances in our missile defense technology, particularly with regard to land- and sea-based interceptors and the sensors that support them. Our new approach will, therefore, deploy technologies that are proven and cost-effective and that counter the current threat, and do so sooner than the previous program. Because our approach will be phased and adaptive, we will retain the flexibility to adjust and enhance our defenses as the threat and technology continue to evolve.

To put it simply, our new missile defense architecture in Europe will provide stronger, smarter, and swifter defenses of American forces and America's allies. It is more comprehensive than the previous program; it deploys capabilities that are proven and cost-effective; and it sustains and builds upon our commitment to protect the U.S. homeland against long-range ballistic missile threats; and it ensures and enhances the protection of all our NATO allies.

This approach is also consistent with NATO missile—NATO's missile defense efforts and provides opportunities for enhanced international collaboration going forward. We will continue to work cooperatively with our close friends and allies, the Czech Republic and Poland, who had agreed to host elements of the previous program. I've spoken to the Prime Ministers of both the Czech Republic and Poland about this decision and reaffirmed our deep and close ties. Together we are committed to a broad range of cooperative efforts to strengthen our collective defense, and we are bound by the solemn commitment of NATO's Article V that an attack on one is an attack on all.

We've also repeatedly made clear to Russia that its concerns about our previous missile defense programs were entirely unfounded. Our clear and consistent focus has been the threat posed by Iran's ballistic missile program, and that continues to be our focus and the basis of the program that we're announcing today.

In confronting that threat, we welcome Russians' cooperation to bring its missile defense capabilities into a broader defense of our common strategic interests, even as we continue to—we continue our shared efforts to end Iran's illicit nuclear program.

Sources: "Remarks by the President on Strengthening Missile Defense in Europe," Diplomatic Reception Room, White House, September 17, 2009, on *Johnson's Russia List*, September 19, 2009, www.cdi.org/russia/johnson. See also "Fact Sheet on U.S. Missile Defense Policy: A 'Phased, Adaptive Approach' for Missile Defense in Europe," White House Office of the Press Secretary, September 17, 2009, on *Johnson's Russia List*, September 19, 2009, www.cdi.org/russia/johnson.

Moreover, Russia's *Interfax* reported that Russian leaders had decided to reverse their decision to place short-range Iskander antiaircraft missiles and strategic bombers in Kaliningrad, near Poland. Polish defense minister Radoslaw Sikorski applauded this decision as a significant improvement in Poland's security situation, and he welcomed the U.S. decision to send Patriot missile batteries to Poland instead.[81]

Just a few days after the announcement of the policy change, both Obama and Medvedev traveled to New York to address the opening session of the UN General Assembly. During their stay, they met privately at the Waldorf Astoria Hotel. Media reports indicated that, in their private meeting, Medvedev agreed to greater UN pressure on Iran, which Russian pundits interpreted as a response to Obama's abandonment of the Polish/Czech ABM system.[82] According to Medvedev, "We believe we need to help Iran to make a right decision. As to . . . sanctions, Russia's belief is very simple, and I stated it recently. Sanctions rarely lead to productive results. But in some cases sanctions are inevitable. Finally, it is a matter of choice." Furthermore, two days later, in an address at the University of Pittsburgh, Medvedev said Russia was ready to significantly cut its number of nuclear delivery vehicles and that the time may have come for tougher sanctions on Iran.[83] White House officials were extremely pleased with his remarks, seeing a shift in position they had long desired. According to the National Security Council's Russia expert, Michael McFaul, "To me, that's a very big change in their position. I can't improve on what President Medvedev said.... It was not that long ago where we had very divergent definitions of the threat and definitions of our strategic objectives vis-à-vis Iran."[84] In a press conference after their meeting, McFaul told reporters that he believed Obama and Medvedev now shared a two-track approach, with diplomacy being the preferred track but with coercive sanctions as a fallback in case Iran did not cooperate.[85]

There were notes of caution, however. For example, while Prime Minister Putin called Obama's decision on the ABM system in Europe brave, he also added that he now expected other brave decisions from Obama, such as ending all trade barriers between the countries and championing Russia's joint bid with Kazakhstan and Belarus to join the WTO.[86] Russian military experts agreed that an ABM system based on the U.S. Navy's Aegis system would not threaten Russia, but they also expressed concerns that technological upgrades in the weapons and radars suggested by Obama could potentially threaten Russian interests, particularly if they involved space-based weapons. Similarly, although Russian legislators expressed appreciation for the decision, calling it a victory for common sense, they also warned that no deal had been struck with the United States in this regard and that reciprocal Russian policy shifts regarding Iran should not be expected in Washington.[87] Focusing on Russia's increasing reliance on its nuclear forces for security as it downsized its conventional forces, one Russian defense analyst went so far as to call Obama's linkage of Russia to his calls for a nuclear free world "idiotic.... They strengthen those in Russia who said you can't believe him—that he is laying traps for us."[88] And in October, Russian officials expressed concern that the possible use of an early-warning radar in Ukraine as part of an anti-Iranian missile defense system could hurt U.S.-Russian relations.[89]

Phase V: (Protracted) Endgame, November 2009–April 2010

In the wake of the missile defense decision, the Obama administration focused on efforts to conclude the START II agreement as the central and most tangible prize of efforts to reset U.S.-Russian relations. However, hopes that it would be completed by December, when the earlier START provisions expired, swiftly disappeared.

Negotiations moved forward in November when Russian and U.S. negotiators met for an eighth time to work on START II. According to Russia's chief of the General Staff, Gen. Nikolai Makarov, one stumbling point was the fact that the U.S. side wanted to continue on-site monitoring of the construction of Russia's Topol and Topol-M missile systems. The Russians saw such inspections as an affront that had been forced on Russia in the last agreement, and so the Russian side resisted on-site monitoring in Russia unless similar on-site monitoring was allowed in the United States.[90] According to one account, the Russians stalled in the late fall and early winter, convinced that Obama "would be so eager to have a new treaty by the time he traveled to Oslo later that month to accept his Nobel Peace Prize that he would accept concessions."[91] Even direct meetings between Obama and Medvedev while both were attending the Asia-Pacific Economic Cooperation (APEC) meetings a short time later in Singapore failed to produce agreement. The two could not break the deadlock, and Obama would not concede in advance of his trip to Oslo.[92]

Obama and Medvedev met again in December during the UN climate change conference in Copenhagen. Accord to press accounts, the two leaders came very close to resolving their key differences. They agreed that:

> They would cut deployed warheads to 1,550 per side, down from the current limit of 2,200. They would cut deployed heavy bombers and missiles to 700 each. They would conduct 18 inspections a year, up from 10 originally proposed by Moscow. Even on the technical telemetry issue, they found agreement. "Let's just do it on an annual basis," Mr. Obama proposed spontaneously. "I don't see any problem with that," Mr. Medvedev said. Mr. Obama turned to his own advisers and asked, "You guys good with that?"[93]

Optimistic about what appeared to be a critical breakthrough, U.S. negotiators followed with a trip to Moscow in January to address the remaining issues. During these talks, which included Gen. James L. Jones, the national security adviser; Adm. Mike Mullen, the chairman of the Joint Chiefs of Staff; Rose Gottemoeller, the lead START II negotiator; Michael McFaul, the president's Russia adviser; and Gary Samore, the nonproliferation adviser, the two sides agreed to cap launchers at eight hundred each, and the U.S. team left believing they had completed the agreement. When they discussed the results with President Obama on their return, they reported "we're done sir."[94]

Yet another delay ensued. Returning again to the issue of missile defense, the day after what had appeared to be the final breakthrough, a lead Russian negotiator told Rose Gottemoeller that any agreement had to include a commitment to lock missile defense plans to their current status. According to one account, "The renewed dispute intensified two weeks later when Romania unexpectedly announced that it would host interceptors from the new system, putting the reconfigured missile defense system right in Russia's geopolitical backyard."[95] These delays apparently also resulted in a conversation between Clinton and Lavrov, in which she urged the Russian foreign minister to speed up the pace of negotiations and help break the impasse.[96] However, on February 24, 2010, Medvedev telephoned Obama to raise the issue and insist that a joint statement on missile defense be included in the treaty. Obama reportedly objected angrily, "Dmitri, we agreed. . . . We can't do this. If it means we're going to walk away from this treaty and not get it done, so be it. But we're not going to go down this path."[97] According to Dmitri V. Trenin, director of the Carnegie Moscow Center, Russian leaders again calculated that Obama would agree to their demands in order to secure the agreement in advance of international nuclear summit meetings planned for April. "They believed Obama could be put under pressure and concessions could be extracted from him. . . . He needed the treaty more than the Russians in the short term."[98]

They calculated incorrectly. Instead, Obama dispatched negotiators for further talks. In mid-March the deal was reached, with the two sides agreeing to issue separate statements on missile defense at the signing ceremony. According to one account:

> Ultimately, Russia backed down. Mr. Medvedev called Mr. Obama on March 13, and Secretary of State Hillary Rodham Clinton then traveled to Moscow. Negotiators finished drafting their separate statements on Tuesday, with Russia warning that it reserved the right to withdraw from the treaty if it deemed American missile defenses a threat, while the United States said it would build the defenses as it saw fit but was not making a target of Russia.[99]

Conclusion: Reset?

On April 8, 2010, Presidents Obama and Medvedev met in Prague and signed a new START treaty. The agreement, to cover a ten-year period from its entry into force, would reduce the nuclear arsenals of each side by about one-third when approved by the legislatures of both countries; it included verification measures and limits on launchers. At the signing ceremony, the two presidents met for nearly ninety minutes to discuss a wide range of additional issues, including civil unrest in Kyrgyzstan and sanctions against Iran.[100] The hope for progress and cooperation on these and other matters in the wake of the successful nuclear accord was high. In a gesture fraught with symbolism and what appeared to be a sign of good faith, Russia invited U.S. troops to participate for the first time in Moscow's annual Victory Day parade on May 9, celebrating the Russian victory over German fascism in World War II.[101] Thus, more than a year after they were initiated, a real reset in U.S.-Russian relations seemed possible. In a telephone conversation near the end of the fifteen-month marathon, Presidents Medvedev and Obama reportedly congratulated themselves on their breakthrough: " 'If you want something done right,' Mr. Medvedev began in English, and Mr. Obama finished his thought: 'you do it yourself.' "[102]

Key Actors

Joe Biden   U.S. vice president whose candid comments on the weakness of the Russian state and society jeopardized the warming relationship between the two regimes.

George Bush, Bill Clinton, George W. Bush   U.S. presidents who presided over a deteriorating U.S.-Russian relationship.

Hillary Rodham Clinton and Sergei Lavrov   The U.S. secretary of state and Russian foreign minister, respectively, who pressed for each country's national interests in the START II negotiations.

Robert Gates   The U.S. defense secretary who said setbacks in Iran's long-range missile program allowed him to change his previous support for a missile defense system in Poland and the Czech Republic to favor a more mobile system located closer to Iran.

Dmitry Medvedev   Russian president who reached out to the United States to change the direction of the relationship.

Barack Obama   U.S. president who pledged to change the U.S.-Russian relationship.

Boris Yeltsin, Vladimir Putin   Russian presidents who presided over a deteriorating U.S.-Russian relationship.

Notes

1. For more on this period, see Robert H. Donaldson and Joseph L. Nogee, *The Foreign Policy of Russia: Changing Systems, Enduring Interests*, 4th ed. (Armonk, N.Y.: M. E. Sharpe, 2009), and Stephen K. Wegren and Dale R. Herspring, eds., *After Putin's Russia: Past Imperfect, Future Uncertain*, 4th ed. (Lanham, Md.: Rowman and Littlefield, 2009).

2. James Martin, Center for Nonproliferation Studies at the Monterey Institute of International Studies, "Russia: Gore-Primakov (Gore-Chernomyrdin) Commission (GCC)," Nuclear Threat Initiative Web site, www.nti.org/db/nisprofs/Russia/forasst/otherusg/gcc.htm.

3. "Fact Sheet—Bosnia: NATO Involvement in the Balkan Crisis," Fact Sheet 95/11/01, Bureau of Public Affairs, U.S. Department of State Web site, http://dosfan.lib.uic.edu/ERC/bureaus/eur/releases/951101BosniaNATO.html.

4. BBC News, "World: Europe: Russian Troops Camp in Pristina," June 12, 1999, BBC Web site, http://news.bbc.co.uk/2/hi/europe/367490.stm.

5. "NATO Enlargement," NATO Web site, www.nato.int/cps/en/natolive/topics_49212.htm.

6. BBC News, "World: Europe: Russian Troops Camp in Pristina," June 12, 1999, BBC Web site, http://news.bbc.co.uk/2/hi/europe/367490.stm.

7. "NATO Enlargement," NATO Web site, www.nato.int/cps/en/natolive/topics_49212.htm. For more on this, see Ronald D. Asmus, *A Little War That Shook the World: Georgia, Russia, and the Future of the West* (New York: Palgrave Macmillan, 2010).

8. Chris Baldwin, Reuters, "Putin Says Russia Threatened by 'Unipolar World,'" November 4, 2007, www.reuters.com/article/idUSL0449803320071104.

9. "The War in Iraq: Legal Issues," Human and Constitutional Rights Resource Web site, www.hrcr.org/hottopics/Iraq.html.

10. Jamie McIntyre and Ryan Chilcote, "Pentagon: Russia Fed U.S. War Plans to Iraq; Russian Official: Report Unfounded," CNN, March 26, 2006, www.cnn.com/2006/WORLD/meast/03/25/saddam.russia/index.html.

11. "Target Iran: Countdown Timeline," Global Security Web site, www.globalsecurity.org/military/ops/iran-timeline.htm.

12. William Douglas and Jonathan S. Landay, "Putin Expands Missile Defense Offer but Division Remains," McClatchy Newspapers, July 2, 2007, www.mcclatchydc.com/2007/07/02/17556/putin-expands-missile-defense.html.

13. Peter Baker, "U.S.-Russia Relations Chilly Amid Transition—Stalled Nuclear Pact Is Just One Sign of Unease," *Washington Post*, March 1, 2008, A1.

14. Peter Baker, "Aiming to Ease Tensions, without U.S.-Russia Pact," *Washington Post*, April 6, 2008, A20.

15. Kevin Sullivan, "Overseas, Excitement over Obama; In Presumptive Nominee, Many See Chance for New Direction and New Attitude," *Washington Post*, June 5, 2008, A10.

16. Peter Finn, "Russian Air, Ground Forces Strike Georgia—Military Action Follows Georgian Offensive to Reassert Control over Separatist South Ossetia," *Washington Post*, August 9, 2008, A1.

17. Peter Finn, "Delegation Led by U.S. Senators Detained Briefly at Russian Airport," *Washington Post*, August 29, 2005, A16; Joby Warrick, "U.S. to Aid Ukraine in Countering Bioweapons—Pact Focuses on Security at Labs—Russia Apologizes for Delay of Senate Delegation," *Washington Post*, August 30, 2005, A11.

18. Peter Finn, "Russia Pumps Tens of Millions into Burnishing Image Abroad," *Washington Post*, March 6, 2008, A1.

19. "Analysis: Russia Ready to Work with NATO," BBC News, February 2, 2009, www.bbc.co.uk/.

20. "Medvedev Calls for Better Relations with U.S., Ex-Soviet Countries," *PRIME-TASS* report, September 25, 2009, on *Johnson's Russia List*, September 25, 2009, www.cdi.org/russia/johnson.

21. Jim Hoagland, "Obama vs. Clenched Fists," *Washington Post*, February 22, 2009, A19.

22. Craig Whitlock, " 'Reset' Sought on Relations with Russia, Biden Says," *Washington Post*, February 8, 2009, A18.

23. David S. Broder, "Biden Is Surprised at Criticism of Plan," *Washington Post*, February 11, 2009, A6.

24. Karen DeYoung, "U.S. Envoy Indicated Flexibility with Russia on Missile Defense," *Washington Post*, February 14, 2009, A8; Jackson Diehl, "A 'Reset' That Doesn't Compute," *Washington Post*, February 23, 2009, A13.

25. Michael A. Fletcher, "Obama Makes Overtures to Russia on Missile Defense," *Washington Post*, March 3, 2009, A2.

26. Philip P. Pan, and Karen DeYoung, "Russia Signaling Interest in Deal on Iran— Still, Obama Effort Faces Obstacles," *Washington Post*, March 18, 2009, A10.

27. Karen DeYoung, "Obama Team Seeks to Redefine Russia Ties—U.S. Aiming at Strategic Goals with Proposals on Arms Reduction, Missile Defense, Economic Support," *Washington Post*, March 4, 2009, A11.

28. Michael A. Fletcher, "Obama Makes Overtures to Russia on Missile Defense," *Washington Post*, March 3, 2009, A2.

29. "No Deal—Barack Obama and Dmitry Medvedev Offer Welcome Clarity on Iran and Missile Defense," *Washington Post*, March 4, 2009, A14.

30. Paul Reynolds, "Pressing the U.S.-Russia Reset Button," BBC News, March 5, 2009, www.bbc.co.uk/.

31. "Button Gaffe Embarrasses Clinton," BBC News, March 7, 2009, www.bbc .co.uk/.

32. Glenn Kessler, "Clinton 'Resets' Russian Ties—and Language," *Washington Post*, March 7, 2009, A6.

33. Philip P. Pan, and Karen DeYoung, "Russia Signaling Interest in Deal on Iran— Still, Obama Effort Faces Obstacles," *Washington Post*, March 18, 2009, A10.

34. "RF, U.S. Have Disagreements on START Talks—Gen. Staff Chief," *ITAR-TASS* report, November 12, 2009, on *Johnson's Russia List,* November 13, 2009, www.cdi.org/ russia/johnson.

35. Philip P. Pan, "Mevedev 'Counting on a Reset' with U.S.—Russia Again Raises Missile Shield Issue," *Washington Post*, March 21, 2009, A10.

36. Anne Applebaum, "For Russia, More than a 'Reset,' " *Washington Post*, March 24, 2009, A13.

37. "Clinton Urges Russia to 'Push Hard' for Arms Treaty," *Ria Novosti*, February 24, 2010, http://en.rian.ru.

38. Jonathan Weisman and Peter Spiegel, "Cost Concerns Propelled U.S. Missile Pivot: Obama Decision Is Aimed at Saving Pentagon Funds While Helping Nonproliferation Push; Shift Was Years in the Making," *Wall Street Journal*, September 19, 2009, on *Johnson's Russia List*, September 20, 2009, www.cdi.org/russia/johnson.

39. See Jackson Diehl, "A World of Trouble for Obama," *Washington Post*, April 20, 2009, A15; "Another Summer in Georgia—Once Again Russia Masses Troops and Stages Provocations," *Washington Post*, June 4, 2009, A20; Misha Dzhindzhikhashvili, Associated Press, "U.S.-Russian Tensions Rise over Georgia," *Washington Post*, July 14, 2009, www.washingtonpost.com/.

40. Tom Esslemont, "UN Monitors to Leave Georgia," *BBC News*, July 15, 2009, www.bbc.co.uk/.

41. Misha Dzhindzhikhashvili, Associated Press, "U.S.-Russian Tensions Rise over Georgia," *Washington Post*, July 14, 2009, www.washingtonpost.com/.

42. David Ignatius, "What a 'Reset' Can't Fix," *Washington Post*, July 5, 2009, A19.

43. "Why Obama Visited Russia: Experts Claim That the Main Objective of U.S. President Barack Obama's Visit to Moscow Was to Identify a Key Counterpart to Deal With," *Argumenty Nedeli* 31, August 7, 2009, on *Johnson's Russia List*, August 7, 2009, www.cdi.org/russia/johnson; "President Dmitry Medvedev Told CNN He Felt Comfortable Communicating with Barack Obama," *ITAR-TASS* Report, September 20, 2009, on *Johnson's Russia List*, September 21, 2009, www.cdi.org/russia/johnson; Michael A. Fletcher and Philip P. Pan, "U.S.-Russia Summit Brings Series of Advances," *Washington Post*, July 8, 2009, A6.

44. Jim Hoagland, "The Two Faces of Russia," *Washington Post*, September 20, 2009, on *Johnson's Russia List*, September 20, 2009, www.cdi.org/russia/johnson.

45. Misha Dzhindzhikhashvili, Associated Press, "U.S.-Russian Tensions Rise over Georgia," *Washington Post*, July 14, 2009, www.washingtonpost.com.

46. David J. Kramer, "Resetting U.S.-Russian Relations: It Takes Two," *The Washington Quarterly* 33 (1, January 2010), www.twq.com/10january/index.cfm?id=375.

47. Gregory L. White and Marc Champion, "No Quick Thaw in Russia Ties," *Wall Street Journal*, September 18, 2009, on *Johnson's Russia List*, September 19, 2009, www.cdi.org/russia/johnson.

48. Misha Dzhindzhikhashvili, Associated Press, "U.S.-Russian Tensions Rise over Georgia," *Washington Post*, July 14, 2009, www.washingtonpost.com; Tom Esslemont, "UN Monitors to Leave Georgia," *BBC News*, July 15, 2009, www.bbc.co.uk/.

49. Philip P. Pan, "Georgia's Saakashvili Seeking U.S. Weapons to Deter Russia," *Washington Post*, July 22, 2009, A8.

50. Samuel Charap, "Anxiety and Recommitment in Russia's Neighborhood," Center for American Progress, July 21, 2009, www.americanprogress.org.

51. Associated Press, "Obama Administration Says Russia Could Join NATO," July 29, 2009, www.ap.org/.

52. Dan Robinson, "U.S. Lawmakers Concerned About 'Reset' of U.S.-Russian Relations," *Voice of America*, July 31, 2009, on *Johnson's Russia List*, July 31, 2009, www.cdi.org/russia/johnson; Walter Pincus, "U.S. Takes Steps to Boost Security Cooperation with Russia," *Washington Post*, July 31, 2009, A17.

53. "Mr. Biden's Diplomacy—The Vice President Pays Important Visits to Ukraine and Georgia," *Washington Post*, July 25, 2009, A16.

54. Sabina Zawadzki, Reuters, "Stop Infighting, Biden Tells Ukraine's Leaders," July 22, 2009, www.reuters.com/.

55. "Mr. Biden's Diplomacy—The Vice President Pays Important Visits to Ukraine and Georgia," *Washington Post*, July 25, 2009, A16. See also Philip P. Pan, "Biden Offers Georgia Solidarity—Russian Invasion in 2008 Decried," *Washington Post*, July 24, 2009, A12.

56. "Biden Takes Aim at Russia," *Washington Post*, July 26, 2009, A8.

57. "Biden's Russia Blunder," *Los Angeles Times*, July 28, 2009, www.latimes.com.

58. Lynn Berry, Associated Press, "Vice President Biden Hits Nerve in Russia," July 27, 2009, www.ap.org/.

59. Yevgeniy Aleksandrovich Klochikhin, "From Multipolar World to Multipartner One," *Nezavisimaya Gazeta*, August 3, 2009, on *Johnson's Russia List*, August 3, 2009, www.cdi.org/russia/johnson.

60. "Russian News Agency Carries Fuller Account of Medvedev-Obama Phone Conversation," *Interfax* report on *Johnson's Russia List*, August 5, 2009, www.cdi.org/russia/johnson.

61. "Georgia Issue No Longer Impedes RF-West Relations-Lavrov," *ITAR-TASS* report on *Johnson's Russia List*, August 5, 2009, www.cdi.org/russia/johnson.

62. "Russia Accuses Georgia of Trying to Destabilize Caucasus," *Ria Novosti* report on *Johnson's Russia List*, August 5, 2009, www.cdi.org/russia/johnson.

63. "Russia Will Not Shut Eyes to USA Supplying Arms to Georgia—Top Diplomat," *Interfax* report on *Johnson's Russia List*, August 5, 2009, www.cdi.org/russia/johnson.

64. Indira Bartsits, "Putin Promises Military Backing for Abkhazia," *Agence France-Presse*, August 12, 2009, on *Johnson's Russia List*, August 12, 2009, www.cdi.org/russia/johnson; Philip P. Pan, "Putin Visits Breakaway Georgian Region, Unveils Plan for Military Base," *Washington Post*, August 13, 2009, A8.

65. David J. Kramer, "Resetting U.S.-Russian Relations: It Takes Two," *The Washington Quarterly* 33, no. 1 (January 2010), www.twq.com/10january/index.cfm?id=375.

66. E.g., "DoD Official on Military Cooperation with Georgia," *Civil Georgia* report on *Johnson's Russia List*, August 5, 2009, www.cdi.org/russia/johnson; "U.S. Renders Military Assistance to Georgia but Does Not Supply Weapons—Vershbow," *Interfax* report on *Johnson's Russia List*, August 12, 2009, www.cdi.org/russia/johnson.

67. *Interfax* report on *Johnson's Russia List*, July 22, 2009, www.cdi.org/russia/johnson.

68. "Russians Blame Georgia, USA for War over South Ossetia—Poll," *Interfax* report on *Johnson's Russia List*, August 4, 2009, www.cdi.org/russia/johnson.

69. Dan Robinson, "U.S. Lawmakers Concerned About 'Reset' of U.S.-Russian Relations," *Voice of America*, July 31, 2009, on *Johnson's Russia List*, July 31, 2009, www.cdi.org/russia/johnson; Robert Wexler, "Opening Statement: The Reset Button Has Been Pushed: Kicking Off a New Era in U.S.-Russian Relations," Hearings before the House Foreign Affairs Subcommittee on Europe, July 28, 2009, on *Johnson's Russia List*, July 29, 2009, www.cdi.org/russia/johnson.

70. Jonathan Weisman and Peter Spiegel, "Cost Concerns Propelled U.S. Missile Pivot: Obama Decision Is Aimed at Saving Pentagon Funds While Helping Nonproliferation Push; Shift Was Years in the Making," *Wall Street Journal*, September 19, 2009, on *Johnson's Russia List*, September 20, 2009, www.cdi.org/russia/johnson.

71. Robert M. Gates, "A Better Missile Defense for a Safer Europe," *New York Times*, September 20, 2009, on *Johnson's Russia List*, September 20, 2009, www.cdi.org/russia/johnson; "Remarks by the President on Strengthening Missile Defense in Europe," Diplomatic Reception Room, White House, September 17, 2009, on *Johnson's Russia List*, September 19, 2009, www.cdi.org/russia/johnson.

72. Ben Feller, Associated Press, "Obama: Missile Defense Decision Not About Russia," September 20, 2009, on *Johnson's Russia List*, September 20, 2009, www.cdi.org/russia/johnson.

73. Jonathan Weisman and Peter Spiegel, "Cost Concerns Propelled U.S. Missile Pivot: Obama Decision Is Aimed at Saving Pentagon Funds While Helping Nonproliferation Push; Shift Was Years in the Making," *Wall Street Journal*, September 19, 2009, on *Johnson's Russia List*, September 20, 2009, www.cdi.org/russia/johnson.

74. Robert M. Gates, "A Better Missile Defense for a Safer Europe," *New York Times*, September 20, 2009, on *Johnson's Russia List*, September 20, 2009, www.cdi.org/russia/johnson.

75. Jonathan Weisman and Peter Spiegel, "Cost Concerns Propelled U.S. Missile Pivot: Obama Decision Is Aimed at Saving Pentagon Funds While Helping Nonproliferation Push; Shift Was Years in the Making," *Wall Street Journal*, September 19, 2009, on *Johnson's Russia List*, September 20, 2009, www.cdi.org/russia/johnson.

76. "Report: U.S. to Scrap E. Europe Missile Shield Bases," *Agence France-Presse*, August 27, 2009, on *Johnson's Russia List*, August 27, 2009, www.cdi.org/russia/johnson; Jonathan Weisman and Peter Spiegel, "Cost Concerns Propelled U.S. Missile Pivot: Obama Decision Is Aimed at Saving Pentagon Funds While Helping Nonproliferation Push; Shift Was Years in the Making," *Wall Street Journal*, September 19, 2009, on *Johnson's Russia List*, September 20, 2009, www.cdi.org/russia/johnson.

77. Gregory L. White and Marc Champion, "No Quick Thaw in Russia Ties," *Wall Street Journal*, September 18, 2009, on *Johnson's Russia List*, September 19, 2009, www.cdi.org/russia/johnson; Mary Beth Sheridan and Philip P. Pan, "Obama Missile Decision May Smooth U.S.-Russia Arms Talks," *Washington Post*, September 21, 2009, A7.

78. Philip P. Pan, "A Cautious Russia Praises Obama Move," *Washington Post*, September 18, 2009, on *Johnson's Russia List*, September 19, 2009, www.cdi.org/russia/johnson.

79. Vladimir Soloviov, Alexander Gabuyev, and Nargiz Asadova, "Curtailment of the ABM System in Europe Requires a Symmetric Response from Russia," *Kommersant*, September 18, 2009, on *Johnson's Russia List*, September 19, 2009, www.cdi.org/russia/johnson; "ROAR: New Bargaining Looms as U.S. Scraps Missile Shield Plan," *Russia Today*, September 18, 2009, www.russiatoday.com.

80. BBC Monitoring, "Expert Ponders Price Russia May Pay for U.S. Decision on ABM," Center TV, September 20, 2009, on *Johnson's Russia List*, September 19, 2009, www.cdi.org/russia/johnson.

81. "Russia's Plan to Abandon Missile Project Good for Poland—Defence Minister," PAP (Polish Agency Press), September 18, 2009, on *Johnson's Russia List*, September 20, 2009, www.cdi.org/russia/johnson; Gleb Bryanski, Reuters, "Russia's Putin Hails U.S. Shield Move, Calls for More," September 18, 2009, on *Johnson's Russia List*, September 19, 2009, www.cdi.org/russia/johnson.

82. Andrei Terekhov, "Dmitry Mevedev's Response: Russia Appeared to Have Promised Washington Support in Dealing with Iran," *Nezavisimaya Gazeta*, September 25, 2009, on *Johnson's Russia List*, September 25, 2009, www.cdi.org/russia/johnson.

83. "Medvedev Calls for Better Relations with U.S., Ex-Soviet Countries," *PRIME-TASS* report, September 25, 2009, on *Johnson's Russia List*, September 25, 2009, www.cdi.org/russia/johnson.

84. Josh Gerstein, "W.H. Hails Russia/Iran Breakthrough," www.politico.com, September 23, 2009, on *Johnson's Russia List*, September 25, 2009, www.cdi.org/russia/johnson.

85. "Press Briefing by Gary Samore, National Security Council Coordinator for Arms Control and Non-Proliferation; Ambassador Alex Wolff, Deputy Permanent Representative to the United Nations; and Mike McFaul, Senior Director for Russian Affairs on Thursday's UN Security Council Meeting and the President's Meeting Today with President Medvedev of Russia," The White House, Office of the Press Secretary, September 23, 2009, on *Johnson's Russia List*, September 25, 2009, www.cdi.org/russia/johnson.

86. Gleb Bryanski, Reuters, "Russia's Putin Hails U.S. Shield Move, Calls for More," September 18, 2009, on *Johnson's Russia List*, September 19, 2009, www.cdi.org/russia/johnson.

87. Philip P. Pan, "A Cautious Russia Praises Obama Move," *Washington Post*, September 18, 2009 on *Johnson's Russia List*, September 19, 2009, www.cdi.org/russia/johnson.

88. Jim Hoagland, "Nuclear Pushback," *Washington Post*, September 27, 2009, A2.

89. Reuters, "Russia," *Washington Post*, October 16, 2009, A10.

90. "RF, U.S. Have Disagreements on START Talks—Gen. Staff Chief," *ITAR-TASS* report, November 12, 2009, on *Johnson's Russia List*, November 13, 2009, www.cdi.org/russia/johnson; Peter Baker, "Twists and Turns on the Way to Arms Pact with Russia," *New York Times*, March 26, 2010, www.nytimes.com/2010/03/27/world/europe/27start.html.

91. Baker, "Twists and Turns on the Way to Arms Pact with Russia."

92. "Medvedev, Obama to Continue Efforts to Settle START Issue—Official," *ITAR-TASS* report on *Johnson's Russia List*, November 13, 2009, www.cdi.org/russia/johnson.

93. Baker, "Twists and Turns on the Way to Arms Pact with Russia."

94. Ibid.

95. Ibid.

96. "Clinton Urges Russia to 'Push Hard' for Arms Treaty," *Ria Novosti*, February 24, 2010, http://en.rian.ru.

97. Baker, "Twists and Turns on the Way to Arms Pact with Russia."

98. Ibid.

99. Ibid.

100. Dinah Spitzer, "Obama, Medvedev Get Off to Fresh START," *USA Today*, April 8, 2010, www.usatoday.com/news/world/2010-04-08-obama-us-russia-nuclear_N.htm.

101. Ellen Berry, "Surprising Guests in a Russian Parade: American Troops," *New York Times*, May 7, 2010, A4.

102. Baker, "Twists and Turns on the Way to Arms Pact with Russia."

7 Maritime Piracy as a U.S. Foreign Policy Problem: The Case of the *Maersk Alabama*

Peter Lehr

Before You Begin

1. What is piracy, and which forms does it take?

2. Why (and where) did piracy reemerge after the end of the cold war?

3. Why did ship owners initially ignore piracy in general, and then the first wave of Somali piracy?

4. What can be done to tackle piracy at sea? What are the advantages and disadvantages?

5. What can be done to tackle piracy on the land? What are the advantages and disadvantages?

6. With regard to the *Maersk Alabama* case, what were the "unknown unknowns" Washington had to deal with?

7. Compared to similar cases, was the *Maersk Alabama* incident nothing but a lucky break?

8. Until modern history, sailors even on commercial vessels were armed and prepared to defend themselves. In your opinion, should sailors be armed again to tackle modern piracy on their own?

Introduction: Piracy Defined

According to the United Nations' (UN) definition, as laid down in the UN Convention on the Law of the Sea (UNCLOS), *piracy* can be defined as:

> [Any] illegal acts of violence or detention, or any act of depredation, committed for private ends by the crew or the passengers of a private ship or a private aircraft and directed (i) on the high seas, against another ship or aircraft, or against persons and property on board of such ship or aircraft; (ii) against a ship, aircraft, persons or property in a place outside the jurisdiction of any State. . . .[1]

There are three expressions readers should take note of: "private ends," "high seas," and "outside the jurisdiction of any state." The first, *private ends*, virtually excludes any act of maritime terrorism since such acts are usually committed for political ends. The other two restrict acts of piracy to the high seas. Any other piratical acts committed in waters under the jurisdiction of any state are thus, strictly speaking, not piracy but maritime burglary or assault. Interestingly, until very recently most acts we would call "piracy" actually occurred in zones under the jurisdiction of a state. Thus, for practical reasons, the International Maritime Bureau's (IMB) more comprehensive definition of the term seems to be preferable:

> An act of boarding or attempting to board any ship with the intent to commit theft or any other crime and with the intent or capability to use force in the furtherance of that act. This definition thus covers actual or attempted attacks whether the ship is berthed, at anchor or at sea. Petty thefts are excluded unless the thieves are armed.[2]

Furthermore, acts of piracy need to be defined with regard to their seriousness—for the crew, their lives and property, and for the vessel itself. Generally, the following types of modern piracy are discernible.

Low-Level Armed Robbery (LLAR)

Maritime robbery is usually conducted in territorial waters close to the coast, or in the harbor area if harbor security is lax. This form of piracy is usually rather opportunistic, with no connection to organized crime.

Medium-Level Armed Assault and Robbery (MLAAR)

If the attack is violent and the crew of the ship detained or locked up, the IMB talks of medium-level armed assault and robbery. The perpetrators usually take the content of the ship's safe, the property of the crew, and perhaps some high-value goods if they are easily transportable.

Major Criminal Hijack (MCHJ)

In this case, the target ship gets hijacked and either converted for the purpose of illegal trading, or taken to a safe anchorage to be released after ransom has been paid. In the former case, the crew is detained or killed, the cargo offloaded and sold somewhere, and the ship reregistered with fraudulent papers.

While LLAR is bad enough, the other two are definitely worse, since in these cases there usually is a strong connection with transnational organized crime.[3] This implies that we also have to take a look at the organizational forms of piracy.

Opportunistic Piracy

This petty, "ad-hoc" form of piracy still is the most common. Perpetrators of opportunistic piracy usually are small gangs of fishermen, bolstering their income by attacks at knifepoint rather than gunpoint. The typical "loot" may include the catch of a luckier trawler, the valuables of an unsuspecting crew, the contents of the master's safe, or anything else the part-time pirates deem to be of value.

Professional Piracy

This form of organized piracy could be seen as "maritime transnational organized crime," either on a predatory level, or—in the case that there is a functioning, albeit weak, state—on a parasitical level.[4] Although membership may be fluctuating, there is at least a core of individuals planning raids, recruiting crew members, and possibly even taking part in an attack as "pirate captains." Such kinds of "pirate syndicates" exist in the South China Sea, for example, but the most prominent professional pirate gangs currently operate from Somali bases.

Sanctioned Piracy

This form of piracy is not exclusively carried out for private gains any longer but also includes political objectives. If the sanctioning comes from a legitimate state actor, this form of piracy is usually referred to as "privateering"; in the case of an illegitimate substate actor such as an independence movement, the phenomenon should rather be called "political piracy." In this case, the main objective is to fund a guerrilla war against a government.

However, as Robert J. Antony cautions on the basis of a historical example, "These three forms of piracy . . . have not necessarily been exclusive. Sanctioned piracy . . . has often merged with professional piracy, and opportunistic piracy has continued even when the other forms of piracy were flourishing."[5]

Background: The Reemergence of (Maritime) Piracy as a Threat to International Security

Until about a decade ago, the phenomenon of maritime piracy was perceived to be yesteryear's problem. If it came to our attention at all, it was usually in the shape of a novel such as Robert Louis Stevenson's *Treasure Island,* or as a Hollywood movie—the *Black Pirate* (1926) starring Douglas Fairbanks being an early example, and the *Pirates of the Caribbean* franchise starring Johnny Depp the most recent. This problem seemed to be so obsolete that the term itself came to be associated more with various forms of intellectual property theft than with the maritime crime from which it originates. Thus anybody interested in "real" piracy was well advised to use the search parameters *maritime* plus *piracy* when researching the topic on the Internet to avoid wading through scores of pages before hitting a relevant result.

However, as these largely fictionalized works imply, piracy was a serious threat to international shipping in the past. It is impossible to say when the first act of piracy occurred, but we can trace it back all the way to ancient history. For example, the Egyptian Nile Delta was repeatedly raided by the so-called "sea people," disrupting everyday life so seriously that Pharaoh Ramses III had to battle them in 1190 BCE. About one thousand years later, Julius Caesar himself was held captive by Aegean pirates between the years 75 and 74 BCE, and only released after ransom had been paid.

Piracy was also endemic along the coasts of the so-called Maritime Silk Road, a network of maritime trade routes connecting the Mediterranean with India and China via the Red Sea, the Persian Gulf, the Arabian Sea and the Bay of Bengal, the Straits of Malacca, and, finally, the South China Sea. For example, in the South and East China Seas of the sixteenth century, the pirates of Fujian, and especially Coxinga (Kuo-hsing-yeh), the "Masters of the Seas," became notorious for their audacious raids on Chinese coastal areas from their strongholds on what today is Taiwan.[6] In the eighteenth and nineteenth centuries, the South China Sea again gained notoriety for the annual raids of organized Ilanun and Balanini pirate fleets mostly hailing from the Sulu islands (nowadays part of the Philippines). Their organized raids in search of slaves and plunder were so predictable that the monsoon that brought them was called "the pirate wind."[7]

In Northern European waters, in the North and the Baltic Seas, Klaus Stoertebeker and the Victual Brothers made names for themselves in the late fourteenth century, until they were successfully hunted down and decisively defeated by Hanseatic fleets.[8] In the Atlantic Ocean, the real "pirates of the Caribbean" were active from the sixteenth century onwards. These pirates emerged as a "by-product" of the Age of Discovery, of which Vasco da Gama (1469–1524) for Portugal and Christopher Columbus (1451–1506) for Spain are probably the most famous actors. The vast amounts of gold and silver discovered in the "New World" (nowadays Latin America) by Spanish conquerors were shipped to the Spanish motherland with annual convoys of galleons. These heavily laden, cumbersome vessels formed tempting targets for the quick and nimble vessels preferred by the navies of Spain's enemies. During the late seventeenth century, the bulk of these vessels sailed under a national flag—usually British or French—and were thus, strictly speaking, not pirates but privateers. Their relentless attacks both at sea and on land earned themselves the status of national heroes in their home countries, and the label of pirates as well as "enemies of all mankind" by Spain—the British seafarers Sir Walter Raleigh and Sir Francis Drake being just two examples. During the eighteenth century, the pretentions of being privateers, not pirates, were done away with, and the "golden age" of piracy ran its course. This is the era to which most novels and Hollywood movies refer. The golden age of piracy culminated in the short-lived Republic of Libertatia—a pirate colony existing for about twenty-five years in Madagascar in the late seventeenth century.[9]

Also noteworthy, especially in the context of U.S. responses to piracy, are the raids of the Barbary Coast pirates in the late eighteenth and early nineteenth centuries. These brands of Mediterranean pirates operated from bases along the Northern African coast of the Mediterranean, especially from the cities of Algiers and Tripoli. These statelets were nominally part of the Ottoman Empire but governed by Beys (or Deys) as they saw fit. Piracy was seen both as a seaborne crusade against Western infidels and as a continuation of the Bedouins' caravan raids on the sea—both viewed as utterly noble enterprises. Of course, piracy was also a very profitable business, filling the coffers of the ruling aristocracies with ransom monies paid in order to free the hostages. As such, the pattern of Barbary Coast piracy was roughly comparable to modern-day Somali piracy, a point to which we shall return in the conclusion. The Barbary Coast pirates were eventually defeated in two wars: the First Barbary Coast War (also known as the Tripolitan War) of 1804–1805, and the Second Barbary Coast War (also known as the Algerine or Algerian War) of 1815. In its first out-of-area operations, the newly formed U.S. Navy participated in both wars, and was responsible for the decisive victory during the second.

With the advent of steamships, usually outrunning as well as massively outgunning any pirate vessel they encountered, piracy finally met its fate at some date in the nineteenth century when the last pirate ship had been sunk—or so it seemed. The Barbary Coast states of the Mediterranean were finally defeated; the whole of the Indian Ocean was turned into a British lake, courtesy of the Royal Navy; the Caribbean became a backwater of diverse colonial powers; and the waters of the Asia-Pacific, including the South China Sea, were being heavily patrolled by warships of several Western fleets. Thus, in the twentieth century, piracy slipped from the radar screen, surviving as a kind of "maritime mugging" in certain areas without being noticed or reported. This is not very surprising: two world wars and a following cold war with the threat of mutual assured destruction based on vast nuclear arsenals monopolized security discussions, pushing everything else to the sidelines. But after the end of the cold war, the demise of the Soviet Union, and the inauguration of a new world order of peace (which, of course, died still in its infancy), piracy came back with a vengeance.

The new wave of maritime piracy emerging during the late 1980s and 1990s can largely be explained by two push-and-pull factors:

- The wave of globalization and liberalization after the end of the cold war brought about a vast increase in international trade at sea. Thus an increasing number of ships transported an equally increasing number of goods—often of high value—which translates into more (potential) targets for criminal activities.
- Parallel to that, the end of the cold war and the demise of the Soviet Union as the second world superpower brought about a general withdrawal of warships, especially in the Asia-Pacific and the Indian Ocean. A lower interest in maritime affairs and a lower number of patrolling warships meant lower security for licit forms of trade and higher security for illicit activities.

If one takes a closer look at the data available, one cannot help noticing that nowadays, the majority of acts of piracy occur in an area stretching from the Arabian Sea (Somali Basin) and the Bay of Bengal all the way through the Strait of Malacca and the South China Sea up to the Hong Kong-Luzon-Hainan Triangle, in the mid-1990s known as the HLH-Terror Triangle. The occurrence of so many acts of piracy along the trade routes of the former Maritime Silk Road can be explained tentatively by the following facts.

Density of Traffic

The Mediterranean, Arabian Sea, Bay of Bengal, Malacca Straits, and South China Sea as parts of the former Maritime Silk Road are interconnected by some of the world's most important sea lines of communication, dubbed "iron highways" because of the density of traffic. For example, the Gulf of Aden is passed by approximately twenty-five thousand ships per year, and the Straits of Malacca by about fifty thousand ships per year.[10]

Topographical Factors

With regard to the Straits of Malacca and the South China Sea, the literally thousands of mostly uninhabited islands and islets and the heavily indented coastlines with dense Mangrove forests can be used for ambush as well as shelter and protection against potential pursuers. Also, the narrowness of the Malacca Straits forces ships to navigate very slowly, thus facilitating attacks.

Territorial Disputes and Sovereignty Issues

With regard to the South China Sea, territorial waters in this area are still disputed; claimants are the People's Republic of China, the Philippines, Vietnam, Malaysia, and Brunei Darussalam. Also, due to unresolved sovereignty issues, some coastal states do not allow their neighbors' maritime law enforcement agencies to pursue a suspected pirate vessel into their sovereign waters.

Lack of Assets

Some coastal states simply do not have the means to effectively police their territorial waters or turn a blind eye to piratical activities of parts of their own naval forces. In the case of Somalia as a failed state, the absence of an effective government enables the pirates to operate with impunity—with the exception of Somaliland and Puntland.

Organized Crime and Corruption

The presence of crime syndicates in many important ports provides the logistical background necessary for laundering money or selling off the stolen cargoes, or even the ships themselves. Also, for various reasons, harbor authorities and naval personnel often turn a blind eye toward acts of piracy or even encourage them.

History and Culture

The former Maritime Silk Road has a history of piracy, going all the way back to the early centuries of the present era. In a sense, even today, for many fishermen piracy still is part and parcel of their culture, and something they resort to without major qualms on an ad-hoc basis if an industrial fishing fleet from, say, Japan or Thailand has turned their waters into a barren, maritime wasteland due to their drag nets, the so-called Walls of Death. Of course, this also means that organized crime willing to dabble in piracy finds a convenient base for recruitment.

Taken together, these factors present modern-day pirates with an attractive opportunity, especially (but not only) in the waters described above.

Additionally, pirates so far could count on the support of very strange allies, at least prior to the recent spate of Somali pirate attacks. In many cases, ship owners explicitly ordered their ship masters not to report pirate attacks—either officially or unofficially—for fear of rising property and indemnity charges on the one hand[11] and lengthy official investigations on the other, during which the respective ship would have to remain in harbor, thus losing money for the owner—roughly $25,000 per day.[12] From the ship owners' perspective, piracy-related losses used to be seen as negligible transaction costs, amounting to less than 1 percent of total income generated by maritime trade,[13] while measures to "harden" their ships would have been very expensive.[14] Of course, from a crew's perspective, the costs were not so negligible: their lives and their property were at stake, so for them, pirate attacks were far from anonymous transaction costs—they got very personal. It is not surprising, therefore, that associations like the National Union for Marine, Aviation and Shipping Transport Officers (NUMAST)[15] or the Baltic and International Maritime Council (BIMCO)[16] were among the first to put piracy on the international agenda and to point out that pirates should neither be ridiculed nor celebrated as new kinds of maritime "Robin Hoods"—as had been done again and again by sensationalist media coverage during the last decade.

The Rise of Somali Piracy

As indicated above, the worst piracy "hotspots" during the 1990s and the first years of the new millennium were situated in maritime Asia: the South China Sea and the Straits of Malacca. With regard to the pirates' activities, all three types introduced above could be observed, including cases of MCHJ where whole crews were killed. Also, with regard to the definitions provided above, one special form of piracy could be observed that was not committed for private ends, but rather for political purposes: "political piracy" conducted by raiders of the Sumatra-based Free Aceh Movement (Gerakan Aceh Merdeka, GAM). In this special case, usually Malaysian-registered trawlers fishing in the Straits of Malacca were hijacked for ransom in order to fund GAM's costly guerrilla war against the Indonesian government.[17]

However, with all attention on these Southeast Asian piracy hotspots, and on some pockets of activity off the Niger Delta, one emerging piracy hotspot went largely unnoticed outside a fairly small group of maritime specialists: the coasts of Somalia and, initially, the Gulf of Aden. From the very early stages of

Timeline
Somali Piracy

1190 BCE	Egyptian pharaoh Ramses III battles the "sea people" who repeatedly raid the Egyptian Nile Delta.
16th–18th centuries	The golden age of piracy in the Caribbean, Indian Ocean, and South China Seas.
1804–1805	U.S. Navy participation in the First Barbary Coast (or Tripolitan) War against pirates from North Africa; Lt. Stephen Decatur becomes a national hero for burning the captured USS *Philadelphia* to prevent its usage by pirates.
1815	Second Barbary Coast War (also known as the Algerine or Algerian War), with the U.S. Navy responsible for the decisive victory.
Early 1990s	Cold war ends, navies downsize, global maritime traffic increases, and piracy becomes a major problem again.
2005	Multiple tramp steamers are captured for ransom off the Somali coast, and an attack on the U.S.-operated cruise liner *Seabourn Spirit* is foiled when the ship outruns the pirates.
April 2008	The French luxury yacht *Le Ponant* is captured and ransomed for $2 million.
September 2008– February 2009	The Ukrainian-operated M/V *Faina* and its cargo of main battle tanks is captured and subsequently released for a ransom of $3.2 million.
November 2008– January 2009	The Saudi supertanker *Sirius Star* is captured and subsequently released for a ransom of $3 million.
April 2009– August 2009	The German-owned *Hansa Stavanger* is captured and subsequently released for a ransom of $2.7 million.

April 8, 2009	The U.S.-flagged *Maersk Alabama* is boarded by four Somali pirates from a small skiff that is swamped by the *Maersk Alabama*'s maneuvering. The crew captures the pirate leader after the pirates capture the ship's captain, Richard Phillips. After agreeing to swap Captain Phillips for the pirate leader and a lifeboat, the pirates renege on the deal, keeping the lifeboat and the captain.
April 9, 2009	The USS *Bainbridge*, a guided missile destroyer, arrives on the scene and the *Maersk Alabama* proceeds on to its destination—Mombasa, Kenya.
April 9–10, 2009	During the night, Captain Phillips jumps overboard from the lifeboat to escape but is recaptured by the pirates.
April 10, 2009	Two more U.S. warships arrive on the scene, the frigate USS *Halyburton* and the amphibious assault ship USS *Boxer.* White House and Pentagon officials make the decision not to allow the lifeboat to reach the Somali coast. President Barack Obama directs the naval commander on the *Bainbridge* to seek a peaceful outcome if possible but authorizes the use of force if lives are endangered.
April 11, 2009	A U.S. Navy Sea, Air, and Land (SEAL) team arrives on the scene.
April 12, 2009	The pirate leader comes on board the *Bainbridge* for medical treatment. When one of the pirates on the lifeboat is seen pointing an assault rifle at Captain Phillips, the order is given to fire, and the SEAL snipers shoot and kill the remaining three pirates.
April 21, 2009	The pirate leader Abdelwali Abdulkadir Muse arrives in New York City to stand trial on piracy charges.
October 24, 2009	The U.S. government announces that surveillance drones carrying missiles have begun patrolling the Indian Ocean in search of pirates.

(continued)

Timeline *(continued)*
Somali Piracy

April 1, 2010	The frigate USS *Nicholas* is attacked by a pirate skiff in the Indian Ocean. It returns fire, disables the skiff, and captures its three-man crew. After sinking the skiff, the *Nicholas* captures a pirate "mother ship" and takes two more suspects into custody.
May 5, 2010	The Russian-flagged oil tanker *Moscow University* is captured.
May 6, 2010	The *Moscow University* is recaptured by Russian commandos. Following the action all the pirates die, either from loss of life at sea or from possible Russian military reprisals.
May 18, 2010	Abdelwali Abdulkadir Muse pleads guilty to hijacking and kidnapping charges.

Somali piracy in the 1990s, just one type of piracy could be observed: MCHJ with the intention to hold the ship and crew for ransom.[18]

The main reason behind this "benign neglect" is the fact that, initially, only smaller, mostly local vessels came under attack: trawlers allegedly involved in illegal fishing activities in coastal waters, older tramp ships with no fixed schedules, and local traffic. For the latter category, the Kenyan-based Motaku Shipping Agency is an excellent example: several of its vessels, chartered by the UN World Food Program, fell prey to pirates in 2005, prompting the company to call for outside help.[19] Although bodies such as IMB, BIMCO, and NUMAST also lobbied for international naval operations to tackle the worsening problem, these initiatives did not lead to robust action. The UN passed some resolutions, and general advice was given to vessels on international voyages to stay as far away from these dangerous waters as possible—not very helpful in the confined waters of the Gulf of Aden, in any case. Interestingly, even the brazen but unsuccessful attack on the cruise liner *Seabourn Spirit* in November 2005 managed to put Somali piracy on the agenda only very briefly: after a couple of weeks, international attention turned elsewhere—especially after it became clear that this attack was piracy pure and simple, and not an attempted act of maritime terrorism aimed at "us" (i.e., wealthy Western vacationers), not "them" (i.e., sailors from Kenya, Pakistan, the Philippines, Kiribati, etc.).

Only the most recent wave of Somali piracy prompted international actors to intervene. This current wave of piracy was triggered by the successful hijacking of the French luxury yacht *Le Ponant* in spring 2008. The fact that the pirates netted a ransom of $2 million did not go unnoticed—either by international media covering the story or by Somali militiamen, clan fighters, and fishermen. In short, this act of piracy resulted in a kind of Somali "gold rush," or "feeding frenzy" (to use a more appropriate maritime simile): scores of willing recruits—young militia- and fishermen mostly in the age range of twenty to twenty-five years[20]—flocked to the pirates' lairs to get a piece of the action and a share of the booty. As a result, the frequency of acts of piracy—both successful and unsuccessful—rose from one or two attacks per month to several attacks per week. Somali pirates' milestones include the attack on the main battletank–carrying M/V *Faina* (captured September 25, 2008; released February 6, 2009; reported ransom $3.2 million), the Saudi supertanker *Sirius Star* (captured November 15, 2008; released January 9, 2009; reported ransom $3 million), the German-owned *Hansa Stavanger* (captured April 3, 2009; released August 3, 2009; reported ransom $2.7 million), the U.S.-flagged *Maersk Alabama* (attempted hijack April 8, 2009), and the Russian-flagged oil tanker *Moscow University* (captured May 5, 2010; recaptured May 6, 2010). However, as we shall discuss later on in some detail, the latter two hijacks went less than smoothly for the pirates.

There is, however, yet another milestone that needs to be mentioned: originally only capable of striking near their own coasts, the current generation of Somali pirates extended their reach to more than 1,000 nautical miles (1,800 kilometers) off their own shores—attacking ships in Seychellois waters, the Mozambique Channel, near the coasts of Oman, and even off the west coast of India. In a sense, the pirates' vastly extended raids (both in terms of duration and distance covered) can be explained as a result of more frequent antipiracy operations in their former hunting ground, the Gulf of Aden. Nevertheless, for the first time since the nineteenth century, international shipping is again confronted by high-seas piracy: prior to the current wave of Somali piracy, pirates used to attack in confined waters or anywhere near their own shores. Thus basically all vessels voyaging through the Northern Arabian Sea, also known as the Somali Basin, are potential targets now, not only those situated in the Gulf of Aden or in Somali waters. To counter this renewed threat of high-seas piracy, robust action seems to be the order of the day.

Responding to Maritime Piracy

Broadly speaking, antipiracy operations—at least those going beyond the stage of lofty but meaningless declarations—can be divided into "from the sea" and "at sea" measures. They range from land strikes to blockades to special forces operations against known pirates or pirate bases in the first category, and from defensive and offensive measures for individual ships to capturing pirates and sinking their boats in the second. Also, these options involve, to a certain degree, relearning the lessons of history: as was stated in the introduction, piracy is not exactly a new phenomenon—and neither, therefore, are antipiracy operations.

At Sea: Robust Measures against Pirates

Although it may sound rather obvious, the first line of defense against pirate attacks is preventing the pirates from boarding in the first place. Whether some shippers like it or not, outfitting vessels with at least defensive devices such as rolls of razor wire, keeping antipiracy watch all the time in the whole of the Northern Arabian Sea, and staying close to warships—i.e., sailing in a convoy—may well be the order of the day.

Another option would be to employ armed security guards or even escort vessels from private security firms in order to be able to *actively* defend a vessel from being boarded. Although this is quite an expensive solution, it may well make sense at least for vessels transporting high-value cargo, or private luxury yachts such as the hapless *Le Ponant*. Yet another option with regard to active defense (but without incurring the high costs involved in hiring a team of specialists from a private security corporation) would be to form "specially trained security teams from the ship's crew, led by a highly trained licensed officer."[21] Many seafarers' organizations and bodies such as the International Maritime Organization are opposed to such an option for a variety of good reasons, be they legal, liability/insurance-related, or practical.[22] Such a drastic action also does not always make sense. Consider a ship under a flag of convenience, for example. For one thing, such vessels tend to be rather economically manned: there are just enough crew members to carry out the usual tasks involved in operating a ship, but hardly enough to maintain proper antipiracy watches. How could such overworked crews find the time for weapons training? And why should they be prepared to defend their ship in the first place as long as there still is a decent chance to survive an attack when offering no resistance? Also, nobody would be too keen to start a gun battle on board a tanker carrying aviation fuel, chemicals, ammonium nitrate, or any other hazardous material.

Still, ships of certain nations are known to be well armed, and thus hardly ever attacked by pirates.[23] In the United States, at least, some ship owners seem to reassess the risks involved in arming sailors. The *Washington Times,* for example, reported the following:

> Many ship owners appreciate that armed crews would protect their ships, cargo and personnel. In May 5 [2009] Senate testimony, Philip J. Shapiro, chief executive officer of Liberty Maritime Corp., said: "In light of the recent threats to U.S. merchant mariners, we respectfully request that Congress consider clearing the obstacles that currently block ship owners from arming our vessels."[24]

At the time of writing, this debate is still ongoing. The majority of seafarers—especially those outside the United States—do not like to be armed, pointing out that they are transport workers, not marines or naval reserves. A minority, however, is willing to give it a try, dismissing the usual argument that this would lead to an escalation of violence by pointing out that this already happened anyway. Therefore, this drastic course of action at least needs more careful consideration, instead of a knee-jerk rejection.

Here, naval forces finally appear on the radar screen. It should not be forgotten that the very raison d'être for naval forces is to protect one's own trade. As of today, more than two decades after the end of the cold war and still under the lingering impression of September 11, 2001, Western navies seem to be rediscovering their duties with regard to securing the maritime domain. Thus NATO currently operates a squadron named Combined Task Force (CTF) 151; the European Union has its own tasked force on station under the name Operation Atalanta; and a variety of other countries, including China, Japan, South Korea, and India, participate in ventures such as the Contact Group on Piracy off the Coast of Somalia (CGPCS) and Shared Awareness and Deconfliction (SHADE).[25]

With regard to Somali piracy, this shift of focus resulted in the creation of secure maritime corridors patrolled by warships, and even in the (re-) establishment of convoys protected by warships. Using airborne platforms such as helicopters, maritime patrol aircrafts (MPA), and even unmanned aerial vehicles (UAV, also known as drones), warships on antipiracy patrol try their best to spot suspicious activities and to interdict a pirate attack before a ship gets boarded. Suspected pirate mother ships—usually trawlers or local "dhows"—are stopped, boarded, and inspected by vessel boarding and security teams, usually covered by an armed helicopter acting as a disincentive for any "hasty" actions from the other side. If evidence pointing at criminal intent (arms and ammunition, ladders, ropes with a grapnel attached, etc.) is found, the crew of the vessel is apprehended for further investigation. Their boat is usually sunk by gunfire. However, experience shows that the crew of suspected pirate vessels is rather quick in throwing all the evidence, including their arms, overboard well before being boarded. The possession of arms can be explained as protection against pirates in any case. Thus bringing pirates to justice is much more difficult than it may look at first glance.[26]

As a measure of last resort, i.e., in the case a commercial vessel has already been boarded by pirates, counterattacks by naval special forces could be feasible under certain circumstances. However, as we shall demonstrate in the section on the *Maersk Alabama* and similar cases, such "direct action" may well lead to casualties.

From the Sea: Attacking the Pirates' Land Bases

More robust action against Somali pirates from the sea would include a variety of responses, including special forces operations to recapture hijacked ships at anchor in or near pirate ports; a blockade of known pirate lairs; and, *in extremis,* even land strikes against known pirate bases or individual pirates themselves.

The first option would be to recapture hijacked vessels at anchor in or near pirate lairs. One of the U.S. Navy's earliest heroes, Commodore Stephen Decatur, made a name for himself as a lieutenant doing exactly that: during the First Barbary War (1801–1805), in the Battle of Tripoli Harbor in July 1804, Decatur and his small team of sailors sneaked into the harbor on board a captured Tripolitan vessel, successfully boarded the captured frigate USS *Philadelphia,* and set it on fire—thus denying its use to the pirates.[27] However, such actions entail a very grave risk to the security of the hostages, who may well be killed in retribution. In the case of the USS *Philadelphia,* this formidable warship had to be taken from the pirates at nearly any price. If, for any reasons, today's Somali pirates would succeed in capturing a modern warship, a similar course of action would have to be taken. With regard to recapturing hijacked commercial vessels, however, such daring missions have so far been restricted to vessels still at sea. It should also be noted that contrary to the case of the Barbary Coast piracy, where dozens of hostages perished due to ill treatment, the hostages of Somali pirates are usually well treated and not harmed. Since they stand a very good chance of surviving their ordeal—as long as ransom is paid, of course[28]—ship owners and naval commanders are not very keen to endorse risky operations.

Another option to combat piracy would be a blockade of the coast—or at least parts of it. Again, this is taking a page from the history book: blockades are time-honored measures to bottle up enemies in their own ports. In 2009 the Spanish navy officially tabled this idea after it had been unofficially discussed for about a year. One should hasten to add that, with regard to the 3,300-kilometer coastline of Somalia, this is neither an easy task nor a "silver bullet" with which to eradicate Somali piracy once and for all. As Royal Navy commander Mike Jager stated after the hijack of the Greek tanker *Maran Centaurus* in November 2009, "Patrolling the whole coast of Somalia is like policing the East Coast of America with five police cars."[29] It thus sounds like a good idea to concentrate these "five police cars" at the most notorious neighborhoods in an effort to interdict criminal activities emanating from them. At the moment, only the possibility of blockading major ports involved in piratical actions is under discussion. However, pirates do not necessarily need sophisticated infrastructure to launch their raids, and they could make use of Yemeni ports for their mother ships in any case—as they (allegedly) already do. Nevertheless, establishing an exclusion zone beyond which any vessel would be stopped and searched would at least restrict the pirates' room to maneuver, and add yet another price tag on their operations.

Some observers even lobby for preventive land strikes in addition to more robust action at sea. The objective of such strikes would be to destroy the pirates' infrastructure, and to eliminate known high-profile leaders of pirate gangs. Supporters of this tactic cite the targeted killing of al-Shabaab leader Aden Hashi Ayrow in May 2008 as an example. Another one cited in this context is the September 2009 strike against Saleh Ali Saleh Nabhan, a Kenyan involved in the Mombasa hotel bombing of November 2002. More related to piracy, the French land strike at pirates involved in the *Le Ponant* hijack is also mentioned in this regard.

Broadening the scope of land strikes to include the destruction of pirates' infrastructure would be the next logical step: without suitable boats, no piracy—for the hardliners, it's as simple as that. Such a strategy would be roughly comparable to the actions against the North African Barbary Coast pirates during the first decades of the nineteenth century: after having ransomed captured sailors for many years, a squadron of the fledgling U.S. Navy bombarded the harbors used by the pirates in what is now known as the First Barbary War (1801–1805), culminating in Decatur's daring raid in the famous Battle of Tripoli Harbor in July 1804.[30] Another example would be the so-called

Arrow War (also known as Second Opium War) of 1856–1860—one of the very rare cases in which a wave of piracy was used as a pretext for a war.[31]

"Doing a Decatur" would come with a considerable risk, however. First of all, it could lead to "collateral damage": even in the case of targeted killings, innocent bystanders could get killed; and in the case of air strikes against the pirates' infrastructure, it is to be expected that the wrong targets might get hit. Furthermore, it could drive the pirates into the arms of militant Islamists such as al-Shabaab—an outfit allied with al Qaeda and aspiring to be "al Qaeda at the Horn of Africa." As such, a "quick fix" in the shape of land strikes could create a problem much worse than piracy: maritime terrorism. True, so far there is only circumstantial evidence for contacts between pirates and al-Shabaab. Still, one should keep in mind that the country's geo-strategic location athwart major sea lines of communication and in the vicinity of a formidable maritime choke point, the Bab el-Mandeb, makes it a formidable launchpad for acts of maritime terrorism. One should also keep in mind that the three al Qaeda–related maritime suicide attacks actually took place in the waters of the Gulf of Aden: the aborted attack on the USS *The Sullivans* in January 2000, the successful attack against the USS *Cole* in October 2000, and the also successful attack on the supertanker M/V *Limburg* in October 2002.

The *Maersk Alabama* Incident

With an overall length of roughly 155 meters, a deadweight tonnage of about 17,500 tons, and a capacity of about 1,400 TEU (twenty-foot equivalent unit), the A-Class container ship M/V *Maersk Alabama* is a comparatively small vessel of a type generally used for feeder lines and not the main transport routes.[32] Launched in 1998 in Keelung, Taiwan, as *Alva Maersk,* it was reflagged as a U.S. vessel in 2004, renamed, and home-ported in Norfolk, Virginia, as part of the Maritime Security Program (MSP).[33] On the day of the hijack, April 8, 2009, the ship was on its way to Mombasa, Kenya, carrying four hundred containers of food aid. It came under attack after having passed the Horn of Africa, about 240 nautical miles off the Somali Puntland coast. A group of four Somali pirates approached on a skiff, clearly intending to board. The chief engineer, Mike Perry, and the first assistant engineer, Matt Fisher, changed course in an attempt to discourage the four pirates from climbing on board, but to no avail: although they succeeded in flooding the skiff, thus reducing its maneuverability, the four pirates got on board.[34]

Most of the well-trained, exclusively U.S. crew of twenty assembled in the "secure room"—a room purposely hardened for such an event—after having transferred the main engine controls from the bridge to the engine room. The chief engineer chose to stay outside the secure room, armed with a knife, in the hope of ambushing the pirates in case they ventured down to the engine room, looking for the rest of the crew.[35] However, the master, Capt. Richard Phillips, and assistant technical manager (ATM), Zahid Reza, were captured by the pirates.[36] Chief Perry's and the crew's chance came when ATM Reza volunteered to lead one of the pirates—their leader—down to the engine room: with the help of Reza, they managed to wrestle the pirate down.[37] The crew then offered a swap of hostages—the captured pirate for Captain Phillips. The three pirates agreed to this offer, but in the end did not honor it. The following quote describes the dramatic events:

> Capt. Phillips offered himself as a hostage to safeguard the crew. The pirates demanded a boat, fuel and food. The two sides agreed to exchange hostages. Once the pirates settled in to a bright orange, enclosed lifeboat, the crew released their hostage. But the pirates refused to let Capt. Phillips free and maneuvered the lifeboat free of the *Maersk Alabama* with the captain aboard.[38]

Thus a very peculiar hostage situation enfolded: four pirates with one hostage in a twenty-eight-foot lifeboat—life-threatening for the hostage, confronted by four pirates armed with assault rifles, but also awkward for the pirates crammed into the covered lifeboat.

To deal with this hostage situation, the nearest U.S. warship, the USS *Bainbridge,* was dispatched to the *Maersk Alabama's* position. It arrived early in the morning of April 9. Contact with the pirates was established via a walkie-talkie and a satellite phone, and hours of protracted negotiations started. In the meantime, the *Maersk Alabama* was ordered to proceed to Mombasa as planned, with a team of armed guards from the *Bainbridge* on board. From this moment on, four pirates on a lifeboat plus a hostage were confronted by a warship, while the *Maersk Alabama* was not part of the story any longer.

Initially, it was hoped that the pirates would give up, release their hostage, and surrender their weapons. However, that quickly turned out not to be the case: the four pirates, knowing that word of their botched attack had spread among their fellow pirates, obviously hoped that a hijacked freighter with around two dozen pirates on board would come to their rescue. Initially, they were right in their assumption: pirates on board the captured German freighter *Hansa Stavanger* indeed directed the crew to sail the vessel to the lifeboat's position. However, without having a clear idea of the lifeboat's exact position, they steamed around for several hours without even coming near it, and then gave up, returning to their original coast-bound course. Allegedly, pirates on board three other hijacked vessels also threatened to come to their fellow pirates' rescue, but could not follow up on these threats since they had no clue about the lifeboat's position either.

For U.S. Navy commander Frank Costello as the commanding officer of the USS *Bainbridge,* the nonappearance of pirate reinforcements meant that an already tense situation would at least not get worse: during the night of April 9–10, Captain Phillips had made a desperate attempt to escape, jumping overboard in an attempt to swim away from the lifeboat. He was quickly followed by two pirates who, both far younger men, outswam him and forced him back to the boat. Under the suspicion that the captain had managed to establish contact with the warship, the pirates then threw a mobile phone and the walkie-talkie overboard. The captain's escape attempt, his recapture, and the ditching of the phones were closely watched from the *Bainbridge* through night-vision goggles.[39] However, there was nothing that could be done to help the captain without endangering his life.

Two more U.S. warships arrived at the scene on Friday, April 10: the frigate USS *Halyburton* and the amphibious assault ship USS *Boxer.* Communications and negotiations with the pirates were still handled by the USS *Bainbridge,* whose officers were supported by an experienced FBI hostage negotiator via satellite. Also in the loop were the Pentagon and the White House: President Barack Obama, faced with the first international crisis of his presidency, took as keen an interest in the incident as did his predecessors Thomas Jefferson and James Madison during the two Barbary Coast Wars.

Washington was faced with a series of open questions—"known unknowns" and "unknown unknowns," to paraphrase former secretary of defense Donald Rumsfeld:

- Who were the pirates, and what was their clan affiliation? Could clan elders be contacted to assist in negotiations to bring the hostage crisis to an end?
- Were the pirates in contact with any other actors—clan elders, pirates, militants—and if so, who were they? Could they be contacted and persuaded to assist in bringing the crisis to an end, or would they need to be cut out of the communications loop (if possible) to stop them from egging the pirates on?
- Were the pirates associated with any of the Islamist movements active in Somalia, especially al-Shabaab? Thus would any political demands

complicate the negotiations? Or was there a danger that the captain would be killed/beheaded once the lifeboat reached the shore?

- How much fuel, and how much food and water, was on board the lifeboat? When would the situation become desperate for the pirates and, of course, the hostage?
- Did the hostage, Captain Phillips, have any known medical condition requiring urgent or at least regular treatment?
- Which options were available to stop the lifeboat before it reached the shore? How much force could be used to end the crisis at sea?
- What should be done if other hijacked vessels in the hands of pirates were to arrive on the scene? Should they be engaged, thus threatening the lives of an unknown number of hostages on board those vessels? Or should the pirates in the lifeboat be allowed to join them, and to take Captain Phillips with them?[40]

After carefully assessing the situation, and weighing all available options, on Friday, April 10, at 0700 EST[41], the following decisions were made:

- The lifeboat was to be prevented from reaching the shore.
- The primary objective of all direct actions was disabling the lifeboat.
- Any direct action to resolve the crisis by force was not feasible before the evening of Saturday, April 11, when a SEAL team would arrive at the scene.[42]

The names of the four pirates were established without problems, and their clan elders volunteered to assist, just as was hoped. After protracted and complicated negotiations with the pirates—recorded messages were transmitted from the *Bainbridge* via loudspeaker—during which the pirates did not make any efforts to get nearer to the shore, the clan elders offered the following suggestions to solve the crisis:

- The pirates should be allowed to get ashore.
- As soon as they reach the shore, Captain Phillips would be released.
- No demands for ransom would be made.

All the elders obviously wanted was to get their young men back: the "lure of easy money" obviously tempted (and still tempts) many young Somalis to try their luck as pirates with only little or no navigational experience—thus an unknown number of these self-made pirates perish at sea without a trace.[43] However, the elders' suggestions were deemed to be unacceptable. Considering that the pirates already broke a similar promise, this very probably was a wise decision: according to available intelligence, pirate groups from the ports of

Eyl, Garaad, and Hobyo were planning to come to their comrades' rescue as soon as the lifeboat would be nearer to the coast.[44]

Hoping that reinforcement was on its way, and getting more and more agitated after running out of Qat (a mild narcotic), the pirates broke up negotiations and made renewed efforts to reach the coast. They even transmitted a message to the elders, telling them, "We don't need you and will not listen, we are in Allah's hands."[45]

In order to prevent the lifeboat from reaching the shore, the *Bainbridge* maneuvered into a blocking position, while the USS *Halyburton* attempted to flood it with water, firing water cannons at the tiny vessel. In addition, a Seahawk helicopter was dispatched to hover over the craft to further intimidate the now rather exhausted pirates. Still, U.S. officials, both in Washington and on board the warships, hoped that the crisis situation could be brought to an unbloody end.

When a boat full of SEALs ventured nearer to the lifeboat and divers attempted to disable the lifeboat's screw, the situation escalated. The pirates opened fire at the approaching boat, and the SEALs fired back: not to kill, but to scare the pirates into abandoning the firefight—which they did.

The last, and rather unexpected, chance for a peaceful resolution of the hostage crisis came on Easter Sunday, April 12, when the pirate leader, Abdelwali Abdulkadir Muse (otherwise known as Ina Wale), asked for permission to come on board the *Bainbridge* to receive medical treatment. After being treated, he was provided a loudspeaker in the hope that he could convince his remaining three comrades to surrender. Unfortunately, after some discussions, they decided not to surrender.

Meanwhile, the lifeboat had run out of fuel. The *Bainbridge* offered to take the craft in tow, presumably to help the pirates on board to reach the shore, but in reality hoping that a swift tow would result in making the three Somalis seasick, thus softening them up and preparing them for a surrender.[46]

In a sense, the tactic worked: the three pirates asked the *Bainbridge* to stop towing them through the choppy waters: indeed, they felt seasick. The *Bainbridge* then offered the pirates to tow the boat nearer to its hull, presumably to get it into calmer waters. The pirates agreed to that. What they did not know was that the White House had already given orders for direct action to bring the crisis to an end. SEAL snipers were already in position and taking aim at the three pirates. Suddenly, all three were clearly visible to the snipers: one of them could be seen inside the boat, pointing an assault rifle at the head of Captain Phillips, and the other two stuck their heads out of the boat's windows to get fresh air.

At that moment, the SEAL snipers opened fire, killing all three of them, while two SEALs rappelled down from a Seahawk helicopter to secure the craft. Captain Phillips turned out to be unharmed. The hostage crisis was over.[47] Less than two weeks later, the pirate leader, Abdelwali Abdulkadir Muse, arrived in New York City to stand trial on piracy charges. On May 18, 2010, he pleaded guilty to hijacking the ship and kidnapping the captain in return for a plea agreement that would have him serve no more than thirty-three years and nine months in jail.[48]

Implications of the *Maersk Alabama* Rescue for Antipiracy Operations

The *Maersk Alabama* case is not the only incident in which a decision was made to recapture a hijacked vessel to free hostages by the use of (deadly) force. In September 2008, for example, the French navy's *Commando Hubert* successfully retook a hijacked private yacht, killing one pirate and capturing six, while rescuing the two hostages, Jean-Yves and Bernadette Delanne. Also, in the case of the *Le Ponant* hijack in April 2008, French commandos hunted down and arrested suspected pirates on land—but only after the release of the hostages. On April 1, 2010, the frigate USS *Nicholas* was attacked by a pirate skiff in the Indian Ocean. It returned fire and disabled the skiff. Three pirate suspects were captured. After sinking the skiff, the *Nicholas* captured a pirate "mother ship" and took two more suspects into custody.[49] Further bolstering the U.S. military effort in the area was the decision in October 2009 to use missile-carrying drone aircraft operating out of the Seychelles to patrol for pirates in the waters off the Somali coast.[50]

The most recent case at the time of writing (June 2010) is a successful operation of a Russian commando team on May 6, 2010: operating from the Russian destroyer *Marshal Shaposhnikov*, this team recaptured the oil tanker *Moscow University*, which had been hijacked by eleven Somali pirates the day before about five hundred nautical miles off the Somali coast. One pirate was killed during this operation, and the other ten surrendered. Comparable to the early stage of the *Maersk Alabama* case, the crew locked themselves in two secure rooms, the radar room and the engine room. But, unlike the *Maersk Alabama* case, none of the crew members fell into the hands of the attacking pirates. Thus, in the absence of a human bargaining chip and threatened by well-armed Russian naval commandos, all the pirates could do was give up. The aftermath of this successful action, however, is under dispute: Russian sources claim that the pirates were set adrift in an inflatable boat and then simply perished at sea. Other sources claim that the pirates had been summarily executed by the Russian commandos, drawing attention to Russian president Dmitry Medvedev's statement that "[we'll] have to do what our forefathers did when they met the pirates."[51]

Thus, the alleged Russian penchant for drastic action aside, special forces operations to recapture a pirated ship and to free the hostages are an option that should be kept in mind—at least under special circumstances.

On the other hand, the two following operations illustrate the risk of using direct action against pirates on board a captured ship in possession of hostages. Again, a French commando is involved in the first case. In April 2009, the French yacht *Tanit* with five crew members on board was captured by Somali pirates. As in the very similar case the year before, French commandos stormed the hijacked vessel. In the ensuing shootout, not only two pirates but also one of the hostages, Florent Lemacon, were killed. As the Associated Press reported after the incident, "The death of the skipper, Florent Lemacon, marked the first time a hostage had been killed and illustrated the risks of such raids."[52]

With regard to the hijacked German-flagged freighter *Hansa Stavanger* (captured April 3, 2009; released August 3, 2009), an antipiracy raid by a team of the well-known GSG-9 special (police) force was planned to recapture the freighter and free the hostages. However, although the elite team was waiting on board the USS *Boxer*, ready to strike, the mission was canceled: the risk was deemed to be too high. Apparently, there were at least thirty pirates on board the freighter, and six of the hostages were always kept below deck—out of sight, and out of reach, of the rescue team. A *Spiegel* report illustrates the difficulty of this operation:

> The situation couldn't have been more difficult. [Walter] Lindner [German ambassador in Nairobi] weighed his options. He could send the helicopters, but the pirates would hear them approaching and possibly kill the hostages. Instead, he devised a combination approach. The frogmen would approach the *Stavanger* first, bringing along inflatable dinghies and their underwater tractors. Then they would use suction equipment to climb up the ship's side. The pirates would likely open fire and the frogmen, facing a hail of bullets, would seek to protect the hostages. Only then would the helicopters arrive. But there were at least two groups of hostages. The frogmen could quickly reach the hostages on the bridge, but the labyrinthine passageways below deck on a typical freighter could become a death trap.[53]

Canceling the mission was not an easy decision, no doubt. But estimates were that at least six hostages and several GSG-9 members would either have been killed or injured during such a raid. However, it left a bad taste, as the *Spiegel* did not fail to point out: "This could have serious consequences. German sailors can now expect to become prime targets for pirates, in contrast to their French or American counterparts, whose governments have not hesitated to use force to rescue their citizens."[54]

The difficulty of tackling pirates with offensive actions after boarding could also be seen in an incident earlier that year, when an Indian navy frigate engaged and sank a trawler off the coast of Yemen. The Thai trawler had been captured by pirates earlier, to be used as a "mother ship." When hailed by the Indian frigate, the pirates threatened to open fire at the warship, so the Indian vessel opened fire fist and sank the trawler. Unbeknownst to the commander of the frigate—and still denied by the Indian navy—the sixteen original Thai crew members were still on board as hostages. Only one of them survived, by jumping overboard before the trawler detonated and sunk. This case is a clear incident of the Clausewitzian "fog of [naval] war" principle. It can be taken for granted that the same principle will be in force in any other offensive action against the pirates after they successfully boarded their prey: some crucial information will be unavailable, some facts not known, and things may simply go wrong. In all probability, Florent Lemacon was killed by a French bullet. Thus it is fair to say that any operation against pirates in possession of a number of hostages will be a bit of a gamble with rather high stakes.

Conclusion: Relearning the Lessons from History

The *Maersk Alabama* case is important not with regard to the action itself—that spectacular rescue operation could have gone wrong. Rather, it is important in that it prompted the still-new Obama administration into action: the *Maersk Alabama* was the first U.S.-flagged vessel hijacked by pirates since the early years of the 1800s. Thus old recipes for fighting this menace had to be reexamined in a hurry.

Remarkably, U.S. foreign policy—which seems to be reinvented by every new administration—remained rather consistent with regard to antipiracy operations, from the first encounters during the last decades of the eighteenth century and the Barbary Coast Wars all the way to the *Maersk Alabama* crisis two centuries later. Furthermore, the declarations of all U.S. presidents who had to deal with or referred to piracy one way or the other sound very similar: they put this kind of maritime crime into the same category as slavery and terrorism. For example, in December 1901 and in the aftermath of the assassination of President William McKinley by an anarchist terrorist, newly elected president Theodore Roosevelt also referred to piracy (and to slavery) when condemning anarchist terrorism:

> Anarchy is a crime against the whole human race; and all mankind should band against the anarchist. His crime should be made an offense against the law of nations, like piracy and that form of manstealing known as the slave trade; for it is of far blacker infamy than either. It should be so declared by treaties among all civilized powers.[55]

As Mikkel Thorup points out, this was echoed very closely by the administration of President George W. Bush in September 2002:

> [Using] the full influence of the United States, and working closely with allies and friends, to make clear that all acts of terrorism are illegitimate so that *terrorism will be viewed in the same light as slavery, piracy, or genocide:* behavior that no respectable government can condone or support and all must oppose.[56]

Thorup, albeit with important qualifications, argues that the first war on terrorism was not the war on anarchist terrorism, but the war on piracy—the Barbary Coast piracy—at the beginning of the nineteenth century.[57] While this is debatable, it is true that even one of the earliest scholars on terrorism, Paul Wilkinson, linked piracy and terrorism when he condemned the terrorists' efforts to legitimize their actions:

> But in reality they are *hostes humani generis.* Any civilized society has an obligation to do everything possible to suppress this scourge, just as our forefathers had to act boldly to suppress crimes such as piracy and slavery.[58]

Against the backdrop of the current debate around the securitization of piracy, it should thus be highlighted that it is actually not piracy that gets dragged into the orbit of the war on terrorism in order to justify actions taken and money spent. Rather, it is the other way around: as the quotes above demonstrate, the "infamy" of piracy was used to justify even more drastic action against terrorism as an even bigger infamy. But this aspect would merit a special treatment in another chapter. Suffice it to argue that Thorup is quite right to set the record straight.

In sum, the lessons provided by the *Maersk Alabama* and similar cases go far beyond the immediate action. Rather, they force us to reexamine historical approaches to counterpiracy operations. And here we encounter yet another inconvenient truth: long-term solutions to the problem of piracy can only be found on land—this is where the root causes of piracy are situated, and this is where they need to be addressed. This point is well made by Andrew Lambert, who opines, "[Because] pirates—like all other people—must live on the land, it is on the land that they must often be stopped; naval power alone is not sufficient to fight piracy."[59] Since even a pirate lives on the land, this is where he has to be attacked—be it by "direct" action (i.e., targeted killings), "indirect" action (i.e., reestablishing law and order on the land, inaugurating welfare policies), or a mixture of both. Unfortunately, such actions take a long time, especially in the context of Somalia as a failed state. Until then, "quick fixes" in the shape of "robust action" at sea may be the order of the day.

Key Actors

Abdelwali Abdulkadir Muse   Leader of the pirates who attempted to hijack the *Maersk Alabama* and kidnap its captain. Later pleaded guilty to hijacking and kidnapping charges in federal court in New York City.

Barack Obama   President who gave orders to the navy to end the *Maersk Alabama* incident peacefully if possible, but to use force if there was a risk of loss of life.

Mike Perry   Chief engineer, who as part of the bridge crew of the *Maersk Alabama* was responsible for swamping the pirate skiff and later wounding and helping capture the pirate leader.

Richard Phillips   Captain of the *Maersk Alabama*, was captured by the pirates and held hostage on a lifeboat for four days before being rescued.

Zahid Reza   Assistant technical manager of the *Maersk Alabama* who helped capture the pirate leader.

Three unnamed navy SEALs   Sniper team members who killed the three pirates holding Captain Phillips hostage on a lifeboat.

Notes

1. United Nations Convention of the Law of the Sea, Article 101, www.un.org/Depts/los/convention_agreements/texts/unclos/unclos_e.pdf.

2. International Chamber of Commerce, *Piracy and Armed Robbery against Ships; Annual Report, 1 January–31 December 2006* (London: International Maritime Bureau, 2007).

3. This is suspected by the Ministry of Foreign Affairs of Japan; see Chapter II, Section 4.D., "Piracy and Armed Robbery against Ships," in *Diplomatic Bluebook 2001*, www.mofa.go.jp/policy/other/bluebook/2001/chap2-4-d.html (downloaded September 23, 2004).

4. For a classification of (land-bound) transnational organized crime, see Peter A. Lupsha, "Transnational Organized Crime versus the Nation-State," *Transnational Organized Crime* 2 (Spring 1996).

5. Robert J. Antony, "Piracy on the South China Coast through Modern Times," in Bruce A. Elleman, Andrew Forbes, and David Rosenberg, eds., *Piracy and Maritime Crime: Historical and Modern Case Studies*, Naval War College Newport Papers, no. 35 (Newport: Naval War College Press, 2010).

6. See, for example, Jonathan Clements, *Coxinga and the Fall of the Ming Dynasty* (Phoenix Mill: Sutton Publishing Ltd., 2005).

7. See Owen Rutter, *The Pirate Wind: Tales of the Sea-Robbers of Malaya* (Singapore et al.: Oxford University Press, 1986).

8. See, for example, Matthias Puhle, *Die Vitalienbrüder: Klaus Störtebeker und die Seeräuber der Hansezeit* (Frankfurt am Main: Campus Verlag, 1992).

9. Whether this republic actually existed or not is still under dispute. See, for example, Frank Sherry, *Raiders and Rebels: The Golden Age of Piracy* (New York: Hearst Marine Books, 1986).

10. U.S. Energy Information Administration, *World Oil Transit Chokepoints: Malacca*, www.eia.doe.gov/emeu/cabs/World_Oil_Transit_Chokepoints/Malacca.html (accessed June 6, 2010).

11. For example, after the *Limburg* (maritime terrorist) attack of October 2002, insurance rates for ships bound for Yemen tripled.

12. This is the average operation cost for a merchant ship per day.

13. An overview of the economic side of the problem is provided by Jack A. Gottschalk and Brian P. Flanagan, *Jolly Roger with an Uzi: The Threat and Rise of Modern Piracy* (Annapolis: U.S. Naval Institute Press, 2000), 86–93.

14. A 2003 Organisation for Economic Co-operation and Development estimate of overall costs for ship operators (prior to the emergence of Somali piracy) amounted to $1.3 billion, with annual operating costs of roughly $730 million.

15. See homepage, www.numast.org/ (especially for views on piracy under "NUMAST Campaigns").

16. Called "the world's largest shipping organization"; see homepage, www.bimco.dk/.

17. See J. N. Mak, "Pirates, Renegades, and Fishermen: The Politics of 'Sustainable' Piracy in the Strait of Malacca," and Jeffrey Chen, "The Emerging Nexus between Piracy and Maritime Terrorism: A Case Study of the Gerakan Aceh Merdeka (GAM)," both in Peter Lehr, ed., *Violence at Sea: Piracy in the Age of Global Terrorism* (New York: Routledge, 2006).

18. Peter Lehr and Hendrick Lehman, "Somalia—Pirates' New Paradise," in ibid.

19. Ibid.

20. See, for example, Robyn Hunter, "Somali Pirates Living the High Life," *BBC News, World, Africa*, October 28, 2008, http://news.bbc.co.uk/1/hi/world/africa/7650415.stm (accessed May 8, 2010).

21. Jeffrey Kuhlmann, "Piracy: Understanding the Real Threat," *Counterterrorism: Journal of Counterterrorism and Homeland Security International* 15, no. 4 (Winter 2009/2010): 36.

22. Ibid.

23. Israel and Russia are usually mentioned in this context.

24. "Arming Sailors: Gun-free Zones are Dangerous at Sea," *Washington Times,* May 11, 2009, www.washingtontimes.com/news/2009/may/11/arming-sailors/ (accessed June 8, 2010).

25. Foreign and Commonwealth Office, "The International Response to Piracy," May 5, 2010, www.fco.gov.uk/en/global-issues/conflict-prevention/piracy/international -response (accessed June 17, 2010).

26. See, for example, Eugene Kontorovich, "A Guantanamo Bay on the Sea: The Difficulty of Prosecuting Pirates and Terrorists," *California Law Review* 2010, www .californialawreview.org/assets/pdfs/98-1/Kontorovich.pdf (accessed June 17, 2010).

27. An easily readable description of this war can be found in Joshua E. London, *Victory in Tripoli: How America's War with the Barbary Pirates Established the U.S. Navy and Shaped a Nation* (Hoboken, N.J.: John Wiley and Sons, 2005).

28. At the time of writing (June 2010) the British couple, Paul and Rachel Chandler, hijacked in October 2009 on board their yacht *Lynn Rival,* are still in captivity. Allegedly, officials from the British Foreign and Commonwealth Office interfered with ransom negotiations that were just about to be successfully concluded.

29. "Patrolling the Sea for Piracy Is Like Policing America's East Coast with Five Police Cars," *The Times,* December 1, 2009.

30. An easily readable description of this war can be found in London, *Victory in Tripoli.*

31. See the interesting case study of Bruce A. Elleman, "The Taiping Rebellion, Piracy, and the Arrow War," in Elleman, Forbes, and Rosenberg, eds., *Piracy and Maritime Crime.*

32. Today's top-of-the-line ultra-large container ship *Emma Maersk,* for example, has an overall length of 397 meters, a deadweight tonnage of 157,000 tons, and a capacity of more than 11,000 TEU.

33. The MSP aims at maintaining a core of U.S.-flagged commercial vessels to be used as auxiliaries in times of crisis—for example, strengthening the U.S. Navy's sealift capacity. Such vessels are U.S.-crewed only.

34. Chip Cummins and Sarah Childress, "On the *Maersk*: 'I hope if I Die, I Die a Brave Person'," April 16, 2009, http://online.wsj.com/article/SB123984674935223605 .html (accessed June 13, 2010).

35. Ibid.

36. Ibid.

37. Ibid.

38. Ibid.

39. Ibid.

40. This list of questions is based on a contribution to the Centre for the Study of Terrorism and Political Violence conference, "War and Terrorism," University of St. Andrews, January 2010.

41. Cummins and Childress, "On the *Maersk*."

42. Ibid.

43. This was pointed out in the contribution to the "War and Terrorism" conference.

44. Cummins and Childress, "On the *Maersk*."

45. Ibid.

46. Ibid.

47. "Hostage Captain Rescued; Navy Snipers Kill 3 Pirates," CNN.com/world, April 12, 2009, http://edition.cnn.com/2009/WORLD/africa/04/12/somalia.pirates/index.html (accessed May 8, 2010).

48. Ray Rivera and Benjamin Weiser, "Somali Man Pleads Guilty in 2009 Hijacking of Ship," *New York Times*, May 19, 2010, A21.

49. "Suspected Pirates Nabbed after Skirmish with U.S. Navy Ship," CNN, www.cnn.com/2010/WORLD/africa/04/01/navy.pirates/index.html (accessed June 20, 2010).

50. "Off East African Coast, U.S. Drones Patrol in Hope of Stemming Piracy," *Boston Globe*, October 24, 2009, www.boston.com/news/world/africa/articles/2009/10/24/us_drones_patrol_east_african_coast_in_hope_of_stemming_piracy/ (accessed June 20, 2010).

51. Mansur Mirovalev, "Russia Says Freed Pirates Didn't Reach Land," Associated Press, May 11, 2010; see, for example, the *Boston Herald*, www.bostonherald.com/news/international/europe/view/20100511russia_says_freed_pirates_didnt_reach_land/ (accessed June 17, 2010).

52. Christian Curtenelle, "Uncertainty Surrounds Death in French Piracy Raid," Associated Press, April 17, 2009, www.blnz.com/news/2009/04/17/Uncertainty_surrounds_death_French_piracy_5492.html (accessed June 8, 2010).

53. "Mission Impossible: German Elite Troop Abandons Plan to Free Pirate Hostages," *Spiegel Online International,* May 4, 2009, www.spiegel.de/international/germany/0,1518,622766,00.html (accessed June 8, 2010).

54. Ibid.

55. As quoted by Richard Bach Jensen, "The United States, International Policing, and the War against Anarchist Terrorism, 1900–1914," *Terrorism and Political Violence* 13, no. 1 (Spring 2001): 15–46.

56. National Security Strategy of the United States of America 2002, as quoted by Mikkel Thorup, "Enemy of Humanity: The Anti-Piracy Discourse in Present-Day Anti-Terrorism, *Terrorism and Political Violence* 21, no. 3 (July–September 2009): 401–411. Emphasis by Thorup.

57. Ibid.

58. As quoted by Thorup, "Enemy of Humanity."

59. Andrew Lambert, "The Limits of Naval Power: The Merchant Brig *Three Sisters*, Riff Pirates, and British Battleships," in Elleman, Forbes, and Rosenberg, eds., *Piracy and Maritime Crime.*

8 National Security Surveillance: Unchecked or Limited Presidential Power?

Louis Fisher

Before You Begin

1. How does the Constitution balance the needs of national security against the rights and liberties of the individual?

2. In the field of national security, does the president possess "inherent" powers that are immune from legislative and judicial controls?

3. Which principles should guide government in balancing the need for national security wiretaps against the constitutional right of privacy?

4. If Congress legislates in the area of foreign intelligence surveillance and selects a procedure that is "exclusive," can the president ignore the statutory command?

5. Is it sufficient for the president to notify eight lawmakers and have them briefed about national security wiretaps conducted without a judicial warrant?

6. What role should federal courts play in supervising and approving national security wiretaps?

Introduction

On December 16, 2005, the *New York Times* reported that in the months following the September 11 terrorist attacks, President George W. Bush secretly authorized the National Security Agency (NSA) to listen to international calls involving Americans and others inside the United States without a court-approved warrant. The agency had been monitoring international telephone calls and international e-mail messages over the past three years in an effort to obtain evidence about terrorist activity.[1]

NSA's statutory purpose, however, was to spy on communications abroad, not on American citizens or domestic activities. During the Nixon

---

Note: The views expressed here are those of the author and do not represent any government agency.

administration, it had crossed the line by engaging in domestic surveillance. After September 11, NSA violated the Foreign Intelligence Surveillance Act (FISA) of 1978, which requires the executive branch to seek warrants from the FISA court to engage in surveillance in the United States. NSA's activity raised the fundamental issue of whether the administration could violate statutory restrictions (FISA) by invoking "inherent" powers supposedly available to the president under Article II of the Constitution or even claim extraconstitutional powers.

Background: Previous Illegal NSA Activities

In 1967, when the U.S. Army wanted NSA to eavesdrop on American citizens and domestic groups, the agency agreed to carry out the assignment. NSA began to put together a list of names of opponents of the Vietnam War. Adding names to a domestic "watch list" led to the creation of Minaret—a tracking system that allowed the agency to follow individuals and organizations involved in the antiwar movement.[2] NSA was now involved in a mission outside its statutory duties, using its surveillance powers to violate the First and Fourth Amendments.

On June 5, 1970, President Richard Nixon met with the heads of several intelligence agencies, including NSA, to initiate a program designed to monitor what the administration considered radical individuals and groups in the United States. Joining others at the meeting was Tom Charles Huston, a young attorney working at the White House. He drafted a forty-three-page, top-secret memorandum that became known as the Huston Plan. Huston put the matter bluntly to President Nixon: "Use of this technique is clearly illegal; it amounts to burglary."[3] His plan required NSA to use its technological capacity to intercept— without judicial warrants—the communication of U.S. citizens using international phone calls or telegrams.[4] Although Nixon, under pressure from FBI director J. Edgar Hoover, withdrew the Huston Plan, NSA had been targeting domestic groups for several years and continued to do so. Huston's blueprint, kept in a White House safe, became public in 1973, after Congress investigated the Watergate affair, and provided documentary evidence that Nixon had ordered NSA to illegally monitor American citizens. To conduct its surveillance operations, NSA entered into agreements with U.S. companies, including Western Union and RCA Global. U.S. citizens, expecting that their telegrams would be handled with utmost privacy, learned that American companies had been turning over the telegrams to NSA.[5]

Timeline

National Security Surveillance

October 25, 1978	Congress enacts the Foreign Intelligence Surveillance Act (FISA) to authorize and control national security surveillance.
September 11, 2001	Terrorists attack the United States, after which President George W. Bush authorizes warrantless national security surveillance (called the Terrorist Surveillance Program, or TSP).
December 16, 2005	The *New York Times* breaks the story on the existence of the TSP.
July 20, 2006	A federal district judge in California denies the government's motion to have a case dismissed that challenges the TSP.
July 25, 2006	A federal district judge in Illinois dismisses a lawsuit against a Bush administration program that involves the collection and monitoring of phone numbers.
August 17, 2006	A federal district judge in Michigan rules that the TSP violates the Constitution and federal statutes. She is reversed by the Sixth Circuit, and on February 19, 2008, the Supreme Court declines to take the case.
May 1, 2007	In congressional testimony, the director of national intelligence, Michael McConnell, appears to revive the administration's reliance on inherent powers after it had announced, earlier in the year, that it would abide by FISA.
July 2, 2008	A federal district court holds that FISA preempts the state secrets privilege offered by the administration to block court action.
July 10, 2008	Congress enacts legislation to provide immunity to the telecoms that assisted in NSA surveillance.
2009	Litigation continues against NSA, especially in *Al-Haramain Islamic Foundation, Inc. v. Bush.*

After the disclosure of the illegal NSA activities by the Church Committee, the agency supposedly underwent a sea change in attitude toward the statutory and constitutional issues and vowed to remain within the bounds of U.S. law.[6] Whatever lessons the agency learned in the 1970s were forgotten or subordinated decades later, especially in the period after September 11.

Establishing Limits on Wiretaps

Presidential authority to engage in eavesdropping for national security purposes without obtaining a warrant from a judge had never been properly clarified by statute or by judicial rulings. In this legal vacuum, presidents often expanded their powers in time of emergency. On May 21, 1940, on the eve of World War II, President Franklin D. Roosevelt sent a confidential memo to his attorney general, Robert H. Jackson, authorizing and directing him to obtain information "by listening devices" to monitor the conversations or other communications "of persons suspected of subversive activities against the Government of the United States, including suspected spies." Roosevelt told Jackson to limit these investigations "to a minimum and to limit them in so far as possible to aliens."[7]

In the landmark case of *Olmstead v. United States* (1928), the Supreme Court decided that the use of wiretaps by federal agents enforcing prohibition to monitor and intercept phone calls did not violate the Constitution. The Court reasoned that the taps—small wires inserted in telephone wires leading from residences—did not enter the premises of the home or office. Without physical entry there was neither "search" nor "seizure" under the Fourth Amendment.[8] This strained analysis drew a scathing dissent from Justice Louis Brandeis, who accurately predicted that technology would soon overwhelm the Fourth Amendment unless the Court met the challenge with open eyes.

Over the next few decades, federal courts wrestled with new forms of technological intrusion, ranging from "detectaphones" (placing an instrument against the wall of a room to pick up sound waves on the other side of the wall) to placing concealed microphones inside homes. Other variations of electronic eavesdropping blossomed. Police used "spike mikes," small electronic listening devices pushed through the wall of an adjoining house until they touched the heating duct of a suspect's dwelling. Law enforcement officers with earphones could listen to conversations taking place on both floors of the house.[9]

In 1967 the Supreme Court put a halt to these practices by returning to basic principles. By a 7–1 decision, it declared unconstitutional the placing of electronic listening and recording devices on the outside of public telephone booths to obtain incriminating evidence. Although there was no physical entrance into the area occupied by the suspect, the Court ruled that the individual had a legitimate expectation of privacy within the phone booth. In a decision broad enough to accommodate technological advances, the Court held that the Fourth Amendment "protects people, not places."[10] In response to this decision, Congress passed legislation in 1968 requiring law enforcement officers to obtain a judicial warrant before placing taps on phones or installing bugs (concealed microphones). If an "emergency" existed, communications could be intercepted for up to forty-eight hours without a warrant, in cases involving organized crime or national security. This legislation on wiretaps and electronic surveillance is often referred to as "Title III authority."

The 1968 statute established national policy on domestic wiretaps. The executive branch claimed that warrantless surveillances for national security purposes were lawful as a reasonable exercise of presidential power. A section of Title III stated that nothing in it limited the president's constitutional power to "take such measures as he deems necessary to protect the Nation against actual or potential attack or other hostile acts of a foreign power, to obtain foreign intelligence information deemed essential to the security of the United States, or to protect national security information against foreign intelligence activities." Nor should anything in Title III "be deemed to limit the constitutional power of the President to take such measures as he deems necessary to protect the United States against the overthrow of the Government by force or other unlawful means, or against any other clear and present danger to the structure or existence of the Government."[11] Congress, feeling an obligation to say something, chose general language to largely duck the issue. It would soon find it necessary to reenter the field and pass comprehensive legislation on national security surveillance.

What pushed Congress to act was a Supreme Court decision in 1972, which held that the Fourth Amendment required prior judicial approval for surveillances of domestic organizations.[12] The Court carefully avoided the question of surveillances over foreign powers, whether within or outside the United States. As to the language in Title III about national security wiretaps, the Court regarded that section as merely disclaiming congressional intent to define presidential powers in matters affecting national security and not to be taken as authorization for national security surveillances.

The FISA Statute

It was now necessary for Congress to pass legislation governing national security wiretaps. In 1973, in announcing a joint investigation by three Senate subcommittees, the lawmakers taking the lead explained: "Wiretapping and electronic surveillance pose a greater threat to the constitutional rights of American citizens than ever before. A recent survey of public attitudes shows that 75 percent of the American people feel that 'wiretapping and spying under the excuse of national security is a serious threat to people's privacy.' "[13] Extensive hearings were conducted to determine the procedures that would simultaneously protect security interests and individual rights. Legislation reported from the Senate Judiciary Committee in 1977 required the attorney general to obtain a judicial warrant authorizing the use of electronic surveillance in the United States for foreign intelligence purposes. Congress was filling a gaping hole. The federal government had never enacted legislation to regulate the use of electronic surveillance within the United States for foreign intelligence purposes, nor had the Supreme Court ever expressly decided the issue of whether the president had constitutional authority to authorize electronic surveillance without a warrant in cases concerning foreign intelligence.[14]

The bill enacted in 1978 was the Foreign Intelligence Surveillance Act. To provide a judicial check on executive actions, it created what is known as the FISA court. The chief justice of the United States would designate seven district court judges to hear applications for, and grant orders approving, electronic surveillance anywhere within the United States. After September 11, Congress increased the number of judges to eleven. No judge designated under this law "shall hear the same application for electronic surveillance under this Act which has been denied previously by another judge designated under this subsection."[15] The chief justice would also designate three judges from the district courts or appellate courts to make up a court of review with jurisdiction to review the denial of any application made under this statute.[16] Significantly, procedures under FISA "shall be the exclusive means by which electronic surveillance, as defined in section 101 of such Act, and the interception of domestic wire and oral communications may be conducted."[17]

The 1978 legislation required the government to certify that "the purpose" of the surveillance was to obtain foreign intelligence information. The USA PATRIOT Act of 2001 changed the requirements placed on federal officers when applying for a search order. The new language allowed application if a "significant purpose" was to obtain foreign intelligence information. The objective was to make it easier to obtain permission from the FISA court, not to bypass it altogether. Legislation after September 11 made other changes to FISA. Under the 1978 law, the attorney general could order emergency electronic surveillance without a warrant provided that he informed a judge having jurisdiction over national security wiretaps and obtained a warrant within twenty-four hours. Congress lengthened the emergency period to seventy-two hours in legislation reported by the Intelligence Committees.[18]

The Administration Responds to the Leak

The Bush administration could have chosen to say nothing about the leak in the *New York Times*; it could refuse either to acknowledge or deny the existence of the surveillance program. That approach is frequently used with public disclosures about other classified operations. In this case, the administration decided to have President Bush publicly defend the program as essential to the protection of U.S. security. One administration official explained that making the president the only voice "is directly taking on the critics. The Democrats are now in the position of supporting our efforts to protect Americans, or defend positions that could weaken our nation's security."[19] Sen. Patrick Leahy, ranking Democrat on the Judiciary Committee, responded to that tactic: "Our government must follow the laws and respect the Constitution while it protects Americans' security and liberty."[20]

During the operation of NSA surveillance, the Bush administration offered to brief eight members of Congress and the chief judge of the FISA court. The lawmakers (called the "Gang of Eight") included the chairs and ranking members of the two Intelligence Committees, the Speaker and minority leader of the House, and the Senate majority and minority leaders. Rep. Nancy Pelosi, Calif., at that time the Democratic leader in the House, acknowledged that she had been advised of the program shortly after it began and had "been provided with updates on several occasions."[21]

On December 17, 2005, in a weekly radio address, President Bush defended what he called the Terrorist Surveillance Program (TSP). He acknowledged that he had authorized NSA, "consistent with U.S. law and the Constitution, to intercept the international communications of people with known links to al Qaeda and related terrorist organizations."[22] His program was, in fact, inconsistent with, and in violation of, statutory law. Gradually it became clear that when President Bush referred to "U.S. law" or "authority," he meant law created within the executive branch, whether or not consistent with law passed by Congress. In his radio address, Bush underscored what he considered to be his independent constitutional powers: "The authorization I gave the National Security agency after September 11 helped address that problem [of combating terrorism] in a way that is fully consistent with my constitutional responsibilities and authorities."[23] He said he had "reauthorized this program more than 30 times since the September 11 attacks."[24] Bush expressed his determination to continue the program as "a vital tool in our war against the terrorists."[25]

In a news conference on December 19, Bush stated: "As President and Commander in Chief, I have the constitutional responsibility and the constitutional authority to protect our country. Article II of the Constitution gives me that responsibility and the authority necessary to fulfill it." He noted that Congress after September 11 had passed the Authorization for Use of Military Force (AUMF) to grant him "additional authority to use military force against Al Qaida."[26] Also on December 19, Attorney General Alberto Gonzales held a press briefing on the NSA program, claiming that "the President has the inherent authority under the Constitution, as Commander-in-Chief, to engage in this kind of activity."[27] When asked why the administration did not seek a warrant from the FISA court, which Congress created as the exclusive means of authorizing national security eavesdropping, Gonzales replied that the administration continued to seek warrants from the FISA court but was not "legally required" to do so in every case if another statute granted the president additional authority.[28] It was the administration's position that the AUMF provided that additional authority.

Gonzales emphasized the need for "the speed and the agility" that the FISA process lacked: "You have to remember that FISA was passed by the Congress in 1978. There have been tremendous advances in technology" since that time.[29] Why did the administration not ask Congress to amend FISA to grant the president greater flexibility, as was done several times after 1978 and even after September 11? Gonzales replied he was advised "that would be difficult, if not impossible."[30] Why not try and put the burden on Congress to pass legislation necessary for national security?

The Sole-Organ Doctrine

On January 19, 2006, the Justice Department produced a forty-two-page white paper defending the legality of the NSA program. It concluded that the NSA activities "are supported by the President's well-recognized inherent constitutional authority as Commander in Chief and sole organ for the Nation in foreign affairs to conduct warrantless surveillance of enemy forces for intelligence purposes to detect and disrupt armed attacks on the United States."[31] Later in the paper, the Justice Department linked "sole organ" to the 1936 Supreme Court decision of *United States v. Curtiss-Wright.*[32]

Nothing in *Curtiss-Wright* supports exclusive, plenary, unchecked, inherent, or extraconstitutional powers for the president. The only question before the Court was the constitutionality of Congress delegating part of its authority to the president to place an arms embargo in a region in South America. The case therefore involved *legislative,* not presidential, power. In imposing the embargo, President Franklin D. Roosevelt issued a proclamation that relied solely on statutory—not constitutional—authority. He acted pursuant to the authority "conferred in me by the said joint resolution of Congress. . . ."[33] The issue in *Curtiss-Wright* was whether Congress could delegate legislative power more broadly in international affairs than it could in domestic affairs. In the previous year, the Court had struck down the delegation by Congress of *domestic* power to the president.[34] None of the briefs submitted to the Court in the *Curtiss-Wright* case discussed the availability of independent, inherent, or extraconstitutional powers to the president.[35]

Nevertheless, in his extensive dicta wholly extraneous to the legal issue before the Court, Justice George Sutherland discussed the availability of inherent and extraconstitutional powers for the president in foreign affairs. His arguments drew from an article that Sutherland had published as a U.S. senator from Utah and from a book that he published in 1919. Sutherland's historical analysis has been dismissed as unreliable and erroneous by many scholars.[36] Sutherland's use of John Marshall's speech in 1800, referring to the president as "sole organ," is a glaring example of a statement made for one limited purpose taken wholly out of context to make the case for a proposition that Marshall never believed at any time in four decades of public life.

On March 7, 1800, in the House of Representatives, Marshall called the president "the sole organ of the nation in its external relations, and its sole representative with foreign nations."[37] The intent was not to advocate inherent or exclusive powers for the president. His objective was merely to defend the authority of President John Adams to carry out an extradition treaty. The president was not the sole organ in formulating the treaty, which required joint action by the president and the Senate. He was the sole organ in implementing it. Article II of the Constitution specifies that it is the president's duty to "take Care that the Laws be faithfully executed." Under Article VI, all treaties made "shall be the supreme Law of the Land."[38]

Once on the Supreme Court as chief justice, Marshall held consistently to his position that the making of foreign policy is a joint exercise by the executive and legislative branches, whether by treaty or by statute, not a unilateral or exclusive authority of the president. With the war power, for example, Marshall looked solely to Congress—not the president—for the authority to take the country to war. He had no difficulty identifying which branch possessed the war power: "The whole powers of war being, by the constitution of the United States, vested in congress, the acts of that body can alone be resorted to as our guides in this enquiry."[39] In an 1804 case, Marshall ruled that when a presidential proclamation issued in time of war conflicts with a statute enacted by Congress, the statute prevails.[40]

In addition to these constitutional arguments, the Justice Department in 2006 looked to statutes as legal justification for NSA eavesdropping. It argued that "Congress by statute has confirmed and supplemented the President's recognized authority under Article II of the Constitution to conduct such warrantless surveillance to prevent catastrophic attacks on the homeland." In responding to the September 11 attacks, Congress enacted the AUMF to authorize the president to "use all necessary and appropriate force against those nations, organizations, or persons he determines planned, authorized, committed, or aided the terrorist attacks" of September 11, in order to prevent "any future acts of international terrorism against the United States."[41] Moreover, although FISA "generally requires judicial approval of electronic surveillance, FISA also contemplates that Congress may authorize such surveillance by a statute other than FISA," and the AUMF, the Justice Department said, met that requirement.[42] Any congressional statute interpreted to impede the president's ability to use electronic surveillance to detect and prevent future attacks by an enemy "would be called into very serious doubt" as to its constitutionality. If this constitutional question "had to be addressed, FISA would be unconstitutional as applied to this narrow context."[43] According to this reading, statutory law could not restrict what the president decided to do under his Article II powers.

There is no evidence that any member of Congress, in voting on the AUMF, thought that it would in any way modify the requirements of FISA or give the president new and independent authority to conduct warrantless national security wiretaps. When Congress decides to amend a statute or grant new powers, it does so explicitly, not by implication. It is a canon of statutory construction that "repeal by implication" is disfavored. Changing law requires specific, conscious, and deliberate action by Congress.

A Hospital Visit

After initiating the Terrorist Surveillance Program, it was the policy of the administration to reauthorize it periodically after internal review of its legality.

In March 2004, the Office of Legal Counsel (OLC) in the Justice Department concluded that the program had a number of legal deficiencies and recommended that it not be reauthorized until changed. The presidential order to reauthorize the program had a line for the attorney general to sign. Attorney General John Ashcroft and Deputy Attorney General James Comey agreed with the OLC analysis and recommendation. At that same time, Ashcroft was hospitalized with a serious illness, placed in intensive care, and had transferred the powers of attorney general to Comey until he could recover and resume the powers of his office.

On the evening of March 10, 2004, in his capacity as acting attorney general, Comey was heading home with his security detail at about 8 o'clock. He received a call from Ashcroft's chief of staff that White House counsel Gonzales and White House chief of staff Andrew Card were on their way to the hospital. Comey thought that Gonzales and Card, knowing of the legal objections that the Justice Department had raised with the TSP, might try to convince Ashcroft to reverse Justice's position and agree to sign the reauthorization form. Comey called his chief of staff and told him to get as many of Comey's people as possible to the hospital immediately. He called FBI director Robert Mueller and asked that he come to the hospital.

When Comey's car reached the hospital, he raced up the stairs to Ashcroft's room and found Mrs. Ashcroft standing by the bed. As Comey explained to the Senate Judiciary Committee on May 15, 2007, he was concerned that, given Ashcroft's illness, there might be an effort to ask him to sign the form and overrule what Justice had decided, when he was in no condition to do that.[44] Comey tried to get Ashcroft oriented to the issue, in preparation for the arrival of Gonzales and Card. Mueller had directed FBI agents not to have Comey removed from Ashcroft's room under any circumstance. OLC head Jack Goldsmith and a senior Justice official, Patrick Philbin, arrived and entered Ashcroft's room.

Within a few minutes Gonzales and Card entered the room. Gonzales, holding an envelope, told Ashcroft why they were there and why they wanted him to approve the reauthorization of the TSP. Ashcroft lifted his head off the pillow and defended the position that Justice had taken. He said his opinion did not matter because he was not the attorney general. Pointing to Comey, he said he was the attorney general. Gonzales and Card, without acknowledging Comey, left the room. At that point Mueller arrived and Comey explained what had happened.[45]

Card then called Comey and told him to come to the White House immediately. Comey said that after the conduct he had just witnessed, he would not come without a witness. Card responded, "What conduct? We were just there to wish him well."[46] Comey called Solicitor General Ted Olson, explained the circumstances, and asked him to accompany him to the White House and witness what was said. Comey and Olson arrived at the White House that evening at 11 o'clock. Comey told the Judiciary Committee that he was very upset and angry because he thought Gonzales and Card had tried to take advantage of a very sick man who lacked the official authority to do what they asked of him.[47]

Card, Gonzales, Comey, and Olson discussed the situation. Card said he had heard reports that there might be a number of resignations at the Justice Department over the incident. Comey said he could not stay if the administration decided to engage in conduct that the Justice Department concluded had no legal basis.[48] Other possible resignations included FBI director Mueller, Comey's chief of staff, Ashcroft's chief of staff, and quite likely Ashcroft.[49] The mass resignations were averted when President Bush met with Comey and Mueller in the Oval Office two days later, in the morning, to receive a briefing on Justice's counterterrorism work. As Comey was leaving, Bush asked to see him privately in a separate room for about fifteen minutes. Bush did the same with Mueller. The result of those two meetings was that Comey understood from Bush that he was to do "the right thing" as he saw it.[50] To Comey, that meant that Justice would not sign the reauthorization form until it was satisfied that the program had been sufficiently altered to pass legal muster. Pending the review by Justice, the White House went ahead with the TSP without the approval of Comey or the Justice Department.[51] After two or three weeks, and the acceptance of changes urged by Justice, the reauthorization form received the signature of the attorney general.[52]

Hayden's Testimony

Michael V. Hayden appeared before the Senate Intelligence Committee on May 18, 2006, to testify on his nomination to be Central Intelligence Agency (CIA) director. Previously he had served as NSA director at the time that the Terrorist Surveillance Program was initiated. At the hearing, Hayden defended the legality of the NSA wiretap program on constitutional, not statutory, grounds. He did not attempt to use the AUMF as legal justification. In recalling his service at NSA after September 11, Hayden told the committee that when he talked to NSA lawyers "they were very comfortable with the Article II arguments and the president's inherent authorities." When they came to him and discussed the lawfulness of the NSA program, "our discussion anchored itself on Article II."[53] The attorneys "came back with a real comfort level that this was within the president's authority [i.e., Article II]."[54] This legal advice was not put in writing, and Hayden "did not ask for it." Instead, "they talked to me about Article II."[55] There is no evidence that the NSA general counsel was asked to prepare a legal memo defending the TSP—no paper trail, no accountability, just informal talks.

Sen. Carl Levin, D-Mich., asked Hayden how he balanced security interests against liberty and privacy concerns. In initiating the TSP, he wanted to know if Hayden understood there was "at least a privacy concern there, whether or not one concludes that security interests outweigh the privacy concerns"? Hayden began by calling September 11 a watershed: "We were taking [steps] in a regime that was different from the regime that existed on 10th September." He had spoken to NSA employees on September 13 "about free peoples always having to decide the balance of security and their liberties, and that we through our tradition have always planted our banner way down here on the end of the spectrum toward security." He said "there are going to be a lot of pressures to push that banner down toward security, and our job at NSA was to keep America free by making Americans feel safe again. So this balance between security and liberty was foremost in our mind."[56] Levin tried to clarify that response: "Does that mean your answer to my question is yes?" Hayden replied: "Senator, I understand there are privacy concerns involved in all of this. There's privacy concerns involved in the routine activities of NSA."[57]

Hayden repeatedly claimed that the NSA program was legal and that the CIA "will obey the laws of the United States and will respond to our treaty obligations."[58] What did Hayden mean by "law"? National policy decided by statute or a treaty? A policy made solely by the president? During the hearing, he treated "law" as the latter—something that can be derived from Article II or inherent powers: "I had two lawful programs in front of me, one authorized by the president, the other one would have been conducted under FISA as currently crafted and implemented."[59] In other words, he had two avenues before him: one authorized by statutory law, the other in violation of it. He told one senator, "I did not believe—still don't believe—that I was acting unlawfully. I was acting under a lawful authorization."[60] He meant a presidential directive issued under Article II, even against the exclusive policy set forth in FISA.

Hearing Hayden insist that he acted legally in implementing the NSA program, a senator said, "I assume that the basis for that was the Article II powers, the inherent powers of the president to protect the country in time of danger and war." Hayden replied, "Yes, sir, commander in chief powers."[61] Hayden implied that he was willing to violate statutory law in order to carry out what he called presidential law. After September 11, CIA director George Tenet asked whether, as NSA director, he could "do more" to combat terrorism with surveillance. Hayden answered, "Not within current law."[62] In short, the administration knowingly and consciously decided to act against statutory policy. It knew that the NSA eavesdropping program it wanted to conduct was illegal under FISA but decided to go ahead.

At one point in the hearing, Hayden referred to the legal and political embarrassments of NSA during the Nixon administration, when it conducted warrantless eavesdropping against domestic groups. In discussing what should be done after September 11, he told one group: "Look, I've got a workforce out there that remembers the mid-1970s." He asked the Senate committee to forgive him for using "a poor sports metaphor," but he advised the group in this manner: "Since about 1975, this agency's had a permanent one-ball, two-strike count against it, and we don't take many close pitches."[63] The TSP was a close pitch. Perhaps with further public disclosures one can answer the question: Did NSA take a close pitch and strike out?

Setbacks in Court

A number of private parties challenged the legality and constitutionality of NSA's eavesdropping. To show the injury necessary to have a case litigated, plaintiffs argued that the contacts they used to have with clients over the telephone were now impossible because of NSA monitoring. To maintain contact, they would have to travel to see clients personally, even in countries outside the United States. The government sought to have all such lawsuits dismissed on the ground that litigation would inevitably disclose "state secrets" injurious to the nation. That argument had been weakened when the Bush administration decided to publicly acknowledge the existence of the TSP and publicly defend its legality.

In a major case in California, decided on July 20, 2006, a federal district judge held that the state secrets privilege did not block action on the lawsuit and that plaintiffs had shown sufficient injury to establish standing. The judge denied the government's motion to have the case dismissed or go to summary judgment on the issue of the state secrets privilege. Under summary judgment, a court does not begin the time-consuming process of depositions and trial but rather goes immediately to the legal issue before it. As a result of the judge's rulings, the lawsuit was allowed to proceed—a significant defeat for the Bush administration.[64]

In this case, the plaintiffs alleged that AT&T and its holding company had collaborated with NSA in conducting a massive, warrantless surveillance program that illegally tracked the domestic and foreign communications of millions of Americans. The plaintiffs charged violations of the First and Fourth Amendments of the Constitution, of FISA, various sections of other federal laws, and California's Unfair Competition Law. In attempting to have the case dismissed, the government advanced three arguments based on the state secrets privilege: "(1) the very subject matter of this case is a state secret; (2) plaintiffs cannot make a prima facie case for their claims without classified evidence and (3) the privilege effectively deprives AT&T of information necessary to raise valid defenses."[65]

To the court, the first step in determining whether a piece of information is a "state secret" requires this judgment: is the information actually a "secret"?[66] The court pointed to public reports about the TSP in the *New York Times* on December 16, 2005. It noted that President Bush, the following day, confirmed the existence of the program and publicly described the mechanism by which the program was authorized and reviewed. Attorney General Gonzales had talked about the program in public briefings and public hearings, and the Justice Department publicly defended the TSP's legality and constitutionality. Based on this public record, the court said, "it might appear that none of the subject matter in this litigation could be considered a secret given that the alleged surveillance programs have been so widely reported in the media."[67]

The court recognized that just because a factual statement has been made public does not guarantee that the statement is true or that the activity was not a genuine secret. Even if a previously secret program has been leaked, verification of the program by the government could be harmful.[68] Also, media reports may be unreliable.[69] However, in this case the administration had "publicly admitted the existence of a 'terrorist surveillance program,' which the government insists is completely legal." Moreover, given the scope of the TSP, the court found it "inconceivable" that it could exist without the acquiescence and cooperation of a telecommunications provider. The size of AT&T and its public acknowledgment that it performs classified contracts and employs thousands who have government security clearances provided enough verifiable public information to avoid adopting the state secrets privilege as an absolute bar to litigation.[70] Under this reasoning, the court concluded that the plaintiffs were entitled "to at least some discovery."[71] As to whether plaintiffs had shown injury and established standing to sue AT&T, the court concluded that they "have sufficiently alleged that they suffered an actual, concrete injury traceable to AT&T and redressable by this court."[72] On those grounds, the court allowed the case to proceed, with each side at liberty to request additional documents to support its position.

A week later, the government prevailed in an NSA case decided in Illinois. A U.S. district court dismissed a class-action lawsuit against a Bush administration program that involved the collection and monitoring of phone numbers rather than actual conversations (the program that the *New York Times* revealed in December 2005). The administration neither confirmed nor denied the existence of this program on phone numbers, and several telephone companies denied that they had given customer calling records to NSA. The district judge noted that "no executive branch official has officially confirmed or denied the existence of any program to obtain large quantities of customer telephone records, the subject of the plaintiffs' lawsuit."[73] By invoking the state secrets privilege, the government this time prevented the plaintiffs from seeking additional facts or documents to establish that they had been harmed or would suffer harm in the future. The judge ruled that the plaintiffs could seek relief only from the elected branches.

In the California case, the federal court merely let the case continue, without deciding on the merits. However, on August 17, 2006, District Judge Anna Diggs Taylor, in Michigan, ruled that the TSP violated the Constitution and federal statutes. Like the judge in California, Taylor took note that the existence of the program, the lack of warrants, and the focus on communications in which one party was in the United States had been admitted by the administration.[74] Contrary to the arguments of NSA, Taylor was persuaded that the plaintiffs were able "to establish a prima facie case based solely on Defendants' public admissions regarding the TSP."[75] As to injury, the plaintiffs had provided documentation that "they are stifled in their ability to vigorously conduct research, interact with sources, talk with clients and, in the case of the attorney Plaintiffs, uphold their oath of providing effective and ethical representation of their clients."[76] Plaintiffs cited additional injury by having to travel to meet with clients and others relevant to their cases.

NSA argued in court that it could not defend itself "without the exposure of state secrets." Judge Taylor disagreed, pointing out that the Bush administration "has repeatedly told the general public that there is a valid basis in law for the TSP." Moreover, NSA contended that the president had statutory authority under the AUMF and the Constitution to authorize continued use of the TSP, and presented that case "without revealing or relying on any classified information."[77] Taylor found that the agency's argument that it could not defend itself in this case "without the use of classified information to be disingenuous and without merit."[78]

Judge Taylor next addressed the constitutional and statutory arguments presented by the plaintiffs, starting with the Fourth Amendment: "The right of the people to be secure in their persons, houses, papers, and effects, against unreasonable searches and seizures, shall not be violated, and no Warrants shall issue, but upon probable cause, supported by Oath or affirmance, and particularly describing the place to be searched, and the persons or things to be seized."

She said that the Fourth Amendment was adopted "to assure that Executive abuses of the power to search would not continue in our new nation."[79] She cited cases that described a private residence as a place where society particularly recognizes an expectation of privacy. Other cases emphasized that executive officers of the government could not be trusted to be neutral and disinterested magistrates or the sole judges of the extent of their prosecutorial powers. In enacting FISA, Congress insisted on a body outside the executive branch—the FISA court—to provide independent review. Yet she concluded that the TSP "has undisputedly been implemented without regard to FISA . . . and obviously in violation of the Fourth Amendment."[80]

The next constitutional issue explored was the principle of separation of powers. Judge Taylor recalled the Framers' resentment of the General Warrants authorized by King George III, which helped to precipitate the break with England. She cited the language of Justice Jackson in the 1952 steel seizure case that emergency power was consistent with free government "only when their control is lodged elsewhere than in the Executive who exercises them."[81] Taylor concluded that President Bush, by acting in a manner forbidden by FISA, functioned outside the law decided by legislative deliberations and attempted to combine the powers of government into one branch.

The Bush administration defended the TSP by relying on the AUMF. Judge Taylor observed that the statute "says nothing whatsoever of intelligence or surveillance." She asked whether the authority for the TSP could be implied in the AUMF. In the cases of FISA and Title III on wiretaps, Congress had adopted those statutes "as the exclusive means by which electronic surveillance may be adopted." Prior warrants must be obtained from judges. FISA allowed for a fifteen-day exception in time of a declared war, but here the government argued that the TSP could function for more than five years without congressional authorization. The implication by the government that the AUMF somehow modified FISA, without direct and explicit amendment, "cannot be made by this court,"[82] said the judge. She also dismissed arguments by the administration that relied on inherent powers and broad readings of Article II and the president's powers of commander in chief. There are no "powers not created by the Constitution. So all 'inherent powers' must derive from that Constitution." The argument that "inherent powers justify the program here in litigation must fail."[83]

Finally, Judge Taylor addressed the government's argument that there were a number of practical justifications for the TSP, including the difficulty of obtaining judicial warrants in a timely manner. She noted that previous decisions by federal courts had rejected "practical arguments" used to justify emergency actions by executive officers, including the lack of judicial competence, the danger of security leaks, and unacceptable delay.[84] She observed that the government had not sought amendments to FISA to alleviate these practical problems. She found the government's argument for "speed and agility," as reason for bypassing statutory and constitutional requirements, to be "weightless."[85]

The government appealed her decision to the Sixth Circuit. On July 6, 2007, the appellate court reversed Judge Taylor on the ground that the plaintiffs lacked standing to bring the suit. Writing for a 2–1 panel, Judge Alice M. Batchelder concluded that if litigation in a state secrets case "would necessitate admission or disclosure of even the existence of the secret, then the case is non-justiciable and must be dismissed on the pleadings," i.e., without proceeding to trial, gaining documents through the discovery process, and reaching the merits.[86] On February 19, 2008, the Supreme Court declined to take this case.

Legislative Remedies

After the *New York Times* disclosed NSA's eavesdropping program, Congress drafted legislation to put the policy on firm legal footing. One element was to impose some type of legislative oversight to replace the skimpy "Gang of Eight" procedure that the Bush administration had followed.[87] However, the administration also was ready to use the *Times* disclosure to press for greater authority, claiming that FISA was out of date and had not kept pace with changing technology. Executive officials testified that it was impractical after September 11 to expect the administration to obtain individual warrants every time it needed to listen to a conversation of someone suspected of being connected with al Qaeda. It urged legislation to recognize by statute what it considered to be the president's inherent authority to conduct warrantless eavesdropping to collect foreign intelligence. Critics of this approach advised Congress that it would be better to have no legislation than to grant the president such sweeping, unchecked power.[88]

By early March 2006, Republicans on the Senate Intelligence Committee said that they had reached agreement with the White House on proposed legislation to impose new forms of congressional oversight. The bill would allow wiretapping without warrants and increase the current three-day limit for emergency surveillance to forty-five days. If the administration found it necessary to exceed forty-five days, the attorney general would have to certify that continued surveillance was necessary to protect the country and explain why the administration would not seek a warrant. His statement would go to a newly created, seven-member "terrorist surveillance subcommittee" of the Senate Intelligence Committee, which would receive full access to details of the program's operations. Democrats attacked the bill as an abdication of legislative power and an effort to bless the NSA program before Congress, and the public, had understood its reach or manner of operation. Sen. John D. Rockefeller IV, D-W.Va., vice chairman of the Intelligence Committee, described the panel as "basically under the control of the White House."[89]

The seven members of the new subcommittee went to the White House to receive a two-hour briefing on the TSP and were scheduled to visit NSA to learn more. Under the rules set by the White House, the seven senators were not permitted to share what they learned with the other eight senators on the Intelligence Committee. Senator Rockefeller had traveled to NSA the previous week and spent almost seven hours getting information from more than a dozen NSA lawyers, policy makers, and technicians. He told reporters he learned more from that visit than from the White House presentation, which consisted of "flip-chart jobs and not very impressive."[90]

In an April 6 appearance before the House Judiciary Committee, Attorney General Gonzales seemed to suggest that warrantless wiretaps could be placed not only on international calls, with one party in the United States, but even on purely domestic calls if they were related to al Qaeda. In response to a question from Rep. Adam Schiff, D-Calif., as to whether the administration thought it had authority to listen to domestic calls without a warrant, Gonzales responded, "I'm not going to rule it out." In previous testimony, he said that the administration had rejected NSA spying on domestic communications because of the fear of public outcry. The Justice Department sought to downplay the significance of his remarks.[91]

As debate on the legislation continued, the hope of reaching an early consensus vanished. Republican leaders thought there would be an advantage in passing legislation just before the November 2006 elections, to allow voters to compare the national security credentials of the two parties, but there were too many bills and too many contradictions. The Senate bill crafted by Sen. Arlen Specter, R-Pa., seemed to many to be too close to what the White House wanted. On the House side, debate was spread among six rival surveillance bills.[92] Strong objections were raised to allowing the FISA court to decide the constitutionality of the NSA program.[93] How would that be done? Secret briefs submitted to the FISA court by the administration, followed by secret oral argument and eventually the release of a declassified, sanitized ruling? Why should constitutional issues be decided in that manner?

With Congress about to recess for the elections, the differences between the various bills were too large to bridge. Members of both parties were reluctant to recognize Article II/inherent powers of the president to conduct warrantless wiretaps. It proved impossible to submit legislation to Bush for his signature.[94] The House managed to pass a bill, 232–191, but it was too unlike the Senate bill to permit quick resolution in conference committee.[95] Democratic victories in the November elections put an end not only to Republican control of Congress but to the Republican-drafted bills on national security surveillance.

Mid-Course Correction?

In the midst of some setbacks in federal courts, the administration announced in January 2007 that it would not continue to skirt the FISA court but would instead seek warrants from it, as required by statute. In a January 17 letter, Attorney General Gonzales informed the Senate Judiciary Committee that on January 10 a judge of the FISA court issued orders authorizing the government "to target for collection international communications into or out of the United States where there is probable cause to believe that one of the communicants is a member or agent of al Qaeda or an associated terrorist organization." As a result of those orders, "any electronic surveillance that was occurring as part of the Terrorist Surveillance Program will now be conducted subject to the approval of the Foreign Intelligence Surveillance Court."[96] This statement seemed to comply with FISA, but did it contemplate a one-time, blanket judicial approval for all future national security wiretaps within this category? Gonzales called these orders "innovative, they are complex, and it took considerable time and work for the Government to develop the approach that was proposed to the Court and for the Judge on the FISC to consider and approve these orders."[97] He concluded: "Under these circumstances, the President has determined not to reauthorize the Terrorist Surveillance Program when the current reauthorization expires."[98]

Coverage by the *New York Times* underscored the altered legal and political climate. The new Democratic-led Congress intended to hold searching investigations of the NSA program, including hearings within a few days to take testimony from Gonzales. Exactly what the FISA court authorized remained classified. Justice Department officials told the *New York Times* that the orders were not broad approval of the TSP but rather a series of orders for individual targets.[99] Precisely what was ordered and what was not would remain private. The administration said it had briefed the full House and Senate Intelligence Committees in closed sessions. Rep. Heather Wilson, R-N.M., who served on the House committee, denied that such briefings had been held. Some sources said that congressional aides had been briefed without lawmakers present.[100]

Gonzales's appearance before the Senate Judiciary Committee on January 18, 2007, provoked further confrontation. He would not agree to provide more documents to explain the decision.[101] He appeared to concede that the administration not only broke the law but knew it had done so: "The truth of the matter is we looked at FISA and we all concluded there's no way we can do what we have to do to protect this country under the strict reading of FISA."[102] There were reports that the FISA court orders would be shown to House and Senate leaders and selected committees, including Intelligence and Judiciary, although access by the latter seemed restricted to chairs and ranking members.[103]

The tentative and possibly temporary accommodation by the administration undermined its position in court that the NSA cases should be considered moot and dismissed. Had the administration entered into a final and binding agreement, or one that could be revisited later and reversed? At a hearing on January 31, 2007, before the Sixth Circuit, one of the judges asked: "You could opt out at any time, couldn't you?" The deputy solicitor general acknowledged the possibility.[104]

Swerving Again: McConnell's Testimony

On May 1, 2007, Director of National Intelligence Michael McConnell testified before the Senate Intelligence Committee and signaled that the administration might not be able to keep its pledge to seek warrants through the FISA court. McConnell had served as NSA director from 1992 to 1996. On the one hand, his written statement appeared to endorse FISA as the foundation for conducting national security wiretaps. The pending bill, he said, "seeks to restore FISA to its original focus on protecting the privacy interests of persons in the United States."[105] He could not "overstate how instrumental FISA has been in helping the IC [intelligence community] protect the nation from terrorist attacks since September 11, 2001."[106] Yet he also stated that FISA's requirement to obtain a court order, "based on a showing of probable cause, slows, and in some cases prevents altogether, the Government's efforts to conduct surveillance of communications it believes are significant to the national security."[107] The Justice Department, in its testimony, objected to what it considered to be the impractical requirement of obtaining a warrant from the FISA court for each national security surveillance. Such an approach was "infeasible" and would impose "intolerable burdens on our intelligence efforts.[108]

Senior officials in the Bush administration told the committee that the president had independent authority under the Constitution to order this type of surveillance without warrants and without complying with statutory procedures. McConnell referred several times to Article II as a source of inherent presidential authority. When asked by Sen. Russ Feingold, D-Wis., whether the administration would no longer sidestep the FISA court, McConnell replied: "Sir, the president's authority under Article II is in the Constitution. So if the president chose to exercise Article II authority, that would be the president's choice." He wanted to highlight that "Article II is Article II, so in a different circumstance, I can't speak for the president what he might decide."[109]

Why would an administration witness tell a congressional committee that Article II is in the Constitution, and that Article II is Article II? Those are obvious—too obvious—points. The apparent message was that Congress can legislate as it likes, but the president need not comply, even if Article II of the Constitution directs the president to "take Care that the Laws be faithfully Executed." McConnell's testimony is similar to that of Michael Hayden, when he was nominated to be CIA director. Both men seemed to be coached to repeat the words "Article II, Article II, inherent, inherent," as though such assertions and claims stated with sufficient frequency would take on substance without further explanation. An assertion is an assertion until the witness offers a persuasive and informed argument, which neither McConnell nor Hayden attempted to do. Moreover, McConnell's testimony, or at least his oral remarks, seemed to undermine the administration's efforts to convince federal courts that pending challenges to the TSP were moot.

The Immunity Issue

On August 5, 2007, just before a scheduled one-month recess, Congress passed an amendment to FISA that gave the administration the discretion it had sought, although only for a period of 180 days. The legislation was called the Protect America Act.[110] A key issue in drafting permanent legislation was whether to grant retroactive immunity to the telecom firms that had provided the technical assistance for NSA surveillance.[111] In October 2007, the Senate Intelligence Committee voted to give the telecoms legal immunity from lawsuit because they had "acted in good faith" and believed the TSP was legal and presidentially authorized.[112] The companies had their own offices of general counsel responsible for independently determining what was legal or not. They could have complied with the law instead of deferring to presidential assertions that were in direct violation of the law. Administration officials stated that the letters to the companies requesting their assistance "said very forcefully" the surveillance program was "being directed by the president, and this has been deemed lawful at the very highest levels of the government."[113] Why would telecoms agree to violate statutory law because executive officials decided that the NSA initiative had been "deemed lawful"?

On February 21, 2008, President Bush argued that "[if] we do not give liability protection to those who are helping us, they won't help us. And if they don't help us, there will be no program. And if there's no program, America is more vulnerable."[114] A week later he said: "You cannot expect phone companies to participate if they feel like they're going to be sued."[115] If the phone companies wanted protection from legal action they could have complied with the procedures set forth in the FISA statute. They were legally at risk because they decided to violate the law.

On July 10, 2008, Congress passed legislation to give the telecoms retroactive immunity. The statutory language is quite unusual. First, the statute reaffirms that the procedures set forth in FISA are the "exclusive means" by which electronic surveillance and interception of certain communications may be conducted.[116]

If FISA establishes the exclusive means, the telecoms (and the administration) should have complied with it. Yet Title VIII of the 2008 statute provides "Protection of Persons Assisting the Government." The title covers civil actions filed in federal or state court that allege that (1) an electronic communications service provider furnished assistance to an element of the intelligence community," and (2) "seeks monetary or other relief from the electronic communications service provider related to the provisions of such assistance."[117]

This type of civil action may not be maintained in court "if the Attorney General certifies to the district court of the United States in which such action is pending" that the company being sued was provided a certification in writing over the period from September 11, 2001, through January 17, 2007, regarding the need to detect or prevent a terrorist attack, and that the company's activity was "(i) authorized by the President; and (ii) determined to be lawful."[118] A blank check to the president? No. The statute provides that the written certification shall be given effect "unless the court finds that such certification is not supported by substantial evidence provided to the court pursuant to this section." A court must conduct an inquiry into the quality and substance of the evidence supporting the certification.

Under these conditions and despite the immunity provision, litigation continues. One of the major cases involves the Al-Haramain Islamic Foundation, based in Oregon. On a routine discovery request, the company obtained a top-secret calling log that showed it was a target of warrantless surveillance. The Treasury Department inadvertently gave the document to Al-Haramain and insisted that the company return it, which it did. On November 16, 2007, the Ninth Circuit ruled that the company could not refer to the document because it was covered by the state secrets privilege, yet allowed the case to move forward on other grounds, including the extensive public disclosures by the Bush administration about the TSP.[119]

The next question in this case was whether a statute passed by Congress (FISA) trumped a program created by the administration (TSP). On July 2, 2008, a federal district court held that FISA preempted the state secrets privilege. In other words, a statutory policy necessarily overrode a claim or assertion by an administration, including the claim and assertion of state secrets. FISA "limits the power of the executive branch to conduct such activities [foreign intelligence surveillance] and it limits the executive branch's authority to assert the state secrets privilege in response to challenges to the legality of its foreign intelligence surveillance activities."[120] Pursuant to this reasoning, the federal court denied the administration's motion to dismiss the case.

The litigation continued into 2009, giving the district judge an opportunity to review a sealed document within the judge's chambers.[121] The next step was to give attorneys representing Al-Haramain access to the sealed document. The judge ordered the Justice Department to provide security clearances to two of the plaintiff's attorneys to enable them to examine classified documents. The dispute escalated in May 2009 when the administration announced that although the two attorneys were suitable for top-secret clearances, executive officials in one or more of the agencies serving in the role as defendants (including the NSA director) are refusing to cooperate with the court's orders because, they assert, plaintiffs' attorneys do not "need to know" the information that the court has determined they do need to know.[122] Access to examine classified documents always include these two steps: clearance and need to know. An individual may have clearance but cannot demonstrate a need to know. In this case, the judge handling the case concluded that the two attorneys did have a need to know, in order to protect the adversary process, only to be told by the defendants (NSA and others) that the judge's determination is incorrect. Of course, this collision raises the question of who runs the courtroom, the judge or the defendants? In such situations what sanctions or penalties may a judge order against the defendants, in this case the Obama administration?[123]

Conclusions

In times of emergency, government officials will push boundaries to do what they think is necessary, whether legal or not. Sometimes their judgments are sound, persuading other branches of government, and the public, to register their support. On other occasions the zeal for quick action and prompt results runs roughshod over fundamental constitutional principles, placing in jeopardy the rights and liberties that government officials are sworn to respect and protect. The TSP was devised to circumvent what some executive officials saw as an outmoded FISA, but if that was their concern they should have come to Congress and ask for remedial legislation. Congress passed many emergency statutes in the months after September 11, including the AUMF and the USA PATRIOT Act. It would not have been difficult for the executive branch to persuade Congress to amend FISA to take account of technological changes after 1978. Many changes had indeed been made to FISA, including some after the September 11 terrorist attacks.

Instead of pursuing a legislative strategy, executive officials preferred to act unilaterally on the basis of inherent presidential power, a field of constitutional law filled with doubts, ambiguities, and open invitations to executive abuse. Claims of inherent presidential power always come at the cost of checks and balances, separation of powers, and the types of structural safeguards the Framers adopted to ensure that a concentration of power does not endanger the liberties of citizens. The very purpose of a Constitution is to confer power and limit it. Inherent power, by definition, recognizes no limits. The principles of government announced in 1787 were sound then, when the Framers drafted the Constitution. They are even more crucial today, when governmental power has grown to dimensions the Founders never imagined.

Key Actors

George W. Bush   As president, he authorized warrantless national security surveillance after September 11 and decided not to comply with the exclusive procedures of the Foreign Intelligence Surveillance Act.

James Comey   Deputy attorney general, acting attorney general during the illness of John Ashcroft.

Alberto Gonzales   White House counsel at the time the warrantless surveillance was authorized; later became attorney general.

Michael V. Hayden   NSA director at the time the Terrorist Surveillance Program was initiated.

Michael McConnell   Previously NSA director and later director of national intelligence; in that capacity oversees all intelligence agencies.

Notes

1. James Risen and Eric Lichtblau, "Bush Lets U.S. Spy on Callers without Courts," *New York Times*, December 16, 2005, A1.
2. James Bamford, *Body of Secrets: Anatomy of the Ultra-Secret National Security Agency* (New York: Random House, 2002), 428–429.
3. Keith W. Olson, *Watergate: The Presidential Scandal That Shook America* (Lawrence: University Press of Kansas, 2003), 16.
4. Bamford, *Body of Secrets*, 430.
5. Ibid., 431–439.
6. Ibid., 440.
7. Louis Fisher and Katy J. Harriger, *American Constitutional Law*, 8th ed. (Durham: Carolina Academic Press, 2009), 731.
8. 277 U.S. 438 (1928).
9. Fisher and Harriger, *American Constitutional Law*, 731–732.
10. *Katz v. United States*, 389 U.S. 347, 351 (1967).
11. 82 Stat. 214 (1968).

12. *United States v. United States District Court,* 407 U.S. 297 (1972).

13. "Warrantless Wiretapping and Electronic Surveillance," Report by the Subcommittee on Surveillance of the Senate Committee on Foreign Relations and the Subcommittee on Administrative Practice and Procedure of the Senate Committee on the Judiciary, 94th Cong., 1st Sess. 2 (February 1975) (Senators Edmund Muskie, Ted Kennedy, and Sam Ervin).

14. Ibid., 7, 9.

15. 92 Stat. 1788, sec. 103(a) (1978).

16. Ibid., sec. 103(b).

17. Ibid., sec. 201(f).

18. 115 Stat. 1402, sec. 314(a) (2001).

19. David E. Sanger, "In Address, Bush Says He Ordered Domestic Spying," *New York Times,* December 18, 2005, 30.

20. Ibid.

21. Ibid.

22. "Bush on the Patriot Act and Eavesdropping," *New York Times,* December 18, 2005, at 30.

23. Ibid.

24. Sanger, "In Address," 30.

25. Ibid.

26. *Weekly Compilation of Presidential Documents,* December 19, 2005, 1885.

27. Press briefing by Attorney General Alberto Gonzales and General Michael Hayden, principal deputy director for national intelligence, 2; available at www.whitehouse.gov/news/releases/2005/12/print/20051219-1.html.

28. Ibid.

29. Ibid.

30. Ibid., 4.

31. U.S. Justice Department, "Legal Authorities Supporting the Activities of the National Security Agency Described by the President," January 19, 2006, 1.

32. Ibid., 6–7.

33. 48 Stat. 1745 (1934).

34. *Panama Refining Co. v. Ryan,* 293 U.S. 388 (1935); *Schechter Corp. v. United States,* 295 U.S. 495 (1935).

35. Louis Fisher, "Presidential Inherent Power: The 'Sole Organ' Doctrine," *Presidential Studies Quarterly* 37 (March 2007): 139, 144.

36. Ibid., 144–150.

37. 10 *Annals of Congress* 613 (1800), cited in *United States v. Curtiss-Wright Corp.,* 299 U.S. 304, 319 (1936).

38. Fisher, "Presidential Inherent Power," 140–142.

39. *Talbot v. Seeman,* 5 U.S. 1, 28 (1801).

40. *Little v. Barreme,* 2 Cr. (6 U.S.) 170, 179 (1804).

41. U.S. Justice Department, "Legal Authorities Supporting the Activities of the National Security Agency," 2.

42. Ibid., 2–3.

43. Ibid., 3.

44. Transcript of May 15, 2007, hearings on U.S. attorneys firings by the Senate Committee on the Judiciary, CQ Transcriptions. The transcript is not numbered, but the remark by Comey appears on page 13.

45. Ibid., 14–15.

46. Ibid., 16.

47. Ibid., 17.

48. Ibid., 19.

49. Ibid., 20–21.

50. Ibid., 21

51. Ibid., 32.

52. Ibid., 43.

53. Hearing of the Senate Select Committee on Intelligence on the Nomination of General Michael V. Hayden to be Director of the Central Intelligence Agency, May 18, 2006, transcript, 35.

54. Ibid., 69.

55. Ibid.

56. Ibid., 32.

57. Ibid., 32–33.

58. Ibid., 74.

59. Ibid., 88.

60. Ibid., 138.

61. Ibid., 144.

62. Ibid., 68.

63. Ibid., 61.

64. *Hepting v. AT&T Corp.*, 439 F.Supp.2d 974 (N.D. Cal. 2006).

65. Ibid., 985.

66. Ibid., 986.

67. Ibid., 989.

68. Ibid., 990.

69. Ibid., 991.

70. Ibid., 992.

71. Ibid., 994.

72. Ibid., 1001. For newspaper stories on this decision, see Arshad Mohammed, "Judge Declines to Dismiss Lawsuit against AT&T," *Washington Post*, July 21, 2006, A9; John Markoff, "Judge Declines to Dismiss Privacy Suit against AT&T," *New York Times*, July 21, 2006, A13.

73. *Terkel v. AT&T*, 441 F.Supp.2d 899, 912 (N.D. Ill. 2006); Adam Liptak, "Judge Rejects Customer Suit over Records from AT&T," *New York Times*, July 26, 2006, A13; Mike Robinson, "Judge Dismisses Lawsuit on AT&T Data Handover," *Washington Post*, July 26, 2006, A6.

74. *American Civil Liberties v. National Sec. Agency*, 438 F.Supp.2d 754, 765 (E.D. Mich. 2006).

75. Ibid.

76. Ibid.

77. Ibid.

78. Ibid., 766.

79. Ibid., 774.

80. Ibid., 775.

81. Ibid., 778 (citing *Youngstown Sheet & Tube v. Sawyer*, 343 U.S. 579, 652 [1952]).

82. Ibid., 779.

83. Ibid., 781.

84. Ibid.

85. Ibid., 782.

86. *ACLU v. National Sec. Agency,* 493 F.3d 644, 650 n.2 (6th Cir. 2007).

87. David D. Kirkpatrick, "Republicans Seek to Bridge Differences on Surveillance," *New York Times,* March 1, 2006, A13.

88. Eric Lichtblau, "Administration and Critics, in Senate Testimony, Clash over Eavesdropping Compromise," *New York Times,* July 27, 2006, A19.

89. David D. Kirkpatrick and Scott Shane, "G.O.P. Senators Say Accord Is Set on Wiretapping," *New York Times,* March 3, 2006, A1.

90. Walter Pincus, "Panel on Eavesdropping Is Briefed by White House," *Washington Post,* March 10, 2006, A4.

91. Dan Eggen, "Warrantless Wiretaps Possible in U.S.," *Washington Post,* April 7, 2006, A3.

92. Jonathan Weisman, "Republican Rift over Wiretapping Widens: Party at Odds on Surveillance Legislation," *Washington Post,* September 6, 2006, A3.

93. Jonathan Weisman, "House GOP Leaders Fight Wiretapping Limits," *Washington Post,* September 13, 2006, A7.

94. Keith Perine and Tim Starks, "House Panels Approve Surveillance Bill," *CQ Weekly,* September 25, 2006, 2556.

95. Eric Lichtblau, "House Approves Powers for Wiretaps without Warrants," *New York Times,* September 29, 2006, A18.

96. Attorney General Alberto Gonzales to Senators Patrick Leahy and Arlen Specter, Chairman and Ranking Member of the Senate Committee on the Judiciary, January 17, 2007, 1.

97. Ibid.

98. Ibid., 2.

99. Ibid., A16.

100. Ibid.

101. David Johnston and Scott Shane, "Senators Demand Details on New Eavesdropping Rules," *New York Times,* January 18, 2007, A18.

102. Ibid. See also Dan Eggen, "Spy Court's Orders Stir Debate on Hill," *Washington Post,* January 19, 2007, A6.

103. Tim Starks, "Oversight Committees to Review Documents on NSA Wiretapping," *CQ Weekly,* February 5, 2007, 402; Mark Mazzetti, "Key Lawmakers Getting Files about Surveillance Program," *New York Times,* February 1, 2007, A11; Dan Eggen, "Records on Spy Program Turned over to Lawmakers," *Washington Post,* February 1, 2007, A2.

104. Adam Liptak, "Judges Weigh Arguments in U.S. Eavesdropping Case," *New York Times,* February 1, 2007, A11.

105. "Modernizing the Foreign Intelligence Surveillance Act," statement by J. Michael McConnell, Director of National Intelligence, before the Senate Select Committee on Intelligence, May 1, 2007, 1.

106. Ibid., 2.

107. Ibid., 5.

108. "The Need to Bring the Foreign Intelligence Surveillance Act into the Modern Era," Statement of Kenneth L. Wainstein, Assistant Attorney General, National Security Division, Department of Justice, before the Senate Select Committee on Intelligence, May 1, 2007, 8.

109. James Risen, "Administration Pulls Back on Surveillance Agreement," *New York Times,* May 3, 2007, A16.

110. P.L. 110-55, 121 Stat. 552 (2007).

111. Helen Fessenden, "Senate Democrats Seek to Regroup Quickly on Surveillance Law Rewrite," *The Hill,* September 11, 2007, 8.

112. Eric Lichtblau, "Senate Deal on Immunity for Telephone Companies," *New York Times,* October 18, 2007, A22; Ellen Nakashima and Shailagh Murray, "Senate Panel Approves New Surveillance Bill," *Washington Post,* October 19, 2007, A2.

113. Eric Lichtblau, "Key Senators Raise Doubts on Eavesdropping Immunity," *New York Times,* November 1, 2007, A16.

114. *Weekly Compilation of Presidential Documents,* vol. 44, 259.

115. Ibid., 291.

116. P.L. 110-261, 122 Stat. 2459, sec. 102 (2008).

117. Ibid., 122 Stat. 2467, sec. 801(5).

118. Ibid., 122 Stat. 2469, sec. 802.

119. *Al-Haramain Islamic Foundation, Inc. v. Bush,* 507 F.3d 1190, 1193 (9th Cir. 2007).

120. In re National Sec. Agency Telecommunications Rec., 564 F.Supp.2d 1109, 1121 (N.D. Cal. 2008).

121. In re National Sec. Agency Telecommunications, 595 F.Supp.2d 1077 (N.D. Cal. 2009).

122. Order, In re National Sec. Agency Telecommunications Rec., MDL Docket No. 06-1791 VRW, May 22, 2009, 3.

123. Jim Abrams, "Access to Top-Secret Papers at Issue in Wiretapping Case," *Washington Post,* May 31, 2009, A3; "U.S. Resists Order In Wiretapping Case," *New York Times,* May 31, 2009, 20; Carrie Johnson, "Showdown Looming on 'State Secrets,'" *Washington Post,* May 26, 2009, A4.

9 Immigration Policy: U.S.-Mexican Relations Confront U.S. Political Realities

Marc R. Rosenblum

Before You Begin:

1. What is the U.S. national interest in immigration policy? Does immigration policy aspire to national goals, or are immigration interests primarily local and parochial?

2. Which interest groups care about immigration policy, and why?

3. How are interest group policy demands regarding immigration related to traditional U.S. party cleavages? What makes partisan cleavages on immigration unlike those on other domestic and foreign policy issues? Why has "comprehensive immigration reform" proven to be such an elusive goal despite the support of recent presidents and congressional leaders?

4. What steps can countries of origin, such as Mexico, take to influence U.S. immigration policy making? Under what conditions do efforts by countries of origin to influence U.S. immigration policy succeed? Have these conditions changed over time?

5. Do the United States and its Caribbean Basin immigration partners share common migration policy goals, or do their migration policy interests mainly conflict?

6. What are the consequences, for the United States and for Mexico and other Caribbean Basin states, of combining open trade and investment policies with restrictive migration controls? Is this combination of policy choices sustainable in the long run?

Introduction

Every twelve years, the U.S. and Mexican political calendars converge as their presidents' four- and six-year terms begin within a month of each other, and analysts on both sides of the border often see these double inaugurations as important opportunities to redefine and strengthen bilateral relations.[1]

Optimism ran especially high in 2000–2001 when Mexico inaugurated its first democratically elected president, Vicente Fox of the National Action Party.[2] Like the new U.S. president, George W. Bush, Fox was a bilingual, former border state governor and business executive. He was also the first Mexican presidential candidate to campaign systematically for votes in the United States. Fox returned to the United States in the fall as president-elect to thank his supporters. Bush broke with recent tradition by making Mexico (rather than Canada) the destination of his first foreign trip as president and then honored President Fox as his first state visitor to the White House.

The two presidents met a total of five times in 2001 alone and quickly agreed to make a priority of addressing the one bilateral issue that most threatened the relationship: migration. Immigration policy topped the agenda at a February summit in Guanajuato, Mexico, after which the two presidents directed Secretary of State Colin Powell and Attorney General John Ashcroft and their Mexican counterparts, Jorge Castañeda and Santiago Creel, to form a special working group to achieve "short and long-term agreements that will allow us to constructively address migration and labor issues between our two countries."[3] These efforts paid off by the September 2001 summit meeting in Washington, D.C.: following the first-ever joint meeting of the full Mexican and U.S. cabinets, the presidents announced a framework for a breakthrough deal based on a new U.S.-Mexican guest worker program and the theme of "shared responsibility" for migration enforcement to preserve orderly migration flows.[4] The presidents also announced a new, bilateral, public-private partnership, to be led by the Treasury and State Departments and their Mexican counterparts, to spur investment and growth in Mexican communities of origin as part of a long-term strategy to reduce emigration pressures.[5]

The September 11 attacks occurred five days later, moving migration negotiations to the back burner, and 2001 was the high-water mark for recent U.S.-Mexican relations, while broader efforts to reform America's immigration system appeared to be stalled. The contrast between Bush's widely praised first trip to the region and his five-country tour in March 2007 is striking. Whereas press accounts of the earlier visit emphasized bilateral friendship and opportunities for greater cooperation,[6] coverage of the latter trip was devoted almost exclusively to protests—occasionally violent—at each of Bush's stops. The new Mexican president, Felipe Calderon, and Guatemalan president Oscar Berger were particularly critical of U.S. migration policy.[7] And although President Barack Obama enjoyed broad popularity in Mexico during the first year of his presidency, migration issues were not on the agenda during his first two visits to Mexico, and Mexicans expressed growing frustration with the administration's slow and unilateral approach to the issue.[8]

Were the complaints warranted? Presidents Bush and Fox had raised expectations for a bilateral approach, and Bush recommitted himself to a guest worker program during his 2004 reelection campaign. Many Mexicans and Latinos within the United States were energized by the U.S. congressional immigration debate in the spring of 2006, when the Senate passed landmark legislation to create new avenues for legal migration (permanent and temporary), move millions of existing undocumented immigrants into legal status, and strengthen enforcement at the border and within the United States. Yet the Senate bill never made it to Bush's desk, and a 2007 bill failed even to pass the Senate. Obama had promised on the campaign trail to push for comprehensive immigration reform during his first year in office, but by early 2010 immigration had not made it onto Congress's agenda, and it appeared unlikely to do so before the November midterm elections. Even though the citizens of Mexico and other countries of origin are the immediate subjects of U.S. immigration legislation, the history of immigration policy making usually has been written by Congress, not the president. As a result, efforts to link immigration to foreign policy compete with Congress's predominantly domestic approach to the issue.

Background: U.S. Immigration Policy Making 1940–2001

The U.S.-Mexican Bracero Program

Rules governing labor migration to the United States were highly restrictive in the decades prior to World War II, as most visas were reserved for the immediate family members of U.S. citizens, and no visas could be issued to contract workers. Restrictions against informal migration were strictly enforced during the Great Depression, including through mass deportations, leading to a net outflow of Mexican immigrants during the 1930s, the only such decade in the history of Mexico-U.S. migration. For these reasons, as the resurgent U.S. economy and the newly instituted military draft led to sharp agricultural labor shortages beginning in 1940, neither a formal nor an informal infrastructure existed to ensure the timely arrival of seasonal migrants to fill those jobs.

Agricultural groups lobbied Congress to restart a World War I–era program under which U.S. employers obtained temporary "guest worker" visas for Mexican laborers. Congress held extensive hearings on such a program during

Timeline
U.S. Immigration Policy and U.S.-Mexican Relations

August 1942	United States and Mexico sign the "bracero" temporary labor migration (guest worker) treaty.
June 27, 1952	Congress passes the Immigration and Nationality Act (INA) over President Harry S. Truman's veto, sustaining a national origins quota system that favors Northern and Western Europe over other regions in the Eastern Hemisphere.
January 1954	U.S.-Mexican "showdown" on the border proves that Mexico is unable to prevent migration outflows; ushers in mature phase of the bracero program, with sharply curtailed rights for temporary workers.
September 1964	Bracero program terminated.
October 3, 1965	INA amended, replacing the national origins quota system with flat cap of twenty thousand visas per country; quotas imposed on Mexico and other Western Hemisphere countries for the first time.
November 1, 1968	United States ratifies 1951 United Nations Convention on Refugees but does not change U.S. immigration law to reflect the convention's requirements.
March 17, 1980	Passage of the Refugee Act, bringing U.S. law into compliance with 1951 United Nations Convention on Refugees.
November 6, 1986	Passage of the Immigration Reform and Control Act (IRCA), increasing border enforcement, making it illegal to employ undocumented immigrants, and offering amnesty to some three million undocumented immigrants.

September 1993	Border Patrol initiates "Operation Blockade" around El Paso; "prevention through deterrence" strategy leads to border fencing and militarization of broad swaths of the U.S.-Mexican border since that time.
September 6, 2001	United States and Mexico sign Partnership for Prosperity, an agreement to target public-private investment toward Mexican emigration communities of origin; they announce plans to negotiate bilateral temporary worker agreement.
January 7, 2004	President George W. Bush proposes general framework for comprehensive immigration reform.
April–November 2005	Three different Senate comprehensive immigration reform bills are introduced; Senate holds seven hearings on immigration reform.
December 16, 2005	House of Representatives passes Border Protection, Antiterrorism, and Illegal Immigration Control Act of 2005.
March 27, 2006	Senate Judiciary Committee votes 12–6 to report the Comprehensive Immigration Reform Act of 2006 to the full Senate.
May 25, 2006	Senate passes Comprehensive Immigration Reform Act of 2006.
June 19, 2006	House announces plans to hold field hearings instead of convening a conference committee to resolve differences between the House and Senate immigration bills.
October 26, 2006	Passage of Secure Fence Act, authorizing seven hundred miles of fencing at the U.S.-Mexico border.
January 23, 2007	President Bush highlights the need for comprehensive immigration reform in his State of the Union address.

(continued)

Timeline *(continued)*
U.S. Immigration Policy and U.S.-Mexican Relations

February–May 2007	Senators from both parties join Secretaries Michael Chertoff and Carlos Gutierrez in negotiations over comprehensive immigration reform.
May 17, 2007	Bipartisan group of senators and cabinet secretaries announce "grand compromise" on immigration reform.
June 28, 2007	Senate fails to support final cloture motion, ending debate on Secure Borders, Economic Opportunity, and Immigration Reform Act of 2007.
February 17, 2009	President Barack Obama reiterates his commitment to pursuing comprehensive immigration reform in an interview on Spanish-language radio.
April 23, 2009	Arizona governor Jan Brewer signs into law the state's Senate Bill 1070, making illegal presence a state crime and requiring law enforcement officers to question anyone they suspect of being an unauthorized immigrant about their immigration status.
July 1, 2009	President Obama delivers a major address on immigration, reiterating his support for comprehensive reform.

spring 1942 but deferred to the Roosevelt administration, which opposed it. Instead, responding to Mexican complaints about the earlier program, the Roosevelt administration initiated negotiations with Mexico to establish a bilateral guest worker program, in which Mexico would be in charge of recruiting workers and representing their interests in the United States. With Mexico threatening to ally with Germany, as the United States prepared to enter World War II,[9] U.S. negotiators were instructed to accommodate Mexican concerns about migrants' rights.[10] Mexico was reluctant to endorse labor outflows because of its own industrialization plans and drove a hard bargain.[11] The resulting agreement is unique in the history of regional relations: a document that favors Mexican over U.S. interests in almost every detail. In particular, Mexican workers (known as *braceros*, as they worked with their *brazos*, or arms)[12] received a guaranteed minimum wage (unlike Americans), along with housing benefits, basic health care, and transportation costs. Mexico also insisted that contracts be signed by the U.S. government, with agricultural employers acting as subcontractors, and Mexico blacklisted the state of Texas, where employers were considered especially likely to mistreat immigrant workers.[13]

The initial bracero agreement was revised a dozen times during the program's twenty-two-year history, and the program went through four distinct stages as a function of evolving policy preferences in Mexico and the United States and of ongoing negotiations between Congress, the president, and Mexico. Direct Mexican oversight of bracero contracts during World War II led to favorable bracero working conditions during the initial phase of the agreement and a rising chorus of grower complaints to Congress. Congress responded in 1948 by proposing legislation to reinstate a more pro-grower, World War I–style program, forcing Mexico to accept a scaled-back oversight role, with contracts signed directly by immigrants and their employers rather than by Mexico and the United States.

A third phase was initiated in 1951, when Mexico threatened to cut off guest worker outflows unless Congress agreed to reestablish state-to-state contracting and crack down on employers of undocumented immigrants (to force employers to participate in the more labor-friendly guest worker program). Congress met Mexico halfway, passing P.L.78, to mandate state contracting, and the so-called Wetback Bill, to make it illegal to aid or harbor undocumented immigrants, but also including the "Texas proviso" in the latter bill, over President Harry S. Truman's objections, explicitly exempting employers of undocumented immigrants from prosecution under the law.[14]

Even so, growers continued to complain about Mexican oversight, and policy makers on both sides of the border objected (for different reasons) to ever-higher levels of undocumented immigration. Thus in 1954 the pro-grower Eisenhower administration demanded substantial reductions in Mexican oversight authority. Mexico objected and threatened to prevent outflows in order to protect its role in the program. President Dwight Eisenhower called Mexico's bluff, however, directing U.S. agents to assist would-be border crossers, occasionally resulting in conflict between U.S. and Mexican border agents as each sought to pull workers to their side of the border.[15] Events quickly proved that ten years of bracero flows had reestablished sufficient linkages for migration to occur with or without Mexico's consent. The showdown at the border ushered in the "mature" stage of the bracero program, in which state-sponsored guest workers were stripped of virtually all legal protections and routinely exploited by unscrupulous employers. Bad publicity about the program, along with increasing sensitivity about worker and minority rights, caused the Eisenhower administration to require more humane treatment of guest workers beginning in the late 1950s, a trend that grew under John F. Kennedy before the program was terminated in 1964.

The Immigration and Nationality Act and Humanitarian Admissions

Legislation governing other migration to the United States operated on a separate track during these years, as Congress and the president clashed about policies governing humanitarian admissions and the balance between domestic and international determinants of migration policy. Congress followed Truman's lead on humanitarian admissions immediately after World War II, passing the Displaced Persons Acts of 1948 and 1950, and eventually authorizing admission for about two hundred thousand Europeans displaced by the war. But Congress also passed the Internal Security Act of 1950, overriding Truman's veto. The law prohibited the admission of former members of the Communist Party, whom Congress viewed as threats to domestic security but Truman viewed as humanitarian cases who also offered valuable propaganda and intelligence resources in the emerging cold war. Truman also opposed Congress's Immigration and Nationality Act (INA) of 1952 on foreign policy grounds because the new law retained the discriminatory national origins quota system and failed to establish a quota for refugee admissions. But Congress again passed the law over the president's veto.

Tight quotas led to a foreign policy crisis in December 1956, when the Soviet Union invaded Hungary. Two hundred thousand refugees fled into neighboring Austria, but the INA limited U.S. immigration from Hungary to 756 visas per year. With Congress in recess, Eisenhower "paroled" fifteen thousand Hungarians into the United States over congressional objections, exploiting a loophole in the 1952 law that Congress intended to be applied on a case-by-case basis for individual migrants. By the time Congress reconvened, returning the refugees to Soviet-occupied Hungary was not a realistic option. Instead, Congress passed the 1957 Refugee-Escapee Act, authorizing Eisenhower's actions post hoc and establishing a precedent that individuals fleeing communist regimes could be admitted at the president's discretion.[16]

Political shifts after 1960 finally brought the domestic and international politics of migration policy into greater harmony. At the international level, the Kennedy administration sought to counter growing Soviet influence in Cuba, Vietnam, and throughout the developing world by more proactively reaching out to the third world, including through the Alliance for Progress in Latin America. At the domestic level, Kennedy and a coalition of northern Democrats and liberal Republicans supported the goals of the civil rights movement. For both these reasons, the Kennedy administration proposed in July 1963 that the INA be revised to eliminate the national origins quota system, establish a permanent refugee quota, and liberalize employment-based admissions rules. Lyndon Johnson took up the cause in his 1964 and 1965 State of the Union addresses and reiterated Kennedy's themes of nondiscrimination in U.S. foreign policy in a special message to Congress accompanying his own legislative proposal in January 1965. Members of Congress viewed the issue in those terms as well, rejecting the 1952 INA as discriminatory and embracing the Kennedy-Johnson reform as a way to burnish the nation's image abroad.[17] After extensive hearings in both chambers during 1964 and 1965, Congress passed a revised set of amendments eliminating the national origins system and establishing a standing refugee quota as Kennedy and Johnson had requested.

U.S.-Mexican Migration Relations 1965–1980s

Migration nonetheless remained a contentious issue in U.S.-Mexican relations. The end of the bracero program in 1964 and the establishment of a universal, per-country admissions quota in 1968 (limiting family-based migration from Mexico for the first time) created an acute supply-and-demand problem for Mexicans seeking legal visas to enter the United States.[18] Mexico appealed repeatedly for a new guest worker program, but memories of the exploitative bracero program caused liberal and labor groups to oppose the proposals, while the willingness and ability of many Mexicans to migrate and work illegally in the United States meant that employers were satisfied with the status quo and thus did not lobby for new visas.

The tables turned following the oil shock of 1973. The Gerald Ford and Jimmy Carter administrations both approached Mexico about restarting guest worker flows in return for privileged U.S. access to Mexican oil. But by now Mexico was flush with oil wealth, and the nationalist Luis Echeverría and Jose Lopez Portillo administrations rejected those overtures.[19] The Carter administration also sought to provide extra visas to Mexican immigrants as part of a broader effort to strengthen U.S.-Mexico ties, but the Mexican visa proposal, like Carter's 1977 effort to pass immigration enforcement and visa reforms, was ignored by the Democratic Congress. As a result, Carter's legacy in this area was limited to his establishment in the White House of an Office of the U.S. Coordinator for Mexican Affairs and, with Jose Lopez Portillo, the establishment of a high-level U.S.-Mexico Consultative Mechanism to promote greater communication on energy, trade, and migration issues.[20]

By the 1980s, the combination of dramatic economic swings in Mexico, attractive job opportunities in the United States, and increasingly sophisticated transnational social networks had resulted in a well-developed system of undocumented Mexico-U.S. migration.[21] And whereas Carter had attempted—unsuccessfully—to use migration legislation as a tool of foreign policy in an effort to strengthen bilateral relations, attention to undocumented immigration instead exacerbated broader conflicts in bilateral relations during the 1980s.[22] Thus members of Congress worried out loud that a wave of "feet people" were poised to invade the United States across the U.S.-Mexican border, and a Reagan administration official testified to Congress in the midst of the immigration debate that members of Mexican president Miguel de la Madrid's family were personally implicated in the drug trade. In this context, even though Sen. Alan Simpson, R-Wyo., made an explicit effort to solicit Mexico's input on pending migration reform legislation, Mexican officials refused an invitation to testify before Congress and remained disengaged from the U.S. policy debate. Likewise, when Congress passed the Immigration Reform and Control Act in 1986, the bill included provisions to strengthen border and worksite enforcement—finally overturning the "Texas proviso"—and an amnesty program for many undocumented immigrants, but it did not include language the Senate had approved two years earlier to expand Mexico's legal visa quota.[23]

Immigration Policy Making after the Cold War

The end of the cold war was seen as a great opportunity to reorient U.S.–Latin American relations in general and U.S. relations with the high-emigration countries of the Caribbean Basin in particular.[24] Incoming presidents Carlos Salinas (December 1988) and George H. W. Bush (January 1989) moved quickly to repair bilateral relations, quickly producing the "Baker plan" for debt relief and eventually producing the breakthrough North American Free Trade Agreement (NAFTA) in 1992. Remaining sources of conflict seemed to fade away. President Bill Clinton signed the NAFTA agreement (over the objections of most congressional Democrats) and convened a 1994 Summit of the Americas that included the head of state from every country in the hemisphere other than Cuba and produced a promise of a hemispheric free trade deal by 2005. Nicaragua's civil war ended with democratic elections in 1990, and El Salvador's civil war ended with a UN-monitored cease-fire in 1991. By the mid-1990s, Mexico was being praised by the Washington community as a model Latin American debtor-state, as it enthusiastically adopted neoliberal economic reforms and peacefully transitioned from a one-party system to a competitive democracy.

Initially, these improvements in regional relations seemed to lay the groundwork for improved regional migration relations as well, as Congress turned its attention from migration control efforts to modernizing the decades-old INA preference system. Congress passed the Immigration Act of 1990 with little fanfare, more than doubling quota numbers for legal permanent migration and dividing the preference system into separate family- and employment-based categories. In contrast with the 1980s, the problems of undocumented immigration and U.S.–Latin American relations did not figure prominently in the debate.

Yet even as Bush and Clinton sought to strengthen regional relations in general, undocumented immigration inflows surged beginning in 1990, and the issue reemerged as a highly salient policy problem. By 1994, undocumented immigration was again the subject of inflammatory media attention, especially following California's passage of Proposition 187, denying social services to illegal immigrants.[25] Congressional Republicans also made migration a theme in their 1994 "Contract with America" campaign, and then candidate Pat Buchanan interjected migration into the 1996 presidential campaign.

Congress responded in 1996 with a trio of highly restrictionist laws: the Welfare Reform Act, which blocked *legal* immigrants from receiving welfare benefits (undocumented immigrants were already ineligible); the Effective Death Penalty and Anti-Terrorism Act, which tightened the asylum application process; and the Illegal Immigration Reform and Immigrant Responsibility Act (IIRIRA), which increased funding for border enforcement, imposed stronger penalties on alien smugglers, and streamlined deportation and exclusion procedures. The new rules governing asylum hearings were applied retroactively, and their primary effect was to threaten with deportation three hundred thousand Salvadoran and Guatemalan civil war refugees who had registered with the INS as part of a legal settlement in 1990.

The legislation put President Clinton in an awkward position, caught between his outreach to Latin America and his effort to define himself as a "new Democrat," including by being tough on immigration.[26] Thus, while generally supporting all three pieces of legislation, Clinton responded to Mexican requests by demanding three important concessions from the Republican Congress: more moderate restrictions on migrants' access to welfare; a lower "deeming requirement," to make it easier for poor migrants to sponsor family members for new visas; and—through a veto threat—reversal of the "Gallegly amendment," which would have allowed states to deny undocumented immigrants access to public schools.[27] In addition, although the Clinton administration embraced "Operation Blockade" in 1993, to fortify the U.S.-Mexican border around El Paso, and more generally pursued a controversial strategy of "prevention through deterrence" that involved substantial new investments in personnel and military equipment at the U.S.-Mexican border,[28] the president also worked with Mexican presidents Salinas and Ernesto Zedillo to create a number of new bilateral institutions designed to minimize the damage to relations from heavy-handed immigration enforcement.[29]

Clinton also responded to Central American lobbying efforts by introducing the Immigration Reform Transition Act, to exempt asylum applications already in the pipeline from IIRIRA's new restrictions. When Congress modified Clinton's bill and passed the Nicaraguan and Central American Relief Act (NACARA), however, it imposed a double standard: pending Guatemalan and Salvadoran applications would be considered under the old rules, as Clinton had proposed, but 5,000 Cubans and 150,000 Nicaraguans would be given a blanket right to adjust their status to legal permanent resident. Clinton reluctantly signed the bill but waited two years to approve regulations implementing the law. The regulations instructed asylum officers to consider Salvadoran and Guatemalan appeals on a case-by-case basis, as Congress had instructed, but—over Congress's objections—to reverse the normal burden of proof, ensuring that most of these applicants would be granted immigration relief.[30] NACARA's benefits were extended to certain Haitian asylum applicants under the 1998 Haitian Refugee Immigration Fairness Act (HRIFA), and the president offered additional benefits to Nicaraguans and Honduran immigrants affected by Hurricane Mitch in 1999.

Immigration Policy since September 11

President Bush Sets the Agenda

If the years after the dual inaugurations of George H. W. Bush and Carlos Salinas held reasons for optimism about integration and migration cooperation, balanced by new pressures for migration control, conflicting pressures were even more intense following the inaugurations of George W. Bush and Vicente Fox. On one hand, six years into the NAFTA period U.S.-Mexican trade and investment had doubled, and optimism ran high as two bilingual, former border state governors and business executives were poised to take office. Both presidents followed through on early pledges to make bilateral migration reform a priority, culminating with the September 2001 Partnership for Prosperity investment deal, aimed at reducing emigration pressures, and the framework agreement envisioning a broader migration deal that would include a Mexico-specific temporary worker program.

On the other hand, the September 11 attacks redefined prospects for bilateral cooperation. After decades of heavy-handed U.S. policies toward Latin America during and before the cold war, Mexicans and others in the region opposed the U.S. intervention in Iraq. Mexico's failure to support U.S. efforts to pass a United Nations Security Council resolution endorsing its military action, in March 2003, drove a significant wedge between the two states. Although Mexicans were initially tolerant of the post–September 11 suspension of migration talks, by the midpoint of Fox's presidency he was increasingly criticized for Bush's failure to follow through on bilateral immigration reform.[31]

Within the United States, immigration policy was subsumed into the war on terrorism. Just six weeks after the September 11 attacks, Congress passes the USA PATRIOT Act, a wide-ranging counterterrorism measure that expanded domestic surveillance and enforcement against money laundering and eliminated barriers to communication among federal law enforcement agencies engaged in foreign and domestic investigations. Although never debated as an immigration bill, the PATRIOT Act also broadened the definition of terrorist activity for the purposes of immigration enforcement and authorized the indefinite detention of non-U.S. citizens. Five years later, Congress passed the REAL ID Act, with limited debate, by appending its provisions to a must-pass authorization bill. REAL ID emerged out of the 2004 Intelligence Reform Bill but eventually focused on three immigration-related provisions: expedited fence building along the U.S.-Mexico border; new restrictions on asylum admissions for "suspected terrorists"; and new federal guidelines on the issuance of state driver's licenses, including a requirement that states verify individuals' immigration status prior to issuing licenses.

These enforcement provisions did not address the core immigration policy issues that had been discussed by Presidents Bush and Fox, nor did they affect undocumented inflows or the availability of legal immigrant workers, the two issues that President Bush had identified in 2000 and 2001 as priorities. Thus in January 2004 Bush held a press conference to place immigration policy back on the national agenda, announcing five core principles for immigration reform: tougher border security, a temporary worker program, temporary legal status for undocumented immigrants already inside the United States, incentives to promote return migration, and a path to permanent legal status and eventual citizenship for some immigrants who chose not to return.[32] The new proposal to "match willing workers with willing employers" became the de facto focus of a summit meeting with President Fox the following week,[33] and the president in his State of the Union address called on Congress to take up immigration reform.[34] Congress failed to do so in 2004, however, as most legislative business gave way to that year's presidential election. President Bush revisited the issue in his 2005 State of the Union address and in subsequent months by repeatedly identifying immigration, along with tax cuts and Social Security reform, as a top legislative goal for his second term.[35]

The Senate Judiciary Committee (Spring 2006)

The Senate took up this challenge, as three competing bills were filed, each of which shared the president's three-legged framework of enhanced enforcement at the U.S. border and worksites, new employment visas for "future flow" immigrants, and some form of legalization for existing undocumented immigrants.[36]

The Senate's work was sidelined in the fall as the Judiciary Committee (in charge of immigration policy) turned its attention to filling two Supreme Court vacancies, and the House stepped into the void by passing James Sensenbrenner's, R-Wis., H.R. 4437.[37] In contrast to the Senate's multiple hearings and extended debate (see below), the House moved quickly. The bill was introduced on December 6, marked up and reported by the Judiciary Committee two days later on a party-line vote, and then debated by the full House for just over a day before passing, 239–182, in a mostly party-line vote on December 16. Also in contrast with the Senate, H.R. 4437 restricted its attention to border and interior enforcement, without addressing future flows or legalizing existing undocumented immigrants. Instead, the House bill included extensive and controversial new provisions to restrict immigrants' access to courts, to expand the definition of *immigrant smuggling* to include acts of humanitarian assistance, and to turn civil immigration violations into felony criminal offenses.

Passage of H.R. 4437 was a wake-up call to supporters of the Senate's more comprehensive approach, especially after the White House issued a strong statement of support for the Sensenbrenner bill during the House debate.[38]

Thus, after completing its work on Supreme Court nominations in late January 2006, the Senate Judiciary Committee began marking up an immigration bill in February. Committee chairman Arlen Specter, R-Pa., drafted a "chairman's mark" (that is, a working draft of a bill not formally filed with the Senate clerk) as the starting point, borrowing elements from all three Senate bills to combine generous employment-based admissions, tough enforcement, and a version of legalization that would allow unauthorized immigrants to remain in the United States (in contrast with the position favored by Republican senators John Cornyn and Jon Kyl) but would not put them on a path to lawful permanent residency and eventual citizenship (in contrast with the position favored by Republican senator John McCain and Democratic senator Ted Kennedy).

Specter's compromise failed to satisfy other advocates of "comprehensive reform," who held firm on a pathway to permanent citizenship and objected to Specter's inclusion of the new enforcement provisions from the Sensenbrenner bill, albeit in modified form. Seven of the eight Democrats on the committee and three of the ten Republicans—that is, a majority of the committee—supported the McCain-Kennedy approach to these issues.[39] But in a break with Senate tradition, Specter threatened to block any committee bill that lacked support from "a majority of the majority" on the committee. Four Republicans were reliable opponents of any legalization scheme or expansion in legal flows, and Specter's position therefore turned Senators Cornyn and Kyl into the swing voters whose support (along with Specter's) would make or break the "majority of the majority" condition.[40]

Two events in mid-March marked a turning point in the committee debate and shifted the focus from the backroom negotiations to the subcommittee markups. First, on March 16 Senate Majority Leader Bill Frist, R-Tenn., imposed a deadline on the Judiciary Committee by offering a bill of his own, which included all of the enforcement provisions in the chairman's mark but none of the new immigration benefits. Frist placed his bill on the calendar for March 28 and pledged to begin floor debate at that time if the Judiciary Committee had not reported a bill. With a recess scheduled the week of March 20, Frist's deadline seemed an impossible hurdle to overcome and a direct affront to Senator Specter and the rest of the committee. Second, in the week leading up to Frist's deadline, a million supporters of comprehensive immigration reform rallied around the country, including over half a million in downtown Los Angeles. The massive show of support—and of opposition to the House's enforcement-only bill—caused a perceptible shift in the debate when the committee reconvened, with California's Democratic senator Dianne Feinstein speaking eloquently, and for the first time, in favor of a McCain-Kennedy-style, broad legalization program for undocumented immigrants.

With Frist's deadline looming, Senator Specter scheduled a marathon markup session for March 27, pledging to keep the committee in session until a bill was agreed to. Sen. Sam Brownback, R-Kan., made a last-ditch effort to forge a compromise between supporters of the McCain-Kennedy bill and Senators Cornyn and Kyl, but when the effort showed no sign of progress Sen. Lindsey Graham, R-S.C., and committee Democrats circumvented the negotiations by forcing votes on a pair of amendments to replace Specter's temporary worker and legalization provisions with language from the McCain-Kennedy bill. In dramatic fashion, both amendments passed with identical 11–7 majorities (all eight Democrats plus the three supportive Republicans). Finally, after six days of markup and many months of work, Senator Specter backed down from his "majority of the majority" threat and joined the committee majority in the 12–6 vote to approve his amended bill.

The Senate Floor (Spring 2006)

The full Senate took up immigration reform two days later, with the committee bill offered as S. 2611, the Comprehensive Immigration Reform Act of 2006. Opponents of the bill introduced a series of amendments that supporters viewed as "poison pills"—amendments that struck at the heart of what reformers hoped to accomplish, but that posed difficult votes with midterm elections looming.[41] Kennedy and other supporters of the committee bill tried to organize votes to defeat the amendments, but the Democratic leadership overruled them and chose instead to exploit a procedural loophole to block votes on any of the disputed amendments during a week of floor debate. Democrats attempted to salvage the bill by filing for cloture—a move that would limit additional amendments and force a vote on final passage—but the cloture move failed on a mainly party-line vote, and the Senate adjourned for its scheduled April recess without taking any substantive votes on the bill.[42]

Even as progress was derailed on the Senate floor, however, behind-the-scenes negotiations resumed. With support from the White House and Senator Frist, Republican senators Hagel, Mel Martinez, Fla., McCain, and Graham sought a compromise with Democrats Kennedy, Barak Obama, Ill., and Ken Salazar, Colo., on a legalization program that would cover enough undocumented immigrants to satisfy Democrats while allowing Republicans to make good on their promise to oppose a broad "amnesty." In a late-night compromise, a two-track system was designed whereby aliens in the country for at least five years would be eligible for the McCain-Kennedy legalization procedure, but aliens with between two and five years of U.S. residence would be required to exit the United States, reenter as guest workers, and apply for green cards from an expanded pool of employment-based visas.[43] Democrats who opposed expanding the temporary worker program (already a source of contention) were mollified by offsetting cuts to visa numbers for new temporary worker flows and improved wage protections.

This "Hagel-Martinez" compromise brought together a bipartisan core group of members who pledged to place their common interest in comprehensive immigration reform ahead of partisan loyalties and to work together to defeat future "poison pill" amendments.[44] Public opinion polls reported unprecedented interest in the issue and a remarkably broad consensus in favor of the Senate bill.[45] Public demonstrations in favor of comprehensive reform continued, with more than three million people eventually marching in opposition to the House's enforcement-only approach and in support of the Senate bill. Broad-based support was reinforced by a broad left-right coalition of interest groups, which coordinated their lobbying activities and worked closely with the expanded McCain-Kennedy-Hagel-Martinez coalition throughout the debate.[46]

With the support of most Democrats and several additional Republicans, the pro-reform coalition fought off eight key amendments striking at the heart of the deal.

The coalition also suffered a handful of defeats from the left (a pair of Jeff Bingaman, D-N.M., amendments to further reduce the size of the temporary worker program and to impose an absolute cap on employment-based permanent visas) and from the right (a Jeff Sessions, R-Ala., amendment to expand border fencing, a revised version of the earlier Kyl-Cornyn amendment to exclude criminal immigrants from the earned legalization program, an Ensign amendment to deny newly legal immigrants access to the Earned Income Tax Credit, and a James Inhofe, R-Okla., amendment declaring English the official language of the United States). With these changes, the amended bill easily survived a cloture vote (73–25) on May 24 and passed the following day by a still-comfortable vote of 62–36.[47]

The House and Senate bills differed in significant ways, however, and further progress would require negotiators to work out a compromise through a House–Senate conference committee.[48] Any sense of inevitability—or even probability—that that would happen evaporated within days of the Senate vote when House leaders announced plans to hold field hearings rather than appoint conferees.

By the time Congress reconvened after its August 2006 recess, party leaders in both chambers had abandoned plans for a bicameral comprehensive reform bill. With the midterm elections looming, leaders felt compelled to "do something" in response to popular demands and settled for passage of the Secure Fence Act of 2006, a bill consisting of the border-area infrastructure language from the earlier House bill but no legalization for unauthorized immigrants and no changes to long-term or temporary visa systems.

The 110th Congress (2007–2008)

Immigration was not a dominant theme in the 2006 midterm elections, but Democratic supporters of comprehensive reform defeated enforcement-only Republicans in thirteen of the fifteen races in which migration played a central role, and new Democratic majorities in both houses of Congress seemed to bode well for comprehensive reform efforts in 2007.[49] Senators Kennedy and McCain met with Representatives Jeff Flake, R-Ariz., and Luis Gutierrez, D-Ill., to negotiate a bicameral, bipartisan starting point for the debate, but McCain pulled out of the talks almost immediately in a dispute over how to set wages for temporary workers, leaving the Senate without a bipartisan bill that could be taken directly to the floor.[50] As in 2005, the Judiciary Committee also failed to take immediate action on an immigration bill, in this case because of its preoccupation with the scandal surrounding the Bush administration's dismissal of several U.S. attorneys.

President Bush revived the reform agenda in March by initiating a new round of bipartisan negotiations, tapping Arizona senator Jon Kyl as the lead Republican negotiator. Cabinet secretaries Michael Chertoff (Department of Homeland Security) and Carlos Gutierrez (Department of Commerce) also joined the talks. But with the 2008 primary campaign already under way, key Republican moderates backed out of the pro-reform coalition, beginning with McCain's decision to pull out of the bicameral negotiations in January. Over the next four months Lindsay Graham, Sam Brownback, Mel Martinez, and Chuck Hagel—all of whom found themselves in sensitive political positions in the 2008 elections—tacked sharply to the right on immigration and publicly distanced themselves from bipartisan negotiations on a comprehensive bill.[51] The stakes were raised when McCain, Graham, Martinez, and Arlen Specter— the key Republican sponsors of the 2006 bill—circulated a "Dear Colleague" letter in May promising to filibuster any bill that came to the floor other than through the Jon Kyl–Ted Kennedy process.[52]

This threat proved decisive, and the Kyl-Kennedy process became the key to immigration reform in the 110th Congress.[53] Republican negotiators took advantage of their enhanced leverage to demand changes to how the 2006 Senate-passed bill approached permanent visa rules, a temporary worker program, and worksite enforcement provisions. But in what authors described as a "grand compromise," the resulting proposal also included more generous legalization provisions for undocumented immigrants than had passed the previous year (see Box 9.1). In response to complaints about the 2006 bill, the 2007 deal also included "enforcement triggers," ensuring that legalization and temporary worker programs would go into effect only after border security and worksite enforcement benchmarks were met.

The compromise was offered on the Senate floor in May as the Secure Borders, Economic Opportunity, and Immigration Reform Act of 2007 (S. 1348). In a process reminiscent of the *second* round of the 2006 debate, the bill was the subject of nine full days of intense debate. Over three hundred amendments were filed and thirty-one voted on, resulting in several significant changes from the left (imposing a five-year sunset on the temporary worker program and cutting its size in half) and from the right (imposing additional enforcement triggers, increasing the penalties in the legalization program, outlawing bilingual ballots and other government documents, and stripping legal protections for migrants applying to be legalized). As before, a bipartisan group of senators met daily and stuck together to defeat amendments they saw as poison pills, including proposals to eliminate the temporary worker program, to expand state and local enforcement of immigration laws, to eliminate the legalization program, to exclude new classes of criminal immigrants, to impose a sunset on the new point system, and to create additional family visas. Yet when Democrats filed cloture at the end of the second week, opponents of the bill demanded votes on additional amendments, and Republican supporters of the bill joined them to defeat the cloture motion, 33–63.

Once again, the defeat of the bill was followed by a new round of backroom talks. Senate leaders reached agreement in June on a list of thirteen additional amendments from each party to be voted on, after which Republicans promised to deliver the votes needed for cloture. In this case, as in the *first* round of the 2006 debate, substantive debate on the merits of the bill gave way to a procedural dispute over the leaders' use of controversial procedural tactics for blocking debate on additional amendments.[54] Yet it was a substantive issue that brought down the bill, as hard-liners strategically voted with a group of

Box 9.1 The Debate over Immigration Reform

Congressional debate about immigration reform during 2005–2010 focused on four key issues:

Legalization of Undocumented Immigrants

About eleven million unauthorized immigrants live in the United States, including about eight million unauthorized workers, over 5 percent of the U.S. workforce. Advocates of legalization argued that deportation of so many people would be too costly and too disruptive—for employers and for U.S. citizen relatives of the undocumented—to be practical. "Comprehensive" reform bills therefore proposed to allow undocumented immigrants to earn legal status by working and paying taxes, learning English and passing a civics test, and paying fees. Fees and work requirements were lower in the 2009 House CIR-ASAP bill than in the 2006 and 2007 Senate bills. Opponents criticized any path to legal status as "amnesty," and argued that it rewarded law-breakers and was unfair to others waiting in line to enter legally. "Enforcement-only" bills therefore sought to deport the unauthorized or to create a climate in which unauthorized immigrants would self-deport, a strategy described as "enforcement through attrition."

Temporary Workers

About four hundred thousand new low-skilled, undocumented workers entered the U.S. workforce each year prior to the economic downturn beginning in 2008. Supporters of comprehensive reform argued that admitting a similar number of legal workers each year would reduce the "jobs magnet" that attracts undocumented immigrants. But critics from the left worried that *temporary* workers also would be easily exploited, and pointed to the mature version of the bracero program as evidence. The 2006 Senate bills therefore would have allowed temporary workers eventually to transition to permanent legal status. The 2007 Senate bill would have required almost all temporary workers to return home after two years, a point of contention for both immigration advocates and immigrant employers. The 2009 House bill did not include a new temporary worker program, but would create a new visa program for countries that are important sources of unauthorized immigration.

Legal Permanent Visas

The United States issues about eight hundred thousand "green cards" per year to the foreign families of U.S. citizens and legal permanent residents, and to foreign workers when U.S. businesses cannot find an American worker to fill a particular position. Individuals with green cards may apply for U.S. citizenship after five years. The waiting lists for employment green cards may be as long as several years, and some family members must wait more than twenty years for a green card. The 2006 Senate bill would have doubled the number of family green cards available to reduce this backlog and meet future demand, and would have more than doubled the number of employment-based cards. The 2007 Senate bill would have provided a temporary increase in family green cards to clear the existing backlog, and then eliminated most categories of both family and employment migration, replacing them with a "point system" that would provide green cards on the basis of immigrants' education and skills. The 2009 House bill would have provided modest increases in family- and employment-based flows, while exempting some employment-based immigrants from visa limits.

Enforcement

All three comprehensive reform bills would have established a universal electronic eligibility verification system (EEVS), a system for employers to confirm workers' legal status by comparing their identity documents to a national legal worker database, but important differences existed with respect to how an EEVS should be structured. The 2006 and 2007 Senate bills also would increase fencing and add new military infrastructure to the U.S.-Mexico border, and would streamline the removal of unauthorized aliens from within the United States by further limiting their access to courts. In addition to these changes, the 2005 House enforcement-only bill would have made it a criminal offense, rather than a civil violation, to be in the United States without a visa.

moderate Democrats and Republicans who opposed the REAL ID Act to strike language linking the bill to still-controversial license provisions.[55] With this change to the bill's enforcement provisions, remaining Republican support for the bill collapsed, and despite a flurry of last-minute calls from President Bush and Secretaries Chertoff and Gutierrez, thirty-seven Republicans joined sixteen Democrats to vote against cloture and kill the bill.

The Obama Administration and the 111th Congress (2009–2010)

President Obama was a cosponsor of the McCain-Kennedy bill in 2006 and an outspoken backer of comprehensive immigration reform in 2007; and as a presidential candidate Obama promised Latino audiences that he would push for immigration reform during his first year as president.[56] The president appointed backers of reform to key cabinet and White House positions, and reiterated his intention to move quickly on immigration in a February 2009 interview on a nationally syndicated Spanish-language radio interview, and again in an April 2009 statement by White House staff.[57] Thousands of Latinos marched in support of reform in May Day rallies around the country, and in June the president gathered congressional leaders at the White House to provide a push to the legislative process. With Democrats now in control of both chambers of Congress—briefly including a supermajority of sixty votes in the Senate—reform advocates had high hopes almost a decade after Presidents Fox and Bush first discussed the issue that comprehensive immigration reform might finally move from concept to legislation.

Yet even though Democratic leaders at both ends of Pennsylvania Avenue saw immigration reform as an important way to solidify their support among Latinos and other pro-immigration ethnic groups, the broader political context made immigration reform more challenging than it had been during the Bush years. The U.S. recession in 2008–2009 and continued high unemployment in 2010 hardened opposition to liberal immigration policies and weakened business groups' (and Republicans') demand for a new temporary worker program. Long-simmering violence at the U.S.-Mexico border erupted in a series of high-profile drug-related killings, prompting a warning from the Pentagon in December 2008 that Mexico was potentially at risk of "a rapid and sudden collapse."[58] A general mistrust of Congress and "big government" resonated with a populist critique that immigration reformers were out of touch with the concerns of most Americans, making immigration reform a core issue for the emerging "tea party" movement that rose to prominence in 2009.[59] And after Democrats passed sweeping health care legislation on a party-line vote in the Senate and without Republican support in the House, congressional politics became increasingly polarized along party lines, making it especially difficult for Democrats to pass controversial legislation.

Thus Obama moved cautiously on immigration in 2009–2010, mainly continuing his predecessor's commitment to tough immigration enforcement at the border and within the United States as a precondition for broader reform. In three meetings with Mexican president Felipe Calderón (plus one meeting in January 2009, prior to Obama's inauguration), the presidents focused primarily on security concerns and Mexico's war on drugs—issues that also dominated the agenda for a high-level working group formed in March

2009 to coordinate U.S.-Mexico border issues among the U.S. Departments of Homeland Security, Justice, and State.

In the House, Rep. Luis Gutierrez (who had cosponsored the House version of the McCain-Kennedy bill in 2006, and worked with Republican Jeff Flake on the STRIVE Act in 2007) abandoned his previous bipartisan approach and introduced the Comprehensive Immigration Reform for America's Security and Prosperity Act of 2009. The CIR-ASAP bill combined more generous legalization provisions then earlier bills with new employment verification requirements, but did not include other tough enforcement measures or a new temporary worker program (see Box 9.1 on pages 278–279). Liberal Democrats lined up to support the bill, but centrist Democrats were reluctant to take up any immigration reform; and Democratic leaders announced that they would not take up the issue unless the Senate acted first to pass a bill—and that they would hesitate to debate the issue at all if its action could not be completed before the summer recess.

Senate action on immigration moved more slowly than in previous sessions, and featured a changed cast of characters, most notably due to the death of Senator Kennedy, who had been the driving force behind the Senate's immigration reform efforts for more than forty years.[60] Sen. Charles Schumer, D-N.Y., took over leadership of the Immigration Subcommittee and worked with Lindsay Graham, R-S.C., to draft a bill capable of gaining bipartisan support. After a year of negotiations, Schumer and Graham reiterated their support for a three-legged approach to comprehensive reform, emphasizing the need for a biometric national ID as an element of enhanced enforcement;[61] but they remained divided on how to structure a legalization program and on the details of a new temporary worker program and failed to file a bill. Senator Schumer and Democratic leaders published a twenty-six-page outline of a bill the following month, but with no Republican support they too failed to file a bill or to schedule hearings or floor debate.

In the absence of congressional action, the most important developments during the first two years of the Obama administration were new forms of immigration enforcement, resulting in a record 387,000 deportations in 2009 and a projection for 400,000 deportations in 2010. In an effort to target criminal aliens, the administration expanded the so-called 287(g) program, signing partnership agreements with seventy-one state and local law enforcement agencies to work with the Department of Homeland Security to enforce immigration law. And it expanded the Secure Communities Program, which uses biometric screening to identify unauthorized immigrants in local jails, from a handful of jurisdictions in 2008 to 470 jurisdictions by the summer of 2010, with plans to implement the program in every jail in the country by 2013. The administration also shifted its focus from unauthorized workers to their employers, scaling back workplace raids that had been a focus of enforcement during the final years of the Bush administration, and instead auditing the records of almost three thousand employers, resulting in a record $6.4 million in fines for unauthorized employment. And in July 2010 Obama deployed 1,2000 National Guard troops to the border to reinforce migration enforcement as well as newer initiatives to crack down on southbound flows of bulk cash and firearms.

While immigrant advocates opposed some of these enforcement efforts—including Latinos, who had turned out in record numbers to vote for Obama—the most controversial developments during the first years of the Obama administration occurred at the local and state levels. Frustrated by the congressional stalemate and the perception that unauthorized immigrants were contributing to the economic downturn, forty-eight states passed 353 laws and resolutions addressing immigration issues in 2009 (twenty of which were vetoed), up from 206 in 2008 (with three vetoes), 240 in 2007 (twelve vetoes), 84 in 2006 (six vetoes), and 38 in 2005 (six vetoes).[62]

The most important of these state measures was Arizona's Senate Bill 1070, which would make it a state crime (rather than a civil offense, as under federal law) to be in the state without authorization and would require law enforcement agents in the state to question people about their immigration status if the officer has probable cause to suspect the person is an unauthorized immigrant. Seven different plaintiffs filed lawsuits to block the Arizona law, including the Obama administration, which claimed that the law was preempted by federal immigration legislation, and that enforcement of Senate Bill 1070 would damage U.S. foreign relations with Mexico and other countries of origin, a position supported by Mexico's controversial decision to file an *amicus curia* brief opposing the Arizona law. While the final outcome of these legal battles remains unresolved, District Judge Susan Bolton issued a temporary injunction in July 2010 that blocked the most important elements of SB1070, a decision likely to remain in effect pending an expected Supreme Court review of the Arizona law in 2011.

Conclusion: Continued Obstacles to Reform

U.S. regional relations since the end of the cold war have been dominated by greater economic and political integration, and the NAFTA agreement is often held up as a model for the entire hemisphere. Immigration relations were a conspicuous outlier from this trend during the 1990s, as increasing trade and investment flows were met with a new focus on border enforcement and a broader trend toward the criminalization of undocumented migration. Why did Mexico drop out of the 2006 immigration debate after receiving so much attention from Bush in 2000–2001? And why did repeated efforts to pass immigration reform legislation fail during the Bush years and the first year of the Obama administration?

On one level, the failure to follow through on the promise of bilateralism should come as no surprise. As the preceding historical review suggests, the early years of the bracero program were uniquely characterized by bilateralism on migration policy. At the time, the United States needed Mexican support to restart migration flows and to ensure reliable access to Mexican labor during a period of war-induced shortages, and Mexico needed U.S. support to ensure that the state played a direct role in managing the program and in protecting the rights of Mexican workers within the United States. At other times, either the United States (1950s, 1960s) or Mexico (1970s) or both (1980s) have perceived their interests as best served by unilateral or even *laissez-faire* approaches to migration control, so that the objective conditions for a bilateral immigration deal have rarely been present.

Yet on another level, the failure of the United States and Mexico to follow through on the promise of 2001, reiterated in 2005, is surprising because the contemporary period resembles the early bracero years in that both Mexico and the United States have self-interested reasons to favor bilateralism. From the Mexican perspective, bilateralism is an attractive strategy for reducing the unacceptable level of violence at the U.S.-Mexican border, a top priority for a democratic Mexico eager to demonstrate its effectiveness. From the U.S. perspective, a bilateral deal offers the greatest promise with regard to both immigration control and the U.S. war on terrorism. And ruling factions in both countries see an immigration deal as an attractive way to solidify regional support for free markets and U.S. economic institutions.

Yet Presidents Bush and Fox both deferred to Congress on the specifics of an immigration proposal, and congressional immigration leaders view immigration from an overwhelmingly domestic perspective. Mexico's episodic efforts to influence U.S. immigration policy have been indirect (for example, mobilizing Mexicans within the United States or seeking to shape the public debate) or made through Mexican ties to the executive branch. As a result, Mexico has weak connections to U.S. congressional actors who are influential in the making of immigration legislation, and few Congress members gave any thought to opportunities for bilateralism as legislative details were finalized. Adding a Mexican dimension to the deal also would have created new sources of opposition to an already fragile compromise.

More generally, why did immigration reform efforts fail so spectacularly in 2006 and 2007, despite widespread popular demands for reform and the rough popular consensus in favor of the Senate's reform bill; and why has Congress been so reluctant to take up the issue in 2009–2010? In short, reform efforts ran into a truism about immigration politics: that they are characterized by cross-cutting cleavages, which confound stable partisan coalitions. Democrats were divided between the desire to appeal to Latino voters, who favored generous comprehensive reform, and the desire to appear tough on national security by backing a House-style, enforcement-only bill. Some Democrats also objected to the Senate bill's temporary worker provisions, which labor unions traditionally have opposed, and which became even more controversial as unemployment hovered above 9 percent in 2009–2010. With Democrats facing substantial losses in the 2010 midterm elections, most vulnerable members saw any vote on legalization of other immigration benefits as far too risky.

Republicans were equally divided. President Bush had made support for comprehensive immigration reform a central theme of his second term, national party leaders saw pro-immigrant reforms as a unique opportunity to solidify Bush's tentative gains with Latino voters, and traditionally Republican business and mainline religious groups were strong backers of comprehensive reform. But grassroots social conservative groups like the Eagle Forum, anti-immigration advocates like the Federation for American Immigration Reform (FAIR) and the Minutemen, evangelical groups like the Christian Coalition, and the burgeoning populist Tea Party movement all brought significant restrictionist pressure to bear on Republican members. The few remaining Republican moderates faced persistent pressure over immigration issues, including in Utah, where Bob Bennett was defeated at the party's convention in May 2010, and in Arizona, where John McCain faced an August primary challenge from long-time immigration hard-liner J. D. Hayworth.

Thus, with both parties internally divided, strategists on both sides of the aisle saw political reasons to avoid immigration issues during the run-up to elections in 2006, 2008, and 2010. In 2006 Democratic leaders believed that the majority Republicans would be blamed if Congress failed to pass immigration reform, reinforcing the Democratic campaign theme of a "do-nothing" Congress. Republicans recognized that voters wanted action on immigration policy, but many considered the price of inaction to be lower than that of supporting *amnesty,* a term that hard-liners defined to include almost any policy short of mass deportation. Ironically, the Democratic takeover of Congress in 2007 and the White House in 2009 reinforced these dynamics, as Democrats were reluctant to take a firm position on immigration, and Republicans generally refused to cooperate on any Democratic legislation.

Finally, Presidents Bush and Obama both failed to exercise effective leadership on the issue. President Bush spoke out in favor of reform on a number of occasions, including in a rare primetime address on May 15, 2006, timed to coincide with the start of the second round of Senate debate that year, but he never explicitly endorsed that year's Senate bill, and his lobbying efforts in 2006 and 2007 were undermined by his low approval ratings.[63] Similarly, while President Obama repeatedly expressed commitment to immigration reform in general, including in a major speech at American University in April 2010, he too refused to commit to a specific legislative approach, and never placed immigration reform ahead of competing agenda items like health care reform, a jobs package, financial regulation, or an energy bill. With economic recovery lagging and the campaign season looming, prospects for immigration reform remained doubtful in the summer of 2010.

Key Actors

George W. Bush   President, placed immigration reform on the agenda in 2001, 2005, and 2007 but was criticized by supporters of reform efforts for failing to push hard enough to pass bills in 2006 and 2007.

Michael Chertoff   Secretary of homeland security, key negotiator and spokesman for the Bush administration during debates over the Comprehensive Immigration Reform Act of 2006 (McCain-Kennedy bill) and the Secure Borders, Economic Opportunity, and Immigration Reform Act of 2007 (Kennedy-Kyl bill).

Vicente Fox   President of Mexico (2000–2006), joined President Bush in pressing for immigration reform in 2001 but was sidelined from U.S. immigration debate after the September 11 attacks.

Carlos Gutierrez   U.S. secretary of commerce, key negotiator and spokesman for the Bush administration during debate over the Comprehensive Immigration Reform Act of 2006 (McCain-Kennedy bill) and of the Secure Borders, Economic Opportunity, and Immigration Reform Act of 2007 (Kennedy-Kyl bill).

Edward Kennedy   Senator, D-Mass., coauthor of the Comprehensive Immigration Reform Act of 2006 (McCain-Kennedy bill) and the Secure Borders, Economic Opportunity, and Immigration Reform Act of 2007 (Kennedy-Kyl bill).

Jon Kyl   Senator, R-Ariz., leading opponent of Comprehensive Immigration Reform Act of 2006 (McCain-Kennedy bill); coauthor of Secure Borders, Economic Opportunity, and Immigration Reform Act of 2007 (Kennedy-Kyl bill).

John McCain   Senator, R-Ariz., coauthor of Comprehensive Immigration Reform Act of 2006 (McCain-Kennedy bill); supporter of the Secure Borders, Economic Opportunity, and Immigration Reform Act of 2007 (Kennedy-Kyl bill).

Janet Napolitano   Secretary of homeland security, leader of the Obama administration's efforts on immigration reform and on binational efforts with Mexico to improve border security.

James Sensenbrenner   Representative, R-Wis., author of the Border Protection, Antiterrorism, and Illegal Immigration Control Act of 2005 (Sensenbrenner bill).

Arlen Specter   Senator, R-Pa., primary Republican cosponsor of the Comprehensive Immigration Reform Act of 2006 (McCain-Kennedy bill) and of the Secure Borders, Economic Opportunity, and Immigration Reform Act of 2007 (Kennedy-Kyl bill).

Notes

1. See, e.g., Jorge I. Domínguez and Rafael Fernández de Castro, *The United States and Mexico: Between Partnership and Conflict* (New York: Routledge, 2002); Cathryn Thorup, "U.S. Policy toward Mexico: Prospects for Administrative Reform," in *Foreign Policy in U.S.-Mexican Relations*, ed. Rosario Green and Peter H. Smith (La Jolla: University of California, San Diego Center for U.S.-Mexican Studies, 1989), 129–157.

2. Robert Leiken, "With a Friend Like Fox," *Foreign Affairs* 80, no. 5 (2001): 91–104.

3. White House, "Joint Statement by President George Bush and President Vicente Fox: Towards a Partnership for Prosperity," February 16, 2001, www.whitehouse.gov/news/releases/2001/02/20010220-2.html (accessed May 7, 2007).

4. The negotiating framework identified four goals: "matching willing workers with willing employers; serving the social and economic needs of both countries; respecting the human dignity of all migrants, regardless of their status; recognizing the contribution migrants make to enriching both societies; [and] shared responsibility for ensuring migration takes place through safe and legal channels." The high-level working group was instructed to work out the details for an agreement focused on border safety, a temporary worker program, and a strategy for legalizing the status of undocumented Mexicans in the United States. See White House, "Joint Statement between the United States of America and the United Mexican States," September 6, 2001, www.whitehouse .gov/news/releases/2001/09/20010906-8.html (accessed May 7, 2007).

5. White House, "Fact Sheet: Partnership for Prosperity," September 6, 2001, www .whitehouse.gov/news/releases/2001/09/20010906-7.html (accessed May 7, 2007). Analysts had long identified such a program as the most promising strategy for reducing undocumented outflows, though the politics of such a program are difficult because economic growth may increase emigration pressures in the short run, before reducing

them in the long run. See U.S. Commission for the Study of International Migration and Cooperative Economic Development (Asencio Commission), *Unauthorized Migration: An Economic Development Response* (Washington, D.C.: U.S. Government Printing Office, 1990).

6. Elliot B. Smith, "Neighborly Visit for Bush, Fox," *Chicago Sun Times*, February 18, 2001, A34.

7. James C. McKinley Jr., "From Mexico also, the Message to Bush Is Immigration," *New York Times*, March 14, 2007, A12.

8. Ioan Grillo, "Obama in Mexico: No Hero's Welcome," *Time,* April 17, 2009; Diego Graglia, "Disappointment in Mexico as Obama Says Immigration Reform Will Have to Wait," *Feet in 2 Worlds*, August 11, 2009, http://feetin2worlds.wordpress .com/2009/08/11/in-guadalajara-obama-tells-mexican-president-immigration-reform-will-have-to-wait/ (accessed February 14, 2010).

9. In addition to a controversy about heavy-handed migration enforcement during the 1930s, bilateral relations were strained as a result of Mexico's 1938 expropriation of U.S. oil holdings. When the two sides were unable to agree on a compensation package for U.S. firms, the United States boycotted Mexican oil sales, and Mexico responded by boosting its exports to Germany.

10. U.S. Department of State, *Foreign Relations of the United States*, vol. 6 (Washington, D.C.: U.S. Government Printing Office, 1943), 538–544.

11. David Fitzgerald, "Inside the Sending State: The Politics of Mexican Emigration Control," *International Migration Review* 40, no. 2 (Summer 2006): 259–293.

12. "The Bracero Program," *Rural Migration News* 10, no. 2 (April 2003), http:// migration.ucdavis.edu/rmn/more.php?id=10_0_4_0 (accessed June 2, 2007).

13. On the bracero program and U.S.-Mexican relations generally, see Richard B. Craig, *The Bracero Program: Interest Groups and Foreign Policy* (Austin: University of Texas Press, 1979); Marc R. Rosenblum, "The Intermestic Politics of Immigration Policy: Lessons from the Bracero Program," *Political Power and Social Theory* 17 (2005): 141–184.

14. Kitty Calavita, *Inside the State: The Bracero Program, Immigration and the I.N.S.* (New York: Routledge, 1992); Stephen W. Yale-Loehr, "Testimony before the House Judiciary Committee, Subcommittee on Immigration," April 24, 2007, http://judiciary .house.gov/media/pdfs/Yale-Loehr070424.pdf (accessed May 7, 2007).

15. "Braceros Riot at the Border," *New York Times*, January 24, 1954, A10.

16. Gil Loescher and John A. Scanlan, *Calculated Kindness: Refugees and America's Half-Open Door, 1945 to the Present* (New York: Free Press, 1986); Daniel J. Tichenor, *Dividing Lines: The Politics of Immigration Control in America* (Princeton: Princeton University Press, 2002).

17. Cheryl Shanks, *Immigration and the Politics of American Sovereignty, 1890–1990* (Ann Arbor: University of Michigan Press, 2001).

18. Douglas Massey, Jorge Durand, and Nolan J. Malone, *Beyond Smoke and Mirrors: Mexican Immigration in an Era of Free Trade* (New York: Russell Sage Foundation, 2002).

19. Carlos Rico, "Migration and U.S.-Mexican Relations, 1966–1986," in *Western Hemisphere Immigration and United States Foreign Policy*, ed. Christopher Mitchell (College Park: Pennsylvania State Press, 1992), 3–25.

20. Salvador Campos Icardo, "Progress in Bilateral Relations," *Proceedings of the Academy of Political Science* 34, no. 1 (1981): 28–31; Thorup, "U.S. Policy toward Mexico."

21. Massey, Durand, and Malone, *Beyond Smoke and Mirrors.*

22. In particular, bilateral relations were strained by disagreements over conflicting U.S. and Mexican approaches to resolving civil wars in Nicaragua, Guatemala, and El Salvador; by Mexico's 1982 debt default and subsequent economic crisis; by the slow pace of Mexico's electoral reform; and by the conflict over the U.S. war on drugs. See Marc R. Rosenblum, *The Transnational Politics of U.S. Immigration Policy* (La Jolla: University of California, San Diego Center for Comparative Immigration Studies, 2004).

23. Ibid.

24. See Peter Hakim, "The Uneasy Americas," *Foreign Affairs* (March/April 2001): 46–61.

25. See, for example, Thomas Elias, "Proposition 187 Fans the Flames of Intolerance," *Houston Chronicle*, December 11, 1994, A1.

26. Clinton's pro-enforcement position was also a legacy of his experience as governor of Arkansas, where riots in 1980 by twenty-one thousand Cuban Marielitos temporarily housed at Arkansas's Fort Chaffee contributed to Clinton's defeat in his gubernatorial reelection campaign.

27. The Gallegly amendment had passed by a comfortable margin of 257–163, and substantial presidential effort was required to strip the provision from the bill. See Rosenblum, *The Transnational Politics.*

28. See Deborah Waller Meyers, "U.S. Border Enforcement: From Horseback to High Tech," Migration Policy Institute Insight #7 (Washington, D.C.: Migration Policy Institute, 2005).

29. These efforts included a new U.S. border crossing card program for local migration, a bilateral "memorandum of understanding" emphasizing human rights over law enforcement, a joint training program for U.S. and Mexican border guards, "mechanisms of consultation" between U.S. enforcement agents and Mexican consuls to improve border-area bilateral communications, "border liaison mechanisms" to govern deportation procedures, and new programs to link migration control efforts to Mexican economic development programs. See Rosenblum, *The Transnational Politics.*

30. Ibid.

31. Jorge Castañeda, "The Forgotten Relationship," *Foreign Affairs* (May/June 2003): 67–81; Peter Hakim, "Is Washington Losing Latin America?" *Foreign Affairs* (January/February 2006): 39–53.

32. White House, "Fact Sheet: Fair and Secure Immigration Reform," January 7, 2004, www.whitehouse.gov/news/releases/2004/01/20040107-1.html (accessed May 7, 2007).

33. White House, "President Bush, President Fox Meet with Reporters in Mexico," January 12, 2004, www.whitehouse.gov/news/releases/2004/01/20040112-7.html (accessed May 7, 2007).

34. White House, "State of the Union Address," January 20, 2004, www.whitehouse.gov/news/releases/2004/01/20040120-7.html (accessed May 7, 2007).

35. White House, "State of the Union Address," February 2, 2005, www.whitehouse.gov/news/releases/2005/02/20050202-11.html (accessed May 7, 2007).

36. Sens. John McCain, R-Ariz., and Edward Kennedy, D-Mass., introduced S. 1033 in March, the Secure America and Orderly Immigration Act. Sens. John Cornyn, R-Texas, and Jon Kyl, R-Ariz., introduced S. 1438 in July, the Comprehensive Enforcement and Immigration Reform Act; and Sen. Chuck Hagel, R-Neb., introduced a package of four separate bills, S. 1916–S. 1919, in October.

37. The Border Protection, Antiterrorism, and Illegal Immigration Control Act of 2005.

38. White House, "Statement of Administration Policy: H.R. 4437—Border Protection, Antiterrorism, and Illegal Immigration Control Act of 2005," December 15, 2005, http://www.whitehouse.gov/sites/default/files/omb/legislative/sap/109-1/hr4437sap-h .pdf (accessed May 28, 2007).

39. Sen. Diane Feinstein, Calif., was the only Democrat on the committee who opposed the McCain-Kennedy guest worker and legalization language. Among Republicans, Lindsay Graham, S.C., and Sam Brownback, Kan., were original McCain-Kennedy cosponsors, and Mike DeWine, Ohio, was a strong supporter.

40. Republicans Jeff Sessions, Ala., and Tom Coburn, Okla., were the two most reliable anti-immigration votes in the Senate, and Charles Grassley, Iowa, and Orrin Hatch, Utah, were also considered safe votes against comprehensive reform.

41. For example, Sen. Johnny Isakson, R-Ga., offered an amendment to require that implementation of the legalization and guest worker provisions could only be "triggered" once the president certified that the U.S.-Mexican border was "sealed and secured." Hard-liners saw this as consistent with the premise that comprehensive reform combined legalization and new legal flows with real enforcement, but supporters of the bill worried that the Isakson language established an impossible standard and that the new benefits would be postponed indefinitely.

42. Six Democrats crossed party lines to vote against cloture. Even solid Republican supporters of comprehensive reform, such as John McCain and Lindsay Graham, voted against cloture based on their conviction that the Democrats were violating Senate norms by blocking votes on the disputed amendments.

43. These "touch-base returns" provided Republicans some political cover against the charge of amnesty because immigrants would reenter in legal status before getting on a path to citizenship. As in the Judiciary Committee and McCain-Kennedy bills, aliens in the country for less than two years were denied legalization.

44. The core group included Republican senators Brownback, DeWine, Graham, Hagel, Martinez, McCain, and Specter, and Democratic senators Durbin, Kennedy, Lieberman, Menendez, Obama, and Salazar. The group met daily during the second floor debate to map out legislative strategy and to agree on coalition positions on each of the expected amendments.

45. A July Tarrance Group poll found that 11 percent of respondents identified candidates' positions on illegal immigration as the most important issue determining their vote in the fall, the highest figure ever reported on this question. Three separate polls conducted by CNN in April and May and by CBS in May found between 75 percent and 79 percent of respondents supporting the Senate's legalization provisions. Even strong majorities of Republican voters favored the Senate plan—75 percent in a June Tarrance Group poll—while only 47 percent supported the House's enforcement-only approach.

46. Key interest groups supporting the comprehensive Senate bill included the U.S. Chamber of Commerce, the Essential Workers Immigration Coalition (EWIC, itself a coalition of business groups employing low-skilled immigrant workers), the U.S. Conference of Catholic Bishops, the National Council of La Raza, the National Immigration Forum, the American Immigration Lawyers' Association, and the Service Employees International Union.

47. Four out of forty-three Democrats crossed party lines to oppose the bill, and twenty-three out of fifty-five Republicans supported it; two Democrats were absent.

48. The House bill ran 256 pages in legislative format, compared to 795 for the Senate's. More fundamentally, while the bills included broadly similar enforcement provisions—increasing border infrastructure and personnel, strengthening document security, requiring employers to participate in an electronic employment eligibility verification system—the House bill made undocumented immigrants into felons, whereas the Senate offered them legal status. The Senate bill also promised a dramatic expansion in both temporary and permanent legal immigration, while the House offered none.

49. Chris Dorval and Andrea LaRue, "Immigration Fails as Wedge Issue for GOP; Succeeds in Expanding Base for Democrats," Immigration 2006.org press release, November 8, 2006, www.immigration2006.org/index.html (accessed May 29, 2007).

50. Gutierrez and Flake agreed to the wage standard favored by Kennedy, and filed the Security through Regularized Immigration and a Vibrant Economy (STRIVE) Act of 2007 (H.R. 1645) in March.

51. Senators Brownback, Hagel, and McCain were all considering presidential runs; Graham was up for reelection for his seat in conservative South Carolina; and Martinez was the new chairman of the Republican Senate Campaign Committee. Republican staffers acknowledged that the 2008 election loomed large in the immigration negotiations, and Democrats involved in the negotiations charged, at a minimum, that McCain's physical absence from the Senate in favor of the campaign trail prevented him from playing a moderating role. Staffers for hard-line Republicans were quick to explain McCain and others' shift as a political decision, as one explained: "Would you want to stand up there next to Tom Tancredo and explain to our voters why you supported Kennedy's amnesty bill?"

52. McCain et al., 2007.

53. The liberal pro-immigration groups saw the bill's legalization provisions as their only opportunity to relieve their constituents from the looming threat of deportation, and while they urged pro-migration senators to demand changes to the point system, guest worker program, and enforcement provisions, only the most hard-line labor unions and the most liberal immigrant groups urged members to vote against the bill.

54. As part of the leadership deal to hold votes only on the predetermined list of amendments, Senator Reid employed an obscure "clay pigeon" procedure, breaking a single massive amendment into twenty-six separate "divisions," each receiving an independent vote without allowing consideration of other amendments.

55. At least eight of the Republicans voting to eliminate the REAL ID language had voted in favor of the license provisions and other tough enforcement provisions in the past; their votes were for immigration hard-liners voting "strategically" to weaken the bill—against their true preferences—in order to break up the bill's winning coalition.

56. Bennett Roth, "Obama, McCain Address Hispanics," Houston Chronicle, July 8, 2008.

57. Julia Preston, "Obama to Push Immigration Bill as One Priority," New York Times, April 8, 2009.

58. United States Joint Forces Command, "The Joint Operating Environment 2008: Challenges and Implications for the Future Joint Force," 36, www.jfcom.mil/newslink/storyarchive/2008/JOE2008.pdf (accessed February 14, 2010).

59. Patrik Johnson, "Immigration Reform Pitch Morphs Tea Party Protests," Christian Science Monitor, November 14, 2009.

60. Three Democratic senators who had been outspoken supporters of immigration reform in 2006–2007 left Congress for the executive branch: President Obama and Secretaries Hillary Clinton and Ken Salazar. Republicans Chuck Hagel and Mel Martinez retired from Congress, Mike DeWine lost his reelection bid, and Arlen Specter changed parties.

61. Charles E. Schumer and Lindsey O. Graham, "The Right Way to Mend Immigration," *Washington Post*, March 19, 2010, A22.

62. National Conference of State Legislatures, "2009 State Laws Related to Immigrants and Immigration," National Conference of State Legislatures, December 1, 2009, www.ncsl.org/default.aspx?tabid=19232 (accessed July 27, 2010). While most of these laws provided for enhanced immigration enforcement or reduced immigrant benefits, about a third of the state laws were resolutions celebrating immigration or other measures that supported immigrants, including, for example, by expanding access to certain benefits or restricting the state's role in enforcement.

63. Nicole Gaouette, "House GOP Not Budging on Border," *Los Angeles Times*, May 24, 2006, A1.

10 The Global Financial Crisis: Governments, Banks, and Markets

Thomas D. Lairson

Before You Begin

1. What are the long-term and short-term causes of the financial crisis?

2. Whose actions and decisions contributed to the crisis?

3. Why did governments intervene in the economy and bail out banks?

4. What are some potential negative consequences of such actions?

5. What foreign policy choices are involved in efforts to solve problems created by the crisis?

6. How do the efforts to create a new regulatory regime affect power relations and foreign policies?

7. Does the concept of state capitalism expand our understanding of financial statecraft?

Introduction

The interactions among powerful states during the time of the global financial crisis—August 2007 to April 2010—were during a time of great drama. The collapsing values of equities, real estate, and currencies combined with the potential for bankruptcy of the financial and credit systems of many nations to create considerable fear and anxiety. Questions were raised about a possible repeat of the depression of the 1930s and about the viability of capitalism itself. The chance of a global economic system spiraling out of control was not small, and political and ministerial leaders made decisions in an atmosphere of genuine crisis. Missteps could have catastrophic consequences.[1]

In the end, there was much reason for worry. The cost of the crisis in various forms of governmental support was $15 trillion, equal to nearly one-quarter of the global gross domestic product (GDP).[2] In addition, the losses in home equity and in investments (potentially recoverable) were as much as $28 trillion.[3] Financial institutions sustained several trillion dollars in losses, as would many firms operating in other areas of the economy. Unemployment rates around the world rose substantially, driven up by the severe economic downturn that followed.

The origins of the crisis in the United States, hitherto the nation providing leadership in global affairs and the nation perhaps most damaged by the crisis, complicated a global response to the crisis. The rapid accumulation of economic resources by China, and its relative insularity from the crisis, created the potential for a stunning shift of global power away from the United States. Tracing the sources and consequences of the crisis illuminates the capacities of governments, the power of financial interests, and the political and power relationships between the United States and China; it also raises important questions about the sustainability of contemporary forms of capitalism.

Background: Financialization of the Global Economy

The global economic crisis emerged out of a three-decade era of financialization: a rapid global expansion of financial transactions that assumed a vastly greater size and geographic scope.[4] This has generated substantial changes in the structure of the financial industry and greatly intensified global competition.[5] The political leadership for this effort came from the government and financial industry of the United States, which pressed hard over thirty years for a liberalization of national policies for the movement of goods and money.

Globalization involves a rapid expansion of trade relative to domestic production but also leads to a tighter integration of global financial markets, increasing the potential for changes in one market to cascade across the system and affect many nations and markets. The financial crisis of 2007–2010 was by no means the first during this era of globalization; indeed, the expansion of markets and number of market players seem to be associated with an increase in the frequency of such crises. Financial crises involving governmental borrowing from global banks occurred in 1982, 1994, 1998, 1999, and 2001; crises involving private sector borrowing occurred in the United States from 1988–1991 and in Asia from 1997–1998; global stock market collapses took place in 1987 and 2000; and the massive collapse of stocks, real estate, and debt instruments came upon us in 2007–2010.[6]

This era of globalization and financialization was also one in which governmental responsibilities for regulatory oversight of financial institutions changed character: both expanding in consistency across nations and contracting in practice within many nations.[7] Though international efforts to

Timeline
The Global Financial Crisis

March 1973	Bretton Woods system of fixed exchange rates ends and a system of floating exchange rates for many nations' currencies begins. This opens the way to large foreign exchange markets and futures markets.
August 1982	Mexico declares a default on its foreign debt. After years of rapid growth and rising debt from large budget deficits, the Mexican government is forced to default when oil prices begin to fall. The loans to Mexico come from large U.S. banks, creating a systemic crisis. The Reagan administration, in conjunction with the International Monetary Fund (IMF), provides loans and helps extend the payment schedule for Mexican debt.
October 1982	Garn–St. Germain Depository Institutions Act of 1982. Provides for a substantial deregulation of savings and loan banks, reducing capital requirements and eliminating restrictions on investment options.
October 1987	Global stock market collapse. After several years of rapid increases in prices, the stock market suffers a large and rapid decline (U.S. markets fall 23 percent in one day). The newly appointed chairman of the Federal Reserve, Alan Greenspan, acts quickly to lower interest rates and increase the money supply to restore confidence and prevent a systemic crisis.
August 1989	Establishment of the Resolution Trust Corp. Facing a substantial disintegration of savings and loan banks, President George H. W. Bush and Congress create an agency with $150 billion to purchase the bad assets of the banks and close many of them.
December 1994	Mexican peso crisis. Limited financial crisis involves large budget deficits, repayment of governmental debt, and the collapse of the Mexican peso. The Clinton administration provides loans to Mexico to support the peso.

July 1997–June 1998	Asian financial crisis. Beginning in Thailand and spreading to many Asian nations, the crisis focuses on current account deficits, exchange rates, and levels of private and governmental debt. Supported by the U.S. government, the IMF provides loans to several Asian nations.
June 1998	Russian financial crisis. Linked to the Asian financial crisis, the focus is on debt repayment, government default, and collapse of the Russian currency—the ruble. Supported by the U.S. government, the IMF provides loans to support the ruble.
September 1998	Long-Term Capital Management (LTCM) crisis. Led by Nobel Prize–winning economists, this large hedge fund uses sophisticated investment strategies, based on high levels of leverage. The failure of these strategies, mostly from the Russian financial crisis, brings on fears of a systemic crisis and leads the New York Federal Reserve to arrange loans by major Wall Street firms to prevent a loss of confidence.
November 1999	Gramm-Leach-Bliley Act. Repeals important parts of the Depression-era regulation of U.S. banks, the Glass-Steagall Act, which prevents the combination of commercial and investment banks. With these restrictions removed, new financial institutions combining various parts of finance, such as insurance, banking, and investment, are created.
March 2000	Dot-com stock market crash. Collapse of stock prices, especially of information technology companies, following years of very large price increases.
December 2000– December 2001	Argentine financial crisis relating to international debt repayment and breakdown of fixed exchange rate. Supported by the U.S. government, the IMF provides loans to support the Argentine peso.
September 2001	World Trade Center attacks. With the U.S. economy already weakened by the stock market declines, this event leads the Federal Reserve under Alan Greenspan to lower interest rates to nearly zero and boost the money supply to promote economic growth.

(continued)

Timeline *(continued)*
The Global Financial Crisis

2002–2006	Rapid expansion of subprime mortgage loans and increases in house prices tied to expansion of collateralized debt obligations (CDOs) and credit default swaps (CDSs). This is fueled by low interest rates and large financing of the U.S. budget deficit by China. Debt levels for households, governments, and businesses rise substantially across much of the world.
June 2004	Federal Reserve begins a three-year process of raising interest rates. This affects homeowners with subprime mortgages who begin to default and enter foreclosure in larger and larger numbers. House prices peak and begin to fall in 2006.
August 2007	Federal Reserve begins to lower interest rates based on worries about the effects of declining home prices on the derivatives market.
March 2008	Facing bankruptcy, Bear Sterns is sold to JP Morgan Chase in a deal engineered by the Federal Reserve.
April 2008	Unemployment levels begin to rise from 5 percent to 10 percent by October 2009. This leads to more foreclosures and more declines in housing prices.
July–September 8, 2008	The potential failures of Fannie Mae and Freddie Mac lead first to direct support by the U.S. government, and when that fails to the September 8 takeover of these firms by the U.S. government.
September 14, 2008	Merrill Lynch, the world's largest brokerage firm, is sold to Bank of America in a sale engineered by Secretary of the Treasury Henry Paulson. Facing massive losses from derivatives trading, Merrill Lynch is deemed too big and too interconnected to fail.

September 15, 2008	Lehman declares bankruptcy after the Federal Reserve is unable to find a buyer. Beset by huge losses from derivative investments, Lehman's collapse sends a shock wave through financial markets.
September 16, 2008	Reversing course, the Federal Reserve acts to provide emergency lending to AIG of $85 billion (eventually $182 billion). Deeply involved in the CDOs and CDSs, AIG is too big and too interconnected to be allowed to fail.
September 19–October 15, 2008	Secretary Paulson proposes that Congress create a $700 billion fund for a Troubled Asset Relief Program (TARP). Congress first rejects the proposal, but on October 3 passes the law and President George W. Bush signs it. On October 15 the terms for application of the fund are modified.
September 2008–February 2010	Federal Reserve initiates a multitrillion-dollar program to inject liquidity into financial institutions by purchasing bad assets and sustaining global liquidity through arrangements with other central banks.
October 2008	The banking system in Iceland collapses and is nationalized by the government.
October 2008	The British government enacts a 500 billion pound rescue package for British banks.
November 9, 2008	China announces a $586 billion stimulus package to bolster its economy.
November 14, 2008	Leaders of the G-20 meet in Washington, D.C.
December 19, 2008	President Bush announces that TARP funds will be used to help U.S. automakers.
February 17, 2009	President Barack Obama signs a $787 billion stimulus plan for the U.S. economy.

(continued)

Timeline *(continued)*

The Global Financial Crisis

April 2, 2009	Leaders of the G-20 meet in London.
June 2009	President Obama proposes new banking regulation legislation.
September 20, 2009	Leaders of the G-20 meet in Pittsburgh.
December 2009– May 2010	Greece faces possible default on sovereign debt unless a lending package from the IMF and European Union (EU) can be arranged. The crisis in Greece has substantial potential for spreading to other European nations and thereby creating a global crisis.

coordinate regulatory rules for banking increased, the effect of those rules can only be understood in terms of an overall relaxation of regulatory restraints across many nations and a decline in effective regulatory consistency.

Perhaps the most striking element of the financialization of the global economy was innovations in the types of financial instruments and in the processes by which investments were made. Ever since the end of fixed exchange rates for most advanced nations in the 1970s, foreign exchange markets and especially futures markets have grown enormously. By mid-2007, daily turnover in these markets was over $3 trillion, more than three-fourths of which involved dollars, euros, yen, and pound sterling.[8]

Using much of the same logic as foreign exchange futures, complex derivatives were developed and expanded as primary trading instruments in global financial markets.[9] A derivative is a security whose value is a time-based result of the value of some other security, asset, or event. Derivatives usually are highly leveraged so that small changes in the value of the underlying asset lead to large changes in the value of the derivative. A derivative could be based on a stock price or on the flow of income coming from bundling together a variety of mortgages on houses (collateralized debt obligations, or CDOs). Even more exotic derivatives are credit default swaps, which are insurance policies that pay off in the event that a particular borrower fails to pay the interest or principal of a bond. These are securitized and traded in shadow markets, based on the market-based risk of defaulting on a bond.[10] In 2008, before the financial crisis had begun in earnest, total global derivatives contracts pending (excluding foreign exchange) were over $600 trillion, or about nine times the entire global GDP for 2008.[11]

Financialization was also enhanced by the enormous globalization of production, in particular the shift of manufacturing to several Asian nations and the resulting imbalances of trade. Competitive complementarities among the economies of the U.S. and several Asian states led to large and persistent imbalances in the global economy.[12] U.S. firms shifted manufacturing capabilities to Asia through foreign direct investment and then exported these products back to eager U.S. consumers, thereby creating large and growing trade deficits for the United States. However, surplus nations in Asia often chose to retain the accumulating dollars as foreign exchange reserves rather than exchange them and push up the value of their currency. Moreover, high growth rates over several decades meant much higher incomes for Asians. When combined with high savings rates, the foreign exchange reserves produced an enormous pool of capital for investment. High budget deficits and large private borrowing in the United States created a large demand for money. But low savings rates in the United States (the flip side of high consumption levels) meant U.S. funds could not meet this demand. Much of the Asian capital pool found its way back into purchases of U.S. government debt and an unlikely supply of capital from "poor" nations to "rich" nations.[13] Many of these investment decisions were the result of choices made by Asian governments. Thus the globalization of production and trade combined with financialization to see initial flows of U.S. investment into Asia to finance production of goods for sale in the United States. U.S. money then flowed to Asia to pay for the products and then flowed back to the United States in exchange for debt. The United States financed much of its consumption spree with debt owed to Asian governments.[14]

Globalization and financialization created many important consequences that contributed to the global economic crisis.[15] Perhaps most significant were the vast size of the markets and the giant role in those markets of highly leveraged assets vulnerable to risks not appreciated by most investors.[16] Some scholars and analysts trace the crisis to the rise of "money manager capitalism," a system involving highly leveraged investments aiming at maximizing

Table 10.1 Global Imbalances from U.S. Current Account, 1999–2008

Year	U.S. current account total ($ U.S. millions)	U.S.-Asia current account ($ U.S. millions)	U.S.-China current account ($ U.S. millions)	U.S.-China % total current account	U.S.-Asia % total current account
1999	−301,630	−216,071	−72,743	24.1	71.6
2000	−417,426	−246,690	−88,043	21.1	59.1
2001	−398,270	−225,945	−88,658	22.3	56.7
2002	−459,151	−249,558	−109,899	23.9	54.3
2003	−521,519	−260,713	−131,825	25.3	50.0
2004	−631,130	−325,465	−172,343	27.3	51.6
2005	−748,683	−377,908	−219,196	29.3	50.5
2006	−803,547	−437,434	−259,490	32.3	54.4
2007	−726,573	−452,594	−293,105	40.3	62.3
2008	−706,068	−430,534	−308,474	43.7	61.0

Source: Author's calculations, based on data from the Bureau of Economic Affairs, www.bea.gov/international/bp_web/simple.cfm?anon=71&table_id=10&area_id=35.

profits even as investment managers have incentives to underestimate the risk of loss.[17] Also, imbalances of trade and finance were inherent in a system based on dramatic asymmetries of capabilities and interests, as between the United States and China. These imbalances were unsustainable in the long run but continued as a result of the preferences of powerful states and actors. Finally, the vast size of both markets and profits generated interests in governments and private actors intensely committed to preserving and extending the system.[18]

The global economic crisis emerged out of a particular global regime of political economy, involving trade and production, global finance and investment, deregulation, and political relations that began to emerge in the 1970s. The explosion of global finance created high demand for new investment opportunities, which was increasingly met with exotic derivatives that were thought to manage risk even while providing high returns. These securities rested on the ability to expand high-risk home mortgage lending based on expectations of rising home prices. An unprecedented rise in public and private debt in the West was financed in significant part by the resources of relatively poor nations selling manufactured products to rich nations.

Background: The Nature of Financial Markets

Scholars have debated the degree to which financial markets are prone to instability and crisis or whether crises are the result of factors outside of markets that affect them negatively. This debate has considerable implications for whether governments accept a limited or proactive role in regulating markets.[19]

On one side are those with a strong belief in the efficacy of free markets for allocating resources (in this case, capital) rationally and efficiently to those best able to use it. Such a view counsels minimal efforts to regulate or manage markets by government, believing such actions always make things worse in terms of efficiency. This assertion rests on one of two alternative assumptions: that market participants are themselves rational and their choices produce the efficient allocation of resources, or, alternatively, that markets are themselves rational and always reflect the best available information. Consequently, free markets always generate a "correct" price.[20]

Countering this position is a collection of scholars who study markets and market crises and those who examine the actual behavior of market participants. The examination of past market panics reveals a set of common features, including a strong tendency for investors to follow and emulate winners, especially when a new and successful product or technology emerges. When this coincides with substantial expansion of credit and several markets are interdependent, the resulting overinvestment can ultimately lead to panic-selling in an effort to escape losses. The consequent cascading of prices across several markets leads to damage to the entire economy.[21] Others have looked at the behavior of market participants, finding considerable evidence for the view that many investors exhibit significant limits to rationality and invest based on emotion as much as clear calculation.[22] One study modeling a stock market composed of players with limited information who form expectations based on the expectations of others found a high frequency of booms and busts in prices.[23]

Background: Regulatory Environments

Financial markets and banking systems have been regulated by governments since the 1930s and even earlier. Central banks (all government-controlled) were designed to manage the money supply in part through the ability to regulate the lending behavior of private banks. Various government institutions have long been involved in guaranteeing banking deposits and in regulating the activities of investment banks and stock markets. But the degree of enforcement of these restrictions has varied according to the government in power and in terms of political and ideological trends. And the ability of central bankers to manage monetary policy to promote economic growth without either inflation or financial crises has been questioned.[24]

During the era of rapid globalization after the 1970s, governments generally retreated from strict regulations and enacted new rules that reduced or eliminated barriers to the international movement of money. This included flexible or floating exchange rates, eliminating controls on capital movements, broadening investment options for banks, and opening financial markets to foreign competition. Financial policies coincided with the privatization of state-owned enterprises, reductions in welfare spending, and the liberalization of trade.[25] At the same time, not all advanced or developing nations were equally committed to such policies. For example, in Europe liberalization of capital was related to constructing an integrated regional market and a single currency requiring more rules to manage and coordinate policies and actions.[26]

Governments and global financial firms interact in more than just a regulatory setting; choices and policy actions are deeply embedded in political and power relations. Government macroeconomic policies are greatly affected by the actual and anticipated reactions of stock, bond, and foreign exchange markets. Even more important, capital is the lifeblood of a capitalist economy, and those who control its allocation have enormous structural power.[27] The rate of economic growth is contingent on the effectiveness of financial firms in providing capital in sufficient volume to those who can best use it for economic activity. This structural power means two things: first, governments and financial firms must engage in a de facto partnership that both regulates and enhances the competitiveness of the financial sector; second, this requires substantial forms of political governance to prevent abuse and errors from damaging national and global economies, but not so much as to harm growth itself. Regulators are conscious of the possibility that controls on the actions of financial actors can reduce opportunities for profit and innovation.[28] Therefore, the nature and application of regulations are both a necessity and a negotiated outcome between financial and political interests.

The financialization of the world economy in recent decades means that regulation of financial institutions must be coordinated across many nations to be effective in protecting the financial system from cascading processes of crisis-induced breakdown. The core of the international coordination of regulation has been a series of negotiated rules designed to manage the consequences of bank failures. Each is named for the agreements reached in Basel,

Switzerland, among central bank officials of the richest nations.[29] The first was in 1988 (Basel I), the second in 2004 (Basel II), and the most recent and pending agreements in 2009. National governments are responsible for enacting these rules and enforcing them.[30]

The development of regulatory rules and enforcement practices takes place within political and power environments and reflects the structural power of financial institutions in providing the capital for economic growth. In addition, the rapid globalization of finance increased competition among financial firms. After the 1970s, the regulatory environment had been increasingly defined by a deepening elite consensus in the United States and Great Britain on the value and effectiveness of freer markets for trade and finance. This meant the considerable international power of the United States was behind the move to freer markets. Sometimes referred to as the "Washington consensus," these views called for less regulations and restrictions based on the assertion that free markets were self-regulating. This meant the economic gains from free and unregulated markets were not at significant risk from a financial collapse because market players themselves were the best judges of the riskiness of their decisions and would adjust their actions accordingly.

Regulatory decisions in the decades leading up to the crisis reflected this thinking. We see considerable evidence of change in government thinking: moving from a regime of intrusive examination and regulation developed in the 1930s to one in which financial institutions themselves defined and measured the risk associated with their actions. An important dynamic in this process was competition between New York and London to attract financial business by creating an environment most favorable to business. This meant a "race to the bottom" in enforcing regulations and in deregulation of finance.[31] This competition came against a background of increasing quantitative sophistication in measuring and managing risk.[32] Moreover, in a series of steps the U.S. government loosened restrictions on the sources of funds and on the investment options for banks. This culminated in the 1999 repeal of the Glass-Steagall Act of 1933 that restricted banks to commercial banking and prevented them from acting as investment banks. Over the years after 1980, banks became multipurpose and complex financial firms operating in virtually all of the rapidly expanding global financial arenas.[33]

The efforts at international regulatory coordination reflect the shifting environment of global finance. The focus of the Basel agreements has been on defining calculations for capital adequacy: How much reserves should banks keep as protection against failure? This question has increasingly been defined by the nature of the evolving partnership between governments and banks. That partnership has focused on government guarantees of depositors and even guarantees for the losses of some banks. Over time, this means the "acceptable" level of capital for banks has declined dramatically. In the 1970s and before Basel, the largest banks normally operated with 5 percent of capital, declining to about 4 percent.[34] The Basel I agreements focused on defining a set of risk categories for bank assets (loans and investments) and required that a certain level of liquid reserves be held as protection against losses.[35] The Basel II agreement in 2004 redefined the risk categories but, most important, placed responsibility for assessing the risk in the hands of the banks themselves. This was premised on assumptions about the validity of new efforts to quantify, with great precision, the risk of loss associated with particular kinds of assets.[36]

Trajectory of the Global Financial and Economic Crisis

Explanation and Summary

The best explanations for the crisis focus on the factors that contribute to the inherent instability of financial markets, and that then show how policies and actions of firms and governments contributed to creating and intensifying those circumstances to the point that a systemic crisis erupted:

- Financial markets are inherently unstable. This is especially the case when markets expand rapidly in size and incorporate new players with less investment sophistication. Couple this with an expansion of credit and rising prices, and asset bubbles are a likely result. In markets such as banking systems, with high levels of interdependence from cross investments and cross lending, there is a high potential for downward price cascades when these bubbles pop. The inherent instability of financial markets is enhanced because of the role of confidence in the ability of the various firms to repay their debt. Substantial doubt about repayment leads to panicked efforts to get money from possibly bankrupt firms—a "run" on the banks. Loss of confidence can also produce a breakdown in the continuous process of credit allocation that is the heart of financial capitalism, and when credit stops flowing the negative consequences cascade even further.
- More specific to this crisis, the deregulation of financial markets spread over several decades led to many financial innovations that required much higher leverage and thus risk-taking. Financial markets in the decade after 1999 became much more interdependent, took on much more debt, and assumed much greater risk. The leveraging of securities based on subprime (high-risk) mortgages is but one example of this.

- The monetary policy of the Federal Reserve, combined with global financial imbalances, supplied large amounts of cheap credit to the investing community. Seeking higher returns, higher risk investments were made that created an increasing potential for a bubble.

These features of an explanation for the crisis can be seen in a brief review of the events of the crisis.

The global financial crisis began with a small downturn in the price of homes in the United States, mostly resulting from increasing foreclosures that followed a rise in interest rates. A large number of mortgage borrowers were unable to make the changing payments on their mortgages. These declines reduced the value of and confidence in the large system of derivative securities, the value of which was based on these mortgages. Once derivatives came under doubt, the viability of the banks and investment institutions (such as hedge funds) with large positions in these securities also came under doubt. This doubt was confirmed as some of the weakest firms began to fail, which created a significant financial panic in which confidence in all lending broke down. Firms that in a normal market were solvent became insolvent in a panicked environment, as all creditors wanted payment at once. The government chose to step into the situation with funding to restore confidence and stop the panic that could lead to a breakdown of the entire global financial system. Large sums were used to purchase bad assets, support the liquidity of failing firms, and place the government into the position of lender of last resort. Once the financial collapse began to drag down purchasing power of consumers and thereby led to a rapid decline of the overall economy, the governments of many countries began to act to shore up the economy through stimulus spending. In the aftermath of the immediate crisis, nations continue to consider how to act to prevent a future crisis.

Crisis Sequence

The near-confluence of the bursting of the "dot-com" bubble in 2000 and the attacks of September 11, 2001, created a significant economic downturn in the U.S. economy. The Federal Reserve responded with a policy of easy money, lowering interest rates to near zero. Interest rates were similarly low in most other advanced economies. In addition, global liquidity—the supply of investment funds looking for returns—continued at a rapid rise. There was considerable political pressure from the U.S. Congress to expand mortgage loans, especially to low-income borrowers. This led to Fannie Mae and Freddie Mac (government-sponsored, but private firms) providing backing to mortgages of questionable value and then to rapid growth of exotic financial instruments tied to mortgages. This flow of funds to housing led to a rapid increase in house prices.

In the years leading up to the crisis, the amount of debt in the United States reached levels not seen for seventy-five years.[37] But in much of the developed world debt levels were even higher. By 2007 total indebtedness in the United States and across the nations of Europe was three times the size of GDP, a ratio that surpassed the record set in the years of the Great Depression. From 2001 to 2007 alone, U.S. domestic financial debt grew to $14.5 trillion from $8.5 trillion, and home mortgage debt ballooned to almost $10 trillion from $4.9 trillion, an increase of 102 percent. A very large proportion of the mortgage debt increase came from subprime loans, among the riskiest of these loans. In Europe, debt reached similar proportions of GDP, driven as much by business borrowing as by home mortgages. Britain was the largest borrower; even after the crisis, borrowing rose to 350 percent of GDP.[38] A very large and increasing portion of the government debt was held by Asian governments eager to sustain trade surpluses by holding dollar assets.

Directly connected to this vast increase in debt was the even larger expansion of derivatives, the value of which was often tied to the value of the income streams from the debt. These derivatives were themselves leveraged, usually traded in dark markets where values were not publicly known, and mostly carried by firms operating in nonregulated settings and in off-the-books accounts. This "shadow market" was designed to attract global investments seeking higher returns, and was usually rated as very safe based on the theory that the issuers of derivatives had been able to manage and reduce the risks of such securities.[39]

Financialization of the global economy had a major consequence: it created a vast global pool of investment capital constantly searching for higher-yielding but safe investments. One estimate from an IMF official is that this pool totaled about $70 trillion.[40] The major players in these securities were the investment bank wings of the great banks and insurance companies: JP Morgan Chase, Citigroup, Goldman Sachs, AIG, Bear Sterns, Lehman, Merrill Lynch, Bank of America, and Wachovia. Also deeply involved were numerous global investment firms seeking to raise yields.

Much of the decision making regarding lending for homes and creating a variety of securitized instruments built on home mortgages was premised on the long-term trend for steadily rising home prices. The large expansion of funding for homes began by 2003 to drive home price increases well above this long-term trend line. The rising prices of houses and the easily available credit pulled more persons into borrowing to purchase a house, thereby driving up prices even further and pulling more persons into the process. Expansion of the number of mortgages also supported an expansion of the derivative securities built on mortgages. Banks and investment firms seeking better yields purchased enormous amounts of the derivatives relating to mortgages, with confidence provided by the high ratings given by agencies such as Moody's.[41] For two to three years an expanding but unsustainable bubble of lending, buying, and securitization continued.

In the summer of 2004, the Federal Reserve began to reverse its policy of extremely easy credit by raising the discount rate, leading to a process of steadily increasing interest rates that took the discount rate from 2 percent in 2004 to 6.25 percent in 2006.[42] Interest rates throughout the economy rose, including the adjustable rates on many subprime mortgages. Many borrowers had also been borrowing a portion of the interest payments for their mortgage. So when the adjustment of mortgage payments included not only higher interest, but now payment for the old accruing interest, new payments were much higher. Housing prices peaked in many parts of the United States in 2005–2006 and then began to fall as more and more homeowners defaulted on their mortgages, taking them into foreclosure.[43]

The decline in house prices and rise in mortgage foreclosures slowly began to unwind the derivatives market along with placing a new drag on the overall economy. Even small increases in unemployment contributed to the emerging housing crisis as problems in one area began to feed back into other areas. In mid-2007, some U.S. and European high-profile hedge funds and banks with large investments in derivations linked to subprime loans declared bankruptcy, with others making ominous announcements about the value of these investments. The result was a 90 percent collapse in new issues of derivatives of CDOs by the end of 2007.

The first large bank failure was the British bank Northern Rock, which was taken over by the government. Several central banks responded with efforts to boost the money supply and lower key interest rates. The U.S. government also attempted to stem the tide with a series of similar but ultimately ineffectual actions. The global credit system began to break down, as many lenders were unable to judge the risks and simply stopped extending credit.

By March 2008, the reinforcing cycles of declining home prices and foreclosures, collapsing derivative values, and bankruptcy for banks and investment firms reached a crisis level when the major Wall Street investment bank Bear

Sterns faced bankruptcy. In an arrangement engineered and partly financed by the Federal Reserve, Bear Sterns was purchased by JP Morgan Chase. This action was taken to prevent losses by Bear Sterns from creating a cascade of losses by other large financial firms.[44] Even so, the process increased fears of a massive crisis. In the late spring of 2008, the financial crisis began to have a significant impact on unemployment, with rates beginning a rapid rise from 5 percent in April 2008 to above 10 percent in late 2009.[45]

Though these are government-sponsored enterprises, Fannie Mae and Freddie Mac are also private and profit-oriented firms in an arrangement coming out of the effort to privatize government enterprises. These enterprises issued bonds and provided guarantees for mortgages and hedge contracts totaling more than $7 trillion in July 2008. The operations of Freddie and Fannie show the deep and profound interconnections in global financial markets, with these obligations held by purchasers such as banks, state and local governments, insurance companies, and foreign governments. Fannie and Freddie began to collapse under huge losses in mid-2008. In July 2008, the U.S. government, led by Secretary Henry Paulson, reversed its previous position on providing backing to Freddie and Fannie and provided billions of dollars in support. This came as confidence in the financial system was threatened by the potential failure of the two firms. Soon, however, this proved insufficient, and these two privatized, government-sponsored entities were taken over by the government on September 8, 2008.[46]

The takeover of Freddie and Fannie ushered in the most intense period of the crisis, in which the deep fragility of the global financial system was nakedly exposed and in which government ingenuity in saving this system was severely tested. Policy actions throughout the crisis were premised on the proposition that some financial institutions were so deeply linked to other firms that failure would set off a panic and produce a set of domino-like failures that could not be controlled and would lead to a terrible depression. This view was tested by the decision not to rescue Lehman, perhaps the largest underwriter of sub-prime mortgage–backed securities, which declared bankruptcy on September 15.[47] This decision brought on the feared nightmare scenario with rising panic, collapsing financial firms, and a near-disintegration of the U.S. credit system.[48]

In quick order, government policy makers at the Treasury and Fed reversed their position. After Lehman filed for bankruptcy and panic levels rose, a government-arranged deal allowed Bank of America to purchase the venerable Merrill Lynch, and the insurance giant AIG was rescued with an $85 billion government loan.[49] The panic in financial markets that followed was evident in rapid and large declines in global stock markets.[50] A global run on money market funds indicated not only a rush to liquidity but widespread fears that all financial institutions were on the brink of collapse. A global financial panic was in the offing, as Secretary Paulson stated: "We're at the precipice."[51]

Recognizing the new level of potential disaster, almost immediately the Fed and U.S. Treasury began to press for new capabilities to stem the crisis. Secretary Paulson proposed that Congress authorize creation of a $700 billion fund to purchase the troubled (some would say toxic) assets of financial firms in order to clear the way for these firms to avoid bankruptcy and resume lending. After initially failing in the U.S. House, which prompted a dramatic drop in U.S. stocks, the bill authorizing funding for the Troubled Asset Relief Program (TARP) passed the Congress.[52] Soon these funds were being used to purchase preferred stock and thereby government ownership positions in these firms. In addition, the program was extended to nonbank financial institutions.

A much larger and unprecedented effort was undertaken by the Federal Reserve, under Bush appointee Ben Bernanke, who moved aggressively into uncharted waters involving use of the monetary power of a central bank. The Fed used its ability to create money to purchase assets directly in markets so as to inject liquidity into the most fragile areas of financial markets. This involved guarantees of money market funds; liquidity for commercial paper markets; $1.25 trillion in purchases of mortgage-backed securities (derivatives, usually CDOs); $300 billion of special purchases of longer-term Treasury bonds; $175 billion purchases of debt of Freddie and Fannie; swap agreements with foreign central banks to provide dollar liquidity in global markets; a PDCF (Primary Dealer Credit Facility), which provides short-term loans to investment banks; and a Term Securities Lending Facility (TSLF), which provides liquidity in credit card, student loan, auto loan, and home equity loan markets.[53] The collective effects of these efforts demonstrate the capacity of the U.S. central bank for rapid and innovative actions in the face of a crisis. Perhaps more important, such capabilities involve a significant extension and deepening of the essential partnership between the central bank and private finance in the governance and operation of contemporary capitalism.

In October 2008, the crisis shifted to Europe and focused on Iceland, the smallest member of the EU and the one most exposed to global finance and the effects of the financial crisis. Faced with a panic run on its banks, Iceland nationalized its banking system and prevented withdrawals. Other European nations were forced to guarantee the banking deposits of their nation's banks, and some bank takeovers occurred. A pan-Euro area meeting in mid-October produced a set of common principles for responding to the crisis. Outside of Europe, the Korean government acted to protect its banks with a $130 billion commitment, and the IMF moved to provide support to several nations.[54]

A backwash effect of the crisis emerged in Europe only later, when in 2010 confidence in the national debt of several nations came into question. Focused initially on the fiscal problems in Greece, with national debt at 113 percent of GDP and a budget deficit at almost 13 percent of GDP, nations in the EU (especially Germany) and the IMF were called on to provide loans to permit Greece to make interest payments, refinance its debt, and avoid default. The crisis came to a head as rating agencies downgraded the sovereign debt of Greece, Portugal, and Spain in late April 2010. Funds to restore confidence in all three nations were projected to reach as high as $500 billion, which generated considerable diplomatic interaction among international organizations and states.[55] The issues were familiar, with opposition to bailout for countries unable to control their spending countered by fears that doing nothing would metastasize into a crisis for the EU and the euro.[56]

The economic effects of the financial crisis became most apparent in the fall of 2008, when the economy began a steep slide. Much of this was the result of the near-collapse of the credit system. Companies facing declines in sales, along with those unable to finance their normal operations, instituted massive layoffs. This led to rapid and steep increases in unemployment and an equally rapid and steep decline in GDP and in global trade, the sharpest and deepest since before the 1960s.[57] Unemployment jumped quickly, with hundreds of thousands of jobs lost each month.

The transition from the Bush to the Obama administration in early 2009 came in the midst of ongoing and continuing economic deterioration. Perhaps most disturbing was the rapid acceleration of job losses and the consequent rise in unemployment. In the four months from December 2008 to March 2009, the U.S. economy lost jobs at the rate of more than seven hundred thousand per month, with a total for that time of almost three million lost jobs.[58] Analysts commonly asserted the possibility of a depression that would rival that of the 1930s. The Obama administration, operating with traditional macroeconomic thinking, acted quickly to increase government spending in order to boost economic demand and blunt the downturn. Congress passed a $787 billion stimulus package of spending increases and tax cuts in February 2009. By the end of 2009, most analysts concluded the stimulus had made a significant contribution to a return to economic growth and had saved or created many jobs.[59] The rapid loss of jobs in early 2009 had been reversed in early 2010. Though the unemployment rate remained very high, the U.S. economy began creating jobs.[60]

The crisis did not affect all nations in the same way and to the same extent. The degree to which a nation experienced an economic downturn was influenced by the level of involvement in the global financial boom and by the ability to adjust to adversity. This is especially true for emerging economies. The nations with a combination of rapid growth in debt, including governmental debt, and an exchange rate of low flexibility suffered the worst. Trade levels were less important for generating economic declines.[61]

Almost all of the most advanced economies adopted a stimulus program to counteract the downturn. However, there was considerable variance in the size and in the emphases of these programs, with the typical size at about 2.5 percent of GDP. Among rich nations, the U.S. stimulus was the largest in absolute and proportional terms, at $787 billion and 5.5 percent of GDP. The emphasis of this program was on income maintenance and tax cuts, with substantial spending for infrastructure.[62] The programs for Norway, Italy, France, and Switzerland were below 1 percent of GDP, while those for Canada, Korea, Australia, and New Zealand were between 4 percent and 5 percent of GDP. The stimulus programs for several emerging economies were dramatically larger as a proportion of GDP. For example, China ($585 billion, 19 percent of GDP), Brazil ($152 billion, 15 percent of GDP), and Russia ($101 billion, 8 percent of GDP) dwarf that of many richer nations.[63] An important effect of the combination of new spending and declining tax revenues from the large recession is a massive increase in fiscal deficits. This is not surprising, given patterns from previous financial crises.[64]

The substantial Chinese stimulus plan appears to have been very successful in quickly reviving the Chinese and perhaps even Asian economies. Announced in November 2008, the $586 billion effort confronted several months of rapid declines in Chinese exports, rising unemployment, and a shrinking economy. China's enormous dependence on exports to rich nations presented a serious threat when those nations fell into deep recession. The stimulus plan involved expanded government spending and equally large increases in bank lending (Chinese banks are state-owned) and investment by state-owned firms. The focus of the spending was on infrastructure (roads, airports, power grid), earthquake recovery (housing for the poor), health care, education, and tax reform to spur business investment.[65] The speed of the Chinese recovery is partly the result of structural differences in Chinese capitalism, in which large and strategic parts of the economy are state-owned and state-influenced and can be coordinated quickly with state policies. Furthermore, the Chinese economy has low levels of debt (government and private) and high savings providing a flush of funding.[66] Though the rate of economic growth in China was cut from about 12 percent to 7 percent on an annualized basis, and from 14 percent to 2 percent on a quarter-to-quarter basis, by early fall 2009 economic recovery was clearly in place. The Chinese decline, though significant, was far less difficult than that of the United States.[67] Equally impressive and significant has been the rapid and steep recovery in other emerging economies.[68]

Perhaps the most striking result of the global financial crisis was that the impending and expected global depression did not happen, in spite of the severe damage done to the banking and financial industry and the spillover into damage to the remainder of the economy. The reason is that government efforts to blunt financial collapse through injections of money into banks via central bank actions and into demand stimulus through government fiscal policies were large enough to work. Nonetheless, the loss of production and the massive increase in unemployment have inflicted severe pain and perhaps permanent damage. There remain lasting and unresolved legacies from the crisis: huge fiscal deficits, uncertainty about how to change institutions to reduce the chances of future financial crises, negative effects on the world's poorest, a reshuffling of power relations, and determining how to redesign the economic system for sustained and more equitable growth.[69]

Foreign Policy Arenas

The global financial crisis has important effects on a wide array of global issues, organizations, political struggles, and power relationships; these are distributed across a set of crucial foreign policy arenas. The global financial crisis affects foreign policy choices, the definition of problems and issues, and short- and long-term power relationships; it also restructures strategic relations. We will examine these arenas as a way of identifying the consequences of the economic crisis for foreign policy and global political economy. The arenas include economic prosperity and global security, global cooperation and coordination, U.S.-China relations, and changes in the nature of capitalism.

Implications for Economic Prosperity, Security, and Power

The ability of the United States to preserve its national security through economic prosperity for itself, its allies, and the many nations linked together through global economic relationships was significantly tested and probably damaged by the economic crisis. Many issues are linked to this broad question:

- the role of the dollar as key currency;
- global competitiveness of U.S. firms;
- continuing growth of U.S. GDP and finance-led globalization;
- credibility of free market ideology;
- U.S. global economic and political leadership position; and
- redistribution of global power.

The global financial crisis of 2008–2009 created significant questions for each of these areas. Equally important, the crisis demonstrated the scale and depth of global financial markets and the degree of global interdependence, upon which the economic security of most nations rests. Also of profound importance is the differential impact of the crisis and the speed and size of the economic recovery by different nations, the most important being China.[70]

The crisis reopened and redefined some of the most basic questions of political economy and global politics: Can existing forms of cooperation among governments, in conjunction with global organizations, provide the political governance adequate to manage global markets? Is the goal of expanding economic openness, especially for capital, appropriate for most nations? What new forms of governance and regulation are needed? Does the crisis demonstrate convincingly the importance of state capitalism, in various forms of public-private partnerships, as the dominant system of political economy for all advanced nations? Can nations devise effective forms of governance for the deepening levels of globalization and the interdependence that develops new forms and effects?

Role of the Dollar as Reserve Currency

After World War II, the Bretton Woods institutions enshrined the U.S. dollar as the key currency, which meant many nations were willing to hold dollars instead of exchanging them for their own currency. A normal nation would find that operating a long-term current account deficit, as the United States has done, would result in a large depreciation of its currency. But the United States has mostly avoided this fate and has consistently used this enormous advantage to pursue its foreign policy and domestic economic goals and shift an important part of the costs to other nations.[71] The large imbalances in trade between the United States and Asia are the latest round in this process.

Many of the nations that have borne the burden of holding dollars have preferred some alternative model in which multiple reserve currencies exist. Expectations of a significantly changed role for the dollar can be found beginning in the 1960s, yet the United States has been able to continue benefiting from its key currency. Several things stand in the way of change, including the global weight of the U.S. economy and its capital markets, and the absence of a viable alternative to the dollar. Nonetheless, in the years leading up to the financial crisis there were many predictions of coming limits to a willingness to hold dollars and a financial crisis resulting from panic-selling of dollars.[72]

To what extent, if any, has the global economic crisis brought about circumstances for a change in the global role of the U.S. dollar? Perhaps the main political element in the role of the dollar is the determined effort of the United States and its political and financial leaders to retain the dollar as the key currency. The gains from this position are simply too great to give them up willingly. Of course, the increasingly bald abuse of the dollar has alienated many nations, especially when this contributes to financial and economic crisis.

The financial crisis could undermine the role of the dollar if it affected negatively the market power or political power relationships that have supported the dollar for decades.[73] The financial industry of the United States continues to hold a dominant position in global markets, one that both facilitates the dollar as key currency and serves as a barrier to any alternative currency.[74] The global scale and liquidity of U.S. financial markets is unmatched. However, the giant imbalances in the U.S. current account (though in decline as a result of the global economic downturn) continue to raise questions about the stability of the dollar. The position of the dollar has also been supported by the political economy of U.S. trade, in which mostly Asian nations are able to expand exports to the United States and then pay for the exports by holding U.S. dollars.[75] This permits cheap products for U.S. consumers and rapid growth for Asian exporters. The financial crisis demonstrated the risks of such an arrangement but did not lead to a large decline in the dollar. But certainly, a central element underlying many of the negotiations for rebalancing the U.S. and Asian economies (discussed below) will be the dollar's key currency role.[76]

Global Policy Coordination

The globalization of the world economy and the expanding weight of financial transactions in this process engage contradictory pressures regarding the international coordination of policies for the management of the new economic relationships. The inherent instability of financial markets and the potential for financial crisis is a constant threat lurking in the background that frequently emerges as a dramatic and real challenge. Typically, the pressure for new global regulatory efforts and for economic policy coordination is highest in the immediate aftermath of such events. More often in the forefront of thinking are the gains to be had from the expansion of financial markets. The political and financial leadership of the United States has aggressively sought those gains for decades through policies and negotiations pressing for deregulation and lax interpretation of existing rules. Any coordination arises from a "follow the leader" process, where the United States sets the standards and others follow along. The current financial crisis has created loud demands for reform and new regulation, usually tempered by fears of undermining the profits and competitiveness of U.S. finance.[77]

Three arenas have been the focus of efforts at global policy coordination: interactions among central bankers, the expansion of the economic forum for political leaders from the G-8 (the seven largest industrial economies and Russia) to the G-20 (the twenty largest economies, including some large but developing states like China, India, and Brazil), and discussion of regulatory policies in the Financial Stability Board. Of equal importance are the deliberations in national governments about economic and regulatory policies.

The financial crisis has affected the power relations among the various players in making policy, mainly by enhancing the importance of central banks. Financial crises create intense fears about the possible collapse of an always fragile financial system leading to dramatic systemic effects. The financial system depends on high levels of confidence in the ability to be paid back among the myriad financial institutions that are constantly engaged in massive monetary transactions with one another. Central banks have long had as a central purpose the management of financial systems in crisis, based in large part on the ability to affect interest rates and create money. In a crisis, central banks can act with some independence of normal political processes and possess the knowledge and resources to affect outcomes. It was central bankers who were able to act most quickly and decisively to address the crisis, and can probably be credited with stopping the momentum toward the abyss generated by the collapse of confidence in global finance. Though the U.S. Federal Reserve certainly made many mistakes and failed to act in anticipation of the crisis, its actions afterward were bold and effective.

The current financial crisis, because of its scale and intensity, has led to a rapid expansion of the economic and political role of central banks. Once the crisis subsided, however, other actors involved in financial statecraft have sought to reestablish their role and power.[78] Much of the subsequent struggle over the nature of the new regulatory regime was the result of different actors seeking to reassert or extend their authority.

A near-immediate result of the financial crisis was a shift of the locus of efforts to coordinate international political efforts to manage economic issues such as a financial crisis from the G-8 to the G-20. This reflects the opening of the club to a much bigger group of formerly poor and now emerging nations. The G-8 has traditionally been an informal and "clubby" setting for "fireside chat" discussions among the leaders of the richest nations. It has had some successes in arranging for the public coordination of policy initiatives among these nations. But it is a forum rather than an organization. And the new size of the group, while commendable in recognizing the importance of new, emerging economies, may be too large for effective discussion and decision.[79]

The G-20 met in November 2008 and in April and September 2009 to address the ongoing financial crisis.[80] The results of these meetings were limited but important. A set of principles to guide efforts to resolve the crisis were adopted, discussion of economic stimulus plans produced some baseline agreement, substantial new resources were committed to the IMF, and arrangements for coordinating financial regulation were strengthened.

Though recognizing the importance of international cooperation in economic policy, the G-20 was able to agree only on a set of broad principles relating to the stimulus. The United States in the April meeting was the strongest advocate of a large stimulus, mainly to help it deal with a major economic downturn. The stimulus plans (monetary and fiscal) need coordination. If all nations stimulate, they boost each other. When some do and others do not, imbalances in global economic relations can occur. This includes larger variation in interest rates, which affect capital flows and trade, and the potential for differences in prices, which can affect trade and competitiveness. The effort to coordinate the size of a stimulus floundered on the large differences in the effects of the financial crisis and on the differences in the commitment to restraint in expanding the size of fiscal deficits. But most nations did enact some stimulus.[81]

The effort to achieve greater coordination of financial regulation has achieved some successes but remains mired in uncertainty. The previous U.S. approach to deregulation and limited application of existing regulatory rules has been completely discredited, at least outside the United States. Though the United States may be able to develop a more effective regulatory regime, its ability to coordinate adoption across many nations is in doubt unless there is considerable movement toward a model more acceptable elsewhere.

Regulatory decisions come against a backdrop of global competition among banks, and competition among nations for being the locations for financial firms and their operations. Affecting these location decisions by banks are a number of considerations, among which are the regulatory standards of the nation. Competition between London and New York was fierce in the years before the crisis, but with a new regulations environment in the offing states cannot help but consider the effect on financial firms who can vote with their feet.[82]

The focal point for international coordination of new arrangements for financial regulation is the Financial Stability Board. This international organization is composed of senior representatives of national financial authorities (central banks, regulatory and supervisory authorities, and ministries of finance), international financial institutions, standards-setting bodies, and committees of central bank experts. It was initially created as the Financial Stability Forum (FSF) following the 1997 Asian financial crisis. The FSF worked on developing measures to promote global financial stability, though the record of success before 2007 was limited.[83] Nonetheless, the FSF was able to act during the current crisis to formulate a series of proposals that won the support of national leaders and as a result was converted into the Financial Stability Board in April 2009.[84]

Whether a new regulatory environment emerges, coordinated across nations, is unclear. In mid-2010, multilateral regulatory coordination awaits the outcome of political struggles over regulation within nations, primarily the United States.[85] The main issues include enforcing larger capital requirements for banks, separating the commercial and investment parts of financial firms, deciding whether to create new forms of consumer protection, figuring out how to reduce the chances of future bailouts of large firms, and determining the locus of responsibility for any new regulatory rules.

The negotiation of a new regulatory regime raises questions about the fate of broader efforts by the United States in organizing and coordinating efforts to promote globalization. The United States has been the primary leader over the past three decades in advancing the process of globalization, often negotiating greater openness for trade and finance and stronger rules and institutions for managing global systems. The crisis may have severely damaged this process. Negotiations for a new trade agreement—Doha—were already in doubt, with bilateral free trade agreements now the main substitute. China has been supporting stronger regional arrangements in Asia and is now in a better position to advance its conception of that area. Many nations now have a much greater space to advance protectionist measures. The U.S. notion of unrestricted capital flows has been arrested by events, and the main question now is the extent of new restrictions that will be adopted.

U.S.-China Relations

Long before the crisis began, the deepening economic interdependence between China and the United States had prompted the term *Chimerica* to reflect the degree of these connections.[86] Much of this centered around the trade and financial imbalances of this relationship, with the large Chinese trade surplus with the United States offset by the willingness of the Chinese to hold U.S. dollar–denominated assets, especially U.S. government debt. The financial crisis has only accentuated this relationship: U.S. budget deficits have tripled from an already very high level and the threat of a declining dollar or even a downgrading of U.S. debt increases.[87] A crucial and unusual feature of this relationship—the financial part of it—is that almost all Chinese purchases of U.S. Treasury bonds are by the Chinese government and not by private Chinese actors. This is not a free market relationship.[88] Moreover, the massive Chinese current account surplus is partly a result of the exchange rate policies of the Chinese government that produce a close but not fixed exchange rate between the Chinese currency—the renmimbi (RMB)—and the dollar.[89] At a deeper level, the financial crisis has accentuated examination of the global subsidies provided to sustaining high levels of U.S. consumption for many years. These subsidies have come from Europe as well as from Asia.

Estimates of the size of China's holdings of foreign assets vary because of limited transparency from Chinese sources (see Figure 10.1). The $2.3 trillion of Chinese-held foreign assets in the spring of 2009 included approximately $1.5 trillion of dollar assets, or about two-thirds of these foreign assets. These dollar assets are composed of approximately $1.25 trillion in U.S. government debt, with the remainder primarily in U.S. corporate debt and equities. During the most intense period of the crisis, Chinese holdings of U.S. government debt rose sharply, perhaps as part of a broader trend of a "flight to safety."[90]

Any realistic strategy for fixing the global imbalances built up over several decades will require a coordinated effort gradually to shift macroeconomic arrangements in the United States and in Asia.[91] In the United States, consumption must fall and savings must rise; in China, the reverse must happen. There is an enormous gap between the savings rates in the two nations, which fuels high consumption in the United States and low consumption in China.

Figure 10.1 Chinese Foreign Assets, including Hidden Reserves, 2000–2009

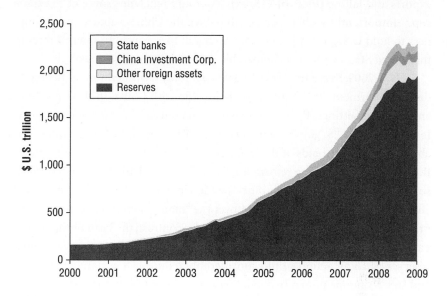

Source: Brad W. Setser and Arpana Pandey, "China's $1.5 Trillion Bet: Understanding China's External Portfolio," Council on Foreign Relations Working Paper, May 2009, 3. Copyright © 2009 by the Council on Foreign Relations, Inc., www.cfr.org. Reproduced by permission.

The result of rebalancing this arrangement should be a decline in the large trade volume and resulting financial imbalances between them.[92] However, forcing such a set of changes will be painful and will require substantial structural and institutional change. For U.S. economic growth to continue, increasing saving in the United States must be offset by increased exports, which may require considerable investment in improving U.S. competitiveness. Moreover, the U.S. government, households, and businesses must engage in a difficult process of reducing reliance on debt.[93] For China, consumers must begin to purchase a larger proportion of Chinese production, which may require some restructuring of Chinese industry.[94]

An associated strategy is to rely primarily on a financial solution, mainly through a significant shift in exchange rates. China has long maintained a controlled exchange rate, mostly pegged to the U.S. dollar but occasionally allowed to adjust. For example, after 2005 the RMB rose in value from 8.1 to 6.8 to the dollar. The United States has threatened to define China as a currency manipulator and has attempted to pressure China to let its currency rise to a market-based level. Should this happen, rising prices of Chinese exports and falling prices of U.S. exports could rebalance some of the trade gap.[95] Importantly, such a change will reduce the Chinese ability and willingness to hold U.S. government debt, which will likely push up interest rates in the United States without a comparable reduction in new borrowing.[96]

In June 2009, Secretary of the Treasury Timothy Geithner went to Beijing to discuss the United States' financial relationship with China. In these meetings and in other settings, the Chinese expressed concern over the value of their investments in U.S. government securities. They also asked many questions about the size and trends of the U.S. budget deficit, including questions about the effects of health care reform on the deficit. The United States has taken some pains to provide reassurance to the Chinese.[97] Earlier, Geithner had challenged the Chinese government over the "manipulation" of its currency to promote the competitiveness of its exports. By contrast, the head of the central bank in China has called for an alternative to the U.S. dollar for international reserves. Such an action would considerably reduce U.S. economic freedom and U.S. economic power. In a more basic sense, the power relationship of the United States and China cannot but be affected when the government of China holds more dollar assets than the U.S. Federal Reserve and vastly more than that of the IMF.[98]

Perhaps the most important and lasting consequence of the financial and economic crisis will be the altered relationship between the United States and China. The enormous accumulation of wealth in China, coming at the expense of U.S. consumption, is an unprecedented event in global affairs. Though the United States retains enormous strengths, the trends of the relationship with China in the thirty years after 1981 have not been favorable. The United States was able to raise its level of consumption and generate GDP growth, but at a large price, primarily through the accumulation of immense levels of debt.[99]

The foreign policy relationship between the United States and China will be deeply colored for years to come by the process of unwinding the effects of that era. Even more significant, the global economic crisis is an important event in the longer-term power shift between the United States and China. This is not a simple "China up and U.S. down" process. Instead, it is better seen as a shift from asymmetrical interdependence favoring the United States, in which U.S. structural power determines outcomes, to a system of mutual dependence, with growing Chinese structural power partly offsetting that of the United States.[100]

Much of China's newfound structural power comes from its form of state capitalism, in which control over financial resources is concentrated in the state. This position greatly enhances the power of the Chinese state in commanding domestic policy and in influencing outcomes in global affairs as well. Put simply, there are no global financial issues that can now be settled apart from China's interests. Moreover, the almost certain diversification of China's financial assets away from the dollar will undermine the power of U.S. financial markets. China is likely to be able to rebalance the structural advantages of U.S. monetary power as a consequence of reducing global imbalances.[101]

Conclusion: State Capitalism

Because the crisis originated in the United States, this has produced considerable criticism around the world of U.S.-style free market capitalism. This cannot be surprising, as U.S. government and business leaders had aggressively pressed their version of capitalism on much of the rest of the world for several decades. In addition to moral condemnations of the system, others have expressed doubts about the viability of such a transactions-based free market system for globalized finance.[102]

Beyond questioning the continuity of Anglo-American-style financial capitalism, we need to examine in more depth the actual workings of such a system. The global financial crisis operates much like lightning on a dark night to illuminate arrangements previously unclear. Specifically, it has served to highlight the relationships of states, financial firms, and global markets in ways that had been largely obscured by the rampant free market rhetoric related to globalization. The pronouncements about the decline of the state and the capabilities of free markets ring as hollow ideology in the face of the clear dependence of the largest financial firms and the entire capitalist system on state support and bailout when times get tough.[103] Much clearer from the crisis is a more accurate picture of the nature of contemporary capitalism, namely the undeniable partnership of states and firms that provides the real governance for globalization.[104] We need to expand our categories of analysis to include the long-standing and expanding role of state capitalism in our understanding of the global economy. For our purposes, the rise of state capitalism increases the role of negotiated outcomes for global economic and financial relationships. These negotiations take place among nations and firms, and are a complex mixture of market-regarding and market-managed arrangements.[105]

State capitalism refers to state-organized and state-directed operations to manage markets, often in cooperation with the largest firms, and thereby promote and manage the governance and functioning of capitalism. These arrangements differ across the world, but the underlying similarity is the deep and profound role played by the central government as a player in capitalism, including the operation of state firms.[106] The concept of state capitalism expands our thinking beyond the simplicities of the liberal state and permits us to reexamine the relationships among firms and nations as different forms of state capitalism.[107]

For example, in all capitalist economies the aggregation and allocation of finance capital is the lifeblood of the economy, and for more than a century governments have assumed a central role in regulating this process and in providing emergency resources when these inherently fragile markets break down. The current financial crisis is simply the latest of many examples of this process, and we should not be surprised that banks and the economic stability of capitalism require this role for government. At the same time, financialization has augmented the role for private finance, as well as the financial operations of states themselves. The financial "power brokers" now include an unlikely set of players, with Goldman Sachs, the Chinese central bank, hedge funds, state petrodollar funds, and other sovereign wealth funds all in a new game of global finance.[108]

Furthermore, the processes of financialization and globalization that contributed to the crisis were a result of the interaction of two different forms of state capitalism: U.S. "market-emphasis capitalism" and Asian "state-emphasis capitalism."[109] In the midst of this process of development, another financial crisis occurred—the Asian financial crisis of 1997–1998.[110] Each crisis was the result of excesses and problems in state capitalism: overconsumption and debt in the current case and overinvestment and debt in the earlier case. And in each instance the government was deeply involved both in creating the problems and in saving the economic system from collapse. The large fiscal stimulus used to stabilize the impending economic depression is hardly surprising. Governments have long provided between one-quarter and one-half of the spending that drives all capitalist economies.

The really interesting and relevant question is not whether governments should be involved in managing capitalism, but in what ways governments can increase competitiveness and economic growth without generating economic and financial crises. The overheated rhetoric about free markets does little to define and evaluate the real issues and choices for policy. It not only misunderstands the actual nature of markets but also ignores the role of states in capitalist economies, a role that the financial crisis makes clear will only increase and deepen. We can better understand economic statecraft when we see it as interactions of different forms of state capitalism.

Key Actors

AIG, Morgan Stanley, Lehman Brothers, Bear Stearns, Bank of America, Goldman Sachs, and various hedge funds   Investment firms heavily involved in the subprime mortgage market and its derivative investments, and thus heavily damaged by the collapse of the housing bubble.

Ben Bernanke   Chairman of the Federal Reserve Board, worked creatively to restore liquidity to the U.S. credit and financial markets.

Fannie Mae   The Federal National Mortgage Association, a government-sponsored enterprise that purchases and secures home mortgages. It came under heavy industry and political pressures in the 1990s to expand home loans to more Americans and, as a result of the subprime mortgage crisis, was taken over by the U.S. government.

Financial Stability Board   Originally created as the Financial Stability Forum following the Asian financial crisis of 1997–1998, this entity—comprised of representatives of national financial authorities, international organizations, and financial experts—helps to coordinate international regulation seeking to prevent future financial crises.

Freddie Mac   The Federal Home Loan Mortgage Company, a government-sponsored enterprise that buys home mortgages and bundles them into mortgage-backed securities, which it then sells to investors. As a result of the subprime mortgage crisis, the company was taken over by the U.S. government.

Timothy Geithner   Secretary of the Treasury under President Barack Obama and former president of the New York Federal Reserve, defended the Obama stimulus program and sought Chinese assistance in coordinating the two countries' financial and economic policies.

International Monetary Fund (IMF)   The United Nations–based international organization created to help countries experiencing runs on their currency. Following the global financial crisis, it is the international entity most likely to coordinate new regulation or supervision of global financial markets.

Henry Paulson   Secretary of the Treasury under President George W. Bush, advocated a governmental bailout of Fannie Mae, Freddie Mac, and the $700 billion Troubled Asset Relief Program.

Notes

1. For a sense of the crisis atmosphere, see Todd Purdum, "Henry Paulson's Longest Night," *Vanity Fair*, October 2009, www.vanityfair.com/politics/features/2009/10/henry-paulson200910.

2. Matthew Valencia, "The Gods Strike Back: A Special Report on Financial Risk," *The Economist*, February 13, 2010, 1.

3. Charles Roxburgh et al., *Global Capital Markets: Entering a New Era* (McKinsey Global Institute, 2009), 7.

4. Ronald Dore, "Financialization of the Global Economy," *Industrial and Corporate Change* 17, no. 6 (December 2008): 1097–1112. See also Gerald Epstein, ed., *Financialization of the World Economy* (Aldershot, U.K.: Edward Elgar, 2005). From the 1980s to 2005, gross international capital flows increased from 4 to 6 percent of global GDP to more than 16 percent. Richard Deeg and Mary O'Sullivan, "The Political Economy of Global Finance Capital," *World Politics* 61, no. 4 (October 2009): 731.

5. Arnould Boot and Matej Marinc, "The Evolving Landscape of Banking," *Industrial and Corporate Change* 17, no. 6 (December 2008): 1173–1203.

6. For a detailed overview of the savings and loan crisis, see Michael A. Bernstein, "The Contemporary American Banking Crisis in Historical Perspective," *The Journal of American History* 80, no. 4 (March 1994): 1382–1396. Over the period of greatest globalization—1980–2010—financial crises happened about every three years.

7. For a review of deregulation in the United States from 1980–2008, see Fiona Tregenna, "The Fat Years: The Structure and Profitability of the U.S. Banking Sector in the Pre-Crisis Years," *Cambridge Journal of Economics* 33 (2009): 610–611. An overview of the movement toward deregulation in the United States, including finance, is by Joshua Green, "Inside Man," *The Atlantic*, April 2010, www.theatlantic.com/magazine/archive/2010/04/inside-man/7992.

8. Bank for International Settlements, *Survey of Foreign Exchange and Derivatives Markets*, April 2007, 5–7.

9. For a readable and thorough discussion of derivatives, see Randall Dodd, "Derivatives Markets: Sources of Vulnerability in U.S. Financial Markets," in Epstein, ed., *Financialization of the World Economy,* 149–180. A more sophisticated review is by Robert C. Merton, "Observations on the Science of Finance in the Practice of Finance," MIT World, http://mitworld.mit.edu/video/659. An analysis of financial innovations is by Saskia Sassen, "Mortgage Capital and Its Peculiarities: A New Frontier for Global Finance," *Journal of International Affairs* 62, no. 1 (Fall 2008): 187–212.

10. For an excellent short description of the derivatives associated with the financial crisis, see Dave Kansas, *The Wall Street Journal Guide to the End of Wall Street as We Know It* (New York: HarperCollins, 2009), 25–46. A particularly dangerous and even fraudulent security was the synthetic derivative. This was a derivative linked to credit default swaps (CDS), in which the security was based on the value of insurance policies that paid off if CDOs went bad. This permitted two different investments: one a bet that the mortgage-backed CDOs would succeed, the other that they would fail. Joe Nocera, "A Wall Street Invention Let the Crisis Mutate," *New York Times*, April 16, 2010, www.nytimes.com/2010/04/17/business/17nocera.html?ref=global-home.

11. Recent data on the size and composition of derivative markets come from Bank for International Settlements, "Detailed Tables on Semiannual OTC Derivatives Statistics at End-June 2009," www.bis.org/statistics/derdetailed.htm. See specifically Table 19: "Amounts Outstanding of Over-the-Counter (OTC) Derivatives." See also Dore, "Financialization of the Global Economy," 1099. Measuring the flows of derivative investments across borders shows figures of $5 trillion annually. See Ceyla Pazarbasioglu et al., "The Changing Face of Investors," *Finance and Development* 44, no. 1 (March 2007), www.imf.org/external/pubs/ft/fandd/2007/03/pazar.htm.

12. Maurice Obstfeld and Kenneth Rogoff, "Global Imbalances and the Financial Crisis: Products of Common Causes," October 2009, www.economics.harvard.edu/

faculty/rogoff/Recent_Papers_Rogoff; Simon Cox, "The Long Climb," *The Economist*, October 1, 2009, www.economist.com/specialreports/displaystory.cfm?story_id=E1_TQVPDDJP.

13. In 2009 China and Japan combined owned more than $1.5 trillion of U.S. government debt. "A Wary Respect," *The Economist*, October 24, 2009, 5. See also Pazarbasioglu et al., "The Changing Face of Investors." China's dollar assets in 2009 totaled over $2.3, which includes investment in other U.S. government and agency debt of $1.5 trillion. Brad Setser and Arpana Pandey, "China's $1.5 Trillion Bet," Council on Foreign Relations Working Paper Update, May 2009.

14. The size of the imbalances is astonishing. The cumulative U.S. current account deficit from 1999 to 2007 was $4.6 trillion and gross U.S. foreign debt reached $13.4, a four-fold increase from 1998. Bank for International Settlements, *Annual Report*, June 2009, 5. Giselle Datz, "Governments as Market Players: State Innovation in the Global Economy," *Journal of International Affairs* 62, no. 1 (Fall 2008): 35–49; Gregory Chin and Eric Helleiner, "China as a Creditor: A Rising Financial Power?," *Journal of International Affairs* 62, no. 1 (Fall 2008): 87–102; Paul Bowles and Baotai Wang, "The Rocky Road Ahead: China, the U.S., and the Future of the Dollar," *Review of International Political Economy* 15, no. 3 (August 2008): 335–353; Mark Lander, "Dollar Shift: Chinese Pockets Filled as Americans' Emptied," *New York Times*, December 25, 2008; Knowledge@Wharton, "Attached at the Wallet: The Delicate Financial Relationship between the U.S. and China," April 29, 2009, http://knowledge.wharton.upenn.edu/article.cfm?articleid=2230; Eswar Prasad et al., "The Paradox of Capital," *Finance and Development* 44, no. 1 (March 2007), www.imf.org/external/pubs/ft/fandd/2007/03/prasad.htm. Debt levels have risen dramatically in almost all advanced countries in the past twenty years. See Susan Lund et al., "The Looming Deleveraging Challenge," *McKinsey Quarterly*, January 2010, 3.

15. For the contrary view that global imbalances were not related to the financial crisis, see Michael Dooley et al., "Breton Woods II Still Defines the International Monetary System," *Pacific Economic Review* 14, no. 3 (2009): 297–311.

16. For an analysis of the effort to measure and manage risk, see Felix Salmon, "Recipe for Disaster: The Formula That Killed Wall Street," *Wired*, February 23, 2009, www.wired.com/techbiz/it/magazine/17-03/wp_quant?currentPage=all.

17. L. Randall Wray, "The Rise and Fall of Money Manager Capitalism: A Minskian Approach," *Cambridge Journal of Economics* 33 (2009): 807–828.

18. Simon Johnson, "The Quiet Coup," *The Atlantic*, May 2009, 46–56. For a longer-term perspective on the political power of finance, see Gerard Dumenil and Dominique Levy, *Capital Resurgent* (Cambridge: Harvard University Press, 2004). For an examination of enterprise capitalism versus speculative capitalism, see Wray, "The Rise and Fall of Money Manager Capitalism."

19. A readable review of this debate is by John Cassidy, *How Markets Fail* (New York: Farrar, Straus, and Giroux, 2009).

20. Knowledge@Wharton, "Efficient Markets or Herd Mentality: The Future of Economic Forecasting," November 11, 2009, http://knowledge.wharton.upenn.edu/article.cfm?articleid=2383.

21. Charles Kindleberger et al., *Manias, Panics, and Crashes: A History of Financial Crises* (New York: Wiley, 2005).

22. George Akerlof and Robert Shiller, *Animal Spirits* (Princeton: Princeton University Press, 2010).

23. W. Brian Arthur et al., "Asset Pricing under Endogenous Expectations in an Artificial Stock Market," in W. Brian Arthur et al., eds., *The Economy as an Evolving Complex System II* (Reading: Perseus, 1997), 15–44. See also Mark Buchanan, "Crazy Money," *New Scientist* 199, no. 2665 (July 19, 2008): 32–35.

24. For an indictment of the policies of the Federal Reserve in managing monetary policy in the years before the crisis, see John B. Taylor, *Getting Off Track* (Stanford: Hoover Institution Press, 2009).

25. Steven Vogel, *Freer Markets, More Rules* (Ithaca: Cornell University Press, 1996); Eric Helleiner, *States and the Reemergence of Global Finance* (Ithaca: Cornell University Press, 1994).

26. Rawi Abdelal, *Capital Rules* (Cambridge: Harvard University Press, 2007).

27. Layna Mosley, *Global Capital and National Governments* (Cambridge: Cambridge University Press, 2003); Susan Strange, *Mad Money: When Markets Outgrow Governments* (Ann Arbor: University of Michigan Press, 1998).

28. Not only do regulations need address the riskiness of financial lending and investing practices, but the use of borrowed funds to expand leverage and thus potential profit margins creates the additional risk for failures to cascade across financial systems. This second form of risk is referred to as "systemic risk." The current financial crisis should have settled any questions about whether such risk exists.

29. Daniel K. Tarullo, *Banking on Basel: The Future of International Financial Regulation* (Washington, D.C.: Peterson Institute, 2008), 15–44.

30. "Base Camp Basel," *The Economist*, January 23, 2010, 66–68.

31. Knowledge@Wharton, "A 'Race to the Bottom': Assigning Responsibility for the Financial Crisis," December 9, 2009, http://knowledge.wharton.upenn.edu/article .cfm?articleid=2397.

32. Valencia, "The Gods Strike Back." The chairman of the Federal Reserve from 1987–2006, Alan Greenspan, was an aggressive proponent of the self-regulatory effectiveness of firms and markets.

33. Tarullo, *Banking on Basel*, 33–35; James R. Barth et al., "The Repeal of Glass-Steagall and the Advent of Broad Banking," *Journal of Economic Perspectives* 14, no. 2 (Spring 2000): 191–204.

34. This compares with a capital ratio of 15 percent in the 1920s. Tarullo, *Banking on Basel*, 31–32.

35. For details on Basel I, see ibid., 45–85.

36. For details on Basel II, see ibid., 87–130. At the onset of the global financial crisis, the Basel II rules were still in the implementation stage in most countries. Salmon, "Recipe for Disaster."

37. Debt had become the major driving force of economic growth in advanced nations from the early 1980s. Debt became a substitute for savings: saving is painful, debt is easy. The economic problems in the 1970s were "solved" by increasing debt, at first governmental and later household and corporate. The increasing levels of debt contributed to the rise of finance in the U.S. economy and to financialization of the global economy. Much of the funding for U.S. debt was supplied at first by Japan and later by other Asian nations, especially China. Debt was used to expand consumption in the United States. Between 1982 and 2005, consumption as a percentage of U.S. GDP rose from 61 percent to 71 percent, and personal savings fell from 10 percent of income to nearly zero. See U.S. Department of Commerce, Bureau of Economic Analysis, www .bea.gov and www.bea.gov/national/nipaweb/PrintGraph.asp?Freq=Year.

38. Roxburgh et al., *Global Capital Markets*, 21–22; Anastasia Nesvetailova and Ronen Palan, "A Very North Atlantic Credit Crunch: Geopolitical Implications of the Global Liquidity Crunch," *Journal of International Affairs* 62, no. 1 (Fall 2008): 165–185.

39. Dodd, "Derivatives Markets."

40. Chicago Public Radio, *This American Life*, episode transcript, program no. 355, "The Giant Pool of Money," March 2008, www.pri.org/business/giant-pool-of-money .html. See also Roger Altman, "The Great Crash, 2008: A Geopolitical Setback for the West," *Foreign Affairs* 88, no. 1 (January–February 2009): 2–14.

41. Roger Lowenstein, "Triple A Failure," *New York Times*, April 27, 2008, http:// query.nytimes.com/gst/fullpage.html?res=9900EFDE143DF934A15757C0A96E9C8B63.

42. Federal Reserve Bank of New York, www.newyorkfed.org/markets/statistics/ dlyrates/fedrate.html.

43. For data on the differential impact of foreclosures through early 2008, see Helen Fairfield, "In the Shadow of Foreclosures," *New York Times*, April 6, 2008, www.nytimes .com/2008/04/06/business/06metricstext.html.

44. Associated Press, "In Bear Bailout, Fed Says It Tried to Avert Contagion," *New York Times*, June 28, 2008, www.nytimes.com/2008/06/28/business/28fed.html?_r=1.

45. For data on unemployment in the United States, see the Bureau of Labor Statistics database, http://data.bls.gov/PDQ/servlet/SurveyOutputServlet?series_ id=LNS14000000.

46. Stephen Labaton, "Scramble Led to Rescue Plan on Mortgage," *New York Times*, July 15, 2008, www.nytimes.com/2008/07/15/washington/15fannie.html.

47. Knowledge@Wharton, "Lehman's Demise and Repo 105: No Accounting for Deception," March 31, 2010, http://knowledge.wharton.upenn.edu/article.cfm? articleid=2464.

48. Lehman was not rescued because the Fed and U.S. Treasury hoped its collapse could be contained and because they expected other Wall Street firms to buy it. Driving these conclusions was a political backlash from free market "conservatives" in Congress and the Bush administration who opposed government bailouts of private firms. The expectations and hopes were wrong on all counts.

49. Gretchen Morgenson, "Behind Insurer's Crisis, Blind Eye to a Web of Risk," *New York Times*, September 27, 2008, www.nytimes.com/2008/09/28/business/28melt.html; Michael J. de la Merced and Andrew Sorokin, "Report Details How Lehman Hid Its Woes as It Collapsed," *New York Times*, March 12, 2010, www.nytimes.com/2010/03/12/ business/12lehman.html?hp.

50. Between September 2008 and the bottom in March 2009, U.S. stock markets fell about 44 percent in value. Shares in other global markets fell by similar amounts, except for China, where shares fell by "only" 30 percent and bottomed in November 2008. During one week in October 2008, U.S. stocks fell by 22 percent.

51. James B. Stewart, "Eight Days," *The New Yorker* 85, no. 29 (September 21, 2009).

52. For details on the events of this period, see Stewart, "Eight Days." For an analysis of past congressional votes on financial rescue packages, see J. Lawrence Broz, "Congressional Politics of Past Financial Rescues," *American Journal of Political Science* 49, no. 3 (July 2005): 479–496. For an analysis of congressional voting in 2008, see Atif Mian et al., "The Political Economy of the U.S. Mortgage Default Crisis," http://papers.ssrn .com/sol3/papers.cfm?abstract_id=1291524.

53. For details, see www.federalreserve.gov/monetarypolicy/bst_crisisresponse.htm; www.federalreserve.gov/monetarypolicy/bst_liquidityswaps.htm; www.newyorkfed.org/markets/pdcf_faq.html; www.newyorkfed.org/markets/tslf_faq.html.

54. For details of the sequence of actions, see Dick Nanto, "The U.S. Financial Crisis: The Global Dimension with Implications for U.S. Policy," Congressional Research Service, January 30, 2009, 66–76. For discussion of different levels of financial crisis impact, see Jorge Ivan Canales-Kriljenko et al., "A Tale of Two Regions," *Finance and Development*, March 2010, 35–36.

55. Landon Thomas Jr. and Nicholas Kulish, "Europe Looks to Aid Package as Spain's Debt Rating Is Cut," *New York Times*, April 28, 2010, www.nytimes.com/2010/04/29/business/global/29euro.html?src=un&feedurl=http%3A%2F%2Fjson8.nytimes.com%2Fpages%2Fbusiness%2Findex.jsonp. Spain's (54 percent) and Portugal's (77 percent) overall debt levels are considerably lower than Greece's, but current budget deficits are roughly comparable.

56. Nicholas Kulish, "Merkel Tested as Escalating Greek Crisis Hurts Euro," *New York Times*, April 28, 2010, www.nytimes.com/2010/04/29/world/europe/29germany.html?hp.

57. Richard Baldwin, ed., *The Great Trade Collapse: Causes, Consequences, and Prospects* (Geneva: Center for Trade and Economic Integration, 2009); Organisation for Economic Co-operation and Development (OECD), *Policy Responses to the Economic Crisis: Investing in Innovation for Long-Term Growth*, June 2009, 9, https://community.oecd.org/docs/DOC-1445;jsessionid=206DDE587C481A1C59FF01875C366D96; Dick Nanto, "The Global Financial Crisis: Foreign and Trade Policy Effects" (Washington, D.C.: Congressional Research Service, April 7, 2009), 6.

58. Bureau of Labor Statistics, www.bls.gov/cps/tables.htm. The total job loss through early 2010 was more than eight million.

59. The turnaround in the U.S. and global economy corresponds closely with the passage of the stimulus bill. Jackie Calmes and Michael Cooper, "New Consensus Sees Stimulus Package as Worthy Step," *New York Times*, November 20, 2009, www.nytimes.com/2009/11/21/business/economy/21stimulus.html?_r=1. See also David Leonhart, "Judging Stimulus by Jobs Data Reveals Success," *New York Times*, February 16, 2010, www.nytimes.com/2010/02/17/business/economy/17leonhardt.html. For details on the actual spending in the stimulus program, see www.recovery.gov/Pages/home.aspx.

60. Catherine Rampell and Javier Hernandez, "Signaling Jobs Recovery, Payrolls Surged in March," *New York Times*, April 2, 2010, www.nytimes.com/2010/04/03/business/economy/03jobs.html?hpw.

61. Pelin Berkman et al., "Differential Impact," *Finance and Development* (March 2010): 29–31.

62. A breakdown of the U.S. stimulus spending is available at: www.theatlantic.com/slideshows/feds/; additional data are available at: www.theatlantic.com/past/docs/images/issues/200905/fed-map.gif.

63. OECD, *Policy Responses to the Economic Crisis*, 17–24.

64. Carmen Reinhart and Kenneth Rogoff, "The Aftermath of Financial Crises," *American Economic Review* 99 (May 2009): 466–472. This material is also available in draft form at: www.economics.harvard.edu/faculty/rogoff/Recent_Papers_Rogoff.

65. For details on the Chinese stimulus, see "A Time for Muscle-Flexing," *The Economist*, March 19, 2009, www.economist.com/displayStory.cfm?Story_ID=E1_TPPNGDRN; "Reflating the Dragon," *The Economist*, November 13, 2008, www.economist.com/

displayStory.cfm?Story_ID=E1_TNGDGJJR; "Lending Binge," *The Economist*, August 6, 2009, www.economist.com/displayStory.cfm?story_id=14161839.

66. "Perhaps a Reason to Be Cheerful?," *The Economist*, February 19, 2009, www .economist.com/business-finance/displaystory.cfm?story_id=E1_TPTQVRQJ; "Follow the Money," *The Economist*, August 27, 2009, www.economist.com/displayStory .cfm?story_id=14327673.

67. "A Fine Balancing Act," *The Economist*, July 16, 2009, www.economist.com/ displayStory.cfm?story_id=14041646; "On the Rebound," *The Economist*, August 13, 2009, www.economist.com/displayStory.cfm?story_id=14209825; Knowledge@Wharton, "After China's RMB 4 Trillion Stimulus, Now What?," January 20, 2010, www .knowledgeatwharton.com.cn/index.cfm?fa=viewfeature&languageid=1&articl eid=2168.

68. "Counting Their Blessings," *The Economist*, December 30, 2009, www.economist .com/business-finance/displaystory.cfm?story_id=15172941.

69. Shaohua Chen and Martin Ravillion, "The Impact of the Global Financial Crisis on the World's Poorest," VoxEU.org, April 30, 2009, www.voxeu.org/index.php? q=node/3520.

70. For an overview of the relationship of financial crises to global politics, see Benn Steil and Robert Litan, *Financial Statecraft: The Role of Financial Markets in American Foreign Policy* (New Haven: Yale University Press, 2008), 81–158.

71. An excellent overview of the dollar as key currency is Eric Helleiner and Jonathan Kirshner, "The Future of the Dollar: Whither the Key Currency?," in Helleiner and Kirshner, eds., *The Future of the Dollar* (Ithaca: Cornell University Press, 2009), 1–23. See also David Andrews, ed., *International Monetary Power* (Ithaca: Cornell University Press, 2006).

72. Paul Krugman, "Will There Be a Dollar Crisis?," *Economic Policy* 51 (2007): 437–467.

73. This analysis relies on the insights of Helleiner and Kirshner, *The Future of the Dollar*.

74. Benjamin Cohen, "Dollar Dominance, Euro Aspirations: Recipe for Discord?," *Journal of Common Market Studies* 47, no. 4 (2009): 741–766.

75. This is not a new situation; for decades several nations have held U.S. dollars to pay for U.S. trade deficits.

76. Benjamin Cohen, "The Future of Reserve Currencies," *Finance and Development*, September 2009, 26–29, considers the potential for a fragmented reserve currency world.

77. David A. Singer, *Regulating Capital* (Ithaca: Cornell University Press, 2007), 67–95.

78. Nicholas Bayne, "Financial Diplomacy and the Credit Crunch: The Rise of Central Banks," *Journal of International Affairs* 62, no. 1 (Fall 2008): 1–16.

79. Martin Donnelly, "Making Government Policy: A Case Study of the G8," in Nicholas Bayne and Stephen Woolcock, eds., *The New Economic Diplomacy* (Aldershot, U.K.: Ashgate, 2007), 93–103. See also Nicholas Bayne, *Staying Together: The G8 Summit Confronts the 21st Century* (Surrey: Ashgate, 2005). The G-7 includes Canada, France, Germany, Italy, Japan, the United Kingdom, and the United States. The G-8 is the G-7 plus Russia. The G-20 adds Argentina, Australia, Brazil, China, India, Indonesia, Mexico, Saudi Arabia, South Africa, South Korea, and Turkey. The G-20 provides a forum for discussions among three groups: national political leaders, finance ministers,

and central bank governors. The first G-20 was composed of finance ministers in the wake of the Asian financial crisis.

80. A G-20 meeting occurred in June 2010 in Toronto and is scheduled for November 2010 in Seoul.

81. One area of failure for the G-20 was in getting nations to carry through on the pledge not to enact additional protectionist measures. See Gideon Rachman, "A Modern Guide to G-ology," *The Economist*, November 13, 2009, www.economist.com/theworldin/displaystory.cfm?story_id=14742524; Simon Cox, "A Fine Balance: The Ins and Outs of the Stimulus Packages," *The Economist*, October 1, 2009, www.economist.com/specialreports/displaystory.cfm?story_id=E1_TQVPDTGN; David McCormick, "Picking Up the Pieces: The Global Crisis and Implications for U.S. Economic Policymaking," in Nicholas Burns and Jonathan Price, eds., *The Global Economic Crisis* (Washington, D.C.: Aspen Institute, 2009), 105–120.

82. "Foul-weather Friends," *The Economist*, December 17, 2009, www.economist.com/business-finance/displaystory.cfm?story_id=15124793. Japan has resisted the creation of more strict regulatory rules because this could hurt the competitive position of its banks. Hiroko Tabuchi, "Japan's Banks Object to Adopting Restrictions Like Those in Europe and the U.S.," *New York Times*, April 23, 2010, B5.

83. Daniel Drezner, *All Politics Is Global: Explaining International Regulatory Regimes* (Princeton: Princeton University Press, 2007).

84. Enrique Carrasco, "The Global Financial Crisis and the Financial Stability Board: The Awakening and Transformation of an International Body," University of Iowa Legal Studies Research Paper No. 10-06, January 2010, http://ssrn.com/abstract=1543508. See also Bayne, "Financial Diplomacy and the Credit Crunch," 10–11. The Web site for the Financial Stability Board is www.financialstabilityboard.org. A list of institutions represented on the FSB can be found at www.financialstabilityboard.org/members/links.htm.

85. Carrasco, "The Global Financial Crisis."

86. Moritz Schularick, "How China Helped Create the Macroeconomic Backdrop for Financial Crisis," *Financial Times Blog*, February 24, 2009, http://blogs.ft.com/economistsforum/2009/02/how-china-helped-create-the-macroeconomic-backdrop-for-financial-crisis/; Niall Ferguson and Moritz Schularick, "Chimerica and the Global Asset Boom," *International Finance* 10, no. 3 (2007): 215–239.

87. A podcast regarding these issues is provided by Brad Setser, "China's Difficult Choices," Council on Foreign Relations, June 2, 2009, www.cfr.org/publication/19546/chinas_difficult_choices.html.

88. Brad Setser, "China: The New Financial Superpower," Council on Foreign Relations, August 3, 2009, http://blogs.cfr.org/setser/2009/08/03/china-new-financial-superpower-%E2%80%A6; Brad Setser, "China: Creditor to the Rich," *China Security* 4, no. 4 (Autumn 2008): 17–23. The United States and China have developed a kind of G-2 forum for discussion of economic issues, now named the "Strategic and Economic Dialogue."

89. Brad Setser, "A Neo-Westphalian International Financial System?," *Journal of International Affairs* 62, no. 1 (Fall/Winter 2008): 21.

90. Setser and Pandey, "China's $1.5 Trillion Bet," 15–16. Additional data are available at: http://blogs.cfr.org/setser/2009/01/03/secrets-of-safe-part-1-look-to-the-uk-to-find-some-of-chinas-treasuries-and-agencies. See also Knowledge@Wharton, "Attached at the Wallet: The Delicate Financial Relationship between the U.S. and China," April 29, 2009, http://knowledge.wharton.upenn.edu/article.cfm?articleid=2230. A significant

part of Chinese holdings in September 2008 were in the debt of Freddie Mac and Fannie Mae. The role this played, if any, in the decision by the Fed to purchase assets of these government-related entities is unclear.

91. Some of the pathways for change are discussed in Oliver Blanchard and Gian Maria Milesi-Ferretti, "Global Imbalances in Midstream?," IMF Staff Position Note SPN 09/20, December 22, 2009.

92. For details on U.S. savings, see David Leonhart, "To Spend or Save? Trick Question," *New York Times*, February 10, 2009. For analysis of the needed changes in the U.S. economy, see Greg Ip, "Time to Rebalance," *The Economist*, April 2009, www.economist .com/surveys/displaystory.cfm?story_id=15793036. For changes in China, see Simon Cox, "The Hamster Wheel," *The Economist*, October 3, 2009, www.economist.com/ specialreports/displaystory.cfm?story_id=E1_TQVPDDSS.

93. Susan Lund et al., "The Looming Deleveraging Challenge," *McKinsey Quarterly*, January 2010, 1–7.

94. Kai Guo and Papa N'Diaye, "Employment Effects of Growth Rebalancing in China," IMF Working Paper, WP/09/169 (August 2009).

95. During 2010, evidence grew of a Chinese willingness to allow some limited rise in the value of the RMB. Keith Bradsher, "China Seems Set to Loosen Hold on Its Currency," *New York Times*, April 9, 2010, A1, A3. China will be wary of this strategy, remembering the damage to the Japanese economy as a result of a significant revaluation of the yen-dollar relationship in the 1980s.

96. Moritz Schularick, "The End of Financial Globalization 3.0," *The Economists' Voice*, January 2010, 1–5, www.bepress.com/ev; Brad Setser, "Debating the Global Roots of the Current Crisis," VoxEU.org, January 28, 2009, www.voxeu.org/index.php? q=node/2915.

97. Bill Powell, "Chinese Give Tim Geithner a Warm Welcome—to a Point," CNNMoney.com, June 2, 2009, http://money.cnn.com/2009/06/02/news/economy/ gethner_goes_to_china.fortune/index.htm.

98. Setser, "A Neo-Westphalian International Financial System?," 18. Of course, the Fed has the special advantage of creating money with a computer keystroke.

99. Stephen Cohen and J. Bradford Delong, *The End of Influence: What Happens When Other Countries Have the Money* (New York: Basic Books, 2010). For an examination of the use of financial power in international politics, see Jonathan Kirshner, *Currency and Coercion* (Princeton: Princeton University Press, 1997); David M. Andrews, ed., *International Monetary Power* (Ithaca: Cornell University Press, 2006).

100. For an examination of U.S.-China relations in light of the financial crisis, see Daniel Drezner, "Bad Debt: Assessing China's Financial Influence in Great Power Politics," *International Security* 34, no. 2 (Fall 2009): 7–45. See also Matthew Burrows and Jennifer Harris, "Revisiting the Future: Geopolitical Effects of the Financial Crisis," *Washington Quarterly* 32, no. 2 (April 2009): 27–38.

101. Gregory Chin and Eric Helleiner, "China as a Creditor: A Rising Financial Power?," *Journal of International Affairs* 62, no. 1 (Fall 2008): 87–102. China's rising structural power also derives from its expanding political and economic relationships around the world.

102. Eric Pfanner, "Criticizing Capitalism from the Pulpit," *New York Times*, September 25, 2008, www.nytimes.com/2008/09/26/business/worldbusiness/26euro .html; Willem Buiter, "Lessons from the North Atlantic Financial Crisis," unpublished paper available at: www.nber.org/~wbuiter/public.htm.

103. One estimate for the current crisis places the injection of state resources into the "private" economy in the United States, Britain, and the EU at $14 trillion. Andrew Haldane, "Banking on the State," *BIS Review* 139 (2009): 1.

104. Perhaps the clearest evidence for the partnership of states and firms comes from the financial crisis itself, which exposed the long-standing but previously under-reported interactions between government officials and private firms. See Jo Becker and Gretchen Morgenson, "How Geithner Forged Ties to the Financial Club," *New York Times*, April 27, 2009, http://dealbook.blogs.nytimes.com/2009/04/27/geithner-as-member-and-overseer-forged-ties-to-finance-club/?scp=2&sq=jp%20becker%20overseer&st=Search; Green, "Inside Man," 36–51; Simon Johnson and James Kwak, *13 Bankers* (New York: Pantheon, 2010).

105. The enormous buildup of Chinese state-owned dollar assets, including the global investment of those assets, involves substantial forms of negotiation and partnership among China, the United States, and global financial firms. Setser, "A Neo-Westphalian International Financial System?"

106. For example, states in Asia have come to act as investors in the global economy seeking to increase investor yields. Datz, "Governments as Market Players," 35–49.

107. Ian Bremmer, "State Capitalism and the Crisis," *McKinsey Quarterly*, July 2009, 1–6; Ian Bremmer, "State Capitalism Comes of Age," *Foreign Affairs* 88, no. 3 (May–June 2003): 40–56.

108. Charles Roxburgh et al., "The New Power Brokers," McKinsey Global Institute, July 2009.

109. Eric Helleiner, *States and the Reemergence of Global Finance* (Ithaca: Cornell University Press, 1994).

110. Miles Kahler, ed., *Capital Flows and Financial Crises* (Ithaca: Cornell University Press, 1998); T. J. Pempel, *The Politics of the Asian Financial Crisis* (Ithaca: Cornell University Press, 1999).

11 Why Do We Still Have an Embargo of Cuba?

Patrick J. Haney

Before You Begin

1. What is the "embargo" of Cuba? Why was it first put in place? By whom, and by what authority?

2. When the cold war ended, there were arguments both for and against ending the embargo. Why did it continue?

3. How did Congress start to get "control" of the embargo? And how is it that presidents since then have still been able to adjust the policy?

4. Presidents Bill Clinton, George W. Bush, and Barack Obama seem so different; would you say that their policies toward Cuba were equally different, or more consistent than you might have expected?

5. What other means of "promoting democracy" have we seen used toward Cuba? What about other countries?

6. Do you agree with the idea of using economic sanctions and embargoes to try to force political change in other countries? Do you think we should have an embargo of Cuba?

Introduction

In 1959 Fidel Castro came to power in Cuba; within a year President Dwight D. Eisenhower, followed later by further restrictions by President John F. Kennedy, would begin to put in place the economic embargo of Cuba. Castro's turn toward the Soviet Union during the cold war was anathema to U.S. interests generally and in the Western Hemisphere in particular—especially given the location of the island just ninety miles from Florida. Following the failed attempt to overthrow Castro with the Bay of Pigs invasion, U.S.-Cuban relations became locked in the same deep freeze as the rest of the cold war. Between 1989–1991 the cold war ended, but the embargo survived. Aging and frail, Castro relinquished power to his brother, Raúl, in 2008; but the embargo continues. It has outlived the cold war, seen most of its early justifications fade, and has continued under presidents from both political parties—including one, Barack Obama, who won office without appealing to the hard-line pro-embargo exiles in Florida. Why is this? Why is there still, so long after the end of the cold war, an embargo of Cuba?

It is important to realize that the "embargo" of Cuba is not a single policy, but a package of policies that have changed over the years, sometimes made stronger, sometimes made weaker. The embargo includes, among other things, a ban on trade and commercial activity with Cuba, although some sales of food and medicine have been allowed since 2000; a ban on travel to Cuba by most Americans unless licensed to go under certain circumstances; restrictions on Cuban Americans' travel and aid to their family members still in Cuba (which President Obama recently lifted); a policy on the circumstances under which Cubans fleeing the island may enter the United States (called the "wet foot/dry foot" policy); and radio and TV broadcasting to the island. The famous ban on cigars falls under the prohibition against trade with most items of Cuban origin and actually extends to Americans who might want to smoke a Cuban cigar in a third country, like Canada or Mexico. These elements that make up the embargo, codified into law in the Helms-Burton Act, have been the subject of significant debate since the cold war ended and especially since 2001, and have been altered in interesting ways by Presidents George W. Bush and Barack Obama. They have also been the targets of congressional activism during this period, though none of it would come to fruition in an actual change to the embargo. But let's start at the beginning with a quick review.

Background

The U.S. embargo of Cuba began to take shape by executive order under President Eisenhower when Castro's government moved into alignment with the United States' principal cold war antagonist, the Soviet Union. At first Ike banned all exports to Cuba from the United States except food and medicine. The 1960 election was under way, and Vice President Richard M. Nixon urged Eisenhower to adopt the embargo. The Democratic candidate for president, Sen. John F. Kennedy, D-Mass., criticized the move as "too little, too late" and called for even stricter actions against the Castro government.[1]

In April 1961 President Kennedy approved a CIA-orchestrated invasion at the Bay of Pigs by a group of Cuban exiles that was intended to lead to the overthrow of Fidel Castro. The invasion was a fiasco, and Castro capitalized on the failure to rally Cuban support behind him. The Kennedy administration,

Timeline

The U.S. Embargo of Cuba

January 1959   Fidel Castro's revolutionary forces take over the Cuban government.

October 1960   President Dwight D. Eisenhower imposes an embargo on Cuba, with the exception of food and medicine.

January 1961   Eisenhower ends U.S. diplomatic relations with Cuba.

February 1962   The Kennedy administration tightens the embargo by banning Cuban imports and the reexport of U.S. products to Cuba from third countries under the Trading with the Enemy Act.

February 1963   President John F. Kennedy bans travel to Cuba by U.S. citizens.

November 1974   President Gerald R. Ford authorizes secret talks with Cuban officials on normalizing relations.

August 1975   Ford eases the trade embargo by allowing the subsidiaries of U.S. multinational corporations based in third countries to trade with Cuba.

March 1977   President Jimmy Carter lifts the travel ban on U.S. citizens.

September 1977   The United States and Cuba each open interest sections in the other's capital.

1981   Jorge Mas Canosa and others found the Cuban American National Foundation.

May 1985   Radio Marti begins broadcasts to Cuba.

October 1992   Congress passes the Cuban Democracy Act, tightening the embargo; it is signed by President George H. W. Bush under pressure from the Bill Clinton presidential campaign.

March 12, 1996   President Clinton signs the Cuban Liberty and Democratic Solidarity Act, or "Helms-Burton," into law.

(continued)

Timeline *(continued)*

The U.S. Embargo of Cuba

October 2000	Clinton signs a bill that allows the sale of food and medicine to Cuba.
September 2002	James Cason arrives to head the U.S. Interests Section in Havana.
September 2003	The House of Representatives votes 227–188 to block government spending to enforce travel restrictions to Cuba.
October 2003	The Senate votes 59–36 to block enforcement of travel restrictions (using the same language as the House).
November 2003	A Senate-House conference committee quietly removes the provision blocking Treasury Department enforcement of the travel ban from the spending bill to which it had been attached.
June 2004	President George W. Bush announces new, tighter restrictions on family travel and remittances.
July 31, 2006	Fidel Castro temporarily transfers power to his brother, Raúl, due to illness.
February 2008	Fidel Castro steps aside, Raúl Castro takes power permanently.
April 2009	President Barack Obama reverses the Bush administration's 2004 tighter restrictions on Cuban American family travel and remittances, eliminating most such restrictions altogether; he also announces that U.S. telecommunications companies may seek licenses to do business in Cuba.
December 2009	An American citizen working on contract for the U.S. Agency for International Development who was distributing cell phones and laptop computers to Cuban activists is arrested in Cuba.

[a] Timeline adapted from Patrick J. Haney and Walt Vanderbush, "The Helms-Burton Act: Congress and Cuba Policy," in *Contemporary Cases in U.S. Foreign Policy: From Trade to Terrorism*, 3rd ed., ed. Ralph G. Carter (Washington, D.C.: CQ Press, 2008); see also http://www.state.gov/www/regions/wha/cuba_chronology.html.

seeing no alternative, then set the course for the full embargo of Cuba and a new level of hostility between the United States and Cuba: diplomatic isolation, attempts at sabotage and assassination, and economic strangulation.[2] The Cuban missile crisis in 1962 underscored the significance of Cuba as a Soviet satellite. Through 1962 and the first half of 1963 the Kennedy administration assembled an "economic denial program" that was meant to wreak havoc on the island's economy. Key elements of the embargo started to take shape: they strengthened the effort to prohibit Americans from traveling to Cuba, which the Eisenhower administration had begun in its final days; and using the Trading with the Enemy Act for cover, they prohibited all trade with the island.[3] After Kennedy's assassination and the descent of American foreign policy into the war in Vietnam, the embargo of Cuba became mostly locked in place with the rest of the cold war. The Johnson administration worked to get U.S. allies also to stop trade with Cuba, and the concrete began to set. Even under President Nixon's détente policy with the Soviet Union, which aimed to ease the tensions of the cold war, engaging with Cuba was out of the question.

In August 1974, after Nixon resigned the presidency in the midst of the Watergate crisis, Secretary of State Henry Kissinger met with President Gerald Ford about making an opening to Cuba. Kissinger was concerned that efforts to isolate Cuba were really isolating the United States. Ford agreed, and said at a press conference that the United States would alter the embargo policy if Cuba changed its behaviors toward the United States and toward promoting and supporting revolutions abroad.[4] As a test, the Ford administration began to allow foreign subsidiaries of U.S.-based multinational corporations to trade with Cuba, and there were secret meetings about moving toward normalizing relations between the two countries. When Cuba mostly failed to respond to the overture, and then became involved in the civil war in Angola, the effort seemed like it was headed nowhere. President Jimmy Carter loosened the ban on travel to Cuba and opened "interest sections" as a step toward more normal diplomatic relations, but ultimately Cuban involvement in Africa made further steps toward normalization politically impossible. The Mariel boatlift, in which 125,000 Cubans fled the island by boat for Florida, sealed the deal.

Up to this point, successive presidents' decisions about U.S. policy toward Cuba were perhaps largely driven by their sense, and that of their advisers, of the role of Cuba in the context of the cold war. But a new dynamic was emerging by the time of the Carter administration: growing Cuban American political clout in Florida, and Florida's growing power in the Electoral College. Cuban American voters flocked to the Republican Party following the Bay of

Pigs; they blamed President Kennedy, and by extension the Democratic Party, for the failure. Over time, non-Cuban Hispanic voters tended to be Democratic Party voters by more than 60 percent; Cuban American voters would come to support the Republican ticket for president by far more than that margin. Starting in 1980, a new and powerful lobby group would emerge as well, seeking to represent the views of the community and to press for a tighter embargo and harder line against Castro's Cuba: the Cuban American National Foundation (CANF), founded by the charismatic Jorge Mas Canosa.[5]

The Reagan administration pursued a much tougher line against Cuba, which Ronald Reagan once called a "stooge for the Soviet Union."[6] The administration sought to tighten the embargo and also elicited CANF's help in appealing to the U.S. Congress to take a tougher stance against the Soviets and against revolutionary movements in the Americas. The administration started Radio Marti as a way to beam information into Cuba, as well as the National Endowment for Democracy as a way to help spread democratic movements around the globe; CANF and its leader, Mas Canosa, would be full partners in both endeavors.

When the cold war came to an end between 1989 and 1991, a debate broke out in the United States about the future of the embargo. Some argued that with the Soviet Union now out of the picture, and thus the end of Soviet economic support for Cuba, Castro's government might finally fall to American pressure—so the embargo should be made even tighter and continue. Others argued that the end of the cold war should also mean the end of the embargo; with Cuba no longer a Soviet proxy, relations with the United States should become more normal. Interestingly, the answer would come from Congress, and be wrapped up in presidential electoral politics.[7]

In the 1992 U.S. presidential election Bill Clinton made a grab for the Cuban American voters in Florida and New Jersey, promising to sign legislation that President George H. W. Bush opposed, the Cuban Democracy Act (CDA), which toughened the embargo on the Castro government (the so-called "Track I" of the policy) while trying to reach out to the Cuban people ("Track II"). Clinton Cuba adviser Richard Nuccio recalled that Clinton liked the policy, and also liked the politics of the situation. By tacking to a Republican president's political Right, Clinton hoped to force Bush to spend time and money in Florida that he wouldn't otherwise have to spend, and to make inroads in the Cuban American community that had been largely ceded to Republicans. He didn't have to win over all the Cuban Americans; just more. Indeed, Clinton carried about 20 percent of the Cuban American vote in 1992, up from previous Democratic candidate Michael Dukakis's 5 percent, and he won the White House. In 1996 his vote totals among Cuban Americans would go up yet again, toward 35 percent, and he would win Florida that time as well.[8]

The "purpose" of the embargo began to shift during the 1990s, a necessity of the end of the cold war. The old goalposts included the end of the alliance with the Soviet Union and the end of Cuba's support for revolutionary movements around the world. The fall of the Soviet Union itself, and the concomitant collapse of the Cuban economy that necessitated an end to Cuban military support for revolutions in the Americas and Africa, brought about these ends. New goalposts were constructed, calling for the release of political prisoners, respect for human rights, and the holding of free and fair multiparty elections—in short, the transition to democracy was now the precondition for lifting the embargo.[9]

An immigration crisis in 1994 helped underscore the precariousness of the situation between the United States and Cuba. In what some saw as a repeat of the Mariel boatlift in slow motion, thousands of rafters started to take to the waters of the Florida Straits, drawn in part by the rules of the 1966 Cuban Adjustment Act that admitted most Cubans to the United States in expedited fashion as being by definition "political exiles." The Clinton administration quickly altered the policy, crafting what is still today a controversial compromise policy sometimes called "wet foot/dry foot." Anyone leaving Cuba and making it to U.S. soil—that is, with "dry feet"—would likely still enjoy quick admission to permanent status in the United States. However, those picked up at sea—with "wet feet"—would either be returned to Cuba or likely be held at the U.S. Naval Base at Guantánamo Bay (in Cuba).

Clinton's policy under the CDA, and the previous statements of several in his administration, made some in Congress concerned that he might try to normalize relations with Cuba in his second term. After the Republicans won control of Congress in the 1994 elections, an effort from the Hill to tighten the embargo yet again began in full force, led by Sen. Jesse Helms, R-N.C., and several of his staffers, as well as by the Cuban American members of the U.S. House of Representatives. In 1995 they unveiled the Cuban Liberty and Democratic Solidarity Act, called Helms-Burton for short, after its sponsors in the Senate House, Helms and Rep. Dan Burton, R-Ind. Clinton tried to fight back the bill and was largely successful until the Cuban air force shot down two airplanes over the Florida Straits that were piloted by members of the exile group Brothers to the Rescue, killing four people. Members of the group flew to look for rafters who might be in trouble making their way from Cuba to Florida, so that they could call in the Coast Guard for help. They also flew over Cuba from time to time dropping leaflets, which angered the Cuban government.

Following this action, Clinton had little choice but to accept Helms-Burton, which was strengthened after the shootdown. Two very controversial parts of the bill that had previously been stripped out were now put back. Title III of the bill established a "right to sue" for U.S. nationals who had property seized in Cuba after the revolution. Under Helms-Burton, they could sue foreign companies who did business with this seized property. Title IV required the heads of corporations that do business with Cuba, and their families, to be put on a list so that if they applied for a visa to come to the United States their applications would be rejected. The whole idea was to increase the pressure on the Cuban economy by increasing the pressure on those who would do business with the island. At the last minute, a new section was added to the bill: codification. Helms-Burton would codify into law all elements of the embargo, though it would give some limited room for the president to make adjustments to the rules for family travel and remittances. This would put Congress clearly in the driver's seat of the embargo. To end the embargo would now require an act of Congress. Clinton signed the bill after negotiating a waiver on Title III.[10]

Clinton would make some attempts to increase "people-to-people" contacts in 1998 during the pope's visit to Cuba, easing the embargo in ways that had seemed to many to now be beyond the president's purview. The fact that all of this happened at the same time that the story broke about Clinton's relationship with intern Monica Lewinsky probably helped to take attention away from Cuba. Clinton took more limited initiatives at "people-to-people" contacts again in 1999, including a "home and home" baseball series between the Cuban national team and the Baltimore Orioles in 1999. More people went to Cuba, often licensed as "journalists," but the embargo remained; Congress was in control now. When George W. Bush won the White House in 2000, the pro-embargo Congress would be joined by an equally hard-line president who promised to "fully enforce" Helms-Burton; good thing for the embargo, because things were beginning to change in Congress and in Florida.

Embargo Politics in the George W. Bush Administration

George W. Bush was inaugurated the forty-third president of the United States in January 2001 following a very tight and contested election that drew the eyes of the nation to the state of Florida and its recount. The Cuban American community was a key asset to the Bush team in Florida, both during the election and afterward. Al Gore won less than 20 percent of the Cuban American vote in Florida, well below the 35 percent that the Clinton-Gore ticket pulled in 1996. In a state that officially cast 537 more votes for Bush than for Gore, out of more than five million total ballots cast, it is not an overstatement to say Cuban Americans elected George W. Bush as president. Bush's promises to fully enforce the embargo, and the Helms-Burton law, as well as the Elian Gonzalez affair, turned the community strongly toward Bush.[11] Once in office, President Bush nominated a favorite of the Cuban American hard-line anti-Castro community, Otto Reich, to the top position on the Americas at the State Department. Reich's nomination was blocked in the Senate, and he ultimately received a "recess appointment." Bush also nominated Florida's Mel Martinez to join the cabinet as the secretary of housing and urban development. Clearly, "Bush was rewarding Florida's Cuban American community for helping him win the presidency."[12]

In September 2002 James Cason was dispatched to head the U.S. mission at the Interests Section in Havana. Under Cason, the Interests Section would become far more aggressive in reaching out to dissident groups in Cuba, trying to foment anti-Castro movements on the island. Reflecting on his experience, Cason said that when he was given his orders for the job in Cuba he was told, "You're not at a mission, you're on a mission."[13] Under his leadership, as Daniel Erikson says, the U.S. Interests Section in Havana was transformed into a dissident outreach operation.[14] Cason even erected an electronic tickertape, or message board, outside of the fifth floor of the mission, beaming messages about democracy to passersby.

Bush talked tough about Castro too. While Cuba was not part of the famous "axis of evil" composed of Iran, Iraq, and North Korea that the president announced at his State of the Union address in January 2002, there certainly were whispers that Cuba was in the next tier of states that Bush would like to see transformed, perhaps even by U.S. military might (or the threat thereof). In the summer of 2003, when it appeared that the United States had secured a quick victory with its invasion of Iraq, President Bush praised the work of retired general Jay Garner, who led the initial administration and reconstruction effort in Iraq. Bush reportedly asked Garner (presumably jokingly) if he and his team would now like to "do Iran?" Garner responded that they were going to "hold out for Cuba."[15] To the surprise of many, given the close ties between the administration and the pro-embargo lobby, the first Bush administration went by with very little change to Clinton's Cuba policy as the 2004 elections approached. Most notably, Bush continued to waive the enforcement of a central component of the Helms-Burton law, the "right to sue," which would allow U.S. nationals to sue foreign corporations who do business in Cuba with property that had been seized after the revolution.

The lobbying environment around the embargo changed quite a bit between Republican presidential administrations. CANF's rise to power and string of lobbying and legislative successes of the 1980s had established the foundation, and its charismatic leader, Jorge Mas Canosa, as a key voice—if not *the* key voice—on policy toward Cuba. CANF became far less influential through the 1990s, however. Mas's death in 1997 was a major blow to CANF's power, but in a way CANF's success also was a part of its relative weakening. CANF and the Cuban American community in Florida worked hard to elect a Cuban American to the U.S. House of Representatives, with Republican Ileana Ros-Lehtinen winning a 1989 special election in Miami to fill the seat vacated by Claude Pepper's death. Her campaign manager was Jeb Bush, who would later serve as the governor of Florida and, of course, was the brother of President George W. Bush. Ros-Lehtinen would soon be joined by other Cuban Americans in the House: Florida Republicans Lincoln Diaz-Balart (elected in 1992), his brother Mario (elected in 2002), and New Jersey Democrat Robert Menendez (elected in 1992). Menendez would later be elected to the U.S. Senate, and Cuban American Albio Sires (D) now represents Menendez's old district. Mel Martinez, R-Fla., was elected to the U.S. Senate in 2004, having served in the Bush administration as the secretary of housing and urban development (HUD). Martinez retired in 2009.

The Cuban Americans in Congress became key leaders on Cuba policy as it ran through the Hill. While enjoying a close relationship with CANF and mostly working together across party lines on issues with respect to Cuba, these representatives and senators became far more important to Cuba policy than CANF. This should come as no surprise, with their location closer to power putting them in a better position of influence. But it is worth noting that the way CANF operated in the 1980s, the power it wielded, would wane in the 1990s in part because of this success. Nonetheless, according to a former senior Clinton administration official (1998), CANF's power diminished in the 1990s, but it was still the most powerful lobby group on Cuba policy. In 2001 two dozen members of the CANF board resigned and formed a rival organization, the Cuban Liberty Council. The rift came about for many reasons, but centered on disagreements about whether CANF, under its new leader,

Jorge Mas Santos (Mas Canosa's son), should be willing to moderate its views about engagement with the island. In 2003 the U.S.-Cuba Democracy PAC was formed to push for a transition in Cuba by preserving the embargo through campaign contributions. They would be up and running for the 2004 election, giving out more than $200,000 in campaign contributions to congressional candidates.

By 2003 the embargo's future looked bleak, as members of Congress from both parties began to coalesce around weakening the embargo by ending the travel ban. In 2001 and 2002 the House had voted to cut off all funds for the Treasury Department that would be used to enforce the travel ban, but the Senate did not agree. In 2003, planning the 2004 budget, both houses would agree to end the travel ban, and did so using identical language and knowing full well that President Bush did not want that bill on his desk. When the final budget bill eventually appeared, the end of the travel ban was nowhere to be found, having been removed from the bill by party leadership at the direction of the White House. The bill's author in the House, Jeff Flake, R-Ariz., described what had transpired as "disgusting. Politics have triumphed again over principle. For the same reason we will never have a rational farm policy as long as presidential campaigns begin in Iowa, we will never have a rational Cuba policy as long as presidential campaigns are perceived to end in Florida."[16]

As the 2004 elections neared, with many in the Cuban American community increasingly frustrated with the Bush approach to Cuba, and with Sen. John Kerry, D-Mass., making a play for the new generation of Cuban Americans who are less wedded to the embargo (but also less likely to vote, given their relative youth), Bush started to move to implement a tougher embargo. Bush started the Commission for Assistance to a Free Cuba, chaired by Secretary of State Colin Powell, which focused its recommendations in the summer of 2004 not only on steps the United States would take to help a newly free Cuba, but also on steps the United States would take to hasten the downfall of the Castro regime.[17] A decision was also made to appoint a coordinator for the transition in Cuba in the State Department in 2004; Caleb McCarry would take on this role. Bush also announced a new set of rules that would govern family travel and remittances to the island.[18] The new rules were far stricter, cutting the amount of money that could be sent to family in Cuba, cutting the number of times that family could visit Cuba from once per year to once every three years, and using a far more limited definition of "family" to exclude aunts and uncles and cousins. While these rules upset many in the community, the Bush gamble was that these tighter embargo restrictions would please the older and mostly hard-line Cuban Americans, who are also the most likely to vote.[19]

In crafting this new policy, members of the Bush administration consulted with several pro-embargo exile groups in Miami, including the Cuban Liberty Council, and also with Florida governor Jeb Bush. Interestingly, when asked about the power of the Cuban American National Foundation, which was opposed to these sanctions, a former Bush White House official told reporter Kirk Nielson, "The Foundation, to my knowledge, has zip influence with this administration. . . . This is an organization that has zero access, zero influence in this administration."[20] How times had changed for CANF. Kerry did better among Cuban Americans than Gore had done in 2000—probably closer to how Clinton performed in 1996—but still lost Florida and the election.

For the remainder of the Bush administration Cuba policy seemed stuck in place. The bipartisan movement in Congress to weaken the embargo by ending the travel ban actually started losing votes, perhaps in no small part due to the work of the U.S.-Cuba Democracy PAC and its carefully targeted campaign contributions.[21] Faced with a White House that was opposed to such a move and Republican Party leadership that was determined to remove such language from bills in ways that surprised many Congress watchers, perhaps it is no wonder why votes started to slip away. Adding to the intrigue was Fidel Castro himself. Castro took ill in 2006 and temporarily transferred power to his brother, Raúl. In December 2006 Director of National Intelligence John Negroponte told Congress that Castro was near death and that he would last "months, not years."[22] Facing the end that so many U.S. presidents had waited for, few seemed to want to get out in front of events, and the embargo policy seemed to be set in place awaiting the end. Once again, though, an American president would leave office before Castro would perish.

The 2008 Election and the Obama Approach

If the embargo seemed frozen in time as the 2008 election neared, the political dynamics in South Florida were changing rapidly as the evolution of the Cuban American community seemed to quickly gain speed.[23] Which is not to say that groups that support the embargo of Cuba do not still exist; they do, and have recently been joined by a new player. The U.S.-Cuba Democracy PAC was formed in 2003 in order to push for a democratic transition in Cuba aided by a strict U.S. embargo. The PAC gives money to candidates who favor the embargo, are opposed to looser restrictions, and have already had some real successes.[24] According to the Web site OpenSecrets.org, it contributed over $500,000 to candidates in the 2006 election cycle and over $750,000 in the 2008 election cycle. Nevertheless, the real energy seems to be on the other side.

As the two major parties' candidates for the presidency in 2008 approached Florida and the question of the embargo, they found quickly shifting terrain. While John McCain was an old favorite of the pro-embargo Right, CANF warmly welcomed Barack Obama and his message of keeping the embargo but lifting Bush's restrictions on family travel and remittances. Obama's willingness to meet with foreign leaders we might despise (such as, potentially, Castro) was less of an issue among Cuban Americans than it would have been even just a few years ago, as the community has become increasingly more open to dialogue with the Cuban government.[25] The Obama campaign tried to reach out to the changing generation of Cuban Americans through a variety of social networking techniques and through a special Web site for Cuban Americans.[26] As an example of how the community's views of the embargo were changing, in 2005 the *Miami Herald* released a survey that found 62 percent of Cuban Americans wanted the embargo; just a year later a poll by Bendixen and Associates found that number had shrunk to 53 percent. Cuban Americans were also quickly becoming more open to increased travel and remittances to the island, with younger Cuban Americans and those who came to the United States more recently the most open to these changes. A Florida International University poll in 2007 found that 64 percent of Cuban Americans wanted to return to the pre-2004 rules, and a majority thought *all* Americans should be able to travel to Cuba.[27] Obama's efforts to reach out to this changing community appear to have paid dividends. Obama won the presidency; he won the state of Florida by about 235,000 votes of the more than eight million votes cast; and, according to one exit poll, he won 47 percent of the Cuban American vote.[28] He carried Florida in part by winning the votes of a large majority of Hispanic voters and a heavy dose of Cuban American voters, more than Bill Clinton carried and far more than other Democratic presidential candidates have been able to garner.

What is interesting about that, and telling, is that Clinton earned such support from Cuban Americans in part by promising to be firm on the embargo, firmer even than the incumbent President George H. W. Bush might be—music to the ears of Cuban American voters then. But times are changing, and so too are Cuban American voters. Thus by winning Florida while calling for some loosening of the embargo, and doing well with Cuban Americans while doing so, Obama comes to the White House in a very different position relative to the embargo than most other presidents who won Florida in part by currying favor with embargo hard-liners. Obama won without promising to out-embargo his opponent, John McCain. During the campaign, while saying he did not want to end the embargo yet, Obama promised to reverse the elements of the embargo imposed by President Bush that placed severe restrictions on Cuban Americans who wish to visit and send money to their families in Cuba; he even suggested that he would be willing to talk to our enemies, like Castro. So Obama came to office in a way that led many to expect rapid and even dramatic change in the long-standing embargo policy.

Obama doesn't "owe" the embargo; quite the opposite, he is likely to want to continue to develop links to the more moderate middle and left of the Cuban American community as well as place Cuba policy into a broader framework. Not long after arriving at the White House, President Obama reached out to the Cuban Americans who supported him by dropping the Bush-era restrictions on family travel and remittances to Cuba. In April 2009 Obama announced several changes to the embargo of Cuba—changes that mostly undid what George W. Bush put in place while he was in office from 2001–2009. He changed the rules so as to make it easier for Cuban Americans to visit family members on the island and relaxed limits on sending money to them, technically called "remittances." The Bush administration had tightened these rules before the 2004 election, limiting the amounts of remittances that could be sent, saying people could only visit once every three years, and also very narrowly defining who counts as "family." Obama's changes essentially return these rules to where they were before Bush's tightening in June 2004. Obama will also allow U.S. telecommunications firms to start to provide services to Cubans.

Not much else has changed, however, as the rest of the embargo has so far gone untouched by the Obama administration or the U.S. Congress. The "travel ban" for U.S. citizens remains in place. While there are some circumstances under which Americans can get a "license" to go to Cuba, most Americans continue to be prohibited from going to the island. The efforts by a bipartisan coalition in Congress to end the travel ban (which at one point was a majority of both houses) seems to be stalled, and the impending retirements of Sens. Byron Dorgan, D-N.D., and Christopher Dodd, D-Conn., mean that two of the embargo's fiercest opponents are about to leave Congress. On the other hand, one of the embargo's most strident defenders, Lincoln Dias-Balart, R-Fla, is retiring from the U.S. House of Representatives at the end of 2010. His brother Mario, currently in the House, will move districts and run for his seat, and several candidates from both parties will thus vie for Mario's vacant seat. It is possible, though far from certain, that someone more inclined to dialogue and loosening the embargo will win that seat.

While limited sales of food and medicine are allowed from the United States to Cuba, the restrictions on these sales continue to be difficult, and there continues to be a total ban on other trade. This includes, to the dismay of some, the ban on Cuban cigars for Americans. Before August 2004, Americans visiting Cuba on a U.S. government license could legally return with a limited amount of their favorite Cuban cigars, but that was changed under President Bush. A range of trade, business, and tourism groups have become increasingly activated on the side of lobbying to loosen the embargo over the last ten years, but Cuba is but one of many issues that concern these lobbies.[29]

The arrest of a U.S. contractor working in Cuba to help spread "civil society" one cell phone at a time has also cast a chill on relations.[30] Even though Obama reversed some of the Bush administration embargo moves, he has continued and even increased the effort to promote democracy on the island by reaching out to dissident groups, a move that has angered Raúl Castro. And the domestic politics that surrounds the embargo continues to evolve in interesting ways. On the one hand, the U.S. Cuba Democracy PAC contributed large sums of money to keep the embargo intact through the 2010 election cycle, an election that is likely to lead to significant Democratic losses in the U.S. House of Representatives. And yet, on the other hand, a Bendixen poll released in April 2009 found that now 67 percent of Cuban Americans want to end *all* restrictions on travel to Cuba, up from only 41 percent in 2003. Only 42 percent want to see the embargo continue, down from 61 percent in 2003.[31] Still, since the ultimate question of the embargo is now codified as law, dismantling other elements of the embargo will have to come through Congress, not just from the White House. According to Arturo Valenzuela, Obama's assistant secretary of state for Latin America (who had previously served on the national security council staff under President Clinton), "We are taking it slow. We're not looking to make any sudden change at this time."[32]

There are reports that Obama sent a signal to Raúl Castro through Spain in October 2009, asking the Spanish government to tell Castro, "We're taking steps, but if they don't also take steps it will be very difficult for us to continue."[33] One of the things that the Cuban government wants changed before it moves forward is to be removed from the U.S. list of terror-supporting states. That list, compiled by the Department of State, now includes four countries: Cuba, Iran, Sudan, and Syria. In very recent years both Libya and

North Korea were removed from the list, but Cuba remains. According to the State Department's 2008 *Country Reports on Terrorism*, which discusses among other things why these states are identified as sponsors of terrorism, even though Cuba no longer supports violent movements in Latin America it does provide safe haven for members of terrorist organizations that have operated in the past in the region and in Spain, and also allows several U.S. fugitives to live in Cuba. There is no sign that the United States is considering removing Cuba from the list. And while Assistant Secretary of State Valenzuela has said that the administration is interested in more fluid people-to-people contacts with Cuba,[34] which could signal a willingness to issue more licenses for travel to Cuba, the 2011 budget request that the administration sent to Congress actually asks for more democracy promotion money, which is likely to continue to irritate the Cuban government. The director of national intelligence, Dennis Blair, testified to the Senate Intelligence Committee in February 2010 that the Obama administration does not see much evidence that the Raúl Castro government wants a changed relationship with the United States. It is his view that "President Raúl Castro fears that rapid or significant economic change would undermine regime control and weaken the revolution, and his government shows no signs of easing his repression of political dissidents."[35] Others wonder if the Obama administration's agenda is so full with other matters, both foreign and domestic, that Cuba policy has been shifted to the back burner after a promising start that did not seem to yield many results.[36]

Conclusion

Despite the fact that the Cuban embargo seems to have been around forever, its apparent permanence masks a great deal of fluidity. The purpose behind the embargo has changed over time, especially when the cold war came to an end; the embargo that had been about opposing a Soviet client state now would be about democracy promotion, human rights, and elections. The restrictions that constitute the "embargo" have changed quite a bit over time, sometimes becoming stricter and sometimes looser. At different times food and medicine could be sold to Cuba, at other times such trade was forbidden (it is now allowed under certain circumstances). The right of U.S. citizens to travel to Cuba, not counting Cuban American family travel, has changed over time (currently it is not legal without license). And how Cuban Americans can see their families on the island, how money can be sent to family on the island ("remittances"), and even what counts *as* family, has been the subject of changing rules over time. The legal backing of the embargo has evolved, with the embargo first existing as a set of executive orders that partly relied on the Trading with the Enemy Act for support; after Helms-Burton it was codified into law, and in 2000 a new law also specified the new rules for sale of food and medicine and codified the travel ban. And who is in control of the embargo has changed as well, with it starting as a presidential policy and now existing largely as a matter of law controlled by Congress.

The domestic politics of the embargo have evolved significantly as well. The 1980s saw the rise of the Cuban American National Foundation as a powerful lobby in support of a strict embargo of Cuba. CANF's influence would wane over time even as, and in some part because, Cuban Americans were being elected to Congress. Today a new political action committee has emerged as a major player with contributions to congressional campaigns to bolster the embargo, while business groups have emerged often opposed to the embargo. The Cuban American community, largely centered in South Florida and Union City, New Jersey, has changed, and its views of the elements of the embargo have also changed rapidly in recent years. And U.S. presidents have changed; President Obama is the forty-fourth president of the United States and the eleventh to preside over the Cuban embargo. So much change, while the embargo remains.

So why does the United States still have an embargo of Cuba? Critics of the policy, like Lawrence Wilkerson, longtime aide to former secretary of state Colin Powell, call the Cuban embargo "the dumbest policy on the face of the earth."[37] Proponents of the embargo, like Rep. Lincoln Diaz-Balart, R-Fla., maintain that the pressure of the embargo is a key instrument in helping motivate a democratic transition in Cuba. Part of the explanation probably lies with the fact that both of these opinions exist in abundance in the United States, and since the embargo is the "status quo," it is awfully hard to defeat it. As we saw above, in 2003 it appeared that there were enough votes in both the House and Senate to end the travel ban, which many think would for most intents and purposes "end" the embargo; with all that cash going to Cuba, Cuba would be able to buy so much more from the United States that the very idea of the embargo would become passé. For a variety of reasons, including the activity of the U.S.-Cuba Democracy PAC, the votes seem to have gone the other way in recent years.

While the status quo is a powerful thing, hard to defeat, it is also important to remember that in this case both sides get a vote. Given the domestic political realities in the United States, it would be especially difficult to ease or drop the embargo if the Cuban government actually behaved worse with respect to human rights and political prisoners. Former president Clinton echoed his concern regarding this issue, saying, "They have blown every conceivable opportunity to get closer to the United States; every time we do something, Castro shoots down planes and kills people illegally, or puts people in jail because they say something he doesn't like. I almost think he doesn't want us to lift the embargo, because it provides him with an excuse for the failures, the economic failures of his administration."[38]

Fidel Castro is no longer the "Castro" in charge, and Raúl Castro does not seem more disposed toward taking more steps that would end the embargo than does President Obama. The U.S. policy toward Cuba, as seen in its democracy promotion activities, is to bring an end to the (now Raúl) Castro government. Leaders not willing to help often put themselves out of power, after all. Daniel Erikson, a Cuba expert with the Washington, D.C.–based think tank Inter-American Dialogue and author of a new book about the embargo called *Cuba Wars*, does not expect significant changes by either the United States or Cuba in the near future. "The forces for continuity are extremely strong both in Cuba and in the U.S.," he says.[39]

Key Actors

Brothers to the Rescue   Two planes flown by members of this group are shot down by the Cuban air force in 1996 over the Florida Straits, reviving and strengthening the Helms-Burton Act.

George W. Bush   President of the United States (2001–2009) and proponent of a tough embargo against Cuba.

Fidel Castro   Cuban leader from 1959–2008.

Raúl Castro   President of Cuba, brother of Fidel.

Cuban American National Foundation   Interest group that strongly supported the U.S. embargo against Cuba during the 1980s and 1990s.

Lincoln Diaz-Balart   (R-Fla.) Cuban American member of the U.S. House of Representatives and one of the leaders of the pro-embargo coalition.

Jeff Flake   (R-Ariz.) Supporter of more trade with Cuba and an end to the ban on travel to Cuba from the United States.

Barack Obama   President of the United States (2009–) who has loosened the embargo somewhat by removing restrictions on Cuban American family travel and remittances.

Ileana Ros-Lehtinen   (R-Fla.) First Cuban American elected to Congress and a strong supporter of the embargo.

U.S.-Cuba Democracy PAC   Political action committee founded in 2003 for the purpose of using campaign contributions to help push for a strict embargo of Cuba as a means to influence a democratic transition on the island.

Notes

1. For background on the U.S. embargo, see especially Lars Schoultz, *The United States and the Cuban Revolution: That Infernal Little Cuban Republic* (Chapel Hill: University of North Carolina Press, 2009). See also Donna Rich Kaplowitz, *Anatomy of a Failed Embargo: U.S. Sanctions against Cuba* (Boulder, Colo.: Lynne Rienner, 1998); Philip Brenner, *From Confrontation to Negotiation: U.S. Relations with Cuba* (Boulder, Colo.: Westview Press, 1988); and Gillian Gunn, *Cuba in Transition* (New York: Twentieth Century Fund, 1993).

2. Schoultz, *The United States and the Cuban Revolution*, 173.

3. See ibid., 173–212.

4. Ibid., 261–262.

5. See Patrick J. Haney and Walt Vanderbush, "The Role of Ethnic Interest Groups in U.S. Foreign Policy: The Case of the Cuban American National Foundation," *International Studies Quarterly* 43 (1999): 341–361; see also their book, *The Cuban Embargo: The Domestic Politics of an American Foreign Policy* (Pittsburgh: University of Pittsburgh Press, 2005); and Maria de los Angeles Torres, *In the Land of Mirrors: Cuban Exile Politics in the United States* (Ann Arbor: University of Michigan Press, 2001).

6. Quoted in Schoultz, *The United States and the Cuban Revolution*, 367.

7. See Morris H. Morley and Christopher McGillion, *Unfinished Business: America and Cuba after the Cold War, 1989–2001* (New York: Cambridge University Press, 2002); Haney and Vanderbush, *The Cuban Embargo*; Walt Vanderbush and Patrick J. Haney, "Policy toward Cuba in the Clinton Administration," *Political Science Quarterly* 144 (Fall 1999): 387–408.

8. Interview with the author, June 1, 1998; see also Vanderbush and Haney, "Policy toward Cuba in the Clinton Administration"; and David Rieff, "From Exiles to Immigrants," *Foreign Affairs* 74 (July/August 1995): 76–89.

9. See especially Morley and McGillion, *Unfinished Business*.

10. For more details, see Patrick J. Kiger, *Squeeze Play: The United States, Cuba, and the Helms-Burton Act* (Washington, D.C.: The Center for Public Integrity, 1997); see also Vanderbush and Haney, "Policy toward Cuba in the Clinton Administration"; and Haney and Vanderbush, "The Helms-Burton Act: Congress and Cuba Policy."

11. William Schneider, "Elian Gonzalez Defeated Al Gore," *The Atlantic*, May 2001, www.theatlantic.com/politics/nj/schneider2001-05-02.htm.

12. Paul de la Garza, "Bush Sidesteps Senate, Appoints Reich, Scalia," *St. Petersburg Times*, January 12, 2002, 5A.

13. Quoted in Daniel P. Erikson, *The Cuba Wars: Fidel Castro, the United States, and the Next Revolution* (New York: Bloomsbury Press, 2008), 42.

14. Ibid.

15. Bob Woodward, *State of Denial: Bush at War, Part III* (New York: Simon and Schuster, 2006), 224.

16. Al Kamen, "Photo Op Becomes an Oops," *Washington Post*, November 14, 2003, A27.

17. Erikson, *The Cuba Wars*, 86–89.

18. Ryan Lizza, "Havana John," *The New Republic*, July 26, 2004, 10–11.

19. Kirk Nielsen, "Politics and Policy: With Its Severe New Cuba Regulations, the Bush Administration Alienated Some Miami Exiles, but Not the Ones Who Matter," *Miami New Times*, July 29, 2004, www.miaminewtimes.com/2004-07-29/news/politics-and-policy; see also Wes Allison, "Bush Cuba Policy Stirs Backlash in S. Florida," *St. Petersburg Times,* May 22, 2004, www.sptimes.com/2004/05/22/news_pf/State/Bush_Cuba_policy_stir.shtml.

20. Nielsen, ibid.

21. See Lesley Clark, "Money Affects Cuba Policy," *Miami Herald*, November 16, 2009, www.miamiherald.com/news/southflorida/story/1335580.html.

22. Karen DeYoung, "Castro Near Death, U.S. Intelligence Chief Says," *Washington Post*, December 15, 2006, www.washingtonpost.com/wpdyn/content/article/2006/12/14/AR2006121401476.html.

23. See Erikson, *The Cuba Wars;* much of this section is adapted from Patrick J. Haney, "Ethnic Lobbying in the Obama Administration," in Steven W. Hook and James M. Scott, eds., *American Renewal? New Directions in Foreign Policy* (Washington, D.C.: CQ Press, forthcoming).

24. See Lesley Clark, "Money Affects Cuba Policy," *Miami Herald*, November 16, 2009, www.miamiherald.com/news/southflorida/story/1335580.html; Trevor Rubenzer, "Campaign Contributions and U.S. Foreign Policy Outcomes: An Analysis of Cuban-American and Armenian-American Interests," paper presented at the annual meeting of the International Studies Association, San Francisco, March 29, 2008; and Ian Swanson, "Hard-line Cuba PAC Makes Inroads with House Freshmen," TheHill.com, September 21, 2007, 1–3.

25. David Rieff, "Will Little Havana Go Blue?" *New York Times Magazine*, July 13, 2008, www.nytimes.com/2008/07/13/magazine/13CUBANS-t.html.

26. Organizing for America, http://my.barackobama.com/page/group/Cuban AmericansforObama.

27. Damien Cave, "Democrats See Cuba Travel Limits as a Campaign Issue in Florida," *New York Times*, June 1, 2008, www.nytimes.com/2008/06/01/us/01florida.html?pagewanted=print.

28. Damien Cave, "U.S. Overtures Find Support among Cuban Americans," *New York Times*, April 20, 2009, www.nytimes.com/2009/04/21/us/21miami.html.

29. See Rubenzer, "Campaign Contributions and U.S. Foreign Policy Outcomes."

30. Wilfredo Canci Isla and Juan O. Tamayo, "Economic Crises, 'Spy' Capers among Obstacles to Change," *Miami Herald*, January 31, 2010, www.miamiherald.com/news/americas/cuba/v-print/story/1454253.html.

31. Cave, "U.S. Overtures Find Support among Cuban Americans."

32. Isla and Tamayo, "Economic Crises."

33. Ibid.

34. "U.S. Does Not Necessarily See E.U. Policy Change Toward Cuba as Positive," *Latin American Herald Tribune*, www.laht.com/article.asp?ArticleId=351555&Categor yId=14510.

35. Quoted in Josh Rogin, "U.S.-Cuba Rapprochement? Not Anytime Soon," Foreign Policy.com, February 9, 2010, http://thecable.foreignpolicy.com/posts/2010/02/09/us_ cuba_rapprochement_not_anytime_soon#commentspace.

36. Ibid.

37. Schoultz, *The United States and the Cuban Revolution*, 540.

38. Quoted in ibid., 514.

39. Quoted in Isla and Tamayo, "Economic Crises."

12 U.S.-China Trade Relations: Privatizing Foreign Policy

Steven W. Hook and Franklin Barr Lebo

Before You Begin

1. In what ways did the U.S. policy of engagement with China reflect general changes in U.S. foreign policy after the cold war?

2. How did the composition of Congress and the worldview of the president affect the prospects for trade "normalization" between the United States and the People's Republic of China (PRC)?

3. Which interest groups and nongovernmental organizations became active as advocates or opponents of closer economic relations between the two countries?

4. To what extent did the outcome of the debate on normalization of trade and U.S. support for China's entry into the World Trade Organization (WTO) reflect economic disparities between business interests and nonprofit nongovernmental organizations?

5. What have been the key trends in China's trade relations, particularly those with the United States, since the PRC joined the WTO in December 2001? What have been the responses of key government actors and interest groups to those trends?

6. What does this case tell us generally about the formulation and content of U.S. foreign policy after the cold war? Can the lessons from this case be applied to other foreign policy arenas, such as national security, particularly since the start of the global war on terrorism in September 2001?

Introduction: The Chinese Challenge

Exactly eight years and two months after the People's Republic of China (PRC) joined the World Trade Organization (WTO) on December 11, 2001, the U.S. government under Barack Obama was plunging headlong into deeper engagement with the not-so-sleeping dragon. In an attempt to reconcile ongoing trade disputes and soothe relations with its largest creditor and third-largest export market, the new U.S. presidential administration had already launched two initiatives, including the U.S.-China Strategic and Economic Dialogue (S&ED) under the auspices of the Treasury Department and the U.S.-China Joint Commission on Commerce and Trade (JCCT) under the Office of the United States Trade Representative.[1] In doing so, Obama and Chinese president Hu Jintao agreed upon four goals: (1) achieving sustainable or balanced growth, (2) establishing greater openness in financial systems, (3) boosting trade and investment, and (4) buttressing the financial regulatory system from a structural perspective.[2] High-level talks and negotiations followed on a plethora of issues, from the infringement of U.S. intellectual property rights by Chinese nationals to questions of restricted access to Chinese markets for U.S. pork products.[3] While pragmatic progress was allegedly under way, Chinese backsliding into protectionism remained an omnipresent concern as Pascal Lamy, director general of the WTO, pledged to avert an all-out trade war.[4]

In the meantime, the U.S. trade deficit with China soared to a high-water mark of $268 billion in 2008, before finally falling sharply to $227 billion in 2009.[5] Yet this drop was likely attributable more to a global economic recession than to dawning fiscal rationality or a change in the basic alignment of the bilateral trade relationship. Indeed, while the voracious U.S. citizenry was forced to consume less in 2009 due to hard economic times, U.S. exports to China remained remarkably flat in both 2008 and 2009 at almost $70 billion.[6] Perhaps this decrease in American consumerism also helps to explain the concomitant rise in vocal Chinese disapproval of U.S. spending practices in 2009. Indeed, unlike in 2006, when China was engaged in a full-throttle "charm offensive" with the United States, by 2010 the tables had remarkably turned.[7] The Obama administration found itself continuously attempting to mollify the Chinese, who were increasingly skeptical about U.S. financial security. As quoted in the New York Times, Premier Wen Jiabao explained, "Of course we are concerned about the safety of our assets. To be honest, I am definitely a little worried."[8] The tensions were underscored by Treasury Secretary Timothy Geithner's earlier remarks about Chinese currency manipulation in his Senate confirmation hearings. His Chinese counterpart at the time, Zhao Xiaochuan, openly raised the question of replacing the dollar as the world's reserve currency. Even so, diplomatic talks were generally remarkable for what was not discussed: the two governments steered away from the unbalanced trade relationship in favor of the less divisive question of how to jumpstart the stalled global economy.

It would be a mistake, however, to assume that only economic matters are relevant in this complex trading relationship. Other issues, such as China's military buildup and continuing conflict over Taiwan, have caused the United States to continuously reassess its regional security strategy in East Asia. In this context U.S. officials have had to consider precisely what it means for China to be a "responsible stakeholder" in the international system.[9] That has translated, for instance, into U.S. pressure on China to support weapons nonproliferation efforts in its trading relationships with other states, such as Iran.[10] Likewise, America's close ties with Taiwan, including weapons sales in 2009 along with support for human rights, continue to be sources of tension.[11] Indeed, the Obama administration has reaffirmed that universal freedom and democratization remain at the heart of U.S. foreign policy. As Obama intoned, "America will always speak out for these core principles around the world. . . . These freedoms of expression and worship—of access to information and political participation—we believe are universal rights. They should be available to all people, including ethnic and religious minorities—whether they are in the United States, China, or any nation."[12]

To understand how this new relationship has evolved, in this case we explore the political process that led to establishment of permanent, normal trade relations (PNTR) between China and the United States and U.S. support for China's entry into the World Trade Organization. Both the Chinese leadership and the Clinton administration considered the two steps critical, and both considered Sino-American trade relations a high foreign policy priority. The administration of President Bill Clinton needed support from Congress to deliver the U.S. end of the bargain, however, and gaining it was hardly a sure thing. Private interest groups on both sides of the trade issue mobilized on behalf of their policy preferences as the legislative process unfolded. The mobilization of those interests and the uneven resources they brought to bear in shaping the U.S. decision played key roles in determining the outcome.

From its founding in 1949 through the end of the cold war, the PRC's relations with the United States were overshadowed by ideological competition and the East-West balance of power. China-U.S. tensions moderated in the 1970s, when the Nixon-Kissinger "opening" to China was followed by the rise of the reformist Deng Xiaoping as China's leader. Bilateral relations continued to be plagued, however, by U.S. complaints about China's repression of human rights, neglect of environmental problems, weapons transfers, and maintenance of protectionist trade policies. Conversely, Chinese leaders frequently opposed the United States at the United Nations and openly criticized Washington as "hegemonic."

Upon taking office in January 1993, President Clinton wanted to revive Sino-American relations. He sought specifically to "engage" the PRC, primarily through closer economic ties, in hopes that a more interdependent relationship would benefit U.S. firms and consumers while also eliciting greater cooperation from Beijing on issues of concern to Washington. Clinton's engagement strategy played an important part in his overall foreign policy, which shifted the nation's strategic focus from the military concerns of the cold war to the geoeconomics of a new era. In the president's view, the United States needed to exploit its status as the world's largest economy by making U.S. firms more competitive in the rapidly integrating global marketplace. Toward that end, the Clinton administration identified several "big emerging markets," including China, that warranted special attention in guiding U.S. foreign economic policy.[13]

Engagement required severing the link between China's human rights policies and its status as a trading partner. As Clinton stated in May 1994:

> That linkage has been constructive during the past year. But I believe, based on our aggressive contacts with the Chinese in the past several months, that we have reached the end of the usefulness of that policy, and it is time to take a new path toward the achievement of our constant objectives. We need to place our relationship into a larger and more productive framework.[14]

The president's policy was based on the neoliberal presumption that China's inclusion in global economic and political regimes would encourage Beijing to moderate its internal behavior and conform with international standards. The alternative policy of estrangement—isolating China diplomatically and economically—was viewed as less likely to produce compliance and restraint in Beijing. Beyond increasing bilateral trade and promoting restraint in China's behavior domestically, engagement raised the possibility of also eliciting China's cooperation in solving transnational problems.

A general shift in U.S. foreign policy in the 1990s produced concrete changes in policy formulation. During the cold war, the State and Defense Departments largely controlled the machinations of foreign policy. The end of the cold war not only altered the mission of those institutions, it also raised the profile of other agencies in the shaping of foreign policy. These included the Treasury and Commerce Departments, the Office of the United States Trade

Representative, and a variety of federal agencies in law enforcement, environmental protection, and health and labor policy. As the foreign policy profile of these institutions grew, so did that of groups outside government in the United States and abroad. With a greater capacity to shape the U.S. foreign policy agenda, interest groups on both sides of the engagement debate mobilized in the late 1990s. Their efforts—often highly visible but frequently behind the scenes—typified the increased activism and policy advocacy of hundreds of organizations in myriad issue areas after the cold war.

Business interests in particular benefited directly from the new opportunities inherent in the engagement policy. Dozens of U.S.-based multinational corporations praised and actively supported the strategy. From their perspective, China's population of more than 1.2 billion was a vast potential market for goods and services that could only be tapped if the governments of China and the United States maintained cordial relations. Echoing the Clinton administration's logic, they predicted that expanded economic contacts would force China's leaders to maintain stable relations overseas and to cooperate on political issues.

Many nonprofit nongovernmental organizations (NGOs), meanwhile, strongly opposed engagement. Human rights groups argued that Beijing should not be "rewarded" as long as it defied human rights standards. NGOs focused on the environment demanded that engagement only proceed after the Chinese government implemented stronger measures to protect air and water quality at home and embraced multilateral environmental initiatives overseas. Religious groups also became vocal on the issue, calling attention to the PRC's suppression of spiritual movements and religious institutions. U.S.-based labor groups weighed in, arguing that engagement would lead to the exodus of U.S. jobs and manufacturing capacity to the PRC.

This mobilization of interest groups occurred at a time when Congress was evenly split over China and highly polarized in general.[15] As Figure 12.1 illustrates, an ad hoc coalition of moderate Republicans and Democrats supported normalized trade with China, with overlapping but divergent priorities in mind: for moderate Republicans, the economic opportunities associated with gaining greater access to the world's largest market were compelling. Moderate Democrats thought engaging China through bilateral agreements and multilateral institutions would improve the chances for democratic reform and for gaining the PRC's cooperation in great power diplomacy. This consensus was threatened, however, by congressional critics at each end of the political spectrum. While conservative Republicans retained cold war–type hostilities

Figure 12.1 Congress and Support for U.S.-China Trade

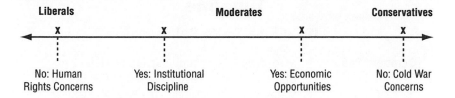

Liberals	Moderates		Conservatives
X	X	X	X
No: Human Rights Concerns	Yes: Institutional Discipline	Yes: Economic Opportunities	No: Cold War Concerns

toward Beijing's communist government and objected to its defiant stance on security issues, liberal Democrats opposed rewarding Chinese leaders who monopolized power, violated human rights, harmed the environment, and exploited labor.

Background: The Course of Sino-American Relations

This reshaping of U.S.-China trade relations occurred more than a half-century after the birth of the PRC in the mid–twentieth century. China, as the world's most populous state and its newest communist country, was then a primary source of concern to Washington. The Sino-Soviet friendship treaty of 1950 and the Korean War exacerbated U.S. apprehension, so that American leaders soon incorporated the PRC into the anticommunist containment policy designed in 1946 to prevent the spread of Soviet influence and power. Asia evolved as an arena of ideological competition in the 1950s and 1960s, with the wars in Korea and Vietnam taking center stage in the global cold war.[16] The United States refused to recognize the communist regime in Beijing and instead considered Nationalist Party exiles in Taiwan the true rulers of China. This policy of nonrecognition lasted until the 1970s, when the Nixon administration initiated bilateral relations with the PRC.

By the time Washington formally recognized the PRC in 1979, when Jimmy Carter was president, key changes in the economic structures of China had occurred. Following the death of Mao Zedong in 1976, Deng Xiaoping, a leader of the growing technocratic movement, assumed power and initiated a series of market-oriented economic reforms geared toward bringing China into the modern era.[17] In 1978 Deng began privatizing a small percentage of state-owned enterprises and overhauled the agricultural sector by permitting the sale of surplus commodities at market prices. The PRC under Deng continued to punish dissidents, however, and to deny political rights in general to the Chinese people.

Timeline

U.S.-China Trade Relations

October 1949	Mao Zedong's communist forces defeat the Chinese nationalist government. The United States refuses to recognize the People's Republic of China (PRC), recognizing instead Nationalist Party exiles in Taiwan as the leaders of China.
February 1972	President Richard Nixon visits Beijing, initiating bilateral relations between the United States and the PRC.
September 1976	Mao dies.
1978	Deng Xiaoping launches a series of market-oriented economic reforms while maintaining strict control over the PRC's political system.
January 1979	President Jimmy Carter formally recognizes the PRC and abrogates the U.S. treaty with Taiwan.
June 1989	Government forces crush pro-democracy protesters in Tiananmen Square. The United States and other governments respond by imposing economic sanctions against China.
May 1994	President Bill Clinton adopts a policy of engagement toward China, arguing that closer economic relations are more likely than isolation to produce cooperation from Beijing.
February 1997	Jiang Zemin assumes leadership of the PRC and continues Deng's policies of economic reform and political repression.
1998	China applies for membership in the World Trade Organization (WTO).
November 1999	Clinton endorses China's entry into the WTO in return for a series of bilateral trade concessions from Beijing.

May 2000	By a vote of 237–197, the House of Representatives approves H.R. 4444, granting permanent normal trade relations (PNTR) to China.
September 2000	The Senate approves the China trade bill by a vote of 83–15.
October 2000	Clinton signs the legislation formally establishing normal trade relations between the United States and China.
November 2001	The WTO approves China's application.
December 2001	China officially joins the WTO.
March 2002	President George W. Bush raises U.S. tariffs on foreign steel, prompting complaints by China and other steel producers and leading to possible sanctions by the WTO.
March 2004	U.S. Trade Representative Robert B. Zoellick files a case with the WTO alleging preferential treatment by China of domestic firms in the electronics industry. The case is subsequently settled outside of the WTO through bilateral negotiation.
2005	China overtakes Britain as the world's fourth-largest economy.
March 2006	U.S. Trade Representative Rob Portman files a case with the WTO alleging that unfair levying of import taxes on U.S. auto parts favors China's domestic manufacturers. The United States and co-complainants subsequently prevail, and China repeals its noncompliant laws in September 2009.
February 2007	U.S. Trade Representative Susan C. Schwab files a case with the WTO alleging preferential treatment by China of domestic firms in the steel, wood, and paper industries.

(continued)

Timeline *(continued)*
U.S.-China Trade Relations

January 2009	China becomes the world's third-largest economy after experiencing 8.7 percent growth from July–September in 2009.[a] It is predicted to overtake Japan to become the second-largest economy possibly by 2010.
2009	The United States receives favorable rulings and/or favorable settlement agreements in five WTO cases against China. For example, U.S. Trade Representative Ron Kirk wins a WTO suit in December, holding China violated trade rules by restricting the domestic distribution of U.S. films, music, and print media.
September 2009	China eases restrictions on film, publishing, entertainment, online games, multimedia, and other foreign investments in the culture industry.

[a] Andrew Jacobs and Bettina Wassener, "China's Growth Picks Up Speed but Raises Concerns," *New York Times*, October 22, 2009, www.nytimes.com/2009/10/23/business/global/23yuan.html.

When the United States recognized the PRC, it adopted a trade policy that required annual review of China's behavior in several areas, including foreign economic relations and the protection of human rights. The reviews rendered China's "most favored nation" (MFN) trade status—which allowed Beijing the same terms of trade accorded other major trading partners of the United States—dependent upon its overall behavior. The MFN reviews became an annual ritual in Congress and were routinely criticized by China's leaders. The Chinese felt that the PRC was being unfairly singled out among U.S. trading partners and that the United States was unduly interfering in their domestic and foreign affairs. Despite the PRC's widely publicized violations of human rights, Congress renewed its MFN trade status every year in the 1980s, largely because of the fast-growing trade between the two states and the rapid growth of the Chinese economy as Deng's economic reforms took effect.[18] Security concerns also figured in U.S. calculations; closer relations with China were seen as vital to containment of Soviet expansionism.

The Chinese government's assault on pro-democracy protesters in Tiananmen Square in June 1989 sparked renewed debate in Congress and the general public regarding human rights in China. Approximately 1,300 protesters were killed in the assault, and thousands more were arrested and imprisoned.[19] Questions regarding the government's treatment of political dissidents, its suppression of political and religious freedoms in Tibet, and its ongoing hostility toward Taiwan were also raised in Congress. Of additional concern to U.S. leaders was the Chinese government's conduct of bilateral trade with the United States. The Chinese domestic market had opened to some foreign goods, particularly high-technology products that facilitated the PRC's modernization drive. China, however, remained largely closed to foreign goods with equivalents that could be produced by Chinese workers. To gain access to Chinese consumers foreign companies had to establish joint ventures with Chinese firms.

U.S. complaints related to a wide range of barriers that prevented U.S.-based firms from competing in the PRC. The most common barriers were high tariffs, which averaged nearly 20 percent on all imports but were much higher on some goods, including automobiles and agricultural products. In addition, the Chinese government imposed a variety of nontariff barriers—such as quotas, import licenses, technical standards, and domestic content provisions—that further discouraged foreign competition. Corporate leaders also complained that the limited number of import-export companies in the PRC further impaired their ability to gain commercial licenses and establish transportation networks in the country.

In October 1991 the White House authorized the Office of the United States Trade Representative to launch the most sweeping market access investigation in that agency's history. In August 1992 the investigation confirmed a wide range of direct and indirect trade barriers hindering U.S. competition. The United States threatened to impose an unprecedented $4 billion in trade sanctions against Beijing if the protectionist measures remained in place. The threat of sanctions was dropped two months later, however, after Chinese officials promised to reform their trade policies and to make their regulations more transparent and understandable to foreign multinational corporations (MNCs) and governments. The symbiotic relationship of mutual need and opportunism between Washington and Beijing led to MFN renewals every year during the Bush administration.

Campaigning against President George H. W. Bush in 1992, Clinton vowed to make MFN status for China genuinely conditional. He viewed the human rights issue as central to U.S. foreign policy and demanded that China's MFN renewal be accompanied by strict legislation requiring reforms in Chinese law and in its behavior at home and overseas. Candidate Clinton promised to impose trade sanctions against China if its leaders did not adhere to internationally recognized standards of human rights. Clinton argued on the campaign trail that Bush had coddled the "butchers of Beijing" and tolerated their repressive rule and persecution of pro-democracy advocates.

Soon after the November 1992 elections, however, Clinton's approach toward China changed. As president he adopted a more cooperative stance based on closer economic ties between the PRC and the United States. Clinton then became a strong supporter of China's entry into the World Trade Organization, the global trade body whose open markets policy he strongly supported. In addition, Clinton endorsed the establishment of normalized trade relations to eliminate the annual reviews of China's MFN status.

Clinton's shift must be placed squarely within the context of the PRC's emergence as a global economic superpower. Between 1979 and 1999 real gross domestic product (GDP) in China grew at an annual rate of 9.7 percent, one of the fastest rates in the world.[20] Between 1978 and 1999 the country's annual trade volume increased in absolute terms from $21 billion to $361 billion. China had become the tenth-largest trading economy by 2000 and was projected by the World Bank to be second only to the United States in total trade by 2020. As China's trade steadily grew, it maintained a large trade surplus—estimated at $21 billion in 1999—and a level of foreign reserves that exceeded $150 billion by 2000. China also became the world's second-largest destination for foreign direct investment (FDI) in the 1990s, attracting more than $45 billion in 1998 alone, primarily from the United States and Japan. This trend reflected strong investor confidence in the sustainability of the Chinese economy, even as real growth in GDP slowed modestly and China's neighbors continued to recover from the regional economic crisis of 1997 and 1998. The scope of private investing in China widened throughout the decade, as the government loosened restrictions on capital transfers and became increasingly receptive to FDI, as well as portfolio investments (that is, trade in stocks, bonds, and international currencies).

The U.S. market was a major stimulant for the Chinese economy. In terms of bilateral trade, China exported more than $81 billion in goods to the United States in 1999. Of this total, $17 billion was in the form of manufactured goods. Footwear, office machines, telecommunications equipment, and apparel were the other major Chinese exports. Bilateral trade grew more lopsided during the 1990s, as China's trade surplus grew each year—from $10 billion in 1990 to nearly $70 billion by 1999. The United States exported just $13 billion in goods to the PRC in 1999, primarily in the form of aircraft, electrical machinery, fertilizers, computers, and industrial equipment.[21] Noticeably absent from this list are automobiles and agricultural products, both of which were subject to rigid trade barriers. It was argued that this would likely change if China were to be granted permanent normal trade relations with the United States. The Agriculture Department estimated that U.S. exports of wheat, rice, corn, cotton, and soybeans to China would have increased by $1.5 billion annually between 2000 and 2009 if barriers had been removed.[22]

The large and growing bilateral trade gap between Beijing and Washington stimulated protests by the U.S. government, which faced strong pressure from labor unions, farmers, and corporate leaders to reverse the imbalance. Many members of Congress and nonprofit NGOs, meanwhile, questioned why the United States continued to tolerate the Chinese government's ongoing violations of human rights, its neglect of environmental standards, and its transfers of military equipment to so-called rogue states. Their criticism was punctuated by the trade disparity, which only widened after the engagement policy was put into practice.

Clinton's Engagement Policy

While calling for improvements in the PRC's human rights record, Clinton argued that U.S.-China trade relations should not depend on political concerns. In May 1994 he renewed China's favorable trade status and by executive order proclaimed that future U.S. trade with China would not be linked directly to human rights. He predicted that U.S. engagement of the PRC, largely through closer economic ties, would elicit greater respect for human rights in China. Toward this end, the basis of U.S.-China trade would be redefined in legislation formalizing the change in policy. When Clinton announced this shift, the link between human rights and trade with China was effectively severed.[23] Concerns over China's human rights policies persisted, however, along with economic tensions. The next year, in 1995,

China exported $48.5 billion worth of goods to the United States, while receiving only $10 billion in U.S. imports.[24] The Clinton administration and Congress, which after the November 1994 midterm elections was dominated by the Republican Party, concluded that a trade war had to be avoided.

Debate over U.S.-China trade intensified in 1995. Human rights groups became more outspoken in February, when Human Rights Watch (HRW) released its annual report, concluding that Chinese officials had failed to improve their human rights record since Clinton's proclamation of the engagement policy. In addition to the human rights and labor groups pressuring Washington, U.S.-based multinationals, which had opposed isolating China for its human rights practices, now pushed for sanctioning China over its trade practices. The bilateral trade deficit had become a serious problem. U.S.-based music and software companies believed they had lost an estimated $500 million in potential profits since the early 1980s as a result of piracy of intellectual property. Even so, many of Clinton's economic advisers believed that a return to estrangement would be more harmful than the potential damage from the problems associated with engagement.

The controversy over intellectual property rights proved especially divisive. Washington threatened a 100 percent tariff on certain items if piracy continued. The result was a $3 billion package of sanctions. In retaliation, Beijing imposed higher tariffs against the U.S. automobile industry, which was already largely denied access to the Chinese market. The Chinese Civil Aviation Administration contracted with European aircraft manufacturers in a deal that exceeded $1.5 billion, spurning Boeing, which had taken its export monopoly in China for granted.[25] U.S. officials also expressed concerns about China's sales of nuclear technologies to developing countries, but the engagement strategy remained intact.[26]

After the death of Deng Xiaoping in February 1997, the new premier, Jiang Zemin, pledged to maintain Deng's formula of economic integration abroad and tight political control at home. Public opinion began to swing against engagement as Chinese officials continued to defy international human rights standards.[27] The PRC's burgeoning trade surplus with the United States provoked outrage among U.S. workers and trade unions. As a result, liberals motivated by human rights and conservatives opposed to the large U.S. trade deficit created ad hoc, anti-engagement coalitions (see Table 12.1). Clinton again argued that economic withdrawal from China would have disastrous consequences for the U.S. economy and would only make matters worse for Chinese dissidents and workers.

Table 12.1 Interest Groups in the U.S.-China Trade Relations Debate

Supporters	Opponents
Business groups	Human rights advocates
Transportation industries	Environmental groups
Telecommunications sector	Religious groups
Financial markets	Trade unions

Proponents of Engagement: Business Groups and MNCs

Outside the U.S. government, most advocates of the Clinton administration's engagement strategy were in the business sector. This was no surprise given the immense size of the Chinese consumer market, which remained largely untapped because of the incremental nature of the country's economic reforms and restrictions on foreign competition. Among the pro-engagement advocates were individual multinational corporations, trade groups, and multisector organizations such as the U.S. Chamber of Commerce. Much of their advocacy took the form of traditional lobbying, but they also committed large sums of money to support the reelection campaigns of like-minded members of Congress and to promote candidates challenging incumbents opposed to normalized trade relations between China and the United States. The groups were also able to advance their interests through soft money donations to the major political parties.

One of the first groups to promote expanded trade with China was the U.S.-China Business Council, which played an active role in commercial relations between Nixon's visit to China in 1972 and formal U.S. recognition in 1979. Created in 1973 as the National Council for U.S.-China Trade, this group consisted of about 270 corporate executives who maintained economic interests in China. In the late 1990s the council supported PNTR status for China and its accession to the WTO. A similar group, the Business Roundtable, composed of the chief executive officers of major U.S.-based multinationals, spent nearly $6 million on an advertising campaign to promote normalized trade relations. Another $4 million was budgeted for campaign contributions in 1996 and 1998 to congressional candidates supporting free trade with China.[28] The U.S. Chamber of Commerce also launched a major effort to support China's entry into the WTO and PNTR status.

Among the most active corporate supporters of normalized trade relations were the transportation industries, primarily aircraft and automotive firms, which eagerly sought greater access to the Chinese domestic market. Boeing was one of the earliest U.S. corporations to do business in China. Following Nixon's 1972 visit, the Chinese Civil Aviation Administration ordered ten passenger jets from the Seattle-based manufacturer. Since then, the Chinese government has purchased about three hundred Boeing aircraft. Despite being snubbed in favor of European contractors in 1996, in 1998 Boeing held a 72 percent market share in China. Commercial flights to and from China increased by more than 20 percent annually from 1988 to 1998, so free trade with China would undoubtedly benefit Boeing.

Meanwhile, the "big three" U.S. automakers contributed large amounts of capital and time to the attempt to open the Chinese automobile market to foreign competition. The Chinese domestic auto market was still in the early stages of development in the 1990s, and importation of foreign-made cars was highly restricted. Nonetheless, the vast potential of the Chinese market attracted great attention from U.S.-based manufacturers. Private automobile purchasing in China grew more than 300 percent in the 1990s, but there remained a vast amount of room for growth in this sector.

General Motors (GM) was the most instrumental among U.S.-based automotive firms in developing the auto market in China. In 1997 GM entered into a joint venture with the Shanghai Automotive Industry Corporation that created nearly two thousand manufacturing and administrative jobs. Together the companies invested $1.5 billion in the project.[29] Predictably, GM strongly supported normalized trade relations and China's entry into the WTO. The Chrysler Corporation, meanwhile, entered the Chinese market in 1987 by forming a partnership with Beijing Auto Works. The 1998 merger of Chrysler and Daimler Benz, the German automaker, was expected to increase the conglomerate's market share in China. By 2000, the Ford Motor Company had yet to maximize its potential in China. Although Ford had entered the Chinese automotive market before the 1949 revolution, its reentry was slow. Ford opened its first dealership on the mainland in 1993, but by 1998 it controlled less than 1 percent of the market in China.[30]

China, like much of the developing world, was also fertile ground for growth in the technology and communications sectors in the 1990s. In this respect U.S.-based corporations played a key role in facilitating China's development and application of information technologies, a cornerstone of its development strategy. The San Diego–based Qualcomm Corporation, for example, partnered with two of the three largest state-owned communications companies, China Telecom and China Unicom, in an effort to develop the Chinese wireless communications market. By 2000 only a small part of the market had been penetrated, but as sharing information becomes a necessity in the rapidly integrating business environment, the use of wireless phones and satellite communications networks will prove vital. Qualcomm's assistance helped standardize the industry by licensing intellectual property and creating a prototype system, Code Division Multiple Access, that all domestic telecommunications firms could use. Not only did Qualcomm reap royalties for its services, but its assistance also made wireless communications more accessible to the business sector. Other major communications and high-technology firms followed Qualcomm into China. Nortel, Motorola, and Lucent Technologies invested in joint ventures with Chinese counterparts. It was commonly estimated at the time that the total wireless market would exceed $16 billion in annual sales once fully exploited.[31]

Other proponents of normalized trade relations came from the financial markets, which may be viewed as something of a collective multinational corporation. Investors can be individual stockholders, corporations, brokerage firms, or mutual fund managers. Recipients of these private investments use the capital to develop new products, expand production, and open new retail outlets. As noted earlier, FDI and portfolio investments played a key role in spurring the PRC's economic growth. As more multinationals set up shop in China, even through the mandated joint ventures with Chinese firms, the country attracted additional private investment. As a result, leaders of U.S.-based financial institutions were among the most ardent supporters of normalized trade relations and Chinese entry into the WTO.

Opponents of Engagement: NGOs and Conservatives

Many conservative members of Congress argued that Clinton's engagement policy would merely reward a "revisionist" Chinese state bent on military expansionism at the expense of U.S. interests. In their view, a policy of isolating the PRC was preferable to one of actively engaging its government. Nonprofit NGOs were also active in the debate, their views in most cases differing strongly from the pro-engagement stance of business-related groups. Among other things, the groups demanded that political, environmental, and labor disputes between China and the United States be resolved before trade relations were normalized. The nonprofit NGOs were highly fragmented because of their wide range of interests and policy preferences. With more limited resources than the corporations and business groups, the NGOs faced an uphill battle in the policy debate. Nonetheless, they posed a strong challenge to the Clinton administration's engagement policy and were able to shape the terms of the legislation that Congress ultimately passed and President Clinton signed.[32]

Lacking the economic clout of business and trade groups, human rights organizations promoted their positions primarily through the release of detailed studies of the Chinese government's human rights conduct. Their reports were especially vital because of the severe press restrictions in the PRC, which prevented Chinese journalists from investigating and exposing human rights violations. In addition to its annual reports on human rights, Human Rights Watch published frequent studies that criticized the PRC's strict control of religion, the news media, and the private affairs of its citizens.[33]

Another human rights NGO that played a major role was Freedom House, based in New York City. Freedom House's annual reports, along with those published by Human Rights Watch, were closely monitored within the U.S. government, by corporate leaders, and by nonprofit interest groups. The reports were especially critical of the Chinese government's human rights policies; the PRC consistently received the group's lowest ranking in its annual surveys of political and civil rights. In its 1997–1998 report, Freedom House declared that the Chinese Communist Party "holds absolute power, has imprisoned nearly all active dissidents, uses the judiciary as a tool of state control, and severely restricts freedoms of speech, press, association, and religion."[34]

Amnesty International (AI) also published reports and sponsored demonstrations to draw attention to human rights abuses in the PRC. Most notably, AI launched a media campaign in 1999 commemorating the ten-year anniversary of the Tiananmen Square massacre and circulated a list of 241 political prisoners still detained by the Chinese government. Members of AI continued to write to political prisoners in China, as well as to government officials, urging the prisoners' release. While remaining nonpolitical, AI cited continuing human rights abuses as evidence that the engagement policy had failed.[35]

NGOs also expressed concern that the engagement policy ignored the environment in China, where air and water pollution had steadily worsened during the country's modernization drive. This trend was especially regrettable given that environmental quality was a noneconomic issue on which the Chinese and U.S. governments could potentially agree. China, however, made a Faustian bargain on the environment to achieve economic growth.[36] In particular, it relied on coal-burning power plants as the primary source of electricity, a practice that led to high levels of fossil fuel emissions that affected air quality far beyond China's borders. Greenpeace, arguably the most influential environmental group in the world, urged the U.S. government to include environmental provisions in any legislation to normalize trade relations and in any U.S. endorsement of Chinese entry into the WTO. Also of concern was the worsening water quality in the Dongjiang River, the Pearl River Delta, and the South China Sea. Greenpeace joined other environmental NGOs in opposing the massive Three Gorges Dam in Hubei Province, which forced the relocation of approximately 1.5 million people by January 2010.

Most of these environmental concerns remained outside the PNTR and WTO debates, primarily because of the Chinese government's rejection of foreign interference in what it considered its sovereign authority over internal economic development. The environmental groups succeeded, however, in raising the profile of these issues and putting pressure on U.S.- and foreign-based corporations to consider the ecological effects of their projects in China. As in other parts of the world, the environmental groups were most effective in appealing directly to public opinion through Internet campaigns and the sponsorship of mass protests and demonstrations.[37]

Religious groups in the United States were also active in the debate over trade relations with China. Of particular concern to them was the persecution of individuals and groups that expressed support for religious principles and institutions. By their nature, such expressions are contrary to the ideology of the Chinese Communist Party. "Freedom of religion is under threat in China," proclaimed the United Methodist Church's General Board of Church and Society. "Catholic churches, mosques, Buddhist temples and indigenous religions are being harassed. . . . We call on Congress to vote against the extension of permanent normal trade relations to China until substantial improvements in religious freedom are achieved."[38]

The groups were particularly outraged at the Chinese government's outlawing in July 1999 of Falun Gong, a spiritual movement that promotes "truthfulness, benevolence, and forbearance," primarily through the ancient meditative practice of *qigong*. Government officials in China labeled Falun Gong a "cult" whose leaders were organizing politically, and illegally, in opposition to the Communist Party. An estimated ten thousand Falun Gong followers surprised Chinese authorities in April 1999 by surrounding the government compound in Beijing to protest their lack of official recognition. The group was officially banned in July, and Chinese authorities arrested large numbers of its followers, closed its facilities, and confiscated its literature.[39]

American labor groups were vocal in their opposition to engagement. These groups sought to sway public opinion against normalized trade relations with

China through public information campaigns and public demonstrations. In an unusual show of unity, more than ten thousand labor union advocates from different industrial sectors held a rally in April 2000 at the U.S. Capitol. Their demonstration was designed to convince undecided members of Congress that public opposition to normalized trade relations was extensive and that normalized relations would have real human cost in the form of displaced workers. Their presence also reminded office seekers that the trade unions represented a large and potentially crucial voting bloc.

The AFL-CIO and the United Auto Workers (UAW) led in promoting the trade union position, often invoking reasons beyond the economic self-interest of their members. AFL-CIO president John Sweeney frequently spoke out against Chinese entry into the WTO and normalized trade relations. Testifying to Congress in March 2000, Sweeney argued that an affirmative vote on PNTR "would reward the Chinese government at a time when there has been significant deterioration in its abysmal human rights record."[40] The AFL-CIO devoted much of its lobbying effort—and its budget—to the China trade issue. Advertisements it ran in eleven congressional districts were crucial in garnering public support for its position. For its part, the UAW initiated a lobbying campaign to oppose PNTR for similar reasons and cited the use of child labor and forced labor by political prisoners as justification for a reversal in U.S. trade policy. Of particular concern to the UAW was the opposition of the Chinese government to the formation of independent trade unions in the country.

With the U.S. trade deficit widening in China's favor, labor leaders also argued that normalized trade relations would jeopardize the country's long-term economic growth and harm thousands of firms as well as workers. Labor cited piracy of intellectual property, global environmental destruction, and the treatment of workers in China as additional reasons to oppose PNTR and China's entry in the WTO. Their primary emphasis as they pressed the issue before Congress, however, was on the effects of normalized trade relations on their members. This appeal carried considerable weight among members of Congress who represented urbanized districts with large blue-collar populations.

Final Debates and Congressional Action

As the antagonists for and against engagement tussled, the U.S. government played a paradoxical role in informing the debate. While the White House promoted the cause of engagement, the State Department released annual reports that were consistently critical of the Chinese government. According to the department's 1999 report:

> The Government's poor human rights record deteriorated markedly through-out the year. The government intensified efforts to suppress dissent, particularly organized dissent. . . . Abuses included instances of extrajudicial killings, torture and mistreatment of prisoners, forced confessions, arbitrary arrest and detention, lengthy incommunicado detention, and denial of due process.[41]

The State Department's findings were affirmed by human rights NGOs. Freedom House's review of human rights in China during 1999 noted that Chinese "authorities escalated a crackdown on political dissidents, labor and peasant activists, and religious leaders."[42] To President Clinton, the arguments of the nonprofit NGOs and the State Department only strengthened his argument that the Chinese government should be engaged. Thus in 1999 and 2000 the president intensified his efforts to apply the engagement policy by supporting Chinese accession to the WTO and normalized trade relations between China and the United States.

China's Drive for WTO Membership

The WTO had barely come into existence when Chinese officials declared their interest in joining. They took the first step in that direction in 1995 by forming a working party to prepare a formal application. That part of the process was completed in 1998, after which China began formal negotiations for membership. All WTO applicants must undergo a two-part screening. First, they negotiate directly with the WTO on compliance with the trade body's regulations for open markets, protection of foreign firms and capital, and transparency of commercial regulations. These terms were originally set forth in the 1947 General Agreement on Tariffs and Trade (GATT), which was revised several times before becoming the World Trade Organization after the completion in 1994 of the Uruguay Round of global trade talks. In the second phase, WTO applicants negotiate directly with their primary trading partners. These bilateral negotiations are often the primary hurdle facing prospective WTO members. Chinese officials acknowledged that gaining the blessing of the United States would be its highest hurdle in the WTO accession process. Once applicants complete bilateral talks, they draft a protocol of accession to be considered by WTO member states (which numbered 135 at the time China's application was under review). Two-thirds of the states must approve the protocol for the applicant to gain entry into the organization.

Talks between Chinese and U.S. trade negotiators progressed early in 1999 despite a series of unrelated political controversies and diplomatic crises that strained relations. The full extent of the 1996 presidential campaign scandals over illegal contributions, many of which involved Chinese citizens, was widely known by 1998. The scandals provoked charges in Congress of undue Chinese influence in the Clinton administration. Making matters worse, U.S. bombers mistakenly destroyed the Chinese embassy in Belgrade in May 1999 as part of the North Atlantic Treaty Organization's effort to stem Serbia's crackdown against Kosovo. Chinese officials condemned the attack, and some even alleged that the bombing was deliberate. Trade talks were suspended for four months after the incident, and during that time the two governments again clashed over Taiwan's status, weapons proliferation in North Korea, and other regional issues.

These incidents compelled Clinton to step up his efforts to conclude a trade pact with China. Talks resumed in September 1999, leading to a comprehensive bilateral agreement that was signed by both governments in November. Under the terms of the deal, the United States endorsed China's WTO membership in return for a wide range of Chinese concessions on bilateral trade. Among other concessions, Chinese leaders agreed to the following:

- allow full trading and distribution rights to U.S. firms doing business in China;
- reduce average tariffs on "priority" agricultural goods from 32 percent to 15 percent by 2004;
- phase out quotas on foreign versus domestically produced goods and suspend other nontariff barriers;
- permit greater access to the Chinese market by U.S.-based automobile companies by 2006; and
- improve the treatment of foreign firms operating in China.[43]

The Chinese government had long acknowledged that reaching a trade accord with the United States was essential if its goal of obtaining WTO membership was to be accomplished. If China had joined the trade body without a positive U.S. vote, its ability to play a meaningful role would have been greatly limited, and chronic differences between China and the United States would have remained. Thus the WTO served a useful function for U.S. officials, whose efforts to gain Chinese cooperation on bilateral trade had previously been frustrated.

While negotiating with the United States, Chinese officials were simultaneously engaged in trade talks with other industrialized countries in their drive for WTO accession. Of particular interest was the European Union (EU), whose progress toward regional economic integration had taken a great leap forward in 1999 with the introduction of the euro as a common currency. Under the terms of the 1992 Maastricht Treaty, the major European states (except for the United Kingdom) agreed to coordinate all facets of their fiscal and monetary policies. Such coordination included the conduct of trade relations, which the union would pursue with one voice. A "bilateral" trade deal between the EU and the PRC was within reach, although EU members demanded many of the same market-opening concessions that China had granted the United States. The China-EU accord was reached on May 19, 2000, when the EU formally endorsed China's bid to join the WTO in return for promised reforms in the PRC's trade practices. Through this single agreement, Beijing garnered the blessings of France, Germany, Italy, and twelve other Western European countries. The pact with the Europeans added momentum to China's drive for permanent normalized trade relations with the United States, an issue soon to be before Congress.

The PNTR Debate in Congress

Under U.S. law, Congress was not required to play a direct role in the bilateral negotiations on U.S. support for China's WTO membership. Congress was also not required to ratify the pact signed by President Clinton. That did not mean, however, that Congress was irrelevant to the process. To the contrary, given its other constitutional powers to regulate trade—specifically its authority to grant or deny "normal" status to U.S. trading partners—Congress effectively held the key to China's entry into the WTO. Furthermore, legislation passed during the cold war imposed explicit conditions on U.S. trade with communist states. Those conditions would violate the basic principle of the WTO that terms of trade among all its members be maintained consistently and unconditionally. For that reason, a bilateral trade agreement between the United States and China approved by both houses of Congress was the last major hurdle in Chinese membership in the multilateral WTO. The Clinton administration, therefore, directed its efforts early in 2000 toward gaining Congress's approval for PNTR with Beijing.

Clinton assigned lobbying duties to Secretary of Commerce William Daley and the deputy chief of staff, Stephen Ricchetti. The president also recruited former presidents Gerald Ford, Jimmy Carter, and George H. W. Bush to endorse the bill, along with Federal Reserve Chairman Alan Greenspan and leading foreign policy advisers in the State and Defense Departments. Clinton's sense of urgency owed much to the setbacks and frustrations that plagued his second term in office. His impeachment by the House of Representatives for the Monica Lewinsky sex scandal had crippled Clinton domestically. In foreign policy, his goal of achieving a comprehensive Middle East peace treaty was proving beyond reach, and his conduct of the military intervention in Kosovo received more criticism than praise. Clinton, therefore, looked to the China trade pact to define his legacy in foreign affairs.

Fortunately for Clinton, the political winds in Congress were in his favor. Under the trade bill introduced on May 15 in the House of Representatives (H.R. 4444), the United States would extend PNTR status to China upon its accession to the WTO. In approving the bill on May 17, the House Ways and Means Committee included an "anti-import surge" amendment that protected U.S. firms in the event of sudden increases in Chinese imports of specific commodities. The House Rules Committee further amended the bill on May 23. Among other provisions of the amended bill, a commission would be established to monitor and report on the PRC's human rights and labor practices. In addition, the U.S. trade representative would annually evaluate China's compliance with WTO regulations, and a special task force would confirm that Chinese exporters were not shipping goods manufactured by prison laborers to the United States. Finally, the House bill called for increased technical assistance to the PRC's efforts to enact legal reforms, and it urged the WTO to consider Taiwan's application to join the trade body immediately after China's accession.

Lobbying efforts peaked as the bill awaited a final vote in the full House. On the day before the vote was taken, about 200 business lobbyists met on Capitol Hill to coordinate their strategy for swaying undecided members.[44] On May 24, the House approved H.R. 4444 by a vote of 237–197. Although a majority of the 224 Republicans in the House voted for the bill, most of the 211 Democrats voted against it. Opponents came largely from urban areas with large populations of industrial workers and a strong labor union presence. On both sides of the aisle, support was primarily from members representing suburban or rural districts. Approval in the Senate was virtually assured, although its timing was uncertain given the Senate's approaching summer recess, other legislation on its schedule, and the distraction of a presidential election campaign.

Many prominent senators opposed the measure, although Senate approval was considered a given. Sen. Paul Wellstone, D-Minn., for example, spoke out against normal trade with China because of the PRC's continuing repression of human rights and religious freedoms. Republican critics included Fred

Thompson, R-Tenn., who sought without success to include an amendment that would link PNTR to Chinese restraint on nuclear weapons proliferation. Jesse Helms, R-N.C., chairman of the Committee on Foreign Relations, argued that PNTR status would reward Chinese leaders for maintaining the communist system he had long condemned. As in the House, supporters and opponents of PNTR crossed party lines to an extent otherwise unseen in the 106th Congress.

As the Senate vote approached in September 2000, the lobbying by interests on both sides of the China trade issue resumed, although with less intensity than before the House vote. Among pro-PNTR interest groups was the American Electronics Association, one of the largest and most influential high-tech trade associations in the United States, which stepped up its lobbying campaign in early September. Representing small and medium-sized industrial firms, the National Association of Manufacturers met with Senate Majority Leader Trent Lott, R-Miss., and Sen. John Breaux, D-La., and received their assurances that the bill would be approved. Once their position was made known, other business groups relaxed their lobbying efforts.[45]

The Senate was under strong pressure from the Clinton administration and business groups to pass the legislation without amendments. Clinton warned senators that amendments to the bill would force a new round of negotiations—first with the Chinese government and then with the House of Representatives. The outcome of those talks would be highly uncertain, and the legislation would be in the hands of a new Congress and a new presidential administration in 2001. The Senate soundly rejected a series of proposed amendments linking China's trade status to improvements in human rights, religious freedom, labor standards, and weapons proliferation. The final bill, identical to that passed by the House, moved quickly toward a vote on the Senate floor.

As expected, the Senate approved the measure on September 19 in an 83–15 vote and sent it to the White House for Clinton's signature. Again, support and opposition to the bill had crossed party lines to an unusual extent, with seven Democrats joining eight Republicans in opposing the legislation. Whereas the Democrats were primarily concerned with labor issues, Republican opponents most often cited the security threat posed by the PRC. Critics of China in both parties raised concerns about human rights. Clinton signed the legislation on October 10, and normalized U.S.-China trade relations became a reality.

Having gained the blessing of the world's foremost economic power, China joined the WTO on December 11, 2001. Its government then embarked on a series of economic reforms, to be phased in over the following decade, that would align the nation's trade policies with WTO standards and those of other member states. Among other commitments, Chinese officials agreed to reduce average tariff levels on industrial as well as agricultural products to 8.9 percent and 15.2 percent, respectively, by 2010.[46] The PRC also pledged to limit subsidies for agricultural production, grant full trade and distribution rights to foreign enterprises, respect intellectual property rights, and open its banking system to foreign-based financial institutions. Taken together, once enacted these reforms would remove the barriers to the entry of goods, services, and foreign investments into China.

Conclusion: The Privatization of Foreign Policy

China's entry into the WTO was followed by rapid increases in its overseas trade. Between 2001 and 2008, China's overall trade increased five-fold, from $510 billion to $2.56 trillion.[47] The volume of Chinese imports and exports grew at roughly the same levels until 2005, when exports grew over the previous year by more than 28 percent ($762 billion), whereas imports grew by only 18 percent ($660 billion).[48] This eventually evened out by 2008, which for the first time saw exports grow more slowly than imports, or 17.2 percent ($1.43 trillion) to 18.5 percent ($1.13 trillion), respectively, probably due to the global economic downturn.[49] Preliminary data suggest that the Chinese economy's real growth, as measured by GDP, continued at an annual average rate of about 9 to 10 percent through 2009.[50] Such robust growth, which China had enjoyed in previous years while its neighbors endured a protracted economic crisis, also stood in stark contrast to the recessions experienced by Western economies, including that of the United States. Significantly, China had become the world's leading recipient of FDI by 2002, and it retained its status as one of the top destinations for FDI thereafter.[51]

Among the key factors in this surge in China's global trade was the United States, whose imports from China grew from $100 billion in 2000 to an estimated $338 billion in 2008.[52] Exports from the United States to China also increased during the same period, from $16 billion to about $71.5 billion. The growth in U.S. exports was welcomed in Washington, but the resulting annual trade deficits, the largest ever recorded between two trading partners, fueled renewed charges that China was shirking its commitment to open markets.[53] According to the Office of the United States Trade Representative, in many economic sectors China by 2009 "has yet to fully implement important commitments, and in other areas, significant questions have arisen regarding

China's adherence to ongoing WTO obligations, including core WTO principles."[54] As noted above, the United States continues to successfully file WTO complaints against China, resulting in positive if incremental improvements in reducing domestic restrictions in areas such as intellectual property–laden U.S. products in the film, publishing, and entertainment industries.[55]

The large and protracted trade imbalance has provided ammunition to U.S. critics of normalized trade relations and China's WTO membership. These critics also have emphasized the most recent human rights reports, which indicate little or no improvement in China's record since it joined the WTO. Freedom House, for example, concluded in its 2009 report that "[d]espite expectations that it would enact at least symbolic human rights improvements during its year as host of the Olympic Games, the Chinese government in 2008 increased restrictions on online writers, human rights lawyers, democracy activists, migrant workers, and individuals seeking to petition the central government on abuses by local officials. Religious and ethnic minorities were also subjected to stepped-up repression, including a number of high-profile deaths."[56] According to Catherine Baber of Amnesty International, "China's so-called economic 'miracle' comes at a terrible human cost—rural migrants living in the cities experience some of the worst abuse in the work place."[57]

American importers in particular have had a difficult time ensuring that workers' rights are not abused, as many factories in China have simply developed more sophisticated methods for hiding violations.[58] Labor unions in the United States claimed that such findings prove that Clinton's logic of inducing reform in China through engagement was unfounded. Although the AFL-CIO repeatedly and often unsuccessfully petitioned the administration of George W. Bush to put greater pressure on China, the Obama administration appears to be more receptive.[59] For instance, upon a favorable ruling from the International Trade Commission in 2009, the president imposed "an increased duty on tires from China for three years" amounting to "35 percent in the first year, then 30 percent and 25 percent in each of the following years."[60] The AFL-CIO's blog responded with jubilation, noting that "[t]oday, President Obama made clear that he will enforce America's trade laws and stand with American workers. The President sent the message that we expect others to live by the rules, just as we do."[61]

Despite these findings, pro-engagement groups in the United States continue to favor closer bilateral trade ties with China. The U.S.-China Chamber of Commerce, for example, published articles on possible ways the two countries might cope with the global financial recession through bilateral trade arrangements.[62] Similar positions are adopted by the U.S.-China Business

Council and other trade groups with a material stake in bilateral trade who are thus opposed to China's "indigenous innovation" policies, which help to insulate Chinese firms from competition by "includ[ing] unique requirements that [various products'] intellectual property be developed and owned in China, and that any trademarks be originally registered in China."[63] This general approach is largely accepted by the administration, whose Office of China Affairs under the supervision of the U.S. Trade Representative, Ron Kirk, works toward closer trade ties with China while recognizing the need "to identify areas where China is not fully honoring its WTO commitments, and developing and implementing strategies to enforce them."[64]

Although the continued centrality of the bilateral trade relationship between the United States and China is beyond dispute, China's global ambitions are much broader than this picture might suggest. The PRC has adopted international engagement as a key component of its own foreign policy agenda and has demonstrated a willingness to deal not only with the democratic allies of the United States, but with more controversial governments in Iran, Syria, and Libya.[65] In addition to ongoing tensions with Japan,[66] China has begun to emerge as a competitor of the United States in Asia, as evidenced by its 2005 participation in the East Asian Summit with sixteen regional powers and its signing of a free trade agreement with the Association of Southeast Asian Nations (ASEAN) in November 2004. China has continued on this trajectory, deepening and expanding relations with other member states in the region.[67] Other examples of China's expanding global reach, which is often aimed at satisfying its voracious energy appetite, include a liquid natural gas agreement with Australia, negotiations with African states rich in resources such as the Sudan, and energy agreements with Venezuela and Brazil.[68] Without a doubt, Clinton's neoliberal engagement strategy has resulted in a much stronger Chinese economy with profound global implications.

The continuing debate over U.S.-China trade relations serves as a microcosm of a larger phenomenon in the formulation of post–cold war U.S. foreign policy. A variety of new issues, actors, and policy calculations emerged in the 1990s to replace the challenge that the Soviet Union formerly posed. Of particular concern to this study is the heightened stature of foreign economic relations on the policy agenda of the first post–cold war administration. With the easing of security concerns, U.S. leaders identified competitiveness in the rapidly integrating global economy as a pressing national interest. A related trend was the growing role of international and domestic nonstate actors seeking to promote their interests in this more fluid, pluralistic environment. The global war on terrorism, while altering the strategic environment since September 2001, has not altered this more general shift in world politics.

All these elements greatly complicate the U.S. policy-making environment, which had already been altered by the diffusion of foreign policy responsibilities beyond the State and Defense Departments. As the foreign affairs bureaucracy has grown to empower economic-oriented agencies, such as the Treasury and Commerce Departments, the opportunities for private interest groups to penetrate the policy-making process have greatly increased. This trend is reflected in Congress, whose committees concerned with foreign economic relations are a focus of heightened interest group lobbying and political pressure. The outcome of this legislative process reflects the more complex setting in which "intermestic" issues—those crossing foreign and domestic boundaries— dominate the agenda. In this respect, the debate over U.S.-China trade relations typifies the new and more complex era in U.S. foreign policy.

Key Actors

Amnesty International   Nongovernmental organization, opposed to the Clinton administration policy of engagement with China because of Beijing's political repression of dissidents.

Bill Clinton   President, an advocate of engagement and normalized trade relations with China.

General Motors Corporation   The largest U.S.-based automaker and a proponent of normalized trade relations with China; involved since 1997 in a joint venture with Shanghai Automotive Industry Corporation.

Human Rights Watch   Nongovernmental organization whose annual reports highlighted ongoing political repression in China despite closer economic relations with the United States.

Qualcomm Corporation   A San Diego–based business, proponent of normalized trade relations with China; partnered with two Chinese companies to modernize the country's telecommunications network.

John Sweeney   AFL-CIO president, an outspoken opponent of normalized trade relations on the basis of Chinese trade restrictions, the country's human rights record, and the potential loss of jobs in the United States.

United Methodist Church   Issued a report condemning the Chinese government's crackdown on religious freedom and opposing closer trade relations.

U.S.-China Business Council   An industry-based group strongly in favor of engagement.

Notes

1. For the Strategic and Economic Dialogue, see www.ustreas.gov/initiatives/us-china/; for the U.S.-China Joint Commission on Commerce and Trade, see www.ustr .gov/about-us/press-office/fact-sheets/2009/october/us-china-joint-commission-commerce-and-trade.

2. David Lovevinger, "U.S.-China Relations: Maximizing the Effectiveness of the Strategic and Economic Dialogue," September 10, 2009, www.treas.gov/press/releases/ tg292.htm.

3. Office of the United States Trade Representative, "2009 Report to Congress on China's WTO Compliance," December 2009.

4. See Bradley S. Klapper, "WTO Chief: U.S.-China Trade Friction Rising," *Huffington Post,* January 21, 2010.

5. U.S. Census Bureau, Foreign Trade Division, Data Dissemination Branch, www .census.gov/foreign-trade/balance/c5700.html#2009.

6. Ibid.

7. Kerry Dumbaugh, Congressional Research Service, "China-U.S. Relations: Current Issues and Implications for U.S. Policy," November 20, 2009.

8. David Leonhardt, "The China Puzzle," *New York Times,* May 17, 2009.

9. Kerry Dumbaugh, Congressional Research Service, "China-U.S. Relations: Current Issues and Implications for U.S. Policy," September 22, 2006, 3–5.

10. Ibid., 20.

11. Peter Nicholas, "Obama Chides China over Human Rights," *Los Angeles Times,* November 16, 2009, http://articles.latimes.com/2009/nov/16/world/fg-obama-shang-hai16.

12. Chris Good, "Obama Goes There: Talking Human Rights in China," *The Atlantic.com,* November 16, 2009, http://politics.theatlantic.com/2009/11/obama_goes_ there_talking_human_rights_in_china.php.

13. Jeffrey E. Garten, *The Big Ten: The Big Emerging Markets and How They Will Change Our Lives* (New York: Basic Books, 1997).

14. White House, Office of the Press Secretary, press conference transcript, May 26, 1994.

15. For an elaboration on this domestic balance of power, see the various essays in Scott Kennedy, ed., *China Cross Talk: The American Debate over China Policy since Nationalization* (Lanham, Md.: Rowman and Littlefield, 2003).

16. For an elaboration, see Steven W. Hook and John Spanier, *American Foreign Policy since World War II,* 15th ed. (Washington, D.C.: CQ Press, 2000), 68–79.

17. See Andrew Nathan, *China's Transition* (New York: Columbia University Press, 1997).

18. China's economic output grew by an average of 10 percent annually in the 1980s, with much of this growth based on foreign commerce. See Claude E. Barfield, "U.S.-China Trade and Investment in the 1990s," in *Beyond MFN: Trade with China and American Interests,* ed. James R. Lilley and Wendell L. Willkie II (Washington, D.C.: AEI Press, 1994), 63.

19. William R. Keylor, *The Twentieth Century World: An International History,* 3rd ed. (New York: Oxford University Press, 1996), 479–480.

20. The figures in this section are derived from Wayne M. Morrison, Congressional Research Service, "China-U.S. Trade Issues," July 20, 2000, 2–5.

21. U.S. Census Bureau, Foreign Trade Division, "U.S. Trade Balance with China," May 7, 2000, www.census.gov/foreign-trade/balance/c5700.html.

22. Department of Agriculture, Economic Research Service, "China's WTO Accession to Significantly Boost U.S. Agricultural Exports," press release, February 2000.

23. See Hook and Spanier, *American Foreign Policy,* 361–363.

24. John T. Rourke and Richard Clark, "Making U.S. Foreign Policy toward China in the Clinton Administration," in *After the End: Making U.S. Foreign Policy in the Post–Cold War World,* ed. James M. Scott (Durham: Duke University Press, 1998), 203.

25. Ibid., 208.

26. During a November 1997 visit to the White House, Jiang Zemin agreed to halt the sharing of nuclear technology with Iran, among other concessions. A similar concern among congressional critics involved the Clinton administration's support for sharing satellite launch technology with China. White House officials certified in May 1999 that such technology exports to China would not harm U.S. firms in this sector or threaten U.S. strategic interests.

27. For a review of the shift in public opinion and its relationship to Sino-American relations, see "Support for NTR/MFN Status," *Americans on Globalization: A Study of Public Attitudes,* Center on Policy Attitudes, University of Maryland, College Park, March 28, 2000, www.pipa.org/OnlineReports/Globalization/appendixa/appendixa.html.

28. Susan Schmidt, "Businesses Ante Up $30 Million," *Washington Post,* October 26, 2000, A26.

29. China Business World Online News Service, "Joint Venture Project with GM," February 25, 1997, www.cbw.com/business/quarter1/automoti.htm.

30. Richard Pastore, "Motorskills: Emerging Markets," *CIO Magazine Online,* September 15, 1998, www.cio.com/archive/enterprise/091598_ford.html.

31. Lester J. Gesteland, "Foreign Firms to Benefit from China Unicom U.S. $16 Billion CDMA Market," *China Online,* December 13, 1999.

32. For more information regarding the impact of NGO pressure on government policies, see Margaret E. Keck and Kathryn Sikkink, *Activists beyond Borders* (Ithaca: Cornell University Press, 1998).

33. For recent critiques, see Human Rights Watch, "China: Release Whistleblowing Doctor. Year-Long Pattern of Harassment Comes to Light," June 10, 2004, http://hrw.org/english/docs/2004/06/10/china8794.htm; and idem, "China: Stifling the Memory of Tiananmen," June 4, 2004, http://hrw.org/english/docs/2004/06/03/china 8732.htm.

34. Freedom House, *Freedom in the World, 1997–1998* (Piscataway, N.J.: Transaction Publishers, 1998), 190–191.

35. *Amnesty International Annual Report, 1999: China,* www.amnesty.org/ailib/aireport/ar99/asa17.htm.

36. Elizabeth Economy, "Painting China Green," *Foreign Affairs* 78 (March/April 1999): 16.

37. For examples of environmental NGOs' Internet lobbying activities, see the Greenpeace Web site, www.greenpeace.org, and that of the Sierra Club, www.sierra club.org.

38. United Methodist Church, General Board of Church and Society, "An Appeal of Conscience by Religious Leaders to Members of the U.S. Congress," September 19, 2000, www.umc-gbcs.org/issues/letter.php?letterid=42.

39. While most religious groups opposed the engagement policy, some sided with the Clinton administration in arguing that toleration of faith would be more likely once

the PRC became more integrated in the global economy. One example was a Quaker group, the Friends Committee on National Legislation, which became active during the 1990s on many aspects of Sino-American relations.

40. Federal News Service, "Prepared Testimony of John J. Sweeney before the Senate Finance Committee," March 23, 2000.

41. State Department, Bureau of Democracy, Human Rights and Labor, *Country Reports on Human Rights Practices, 1999,* February 25, 2000, www.state.gov/www/global/ human_rights/1999_hrp_report/china.html.

42. See the Freedom House Web site, www.freedomhouse.org.

43. Wayne M. Morrison, National Council for Science and the Environment, "U.S.-China Trade Issues," CRS Issue Brief for Congress, January 3, 2001, http://cnie.org/ nle/econ-35.html.

44. Anne E. Kornblut, "House OK's Normalizing China Trade, Bipartisan Vote Praised and Assailed," *Boston Globe,* May 25, 2000, A1.

45. Edward Daniels, "Manufacturing Advocate Confident China Trade Bill Will Pass," States News Service, August 23, 2000.

46. While China's record on reducing tariff barriers remained mixed as of 2010, these twin goals had been achieved. See Wayne M. Morrison, "U.S.-China Trade Issues," CRS Issue Brief for Congress, June 21, 2010, www.fas.org/sgp/crs/row/RL33536.pdf.

47. U.S.-China Business Council, *U.S.-China Trade Statistics and China's World Trade Statistics,* www.uschina.org/statistics/tradetable.html (accessed February 12, 2010).

48. Ibid.

49. Ibid.

50. Andrew Jacobs and Bettina Wassener, "China's Growth Picks Up Speed but Raises Concerns," *New York Times,* October 22, 2009, www.nytimes.com/2009/10/23/business/global/23yuan.html.

51. U.S.-China Business Council, "Foreign Investment in China," February 2010, www.uschina.org/statistics/fdi_cumulative.html.

52. U.S.-China Business Council, *U.S.-China Trade Statistics and China's World Trade Statistics.*

53. Office of the United States Trade Representative, "2009 Report to Congress on China's WTO Compliance," December 2009. Amid these complaints from Washington, interestingly, increasing discontent in China over the status of the trade relationship also grew, as the United States was seen more and more as a brake on China's otherwise unrestrained growth.

54. Ibid., 4.

55. The first complaint against China filed in 2004 with the WTO involved the semiconductor industry; it was settled through bilateral negotiation. David Armstrong, "United States Complains to WTO about China," *San Francisco Chronicle,* February 3, 2007, http://articles.sfgate.com/2007-02-03/business/17233202_1_wto-export-subsidies-us-china-business-council.

56. Freedom House, *Freedom in the World, 2009 Edition—Country Report: China (2009),* www.freedomhouse.org/template.cfm?page=22&country=7586&year=2009.

57. Amnesty International, press release, "China: The Human Cost of the Economic Miracle," March 1, 2007, http://web.amnesty.org/library/Index/ENGASA170092007?open&of=ENG-CHN.

58. Dexter Roberts and Pete Engardio, "Secrets, Lies, and Sweatshops," *Business-Week,* November 27, 2006.

59. AFL-CIO, *The AFL-CIO's Worker's Rights Case against China, Global Economy,* www.aflcio.org/issues/jobseconomy/globaleconomy/chinapetition.cfm (accessed April 5, 2007).

60. James Parks, "Obama Enforces Trade Laws on China Tire Imports," *AFL-CIO Now Blog News,* September 12, 2009, http://blog.aflcio.org/2009/09/12/obama-enforces-trade-laws-on-china-tire-imports.

61. Ibid.

62. U.S.-China Chamber of Commerce, "Opportunities for U.S. and Chinese Companies during Financial Crisis," September 29, 2009, www.usccc.org/newhome/article/Opportunities_for_US&Chinese_Companies_During_Financial_Crisis.pdf.

63. Michael Barbalas et al., "U.S.-China Business Council, International Business Letter on Indigenous Innovation Accreditation Policy," December 10, 2009, www.uschina.org/public/documents/2009/12/indigenous_innovation_letter.pdf.

64. Office of the United States Trade Representative, "U.S. China Trade Facts," February 12, 2010, www.ustr.gov/countries-regions/china. See also Office of the United States Trade Representative, "2009 Report to Congress on China's WTO Compliance," December 2009, www.ustr.gov/webfm_send/1572.

65. Dumbaugh, "China-U.S. Relations," 2006, 16.

66. The National Institute for Defense Studies, Japan, "East Asian Strategic Review," *Japan Times,* 2009, 113–123.

67. Jing-dong Yuan, "China-ASEAN Relations: Perspectives, Prospects, and Implications for U.S. Interests," Strategic Studies Institute, U.S. Army War College, October 2006, www.strategicstudiesinstitute.army.mil/pdffiles/PUB735.pdf.

68. Dumbaugh, "China-U.S. Relations," 2006, 13–18.

13 The Politics of Climate Change: A Consensus for Copenhagen?

Rodger A. Payne and Sean Payne

Before You Begin

1. What is the U.S. national interest regarding climate change? How do leaders balance economic concerns against environmental issues?

2. Which organizations, coalitions, and leaders most influence climate change policy in the United States? What interests do they pursue?

3. What role do cities and states play in shaping American policy on climate change?

4. Will the United States likely play a pivotal role in ongoing negotiations about climate change?

5. Is the United States likely to reduce its greenhouse gas emissions without a formal new climate treaty? What policy processes might lead to a reduction in emissions?

6. To the extent that U.S. reluctance to cut greenhouse gas emissions has been rooted in domestic politics, what are the prospects for future U.S. reductions given recent shifts in political power and business perspectives?

Introduction: The U.S. Perspective

The scientific evidence linking carbon dioxide and other so-called greenhouse gases to global warming is now viewed as overwhelming. That was made abundantly clear in the very troubling "Summary for Policymakers" included in the most recent report of the Intergovernmental Panel on Climate Change (IPCC), which was produced by 2,500 scientists from over 130 countries. The panel's fourth assessment found that the data about global temperature increases are "unequivocal." Moreover, the IPCC declared that "most of the observed increase in globally averaged temperatures since the mid-20th century is *very likely*"—defined as greater than 90 percent likely— "due to the observed increase in anthropogenic greenhouse gas concentrations." The IPCC specifically finds that human fossil fuel consumption and "land-use change"—caused by deforestation, for example—are primarily responsible for an "atmospheric concentration of carbon dioxide in 2005 [that] exceeds by far the natural range over the last 650,000 years."[1]

Unsurprisingly, global climate change is now recognized as a very high political priority item on the international agenda. Sir David King, Britain's former top scientific adviser, has written, for instance, that "climate change is the most severe problem that we are facing today—more serious even than the threat of terrorism."[2] Numerous countries are now debating the most effective and affordable means of heading off disastrous consequences. It is generally agreed that climate change simply must be addressed collectively, since neither the causes nor consequences can be isolated even to a small set of nation-states.

The first major step was taken in February 2005, when the Kyoto Protocol to the Framework Convention on Climate Change (FCCC) went into effect after ratification by 168 countries and the European Union (EU). The treaty requires meaningful reductions in greenhouse gas emissions, as parties committed to reducing emissions by 5.2 percent by 2012. Though the Kyoto deal was struck in 1997, no U.S. presidential administration has ever forwarded it to the Senate for ratification. President Bill Clinton's negotiators aggressively and openly sought significant additions to the agreement, but could not obtain a deal before his term expired. President George W. Bush's administration considered Kyoto "fatally flawed" and refused to partake in ongoing international talks designed to achieve additional reductions.[3] Well in advance of the December 2009 Copenhagen climate summit, the twenty-seven nations of the EU and Japan agreed to cut their greenhouse gas emissions by 20 percent or more from their 1990 levels by 2020.[4] President Barack Obama claims that the United States wants to help the world head off climate change, but the results to date have been modest. Because the United States emits nearly one-fourth of the pollutants that contribute to global warming, it is nearly impossible to imagine an international treaty that can successfully address this worldwide problem without Washington's endorsement and cooperation.[5] Domestic and international politics in large part explain U.S. behavior in climate change negotiations over the past two decades.

Background: The Emergence of the Global Warming Issue

In 1827 French scientist Jean-Baptiste Fourier recognized that Earth's atmosphere traps significant amounts of the sun's heat in much the same way that glass panels trap heat in a greenhouse. It is now well-established science that

Timeline

The Kyoto Protocol

1896	Swedish scientist Svante Arrhenius publishes "On the Influence of Carbonic Acid in the Air upon the Temperature of the Ground."
1957	American oceanographer Roger Revelle warns that humans are conducting a "large-scale geophysical experiment" on the planet by emitting substantial quantities of greenhouse gases.
October 1985	The findings of the first major international conference on global warming, held at Villach, Austria, warn, "As a result of the increasing concentrations of greenhouse gases, it is now believed that in the first half of the next century a rise of global mean temperature could occur which is greater than any in man's history."
June 1988	NASA's James E. Hansen testifies before Congress that "the greenhouse effect is here and affecting our climate now."
November 1988	The first meeting is held of the Intergovernmental Panel on Climate Change, an interdisciplinary group of scientists, scholars, policy makers, and diplomats that regularly issues reports about climate change science, the effects of those changes, and possible means of mitigating the consequences of global warming.
May 12, 1989	President George H. W. Bush announces U.S. support for climate change negotiations.
June 1992	The United Nations Framework Convention on Climate Change (FCCC) is presented to the "Earth Summit" at Rio de Janeiro, Brazil. The treaty does not require states to make binding commitments to reduce greenhouse gas emissions.
October 1992	The United States becomes the first industrialized nation to ratify the FCCC.

March 21, 1994	The FCCC becomes international law three months after the fiftieth ratification.
July 5, 1997	The U.S. Senate passes the Byrd-Hagel Resolution (95–0) opposing U.S. acceptance of any climate change commitment that excludes the developing world or would seriously hurt the U.S. economy.
December 11, 1997	More than 150 nations, including the United States, agree to the Kyoto Protocol to the FCCC. The agreement commits industrialized nations to an average 5 percent reduction in greenhouse gas emissions, using 1990 levels as the base.
November 12, 1998	President Bill Clinton signs the Kyoto Protocol.
March 2001	Bush administration officials declare the Kyoto Protocol "dead" and announce U.S. withdrawal from international negotiations.
June 2002	The European Union and Japan ratify the Kyoto Protocol. Canada joins them six months later.
July 2002	California becomes the first U.S. state to restrict greenhouse gas emissions from motor vehicles.
November 2004	Russia ratifies the Kyoto Protocol, which enters into effect three months later.
December 2005	New York and six other states organize a Regional Greenhouse Gas Initiative to reduce greenhouse gas emissions in the northeastern United States.
August 2006	California requires industry to lower greenhouse gas emissions, committing to 25 percent cuts in current levels by 2020.
January 2007	An industry-backed coalition, the United States Climate Action Partnership, releases a report calling for mandatory reductions in greenhouse gas emissions.
February 2007	California and four neighboring states form the Western Climate Initiative to reduce greenhouse gas emissions.

(continued)

Timeline *(continued)*

The Kyoto Protocol

April 2007	The U.S. Supreme Court rules that carbon dioxide and other greenhouse gases are pollutants, the Environmental Protection Agency (EPA) has the authority to regulate them, and states have the right to sue the EPA to force such decisions.
June 26, 2009	By a 219–212 vote, the House of Representatives passes the American Clear Energy and Security Act, cosponsored by Reps. Henry A. Waxman, D-Calif., and Edward J. Markey, D-Mass.
September 2009	The EPA proposes to focus its first greenhouse gas–permitting requirements on large industrial facilities.
December 2009	Copenhagen summit concludes with a nonbinding U.S. agreement with China, India, and other nations establishing a 2° Celsius limit on future warming and a commitment of $100 billion over ten years to help poor countries adapt to climate change.

carbon dioxide (CO_2), methane, nitrous oxide, and especially water vapor create a greenhouse effect, which modulates the planet's climate. Without this atmosphere, Earth would be cooler by at least 60 degrees Fahrenheit, and life as it is known today would not exist. In the 1890s, however, Swedish scientist Svante Arrhenius and American P. C. Chamberlain identified a potential problem: the buildup of carbon dioxide in the atmosphere because of the burning of fossil fuels. Since the beginning of the Industrial Revolution, the combustion of coal, oil, and natural gas and other human activities have increased carbon dioxide concentrations in Earth's atmosphere by about 35 percent. In 1957 oceanographer Roger Revelle noted, "Human beings are now carrying out a large-scale geophysical experiment of a kind that could not have happened in the past nor be reproduced in the future."[6]

More than half a century has passed since Revelle made his observation, and the scientific community now believes that it has a solid understanding of the results of this grand experiment in atmospheric science. For many years, and after decades of genuinely impressive research, a consensus of scientists have agreed about the phenomenon now commonly known as global warming. The latest IPCC assessment notes the cumulative result of the research, "a *very high confidence* that the globally averaged net effect of human activities since 1750 has been one of warming."[7] Scientists expect climate change to become even more apparent and pronounced through the twenty-first century. As economies and populations grow worldwide, fossil fuel consumption increases. By the year 2100, carbon dioxide concentrations in the atmosphere are expected to be at least double the levels present at the beginning of the Industrial Revolution.

Although no one can be certain of the effects of these developments, many scientists have long warned of the polar ice caps melting at rapid rates, ocean currents changing dramatically, and precipitation and storm patterns shifting significantly. The global consequences of these changes could include severe flooding of coastal areas, disruption of agricultural patterns, emergence of new and threatening disease patterns, creation of millions of "environmental refugees," and great damage to the planet's biological diversity. In other words, the effects of climate change are likely to be numerous, adverse, costly, and potentially severe.[8]

International Negotiations

The ten warmest years of the twentieth century occurred during its last fifteen years. The ten warmest years recorded since 1850 occurred in the twelve-year period from 1997 to 2008.[9] Thus, with ever-increasing urgency, many national governments behave as if global warming is an extremely serious ecological threat to the planet.

In 1988 global warming emerged as a major issue in many countries, including the United States. Temperatures were much warmer than normal, North America experienced major drought, and forest fires raged through Yellowstone National Park. In June 1988, James E. Hansen, director of the National Aeronautics and Space Administration's (NASA) Goddard Institute of Space Studies, made headlines when he declared to the Senate Committee on Energy and Natural Resources, "The greenhouse effect is here and affecting our climate now."[10] Many scientists were publicly critical of that comment, arguing that the assertion was not clearly supported by the available evidence. Nonetheless, after Hansen's testimony, "media coverage of global warming ignited."[11] Many political figures around the world soon began recommending that nations pay more attention to the problem. Prime Minister Margaret Thatcher of the United Kingdom, for example, worried that human activity was "creating a global heat trap which could lead to climatic instability."[12]

In late June 1988, Canada sponsored the Toronto Conference on the Changing Atmosphere, which was attended by hundreds of government officials, scientists, environmentalists, and industry representatives from forty-six countries; among those attending were the prime ministers of Canada and Norway. Later that year, the United Nations Environment Program (UNEP) and the World Meteorological Organization—with the strong support of the United States and other governments—created the Intergovernmental Panel on Climate Change. Holding its first meeting in November 1988, the IPCC engaged nearly two hundred top-notch scientists in assessing global warming by creating working groups on science (chaired by the United Kingdom), impacts (chaired by the Soviet Union), and response strategies (chaired by the United States). In addition to the impressive pool of atmospheric scientists, hundreds of economists, diplomats, and public servants also ultimately participated in IPCC working groups.

Momentum for international action continued to build. In March 1989, France, Norway, and the Netherlands cosponsored a meeting on global environmental issues that was attended by representatives from two dozen countries, including seventeen heads of state. That month, twenty-two nations, including Canada, France, Italy, and Japan, called for the negotiation of a climate change convention; in May 1989, just months into George H. W. Bush's presidency, the United States announced support for such negotiations. In July, the leaders of the Group of Seven (G-7) industrialized countries (Canada, France, Germany, Italy, Japan, the United Kingdom, and the United States) met in Paris, and held what some observers called the "environmental summit." The resulting G-7 declaration "strongly advocate[d] common efforts to limit emission of carbon dioxide and other greenhouse gases."[13]

The IPCC working groups reported their initial findings to the UN General Assembly and the Second World Climate Conference in fall 1990 at Geneva. These first assessments reflected a scientific consensus that the greenhouse effect was real and was being exacerbated by human activity. They also paid immediate policy dividends: on December 21, 1990, the General Assembly adopted Resolution 45/212 establishing the Intergovernmental Negotiating Committee (INC) to serve under its auspices and coordinate bargaining among nations.

Many observers believed that international negotiators intended to model a climate change treaty on the Montreal Protocol. During the 1980s, a series of negotiations led to an agreement to address the class of man-made chemicals known as chlorofluorocarbons (CFCs), which were thinning the atmospheric ozone layer. Under the 1987 Montreal Protocol, a baseline emissions year was established, and then production and use of CFCs were reduced in relation to this target and ultimately banned. Following this precedent, the 1988 Toronto Conference statement recommended that global carbon dioxide emissions be reduced by 20 percent from 1988 levels by the year 2005.[14] In 1990 Prime Minister Thatcher promised that the United Kingdom had "set itself the demanding target of bringing carbon dioxide emissions back to this year's level by the year 2005."[15] Similarly, "a large majority of the industrialized states represented at the conference" meeting in Bergen, Norway, in May 1990 "agreed that they would stabilize the emission of CO_2 and other important greenhouse gases at 1990 levels by the year 2000."[16]

Knowledgeable onlookers realized that despite such commitments, it would be very difficult to duplicate the success of the Montreal Protocol.[17] The stage for that agreement was set in 1985, when a British Antarctic Survey report made worldwide news by establishing the existence of a dramatic "hole" in the ozone layer.[18] The news media helped build public awareness and concern by describing the many potential dangers of the exposure to ultraviolet radiation resulting from ozone depletion. The agreed cause of the ozone hole was CFC emissions. By the mid-1980s, those chemicals were used primarily in the manufacture of foam insulation (about 25 percent of all CFC uses), as aerosol propellants (33 percent), as refrigerants (25 percent), and as cleansers in the electronics industry (16 percent).[19] These uses were not centrally important to the global economy; a small number of countries produced and consumed the overwhelming majority of the chemicals, and only about twenty companies manufactured billions of dollars worth of CFCs. Developing countries produced just 4 percent of CFCs—and China and India together consumed only about 2 percent of the world total. The U.S. Environmental Protection Agency (EPA) had already banned nonessential CFC use in 1978, and in 1986 U.S. industry leader DuPont announced that it could likely develop and market substitutes for CFCs within a decade. The United States even assumed an international leadership role in the negotiations. In all, this was a welcoming context in which to negotiate an agreement.

The economic and political situation facing the INC participants in the 1990s was dramatically different, and negotiators were aware of the substantial barriers to cooperation on global warming. Despite evidence backed by a fairly strong scientific consensus, many Americans continued to contest the need to act upon what they considered uncertain information. Scientists willing to challenge the assembled evidence pointing toward global warming assumed prominent positions in the public debate. Additional resistance stemmed from the consumption of fossil fuels by virtually every nation and the expense and difficulty of adopting substitutes. Coal and petroleum use was and remains integral to the economic livelihood of dozens of countries. Fossil fuels provide power for electricity generation, heating, nearly all automobiles, and a substantial proportion of worldwide industrial activity. Politically potent business interests have strong stakes in the status quo, as do national producers of fossil fuels, such as the members of the Organization of Petroleum Exporting Countries (OPEC).[20]

Despite these challenges, during the 1990s negotiators worked toward a meaningful climate change treaty after the General Assembly created the INC. From February 1991, the INC met five times to draft a Framework Convention on Climate Change in advance of the UN Conference on Environment and Development, which was held in June 1992 at Rio de Janeiro, Brazil. Because INC negotiators knew that the Earth Summit, as the gathering is popularly known, was symbolically important, they effectively operated under a deadline and made rapid progress in the sessions leading up to the June conference. During the negotiations, however, the United States refused to agree to targeted greenhouse gas emission reductions and legally binding timetables; therefore, the FCCC did not include such provisions. As the world leader in emissions, the United States could effectively block any requirements by threatening not to go along with the treaty.

In the final FCCC agreement presented at the Rio conference, the industrialized nations (listed in a document designated "Annex I") agreed merely to "aim" to return their greenhouse gas emissions to 1990 levels by the year 2000. The Annex I countries were also charged with developing national policies to mitigate greenhouse gas emissions, although they were allowed the option of "joint implementation." In practice, this meant they could obtain credit for reductions by helping other nations—potentially including those in the developing world—reduce their emissions. The convention also created transparency measures requiring countries to provide to the FCCC secretariat inventories of greenhouse gas emissions and reports on their development of national emission reduction plans. Poor countries had attempted to secure pledges of increased development assistance to help them acquire the means to reduce their emissions, but the agreement did not include a provision for such aid. Yet the world's richest nations were required "to provide new and additional financial resources to meet the agreed full cost" for developing countries to meet their transparency requirements. At the Earth Summit, the Global Environment Facility (GEF) was named as the interim agency to pool and distribute these financial resources. In 1999, after significant restructuring, the GEF became the treaty's permanent financial mechanism.

More than 150 states signed the agreement in Rio, and 193 countries and the EU are members as of July 2010. The United States was the first industrialized nation to ratify the convention, which entered into force in March 1994, three months after the fiftieth ratification. The FCCC established a Conference of the Parties (COP), composed of all member states, which meets regularly to discuss key unresolved issues. At the spring 1995 COP-1 meeting in Berlin, the Alliance of Small Island States (AOSIS) pressed mightily for a protocol that would require emissions reductions. AOSIS diplomats have strong interests in climate change because their nations are vulnerable to future increases in sea level caused by melting polar ice caps. No agreement on emissions reductions emerged from COP-1, however, as very few states were prepared to make a commitment. In December 1995, the IPCC released its Second Assessment Report, which bolstered the arguments of countries seeking firm reduction requirements.[21] Nonetheless, the 1996 COP-2 meeting in Geneva also failed to reach agreement on this issue. The Clinton administration made an important concession, however, by committing the United States to legally binding reductions on greenhouse gas emissions; the precise figures were to be negotiated.

The December 1997 COP-3 meeting in Kyoto, Japan, yielded the first legally binding commitments by countries to reduce greenhouse gas emissions. Under the Kyoto Protocol, countries were assigned varying reduction goals, and the timetable for reaching the goals was expressed as an average over the five years from 2008 to 2012. The United States agreed to a target of a 7 percent reduction in greenhouse gas emissions from the 1990 base year. The actual U.S. obligation to reduce emissions was mitigated significantly by the acceptance of its plan to credit countries for the successful management of so-called carbon "sinks" (mainly forested areas that absorb carbon dioxide) by employing environmentally friendly land-use techniques and innovative forestry practices. The major negotiating parties remained deeply divided about many proposed provisions, and as a result the Kyoto Protocol actually reflected only limited agreement. To their credit, the states overcame most divisions about the specific emissions reductions that would be required and the various gases that the treaty would cover.

The Kyoto deal did not, however, successfully resolve two key U.S. concerns, which were influenced as much by domestic as by international political factors. First, the agreement ignored the U.S. demand that developing countries be required to reduce greenhouse gas emissions. The United States worried that developed states might make significant and costly reductions but see their efforts diluted by states like China and India substantially increasing their fossil fuel consumption and greenhouse gas emissions even as they gained a comparative economic advantage.[22] Poorer countries argued that they should be exempted from making reductions: they had not contributed much to the atmospheric changes that dated back to the start of the Industrial Revolution, and they expelled only a small fraction of the emissions of wealthier countries on a per capita basis.[23] Many nongovernmental organizations agreed that it was unjust for wealthy countries to demand reductions in the use of fossil fuels by the world's most impoverished inhabitants.

Second, the United States strongly favored market-friendly emissions trading and joint implementation plans. Economists often argue that such approaches reduce the costs of pollution abatement because they encourage greater efficiency as compared with regulatory approaches. Most American businesses vulnerable to environmental regulation prefer market-based mechanisms, such as "cap-and-trade" approaches, which typically allow businesses to buy and sell pollution permits in order to meet local, regional, or national caps on pollution. However, influential environmental groups, such as Friends of the Earth, argue against global adoption of such mechanisms. These groups fear that industrialized states will refuse to make any technological or resource-use changes if they have the option of "joint implementation." Polluters from advanced countries might merely build new factories in nonindustrial nations to offset treaty obligations.[24] In the end, resolution of this particular dispute was deferred until future COP meetings.

Domestic politics influenced U.S. positions on these points as Congress seemed determined not to allow the Clinton administration to commit to any real emissions reductions. On July 25, 1997, the Senate voted 95–0 in support of S.Res. 98, cosponsored by Democrat Robert Byrd, from coal-rich West Virginia, and newcomer Chuck Hagel, R-Neb. The nonbinding resolution indicated the sense of the Senate that it would not ratify any protocol that would "result in serious harm to the economy" or that would "mandate new commitments to limit or reduce greenhouse gas emissions for the Annex I Parties, unless the protocol or other agreement also mandates new specific scheduled commitments to limit or reduce greenhouse gas emissions for Developing Country Parties within the same compliance period."[25] The resolution also required that any future agreement forwarded to the Senate for approval be accompanied by a detailed explanation of regulatory or other legal action that would be needed for implementation, as well as a detailed financial analysis of the costs to the economy.

The Clinton administration signed the Kyoto accord in November 1998, but pointed to the Byrd-Hagel resolution and indicated that it would not submit the agreement to the Senate for "advice and consent" until gaining commitments from developing countries not yet covered by the treaty obligations to reduce their greenhouse gas emissions. This delay was globally significant; for the Kyoto Protocol to become binding, it had to be ratified by at least fifty-five countries "which accounted in total for at least 55 per cent of the total carbon dioxide emissions for 1990 of the Parties included in Annex I."[26]

While countries debated whether to ratify Kyoto, they continued to meet to address unresolved issues. In several successive COP meetings through the late 1990s, negotiators engaged in ongoing talks about enforcement of the Kyoto-mandated emissions reductions, emissions trading proposals, and possible credits for greenhouse gas "sinks." In the various meetings, Clinton's negotiators sought both joint implementation and developing-country participation. The parties were apparently close to a deal concerning implementation questions at the November 2000 COP-6 meeting at The Hague, but the bargaining collapsed over the issue of carbon "sinks" and "reservoirs." The United States, Canada, and Japan wanted generous credits for various land uses and forestry practices, whereas the EU nations wanted to limit such credits.[27] The meeting was widely viewed as a failure, and environmental groups largely blamed the United States, which some argued was trying to gain climate credits for ordinary agricultural practices.

Thus, as the Clinton presidency ended, many environmentalists hoped that a new administration would be able both to convince the next Senate to ratify the Kyoto Protocol and to negotiate a follow-on compliance and implementation agreement with the rest of the world.

The Bush–Exxon Mobil Years

Republican George W. Bush entered the White House in 2001 after narrowly defeating Vice President Al Gore in a drawn-out and contentious political process. Gore was an environmentalist and strong supporter of Kyoto. Bush, by contrast, had worked in the oil industry before serving as governor of Texas, and was opposed to the Kyoto accord, claiming that it provided unfair trade advantages to unregulated economic competitors like China.

On the day of Bush's inauguration, the IPCC released a new report on the scientific basis of global warming that predicted temperature increases substantially greater than prior reports had expected.[28] The next round of negotiations on Kyoto was delayed from May until July at the new president's request, so that his administration would have time to evaluate and develop U.S. climate policy. Internally, there was some support in the administration for regulating carbon dioxide, but support for the Kyoto Protocol was weak at best. Secretary of the Treasury Paul O'Neill circulated a memo promoting a comprehensive domestic approach to global warming, but he too thought the treaty reflected bad policy.[29] The new EPA administrator, Christine Todd Whitman, publicly advocated a regulatory approach, which would include carbon dioxide, and by March media reports suggested that the administration might announce a plan to regulate greenhouse gas emissions from power plants.

However, the prospect of a new regulatory scheme met strong opposition from conservatives who were skeptical about climate science and from industry groups that opposed new environmental standards. Faced with the risk of alienating Republican support in an evenly divided Senate, the White House simply dumped the regulatory proposal from the agenda.[30] The president told key Republican senators, "I do not believe . . . that the government should impose on power plants mandatory emissions reductions for carbon dioxide, which is not a 'pollutant' under the Clean Air Act."[31]

It is certainly not surprising that the Bush White House, which openly proclaimed "business-friendly" views, shunned regulatory approaches to climate change. After all, businesses generally oppose regulations, and even the Clinton administration sought market-based mechanisms to implement Kyoto. However, the Bush administration avoided all greenhouse gas emission standards, even those based on market principles. Instead, the White House encouraged voluntary efforts with an emphasis on the development of new technologies. Neither its Climate Leaders nor Climate Vision programs, however, slowed the annual increase in U.S. greenhouse gas emissions.[32] Two weeks after abandoning the domestic plan to regulate emissions, Administrator Whitman further announced that the administration considered the Kyoto Protocol "dead" and that the United States had "no interest in implementing that treaty."[33] Environmentalists and many European governments were furious.

Even as it was avoiding mandatory domestic and international measures, the Bush administration was also manipulating the public debate about the scientific evidence on climate change. For example, the administration stripped the entire global warming section from the final 2002 EPA report on air pollution.[34] Moreover, the *New York Times* in 2005 reported that several government climate reports issued in 2002 and 2003 were suspiciously edited by Philip A. Cooney, the chief of staff for the White House Council on Environmental Quality and a former lobbyist for the American Petroleum Institute (API), the largest trade group representing oil companies. Cooney altered the reports so as to suggest doubt about the "robust" findings of climate experts, and the administration's Climate Change Science Program nonetheless officially issued the edited documents.[35] Rick S. Piltz ultimately resigned as a senior associate in that office, claiming that "politicization by the White House has fed back directly into the science program in such a way as to undermine the credibility and integrity of the program."[36] At a January 2007 House Oversight and Government Reform Committee hearing, the Union of Concerned Scientists (UCS) and Government Accountability Project presented survey results finding that many federal scientists and officials had been subjected to political pressures to downplay the risks of global warming. Francesca Grifo, a UCS senior scientist, testified that the survey "brought to light numerous ways in which U.S. federal climate science has been filtered, suppressed and manipulated in the last five years."[37] Rep. Henry Waxman, D-Calif., a newly empowered committee chair, condemned the apparent "orchestrated campaign to mislead the public about climate change."[38]

The Bush administration was certainly not working alone in trying to shape the domestic debate to its liking. Exxon Mobil Corporation—the largest company in the United States—distributed millions of dollars to dozens of think tanks that the leading British scientific academy, the Royal Society, said "misrepresented the science of climate change by outright denial of the evidence."[39] Exxon Mobil's role can perhaps be readily explained by the fact that its products emit more carbon dioxide than all but five countries. Greenpeace released State Department briefing papers from the period 2001–2004, obtained through a Freedom of Information Act request, revealing that the Bush administration sought the company's "active involvement" on climate policy. One briefing note written for Under Secretary of State Paula Dobriansky claimed that the president "rejected Kyoto in part based on input" from an industry group substantially funded by Exxon Mobil.[40]

The International Community Moves Forward

With U.S. withdrawal from the climate negotiations, the EU grabbed the leadership mantle in hopes of ensuring the Kyoto Protocol's implementation. In June 2001, European environment ministers unanimously passed a resolution affirming their countries' intentions to ratify the treaty, and they began to court Russia and Japan in an effort to put the treaty into force without the United States. At July 2001 COP-6 meetings in Bonn, the strategy seemed to work, as the EU was able to bring the parties together on a compromise over implementation rules. To reach a deal, the Europeans acceded to the Japanese position on carbon-trapping "sinks" and compromised on a Russian desire for emissions trading. These developments likely would have pleased Clinton negotiators, but the Bush administration was unmoved. U.S. officials reiterated complaints that the treaty did not go far enough to require action by developing countries, such as China and India.[41] Under Secretary Dobriansky was booed at the conference when she claimed that the United States remained committed to preventing climate change.[42]

The EU nations collectively ratified the Kyoto Protocol in May 2002, and Japan and Canada followed later that year. After a lengthy bargaining period, Russian president Vladimir Putin was able to extract Europe's backing for his country's accession to the World Trade Organization in exchange for a promise to ratify Kyoto.[43] This meant that the agreement had sufficient Annex I membership, and the treaty became binding on parties in February 2005. The international community proved capable of negotiating and ratifying climate deals without U.S. cooperation. Given the volume of U.S. emissions, however, its future position on this issue remained centrally important. After all, the world lacks a central governing authority to pass and enforce universally binding laws.

Subnational Action

After the Bush administration pronounced Kyoto "dead," many members of Congress fruitlessly pursued legislative means to limit U.S. greenhouse gas emissions. In fact, 511 bills, resolutions, and amendments "specifically addressing climate" change were introduced in Congress from 2001 through 2008.[44] Fully 235 pieces of legislation were introduced in the 110th Congress alone after Democrats took majority control of both chambers. Despite this energetic activity, not a single piece of binding legislation addressing climate change was passed during the Bush years.

Absent federal action on emissions reductions and climate change, numerous local and state governments moved to combat climate change, typically through collective initiatives and often modeled on the goals and mechanisms of the Kyoto Protocol. For instance, over one thousand executives from cities in every state signed the U.S. Mayors Climate Protection Agreement, committing local governments to work independently to meet Kyoto standards and to promote state and national governments to adopt climate legislation.[45]

The Pew Center on Global Climate Change found that states also have been leading the way on climate policy. By 2009, thirty-two states adopted comprehensive climate action plans, and four more are now in progress.[46] California especially has been at the forefront of these efforts. In July 2002, Sacramento passed the first legislation in the United States to restrict greenhouse gas emissions from noncommercial vehicles.[47] The statute required that new "maximum" but "economically feasible" auto emission standards be set by 2005, so as to be incorporated into new car models sold by 2009.[48] "California led the nation with the introduction of the catalytic converter, unleaded gasoline, hybrid vehicles, and now we will lead on global warming," boasted environmental activist Russell Long.[49] California is in a unique position among states because it had strict air quality regulations predating the Clean Air Act. Thus it is the only state that can establish tougher air standards than the federal government, though it must first be granted a waiver by the EPA. Other states are then free to follow stronger California standards rather than weaker national regulations. Rules issued in 2004 under the new clean cars law required a 30 percent cut in emissions from vehicles sold in the state by 2016. Twelve states announced plans to follow California's rules, leading David Doniger of the Natural Resources Defense Council to comment, "That is so much of the market it should reach a tipping point. . . . It won't make sense for the automakers to build two fleets, one clean and one dirty."[50]

The automobile industry, unsurprisingly, was displeased with California's regulations, and in January 2005 sued in federal court to block their implementation. While a decision on the case was delayed pending the outcome of a related Supreme Court case, *Massachusetts v. Environmental Protection Agency,* California responded in 2006 by filing a lawsuit against six automakers for creating a "public nuisance" through their vehicles' carbon emissions. The state explicitly claims that the vehicles are contributing to global warming and harming public health.[51] In December 2007, a federal judge upheld California's law regulating auto emissions, affirming the state's right to establish strict air standards if granted a waiver from the EPA.[52] Later the same month, however, the EPA denied California's waiver—the first time ever in thirty years under the Clean Air Act. Though the denial prompted outcries from states and Congress, then–EPA head Stephen L. Johnson defended the decision: "The Bush administration is moving forward with a clear national solution, not a confusing patchwork of state rules."[53]

Building on the advances made by California's clean car law, many other states began to look for subnational solutions to combat global warming. The first regional plan to gain national attention involved northeastern states, and was initiated by Gov. George Pataki, R-N.Y. In April 2003, Pataki invited the governors of nearby states to participate in developing a "cap-and-trade" program for reducing greenhouse gas emissions. Connecticut, Delaware, Maine, Massachusetts, New Hampshire, New Jersey, Rhode Island, and Vermont joined New York in forming the Regional Greenhouse Gas Initiative (RGGI) and began negotiating a plan loosely based on the Kyoto Protocol to lower emission levels. The ten northeastern and mid-Atlantic state members (Maryland joined in 2007) embraced a plan that caps power plant emissions through 2014 and will reduce them 2.5 percent annually, or by 10 percent in total, by 2018.[54] The initiative held its first permit auction in September 2008, capping emissions from 233 power plants.[55] The RGGI could serve as a model for a national cap-and-trade plan.

In February 2007, the governors of five western states followed the pathway blazed by RGGI and collectively formed the Western Climate Initiative (WCI), through which California, Washington, Oregon, Arizona, and New Mexico have created a plan to reduce greenhouse gas emissions 15 percent below 2005 levels by 2020.[56] The initiative limits the importation of coal-fired power from other states, and in 2012 will open a regional cap-and-trade system targeting electricity producers and large industrial sources of emissions. Since its formation, the WCI has grown to include seven western state partners and four Canadian provinces. Gov. Arnold Schwarzenegger, R-Calif., lauded the agreement as showing "the power of the states to lead our nation."[57]

Jeremiah Baumann, of the Oregon Public Interest Research Group, pointed out that the WCI transmits a very strong "message to business that national regulations are coming."[58] Indeed, California's most recent initiatives provide an indicator of what may be next. In August 2006, California became the first state to require industry to lower greenhouse gas emissions, requiring 25 percent cuts from current levels by 2020, with some reductions beginning in 2012. Schwarzenegger boasted that "our federal government will follow us—trust me."[59] In January 2007, to meet emissions goals, California's Public Utilities

Commission passed new and unprecedented rules banning power companies from buying energy from highly polluting sources, including out-of-state coal-fired plants. In December 2008, California adopted the country's first comprehensive plan to address global warming, which includes energy efficiency measures, renewable energy supports, and a cap-and-trade plan to prepare for greenhouse gas deals with other WCI members.[60]

States won a significant legal victory in 2007 when the Supreme Court issued its decision in the case of *Massachusetts v. Environmental Protection Agency*. The matter began in 1999 when a group of environmental scientists petitioned the EPA to regulate carbon dioxide and other greenhouse gases under the 1970 Clean Air Act, which Congress renewed in 1990. The Bush administration refused to regulate carbon dioxide, however, claiming it was not a pollutant and that the EPA therefore had no authority to impose standards. The EPA rejected the petition in 2003 and questioned the relationship between automobile emissions and global climate change. The agency's decision was upheld in 2005 by a 2–1 ruling in the U.S. Court of Appeals, but California, New York, ten other states, and three cities joined the environmentalists to challenge the ruling. In April 2007, the Supreme Court ruled 5–4 that carbon dioxide and other greenhouse gases are pollutants, that the EPA has the legal authority to regulate emissions, and that states have the right to sue the EPA over its refusal to do so.[61] Despite the ruling, the EPA delayed issuing rules on greenhouse gases and sought public comments, effectively pushing any administrative action on climate change onto the succeeding president.

Business Reconsiders

President Bush called global climate change a "serious challenge" in his January 2007 State of the Union speech, which marked the first time he had referenced the problem in his annual agenda-setting address.[62] However, the administration did not suddenly reverse course and embrace mandatory domestic and international greenhouse gas reductions. Likewise, longtime industry opponents of greenhouse regulations, like Exxon Mobil, continued to fund groups working against regulation while attempting to change their public image.[63] Many other businesses, however, began taking dramatically different positions.

In 2006 ten major corporations, including Alcoa, BP America, Caterpillar, DuPont, General Electric, and Wal-Mart, joined with environmental groups to form the United States Climate Action Partnership (USCAP). Notably,

USCAP's January 2007 report advocated mandatory greenhouse gas reductions. The chair of Duke Energy, Jim Rogers, said at its press conference, "It must be mandatory, so there is no doubt about our actions. . . . The science of global warming is clear. We know enough to act now. We must act now."[64] This message appears to be spreading in the business community, as Apple and a number of utility companies withdrew from the Chamber of Commerce in 2009 because of the group's opposition to domestic climate change policy. Nike and Johnson & Johnson likewise publicly expressed their disapproval.[65]

In the mid-1980s, the Montreal Protocol negotiations gained tremendous momentum once DuPont and other chemical companies abandoned all-out opposition to an ozone accord and signaled their willingness to live with regulation—and to research and develop potentially profitable substitutes for CFCs.[66] Similar bottom-line concerns help explain why some companies are now reversing course on climate change. Many simply want their brand to be "greened," while power companies promoting nuclear energy or other alternatives have more direct financial interests. As company president John Hofmeister explains, "From Shell's point of view, the debate is over. When 98 percent of scientists agree, who is Shell to say, 'Let's debate the science'?"[67] Industry's reversal can also be explained by the unpredictable political situation that the state initiatives have created. Many companies prefer a single national policy, likely based on market mechanisms such as cap-and-trade. Even Exxon Mobil vice president for public affairs Kenneth P. Cohen acknowledges, "One thing heavy industry cannot live with is a patchwork quilt of regulations."[68]

The Obama Era: National Action?

After eight years of federal inaction on climate change, the 2008 U.S. presidential election clearly held the promise of change regardless of which candidate won the presidency. Both major-party candidates, Republican senator John McCain and Democratic senator Barack Obama, had previously cosponsored legislation to reduce carbon emissions. Both candidates also publicly stated the need for increased U.S. cooperation with the international community.[69] Obama, who won the election, had the more ambitious proposal, as his plan called for an 80 percent reduction in greenhouse gases, $150 billion in clean energy investments, and a national cap-and-trade system. Campaigning in New Hampshire in October 2007, Obama stated, "No business will be allowed to emit any greenhouse gases for free. Businesses don't own the sky, the public does, and if we want them to stop polluting it, we have to put a price on all pollution."[70] Environmental groups working on climate change greeted the decisive election results with hopeful optimism. "Elections are about change and this election offers us the greatest opportunity we have ever had to change course on global warming," stated Fred Krupp, president of the Environmental Defense Fund.[71] Two weeks after his victory, Obama told the Bi-Partisan Governors Global Climate Summit, "Few challenges facing America and the world are more urgent than combating climate change. . . . Now is the time to confront this challenge once and for all. Delay is no longer an option. Denial is no longer an acceptable response."[72]

Obama's White House created a new Office of Energy and Climate Change Policy and appointed as its head Clinton's EPA administrator, Carol Browner. Other initial appointments included alternative energy expert and Nobel laureate Steven Chu as secretary of energy, environmental policy analyst John P. Holdren as assistant for science and technology, and experienced environmental regulator Lisa Jackson as EPA administrator. These appointments starkly contrast the oil industry ties of many Bush-era officials.[73] Though overshadowed by a prolonged economic and financial crisis and a contentious battle over health care legislation, the Obama team pursued two distinct tactics for limiting greenhouse gas emissions domestically. The administration has sought to leverage existing regulatory agencies and tools to limit emissions. Additionally, it wants Congress to pass climate legislation.

The new administration acted on climate issues almost immediately with a set of presidential memorandums issued in January 2009. One directed the Department of Transportation (DOT) to establish tougher fuel efficiency standards for vehicles. Another ordered the EPA to reconsider the Bush administration's denial of California's waiver application, which would allow states to set higher restrictions on vehicle greenhouse gas emissions.[74] In February, the Energy Department was directed to implement aggressive efficiency standards for household appliances. The DOT order led to a new national policy announced in May that increased fuel efficiency and limited greenhouse gas emissions from cars and trucks. The new fuel standards resulted from bargaining among the states requesting the EPA waiver, automakers, and the administration. In the deal, California agreed to drop its suit against automakers and also to amend its 2002 car emissions law to conform to the new national standard beginning in 2012.[75] In June, the EPA granted California its waiver to set its own emission standards, and in October the president signed an executive order requiring all federal agencies to set a greenhouse gas emissions reduction target for 2020.

Perhaps the most significant step the administration has taken involves EPA preparation to regulate greenhouse gas emissions directly under the Clean Air Act. In *Massachusetts v. Environmental Protection Agency*, the Supreme Court in 2007 ruled that the EPA could not refuse to regulate greenhouse gases without a scientific basis.[76] Throughout 2009, the Obama administration set into motion the various steps required for the EPA to regulate greenhouse gases. Due to the sometimes arcane proposal, commentary, and oversight procedures involved in creating or changing regulatory rules, the federal bureaucratic process to establish EPA standards moves slowly. However, the agency made steady and incremental progress. In April 2009, the EPA announced that it expected to find carbon dioxide and five other greenhouse gases to be pollutants and a threat to human health and welfare. An "endangerment finding" is a necessary precondition to regulate emissions. When congressional Republicans asked for a delayed finding and questioned the underlying science, Administrator Jackson refused: "We know that skeptics have and will continue to try to sow doubts about the science. . . . But raising doubts—even in the face of overwhelming evidence—is a tactic that has been used by defenders of the status quo for years."[77] In September, the EPA finalized a new rule that requires mandatory reporting of greenhouse gasses from large emitters, beginning in January 2010. The agency also announced a proposal to regulate large emitters, primarily power plants. While the proposed "tailoring rule" exempts small businesses and family farms, the EPA assumed "authority for the greenhouse gas emissions of 14,000 coal burning power plants, refiners and big industrial complexes that produce most of the nation's greenhouse gas pollution."[78] The final endangerment finding was released in December 2009 to coincide with the opening of the Copenhagen climate conference. The timing was not altogether fortuitous, as controversy had erupted in November after e-mail archives "hacked" from the Climatic Research Unit in England seemed to reveal that scientists had engaged in dubious practices that threatened the credibility of their work. However, investigative reports in scientific and media outlets soon revealed that the controversy was greatly overblown and did not significantly challenge the climate change science.[79]

Though the EPA's finding opens the door for new standards limiting greenhouse gas emissions in 2010, a direct regulatory approach is not guaranteed. Administrative rules and regulations are subject to judicial review, so the regulations could be delayed or overturned through litigation.[80] Congress could also act to remove the EPA's authority to regulate greenhouse gases through legislation or simply move to block action via procedural or oversight rules. In January 2010, Sen. Lisa Murkowski, R-Alaska, and thirty-four Republican and three Democratic cosponsors attempted to stop new regulations by introducing a "resolution of disapproval."[81] Even if unlikely to pass, the resolution illustrates the potential power of Congress. Moreover, the White House has repeatedly announced its preference for a legislative solution. As Carol Browner explains, "The best path forward is through legislation, rather than through sort of the weaving together the various authorities of the Clean Air Act, which may or may not end in a cap-and-trade program. You can get the clearest instruction by passing legislation."[82]

While the 111th Congress moved closer to enacting binding climate legislation in 2009 than ever before, the body still fell far short of implementing greenhouse gas controls into law. In June, the House of Representatives passed the first legislation ever seeking to control greenhouse gases. The American Clean Energy and Security Act (ACES), introduced by Reps. Henry Waxman, D-Calif., and Edward Markey, D-Mass., includes support for alternative energy and efficiency targets, but it most significantly establishes an economy-wide cap-and-trade system for greenhouse gases and establishes emission targets—a 17 percent reduction from 2005 levels by 2020 and an 83 percent cut by 2050.[83] The bill faced significant opposition both from House Republicans and private groups, and the final product reflected intense last-minute deal-making and political compromise.

The global warming provisions of ACES were closely modeled on a plan developed and published by USCAP, the coalition of corporations and environmental groups supporting climate change action. Opposition to the bill included high-profile business interests like the U.S. Chamber of Commerce and the American Petroleum Institute, which has long sought to undermine climate science and legislation. API's opposition generated controversy when leaked internal memos revealed "astroturfing"—organized rallies featured member employees to create the appearance of grassroots opposition to legislation.[84] In all, the Center for Public Integrity reported that in 2009, 1,150 companies and private groups hired 2,810 lobbyists on climate change, or "5 lobbyists for every member of Congress." This marked a 400 percent increase from just six years ago.[85]

Strongly opposed House Republicans offered more than four hundred amendments to stall passage. Rep. John Boehner, R-Ohio, the minority leader, delayed a floor vote by reading from a three-hundred-page amendment![86] Despite a personal appeal from President Obama, rural and Midwestern Democrats with vested interests in the status quo, led by Agriculture Committee Chairman Collin Peterson, D-Minn., also forced several last-minute changes before agreeing to vote in the majority. The compromises included provisions stripping the authority of the EPA to regulate greenhouse gases under the Clean Air Act, allowing the Department of Agriculture rather than the EPA to manage carbon offsets for farmers and agribusiness, and requiring the president to impose tariffs starting in 2020 on goods from countries that do not limit greenhouse gas emissions.[87] Primarily because of the limits on the EPA's authority, some environmental groups called on Congress to reject the bill. On June 26, however, the House narrowly passed ACES 219–212, with forty-four Democrats voting against and only eight Republicans voting in favor.

Next, the Senate took up climate change legislation, where it continues to face major obstacles as of this writing. Senate Democrats split the provisions of the House bill into two separate proposals. The less controversial energy provisions are contained in the American Clean Energy Leadership Act, which was passed by the Natural Resources Committee in June 2009. The cap-and-trade provisions, however, were placed in the Clean Energy Jobs and American Power Act, cosponsored by former presidential candidate John Kerry, D-Mass., and Environment and Public Works Committee Chair Barbara Boxer, D-Calif. The Kerry-Boxer bill cleared the committee in November on an 11–1 vote featuring a Republican boycott. The legislation contains notable differences from the House version, setting more ambitious reduction targets—20 percent reduction rather than 17 percent by 2020—and maintaining EPA authority to regulate greenhouse gases.[88]

The bill faces significant challenges. Indeed, given strong Republican opposition, Senate Democrats will struggle to gather the sixty votes needed to ensure cloture and end debate on their proposal. Republicans precluded cloture at an unprecedented rate in the most recent Congress. On climate change, Senate Democrats are split between the members from the coasts and the so-called Brown Dogs from the Midwest and Great Plains, which rely on coal and manufacturing. In August 2009, ten Brown Dog senators sent Obama a letter stating that they would not support any climate legislation lacking trade protections for industries in their states.[89] After the surprising special election of Scott Brown, R-Mass., as the forty-first Republican senator, the climate bills may not come to a vote during 2010. Senator Boxer acknowledged that definitive congressional action on climate change "might not happen, in a year or two, or five or six or eight or 10" years.[90]

Conclusions: Climate Change Policy into the Future

The December 2009 COP-15 climate conference did not yield a comprehensive binding agreement for nations to reduce greenhouse gas emissions throughout the twenty-first century. Rather, President Obama's negotiators achieved with leaders from China, India, Brazil, and South Africa a relatively short Copenhagen Accord. The other COP states merely took note of the accord, which establishes a 2° Celsius maximum on future warming and commits the world to contribute $100 billion annually by 2020 to help poor countries adapt to climate change.[91] Many environmentalists and leaders of small states viewed the conference a failure, but President Obama called the agreement an "unprecedented breakthrough."[92] No one can know if the accord will lead to real emissions reductions, but the inclusion of major developing states is certainly noteworthy, as is the promise of substantial funding to help needy nations. The two largest global sources of greenhouse gases agreed to the new deal. Parties meet again in November 2010 in Cancun, Mexico, and will presumably attempt to strengthen the Copenhagen Accord.

Meanwhile, forces inside the U.S. government will struggle to create measures to limit greenhouse gas emissions and reverse the steady increase in emissions. These past few years, observers witnessed a flurry of new activity as many of the largest U.S. states moved toward regional cap-and-trade plans, the EPA launched an effort to create national standards, and the House of Representatives for the first time passed a piece of climate legislation mandating emissions reductions. Additionally, an increasing number of prominent businesses have announced support for a national plan, and polling data from throughout 2009 indicate that between two-thirds and three-fourths of the American public thinks that the federal government should regulate greenhouse gas emissions in order to reduce global warming.[93] Whatever the policy pathway, reductions in greenhouse gas emissions seem destined to remain on the policy agenda, and ongoing domestic and international political battles will determine the outcomes.

Key Actors

George H. W. Bush   President, favored participation in the negotiation of the Framework Convention on Climate Change but refused to agree to specific emissions reductions.

George W. Bush   President, rejected the Kyoto Protocol because of concerns about the cost of compliance and because it required emissions reductions from advanced countries but not from less-developed nations.

Robert Byrd   Senator, D-W.Va., cosponsored S.Res. 98, which warned that the United States should not abide by a climate agreement that exempted developing countries.

Bill Clinton   President, favored the Kyoto Protocol but did not forward the agreement to the Senate because he knew it would likely meet defeat.

James E. Hansen   Director, NASA's Goddard Institute for Space Studies, outspoken scientist about the threat of global warming for over twenty years.

Edward Markey   Representative, D-Mass., cosponsored first climate legislation to pass either body of Congress.

Barack Obama   President, favors international and domestic limits on greenhouse gas emissions, but has not yet concluded policy actions that secure long-range reductions.

George Pataki   Governor, R-N.Y., worked with governors of other northeastern states to join New York in developing a regional initiative to reduce greenhouse gas emissions.

Arnold Schwarzenegger   Governor, R-Calif., negotiated deals with his state legislature and neighboring states to cut greenhouse gas emissions and develop a regional cap-and-trade plan.

Henry Waxman   Representative, D-Calif., cosponsored first climate legislation to pass either body of Congress.

Notes

1. "Contribution of Working Group I to the Fourth Assessment Report of the Intergovernmental Panel on Climate Change," *Climate Change 2007: The Physical Science Basis, Summary for Policymakers* (Geneva: Intergovernmental Panel on Climate Change, February 2007), 2, 4, and 8, www.ipcc.ch/pdf/assessment-report/ar4/wg1/ar4-wg1-spm.pdf. Emphasis in the original.

2. David A. King, "Climate Change Science: Adapt, Mitigate, or Ignore?" *Science* 303, January 9, 2004, www.sciencemag.org/cgi/content/full/sci;303/5655/176.

3. White House, Office of the Press Secretary, "President Bush Discusses Global Climate Change," June 11, 2001, http://georgewbush-whitehouse.archives.gov/news/releases/2001/06/20010611-2.html.

4. BBC News, "Where Countries Stand on Copenhagen," 2009, http://news.bbc.co.uk/2/hi/science/nature/8345343.stm.

5. Energy Information Administration, U.S. Department of Energy, *Emissions of Greenhouse Gases in the United States* (Washington, D.C.: U.S. Department of Energy, November 2006), 2, ftp://ftp.eia.doe.gov/pub/oiaf/1605/cdrom/pdf/ggrpt/057305.pdf.

6. Spencer Weart, "Roger Revelle's Discovery," *Discovery of Global Warming*, American Institute of Physics, August 2003, www.aip.org/history/climate/Revelle.htm.

7. "Contribution of Working Group I," 5. The study defines this as at least a 9 out of 10 chance. Emphasis in the original.

8. See IPCC, "Summary for Policymakers," *Climate Change 2007: Impacts, Adaptation, and Vulnerability. Contribution of Working Group II to the Fourth Assessment Report of the Intergovernmental Panel on Climate Change*, ed. M. L. Parry et al. (Cambridge: Cambridge University Press, 2007), 7–22.

9. Goddard Institute for Space Studies, "Global Temperature Trends: 2008 Annual Summation," December 16, 2008, http://data.giss.nasa.gov/gistemp/2008/.

10. Robert H. Boyle, "You're Getting Warmer," *Audubon,* November–December 1999, http://audubonmagazine.org/global.html.

11. Craig Trumbo, "Longitudinal Modeling of Public Issues: An Application of the Agenda-Setting Process to the Issue of Global Warming," *Journalism and Mass Communication Monographs* 152 (August 1995): 1–57.

12. Margaret Thatcher, "Speech to the Royal Society," Fishmongers' Hall, London, September 27, 1988, www.margaretthatcher.org/speeches/displaydocument.asp?docid=107346.

13. David Bodansky, "Prologue to the Climate Change Convention," in *Negotiating Climate Change: The Inside Story of the Rio Convention,* ed. Irving M. Mintzer and J. A. Leonard (New York: Cambridge University Press, 1994), 52.

14. Center for Environmental Information, archives of the *Global Climate Change Digest,* vol. 1, August 1988, www.gcrio.org/gccd/gcc-digest/1988/d88aug1.htm.

15. Margaret Thatcher, "Speech at the 2nd World Climate Conference," Geneva, November 6, 1990, www.margaretthatcher.org/speeches/displaydocument.asp?docid=108237.

16. Information Unit on Climate Change, UN Environment Program, "The Bergen Conference and Its Proposals for Addressing Climate Change," May 1, 1993, http://unfccc.int/resource/ccsites/senegal/fact/fs220.htm.

17. See Marvis S. Soroos, *The Endangered Atmosphere: Preserving a Global Commons* (Columbia: University of South Carolina Press, 1997), chap. 6.

18. Richard Elliot Benedick, *Ozone Diplomacy: New Directions in Safeguarding the Planet* (Cambridge: Harvard University Press, 1991), 18–20.

19. Ibid., 119.

20. OPEC's eleven members collectively produce about 40 percent of the world's oil and hold about 75 percent of proven petroleum reserves.

21. IPCC reports are available at www.ipcc.ch.

22. China has emerged as the top source of emissions. See BBC, "Climate Change: Copenhagen in Graphics," November 24, 2009, http://news.bbc.co.uk/2/hi/science/nature/8359629.stm.

23. Per capita, Americans emit four times the greenhouse gases of Chinese people and sixteen times as much as Indians. See International Energy Agency, "CO_2 Emissions from Fuel Consumption, Highlights" 2009, 89–91, www.iea.org/co2highlights/CO2highlights.pdf.

24. Peter Zollinger and Roger Dower, "Private Financing for Global Environmental Initiatives: Can the Climate Convention's 'Joint Implementation' Pave the Way?" 1996, http://pubs.wri.org/pubs_content_text.cfm?ContentID=372.

25. S.Res. 98—"Expressing the Sense of the Senate Regarding the United Nations Framework Convention on Climate Change," *Congressional Record,* June 12, 1997, S5622.

26. See Article 25 of the Kyoto Protocol, http://unfccc.int/resource/docs/convkp/kpeng.html.

27. See Hermann E. Ott, "Climate Change: An Important Foreign Policy Issue," *International Affairs* 77 (2001): 277–296.

28. IPCC, Working Group I, Third Assessment Report, "Summary for Policymakers," *Climate Change 2001: The Scientific Basis* (Geneva: IPCC, 2001), www.ipcc.ch/ipccreports/tar/wg1/index.php?idp=5.

29. Paul H. O'Neill, Memorandum for the President, Department of the Treasury, "Global Climate Change," February 27, 2001. See Ron Suskind, "The Bush Files: Environment, from the Book," *The Price of Loyalty* (author's Web site), http://thepriceofloyalty.ronsuskind.com/thebushfiles/archives/000051.html.

30. Douglas Jehl and Andrew C. Revkin, "Bush, in Reversal, Won't Seek Cut in Emissions of Carbon Dioxide," *New York Times,* March 14, 2001, www.nytimes.com/2001/03/14/politics/14EMIT.html?pagewanted=1.

31. George W. Bush, "Text of a Letter from the President to Senators Hagel, Helms, Craig, and Roberts," White House, Office of the Press Secretary, March 13, 2001, http://georgewbush-whitehouse.archives.gov/news/releases/2001/03/20010314.html.

32. Environmental Protection Agency, "Executive Summary," *U.S. Greenhouse Gas Inventory Reports,* April 2009, ES-4, www.epa.gov/climatechange/emissions/usinventoryreport.html.

33. Eric Pianin, "U.S. Aims to Pull Out of Warming Treaty," *Washington Post,* March 28, 2001, A1.

34. Jeremy Symons, "How Bush and Co. Obscure the Science," *Washington Post,* July 13, 2003, B4.

35. Revkin, "Bush Aide Edited Climate Reports," *New York Times,* June 8, 2005, www.nytimes.com/2005/06/08/politics/08climate.html.

36. Ibid.; Cooney was later hired by Exxon Mobil.

37. H. Josef Hebert, Associated Press, "Lawmakers Hear of Interference in Global Warming Science," *Houston Chronicle,* January 31, 2007, www.chron.com/disp/story.mpl/headline/nation/4513577.html.

38. Ibid.

39. David Adam, "Royal Society Tells Exxon: Stop Funding Climate Change Denial," *The Guardian,* September 20, 2006, www.guardian.co.uk/environment/2006/sep/20/oilandpetrol.business.

40. John Vidal, "Revealed: How Oil Giant Influenced Bush," *The Guardian,* June 8, 2005, www.guardian.co.uk/climatechange/story/0,12374,1501646,00.html.

41. William Drozdiak, "U.S. Left Out of Warming Treaty; EU-Japan Bargain Saves Kyoto Pact," *Washington Post,* July 24, 2001, A1.

42. Associated Press, "U.S. Isolated after Global Warming Deal Reached," *USA Today,* July 23, 2001, www.usatoday.com/news/world/2001/07/23/warming.htm.

43. Peter Baker, "Russia Backs Kyoto to Get on Path to Join WTO," *Washington Post,* May 22, 2004, A15.

44. Pew Center on Global Climate Change, "What's Being Done in Congress," 2009, www.pewclimate.org/what_s_being_done/in_the_congress.

45. United States Conference of Mayors, "Mayors Leading the Way on Climate Protection," 2009, www.usmayors.org/climateprotection/revised/.

46. Pew Center on Global Climate Change, "Climate Change 101: State Action," January 2009, www.pewclimate.org/docUploads/Climate101-State-Jan09_1.pdf.

47. BBC News, "California Gets Landmark Green Law," July 22, 2002, http://news.bbc.co.uk/2/hi/americas/2143615.stm.

48. William Booth, "Calif. Takes Lead on Auto Emissions," *Washington Post,* July 22, 2002, A1.

49. Ibid.

50. Danny Hakim, "Battle Lines Set as New York Acts to Cut Emissions," *New York Times,* November 26, 2005, A1.

51. Sholnn Freeman, "Calif. Sues Six Automakers over Global Warming," *Washington Post,* September 21, 2006, D2.

52. John M. Broder, "Federal Judge Upholds Law on Emissions in California," *New York Times,* December 13, 2007, www.nytimes.com/2007/12/13/washington/13emissions.html.

53. John M. Broder and Felicity Barringer, "E.P.A. Says 17 States Can't Set Emission Rules," *New York Times,* December 20, 2007, www.nytimes.com/2007/12/20/washington/20epa.html.

54. RGGI Inc., "States Initiate Bidding Process for March 2010 CO_2 Allowance Auction," January 12, 2010, www.rggi.org/docs/Auction_7_notice_news_release.pdf.

55. Editorial, "Ten States with a Plan," *New York Times,* September 24, 2008, www.nytimes.com/2008/09/25/opinion/25thu2.html.

56. Pew Center on Global Climate Change, "Climate Change 101: State Action," January 2009, www.pewclimate.org/docUploads/Climate101-State-Jan09_1.pdfwww.

57. Timothy Gardner, "Western States United to Bypass Bush on Climate," Reuters, February 26, 2007, www.reuters.com/article/idUSN2630275420070226.

58. Ibid.

59. Adam Tanner, "Schwarzenegger Signs Landmark Greenhouse Gas Law," Reuters, September 28, 2006, www.truthout.org/article/schwarzenegger-signs-landmark-greenhouse-gas-law.

60. Felicity Baringer, "California Adopts a Plan on Emissions," *New York Times,* December 11, 2008, www.nytimes.com/2008/12/12/us/12emissions.html.

61. Robert Barnes and Juliet Eilperin, "High Court Faults EPA on Inaction on Emissions; Critics of Bush Stance on Warming Claim Victory," *Washington Post,* April 3, 2007, A1.

62. White House, Office of the Press Secretary, "President Bush Delivers State of the Union Address," January 23, 2007, http://georgewbush-whitehouse.archives.gov/news/releases/2007/01/20070123-2.html.

63. David Adam, "ExxonMobil Continuing to Fund Climate Sceptic Groups, Records Show," *The Guardian,* July 1, 2009, www.guardian.co.uk/environment/2009/jul/01/exxon-mobil-climate-change-sceptics-funding.

64. "Companies Spell Out Warming Strategy," MSNBC, January 23, 2007, www.msnbc.msn.com/id/16753192/.

65. Michael Burnham and Anne C. Mulkern, "Enviros Waging 'Orchestrated Pressure Campaign' on Climate Bill—U.S. Chamber CEO," *New York Times,* October 9, 2009, www.nytimes.com/gwire/2009/10/09/09greenwire-enviros-waging-orchestrated-pressure-campaign-28715.html.

66. Soroos, *The Endangered Atmosphere,* 159–161.

67. Steven Mufson and Juliet Eilperin, "Energy Firms Come to Terms with Climate Change," *Washington Post,* November 25, 2006, A1.

68. Quoted in Steven Mufson, "Exxon Mobil Warming Up to Global Climate Issue," *Washington Post,* February 10, 2007, D1.

69. Pew Center on Global Climate Change, "Voter Guide: International Climate Agreements," 2009, www.pewclimate.org/voter-guide/international.

70. Jeff Zeleny, "Obama Proposes Capping Greenhouse Gas Emissions and Making Polluters Pay," *New York Times,* October 10, 2009, www.nytimes.com/2007/10/09/us/politics/09obama.html.

71. Maura Judkis, "Environmental Groups Congratulate Obama on Victory," *Huffington Post,* November 5, 2008, www.huffingtonpost.com/maura-judkis/environmental-groups-cong_b_141601.html.

72. Office of the President-Elect, "President-elect Barack Obama to Deliver Taped Greeting to Bi-partisan Governors Climate Summit," November 18, 2008, http://change.gov/newsroom/entry/president_elect_barack_obama_to_deliver_taped_greeting_to_bi_partisan_gover/.

73. Katty Kay, "Analysis: Oil and the Bush Cabinet," *BBC News,* January 29, 2001, http://news.bbc.co.uk/2/hi/americas/1138009.stm.

74. Bryan Walsh, "Obama's Move on Fuel Efficiency: A Clean Win for Greens," *Time,* January 26, 2009, www.time.com/time/health/article/0,8599,1874106,00.html. See the EPA's "Climate Change" homepage for a complete rundown of recent initiatives, www.epa.gov/climatechange/index.html.

75. Pew Center on Global Climate Change, "Federal Vehicle Standards," www.pewclimate.org/federal/executive/vehicle-standards.

76. Linda Greenhouse, "Justices Say E.P.A. Has Power to Act on Harmful Gases," *New York Times,* April 3, 2007, www.nytimes.com/2007/04/03/washington/03scotus.html?pagewanted=1&_r=1.

77. John M. Broder, "Greenhouse Gases Imperil Health, E.P.A. Announces," *New York Times,* December 17, 2009, www.nytimes.com/2009/12/08/science/earth/08epa.html.

78. Ibid.

79. Editorial, "Climatologists under Pressure," *Nature* 462, December 3, 2009, www.nature.com/nature/journal/v462/n7273/full/462545a.html.

80. Deborah Zabarenko, "SCENARIOS: EPA Rules vs. Congress's Laws on Climate Change," Reuters, December 8, 2009, www.reuters.com/article/idUSTRE5B628820091208.

81. Juliet Eilperin, "Senators Try to Thwart EPA Efforts to Curb Emissions," *Washington Post,* January 22, 2010, www.washingtonpost.com/wp-dyn/content/article/2010/01/21/AR2010012104512.html.

82. Darren Samuelsohn, "Obama Prefers Congress to EPA in Tackling Climate—Browner," *New York Times,* February 23, 2009, www.nytimes.com/cwire/2009/02/23/23climatewire-obama-prefers-congress-to-epa-when-it-comes-t-9800.html.

83. Suzanne Goldenberg, "Barack Obama's U.S. Climate Change Bill Passes Key Congress Vote," *The Guardian,* June 27, 2009, www.guardian.co.uk/environment/2009/jun/27/barack-obama-climate-change-bill.

84. Suzanne Goldenberg, "Oil Lobby to Fund Campaign against Obama's Climate Change Strategy," *The Guardian,* August 14, 2009, www.guardian.co.uk/environment/2009/aug/14/us-lobbying.

85. Marianne Lavelle, "A Case of Lowered Expectations," Center for Public Integrity, November 9, 2009, www.publicintegrity.org/investigations/global_climate_change_lobby/articles/entry/1768/.

86. John M. Broder, "House Passes Bill to Address Threat of Climate Change," *New York Times,* June 26, 2009, www.nytimes.com/2009/06/27/us/politics/27climate.html?_r=2&hp.

87. Greg Hitt and Naftali Bendavid, "Obama Wary of Tariff Provision," *Wall Street Journal,* June 29, 2009, http://online.wsj.com/article/SB124621613011065523.html.

88. Juliet Eilperin, "Democrats Move on Emissions Bill," *Washington Post*, November 6, 2009, www.washingtonpost.com/wp-dyn/content/article/2009/11/05/AR2009110502195.html?hpid=topnews.

89. John M. Broder, "Climate Bill Is Threatened by Senators," *New York Times*, August 6, 2009, www.nytimes.com/2009/08/07/us/politics/07climate.html.

90. Eilperin, "Senators Try to Thwart EPA Efforts to Curb Emissions."

91. Copenhagen Accord, December 2009, http://unfccc.int/files/meetings/cop_15/application/pdf/cop15_cph_auv.pdf.

92. Jim Tankersley, "Obama Hails Copenhagen Deal as 'Unprecedented Break-through,' " *Los Angeles Times*, December 19, 2009, http://articles.latimes.com/2009/dec/19/world/la-fg-obama-climate19-2009dec19.

93. ABC News/*Washington Post* poll, PollingReport.com, 2009, www.pollingreport.com/enviro.htm.

14 The International Criminal Court: National Interests versus International Norms

Donald W. Jackson and Ralph G. Carter

Before You Begin

1. What is the International Criminal Court (ICC), and why do many countries believe that it is needed?

2. Why was the U.S. position so contrary to positions its allies took?

3. Is there merit to the U.S. position in this case? Why or why not?

4. Should the rule of law supersede national interests? Why or why not?

5. What does this case suggest about the future of international law or tribunals in the twenty-first century?

Introduction: The Rise of International Law

From 1989 to 1991, a process of disintegration began that led to the dissolution of the Soviet empire and ultimately of the Soviet Union itself. Some of the early beneficiaries of this change seemed to be international institutions and international law, as was illustrated by Soviet-U.S. cooperation during the 1990–1991 Persian Gulf crisis and war. With the apparent end of the cold war, the U.S.-led international coalition that drove Iraqi forces from Kuwait justified and coordinated its actions through the United Nations (UN) and the application of international law. Events in the late 1980s and early 1990s led President George H. W. Bush to declare that an increasingly democratic "new world order" had arrived, a time when "the international system would be based on international law and would rely on international organizations such as the United Nations to settle international conflicts."[1]

An illustration of this trend toward international institutions—though perhaps not of the new world order envisioned by Bush—occurred on July 17, 1998, when 120 states voted at a UN diplomatic conference in Rome to create the International Criminal Court (ICC), with powers to try perpetrators of genocide, crimes against humanity, and war crimes. Only seven states voted against creating the ICC: China, Iraq, Israel, Libya, Qatar, Yemen, and the United States. Within four years, more than the sixty nations needed for implementation of the court had ratified the agreement. On July 1, 2002, the Rome Statute for the International Criminal Court entered into force, despite the persistent opposition of the United States. How did the United States come to find itself on "the other side" of international law and abandoned by most of its traditional allies?

Background: The Rise of International Tribunals

International courts are not unique to the twenty-first century. The Hague Peace Conference of 1899, convened for the primary purpose of promoting peace and stability by limiting or reducing armaments, also created the Hague Convention for the Pacific Settlement of International Disputes and the Permanent Court of Arbitration.[2] With the League of Nations in 1920 came the Permanent Court of International Justice, which rendered thirty judgments and issued twenty-seven advisory opinions from 1922 to 1946.[3] After World War II, the United Nations created the International Court of Justice (or World Court), but two exceptions to this international court's jurisdiction remained: the court's decisions generally applied only to states, not individuals, and, moreover, it was possible for states, through reservations, to avoid the court's obligatory jurisdiction.[4] The idea for the International Criminal Court did not arise in a political vacuum and was not a dream of idealistic abstractions; rather, it followed a series of precedent-setting tribunals. Between 1919 and 1994, five ad hoc international commissions, four ad hoc international criminal tribunals, and three international or national prosecutions of "crimes" arising during World Wars I and II were convened. The first commission sought to prosecute German and Turkish officials and military officers for war crimes and crimes against humanity during World War I. Crimes against humanity generally consisted of the abusive or murderous treatment of civilians by military personnel. This commission's efforts resulted in a few token convictions in the German supreme court.[5]

After the ineffective United Nations War Crimes Commission was created in 1942, the Allies signed the London Charter for the Prosecution and Punishment of the Major War Criminals of the European Axis, in August 1945. The principles contained in the 1945 agreement were later

Timeline
International Criminal Court

1946	The UN General Assembly passes Resolution 95 (I), recognizing the principles contained in the 1945 London Charter as binding precedents in international law. It also passes Resolution 96 (I), making genocide a crime under international law. Trials are held in Nuremberg and Tokyo of Germans and Japanese accused of crimes against peace, war crimes, and crimes against humanity. In the U.S. Senate, the Vandenberg and Connally amendments ensure congressional support for U.S. acceptance of the jurisdiction of the new International Court of Justice (or World Court).
1989	Sixteen Caribbean and Latin American nations propose a permanent international criminal court for the prosecution of narco-traffickers.
1991	The International Law Commission prepares a draft code of international crimes.
1993	The UN Security Council passes Resolution 808, providing for the establishment of the International Criminal Tribunal for the Former Yugoslavia.
1994	The UN Security Council passes Resolution 955, creating the International Criminal Tribunal for Rwanda. The International Law Commission prepares a draft statute for an international criminal court.
1995	The UN General Assembly creates the Preparatory Committee for the Establishment of an International Criminal Court.
March 26, 1998	Sen. Jesse Helms, R-N.C., sends a letter to Secretary of State Madeleine Albright vowing that any agreement that might bring a U.S. citizen under the jurisdiction of a UN criminal court would be "dead on arrival" in the Senate.

March 31– April 1, 1998	Defense Department leaders meet in Washington, D.C., with military attachés of more than one hundred countries to warn them of the possible jurisdiction of an international criminal court over their soldiers.
June–July 1998	At a conference in Rome, delegates discuss and then vote 120–7 to establish the International Criminal Court.
June 14, 2000	Helms introduces the American Servicemembers' Protection Act (S. 2726), which would prohibit U.S. officials from cooperating with the proposed ICC. Majority whip Tom DeLay, R-Texas, introduces the same measure in the House of Representatives (H.R. 4654).
December 31, 2000	The Clinton administration signs the Rome Statute establishing the ICC, so the United States can be considered an original signatory and participate in decisions about implementation of the new tribunal.
May 6, 2002	The administration of George W. Bush formally declares that it does not intend to submit the Rome Statute to the Senate for ratification and renounces any legal obligation arising from the Clinton administration's signing of the treaty.
July 1, 2002	The Rome Statute for the International Criminal Court enters into force without the participation of the United States, but with more than sixty accessions.
August 2, 2002	The American Servicemembers' Protection Act becomes law with the signature of Bush.
March 11, 2003	The first judges of the ICC are inaugurated, and Philippe Kirsch of Canada, who chaired the diplomatic conference in Rome, becomes the court's first president.
March 24, 2003	Luis Moreno Ocampo of Argentina is elected the first chief prosecutor of the ICC.

(continued)

Timeline *(continued)*

International Criminal Court

July 1, 2003	The Bush administration announces its intention to eliminate military aid to the thirty-five countries that have not signed bilateral agreements exempting U.S. citizens from being rendered to the jurisdiction of the ICC.
January 29, 2007	The ICC announces its first case for prosecution. Thomas Lubanga Dyilo of the Union of Congolese Patriots is charged with three counts of enlisting, conscripting, and using children under the age of fifteen as combat soldiers in the Democratic Republic of Congo.
March 4, 2009	The ICC announces the issuance of arrest warrants for Sudanese president Omar al-Bashir for crimes against humanity and war crimes in the conflict involving the Darfur region of Sudan.
February 3, 2010	The ICC's 2009 decision not to include genocide charges against Omar al-Bashir, due to a legal technicality, is overturned; this opens the possibility that genocide could be added to the charges against him.

recognized as binding precedents in international law by UN General Assembly Resolution 95, of December 11, 1946. The London Charter created the International Military Tribunal (IMT), consisting of four judges (one from each of the four powers—France, the Soviet Union, the United Kingdom, and the United States). The jurisdiction of the IMT included the following crimes:

- crimes against peace—Article 6[a] of the London Charter: planning, preparation, initiation or waging a war of aggression or a war in violation of international treaties or agreements;
- war crimes—Article 6[b] of the London Charter, though the most definitive statement appears in the Charter of the International Military

Tribunal (annexed to the London Charter): violations of the laws or customs of war, to include murder, ill-treatment, or deportation to slave labor of civilian populations in occupied territory, murder or ill-treatment of prisoners of war or persons on the seas, killing of hostages, plunder of public or private property, wanton destruction of cities, or devastation not justified by military necessity; and

- crimes against humanity—Article 6[c] of the London Charter: murder, extermination, enslavement, deportation, and other inhumane acts committed against any civilian population, or persecutions on political, racial or religious grounds in execution of or in connection with any crime within the jurisdiction of the tribunal.[6]

The IMT's role concluded with the Nuremberg trials in 1946. The tribunal found eighteen of twenty-one prominent Nazi defendants guilty; twelve of the eighteen were given the death penalty, and the other six were imprisoned for terms ranging from ten years to life.[7]

With the occupation of Japan, the International Military Tribunal for the Far East (IMTFE) was created in Tokyo in 1946. Its list of punishable crimes was essentially the same as that for the IMT in Germany.[8] The results were generally similar as well: all twenty-five defendants were found guilty; seven were executed, sixteen were given life imprisonment, and two were given shorter prison terms.[9]

The London Charter and the Nuremberg precedent were affirmed in 1946 by the UN General Assembly in Resolution 95 (I). In December 1946 the assembly unanimously adopted Resolution 96 (I), which expressly made genocide—derived from the London Charter's definition of crimes against humanity—a crime under international law. Two years later the General Assembly adopted the Convention on the Prevention and Punishment of the Crime of Genocide.[10] In the United States, the genocide convention was submitted to the Senate for ratification in 1949, but U.S. ratification (with reservations) came almost forty years later, in 1988.

Much of the substantive international criminal law as applied by the IMT at Nuremberg was expanded and codified in the Geneva Conventions of 1949. In 1948 the UN General Assembly invited the International Law Commission to study the possibility of creating an international criminal court with jurisdiction over the crime of genocide and other crimes that might be defined by international conventions. Because of the cold war, however, it was not until 1989 that the idea of an international criminal court was again brought before the General Assembly.[11]

U.S. Concerns

The protection of U.S. sovereignty vis-à-vis international law has been a long-standing issue. In 1945 President Harry Truman had to reassure the Senate that Article 43 of the UN Charter, which obligated members to make available to the Security Council "armed forces, assistance, and facilities," would not rob Congress of its right to declare war. In 1946 it took two amendments to ensure Senate support for U.S. acceptance of the jurisdiction of the World Court. The Vandenberg amendment specified that the court's jurisdiction would not apply to "disputes arising under a multilateral treaty, unless (1) all parties to the treaty affected by the decision are also parties to the case before the court, or (2) the United States specially agrees to jurisdiction."[12] The more famous reservation was the Connally amendment, which drew the line of the World Court's obligatory jurisdiction at "disputes with regard to matters which are essentially within the domestic jurisdiction of the United States of America as determined by the United States of America."[13] In the eyes of its critics, this amendment essentially said that the United States would obey the World Court when the U.S. government happened to agree with it. In 1959 the Connally amendment was revisited, when the American Bar Association's Committee on World Peace through Law tried to repeal it. That effort died when the Senate Foreign Relations Committee voted to postpone the matter indefinitely.[14]

These were not the only instances of U.S. unwillingness to be bound by international law. For example, in 1977 the United States and Panama reached agreement on two treaties that returned sovereignty of the Panama Canal and the Canal Zone to Panama and guaranteed neutral operation of the waterway. In approving the treaties, however, the Senate added the DeConcini amendment, which reserved the right of the United States to intervene militarily in Panama to keep the canal open if the United States (not Panama) decided that such a step was necessary.[15] Not surprisingly, the Panamanians were outraged by this infringement on their national sovereignty, and it nearly scuttled the treaties. More recently, in 1984, when the World Court ruled that the United States was illegally trying to overthrow the government of Nicaragua, the United States announced its withdrawal from the court's jurisdiction, for a period of two years, regarding any of its actions in Central America. To be fair, most countries have also rejected the obligatory jurisdiction of the World Court, and many states that have accepted obligatory jurisdiction have attached reservations to their acceptance.[16]

Creation of the ICC

Unlike the Nuremberg and Tokyo trials, the idea for the permanent International Criminal Court was not something that victors in a war imposed on the vanquished. Instead, the genesis of the ICC came from smaller powers in the international system. In 1989 sixteen Caribbean and Latin American nations suggested international criminal prosecutions for narco-traffickers.[17] In 1990 a committee of nongovernmental organizations, including the World Federalist Movement, prepared a draft statute for an international court and submitted it to the Eighth United Nations Congress on the Prevention of Crime and the Treatment of Offenders. In 1991 the UN International Law Commission prepared a draft code of international crimes. These events culminated in November 1994, when the commission produced its draft statute for an international criminal court.[18]

At that time, the international legal community was reacting to allegations of horrendous human rights violations in civil wars in Yugoslavia and Rwanda. In 1993 UN Security Council Resolution 808 provided for the establishment of the International Criminal Tribunal for the Former Yugoslavia, to "prosecute persons responsible for serious violations of international humanitarian law committed in the territory of the former Yugoslavia since 1991."[19] The International Criminal Tribunal for Rwanda was established by UN Security Council Resolution 955, with jurisdiction starting January 1, 1994. The mandate of the Rwanda tribunal was to prosecute genocide and crimes against humanity.[20] These tribunals were temporary, however, and dealt only with the specific conflicts involved.

In December 1995, the UN General Assembly created a Preparatory Committee for the Establishment of an International Criminal Court. The committee, known as PrepCom, first met in March 1996. Its membership was open to all the member states of the United Nations, UN specialized agencies, and the International Atomic Energy Agency.[21] The Clinton administration had been a strong supporter of the temporary tribunals for Yugoslavia and Rwanda and had pushed the general issue of criminal prosecution for persons accused of war crimes. In 1997 it created the position of ambassador-at-large for war crimes in the State Department and named David Scheffer to the post, thereby making him the top U.S. representative to PrepCom. It is most notable that in his September 1997 address to the UN General Assembly, President Bill Clinton endorsed the establishment of a permanent international criminal court "to prosecute the most serious violations of international humanitarian law."[22]

By April 1998, six PrepCom sessions had been held. The aim of the last meeting was to prepare for an international conference in Rome in summer 1998 to conclude a treaty that would establish the permanent court.[23] The working draft at the last PrepCom meeting was the Zutphen Text, which had been produced during a January 1998 meeting in the Netherlands. That document called for a court that would complement national criminal courts. The crimes within the proposed jurisdiction of the international court were not yet determined, but the proposals included genocide, aggression, war crimes, and crimes against humanity. The definition of these crimes varied in different proposals. The draft statute included bracketed language wherever PrepCom had been unable to reach consensus. Near the completion of the last PrepCom meeting, the 175-page draft statute contained 99 articles and about 1,700 bracketed words or provisions.[24]

The proposals included a listing of sexual offenses under war crimes, including rape, sexual slavery, enforced prostitution, enforced pregnancy, and enforced sterilization. One proposal included war crimes against children—for example, forcing children under the age of fifteen to take part in hostilities, recruiting them into the armed forces, or allowing them to take part in hostilities. Another proposed the inclusion of terrorist actions, while another would have included narco-trafficking. A further issue discussed was criminalizing the use of certain weapons likely to cause "superfluous injury or unnecessary suffering," such as expanding bullets, chemical and biological weapons, land mines, and nuclear weapons.[25]

The most difficult issues touched on in Rome involved delimiting domestic criminal jurisdiction relative to the criminal jurisdiction of the international court and the means by which cases would reach the ICC. The domestic–international jurisdictional issue involved "complementarity," which is the idea that international prosecution ought to occur only when a state fails to take responsibility for its own good faith investigation and prosecution of crimes defined by the statute. The statute provided that a case would be admissible before the ICC only when a domestic judicial system was "unwilling or unable" to conduct the proper investigation or prosecution. In addition, a U.S. proposal on complementarity required the prosecutor for the international court to notify state parties and to make a public announcement when a case had been referred. A state could then step forward and inform the prosecutor that it was taking responsibility for prosecution. In the U.S. proposal, the assertion of domestic responsibility for prosecution would delay international criminal jurisdiction for a period of six months to one year, thus giving home governments more time to try accused individuals. One of the concerns expressed before the PrepCom was the length of this delay.[26]

Other issues concerning the means by which cases might come to the court were more vexing. The draft statute provided that the ICC prosecutor would initiate an investigation only when the UN Security Council referred a case or when a state party that had accepted the jurisdiction of the ICC filed a complaint with the prosecutor. Those favoring a strong ICC wanted the prosecutor to have independent authority to investigate and file charges. At the other end of the controversy were those who, like the United States, preferred that the Security Council determine the agenda of the prosecutor and the ICC. That, of course, would give the United States and the other permanent members of the Security Council a veto over the ICC's jurisdiction. As former president Jimmy Carter noted, "Such a move rightly would be seen by many nations as a means for serving only the interests of the permanent members of the Security Council rather than as an independent arbiter of justice."[27]

The U.S. Reaction

In February 1998 Ambassador Scheffer, who was acting as chief negotiator for the United States on the creation of an international court, identified three issues involving the relationship between a court and the UN Security Council that needed to be addressed. The first issue was the need for the two institutions to operate compatibly, with neither undermining the legitimate pursuits of the other; the second involved the council's power to refer situations to the ICC; and the third was the council's role in assisting the court with the enforcement of its orders. Scheffer also made note of the unique position of the United States in the world. Either alone or in concert with its NATO allies and the United Nations, the U.S. military often "shoulders the burden of international security." As he put it, "It is in our collective interest that the personnel of our militaries and civilian commands be able to fulfill their many legitimate responsibilities without unjustified exposure to criminal legal proceedings."[28] State Department spokesman James Rubin followed up on Scheffer's view, adding, "We need to ensure that, in pursuit of justice, a permanent court does not handcuff governments that take risks to promote international peace and security and to save lives."[29]

In August 1997 Singapore had presented a compromise proposal requiring the Security Council to take an affirmative vote to delay ICC proceedings, so the United States, for example, would have to have the consent of the rest of the council to delay a case. The United Kingdom accepted Singapore's proposal, and for a while it appeared that the United States might be moving in that direction as well.[30] However, Sen. Jesse Helms, R-N.C., chairman of the Senate Committee on Foreign Relations, stopped any such momentum. In a March 26, 1998, letter to Secretary of State Madeleine Albright, he vowed that any compromise that might bring an American citizen under the jurisdiction of a UN criminal court would be "dead on arrival" in the Senate. He declared that there should be no flexibility with respect to a U.S. veto over the court's power to prosecute U.S. citizens.[31] A week later, Helms again publicly encouraged the State Department to take aggressive actions to block the establishment of the ICC.

Helms's letter and public statements were the first warning shots. On March 31 and April 1, 1998, in Washington, D.C., Defense Department leaders held meetings with military attachés of more than one hundred countries. Their message was that an international criminal court could "target their own soldiers—particularly when acting as peace keepers—and subject them to frivolous or politically motivated investigations by a rogue prosecutor or an overzealous tribunal." It was by all accounts quite an unusual briefing for Pentagon officials. According to Frederick Smith, deputy assistant secretary of defense for International Security Affairs, "It was not lobbying; there was no arm-twisting—it was awareness raising."[32]

A contrasting take on the court's ability to prosecute appeared in the *Times of India*. Having read the State Department's comment that "the permanent court must not handcuff governments that take risks to promote peace and security," an Indian columnist considered the conduct of U.S. forces in the My Lai massacre in Vietnam and an alleged massacre of one thousand civilians by U.S. Army Rangers in Mogadishu, Somalia: "Shouldn't the ICC be allowed to prosecute those involved in such crimes? . . . Or, like the Security Council, will it become a victim of double standards?"[33] Going into the 1998 Rome meeting to draft the ICC statute, about forty-two so-called like-minded countries— including Canada, most European nations, and many countries in Africa, Asia, and Latin America—favored a stronger and more independent international court and prosecutor.[34] According to the *Economist*:

> After nearly four years of intense negotiations among some 120 countries, the effort to set up the world criminal court has run smack into the ambivalence that has always been felt by the world's biggest powers about international law: they are keen to have it applied to others in the name of world order, but loath to submit to restrictions on their own sovereignty.[35]

The Rome Conference

In June 1998 representatives from 162 nations gathered in Rome to see whether they could agree on the creation of a permanent international criminal court.[36] The five-week Rome Conference opened with four days of speeches, during which U.S. Ambassador to the United Nations Bill Richardson reiterated the U.S. position that the Security Council should control the work of the ICC by referring critical situations for investigation and by instructing countries to cooperate. The ultimate goal, he said, would be to create a court that "focuses on recognized atrocities of significant magnitude and thus enjoys near universal support."[37] At that time, the United States' position put it in the company of China, France, and Russia, three of the other permanent members of the Security Council; only the United Kingdom had come out in favor of a stronger and more independent court. On the other side with respect to the most critical issues, the group of like-minded countries had by then grown to about sixty members. They were especially intent on creating an independent prosecutor and a court with sufficient jurisdiction and authority to actually bring those who committed human rights crimes to account. More than two hundred accredited nongovernmental organizations monitored the conference. A coalition of these organizations had been working for years in the interest of creating a permanent court. The most prominent were Amnesty International, Human Rights Watch, and the European Law Students Association.

During the conference, an enormous amount of time was spent pursuing the elusive goal of consensus among the 162 nations. In part, consensus was sought because each nation had a single vote in the conference, which meant a simple majority vote would not take into account the relative size, power, or influence of individual countries. Hours were sometimes spent on one clause of one section of one article, with delegates from country after country making statements that usually were repetitive and often only seemed to serve the purpose of giving that delegate the chance to claim a few minutes at the microphone. The U.S. delegation worked hard to persuade its traditional allies to accept U.S. conditions for the treaty, especially during the final week of the conference. Indeed, the behind-the-scenes "buzz" was that the United States was actually threatening poor states with the loss of foreign aid and its NATO allies with a reduction of U.S. military support, including the withdrawal of troops.[38]

Motivated by Senator Helms's "dead on arrival" letter, throughout the conference the "U.S. delegation seemed increasingly gripped by a single overriding concern"—that no American could be tried before the court without the consent of the U.S. government.[39] Philippe Kirsch of Canada, chairman of the Committee of the Whole of the conference, noted about the U.S. delegation:

> It was amazing. Nothing could assuage them. . . . They seemed completely fixated on that Helms/Pentagon imperative—that there be explicit language in the Treaty guaranteeing that no Americans could ever fall under the Court's sway, even if the only way to accomplish that was going to be by the U.S. not joining the treaty. . . . Clearly, they had their instructions from back home—and very little room to maneuver.[40]

Most of the world's countries, however, were more willing than the United States to be subject to the international rule of law. Even the country's most powerful European allies, who had also participated in military "humanitarian" interventions, were far friendlier to the idea of the court than was the United States. The reasons for such differences were no doubt complex, but among them was the fact that since World War II European countries had been moving from the tradition of individual sovereignty toward "European" institutions transcending nationhood. Examples of this trend were the adoption of the European Convention on Human Rights (1950)—and the subsequent empowerment of a European Court of Human Rights—and the emergence of the Court of Justice of the European Union (EU) as a powerful force.

In the last days of the Rome Conference Ambassador Scheffer issued a public plea:

> We stand on the eve of the conference's conclusion without having found a solution. We fear that governments whose citizens make up at least two-thirds of the world's population [chiefly China and the United States] will find the emerging text of the treaty unacceptable. The world desperately needs this mechanism for international justice, but it must be a community, not a club.[41]

The final draft document for an international criminal court was distributed early on July 17 by Chairman Kirsch. It appeared to offer more to the sixty or so like-minded countries that favored a strong court than it did to the United States. The draft provided for obligatory jurisdiction of the court upon ratification of the treaty by a country for the crime of genocide, crimes against humanity, war crimes, and the crime of aggression. The United States was willing to accept obligatory jurisdiction only for the crime of genocide. Jurisdiction over war crimes was limited by a new draft article allowing states that signed the Rome Statute to opt out of the court's jurisdiction over war crimes for a period of seven years following the creation of the court. Consistent with its objective of blocking the creation of an institution that it could not control, or whose jurisdiction it could not veto, the United States sought a comprehensive opt-out provision that would allow it to be permanently exempt from the court's jurisdiction over war crimes. France agreed to support the draft proposal when the seven-year opt-out provision was added. The United Kingdom also supported the draft.

On July 17, the United States again voiced its opposition in the Committee of the Whole to a criminal tribunal beyond its control, when it offered an amendment to the proposal. India also offered amendments that would have made the use of nuclear weapons a war crime and that limited the power of the Security Council over the court. Norway, however, moved to table the proposed amendments, and its motions were adopted. The vote against taking up the U.S. amendment was 113–17. The United States could not even muster the support of its closest allies. In the final conference plenary session, the United States demanded a vote on the draft treaty. The Russian Federation joined France and the United Kingdom in voting for the statute, leaving China and the United States the only permanent Security Council members in opposition. Israel also voted against the draft, in part because it made the relocation of a civilian population in an occupied territory a war crime, a provision too close for its comfort. Iraq, Libya, Qatar, and Yemen also voted against the statute.

As the conference ended, the United States was clearly the big loser. The final vote was 120 countries for the treaty, 7 against, and 21 abstentions. As approved, the court would exercise its jurisdiction over individuals suspected of treaty crimes if the country where the alleged violation occurred or the country of which the accused was a national was a party to the treaty (Article 12). States would accept the jurisdiction of the court on a case-by-case basis. The United States strongly opposed these provisions because they might—as the United States had feared all along—subject American troops to prosecution for alleged crimes committed in countries that had accepted the jurisdiction of the court, without first requiring the consent of the U.S. government.

Most countries felt that there were sufficient safeguards in the treaty to address U.S. concerns. The new court would only take cases involving major human rights violations carried out as part of a plan, policy, or widespread practice, not actions by individuals acting on their own. The court would act only when the appropriate domestic jurisdictions were unable or unwilling to deal with alleged crimes themselves (the complementarity principle).

Early on, the United States had favored a proposal that would have charged the Security Council with referring cases to the court, in part so the U.S. veto in the council could be used to protect U.S. citizens from prosecution. Most countries, however, eventually supported the compromise put forth by Singapore that would allow the Security Council to defer a case for a period of twelve months, with the possibility of extension. The United States eventually accepted this proposal, a version of which was included in the final draft.

The final draft called for a prosecutor with independent power to investigate and initiate prosecutions, as well as for the initiation of cases by a state party or by referral of the Security Council. The United States had fought hard against this provision, but a strong and independent prosecutor was one of the fundamental requirements of the sixty or so like-minded countries. The draft statute did call for a court review panel that would have the power to reject cases arising from an abuse of prosecutorial power, but that safeguard was not enough to satisfy the United States.

The draft also provided for jurisdiction over internal armed conflicts, such as that in Bosnia, which most delegations, including the United States, believed to be absolutely essential for a credible international court. Furthermore, the draft included among war crimes and crimes against humanity the crimes of rape, sexual slavery, enforced prostitution, enforced pregnancy, and enforced sterilization. Aggression was made a treaty crime, but it was left to be defined at later preparatory meetings. This decision was a concession to the members of the Non-Aligned Movement, but the draft did not include the prohibition of nuclear weapons, which the movement also strongly supported. The draft also left out chemical and biological weapons, as a concession to several Arab countries.

The Rome Statute provided that when ratified by at least sixty nations, the new International Criminal Court would enter into force, to be located at The Hague, in the Netherlands, where the ad hoc tribunal for the former Yugoslavia also is located. By April 11, 2002, sixty-six countries had ratified the treaty, and July 1, 2002, was set as the date that the agreement would enter into force.

The rift between the United States and its major European allies over the creation of the court widened and deepened following the Rome Conference and the July 2002 entry into force of the ICC. As of March 2004, ninety-two countries had ratified the Rome Statute, including Afghanistan, Argentina, Australia, Austria, Belgium, Brazil, Canada, Denmark, Finland, France,

Germany, Greece, Hungary, Ireland, Italy, Luxembourg, the Netherlands, New Zealand, Nigeria, Norway, Poland, Portugal, the Republic of Korea, Romania, Serbia and Montenegro, Slovakia, Slovenia, South Africa, Spain, Sweden, Switzerland, and the United Kingdom.[42]

Although Europeans, like the Americans, put their troops in harm's way as peacekeepers in global hotspots, the general consensus among Europeans seems to be that the principle of complementarity protects them from unwanted or unwarranted international prosecution. U.S. government officials have been unwilling to put their trust in this principle. Thus the ICC has been added to a growing list of issues on which the United States and its European friends significantly disagree, among them U.S. dominance of NATO, the sizes and roles of tariffs and trade subsidies, U.S. exports to Europe, capital punishment in the United States, and U.S. withdrawal from the 1972 Anti-Ballistic Missile Treaty so the United States can develop a national missile defense system. Among the most recent differences of opinion have been the efforts of EU members to create a rapid-reaction military force independent of NATO and the opposition (led by France and Germany) to the U.S.-led war against Iraq. The latter had the added effect of creating divisions among EU governments and in some cases splits between official government positions for war and the will of the citizenry, as popular majorities across most of Europe opposed an attack.

Many of the institutional details of the ICC were not finalized at the Rome Conference. Follow-up PrepCom sessions in 2000 sought to complete the rules of evidence and procedure and the specifications for the elements of crimes recognized in principle by the Rome Statute. The United States had to sign the statute by December 31, 2000—the last day for nations to become signatories of the original treaty—in order to participate in future PrepCom meetings. On the last day of 2000, President Clinton instructed Ambassador Scheffer to sign the treaty on behalf of the United States. In a press release, Clinton noted that he still had concerns about "significant flaws" in the treaty, but he hoped that they could be overcome in subsequent negotiations before the court became a reality. He said it was important for the United States to sign the treaty to "reaffirm our strong support for international accountability. . . . With signature, we will be in a position to influence the evolution of the court. Without signature, we will not."[43]

Reaction to the U.S. signature was swift. Human rights groups praised it. Richard Dicker, associate counsel of Human Rights Watch, said Clinton's action had "offered the hope of justice to millions and millions of people around the world by signaling United States' support for the most important international court since the Nuremberg tribunal." On the other hand, Senator Helms warned that the president's "decision will not stand."[44] The incoming administration of George W. Bush also opposed the signature. In a May 6, 2002, letter from U.S. Under Secretary of State John Bolton to UN Secretary General Kofi Annan, the Bush administration formally declared that it would not submit the Rome Statute for Senate ratification and renounced any legal obligations arising from the previous administration's signing of the treaty.[45]

The ICC at the Turn of the Twenty-First Century

UN Secretary General Kofi Annan hailed the adoption of the Rome Statute as a "giant step forward."[46] One of the proponents of U.S. participation in the court has argued that

> America does not commit genocide, war crimes, or crimes against humanity. Nor do our NATO allies. . . . We thus have nothing to fear from the prosecution of these offenses, nothing to make us hesitate when the pleas of the victims of mass slaughter fill our television screens and their plight hounds our conscience.[47]

Furthermore, proponents have pointed out that should American troops cross the line, the principle of complementarity would protect them from international prosecution as long as the United States took action against them.[48] Nonetheless, others have disagreed. One opponent called the treaty "a pernicious and debilitating agreement, harmful to the national interests of the United States."[49] On July 23, 1998, Ambassador Scheffer spoke at a hearing before the Senate Committee on Foreign Relations and outlined the U.S. objections to the Rome Statute. The four main concerns of the United States were as follows:

- the fact that U.S. military personnel could be brought before the ICC prosecutor;
- the degree of Security Council control over prosecutions initiated by the ICC prosecutor;
- the ambiguity of the crimes over which the ICC would exercise jurisdiction, particularly the crime of aggression, which could conceivably extend to some U.S. troop deployments, and the alleged crime of settlement in an occupied territory, which would arguably implicate Israeli leaders for activities in the West Bank and the Gaza Strip; and
- the relationship between the ICC and domestic judicial processes.[50]

Not only did Republican senators Helms and Rod Grams of Minnesota praise Scheffer's remarks, but so did Democratic senators Joseph Biden of Delaware and Dianne Feinstein of California. Republicans and Democrats alike on the committee congratulated Scheffer's resolve to protect U.S. interests in Rome and expressed their contempt for the ICC as created by the Rome Statute.[51] At the hearing, Senator Helms made his position clear: the United States should block any organization of which it is a member from providing funding to the ICC; renegotiate its status of forces agreements and extradition treaties to prohibit treaty partners from surrendering U.S. nationals to the ICC; refuse to provide U.S. soldiers to regional and international peacekeeping operations when there is any possibility that they will come under the jurisdiction of the ICC; and never vote in the Security Council to refer a matter to the ICC.[52]

These concerns about protecting individual members of the U.S. armed forces may have been a stalking horse for another, broader concern. At the end of the hearing, "Helms picked off the examples defiantly[;] he was going to be damned if any so-called International Court was ever going to be reviewing the legality of the U.S. invasions of Panama or Grenada or of the bombing of Tripoli and to be holding any American presidents, defense secretaries, or generals to account."[53] Still, by early August 1998 more than twenty editorials and op-eds had run in major U.S. newspapers broadly supporting the creation of the ICC. These were written by a number of leaders of nongovernmental organizations, as well as by former president Jimmy Carter.[54] One of the treaty's defenders argued that the United States had managed to have powerful national security safeguards added to the treaty:

> First, Rome provides for "complementarity," the idea that the primary responsibility for enforcing the law of war must remain with each nation-state and with national military justice systems. . . . On another point of concern, the Rome Statute provides complete protection for sensitive national security information. . . . Isolated incidents of military misconduct that occur in wartime will not be prosecuted by the court. Rather, the tribunal is charged to focus on war crimes committed "as part of a plan or policy" or as part of "a large-scale commission of such crimes." . . . The Rome Statute also respects our bilateral treaty agreements protecting American troops stationed abroad against any attempted exercise of foreign criminal jurisdiction—the so-called Status of Forces Agreements.[55]

Countering the pro-ICC forces, on the op-ed page of the *Financial Times* Senator Helms wrote, "We must slay this monster. Voting against the International

Criminal Court is not enough. The US should try to bring it down."[56] Another opponent suggested the treaty's wording would have found the United States guilty of war crimes for the bombing campaigns against Germany and Japan during World War II.[57] Others raised the possibility of international prosecution for air strikes such as those against Libya in 1986 and Sudan in 1998.[58]

Controversy continued over who was to receive blame for genocide and other war crimes and what to do after such crimes had occurred. On June 14, 2000, Senator Helms introduced the American Servicemembers' Protection Act (S. 2726), which would prohibit U.S. officials from cooperating with the ICC. That same day, Majority Whip Tom DeLay, R-Texas, introduced the measure in the House of Representatives (H.R. 4654). It mandated that the president ensure that any Security Council resolution authorizing a peacekeeping operation exempt U.S. personnel from prosecution before the ICC. Additionally, it required the president to certify to Congress that U.S. personnel are immunized by each country participating in the operation. The bill proposed that no U.S. military assistance be provided to governments that are parties to the ICC (with the exception of the NATO allies and Israel), although the president could waive this provision. With these "big sticks," Senator Helms denounced "the ICC's bogus claim of jurisdiction over American citizens."[59]

In July 2000 a seven-member panel created by the Organization of African States issued a report blaming Belgium, France, the United States, the Catholic Church, and the UN Security Council for the 1994 slaughter of more than five hundred thousand Tutsis and moderate Hutus by more radical, xenophobic Hutus during the Rwandan civil war. Canadian panel member Stephen Lewis said the United States knew what was going on in Rwanda, but prevented the Security Council from deploying an effective force to stop it, because of the political fallout that ensued after eighteen Americans were killed in the Somalia intervention in October 1993. As Lewis said, "It's simply beyond belief that because of Somalia hundreds of thousands of Rwandans needlessly lost their lives. I don't know how Madeleine Albright lives with it."[60]

Despite the protection that complementarity offered the United States and other nations, Senator Helms wanted to leave nothing to chance. On November 29, 2000, his spokesman held a press conference at UN headquarters in New York. There he said Helms would make passage of the American Servicemembers' Protection Act a top priority in the Congress convening in January 2001. On that same day, a letter signed by a dozen former U.S. foreign policy officials was released, supporting Helms's bill; the letter claimed that U.S. world leadership "could be the first casualty" of the new ICC.[61] Among the signatories were former U.S. secretaries of state James Baker, Henry Kissinger, and George Shultz and former U.S. ambassador to the UN Jeane Kirkpatrick. As the writer James Carroll concluded in the *Boston Globe*, "That James Baker is a party to the Helms campaign signals that an incoming [George W.] Bush administration would prefer to be shackled by a xenophobic Congress than to be constrained by multilateral and equitable agreements with other nations."[62]

On July 12, 2002, shortly after the ICC entered into force and at the behest of the United States, the UN Security Council passed Resolution 1422, which restricted the ICC from commencing or proceeding with investigations or prosecutions of "peacekeepers" and other officials of states not then part of the ICC for a period of twelve months. The U.S. ambassador to the UN, John Negroponte, announced that the United States would continue to seek bilateral agreements exempting U.S. citizens from the jurisdiction of the ICC.[63]

On August 2, 2002, President Bush signed into law the American Service-members' Protection Act (ASPA), which had been included as part of the 2002 supplemental appropriations bill. It provided that the United States cut off military assistance to countries that had not signed bilateral agreements with the United States by July 1, 2003, ensuring that they would not surrender a U.S. citizen to the jurisdiction of the ICC or cooperate with the ICC in the apprehension or rendition of them. The law also, however, authorized the president to waive this provision on grounds of "national interest." The ASPA specifically exempted NATO members and a few other allies but potentially applied to more than fifty other countries. As of June 2003, forty-five countries had signed bilateral agreements; but few of these were adherents to the Rome Statute.[64]

In February 2003, the first eighteen ICC judges were elected, after as many as eighty-five state adherents to the Rome Statute cast thirty-three ballots. The judges took their seats on March 11, 2003, and on that same day career diplomat and attorney Philippe Kirsch of Canada, who had led the Rome Conference in 1998, was elected the first president of the ICC. On March 24, 2003, Luis Moreno Ocampo of Argentina was elected the first chief prosecutor of the ICC. Ocampo, a lawyer experienced in criminal and human rights law and anticorruption programs, participated in the 1980s in the prosecution of the Argentine military leaders alleged responsible for the Falklands War. He also served as president of the Latin American section of Transparency International.[65]

On July 1, 2003, the Bush administration announced its intention to cut off military aid to thirty-five countries that had failed to sign bilateral agreements. At the same time, it granted waivers for varying periods of time to twenty-two countries. As of May 2005, the State Department reported that one hundred bilateral agreements had been signed. However, by late July 2009, one hundred and ten countries had ratified the Rome Statute, including thirty African, thirteen Asian and Pacific, forty-one European, twenty-five Latin American and Caribbean, and one Middle Eastern state. Despite this impressive number of state ratifications, seven of the ten largest states by population—China, India, the United States, Indonesia, Pakistan, Bangladesh, and Russia—have not ratified the statute as of this writing, and Jordan is the only state in the conflict-prone Middle East to have ratified the statute. Thus states representing more than half of the world's population are still refusing to participate in the ICC.[66]

It is also notable that the first situations before the International Criminal Court come from Africa. The crimes involved include war crimes in the Democratic Republic of Congo (the conscription and employment of child soldiers); war crimes and crimes against humanity in Uganda (the use of child soldiers and the rape, assault, and murder of civilians); war crimes and crimes against humanity in the Central African Republic (rape, torture, murder, and pillaging); and war crimes, crimes against humanity, and genocide in Sudan (the death and destruction in Darfur). Twelve arrest warrants have been issued, but so far only four of those indicted are in custody, and no case has yet come to a conclusion.[67]

The most interesting case so far has been the 2009 indictment of Sudanese president Omar al-Bashir for war crimes and crimes against humanity.[68] A perceived legal technicality kept the crime of genocide from being added to the charges. In February 2010, the court reversed its prior interpretation that a genocide indictment was not possible, thereby opening the possibility that genocide charges could be added to the other two indictments.[69] Following these indictments, President al-Bashir traveled without incident to Egypt, Mauritania, Saudi Arabia, and Qatar, but he did not go to New York for the 2009 UN General Assembly meeting. Furthermore, he was asked not to attend international meetings in South Africa, Uganda, Nigeria, and Turkey so as not to put the host country on the spot.[70] Still, numerous state governments—not just other North African states but France as well—press the argument that pursuing his arrest is counterproductive to seeking his cooperation with peace negotiations and peacekeeping operations in Darfur. His case thus frames a fundamental quandary: What is more important, justice for specific victims or peace in the region?

So where does the United States stand regarding the ICC? In October 2008, John Bellinger, the legal adviser to the secretary of state, said at an international law society meeting that the fundamental concerns regarding the ICC had been remarkably consistent across three presidential administrations, and that— absent major political changes—it continued to be unlikely that the United States would ratify the Rome Statute. However, he added that the U.S. government shared the concerns of ICC supporters regarding impunity for serious war crimes and crimes against humanity. Thus the U.S. government adopted a more nuanced approach and was not trying to kill the ICC. Finally, he noted that the U.S. government was prepared to cooperate with ICC prosecutions in appropriate circumstances (Darfur being his cited example), and that it opposed an Article 16 UN Security Council resolution to defer the prosecution of Omar al-Bashir.

The election of Barack Obama to the presidency in 2008 signaled a shift in U.S. government policy in many areas, but that shift is not apparent regarding the ICC. Although a strong proponent of the rule of law, then-Senator Obama said on October 6, 2007:

> The United States has more troops deployed overseas than any other nation and those forces are bearing a disproportionate share of the burden in the protecting of Americans and preserving international security. Maximum protection for our servicemen and women should come with that increased exposure. Therefore, I will consult thoroughly with our military commanders and also examine the track record of the Court before reaching a decision on whether the U.S. should become a State Party to the ICC.[71]

Despite the oft-stated fears of malicious prosecution of U.S. military personnel, part of the unspoken U.S. opposition to the independent operation of the ICC may be the fear of indictments of senior U.S. governmental officials for a variety of war crimes.[72] Such fears may be real, but they may be slightly misplaced. The more likely source of such indictments would be other states' national courts acting on the basis of universal jurisdiction. In 1998 former Chilean general Augusto Pinochet was arrested in Britain on a Spanish indictment for crimes that occurred during his presidency. After being held for over a year, he was released because of health problems and never turned over to Spain. Actions taken by the U.S. government against suspects in the global war on terrorism raised the possibility of similar prosecutions of senior U.S. officials. In 2004 human rights groups sought prosecution in German courts of U.S. Defense Secretary Donald Rumsfeld for war crimes, but the prosecution was dismissed the next year. In 2006 prosecutions in Germany were sought not only against Rumsfeld but also against Director of Central Intelligence George

Tenet and Attorney General Alberto Gonzales for war crimes against detainees. Again, the prosecution was dismissed the following year.[73] In October 2007, several human rights groups filed a complaint in Paris charging Rumsfeld with authorizing torture, an action that was brought under the 1984 Convention against Torture (which has been ratified by both France and the United States).[74] However, the French case against Rumsfeld was dismissed in February 2008.[75] So while no prosecutions of high-level U.S. officials have taken place, the possibility exists that those who gave certain orders—for example, to aggressively interrogate (i.e., possibly torture) detainees—may be held liable at some future point in a court of law. That court may just not be the ICC.

Conclusion: The United States and International Law

Israeli diplomat Abba Eban once said international law was "the law which the wicked do not obey and the righteous do not enforce." Whether the United States has lined up on the side of the wicked or of the righteous in this case probably lies in the eye of the beholder. There is no question that U.S. political culture values the rule of law: Presidents George H. W. Bush and Bill Clinton saw reliance on international law as a mainstay of the post–cold war era. Clinton wanted to use international law to punish war criminals and those guilty of genocide and crimes against humanity, and he said so when he endorsed the creation of the ICC in his UN General Assembly address in September 1997. Yet by the time of the Rome Conference the following summer, U.S. diplomats were swimming against the international tide by trying to ensure some degree of U.S. control over the ICC or its prosecutor. The inability to prevail on this issue produced the final vote that placed the United States in the somewhat unusual company of China, Iraq, Israel, Libya, Qatar, and Yemen. What accounts for this seeming about-face? The answer is national interests in the form of sovereignty concerns in the U.S. Congress.

In 1946 prominent senators had ensured that the World Court would not act contrary to U.S. interests, as defined by the United States. Fifty-two years later congressional emphasis on U.S. national sovereignty at the expense of international law, the United Nations, and a host of nongovernmental organizations reappeared in the ICC case. Once powerful legislators staked out the priority of preserving U.S. sovereignty, the nature of policy making on the issue changed for the Clinton administration. The question was no longer whether the United States could agree with its friends and allies on an important issue in international law, but whether any set of procedures could be found that could ensure Senate ratification of such a treaty. Moreover, the George W. Bush administration was willing to work outside the norms of international law when perceived U.S. national interests seemed to dictate such a course of action. Only time will tell whether Barack Obama, a former law school professor, will be able to do three things: first, challenge the premise that the United States will only support international law when it coincides with narrowly drawn U.S. national interests; second, find ways to redefine U.S. national interests so they coincide with and support the ICC; and third, find ways to convince sufficient numbers of U.S. senators to ratify the Rome Statute.

Key Actors

George W. Bush President, rescinded the Clinton administration's signature of the Rome Statute, signed the American Servicemembers' Protection Act, and ordered the cutoff of military aid to thirty-five countries that refused to sign bilateral agreements protecting U.S. service personnel from possible prosecution by the ICC.

Bill Clinton President, unexpectedly ordered Ambassador David Scheffer to sign the ICC treaty so the United States could be considered an original signatory.

Jesse Helms Senator, R-N.C., the chairman of the Committee on Foreign Relations, was an early and active opponent of U.S. participation in the ICC.

Barack Obama Senator, D-Ill., endorsed the premise that the U.S. military deserved some form of protection from an aggressive or irresponsible ICC prosecutor.

David Scheffer Ambassador-at-large for war crimes, led the U.S. effort to modify the ICC treaty so the United States would have some control over the court's future actions.

Notes

1. John T. Rourke, Ralph G. Carter, and Mark A. Boyer, *Making American Foreign Policy,* 2nd ed. (Guilford, Conn.: Brown and Benchmark, 1996), 87.

2. Sir Arnold Duncan McNair, *The Development of International Justice* (New York: New York University Press, 1954), 4.

3. George Schwarzenberger, *International Law, as Applied by International Courts and Tribunals* (London: Stevens and Sons, 1986), 4:138.

4. Ian Brownlie, *Basic Documents in International Law,* 4th ed. (Oxford: Clarendon Press, 1995), 446. Reservations are legal statements of the conditions under which parties will agree to a treaty. Often during a debate over the ratification of a treaty, states

will declare in advance certain circumstances under which they say a treaty will not apply to them or their actions. Accepting these conditions is the political cost of getting that state to agree to the treaty. "Obligatory jurisdiction" means that states are obliged to obey a court's jurisdiction. With obligatory jurisdiction, the states cannot deny that a court has jurisdiction in a case or matter. Through reservations, states can set the terms and conditions under which they will accept a court's jurisdiction.

5. M. Cherif Bassiouni, "From Versailles to Rwanda in Seventy-Five Years: The Need to Establish a Permanent International Criminal Court," *Harvard Human Rights Journal* 10 (1997): 11–62; Gerhard von Glahn, *Law among Nations: An Introduction to Public International Law* (New York: Macmillan, 1992), 878.

6. Von Glahn, *Law among Nations,* 880.

7. John E. Findling, ed., *Dictionary of American Diplomatic History,* 2nd ed. (New York: Greenwood Press, 1989), 260.

8. Bassiouni, "From Versailles to Rwanda," 34.

9. Findling, *Dictionary of American Diplomatic History,* 259.

10. Von Glahn, *Law among Nations,* 354–357.

11. Michael P. Scharf, *Balkan Justice: The Story behind the First International War Crimes Trial since Nuremberg* (Durham, N.C.: Carolina Academic Press, 1997), 13–15.

12. *Congressional Record,* August 1, 1946, 10618.

13. Von Glahn, *Law among Nations,* 615–616.

14. *Congress and the Nation,* vol. 1, *1945–1964* (Washington, D.C.: Congressional Quarterly, 1965).

15. John T. Rourke, Ralph G. Carter, and Mark A. Boyer, *Making American Foreign Policy* (Guilford, Conn.: Dushkin Publishing Group, 1994), 209–210.

16. Von Glahn, *Law among Nations,* 192.

17. Scharf, *Balkan Justice,* 15.

18. Bassiouni, "From Versailles to Rwanda," 55–56.

19. Ibid., 43.

20. Ibid., 46–47.

21. See the Rome Conference/PrepCom document at www.un.org/law/icc/ prepcomm/ prepfra.htm.

22. Anne-Marie Slaughter, "Memorandum to the President," in *Toward an International Criminal Court?,* ed. Alton Frye (New York: Council on Foreign Relations, 1999), 7.

23. See the Rome Conference/PrepCom document.

24. James Bone, "U.S. Seeks to Limit War Crimes Court," *Times* [London], March 30, 1998.

25. More information on these issues can be found at the Web site of the Coalition for the International Criminal Court, www.iccnow.org.

26. Human Rights Watch, "Justice in the Balance: Recommendations for an Independent and Effective International Criminal Court," 1998, www.hrw.org/reports98/icc.

27. Jimmy Carter, "For an International Criminal Court," *New Perspectives Quarterly* 10 (1997): 52–53.

28. David Scheffer, "An International Criminal Court: The Challenge of Enforcing International Humanitarian Law," address to the Southern California Working Group on the International Criminal Court, February 26, 1998, www.unausa.org/issues/ scheffer.asp.

29. Agence France-Presse, "Paris, Washington in Agreement on UN Genocide Court," April 4, 1998.

30. John R. Bolton, "Why an International Court Won't Work," *Wall Street Journal,* March 30, 1998; John M. Goshko, "A Shift on Role of UN Court? Envoy Suggests U.S. May Alter Demands on Proposed Tribunal," *Washington Post,* March 18, 1998; Barbara Crossette, "U.S. Budges at U.N. Talks on a Permanent War-Crimes Court," *New York Times,* March 18, 1998.

31. Senate Committee on Foreign Relations, "Helms Declares UN Criminal Court 'Dead on Arrival' without U.S. Veto," press release, March 26, 1998.

32. Eric Schmitt, "Pentagon Battles Plans for International War Crimes," *New York Times,* April 14, 1998.

33. Siddharth Varadarajan, "Imperial Impunity: U.S. Hampers World Criminal Court Plan," *Times of India,* April 23, 1998.

34. Alessandra Stanley, "Conference Opens on Creating Court to Try War Crimes," *New York Times,* June 15, 1998, A1.

35. "A New World Court," *The Economist,* June 13–19, 1998, 16.

36. Bertram S. Brown, "The Statute of the ICC: Past, Present, and Future," in *The United States and the International Criminal Court: National Security and International Law,* ed. Sarah B. Sewall and Carl Kaysen (Lanham, Md.: Rowman and Littlefield, 2000), 62. Donald Jackson was an accredited correspondent at the Rome Conference. Statements not otherwise attributed in this section are based either on direct observation or on contemporaneous conversations with conference participants, nongovernmental organization representatives, or journalists.

37. UN press release, L/ROM/11, June 17, 1998.

38. Alessandra Stanley, "U.S. Presses Allies to Rein in Proposed War Crimes Court," *New York Times,* July 15, 1998.

39. Lawrence Weschler, "Exceptional Cases in Rome: The United States and the Struggle for an ICC," in Sewall and Kaysen, *The United States and the International Criminal Court,* 91.

40. Ibid., 105.

41. David Scheffer, press release distributed at the conference, July 15, 1998.

42. Coalition for the International Criminal Court, *ICC Update,* October 2003, www.iccnow.org/publications/update.html.

43. Steven Lee Myers, "U.S. Signs Treaty for World Court to Try Atrocities," *New York Times,* January 1, 2001.

44. "War Crime Pact OK'd by Clinton," *Dallas Morning News,* January 1, 2001, 10A.

45. Coalition for the International Criminal Court, *ICC Monitor,* September 2002, www.iccnow.org/publications/monitor.html.

46. "Permanent War Crimes Court Approved," *New York Times,* July 18, 1998.

47. Kenneth Roth, "Speech One: Endorse the International Criminal Court," in Frye, *Toward an International Criminal Court?,* 31–32.

48. Ibid., 31.

49. John Bolton, "Speech Two: Reject and Oppose the International Criminal Court," in Frye, *Toward an International Criminal Court?,* 37.

50. Slaughter, "Memorandum to the President," 8.

51. Weschler, "Exceptional Cases in Rome," 110.

52. Michael Scharf, "Rome Diplomatic Conference for an International Criminal Court," *ASIL Insight,* June 1998, www.asil.org/insights/insigh20.htm.

53. Weschler, "Exceptional Cases in Rome," 111.

54. For example, see the op-eds in the *Los Angeles Times,* July 17, 1998, B-9; *New York Times,* June 14, 1998, WK14; and *Washington Post,* May 2, 1998, A17; May 13, 1998, A17; May 27, 1998, A-17.

55. Ruth Wedgwood, "Speech Three: Improve the International Criminal Court," in Frye, *Toward an International Criminal Court?,* 63–64.

56. "Personal View: Jesse Helms," *Financial Times,* July 31, 1998.

57. Bolton, "Speech Two: Reject and Oppose the International Criminal Court," 39–40.

58. William L. Nash, "The ICC and the Deployment of U.S. Armed Forces," in Sewall and Kaysen, *The United States and the International Criminal Court,* 156.

59. Coalition for the International Criminal Court, August 29, 2000, www.cicclegal @iccnow.org; United Nations Association–USA, June 20, 2000, www.unausa.org/ dc/ info/dc062000; http://frwebgate.access.gpo/cgi_bin/getdoc.cgi?dbname=107_cong _ public_laws&docid=f:publ206.107.

60. "U.S., Others Blamed for Not Halting Slaughter in Rwanda," *Dallas Morning News,* July 8, 2000, 21A.

61. Myers, "U.S. Signs Treaty for World Court to Try Atrocities."

62. James Carroll, "How Helms Is Sparking a Real Crisis," *Boston Globe,* December 5, 2000, A23.

63. Coalition for the International Criminal Court, *ICC Monitor,* September 2002.

64. Ibid.

65. Coalition for the International Criminal Court, *ICC Monitor,* April 2003, www .iccnow.org/publications/monitor.html.

66. Coalition for the International Criminal Court, www.iccnow.org/documents/ RATIFICATIONSbyRegion_21_July_20091.pdf (accessed January 18, 2010).

67. Coalition for the International Criminal Court, www.iccnow.org/? mod=casessituations (accessed January 18, 2010).

68. International Criminal Court, www.icc-cpi.int/press/pressreleases/406.html (accessed September 30, 2008). "On 14 July 2008, the Prosecutor Luis Moreno-Ocampo, requested Pre-Trial Chamber I to issue an arrest warrant for Omar Hassan Ahmad al-Bashir in the Darfur situation in Sudan. In his Application, the Prosecutor stated that there are reasonable grounds to believe that al-Bashir bears criminal responsibility for genocide, crimes and war crimes committed in Darfur in the past five years. The Application lists ten counts, and alleges among other things that al-Bashir master-minded and implemented a plan to destroy in substantial part the Fur, Masalit and Zaghawa groups, on account of their ethnicity." International Criminal Court, www .iccnow.org/?mod=darfur (accessed September 30, 2008).

69. "ICC Overturns Decision to Exclude Genocide Charges in Al-Bashir Arrest Warrant," www.iccnow.org (accessed February 3, 2010).

70. Marlise Simons, "Sudan's Leader May Be Accused of Genocide," *New York Times,* February 4, 2010, A10.

71. Citizens for Global Solutions, http://globalsolutions.org/08orbust/ quotes/2007/10/31/quote484 (accessed July 24, 2008).

72. While there are many new books on the policies regarding interrogation tech-niques embraced by the Bush administration, two notable ones are Philippe Sands's

Torture Team: Rumsfeld's Memo and the Betrayal of American Values (New York: Palgrave Macmillan, 2008), and Jane Mayer's *The Dark Side: The Inside Story of How the War on Terror Turned into a War on American Ideals* (New York: Doubleday, 2008).

73. *Time,* November 10, 2006, www.time.com/printout/0,8816,1557842,00.html (accessed July 25, 2008).

74. Center for Constitutional Rights, "Donald Rumsfeld Charged with Torture during Trip to France," http:ccrjustice.org/newsroom/press-releases/Donald-rumsfeld-charged-torture-during-trip-france (accessed July 28, 2008).

75. According to the Center for Constitutional Rights, the case was dismissed at the suggestion of the French Ministry of Justice, even though Rumsfeld was at the time a private citizen on a personal visit in France. See "Open Letter Submitted to French Minister of Justice in Rumsfeld Torture Case," www.ccrjustice.org/files/OpenLetter KouchnerDatiFinal.pdf (accessed July 28, 2008).

15 The Rights of Detainees: Determining the Limits of Law

Linda Cornett and Mark Gibney

Before You Begin

1. Why is there so much political contention over the rights of detainees held in connection with the war on terrorism?

2. Why, and on what basis, did the administration of George W. Bush act so aggressively to assert executive privilege in defining the rights of detainees in its war on terrorism?

3. Why, and on what basis, have critics challenged the executive branch's authority to define the rights of detainees without "interference" from Congress or the judiciary?

4. Is the war on terrorism equivalent to other wars—such as World War II or the Vietnam War—that the United States has fought? Does it justify the president's claims to exceptional war powers and military jurisdiction over detainees, or is the "war on terrorism" better understood rhetorically, like the "war on drugs" or the "war on poverty," and better fought in the criminal court system, as with the Oklahoma City bombings?

5. How does the separation of powers play out in this case?

6. What deference, if any, should the courts show the president in executing the war on terrorism? What would constitute the "end of hostilities" in this war and mark the expiration of the president's "war powers"?

7. What role did such nongovernmental organizations as the Center for National Security Studies play in defining the rights of detainees?

8. What role have the news media played in shaping the political controversies surrounding the detainees? Should media outlets have published the classified materials leaked to them, in the interest of transparent government and informed debate?

Introduction: Responding to Terrorism

On September 11, 2001, members of the al Qaeda network hijacked four commercial airliners. Two were flown into the World Trade Center towers in New York, one dived into the Pentagon outside Washington, D.C., and one crashed in a field in Pennsylvania after passengers attempted to wrest control of the plane from the hijackers. The attacks killed approximately three thousand people, unsettled the economy, and shook Americans' sense of security. Shortly thereafter, President George W. Bush promised that the United States would "direct every resource at [its] command, every means of diplomacy, every tool of intelligence, every instrument of law enforcement, every financial influence, and every weapon of war to the disruption and to the defeat of the global terror network . . . before they strike [again]."[1] Under the assumption that extraordinary times call for extraordinary measures, the administration set out to expand its capabilities to execute what it called the "war on terrorism."

On September 14 the president declared a national emergency and requested that Congress give the administration the authority and tools to act decisively on all fronts of this new war.[2] Four days later, Congress responded to Bush's call with S.J. Res. 23, granting the executive branch broad authority to act against those responsible for the attacks of September 11 and to act to prevent future attacks, which the administration interpreted as the authority to combat terrorism whenever and wherever the threat arose. A short four weeks later, on October 24, Congress passed the USA PATRIOT Act—formally the Uniting and Strengthening America by Providing Appropriate Tools Required to Intercept and Obstruct Terrorism Act—to enhance the executive branch's law enforcement and intelligence-gathering capabilities, as well as its authority. Although it is multifaceted, the primary thrust of the act was to broaden the power of executive agencies to define, investigate, detain, and punish terror suspects with lower thresholds of evidence and less judicial oversight.

The administration moved equally aggressively in the international arena. On September 21, 2001, in a nationally televised address before Congress, Bush demanded that the Taliban government in Afghanistan immediately and unconditionally surrender any and all al Qaeda members on its soil, dismantle al Qaeda training camps, and give the United States unfettered access to suspected al Qaeda facilities. When this request was rebuffed, on October 7 the United States initiated a military campaign against Afghanistan, aided by Afghan forces of the Northern Alliance, to depose the Taliban government and root out al Qaeda. On March 19, 2003, the Bush administration carried its war on terrorism to Iraq, largely based on the claim that Iraq possessed weapons of mass destruction. The consequences of the administration's actions have been many and complex; however, one of the most immediate effects of the executive's expanded law enforcement, intelligence, and military efforts and capabilities has been a dramatic expansion in the number and variety of people detained by the government. The nature of these detentions raises the question: What legal rights do detainees in the war on terrorism have? What follows is a depiction of the continuing struggle to answer that question.

Background: Detainees in the War on Terrorism

Detainee, by definition, refers to "any person deprived of personal liberty except as a result of conviction for an offense."[3] The rights of detainees are intrinsically important in a democracy that has traditionally privileged liberty above virtually all other values. The rules governing the state's authority to deprive individuals of their liberty are a central theme in the U.S. Constitution. In addressing issues related to detainees, the Court of Appeals for the Fourth Circuit noted in January 2003 that, indeed, the "Constitution is suffused with concern about how the state will wield its awesome power of forcible restraint. And this preoccupation was not accidental. Our forebears recognized that the power to detain could easily become destructive 'if exerted without check or control.' "[4] The Bush administration's war on terrorism has significantly expanded the number and variety of detainees under the authority of the U.S. government to include the September 11 detainees; foreign "enemy combatants" at Guantánamo Bay, Cuba; prisoners held in American-run prisons in Iraq and Afghanistan; and finally, foreign nationals who have been detained and interrogated as part of a policy known as "extraordinary rendition." An examination of some of the controversies surrounding the rights of detainees brings into stark relief a number of broader, enduring debates about the appropriate balance between national security and civil liberty; the relationship between national interest and international law; and the responsibilities of each of the branches of government in balancing competing interests and values in the making of national security policy.

September 11 Detainees

In the months following the September 11 attacks, U.S. authorities detained approximately twelve hundred foreign nationals, most on visa violations.[5] Many were arrested by the Immigration and Naturalization Service at the direction of Attorney General John Ashcroft and detained as "special interest cases." Some were held for days, weeks, and even months without being charged with a crime. All were denied the opportunity to post bond and given

Timeline

The Rights of Detainees

September 11, 2001 | Al Qaeda members hijack commercial airliners and crash them into the World Trade Center towers and the Pentagon. One plane believed destined for Washington, D.C., crashes in rural Pennsylvania.

September 12, 2001 | The Justice Department begins using federal immigration laws to detain aliens suspected of having ties to the September 11 attacks or connections to terrorism, or who are encountered during the course of an investigation conducted by the Federal Bureau of Investigation.

September 14, 2001 | President George W. Bush declares a state of emergency and vows to devote the full resources of the United States to the "war on terrorism."

September 18, 2001 | Congress passes S.J. Res. 23, "Authorizing Use of United States Armed Forces against Those Responsible for Recent Attacks against the United States."

October 7, 2001 | The United States attacks Afghanistan to overthrow the Taliban government and root out al Qaeda.

October 24, 2001 | Congress passes the USA PATRIOT Act, expanding the executive branch's intelligence-gathering and law enforcement powers.

December 6, 2001 | A broad coalition, led by the Center for National Security Studies, files a lawsuit under the Freedom of Information Act to compel the U.S. government to release information about September 11 detainees.

January 11, 2002 | The Defense Department begins transporting prisoners captured in the course of the war in Afghanistan to U.S. bases in Cuba. Among the prisoners is Yaser Esam Hamdi, a U.S. citizen.

(continued)

Timeline *(continued)*

The Rights of Detainees

January–February 2002	Memoranda from the White House counsel and Justice Department lawyers argue that the prisoners taken in Afghanistan do not qualify for protections under the Geneva Conventions. State Department lawyers strongly dissent. The White House announces that although the prisoners do not merit these legal protections, the Geneva Conventions would govern the actions of U.S. military personnel toward them and in Afghanistan.
February 19, 2002	In *Rasul et al. v. Bush,* the Center for Constitutional Rights files a writ of habeas corpus in the U.S. District Court for the District of Columbia on behalf of Shafiq Rasul and other foreign nationals held at Guantánamo Bay.
March 3, 2002	The U.S. District Court for the District of Columbia dismisses *Rasul* and other Guantánamo Bay suits for lack of jurisdiction. The case is appealed.
May 8, 2002	José Padilla, a U.S. citizen, is arrested as he enters the country at Chicago's O'Hare International Airport. He is detained as a material witness in the September 11 investigations.
June 9–11, 2002	Padilla is designated an "enemy combatant" by order of Bush and is transferred from the U.S. criminal justice system to a navy brig in South Carolina. Lawyers for Padilla and Hamdi file petitions for a writ of habeas corpus in the U.S District Court for the Eastern District of Virginia.
August 2, 2002	Judge Gladys Kessler of the U.S. District Court for the District of Columbia orders the Justice Department to release the names of the September 11 detainees and their attorneys but allows the department to keep other details of their cases secret.
October 2, 2002	Congress passes a joint resolution authorizing the use of U.S. armed forces against Iraq.

January 8, 2003	The U.S. Court of Appeals for the Fourth Circuit overturns the lower court finding in *Hamdi v. Rumsfeld* and rules that the president can designate U.S. citizens enemy combatants and hold them without access to counsel, if the president believes a person's behavior constitutes a threat to national security. The case is appealed to the U.S. Supreme Court.
March 19, 2003	The United States attacks Iraq based on Bush administration claims that Iraq possesses weapons of mass destruction and maintains ties with terrorists who might use such weapons against the United States.
June 17, 2003	The U.S. Court of Appeals for the District of Columbia accepts the Bush administration's contention that "disclosure of even one name could endanger national security" and reverses the lower court ruling requiring the government to release limited information about the September 11 detainees. The U.S. Supreme Court declines, without explanation, to take up the case on appeal.
April 5, 2004	The Center for Constitutional Rights directly files two habeas corpus briefs with the Supreme Court and one in district court on behalf of Rasul and his coplaintiffs.
April 28, 2004	The Supreme Court begins hearing oral arguments in *Hamdi v. Rumsfeld, Rumsfeld v. Padilla,* and *Rasul et al. v. Bush.*
June 28, 2004	The Supreme Court hands down rulings in *Hamdi v. Rumsfeld* and *Rasul et al. v. Bush* that essentially affirm the rights of detainees to due process before a neutral judge to challenge their detention as enemy combatants. The Court rejects Padilla's petition for due process on a technicality.
October 11, 2004	Hamdi is released from U.S. custody and flown to Saudi Arabia.
December 30, 2005	Congress passes the Detainee Treatment Act, which drastically curtails the courts' habeas corpus jurisdiction over detentions at Guantánamo.

(continued)

Timeline *(continued)*

The Rights of Detainees

June 29, 2006	In its decision in *Hamdan v. Rumsfeld,* the Supreme Court strikes down the military commissions President Bush established to try suspected members of al Qaeda.
September 28, 2006	Congress passes the Military Commissions Act, which provides statutory authorization for military commission trials for Guantánamo Bay detainees and eliminates judicial jurisdiction, effectively stripping detainees of the right to file habeas corpus petitions in federal court.
June 18, 2008	In its decision in *Boumediene v. Bush*, the U.S. Supreme Court strikes down the Military Commissions Act, holding that detainees have a constitutional right to habeas protection.

very limited opportunities to communicate with family members or seek legal counsel. The government refused even to release their names, arguing that disclosing such information "would give terrorists a virtual roadmap to [the government's] investigation that could allow terrorists to chart a potentially deadly detour around [its] efforts."[6] Ashcroft further directed chief immigration judge Michael Creppy to close proceedings in deportation hearings of the special interest cases, a policy later ruled unconstitutional by the Court of Appeals for the Sixth Circuit. A broad coalition of civil liberties advocates, led by the Center for National Security Studies, sought to compel the Justice Department to release information about the detainees under the Freedom of Information Act (FOIA). In August 2002, Judge Gladys Kessler of the U.S. District Court for the District of Columbia agreed that although the government's national security concerns were legitimate, "the public's interest in learning the identity of those arrested and detained is essential to verifying whether the government is operating within the bounds of the law."[7] The judge ordered the Justice Department to release the names of the detainees and their attorneys, but allowed the department to keep the details of their cases secret.

In June 2003, the U.S. Court of Appeals for the District of Columbia overturned that decision on appeal, accepting the administration's contention that "disclosure of even one name could endanger national security,"[8] and in general deferring to the executive on questions of national security. The court asserted that "when government officials tell the court that disclosing the names of the detainees will produce harm, it is abundantly clear that the government's top counterterrorism officials are well suited to make this predictive judgment. Conversely, the judiciary is in an extremely poor position to second guess the government's views in the field of national security."[9] The U.S. Supreme Court declined, without explanation, to take up the case on appeal.

The government never charged any of the September 11 detainees with terror-related crimes, and most of them have been released or deported. Regardless, the USA PATRIOT Act substantially increased the Justice Department's authority to detain noncitizens without charge or counsel and, in fact, prescribes mandatory detention for "certified" aliens—that is, people whom the attorney general "has reasonable grounds to believe" represent a security threat or are found by the attorney general and the secretary of state to associate with "foreign terrorist organizations" to commit, incite, prepare, plan, gather information on, or provide material support for, terrorist activities.[10] The legislation also explicitly limits judicial oversight of the executive branch's decisions, but it allows detainees to petition the attorney general for a reconsideration of their status every six months.

Critics warned that the administration's increasingly broad authority to secretly arrest and detain terror suspects is a dangerous precedent and provides opportunities for abuse. An internal Justice Department investigation by Inspector General Glenn Fine seemed to lend credence to those fears. In April 2003, Fine reported "significant problems" with the treatment of the September 11 detainees. For example, while recognizing that the Justice Department was operating under extremely difficult circumstances, he charged that the Federal Bureau of Investigation (FBI) in New York had made too little effort to distinguish between aliens who might have knowledge of terrorist threats and aliens encountered coincidentally, resulting in the detention of minor visa violators under very restrictive conditions. The report decried the FBI's "hold-until-cleared" and blanket "no bond" policies, which kept many of these detainees in confinement for extended periods. Fine also found evidence of a disturbing pattern of physical and verbal abuse by some correctional officers.[11]

The war in Afghanistan produced another category of detainee: enemy combatant. Beginning January 11, 2002, the military started transferring several hundred prisoners to an interrogation facility, dubbed "Camp X-Ray," at Guantánamo Bay, Cuba. Arguing that these detainees represent the "worst of the worst," General Richard B. Myers, chairman of the Joint Chiefs of Staff, described the Guantánamo Bay detainees as "people who would gnaw through hydraulic lines at the back of a C-17 to bring it down."[12] Many of these inmates, some of whom have now been detained for years, were subjected to constant interrogation, surveillance, and severe restrictions on their physical movements. Although the great majority were captured in Afghanistan during or immediately following hostilities there, a sizable number arrived after being turned over to the United States by other governments based on suspected ties to al Qaeda.[13] As of January 2010, approximately 200 men remained imprisoned at Guantánamo. The remainder (about 560) have been released or transferred to other countries (usually to their home governments).[14]

The Bush administration maintained that the detainees at Guantánamo Bay should not have access to U.S. courts or constitutional protections. It based its argument on the grounds that the facility where the detainees were being held is outside the territorial boundaries of the United States and that constitutional protections do not apply extraterritorially. Memos written by Deputy Assistant Attorneys General Patrick Philbin and John Yoo laid out the administration's view. As one former administration lawyer later described it, the base at Guantánamo Bay "existed in a legal twilight zone"—or "the legal equivalent of outer space."[15] Moreover, the government argued, the unprecedented threat that global terrorist networks posed required a suspension of the usual rules governing detainees. Holding prisoners without rights, Solicitor General Theodore Olson argued before the Supreme Court, "serves the vital objectives of preventing combatants from continuing to aid our enemies and gathering intelligence to further the overall war effort."[16]

The Bush administration also claimed exemption from judicial oversight based on the president's powers as commander in chief. The U.S. government classified all of the detainees as "enemy combatants" and steadfastly maintained that only the president can determine who is an enemy combatant and the conditions under which such detainees will be held. In a reply brief in *Rasul et al. v. Bush,* the case challenging the Guantánamo Bay detentions, the government spelled out its position:

The detained petitioners are aliens held abroad. Accordingly, none of their claims—including their premature challenges to the Military Order—are within the subject matter jurisdiction of this Court, or *any* United States court. . . . The extraordinary circumstances in which this action arises and the particular relief that petitioners seek implicate core political questions about the conduct of the war on terrorism that the Constitution leaves to the Commander-in-Chief.[17]

In effect, the administration argued that the chief executive has total discretion over the designation of enemy combatants, that it can hold enemy combatants without benefit of counsel, and with no right to challenge their detention until the "end of hostilities." Moreover, the administration argued that its judgments could not be second-guessed by the judiciary. Allowing detainees access to the federal courts, Olson argued before the Supreme Court, would "place the federal courts in the unprecedented position of micromanaging the executive's handling of captured enemy combatants from a distant zone."[18]

In addition to the position that the Guantánamo detainees were without protection under domestic law, the Bush administration also maintained that as enemy combatants, they were not protected under the Geneva Conventions. In early 2002, Secretary of State Colin Powell and State Department attorneys argued within the administration that the case of each detainee would need to be individually reviewed to determine if the conventions applied to that person. A January 9, 2002, memo from the Justice Department's Office of Legal Counsel argued, however, that the Geneva Conventions did not apply to the detainees. It also stated that the detainees were not covered by the 1996 War Crimes Act, a measure specifying the conditions under which U.S. citizens, including U.S. officials, can be prosecuted for war crimes. In a January 25, 2002, memo, White House Counsel Alberto Gonzales agreed with the Justice Department's interpretation that the Geneva Conventions (as well as the War Crimes Act) did not apply to al Qaeda or Taliban detainees. Following protests by Secretary Powell and his primary legal aide, William Howard Taft IV, the White House responded with a compromise position in February 2002: although the protection of the Geneva Conventions did not apply to captured al Qaeda and Taliban fighters, the United States would adhere to the conventions in its conduct of the war in Afghanistan "to the extent appropriate and consistent with military necessity."[19] Regardless, the government did hold out the promise that at least some of the Guantánamo Bay detainees would receive trials before a military tribunal, although at the same time it maintained that it would not be bound to release any detainees even if the tribunal acquitted any of them.

The conditions under which the Guantánamo detainees were held and interrogated attracted renewed attention when gross abuses of detainees in Iraq's Abu Ghraib prison—where the Geneva Conventions ostensibly *did* apply—came to light in early 2004. Investigations into the Iraqi prisoner abuse scandal suggested that more aggressive interrogation techniques that Defense Secretary Donald Rumsfeld had approved for use at Guantánamo Bay were "exported" to Iraq when officials became frustrated by the paltry quantity and quality of intelligence being generated during a sustained Iraqi insurgency.[20] Of particular interest were a set of interrogation rules developed under Major General Geoffrey Miller that were first employed in Guantánamo Bay but later brought to Iraq.[21] The " '72-point matrix for stress and duress' . . . laid out the types of coercion and the escalating levels at which they could be applied. These included the use of harsh heat or cold; withholding food; hooding for days at a time; naked isolation in cold, dark cells for more than 30 days; and threatening (but not biting) by dogs. It also permitted limited use of 'stress positions' designed to subject detainees to rising levels of pain."[22] The Red Cross issued several reports to U.S. military authorities warning of the conditions at the Guantánamo Bay prison. In addition to potential abuses, the Red Cross specifically stated that the indeterminate nature of the detentions at Guantánamo was taking a heavy psychological toll on detainees and had resulted in thirty suicide attempts since the prison opened.[23]

Subsequent studies revealed that the purported danger and intelligence value of the Guantánamo detainees may have been systematically overstated by the Bush administration. According to the *New York Times*:

> In interviews, dozens of high-level military, intelligence, and law-enforcement officials in the United States, Europe, and the Middle East said that contrary to the repeated assertions of senior administration officials, none of the detainees at the United States Naval Base at Guantanamo Bay ranked as leaders or senior operatives of Al Qaeda. They said only a relative handful—some put the number at about a dozen, others more than two dozen—were sworn Qaeda members or other militants able to elucidate the organization's inner workings. While some Guantanamo intelligence has aided terrorism investigations, none of it has enabled intelligence or law-enforcement services to foil imminent attacks, the officials said.[24]

The article further charged that based on a top-secret study conducted at Guantánamo by the Central Intelligence Agency (CIA), the administration knew as early as September 2002 that "many of the accused terrorists appeared to be low-level recruits who went to Afghanistan to support the Taliban or even innocent men swept up in the chaos of the war."[25]

Abu Ghraib and the Issue of Torture

Another category of detainees consists of those held at various U.S.-run military facilities in Iraq and Afghanistan, where it is estimated that tens of thousands have been incarcerated for various periods of time during the course of both wars. However, there is one name that stands out from all of these: Abu Ghraib. In an April 28, 2004, broadcast of *60 Minutes II*, the entire world was shown the despicable and illegal treatment carried out against detainees at the Abu Ghraib prison in Iraq. The Bush administration immediately protested that the acts depicted were nothing more than the work of a few "bad apples" and vigorously denied that the abuses had deeper roots in policy. Faced with growing public criticism, Bush issued an apology for these atrocities a few days later. After meeting privately with King Abdullah II of Jordan, President Bush told a group of reporters and journalists what he had told the king: "I told him I was sorry for the humiliation suffered by Iraqi prisoners and the humiliation by their families."[26] There followed immediately a veritable flood of apologies from members of his cabinet, including Secretary Powell, national security adviser Condoleezza Rice, and Secretary Rumsfeld.

As the scandal unfolded and investigations into its causes strengthened, particularly in Congress, a paper trail began to emerge tracing the evolution of Bush administration policies regarding the status and treatment of detainees. A number of legal memoranda from Justice Department lawyers and the White House counsel surfaced that interpreted the limitations on the detention and interrogation of prisoners in the war on terrorism extremely narrowly. Indeed, in a leaked memo dated January 25, 2003, White House Counsel Alberto Gonzales advised the president on how to preserve the government's flexibility in the detention and interrogation of suspects:

> As you have said, the war on terrorism is a new kind of war. . . . The nature of the war places a high premium on other factors, such as the ability to obtain information from captured terrorists and their sponsors in order to avoid further atrocities against American civilians, and the need to try terrorists for war crimes such as wantonly killing civilians. In my judgment, this new paradigm renders obsolete Geneva's strict limitation on questioning enemy prisoners and renders quaint some of its provisions.[27]

Other legal memos appear to explore ways to circumvent domestic and international laws prohibiting torture. One emphasizes the evidentiary hurdles to the prosecution of torture:

> To convict a defendant of torture [under federal criminal law], the prosecution must establish that: (1) the torture occurred outside the United States; (2) the defendant acted under the color of law; (3) the victim was within the defendant's custody or physical control; (4) the defendant specifically intended to cause severe physical or mental pain and suffering; and (5) that the act inflicted severe mental pain and suffering.[28]

Each of these requirements presented new opportunities to further narrow the definition of torture. For example, the intent clause was interpreted to require that inflicting severe pain or suffering contrary to the law be the primary *intent* of the defendant. "Thus, even if the defendant knows that severe pain will result from his actions, if causing such harm is not his objective, he lacks the requisite specific intent . . . ; a defendant is guilty of torture only if he acts with the express purpose of inflicting severe pain or suffering." Likewise, the memo argues, federal law "makes plain that the infliction of pain or suffering per se . . . is insufficient to amount to torture. Instead, the text provides that the pain or suffering must be 'severe,'" which government lawyers interpreted to mean "death, organ failure, or the permanent impairment of a significant bodily function."[29] The memorandum further maintains that under the president's authority as commander in chief, torture is lawful as long as it is carried out to protect U.S. national security and that interference by Congress or the courts would be unconstitutional. Another memo, prepared by the Justice Department, explains:

> Even if an interrogation method [might arguably constitute torture under these narrow definitions], and application of the statute was not held to be an unconstitutional infringement of the President's Commander-in-Chief authority, we believe that under current circumstances certain justifications [including military necessity or self-defense] might be available that would potentially eliminate criminal liability.[30]

That memo also attempts to draw a legal distinction between torture, which it acknowledges is illegal, and lesser forms of cruel, inhuman, or degrading treatment or punishment, which the memo claims are to be deplored and prevented but are not so universally and categorically condemned as to be illegal. A lengthy portion of the memo goes on to explore a range of cruel, inhuman, and degrading actions, just short of torture, which Justice Department lawyers argue would not violate domestic and international prohibitions on torture if applied. For example, forcing someone onto their hands and knees and kicking them in the stomach might not be construed as torture, but rape or sexual assault would.[31]

Some groups within the administration were offended by these arguments. There was, reportedly, "almost a revolt" by the military's judge advocates general, or JAGs, including lawyers who report to the chairman of the Joint Chiefs of Staff. In frustration, they made their concerns public, charging that there was "a calculated effort to create an atmosphere of legal ambiguity about how the [Geneva C]onventions should be applied."[32] State Department lawyers also objected. Taft, the State Department's legal adviser, hastily added his own memo to the debate, arguing that the Justice Department's legal advice to President Bush was " 'seriously flawed,' its reasoning 'incorrect as well as incomplete,' and all of it 'contrary to the official position of the United States, the United Nations and all other states that have considered the issue.' "[33]

Although the administration argued that these memos were "theoretical" rather than operational, it has become increasingly clear that the secretary of defense did expand the scope and nature of permissible interrogation techniques and admitted that he hid some detainees from the Red Cross at the request of Director of Central Intelligence George Tenet.[34] It is also undeniable that gross abuses, reported by the Red Cross and confirmed in detail in a report by Major General Antonio Taguba,[35] were rife in Iraq prisons. Although the administration vigorously denied that it in any way condoned torture, some observers have concluded that the atmosphere of legal ambiguity at the very least opened the door for abuses. One report, prepared by three senior army generals and commonly known as the Fay report, after its chair, General George R. Fay, asserts that "a list of interrogation techniques approved by Defense Sec[retary] Rumsfeld for use at the US detention facility at Guantanamo Bay, Cuba, migrated improperly to Abu Ghraib and contributed to some of the abuses there."[36] A four-member independent panel headed by James A. Schlesinger reiterated that "leadership failures at the highest levels of the Pentagon, Joint Chiefs of Staff and military command in Iraq contributed to an environment in which detainees were abused at Abu Ghraib prison and other facilities."[37] Public trust in the administration's appeal for wide latitude in dealing with detainees in the war on terrorism reached new lows in the wake of these revelations.

Although information has been difficult to obtain, there is now strong evidence that the executive branch has also held prisoners in a number of secret detention facilities offshore. Some of those detainees were taken into custody through a process known as "extraordinary rendition," in which the U.S. government has abducted persons suspected of supporting international terrorism—often in collusion with friendly governments—and taken them to other foreign countries for "interrogation" purposes.

The two best known cases involve Maher Arar and Khaled El-Masri. Arar is a dual citizen of Syria and Canada. He was living in Canada when he took a family vacation to Tunis in September 2002. Responding to his employer's request to return, Arar took a plane that had a stopover in New York. There, he was taken aside by immigration authorities and interrogated for more than a week. Following this, Arar was flown to Syria, where he was detained for ten months and subjected to torture throughout the period, before finally being released and allowed to return to his family in Canada. After a full inquiry, the Canadian government exonerated Arar of having any connection to terrorism and awarded him nearly $10 million in restitution. On the other hand, the U.S. government has refused to acknowledge any wrongdoing, and to this day Arar remains on the government's terrorist watch list. Furthermore, Arar's attempt to obtain a remedy under U.S. law has not been successful either. In November 2009, the U.S. Court of Appeals for the Second Circuit ruled that "special factors counseling hesitation" barred Arar's claim that his constitutional rights were violated when American officials sent him to Syria.[38] The U.S. Supreme Court later declined to hear Arar's appeal.

Khaled El-Masri is a German citizen of Lebanese descent who was arrested by Macedonian authorities during a family vacation and turned over to CIA operatives. He was flown to Kabul, Afghanistan, and detained there for five months. While in detention, he was tortured. Ultimately, he was flown to a remote area of Albania and released. El-Masri subsequently filed suit in U.S. district court against former director of central intelligence Tenet, three corporate defendants, ten unnamed employees of the CIA, and ten unnamed employees of the defendant corporations. The government sought dismissal of the suit on the basis of the "state secrets" doctrine—namely, that to defend itself in the case, the government would be forced to disclose sensitive military secrets and operations. This district court ruled in favor of the United States and dismissed his case. On appeal, El-Masri claimed that both the Council of Europe and President Bush himself had publicly acknowledged the existence of the extraordinary rendition program. Thus there was no longer any "secret" to which the "state secrets" doctrine could be applied. The Fourth Circuit Court of Appeals disagreed and upheld the dismissal on the grounds that pursuit of El-Masri's claim might still involve the disclosure of some sensitive military information.

The Legal Wrangling over Guantánamo

At the outset, it was not clear what role (if any) the American judiciary would play in the "war on terrorism." For one thing, there is a long-standing principle in U.S. law that courts will not involve themselves in issues involving the conduct of American foreign policy, and this is particularly true during times of war. One of the most notorious examples in U.S. history was the Supreme Court's ruling during World War II in *Korematsu v. United States*,[39] which upheld the internment of Japanese nationals. However, in the present case, and with some notable exceptions (see the discussion of Arar and El-Masri above), U.S. courts have come to play a vigorous and vital role. We now turn to the (ongoing) tug of war between the political branches, on the one hand, and the U.S. Supreme Court, on the other. Among the questions we will address are the following: How broad is the latitude that the president can expect in the execution of the war on terrorism? Does the doctrine of separation of powers limit judicial oversight of the president's treatment of various categories of detainees, or does it demand it instead? Do the courts have jurisdiction over enemy combatants on territory outside the United States but effectively and fully under U.S. military control? What (if any) are the rights of detainees in Afghanistan and Iraq? What (if any) protections are available for targets of extraordinary rendition?

Rasul et al. v. Bush

Rasul et al. v. Bush was a consolidated action brought by a group of British, Australian, and Kuwaiti nationals being detained by the U.S. government at Guantánamo Bay.[40] Relying primarily on the Supreme Court's decision in *Johnson v. Eisentrager* (1950),[41] the U.S. District Court for the District of Columbia dismissed their suit for want of jurisdiction, holding that aliens detained outside the sovereign territory of the United States may not invoke a petition for a writ of habeas corpus.[42] The Court of Appeals for the District of Columbia affirmed the dismissal, holding that "the 'privilege of litigation' does not extend to aliens in military custody who have no presence in any territory over which the United States is sovereign."[43]

The Supreme Court reversed the court of appeals decision.[44] The majority opinion emphasized the historic purpose of the writ to justify and reaffirm "the federal courts' power to review applications for habeas relief in a wide variety of cases involving Executive detention, in wartime as well as in times of peace."[45] Traditionally, the writ has been seen as the primary protection against executive restraint. The Court affirmed that "[a]t its historical core, the writ of habeas corpus has served as a means of reviewing the legality of Executive detention, and it is in that context that its protections have been strongest."[46] Congress has generally supported this broad interpretation, the Court noted, "extending the protections of the writ to all cases where any person may be restrained of his or her liberty in violation of the Constitution, or of any treaty or law of the United States."[47] The fact that the petitioners are aliens and are located outside the United States did not matter to the Supreme Court.

For the Court, the crux of the matter was the proper scope of *Eisentrager* in defining the rights of detainees. That case arose during the close of the Second World War. The plaintiffs were a group of twenty-one German nationals who had been captured in China for engaging in espionage against the United States. Following a trial and conviction by a U.S. military commission sitting in China, the prisoners were shipped to the Landsberg prison in Germany. Their legal challenges ultimately reached the Supreme Court, which ruled that the detainees were not entitled to any legal remedy under U.S. law.

The Supreme Court in 2004 found important distinctions between the detainees in *Eisentrager* and *Rasul et al.*:

> Petitioners in [*Rasul et al.*] differ from the *Eisentrager* detainees in important respects. They are not nationals of countries at war with the United States, and they deny that they have engaged in or plotted acts of aggression against the United States; they have never been afforded access to any tribunal, much less charged with and convicted of wrongdoing; and for more than two years they have been imprisoned in territory over which the United States exercises exclusive jurisdiction and control.[48]

Justice Anthony M. Kennedy, in a concurring opinion, added that also unlike the *Eisentrager* case, Guantánamo Bay is in every practical respect a U.S. territory, and it is one far removed from any hostilities.[49] Moreover, the detainees at Guantánamo Bay face the possibility of indefinite detention, and without any benefit of a legal proceeding to determine their status, whereas the Germans were tried and convicted by a military tribunal.

Justice Antonin Scalia filed a dissenting opinion, joined by Chief Justice William Rehnquist and Justice Clarence Thomas. For Scalia, the crux of the case was that the Guantánamo Bay detainees are not located within the territorial jurisdiction of *any* federal district court, and thus the protections afforded under the habeas statute do not extend to them. Scalia went on to describe the "breathtaking" and, in his view, frightening consequences of the majority's decision:

> It permits an alien captured in a foreign theater of active combat to bring a [habeas corpus] petition against the Secretary of Defense. Over the course of the last century, the United States has held millions of alien prisoners abroad. . . . A great many of these prisoners would no doubt have complained about the circumstances of their capture and the terms of their confinement.[50]

For good or for ill, the major thrust of this and the other Supreme Court decisions regarding the detainees was to reassert the judiciary's authority in defining and defending due process in the administration's war on terrorism. However, the decisions also highlighted the role of Congress in defining the reaches of both the administration and the judiciary through the legislative process. Because many of the legal controversies that made their way to the courts depended on differing interpretations of previous laws, breaking the stalemate between the executive and judiciary would require new legislation. The legislature was quick to respond to the call. Before the Guantánamo detainees could take advantage of the Court's ruling, Congress passed new legislation that (seemingly) took away the very rights that the courts had granted detainees. Furthermore, the Justice Department had asked the federal appeals court to restrict Guantánamo detainees' access to their lawyers who, the administration charged, were causing threats to security at Guantánamo by "caus[ing] unrest among the detainees and improperly serv[ing] as a conduit to the news media."[51]

Congress Responds

Following the Supreme Court's decision in *Rasul*, in December 2005 Congress passed the Detainee Treatment Act (P.L. 109-148, 119 Stat. 2680), which added a new subsection (e) to the habeas statute, which reads: "Except as provided in section 1005 of the [Detainee Treatment Act], no court, justice, or judge" may exercise jurisdiction over:

(1) an application for a writ of habeas corpus filed by or on behalf of an alien detained by the Department of Defense at Guantanamo Bay, Cuba; or

(2) any other action against the United States or its agents relating to any aspect of the detention by the Department of Defense of an alien at Guantanamo Bay, Cuba who

    (A) is currently in military custody; or

    (B) has been determined by the United States Court of Appeals for the District of Columbia Circuit . . . to have been properly detained as an enemy combatant.

The Detainee Treatment Act (DTA) attempted to limit the judiciary's role to the D.C. Circuit Court, and then only for the purpose of determining whether the designation of "enemy combatant" was supported by the evidence that the administration provided. The only reason the federal courts were able to take up these issues again stemmed from ambiguity in the act about whether or not it would apply to cases pending when the legislation was passed.

The Supreme Court Counters

In June 2006, the Supreme Court took up the matter of the DTA in the case of *Hamdan v. Rumsfeld.*[52] Salim Ahmed Hamdan, allegedly Osama Bin Laden's former chauffeur, was an enemy combatant held at Guantánamo Bay who challenged the legality of the military tribunals the Bush administration created to try the detainees. The Court agreed with the substantive claim that the proposed military commissions were inconsistent with the procedures established under both the Uniform Code of Military Justice and the Geneva Conventions. It also affirmed the Court's authority to hear the case despite provisions in the DTA that eliminated most avenues for judicial oversight in matters related to the detainees. Although the government claimed that the DTA had removed the Supreme Court's jurisdiction, the Court disagreed. Rather, it pointed to a provision of the DTA that stated that subsections (e)(2) and (e)(3) of section 1005 "shall apply with respect to any claim . . . that is pending on or after the date of the enactment of this Act [DTA Sec. 1005(h)]." However, no provision of the DTA stated whether subsection (e)(1) applied to pending cases. The Court found evidence in the legislative record that the omission of pending cases from the exemption from judicial review was purposeful. Therefore, it refused to dismiss Hamdan's suit, while adroitly sidestepping separation of powers issues being raised by both sides of the continuing controversy.

Congress Responds to the Hamdan Decision

Congress responded to *Hamdan* almost immediately by passing the Military Commissions Act of 2006 (P.L. 109-366, 120 Stat. 2600) (2006) (MCA), which the president signed into law on October 17, 2006. Subsection 7(a) of the MCA, entitled "Habeas Corpus Matters," added a new amendment, which reads:

> (1) No court, justice or judge shall have jurisdiction to hear or consider an application for a writ of habeas corpus filed by or on behalf of an alien detained by the United States who has been determined by the United States to have been properly detained as an enemy combatant or is awaiting such determination.
>
> (2) Except as provided in [section 1005(e)(2) and (e)(3) of the DTA], no court, justice, or judge shall have jurisdiction to hear or consider any other action against the United States or its agents relating to any aspect of the detention, transfer, treatment, trial, or conditions of confinement of an alien who is or was detained by the United States and has been determined by the United States to have been properly detained as an enemy combatant or is awaiting such determination.

Furthermore, in a pointed response to the Court's ruling on *Hamdan,* a new subsection (b) provides:

> The amendment made by subsection (a) shall take effect on the date of the enactment of this Act, and shall apply to all cases, without exception, pending on or after the date of the enactment of this Act which relate to any aspect of the detention, transfer, trial, or conditions of detention of an alien detained by the United States since September 11, 2001.

Congress again clearly and consistently favored executive privilege in the conduct of the war on terrorism.

The Supreme Court Counters—Once Again

Not to be deterred, the final word (we believe) on this matter was delivered by the Supreme Court in its decision in *Boumediene v. Bush.*[53] The Bush administration argued that under the provisions of the Military Commissions Act, courts no longer had jurisdiction to hear any claims filed by enemy combatants, and it petitioned the Court to dismiss the case. The Supreme Court declined to do so. Instead, what it did was to reaffirm the importance of having a judicial check over executive actions, and it arrived at this position by ruling for the very first time that detainees at Guantánamo Bay had a constitutional right to habeas corpus protection.

The Court proceeded in three steps. The first consisted of an extended history of the role that habeas corpus has played in both British and American political history as a means of protection against executive abuses. The second step consisted of addressing the claim whether habeas protection extends to non-nationals being detained outside the United States. As noted earlier, the strongest argument against this proposition was that the Supreme Court had already answered this question in *Eisentrager*, when the Court denied habeas corpus protection in a case filed by a group of German soldiers held in a military camp (Landsberg) in occupied Germany. For the majority in *Boumediene*, there were several factors that differentiated between these two situations. For one thing, Guantánamo Bay is under complete American jurisdiction and control, which was not the case with Landsberg. Another rationale is that while the German prisoners had been given a hearing that established their role as combatants, no such proceedings had ever taken place for the Guantánamo detainees. Finally, the Court was also disturbed that many of the claimants had already spent years in prison—with no apparent end in sight.

Finally, the Supreme Court directly addressed the constitutional require-ments for suspending habeas corpus, once it concluded that it was indeed the intention of Congress "to circumscribe habeas review."[54] The U.S. Constitution provides in Article 1, Section 9, that "The privilege of the Writ of Habeas Corpus shall not be suspended, unless when in Case of Rebellion or Invasion the public Safety may require it." Even then, the majority ruled, any suspension of the writ would have to be accompanied by some other means by which executive author-ity could be challenged. In the Court's view, the protections afforded under the Detainee Treatment Act simply did not meet this standard and thus "operates as an unconstitutional suspension of the writ."[55] In its analysis, it pointed to a number of shortcomings in the military tribunals established by the political branches, including the lack of effective legal counsel; the fact that the detainee might not even be aware of critical legal allegations that have been filed against him; and finally, the admissibility of hearsay evidence. Furthermore, although the DTA did establish a level of judicial review through the Court of Appeals for the District of Columbia, the Supreme Court ruled this process inadequate, most notably the fact that the procedure established by Congress did not afford the detainee the opportunity to present relevant exculpatory evidence that was not a part of the record in earlier proceedings.

Boumediene v. Bush is a landmark decision in at least two ways. First, it represents a monument to judicial perseverance. Notwithstanding repeated efforts by Congress and the president, the American judiciary has refused to be sidelined in the government's conduct of the "war on terrorism." In that way, this decision and its progeny have reaffirmed the principle first established by Chief Justice John Marshall in *Marbury v. Madison*: "It is emphatically the province and duty of the judicial department to say what the law is."

Second, *Boumediene* establishes for the very first time that nonresident foreign nationals have rights under the U.S. Constitution. It is not clear how far (literally) the holding in *Boumediene* will be taken, but it is noteworthy that in a subsequent case, *Maqaleh et al. v. Gates*,[56] involving habeas petitions filed by a group of detainees captured outside Afghanistan and then transferred to the Bagram Airfield in Afghanistan, the U.S. District Court for the District of Columbia was willing to extend *Boumediene* and grant habeas hearings—at least with respect to non-Afghan nationals.

The Obama Administration Joins the Debate

The election of Barack Obama to the presidency substantially changed the direction—if not the charged tone—of the debate. Dramatically, on the day he was sworn into office, President Obama promised to close Guantánamo within a year's time. A year later, however, the administration was still weighing its options. In January 2010, a Justice Department–led task force recommended that roughly half of the detainees be repatriated or relocated to a third country; that thirty-five or so be prosecuted in federal courts or reconstituted military tribunals in the United States; and that fifty be detained indefinitely in a new facility in Illinois.[57] Each of these options faces obstacles: few countries are stepping forward to take in the detainees eligible for repatriation or relocation; Republicans and other critics vociferously oppose bringing detainees "to America's heartland" for prosecution or permanent relocation; and human rights groups are equally opposed to the prospect of indefinite detention. The political contest over the future of the detainees continues.

Conclusion

The debate over the rights of detainees has raged so furiously and on so many fronts because the stakes are so high. The fundamental interests and values of the United States hang in the balance. Does terrorism represent a clear and present threat to U.S. national security? Does the threat terrorism poses require limitations on legal rights and freedoms? What is the appropriate trade-off between security and freedom? Does the nature of the threat render international institutions and laws obsolete? What are the proper roles of the president, Congress, and the courts in striking the right balance between competing interests and values? And finally, what does it mean to say that the United States is a nation that follows the rule of law?

Key Actors

John Ashcroft   Attorney general, fundamentally reoriented the Justice Department after September 11, 2001, to give priority to security and to emphasize prevention over prosecution; had primary responsibility over the September 11 detainees.

George W. Bush   President, sought expanded powers for executive agencies based on "war footing" of the country after September 11 and the president's constitutional role as commander in chief.

Colin Powell   Secretary of state, offered views on U.S. obligations under international law that were often contrary to the views of the Justice Department and the Defense Department.

Donald Rumsfeld   Secretary of defense, had primary responsibility for the detention and interrogation of all persons designated "enemy combatants."

U.S. Supreme Court   Court of last resort, ruled on the legal limits of the executive branch's detention policies in the Bush administration's war on terrorism.

Notes

1. "Address to a Joint Session of Congress and to the American Public," September 20, 2001, www.whitehouse.gov/news/releases/2001/09/20010920-8.html.

2. Ibid.

3. "Imprisoned persons," by contrast, refers to people who have been "deprived of personal liberty as a result of conviction for an offense." UN General Assembly, "Body of Principles for the Protection of All Persons under Any Form of Detention or Imprisonment," General Assembly Resolution 43/173, passed December 9, 1988.

4. Opinion written by Chief Judge T. Harvie Wilkinson III, *Hamdi v. Rumsfeld,* 316 F. 3rd 450, 464 (4th Cir. 2003).

5. The number is approximate because the government has never released complete information about the detainees.

6. Steve Fainaru, "Court Says Detainees' IDs Can Be Kept Secret; Panel: 9/11 Realities Outweigh Disclosure," *Washington Post,* June 18, 2003.

7. *Center for National Security Studies et al. v. Department of Justice,* No. 01-2500, www.cnss.org/discoveryopinion.pdf.

8. Fainaru, "Court Says Detainees' IDs Can Be Kept Secret."

9. Neil A. Lewis, "Threats and Responses: The Detainees: Secrecy Is Backed on 9/11 Detainees," *New York Times,* June 18, 2003.

10. USA PATRIOT Act, sec. 41-412.

11. Office of the Inspector General, Justice Department, "The September 11 Detainees: A Review of the Treatment of Aliens Held on Immigrations Charges in Connection with the Investigation of the September 11 Attacks," Washington, D.C., April 2003.

12. Tim Golden and Don Van Natta Jr., "U.S. Said to Overstate Value of Guantanamo Detainees," *New York Times,* June 21, 2004.

13. Neil A. Lewis, "Bush's Power to Plan Trial of Detainees Is Challenged," *New York Times,* January 16, 2004.

14. U.S. Department of Defense, Detainee Affairs Web site, ARB Factsheet, www .defense.gov/news/Jan2006/5pagehandout.html (accessed February 3, 2010).

15. John Barry, Michael Hirsh, and Michael Isikoff, "The Roots of Torture," *Newsweek International,* May 24, 2004.

16. *Rasul et al. v. Bush,* No. 03-334, Brief for the Respondents in Opposition, www .usdoj.gov/osg/briefs/2003/0responses/2003-0334.resp.html.

17. Respondent's Motion to Dismiss Petitioner's First Amended Writ of Habeas Corpus, U.S. District Court for the District of Columbia, March 18, 2002, *Rasul et al. v. Bush,* No. 02-0299 (CKK), www.ccr-ny.org/v2/legal/september_11th/docs/Government ResponseToRasulPetition.pdf (accessed April 23, 2004) (emphasis in original).

18. Patti Waldmeir, "Court Tries to Balance Guantanamo Detainee Rights with Security Goals," *Financial Times,* April 21, 2004.

19. Michael Isikoff, "Memos Reveal War Crimes Warnings," *Newsweek,* May 17, 2004, www.msnbc.msn.com/id/4999734/site/newsweek/site/newsweek.

20. Under mounting pressure from human rights groups as well as Congress, the Defense Department has released a number of previously classified documents outlining the government's interrogation policies. See "Working Group Report on Detainee Interrogations in the Global War on Terrorism: Assessment of Legal, Historical, Policy, and Operational Considerations," March 6, 2003, http://i.a.cnn.net/cnn/2004/ images/06/09/pentagonreportpart1.pdf, and an untitled and incomplete report at http://i.a.cnn.net/cnn/2004/images/06/09/pentagonreportpart2.pdf.

21. General Miller assumed command of the Guantánamo base after interrogators complained that his predecessor was too soft on the detainees.

22. Barry, Hirsh, and Isikoff, "The Roots of Torture."

23. Associated Press, "Guantanamo Suicide Bids May Be Tied to General," MSNBC, June 22, 2004, www.msnbc.msn.com/id/5261632.

24. Golden and Van Natta, "U.S. Said to Overstate Value."

25. Ibid.

26. Elizabeth Bumiller and Eric Schmitt, "President Sorry for Iraq Abuse: Backs Rumsfeld," *New York Times,* May 7, 2004.

27. Alberto Gonzales, memorandum for the president, "Decision Re: Application of the Geneva Conventions on Prisoners of War to the Conflict with Al Qaeda and the Taliban," www.library.law.pace.edu/research/020125_gonzalesmemo.pdf.

28. "Working Group Report on Detainee Interrogations in the Global War on Terrorism: Assessment of Legal, Historical, Policy, and Operational Considerations,"

March 6, 2003, www.ccr-ny.org/v2/reports/docs/PentagonReportMarch.pdf. See also the Memorandum for the General Counsel for the Department of Defense, www.dod.gov/news/Jun2004/d20040622doc8.pdf.

29. "Working Group Report on Detainee Interrogations in the Global War on Terrorism: Assessment of Legal, Historical, Policy and Operational Considerations," April 4, 2003, www.defenselink.mil/news/Jun2004/d20040622doc8.pdf.

30. Jay S. Bybee, "Memorandum for Alberto R. Gonzales: Re Standards of Conduct and Interrogation under 18 U.S.C.§§ 2340–2340A," August 1, 2002, http://news.findlaw.com/wp/docs/doj/bybee80102mem.pdf.

31. Ibid.

32. Barry, Hirsch, and Isikoff, "The Roots of Torture."

33. R. Jeffrey Smith, "Military Legal Advisers also Questioned Tactics," *Washington Post*, June 24, 2004, A7, quoting from Taft, memo to White House counsel regarding comments on the applicability of the Geneva Convention to al Qaeda and Taliban prisoners, February 2, 2002. The Taft memo is available at www.fas.org/sgp/othergov/taft.pdf.

34. Memos are available at www.dod.gov/releases/2004/nr20040622-0930.html.

35. Antonio Taguba, "Article 15-6 Investigation of the 800th Military Police Brigade," made available to the public in May 2004, http://news.findlaw.com/hdocs/docs/iraq/tagubarpt.html.

36. Greg Jaffe, "Army Blames Confusion in Iraq for Iraqi Abuse," *Wall Street Journal*, August 27, 2004, A3.

37. Eric Schmitt, "Defense Faulted by Panel in Prison Abuse," *New York Times*, August 24, 2004, 1.

38. David Cole, "Getting Away with Torture," *New York Review of Books*, January 14, 2010, 39.

39. *Korematsu v. United States*, 323 U.S. 214 (1944).

40. *Rasul et al. v. Bush*, 124 S. Ct. 2686 (2004). Mention must also be made of two companion cases handed down the same day as *Rasul*. The first is *Hamdi v. United States*, 542 U.S. 507 (2004). Yaser Esam Hamdi, who was born in Louisiana but raised in the Middle East, was captured in a war zone in Afghanistan in 2001. After his American citizenship became known, Hamdi was transferred to Guantánamo Bay, but then later taken to a naval brig in South Carolina. The Bush administration claimed the authority to detain Hamdi as an "enemy combatant." In its ruling, the Court held that such detention would have to be accompanied by due process rights, which had not been afforded to Hamdi. In the words of Justice Sandra Day O'Connor, who wrote the majority opinion, the war on terrorism does not provide the president with a "blank check." Following the Court's ruling, in October 2004 Hamdi was released from U.S. custody and flown to Saudi Arabia. He remains there under house arrest. The other companion case, *Padilla v. United States*, 542 U.S. 426 (2004), also involves a U.S. citizen. José Padilla was arrested at O'Hare Airport in Chicago on June 10, 2002, and charged with conspiring with al Qaeda to carry out a terrorist attack in the United States by means of detonating a radioactive bomb. Padilla was then brought to New York, but eventually transferred to a naval brig in Charleston, South Carolina. Padilla's attorney challenged his detention by filing a petition for habeas corpus in New York. In its ruling, the Supreme Court held that because of Padilla's detention in South Carolina the habeas petition was wrongly filed. Padilla ultimately spent three and a half years in solitary confinement as a designated "enemy combatant." Then, in November 2005, a new set of criminal charges was

filed against him. The new indictment made no mention of a "dirty bomb." Rather, Padilla was charged with being a member of a "North American cell group" that worked to support jihadist campaigns in Afghanistan and elsewhere. In August 2007, Padilla and two codefendants were convicted of conspiracy to provide material support for terrorists and sentenced to seventeen years and four months in prison.

41. *Johnson v. Eisentrager,* 339 U.S. 763 (1950).

42. *Rasul v. Bush, Habib v. Bush,* and *Al Odah v. Bush,* 215 F. Supp. 2d 55 (D.D.C. 2002).

43. *Rasul v. Bush, Habib v. Bush,* and *Al Odah v. Bush,* 321 F. 3d 1134 (D.C. Cir. 2003).

44. *Rasul et al. v. Bush* is available at http://caselaw.lp.findlaw.com/cgi-bin/getcase .pl?court=US&navby=case&vol=000&invol=03-334.

45. 124 S. Ct. 2692-93.

46. Id. at 2692 (citation omitted).

47. Id. (referencing Habeas Act of February 5, 1867).

48. *Rasul et al. v. Bush,* 124 S. Ct. 2686, 2693 (2004).

49. Id. at 2700, Justice Anthony Kennedy concurring.

50. Id. at 2706, Justice Antonin Scalia dissenting.

51. William Glaberson, "U.S. Asks Court to Limit Lawyers at Guantanamo," *New York Times,* April 26, 2007, A1.

52. *Hamdan v. United States,* 548 U.S. 557 (2006).

53. *Boumediene v. Bush,* 553 U.S. ___ (2008).

54. 128 S. Ct at 2265.

55. 128 S. Ct 229 (2008).

56. *Maqaleh et al. v. Gates,* Civil Action No. 06-1669, U.S. District Court for the District of Columbia (June 3, 2009).

57. Peter Finn, "Justice Task Force Recommends about 50 Guantanamo Detainees Be Held Indefinitely," *Washington Post,* January 22, 2010.

Conclusion

Ralph G. Carter

Change we can believe in? Despite the rhetoric of Barack Obama's presidential campaign in 2008, the early foreign policy actions of the new administration seem more a difference of style than a sharp change in substance. While Obama reached out in new ways to diverse international audiences and was generally perceived abroad to be more willing to listen than was President George W. Bush, his policies proved to be largely centrist and pragmatic in nature. Thus, with only limited exceptions, most Republicans in Congress found they could usually support the president's requests—at times more easily than could members of the more liberal wing of his own party. Thus the sharp partisan differences found in domestic policy making (see health care reform for an example) were not generally found in foreign policy making. Time will tell whether that pattern remains in place for the rest of his administration.

As in the previous editions of this volume, these case studies illustrate the array of external challenges and opportunities, substantive issues, internal political situations, and policy-making dynamics likely to confront U.S. foreign policy makers well into the twenty-first century. While each of these fifteen cases offers a unique perspective on policy making, patterns can be discerned in the internal and external policy-making environments.

On the Outside: Shifts in External Challenges

Foreign policy is made by those who act in the name of the state, and they do so in relation to the external and internal environments. Although the concept of viewing "the state as an actor in a situation" is not new, it continues to be helpful.[1] The external environment presents either opportunities to embrace or problems to solve. How foreign policy makers react to such external situations often depends on the internal environment. Why they get involved in a situation makes a difference, and how their preferences correspond to those of the people, opinion makers, and the media plays a major role in decision making.

The cold war era was dominated by the politics of national security. To U.S. foreign policy makers, the Soviet threat overrode all other foreign policy issues. Persistent images of a relentless enemy and the potentially catastrophic costs of a policy mistake typically led administration officials to neither seek nor encourage input from others who might know less about the external situation.[2] Although some observers perceived that presidential policy-making preeminence ended with the Vietnam War,[3] most would agree that such presidential preeminence ended with the end of the cold war. Without the threat of nuclear annihilation looming over policy discussions, reasonable people could disagree about what the United States should do in foreign affairs.[4] So in the post–cold war and post–September 11 era, the external situation neither stifles foreign policy debate nor deters the participation of potential policy-making actors. While during the cold war many "realists" seemed to think that only the external environment mattered, there now seems little question that both the external and internal political situations significantly influence U.S. foreign policy makers.

In the present era, fewer traditional external challenges and opportunities confront U.S. foreign policy makers. Financial crises can threaten the viability of even mature states—like Greece and others—and require new responses from international actors like the European Union and the G-20. The global terrorist threat has concentrated itself in a front line called "AfPak" while at the same time fragmenting globally into diverse al Qaeda franchises that operate on their own. Regime change and nation-building, rogue regimes, nuclear proliferation, genocidal civil wars, drug smuggling, and global environmental degradation are but a few other examples of the challenges policy makers face. Other examples are more positive, such as structuring beneficial trade relations, helping people and states through multilateral assistance, and creating new, cooperative international institutions to handle complex problems. For U.S. policy makers, the difficult questions are whether the United States should respond to a given situation, and if so, how?

On the Inside: The New Foreign Policy Challenges

The answers to whether and how the United States should respond are usually found in the internal political situations facing foreign policy makers. As James Scott sums it up, "A changing agenda and increasing interdependence and transnational ties make foreign policy making more like domestic policy making: subject to conflict, bargaining, and persuasion among competing groups within and outside the government."[5] This statement echoes a remark made by President Bill Clinton: "The more time I spend on foreign policy . . . the more I become convinced that there is no longer a clear distinction between what is foreign and domestic."[6] During the cold war, the president and his advisers directed foreign policy, but in the present era members of Congress and other powerful groups have become highly visible participants in the process. There are now numerous actors clamoring to act in the name and best interest of the United States.

Interbranch Leadership: Presidential-Congressional Interactions

In the present period some actions remain clearly presidential, such as decisions to go to war or deploy more troops in a combat zone. In other instances, Congress seems to be calling the tune, such as in establishing Cuba policy, limiting what the president can promise in global climate change talks, setting the parameters of acceptable terms in financial bailouts and stimulus packages, or telling the president he cannot have the immigration reform legislation he wants.

Today presidents and members of Congress openly vie for influence over many policy issues, with each branch doing its best to shape the outcome. The possible results of this pattern of interbranch leadership include cooperation, constructive compromise, institutional competition, or confrontation and stalemate.[7] The cases in this volume illustrate all four of these variants. For example, the Colombian drug case reflects institutional cooperation, the China trade case reveals constructive compromise, institutional competition is at the heart of the climate change case, and confrontation and stalemate mark the immigration reform case. The judicial branch also occasionally becomes a major player in these policy disputes, as the National Security Agency (NSA) eavesdropping and the detainees cases demonstrate.

Each branch of government uses direct and indirect tactics to accomplish its goals. Direct tactics reflected here include members of Congress introducing legislation to change U.S. policy (as in the NSA eavesdropping, immigration reform, Cuban embargo, China trade, global financial crisis, International Criminal Court [ICC], and detainees cases), presidents using the military (as in the terrorism, Iraq, and Colombian aid cases), and promoting diplomatic negotiations (as in the Iranian, North Korean, and ICC cases). Sometimes, when both branches want to "frame" issues in a favorable way, indirect tactics are chosen. Thus, from President Clinton's point of view, Plan Colombia was not about getting the United States into another Vietnam War, but about protecting Americans from the ravages of illegal drugs. Similarly, from Sen. Jesse Helms's perspective, the ICC was not about the United States being a law-abiding member of the international community, but about threats to U.S. sovereignty. Once issues are successfully framed in the negative, as in the latter case, no one wants to be depicted as supporting them. The executive and legislative branches also try to anticipate the reaction of the other, whether it is an administration trying to gauge congressional reactions in cases like immigration reform and ICC participation, or a Democratically controlled Congress testing how much it can press the Obama administration, as in the global financial crisis case.

The actions of other administration officials, and occasionally the courts, also complicate interbranch leadership. Senior administrative officials played pivotal roles in the decisions to pursue war with Iraq, eavesdrop without warrants, and detain enemy combatants. The decisions of the courts were pivotal in deciding the ability of the administration to pursue warrantless wiretaps or to detain enemy combatants and U.S. citizens and immigrants in the war on terrorism.

New Influences: The Societal Actors

Government officials do not act in a political vacuum. They are often the targets of interest group representatives, who usually believe that their concerns are identical to those of the collective nation (as in the Cuban trade, Chinese trade, and detainees cases). The news media report on politics, and how the news is reported can sway public opinion (for example, in the cases of NSA eavesdropping and the detainees). The public's opinion is then used to impress a policy preference on policy makers (as in the Colombian, immigration reform, and Cuban trade cases). In most of these cases, experts who serve as opinion leaders line up on one or both sides of an issue, trying to get their preferred policies enacted. The question becomes, "Who has the ear of policy makers?"

Stimuli: Underlying Factors

Governmental and nongovernmental actors often disagree on foreign policy issues because they respond to different stimuli and thus frame issues differently.[8] For example, in the case of Colombia, one person's "new Vietnam" is another person's "war on drugs." To one person, the China trade issue is a human rights problem, while to another it is a jobs issue. At other times agreement can be reached on the definition of an issue but not on the policy solution. For instance, nuclear proliferation concerns virtually everyone, but should Iran and North Korea be the targets of "hard" or "soft" power responses? As the product of a political process, foreign policy is influenced by what government officials think they should do—enact good policy or garner institutional prestige and stature—and what they think they must do—address the potential preferences of citizens and voters.[9]

Sometimes these differences are simply the products of partisanship and ideology. In the late 1940s and early 1950s, politics seemed to stop "at the water's edge."[10] The last two decades, however, have brought increasingly ideological partisanship to foreign affairs.[11] Cases such as warrantless eavesdropping, immigration reform, and how to get out of Iraq pitted more liberal Democrats against the more conservative Republican administration. Now they pit congressional Democrats against their own copartisan in the White House. Although Obama's preference for centrist foreign policy has dampened this ideological divide in a Democratically controlled Congress, it has not ended it.

Looking to the Future

Each case in this collection touches on the unifying theme that U.S. foreign policy making is becoming more open, pluralistic, and partisan. Responding to increasingly diverse motivations, more and more governmental and nongovernmental actors are getting involved. As foreign policy becomes increasingly intermestic and more like domestic policy, reasonable people can be expected to disagree and try to shape policy based on their own values and attitudes. Such behavior has long been commonplace for "low politics," that is, such intermestic issues as immigration, weapons procurement, and foreign trade. Without the overriding fear of global annihilation, there seem to be few reasons for congressional and societal actors to defer to the president or other officials of the executive branch for many "high politics" issues involving core national interests. These other actors bring their ideas, attitudes, passions, ideological beliefs, and partisanship with them as they try to affect policy making. In terms of any search for consensus, the short-term trends do not look promising as the foreign policy process continues to become more political.

With more open and pluralistic foreign policy making, those who oppose the president's policy preferences will seek to exploit any internal divisions within an administration. Members of Congress, interest groups, nongovern-mental organizations, and media pundits will seek to find policy allies in the administration. It is interesting to observe to what degree officials' loyalties to the president outweigh their occasional differences with his policy preferences. Future presidents will have to find policy positions that feel right to them, keep their administration's officials "on message," and convince the country that their policy prescriptions are the best for the nation.

The 2008 elections paired a Democratically controlled Congress with a Democratic president. Quickly, all concerned realized that this situation did not represent a free pass to create whatever policies they desired. Despite the common partisan tie, the structural differences remained. Even when from the same party, presidents and members of Congress respond to different cues and motivations. Thus, even under the best of circumstances, presidents can be expected to have difficulties with Congress regarding foreign policy. As a noted congressional scholar argues:

> The Constitution establishes a fluid decision process that cannot ensure a cre-ative governmental response to issues that confront the country. The system of separation of powers, with its checks and balances, works to constrain the enactment of public programs. Partisanship (embodied in divided or unified government), the responsiveness of government to electoral considerations, the character of congressional organization, and the quality and commitment of presidential leadership conspire in distinctive ways to create a policy process prone to delay and deadlock.[12]

In such an environment, anything controversial will further complicate policy making. After September 11, 2001, George W. Bush bet his presidency on his war on terrorism. While it began with great domestic and international sup-port, that support began to wane after the invasion of Iraq. For his part, it appears Obama has bet his presidency on recovery from the global financial crisis and some measure of success regarding the defense challenges present in Afghanistan and Pakistan. Winning the Nobel Peace Prize in his first year in office suggests the international arena welcomed his presence in the White House, but only time will tell if his policies prove successful.

Thus some things have not changed in this post–cold war and post–September 11 era. U.S. foreign policy making continues to grow more pluralis-tic, partisan, and political in the twenty-first century. The good news is that U.S. foreign policy is becoming representative of more organized interests and points of view, more democratic in nature, and somewhat more transparent in process. The bad news for policy makers is that the road to foreign policy enactment and successful implementation shows all the signs of being an increasingly bumpy ride. To paraphrase Winston Churchill's seafaring analogy, democracies are like rafts—they are virtually unsinkable, but they proceed slowly and one's feet always get wet. In this more open process, foreign policy making will almost always be slower, but one hopes that it will be surer in its outcomes.

Notes

1. See Richard C. Snyder, H. W. Bruck, Burton M. Sapin, Valerie M. Hudson, Derek H. Chollet, and James M. Goldgeier, *Foreign Policy Decision Making (Revisited)* (New York: Palgrave Macmillan, 2002).

2. See Richard Melanson, *American Foreign Policy since the Vietnam War,* 2nd ed. (Armonk, N.Y.: M. E. Sharpe, 1996).

3. See Thomas Franck and Edward Weisband, *Foreign Policy by Congress* (New York: Oxford University Press, 1979); James M. Scott and Ralph G. Carter, "Acting on the Hill: Congressional Assertiveness in U.S. Foreign Policy," *Congress and the Presidency,* no. 2 (Autumn 2002): 151–169; and Ralph G. Carter, "Congressional Foreign Policy Behavior: Persistent Patterns of the Postwar Period," *Presidential Studies Quarterly* 16, no. 2 (Spring 1986): 329–359.

4. For a good discussion of these themes, see James M. Scott and A. Lane Crothers, "Out of the Cold: The Post–Cold War Context of U.S. Foreign Policy," in *After the End: Making U.S. Foreign Policy in the Post–Cold War World,* ed. James M. Scott (Durham: Duke University Press, 1998), 1–25.

5. James M. Scott, "Interbranch Policy Making after the End," in Scott, *After the End,* 401.

6. Quoted in Ralph G. Carter, "Congress and Post–Cold War U.S. Foreign Policy," in Scott, *After the End,* 129–130.

7. Scott and Crothers, "Out of the Cold," 11.

8. James M. Lindsay, *Congress and the Politics of U.S. Foreign Policy* (Baltimore: Johns Hopkins University Press, 1994).

9. For more on congressional policy motivations, see R. Douglas Arnold, *The Logic of Congressional Action* (New Haven: Yale University Press, 1990); Aage Clausen, *How Congressmen Decide* (New York: St. Martin's Press, 1973); Richard F. Fenno, *Congressmen in Committees* (Boston: Little, Brown, 1973); or John W. Kingdon, *Congressmen's Voting Decisions,* 3rd ed. (Ann Arbor: University of Michigan Press, 1989).

10. See Carter, "Congressional Foreign Policy Behavior."

11. Carter, "Congress and Post–Cold War U.S. Foreign Policy," 128.

12. Leroy N. Rieselbach, "It's the Constitution, Stupid! Congress, the President, Divided Government, and Policymaking," in *Divided Government: Change, Uncertainty, and the Constitutional Order,* ed. Peter F. Galderisi (Lanham, Md.: Rowman and Littlefield, 1996), 129.

Index

Figures and tables are indicated by f and t following page numbers.

477

timeline on, 388–390
U.S. policy on, 387
overview, 386–387
states' action on, 400–403
U.S. perspective, 386–387
White House, science, and big oil and, 399
Climate Change Science Program, 399
Climate Leaders program, 398
Climate Vision program, 398
Clinton, Bill
Bin Laden, air strikes against, 12–18, 31, 40.
    See also Terrorism
China policy of, 356–357, 360–361, 364–372
climate change policy of, 387, 389, 395,
    397, 410
Colombia drug policy of. See Colombia and
    drug trade
Cuba policy of, 335–336, 338–340, 345, 350
foreign policy and, 472
global financial crisis and, 294
ICC and, 419, 423, 431, 438, 439. See also
    International Criminal Court
immigration policy of, 269–270
Iran and, 111, 116–117, 132
military action by, 31
NAFTA and, 268
North Korea policy, 141, 149–151, 153–155,
    164
PNAC letter to, 45
Russia policy of, 168, 169, 193
scandals of, 14, 16, 17, 340, 376
use of military force by, 12
Clinton, Hillary Rodham
AfPak strategy, 28–29
authorization of force and war on
    terrorism, 27, 28, 31
Colombia drug policy, 101
North Korea policy, 161
troop surge, 31
U.S.-Russian relations, 171, 176, 179, 184,
    192, 193
Coalition Provisional Authority, 58
Code Division Multiple Access, 369
Cohen, Kenneth P., 404
Cohen, William, 16
Colombia and drug trade, 74–107
background, 75–84
Bush (George W.) drug policy, 75, 77,
    92–98, 100, 101
    Andean Regional Initiative and Andean
        Counterdrug Initiative, 94–98
    insurgency as new terrorism, 92–94, 100

challenge of, 74–75
Clinton drug policy, 75, 77, 84–92, 100, 101
    congressional passage, 89–92
    Plan Colombia, aid in 2000–2001, 87–88
    resistance, 88–89
key actors in, 101–102
Obama drug policy, 98–100
producer state, Colombia as, 75–84
    control of drug trade, 81–83
    politics and drugs, 79–81
    pre-Clinton U.S. policy, 83–84
U.S. aid to Colombia, timeline of, 76–78
Comey, James, 239–240, 254
Commission for Assistance to a Free Cuba, 343
Comprehensive Immigration Reform Act
    (2006), 263, 274, 281
Conference of the Parties (COP), 395, 397,
    400, 408
Congressional-presidential interactions,
    472–473
Connecticut, environmental policy in, 402
Constitution, war powers under, 12, 18–19
Contract with America, 269
Convention on the Prevention and
    Punishment of the Crime of
    Genocide, 421
Cooney, Philip A., 399
COP-1 meeting (1995), 395
COP-2 meeting (1996), 395
COP-3 meeting (1997), 395
COP-6 meeting (2000), 397
COP-6 meeting (2001), 400
COP-15 meeting (2009), 408
Cornyn, John, 273–275
Costello, Frank, 218
Counterinsurgency and counternarcotics aid,
    75, 92–94. See also Colombia and drug
    trade
Counterterrorism. See Terrorism
Counterterrorism Evaluation Group, 46
Court of Justice of the European Union, 428
Courts, FISA, 230, 234, 236, 248–253.
    See also National Security Agency
    (NSA) eavesdropping
Creel, Santiago, 260
Creppy, Michael, 450
Crimes against humanity, 417, 420. See also
    International Criminal Court (ICC)
Crouch, J.D., 61
Cuban Adjustment Act (1966), 339
Cuban American National Foundation
    (CANF), 335, 338, 342, 344, 345, 349–350

Italy
China and, 375
climate change and, 392
global financial crisis, 311
ICC and, 431
war on terrorism, 24
Ivanov, Sergei, 177

J
Jackson, Lisa, 405–406
Jackson, Robert H., 232
Jager, Mike, 215
Japan
China and, 364, 380
climate change and, 392, 397, 400
Kyoto Protocol and, 389
North Korea and, 139, 141–142, 152–154,
155, 158, 163
JCCT (U.S.-China Joint Commission on
Commerce and Trade), 355
Jiang Zemin, 360, 366
Jihad, 13
Johnson, Lyndon B., 12, 267, 337
Johnson, Stephen L., 402
Johnson v. Eisentrager (1950), 459–460, 464
Johnson & Johnson, 404
Joint Declaration on the Denuclearization of
the Korean Peninsula, 140, 147, 152
Jones, James, 27–30, 32, 191
JP Morgan Chase, 296, 306

K
Kang Sok Ju, 153
Kanter, Arnold, 147
Karasin, Grigoriy, 184
Karimov, Islam, 22–23
Karzai, Hamid, 120
Keane, Jack, 61
KEDO. *See* Korean Peninsula Energy
Development Organization
Kelly, James, 142, 158
Kennedy, Anthony M., 460
Kennedy, Edward, 273–277, 281, 285
Kennedy, John F., 266–267, 333, 334–335,
337–338
Kenya embassy bombing, 13, 14, 16–18
Kerrey, Bob, 17
Kerry, John, 28, 343–344, 408
Kessler, Gladys, 448, 450
Khalilzad, Zalmay, 45
Khamenei, Ali, 109–110, 119, 122, 125–126,
128–130, 132

Khan, A.Q., 111, 118, 124
Khatami, Mohammad, 111, 119, 120,
121, 132
Khomeini, Ayatollah Ruhollah, 111, 114–115,
117, 132
Kim Dae Jung, 153
Kim Gye Gwan, 162
Kim Il Sung, 141, 143, 152, 164. *See also* North
Korea
Kim Jong Il, 141, 143, 149, 153, 158, 163–164.
See also North Korea
Kim Yong Sam, 150
King, David, 387
Kirk, Ron, 362, 380
Kirkpatrick, Jeane, 435
Kirsch, Philippe, 419, 428, 435
Kissinger, Henry, 115, 180, 337, 356, 435
Korean Peninsula Energy Development
Organization (KEDO), 141–142,
152–154, 156, 157, 158, 164
Korean War, 139, 359
Korematsu v. United States (1944), 459
Kosovo, 12, 169, 170, 174–175, 374, 376
Kristol, William, 45
Krupp, Fred, 405
Kucinich, Dennis, 99
Kuwait
ICC and, 416
Iraq invasion of, 40
U.S.-Iranian relations, 116
Kyl, Jon, 273–277, 286
Kyoto Protocol. *See* Climate change

L
Labor groups and China, 371–372, 379
Lambert, Andrew, 225
Lamy, Pascal, 355
Latin America and immigration issues. *See*
U.S.-Mexican relations
Lavrov, Sergey V., 128, 171, 179–180, 184,
191, 193
Leach, Jim, 98
League of Nations, 417
Leahy, Patrick, 87, 88, 96, 99, 102, 235
Lee, Barbara, 20
Lehman Brothers, 297, 306, 308, 323
Levin, Carl, 20, 29, 241
Libby, I. Lewis, 45
LIBERTAD (Cuban Liberty and Democratic
Solidarity Act). *See* Cuba policy
Libya, 417, 429, 434, 438
Lindsay, James M., 43

Local and state action on climate change, 400–403
London Charter for the Prosecution and Punishment of the Major War Criminals of the European Axis, 417–418, 420
Long, Russell, 401
Long-term capital management crisis, 295
Lopez Portillo, Jose, 267
Lott, Trent, 17, 19, 90, 377
Lucent Technologies, 369
Lugar, Richard, 28, 51, 54, 55

M
Maastricht Treaty, 375
Maersk Alabama, 216–223
    incident, 216–221
    rescue, implications for antipiracy operations, 221–223
    timeline, 209
Maine, environmental policy in, 402
Makarov, Nikolai, 191
Al-Maliki, Nouri, 42, 62, 65
Mancuso, Salvatore, 78
Manzullo, Donald, 85
Mao Zedong, 144, 359, 360
Maqaleh v. Gates (2009), 465
Maritime patrol aircraft, 213
Maritime piracy, 200–228
    antipiracy operations, 221–223
    Barbary Coast, 204, 208
    China, 204–206, 208
    defined, 200–202
        high seas, 201
        low-level armed robbery, 201
        major criminal hijack, 201–202
        medium-level armed assault and robbery, 201
        opportunistic piracy, 202
        private ends, 201
        professional piracy, 202
        sanctioned piracy, 202
    history of, 223–225
    jurisdiction, 201
    key actors, 225
    Maersk Alabama incident, 216–223
    reemergence as threat to international security, 202–207
        assets, lack of, 206
        density of traffic, 205
        history and culture, 206–207
        organized crime and corruption, 206
        territorial disputes and sovereignty issues, 206
        topographical factors, 206

response to, 212–216
    land bases, attacking, 214–216
    maritime patrol aircrafts, 213
    measures against, 212–214
    NATO, 213
    at sea, 212–214
    from sea, 214–216
    Somali piracy, rise of, 207–211
    timeline, 208–210
Maritime Silk Road, 205, 206
Markey, Edward J., 390, 407, 410
Marshall, John, 237–238, 465
Martinez, Mel, 274–276, 341–342
Mas Canosa, Jorge, 335, 338, 342
El-Masri, Khaled, 458–459
Massachusetts, environmental policy in, 402
Massachusetts v. Environmental Protection Agency (2007), 401, 403, 406
Mas Santos, Jorge, 343
McCaffery, Barry, 81, 85–86, 100, 102
McCain, John
    AfPak strategy, 29
    climate change policy and, 404
    Cuba policy and, 345–346
    immigration policy and, 273–276, 284, 286
    U.S. intervention in Iraq and, 52
    U.S.-Russian relations, 176
McCarry, Caleb, 343
McChrystal, Stanley, 15, 27–29, 32
McConnell, Michael, 250–251, 254
McCurry, Michael, 17, 151
McFaul, Michael, 176, 190
McGovern, Jim, 93, 96, 98, 102
Mckiernan, David, 27
McKinley, William, 224
Medellín cartel, 80, 83, 94
Medvedev, Dmitry, 128, 171–173, 176–185, 189–193, 222
MEM (Multilateral Evaluation Mechanism), 98
Menendez, Robert, 342
Merrill Lynch, 296, 306, 308
Mexico
    financial crisis, 294
    U.S. relations. *See* U.S.-Mexican relations
MFN. *See* Most favored nation trade status
Midterm elections of 2006, 60–61
Military Commissions Act (2006), 450, 451, 463
Military tribunals. *See* Detainees, rights of
Miller, Geoffrey, 454
Minaret tracking system, 230
Minutemen, 284
Missile defense systems, 173
Missile Technology Control Regime (MTCR), 141, 153

Montreal Protocol, 393, 404
Moreno Ocampo, Luis, 419, 435
Morgan Stanley, 323
Mossadeq, Mohammad, 110, 111, 114
Most favored nation (MFN) trade status, 362, 363–364
Motorola, 369
Mottaki, Manouchehr, 129
Moussavi, Mir Hussein, 129, 133
MTCR. *See* Missile Technology Control Regime
Mueller, Robert, 239, 240
Al Muhajir, Abdullah. *See* Padilla, Jose
Mullen, Michael, 27, 29, 191
Multilateral Evaluation Mechanism (MEM), 98
Munich syndrome, 147
Murkowski, Lisa, 407
Murtha, John, 29
Muse, Abdelwali Abdulkadir, 209, 210, 220–221, 225
Musharraf, Pervez, 22, 26
Myers, Richard, 43, 59, 452

N
NACARA (Nicaraguan and Central American Relief Act, 1997), 270
NAFTA. *See* North American Free Trade Agreement
Nairobi, Kenya embassy bombing, 13, 16–18
Najjar, Mostafa Mohammad, 118, 178
Napolitano, Janet, 286
National Aeronautics and Space Administration (NASA), 391
National Association of Manufacturers, 377
National Commission on Terrorist Attacks Upon the United States (9/11 Commission), 18
National Council for U.S.-China Trade, 367
National Endowment for Democracy (NED), 338
National origin quotas for immigration, 262, 266. *See also* U.S.-Mexican relations
National Security Agency (NSA)
   eavesdropping, 229–258
   administration's response to leak, 232, 235–236
   background, 230–232
   FISA statute, 230, 231, 233–236
   Hayden's testimony and, 240–242, 250, 254
   hospital visit to Ashcroft and, 238–240
   immunity, 251–253
   key actors, 254
   legislative remedies, 246–248
   McConnell's testimony, 250–251

mid-course correction, 248–249
overview, 229–230
previous illegal NSA activities, 230–232
setbacks in court, 242–246, 472
sole-organ doctrine, 236–238
timeline, 231
wiretaps, establishment of limits on, 232–233
National Security Council (NSC), 47, 48
National Union for Marine, Aviation and Shipping Transport Officers (NUMAST), 207, 210
NATO
   in Afghanistan, 15, 24–25, 56–57
   China and, 374
   maritime piracy, 213
   Russia and, 168–170, 174–175
NED (National Endowment for Democracy), 338
Negroponte, John, 344, 435
Neoconservatives ("neocons"), 45, 50, 57
Netherlands
   climate change and, 392
   ICC and, 431
   war on terrorism, 24, 25
New Hampshire, environmental policy in, 402
New Jersey, environmental policy in, 402
New Mexico, environmental policy in, 402
"New Way Forward," 42
New York, environmental policy in, 402
New York Time's reports on NSA eavesdropping, 229, 231, 235–236, 243–244, 246, 249
NGOs. *See* Nongovernmental organizations
Nicaragua
   Colombia and, 99
   ICC and, 422
   immigration policy and, 269–270
Nicaraguan and Central American Relief Act (NACARA, 1997), 270
Nielson, Kirk, 344
Nike, 404
9/11 attacks. *See* September 11, 2001 terrorist attacks
9/11 Commission, 18
Nixon, Richard
   China-U.S. relations and, 356, 359–360, 367–368
   Cuba policy and, 334
   domestic surveillance and, 229–230, 242
   resignation of, 39
   Soviet Union and, 337
   war powers and, 12

Pakistan
    ICC and, 436
    Iran and, 118, 127
    maritime piracy, 211
    North Korea and, 162
    war on terrorism, 12, 15, 22–23, 26–30
Panama Canal, 422
"Paragate" scandal, 78, 98
Partnership for Prosperity, 263, 271
Pastrana, Andrés, 76–77, 82–83, 87, 102
Pataki, George, 402, 410
Patriot Act. *See* USA Patriot Act (2001)
Paulson, Henry, 296, 297, 309, 323
Pelosi, Nancy, 29, 94, 235
Pentagon's Office of Special Plans, 46, 58
People's Republic of China (PRC). *See* China
Pepper, Claude, 342
Perle, Richard, 45
Permanent, normal trade relations (PNTR),
    356, 361, 367, 371, 372, 375–378. *See also*
    China
Permanent Court of Arbitration, 417
Perry, Mike, 216, 225
Perry, William J., 153–154, 164
Persian Gulf War (1991), 13, 44, 52, 58, 416
Peterson, Collin, 407
Petraeus, David, 27, 62–66, 68
Pew Center on Climate Change, 401
Philbin, Patrick, 452
Phillips, Richard, 209, 217, 220–221, 225
Piltz, Rick S., 399
Pinochet, Augusto, 437
Piracy. *See* Intellectual property issues in
    China; Maritime piracy
Plan Colombia, 75, 77–78, 83, 87–88, 94–98,
    473. *See also* Colombia and drug trade
PNAC (Project for the New American
    Century), 45
PNTR. *See* Permanent, normal trade relations
Poland
    ICC and, 431
    Russia and, 169–171, 173–175, 179,
        181–182, 186–189
Portillo, Jose Lopez, 268
Portman, Rob, 361
Postwar occupation of Iraq, 58–66
Powell, Colin
    authorization of force and war on
        terrorism, 21, 22, 41
    on Cheney, 46
    Colombia drug policy and, 92, 97
    Cuba policy and, 343
    detainees' rights and, 453, 455, 466

immigration policy and, 260
international community and impending
    war and, 57
North Korea policy and, 155, 157
U.S. intervention in Iraq and, 41, 43, 48,
    50–51, 68
PRC (People's Republic of China). *See* China
Predator unmanned aerial vehicle, 17, 18
Preemption. *See* Bush Doctrine and U.S.
    interventions in Iraq
PrepCom, 423–425, 431
Presidential-congressional interactions,
    472–473
Presidential Decision Directive 73, 93
Presidential Directive NSPD-24, 48, 49
Presidential powers
    NSA eavesdropping and, 236–238, 247, 248,
        250, 251. *See also* National Security
        Agency (NSA) eavesdropping
    terrorism and, 12
    war powers, 12, 18–19
Project for the New American Century
    (PNAC), 45
Protect America Act (2007), 251
Provincial Reconstruction Teams (PRTs), 24
Putin, Vladimir
    ABM system, 190
    authorization of force and war on
        terrorism, 22
    Kyoto Protocol and, 400
    nuclear standoff between U.S. and Iran, 126
    U.S.-Russian relations, 172, 174–177, 181,
        184, 193

Q

Qanooni, Yunus, 120
Qatar and ICC, 417, 429, 438
Qualcomm Corporation, 368, 369, 381
Quotas for immigration, 262, 266. *See also*
    U.S.-Mexican relations

R

Radio Marti, 335, 338
Rafsanjani, Ali Akbar Hashemi, 121, 133
Rasul v. Bush (2004), 448, 449, 452, 459–463
RCA Global, 230
Reagan, Nancy, 75
Reagan, Ronald
    Colombia drug policy of, 75
    Cuba policy of, 338
    financial crisis, 294
    Iran and, 116–117, 133
    North Korea and, 151